The Blackwell Reader in Judaism

Blackwell Readings in Religion

The Blackwell Readings in Religion series brings together the knowledge of leading international scholars, and each volume provides an authoritative overview of both the historical development and the contemporary issues of its subject. Titles are presented in a style which is accessible to undergraduate students as well as scholars and the interested general reader.

Each volume is designed to be read in tandem with its corresponding Companion, in the series Blackwell Companions to Religions.

Published

1. *Blackwell Readings in Judaism*

Edited by Jacob Neusner and
Alan J. Avery-Peck

The Blackwell Reader in Judaism

Edited by

Jacob Neusner and *Alan J. Avery-Peck*

Blackwell
Publishing

BLACKWELL PUBLISHING
350 Main Street, Malden, MA 02148-5020, USA
108 Cowley Road, Oxford OX4 1JF, UK
550 Swanston Street, Carlton, Victoria 3053, Australia

First published 2001
Reprinted 2005

Library of Congress Cataloging-in-Publication Data

The Blackwell reader in Judaism / edited by Jacob Neusner and Alan J. Avery-Peck.
        p.   cm. — (Blackwell readings in religion ; 1)
    Includes bibliographical references and index.
    ISBN 0–631–20737–6 (alk. paper) — ISBN 0–631–207384–4 (pb. : alk. paper)
    1. Judaism.   2. Rabbinical literature—Translations into English.   I. Neusner, Jacob, 1932–
II. Avery-Peck, Alan J. (Alan Jeffrey), 1953–   III. Series.

BM43 .B54   2000
296—dc21

                                                                                00-050753

A catalogue record for this title is available from the British Library.

Set in 10.5 on 12.5 pt Photina
by Kolam Information Services Pvt. Ltd.
Printed and bound in the United Kingdom
by MPG Books Ltd, Bodmin, Cornwall

The publisher's policy is to use permanent paper from mills that operate a sustainable forestry
policy, and which has been manufactured from pulp processed using acid-free and elementary
chlorine-free practices. Furthermore, the publisher ensures that the text paper and cover board
used have met acceptable environmental accreditation standards.

For further information on
Blackwell Publishing, visit our website:
www.blackwellpublishing.com

Contents

List of Contributors   xii

Preface   xvi

Acknowledgments   xxii

Part I. The History of Judaism   **1**

  1 Defining Judaism *Jacob Neusner*   3

    A. *Louis Jacobs, "Judaism: The Religion, Philosophy, and*
        Way of Life of the Jews"   3
    B. *William Scott Green, "Old Habits Die Hard: Judaism in*
        the Encyclopaedia of Religion"   8

  2 The Religious World of Ancient Israel to 586
    Marvin A. Sweeney   19

    A. *Genesis 15:1–21*   19
    B. *Exodus 13:1–16*   20
    C. *Exodus 15:1–21*   21
    D. *Exodus 20:1–14*   22
    E. *Deuteronomy 15:1–18*   23
    F. *Deuteronomy 16:1–17*   24
    G. *2 Samuel 6:1–19*   25
    H. *2 Samuel 7:1–16*   26
    I. *Isaiah 11:1–16*   27
    J. *Jeremiah 7:1–20*   28
    K. *Psalm 19*   29
    L. *Psalm 132*   30

3   Judaism and the Hebrew Scriptures *Philip R. Davies*   31

   A.   The Habakkuk Pesher *from Qumran (1QpHab), cols. 7–9*   31
   B.   *Josephus,* Antiquities *I:13 (222–236)*   33
   C.   *Philo,* On the Migration of Abraham *1–5 (1–25)*   35
   D.   *Targum Pseudo-Jonathan on Genesis 4*   39

4   Second Temple Judaism *Frederick J. Murphy*   42

   A.   *Ezra and Nehemiah*   42
   B.   *Haggai and Zechariah*   45
   C.   *Daniel*   47
   D.   *1 Maccabees*   49
   E.   *2 Maccabees*   52
   F.   *The Psalms of Solomon*   54
   G.   *Josephus*   55
   H.   *4 Ezra*   58

5   The Formation of Rabbinic Judaism, 70–640 CE
   Günter Stemberger   60

   A.   *B. Git. 56a–b: Yohanan ben Zakkai's Escape from
      Jerusalem*   60
   B.   *M. Abot 1:1–18: The Chain of Tradition*   62
   C.   *Y. Peah 2:6, 17a: Written and Oral Torah*   63
   D.   *Y. Sanhedrin 1:2, 19a: The Ordination of Rabbis*   65
   E.   *Y. Yebamot 12:6, 13a: Rabbis in the Service of the
      Community*   66
   F.   *Leviticus Rabbah 13:5: The Four Kingdoms*   67
   G.   *B. Baba Qamma 83b–84b: Biblical Foundation
      of the Mishnah*   70

6   The Canon of Rabbinic Judaism: The Mishnah
   and the Midrash *Jacob Neusner*   73

   A.   *The Mishnah*   73
   B.   *Martin Jaffee, How the Mishnah Makes a Theological
      Statement: Mishnah Ma'aserot Chapter One*   75
   C.   *The Midrash: Genesis Rabbah: The Rules of History Set
      Forth by Revelation*   79

7   Judaism and Christianity in the Formative Age
   Bruce Chilton   86

   A.   *Matthew 12*   86
   B.   *Thomas (sayings 79–85)*   88
   C.   *Galatians 2*   88

D.	Hebrews 9	90
E.	Justin, The First Apology 1–3	91
F.	Clement of Alexandria, Paidagogos 6.32–6.35	92
G.	Origen, On First Principles 2.11.2–4	94
H.	Eusebius, History of the Church 8.8.1–8.9.6	96
I.	Augustine, The City of God 22.14–22.15	98

8 Judaism in the Muslim World *Sara Reguer* 101

A.	A Late Twelfth Century Curriculum of Advanced Study: Joseph b. Judah ibn 'Aqnin, Tibb al-Nufus	101
B.	Maimonides' Philosophy: Introduction to The Guide of the Perplexed	105

9 Judaism in Christendom *David R. Carr* 114

A.	Solomon ben Isaac on Forced Conversion	114
B.	Judah ha-Levi: Poem on Return to Zion	115
C.	Moses ibn Ezra: Poem on Worldliness	115
D.	Moses ben Nahman: The Disputation at Barcelona	116
E.	Solomon bar Simson on the Mainz Martyrs	117
F.	Abraham ibn Daud of Toledo on Samuel ha-Nagid	118
G.	Maimonides regarding a Hebrew Translation of Guide of the Perplexed	118
H.	Judah ibn Tibbon on Education	119
I.	Joseph ibn Caspi on Education and Philosophy (1332)	121
J.	Solomon ben Isaac's Exegesis of Torah (1105)	121
K.	Testament of Eleazar of Mayence on Piety and Charity (ca. 1357)	122
L.	Maimonides on Law	123
M.	Maimonides on Art and Idolatry	124
N.	Solomon ben Adret on Faith and Reason (Second Half of the Thirteenth Century)	124
O.	Solomon ben Adret's Ban on Study of Philosophy by Youths (1305)	125
P.	The Book of Splendor (The Zohar) (1286)	126
Q.	Wisdom of the Chaldeans	126

10 Philosophy in Judaism: Two Stances *S. Daniel Breslauer* 128

A.	Flavius Josephus: Philosophy Is Judaism; Judaism Is Philosophy	128
B.	Julius Guttmann: Philosophy is Alien to Judaism	129

C. Isaac Husik: Jewish Philosophy in the Past but
    Not the Present   131
D. Philo of Alexandria: Jewish Scripture as Philosophy   132
E. Saadia Gaon: Defending Tradition   135
F. Judah Halevi: The Special Function of the Jews   136
G. Maimonides: The Philosophical Function of Judaism   138
H. Baruch Spinoza: A Modern Critique of Judaism   139
I. Hermann Cohen: Modern Religion out of the Sources
    of Judaism   141
J. Emmanuel Levinas: Translating Judaism into Modern
    Philosophy   142

11 Jewish Piety *Tzvee Zahavy*   145

A. Rules for a Bar Mitzvah   146
B. Dedication of a House   146
C. Laws for Visiting the Sick   147
D. Laws of Purification (Taharah) and Shrouds   149
E. Order of the Wedding Ceremony   152

Part II   The Principal Doctrines of Judaism   157

12 The Doctrine of Torah *Jacob Neusner*   159

A. Warren (Zev) Harvey, "Torah"   160

13 The Doctrine of God *Alan J. Avery-Peck*   173

A. George Foot Moore, "God and the World"   173

14 The Doctrine of Israel *Jacob Neusner*   187

A. Israel as Sui Generis in the Mishnah   187
B. Genesis Rabbah: The Metaphor of the Family, "Israel"   190
C. Israel as Sui Generis in the Yerushalmi's Theory of Salvation 199

15 The Doctrine of Hebrew Language Usage
    David H. Aaron   202

A. The Mishnah and Tosefta: Translations Are Appropriate   202
B. The Talmud: The Language of Liturgy   204
C. The Talmud: Torah Language and Colloquial Speech   207
D. The Midrashic Literature: The Preference for Hebrew   207
E. Mysticism: The Power of Individual Letters   211

Part III   Modern and Contemporary Judaisms   215

16 Reform Judaism *Dana Evan Kaplan*   217

A.	Eugene B. Borowitz, "A Liberal Jewish Approach to Ritual"	217
B.	Walter Jacob, "Standards Now"	220
C.	Eric Yoffie, "Moses, Too, Was Once a Marginal Jew"	222
D.	Henry Cohen, "Rabbinic Officiation and Mixed Marriage Revisited"	225
E.	A Statement of Principles for Reform Judaism	227

17 Orthodox Judaism *Benjamin Brown* — 232

A.	Rabbi Moshe Sofer (The Hatam Sofer): A Testament	232
B.	Rabbi Samson Raphael Hirsch, "Emancipation"	234
C.	Rabbi Avraham Isaac ha-Cohen Kook on the Unity of Contradiction	237
D.	Rabbi A. Y. Kook on Ideological Diversity and Unity	239
E.	Rabbi A. Y. Kook on Secular Zionist Idealism	241
F.	Rabbi Avraham Yesha'ayahu Karelitz on Israel as a New Torah Center	244
G.	Rabbi Avraham Yesha'ayahu Karelitz on Extremism	245
H.	Rabbi Yoel Teitlbaum of Satmar on the Holocaust as Divine Punishment	246
I.	Rabbi Joseph Baer Soloveitchik on the Objectivity of Halakha	247
J.	Rabbi Menahem Mendl Schneerssohn of Lubavitch	251
K.	Yesha'ayahu Leibowitz on Science and Jewish Religion	253

18 Conservative Judaism: The Struggle between Ideology and Popularity *Daniel Gordis* — 256

A.	Emet Ve-Emunah – A Statement of Principles	256
B.	A Responsum on Sabbath Observance	260
C.	Joel Roth: Faculty Paper Urging the Ordination of Women	262
D.	Elliot Dorff: Position Paper on Homosexuality and Sexual Ethics	266

19 New Age Judaism *Jeffrey K. Salkin* — 268

A.	Neil Gillman, "On the New Jewish Spirituality"	268
B.	Arthur Green, "Judaism for the Post-Modern Era"	271
C.	Jeffrey K. Salkin, "What Is Spirituality, Anyway?"	277
D.	Jack Moline, "Is Jewish Renewal Good for the Jews?"	280

Part IV Special Topics in Understanding Judaism   **285**

20 Ethics of Judaism *Elliot N. Dorff*   287

    A. *Jewish Ethics: Aaron L. Mackler, "Cases and Principles in Jewish Bioethics: Toward a Holistic Model"*   287
    B. *Jewish Morality: Seymour Siegel, "A Jewish View of Economic Justice"*   306

21 Women in Contemporary Judaism *Judith R. Baskin*   316

    A. *Tamar Frankiel*, The Voice of Sarah: Feminine Spirituality and Traditional Judaism   316
    B. *Marcia Falk, "Introduction of New Blessings"*   318
    C. *Merle Feld, "Healing After a Miscarriage" and "We All Stood Together"*   320
    D. *Ellen M. Umansky, "Re-Visioning Sarah: A Midrash on Genesis 22"*   322
    E. *Susan Grossman, "On Tefillin"*   323
    F. *Judith Plaskow*, Standing Again at Sinai: Judaism from a Feminist Perspective   326
    G. *Rachel Adler*, Engendering Judaism: An Inclusive Theology and Ethics   329

22 Judaism as a Theopolitical Phenomenon
Daniel J. Elazar   333

    A. *Certificate of Incorporation and Bylaws: Congregation Kehillat Jeshurun, New York (1972)*   333
    B. *Constitution and Bylaws of Monmouth Reform Temple, Monmouth, New Jersey (1988)*   344
    C. *The Covenant of Petah Tikva (1878)*   358
    D. *The Scroll of Independence of the State of Israel (1948)*   359

23 Theology in Contemporary Judaism *Neil Gillman*   363

    A. *Eugene Borowitz*, Renewing the Covenant: A Theology for the Postmodern Jew   363
    B. *Emil Fackenheim*, Quest for Past and Future   364
    C. *Neil Gillman*, Sacred Fragments   365
    D. *Arthur Green*, Seek My Face, Speak My Name   366
    E. *Irving Greenberg, "Voluntary Covenant"*   367
    F. *David Hartman*, A Living Covenant   368
    G. *Will Herberg*, Judaism and Modern Man – God   368
    H. *Will Herberg*, Judaism and Modern Man – Faith   369
    I. *Abraham Joshua Heschel*, God in Search of Man   370

J. *Mordecai Kaplan,* Questions Jews Ask: Reconstructionist
    Answers   372
K. *Franz Rosenzweig, "The Builders: Concerning the Law"*   373
L. *Richard Rubenstein, in* The Condition of Jewish Belief   374
M. *Harold M. Schulweis,* Evil and the Morality of God   375
N. *Michael Wyschogrod,* The Body of Faith: God in the
    People Israel   376

24 Secular Forms of Jewishness *Paul Mendes-Flohr*   378

A. *Michah Joseph Berdichevski, "Wrecking and Building"*   378
B. *Ben Halpern, "Apologia Contra Rabbines"*   381
C. *Yaakov Malkin, "The Faith of Secular Jews"*   394

25 Judaism and Zionism *Yosef Gorny*   397

A. *David Vital,* "The Future of the Jews: A People at the
    Crossroads?"   398
B. *Ben Halpern, "Exile – Abstract Condition and Concrete
    Community"*   399
C. *Nathan Rotenstreich, "The Present-Day Relationship"*   400
D. *Shlomo Avineri, "Israel – A Normative Value of Jewish
    Existence"*   401
E. *Ismar Schorsch, "Making Israel a Light unto the Nations:
    Conservative Zionism Reconsidered"*   403
F. *Eugene B. Borowitz, "What Is Reform Religious
    Zionism?"*   404
G. *Isadore Twersky, "Survival, Normalcy, Modernity"*   405
H. *Henry L. Feingold, "Zionism: A New Course Needed"*   407
I. *Eliezer Schweid, "The Major Goal of Zionism Today:
    To Build the Spiritual Center"*   408
J. *Yosef Gorny, "The Need for a New* Hibbat Zion"   409

26 The "Return" to Traditional Judaism at the End of
    the Twentieth Century: Cross-Cultural Comparisons
    M. Herbert Danzger   411

A. *Return: An Unanticipated Development*   411
B. *Religious Authority in Judaism*   413
C. *Action and Study*   419
D. *Why They Return*   424

List of Abbreviations   432

Index   434

Contributors

Jacob Neusner, Ph.D., Columbia University, is Research Professor of Religion and Theology at Bard College, Annandale-on-Hudson, New York. He is a Life Member of Clare Hall, Cambridge University, and Member of the Institute for Advanced Study in Princeton, New Jersey. He holds sixteen honorary degrees and academic medals.

Alan J. Avery-Peck is Kraft–Hiatt Professor of Judaic Studies at the College of the Holy Cross, Worcester, Massachusetts. He has written broadly on Judaism in the first six centuries CE. Along with Jacob Neusner and William S. Green, he is co-editor of *The Encyclopaedia of Judaism* (1999).

David H. Aaron is Professor of Bible and History of Interpretation at Hebrew Union College–Jewish Institute of Religion, Cincinnati. His publications are in the fields of Biblical and Rabbinic Literature, often with a focus on the transformations of myth and literary motifs.

Judith R. Baskin is Professor and Chair of the Department of Judaic Studies at the University at Albany, State University of New York. Her publications include *Pharaoh's Counsellors: Job, Jethro and Balaam in Rabbinic and Patristic Tradition* (1983) and the edited collections, *Jewish Women in Historical Perspective* (1991; second edn., 1998) and *Women of the Word: Jewish Women and Jewish Writing* (1994).

S. Daniel Breslauer is Professor of Religious Studies at the University of Kansas, Lawrence, Kansas, where he has taught since 1978. His major field of research is modern Jewish thought, and he has most recently published *Toward a Jewish (M)Orality: Speaking of a Postmodern Jewish Ethics* (1998) and *The Seductiveness of Jewish Myth: Challenge or Response* (1997).

Benjamin Brown is lecturer in Jewish Thought at Beit Morasha of Jerusalem and, since 1997, at the Hebrew University of Jerusalem. In 1999–2000, he is also guest-lecturer at Tel Aviv University. He has published several articles on Orthodox Judaism.

David R. Carr is Professor of History at the University of South Florida in Tampa, Florida.

Bruce Chilton is Bernard Iddings Bell Professor of Religion at Bard College and Rector of the Church of St. John the Evangelist. His publications include *God in Strength. Jesus' Announcement of the Kingdom: Studien zum Neuen Testament und seiner Umwelt 1* (1979), *The Isaiah Targum. Introduction, Translation, Apparatus, and Notes: The Aramaic Bible 11* (1987), and *Pure Kingdom. Jesus' Vision of God: Studying the Historical Jesus 1* (1996). With Jacob Neusner, he is also the author of *Jewish–Christian Debates. God, Kingdom, Messiah* (1998).

M. Herbert Danzger is Professor of Sociology at Lehman College CUNY and at the Graduate Center CUNY. His earlier work on community power structure, conflict, and social movements was supported by the National Institute of Mental Health and the National Science Foundation and published in the *American Sociological Review* and elsewhere. His studies of "return" to Jewish traditionalism benefited from two academic years in Israel, first at Bar Ilan University as senior lecturer and then at The Hebrew University of Jerusalem as Fulbright Professor. A portion of his studies of "return" is described in *Returning to Tradition* (1989).

Philip R. Davies is Professor of Biblical Studies at the University of Sheffield and founder and editor of the *Journal for the Study of the Old Testament*. His major interest lies in the Dead Sea Scrolls, on which he has written five books and numerous articles. He is also the author of *In Search of Ancient Israel* (1992) and *Scribes and Schools: The Canonization of the Hebrew Scriptures* (1998).

Elliot N. Dorff is Rector and Professor of Philosophy at the University of Judaism in Los Angeles. He serves as Vice Chair of the Conservative Movement's Committee on Jewish Law and Standards, for which he has written a number of responsa on moral issues. His books include *Contemporary Jewish Ethics and Morality: A Reader* (edited with Louis Newman, 1995) and *Matters of Life and Death: A Jewish Approach to Modern Medical Ethics* (1998).

Daniel J. Elazar was Professor of Political Science at Temple University, Philadelphia, and Senator N.M. Paterson Professor Emeritus of Intergovernmental Relations at Bar Ilan University, Israel. He was the founder and editor of the *Jewish Political Studies Review* and president of the Jerusalem Center for Public Affairs. He was the author or editor of over seventy books including a four-volume study of the *Covenant Tradition in Politics* (1995–8), as well as *Community and Polity*, *The Jewish Polity*, and *People and Polity*, a trilogy on Jewish political and community organization from earliest times to the present.

Neil Gillman is the Aaron Rabinowitz and Simon H. Rifkind Professor of Jewish Philosophy at the Jewish Theological Seminary in New York. He is the author of

Sacred Fragments: Recovering Theology for the Modern Jew and of *The Death of Death: Resurrection and Immortality in Jewish Thought*. He is currently working on a book-length study of images of God in Jewish literature.

Daniel Gordis is Director of the Jerusalem Fellows Program at the Mandel School in Jerusalem, Israel. He is author of *God Was Not in the Fire: The Search for a Spiritual Judaism* (1995), *Does the World Need the Jews? Rethinking Chosenness and American Jewish Identity* (1997), and most recently *Becoming a Jewish Parent: How to Explore Spirituality and Tradition with Your Children* (1999).

Yosef Gorny teaches modern Jewish history at Tel Aviv University and presently is Head of the Chaim Weizmann Institute for Research in the History of Zionism. His main publications in English are: *The British Labour Movement and Zionism 1917–1948* (1983), *Zionism and the Arabs 1882–1948: A Study of Ideology* (1987), and *The State of Israel in Jewish Public Thought: The Quest for Collective Identity* (1994). He has recently completed for publication the book *Between Auschwitz and Jerusalem: The Holocaust and the State of Israel as Components of Jewish Identity*.

Dana Evan Kaplan is the Oppenstein Brothers Assistant Professor of Judaic and Religious Studies in the Department of History at the University of Missouri, Kansas City. He is editor of the forthcoming *Conflicting Visions: Contemporary Debates in Reform Judaism* and author of *The Jewish Community in South Africa during the Mandela Era* (forthcoming), *American Reform Judaism Today* (forthcoming), and *Conversion to Judaism in 19th Century America* (forthcoming).

Paul Mendes-Flohr is Professor of Jewish Thought at the Hebrew University of Jerusalem.

Frederick J. Murphy is Professor of Religious Studies at the College of the Holy Cross, Worcester, Massachusetts. His research interests are New Testament and late Second Temple Judaism and his publications include *The Structure and Meaning of Second Baruch; The Religious World of Jesus: An Introduction to Second Temple Palestinian Judaism; Pseudo-Philo: Rewriting the Bible;* and *Fallen Is Babylon: The Revelation to John*.

Sara Reguer is Chair of the Department of Judaic Studies of Brooklyn College of the City University of New York. Her research interests are in Middle East history, and she currently is completing a book for Columbia University Press on the Jews in the modern Islamic world.

Jeffrey K. Salkin is senior rabbi of The Community Synagogue, Port Washington, New York. He holds a Doctor of Ministry degree from Princeton Theological Seminary and is author of several books on popular theology, including *Being God's Partner: How to Find the Hidden Link between Spirituality and Your Work*. His most recent book is *Searching for My Brother: Jewish Men in a Gentile World*.

Günter Stemberger teaches at the University of Vienna, where he holds the chair of Jewish Studies. His main fields of research and teaching are Rabbinic Literature and the history of the Jews in the pre-Islamic period. His books in English translation are *Introduction to the Talmud and Midrash* (second edn., 1996); *Jewish Contemporaries of Jesus* (1995); and *Jews and Christians in the Holy Land. Palestine in the Fourth Century* (1999).

Marvin A. Sweeney is Professor of Hebrew Bible at the Claremont School of Theology and Professor of Religion at the Claremont Graduate University, Claremont, California. He is author of *Isaiah 1–39, with an Introduction to Prophetic Literature* (1996); *King Josiah of Judah: The Lost Messiah of Israel* (2000); and *The Book of the Twelve Prophets* (2000). He is editor of the *Review of Biblical Literature* and co-editor of the *Forms of the Old Testament Literature* commentary series.

Tzvee Zahavy has taught at the University of Minnesota, the University of California, Berkeley, and the College of William and Mary. His publications include *The Traditions of Eleazar Ben Azariah* (1997), *The Mishnaic Law of Blessings and Prayers: Tractate Berakhot* (1987), *The Talmud of the Land of Israel: Tractate Berakhot* (1989), *Studies in Jewish Prayer* (1990), and *The Talmud of Babylonia: Tractate Hullin* (1992–4).

Preface

The *Reader in Judaism* introduces Judaism in its own words, so affording direct encounter with the ancient, enduring faith of Israel, defined as "the people that know God made manifest in the Torah." That is particularly appropriate, because Judaism is a book-religion, a religion that speaks through, and endures in, the permanent word. This means that, in Judaism, God can be met through the act of reading (to be sure, reading defined in unconventional ways, e.g., reading through singing, praying, analytical discourse in community, and so forth). The *Reader in Judaism* therefore proves a singularly apt way of learning about Judaism in its principal mode of discourse.

How do the *Companion to Judaism* and the *Reader* relate? The essays in the *Companion* expound the topics, and the selections in the *Reader* then illustrate important points with primary sources, in English, to complement the exposition. In this way, we both talk about Judaism and let Judaism speak for itself, in its own mode of formulating and expressing its convictions. While each volume stands on its own, the two work best in tandem, the chapter of the *Reader* side by side with its counterpart in the *Companion*. This close relationship is the result of the three specific purposes that guided our authors in their selection of readings.

First of all, readings have been chosen that will stimulate thought and reflection, affording the possibility, from the case at hand, to generalize about a given theme or problem. Nothing is random, everything purposive. Second, while the readings stand on their own, making their own point and delivering their own message, each also exemplifies an important trait of Judaism in the aspect covered by the chapter at hand. And, third, the readings illustrate the essays in the *Companion* so that the expositions set forth there find nuance and concreteness in the actualities of discourse no longer *about* the faith but *within* its interior reality: in the readings, believers talking to believers are overheard by the rest of us as they transact the negotiations of the religious life.

In most cases, our authors have met these goals by presenting primary sources of participants in the age and phenomenon under discussion; hence there are passages from Scripture, the Dead Sea Scrolls, Rabbinic writings, medieval and modern Jewish philosophy and theology, statements of the modern movements in Judaism, and the like. Still, in some cases, especially those involving broad themes, for instance, the definition of Judaism or Judaism's conception of God, the authors preferred to follow contemporary expositions of issues, perhaps because these are a more efficient manner of setting forth a coherent view of confusing data. The editors hope that readers will find that the selections adopted meet the goal of affording direct access to a living religion, its vitality and power.

How is our larger aspiration for this project realized in the specific readings that have been chosen? First, we wanted our topics to be systematically expounded through primary sources, and that is what the selections in many of the chapters, particularly in Part I, accomplish. Günter Stemberger, for example, sets forth principal doctrines of Rabbinic Judaism in its nascent age through sources that embody those doctrines. Traits of medieval Jewish piety are conveyed in the selections on Judaism in medieval Christendom. Philosophy in Judaism is illustrated through the writings of the philosophers, ancient and modern, whose attitudes toward Judaism's relationship to philosophy are systematically explained in the relevant section in the *Companion*.

Second, selections that expound the central doctrines of normative Judaism, e.g., Torah, God, Israel, and the messiah, areas in which the primary sources are diverse and require extensive interpretation and elaboration, focus on formal scholarly expositions rather than on the primary sources alone. Here the reader has access to the sources and their meaning through classical statements of the theme, presented in the ground-breaking scholarship of the past generation.

Third, we wanted modern and contemporary debate to find a forum here and, from the opening section, differences abound in the debate between Judaism defined principally through ideas Jews hold and Judaism set forth as a system of ideas of the social order, independent of the sociology and secular history of a particular group of people. Not only so, but the contemporary Judaisms – Reform, Orthodox, Conservative, and New Age – are allowed to speak through their practitioners, writing to acutely present-tense audiences in the here and now. Even our special topics – ethics, women's issues, theological–political concerns, constructive theology, secular Jewishness, and Zionism – reflect contemporary and continuing debate on what it means to be Jewish, to live as a Jew, and to create a "Jewish" community, whether in the diaspora, in the modern State of Israel, or of all Jews – whether practitioners of the religion or simply members of a group defined in sociological terms – everywhere.

As in the *Companion to Judaism*, each of our experts in this volume has addressed a broad audience, assuming only an interest in the subject but not a prior knowledge of more than bits and pieces of it, if that. We present not academic essays for specialists but introductions and expositions for any literate person interested in our subject. The authors, further, whether in their own exposition or in their selection of readings, do not take partisan or sectarian positions upon Judaism or its history, theology, and social expressions. They mean to build upon the consensus of contemporary learning and to provide as complete and rounded a view as possible of their topic.

In all, these two volumes together work systematically to organize and place into context the history of Judaism in ancient, medieval, and modern times; identifying and expounding some of its principal doctrines; introducing the more important modern and contemporary Judaisms; and taking up topics of special interest in contemporary Judaic life. In this way the editors mean to identify the focal points of an ancient and contemporary religion, to define a context in which diverse texts and facts of Judaism fit and make sense, so as to accord a view of the whole and facilitate encounter with the parts.

Despite our larger goals, the organization and selection of the topics and illustrative readings in the *Companion* and *Reader* required a measure of selectivity. It goes without saying that we could cover only the more important topics, doctrines, movements, and problems. We are the first to concede that other, equally significant subjects deserved a place in these pages. The four principal parts *could have* included other aspects of Judaism, but we affirm that those to which we have assigned priority belong in any account, however brief, of Judaism. It further goes without saying that we do not attempt a history of the Jews, as an ethnic group, but only portray Judaism. In distinguishing the ethnic group from the religious community, moreover, we do not portray as "Judaism" the sum total of Jews' opinions on various subjects. Rather for our picture of Judaism, its history, doctrines, and movements, we assign priority to Judaism's authoritative writings, to which all the faithful refer. People generally understand that a wide variety of personal opinion mediates what the books say into the actualities of popular practice and belief.

What is the structure of these volumes viewed as wholes? The first three parts of the *Companion* and their counterparts in the *Reader* describe Judaism from two angles, the historical and the theological. These chapters deal with the definition of Judaism — exactly what we are talking about when we speak of that religion? — and its formative history, from Scripture up to and including modern times. Part I narrates the history of Judaism from its formative age, in dialogue with the Hebrew Scriptures, through the complex and diverse world of Second Temple times to the ultimate statement of Rabbinic Judaism as the normative system. We deal here with both the history and the literature of that Judaism. We turn then to the relationships of Judaism with Christianity in the formative age, and Judaism and Christianity and Judaism and Islam in medieval times. In that same historical unit, we discuss Judaism in its philosophical expression, and in its expression in piety and concrete religious life with God.

Then come expositions of the fundamental doctrines of Judaism. God, Torah, and Israel define the principal parts of Judaic theology in the Rabbinic writings of classical and medieval times, and, in Part II, these are set forth as they take shape in the principal documents of the ancient rabbis of the Mishnah, Midrash, and Talmuds. These are the documents to which all later theological and legal authorities referred, however they may have differed in matters of detail, for the fundamental principles of the faith. Because of broad interest in the messiah-theme of Judaism, we included in the *Companion* an exposition of that matter. Finally, we wanted to call attention to the way in which a religion makes its statement through the media of culture, not only through theological categories. Hence how the Hebrew language embodies the theological doctrine of normative Judaism, representing a set of religious choices of formidable cultural consequence, is spelled out.

Among many Judaic religious systems of modern and contemporary times, detailed in Part III, three predominate: Reform Judaism, the first and most important Judaism of modernity, Orthodox Judaism in its western, integrationist mode, and Conservative Judaism. Like God, Torah, and Israel, these are principal, but they do not encompass all of the interesting constructions that have responded to issues of the social order of nineteenth- and twentieth-century Judaism. Modernity presented a new set of questions of a political and cultural order, to which these Judaisms responded, each in a coherent and systematic manner. These are to be compared both to one another and to the classical Rabbinic Judaism to which all make constant reference. Among the twentieth-century Judaisms, we chose the most acutely contemporary of them all, generally called "New Age Judaism," different in its media of expression from Orthodox, Reform, and Conservative Judaism, quite separate from the Rabbinic tradition that sustains the Judaic systems of modernity, and intensely interesting in its own right.

For our survey of contemporary issues of Judaism, in Part IV, we chose the four issues we deemed of most acute relevance to religious life today: ethics, politics, constructive theology, and feminism. These are the topics on which systematic thought in Judaism, mediating between the received tradition and contemporary sensibility, distinguishes itself. So far as religious thinking does not merely recapitulate the received tradition but proposes to contribute to it, it is in these four areas that, as the twenty-first century commences, the world of living Judaism focuses its attention.

Three other special topics find their place not only because of their importance to the Jews as a group but also by reason of their pertinence to the religion, Judaism. The first is secular Jewishness, the definition of ways of "being Jewish," modes of identification as Jews, on other than religious foundations. In some ways, secular Jewishness takes over the theological heritage of Judaism and translates it into the building blocks of culture. In other ways, secular Jewishness proposes to form a social culture out of the traits of Jews as an ethnic community. The importance of secular Jewishness for the study of Judaism lies in the influence that the secular reading of the religious tradition exercises within the framework of the faith, especially in Reform, Conservative, and New Age Judaisms. The second of these three topics is Zionism, which is the movement of national liberation of the Jewish people, regarded as "a people, one people," and which brought about the creation of the State of Israel. Zionism draws heavily upon the Judaic religious tradition and profoundly influences the life of the faith as it is practiced both in the State of Israel and in the diaspora. Hence it demands an important position in any account of Judaism today.

We conclude with a topic that combines interest in religion and theology with a concern for the social group, the Jews. In the recent past, throughout the world of Jewry, a "return" to Judaism has marked a renewal of the faith for Jews formerly divorced therefrom. The interplay of the ethnic group and the religious tradition is worked out in the phenomenon of reversion. A religion that, at the advent of modern times, seemed to face a gloomy future turns out to exercise remarkable power to lead to God through the medium of the Torah people who presented unlikely candidates for religious piety. The return of Jews to Judaism marks the conclusion of modernity. But what now is going to happen, we do not pretend to know.

As noted, we do not claim to have encompassed every topic, even every important one. We have not addressed, among subjects as important as those we have treated, mysticism, the complexities of segregationist Orthodox Judaism, those that reject modern and contemporary learning altogether, and the actual practice of Judaism in various places today – all of them basic subjects. Happily, these and numerous other topics that we could not treat here are set forth in large, systematic essays, comparable to those in the present *Companion* and *Reader*, in the three volumes, 120 chapter-length entries, and 1800 pages, illustrated, of the *Encyclopaedia of Judaism*, published in 1999 under the auspices of the Museum of Jewish Heritage, New York, by E. J. Brill, Leiden–Cologne, and Continuum, New York, and edited by the editors of these books together with William Scott Green. The twenty-six chapters (topics) treated here in this *Reader* are augmented by more than a hundred others. So in these collaborative projects we have done our best to present to coming generations a thorough, balanced, objective, reliable, and proportionate account of Judaism. In the *Companion*, *Reader*, and *Encyclopaedia*, we believe we, together with scores of the best scholars in the subject, Judaism, have fulfilled this task.

The editors express their gratification at working with the fine staff of Blackwell Publishers, which proposed the project to them and cooperated at every stage in the work of organizing, editing, and bringing to realization this complex undertaking. The editors and production managers of the firm reached a high standard of professionalism and made the work a real pleasure. We have worked with many publishers on a variety of complex publishing projects. No editorial staff in our experience has excelled that of Blackwell Publishers. Professor Avery-Peck expresses his thanks to the College of the Holy Cross, and Professor Neusner to Bard College, for sustaining their academic careers and making possible all that they do.

The two editors also point with thanks and pride to the contributors of the essays in the *Companion* and the chapters in the *Reader*. They gave us their best work. They labored under rigid rules: 9,000 words for the *Companion*, 7,000 for the *Reader*. They accepted our requests for revision (often: concision!) and reorganization. They met deadlines responsibly. And they are the ones who in the end realized the project; we could not have done it without each of them. They never disappointed us, and they always kept their promises. Anyone who has ever contemplated undertaking a project comparable to this one will appreciate the weight of those well-earned compliments.

Jacob Neusner, Bard College
Alan J. Avery-Peck, College of the Holy Cross

Acknowledgments

The authors and publishers gratefully acknowledge the following for permission to reproduce copyright material:

Adler, Morris, Jacob Agus, and Theodore Friedman, "A Responsum on the Sabbath," Reprinted from *Tradition and Change* by Mordecai Waxman. Reprinted with permission, The Rabbinical Assembly, New York, 1958;

Adler, Rachel, *Engendering Judaism: An Inclusive Theology and Ethics* (Jewish Publication Society, Philadelphia 1998);

Alexander, Philip S. (ed. and trans.), *Textual Sources for the Study of Judaism* (Barnes & Noble, 1984);

Altmann, Alexander (ed.), *Three Jewish Philosophers* (Jewish Publication Society, New York, 1965);

Borowitz, Eugene, *Liberal Judaism* (Union of American Hebrew Congregations Press, 1984);

Bowker, John, *The Targums and Rabbinic Literature* (Cambridge University Press, Cambridge, 1969);

Brooks, Roger, *The Talmud of the Land of Israel* (University of Chicago Press, 1990);

Cantor, Norman F. (ed.), *The Medieval Reader* (HarperCollins, New York, 1994);

Charlesworth, James, from *The Old Testament Pseudepigrapha*. Copyright © 1983, 1985 by James H. Charlesworth. Used by permission of Doubleday, a division of Random House Inc;

Cohen, Henry, "Rabbinic Officiation and Mixed Marriage Revisited." *Central Conference for American Rabbis Journal*, Winter 1996;

Cohen, Hermann, *Reason and Hope: Selections from the Jewish Writings of Hermann Cohen* (trans. Eva Jospe) (New York, 1971);

Colson and Whitaker (trans.), *On the Migration of Abraham* (Loeb Classical Library edition) (Heinemann, London/Putnam, New York, 1932);

Danzger, M. Herbert, *Returning to Tradition: The Contemporary Revival of Orthodox Judaism* (Yale University Press, New Haven, 1989);

Diament, Carol (ed.), *Zionism the Sequel*. Reprinted by permission of Hadassah, New York, 1998; extracts by Ben Halpern, Nathan Rotenstreich, Shlomo Avineri, Eugene Borowitz, Eliezer Schweid, Isadore Twersky, Henry L. Feingold, and Yosef Gorny by permission of *Sh'ma: A Journal of Jewish Responsibility*;

Dorff, Elliot N., "Position Paper on Homosexuality and Sexual Ethics." Reprinted from *This is My Beloved, This is My Friend* by Elliot Dorff. Reprinted with permission The Rabbinical Assembly, New York, 1996;

Eidelberg, Shlomo (ed.), *The Jews and the Crusaders: The Hebrew Chronicles of the First and Second Crusades* (University of Wisconsin Press, Madison, 1977, copyright courtesy KTAV Publishing House Inc., Hoboken);

Epstein, I. (ed.), *The Soncino Talmud* (The Sincino Press, London, 1938);

Fackenheim, Emil, *Quest for Past and Future* (Indiana University Press, Bloomington, 1968. Copyright 1968 Emil Fackenheim);

Frankiel, Tamar, *The Voice of Sarah: Feminine Spirituality and Traditional Judaism* (Biblio Press, New York, 1990);

Gillman, Neil, "On the New Jewish Spirituality." This article is reprinted with permission from *Sh'ma: A Journal of Jewish Responsibility*, vol. 27, no. 522, 1996;

Gordis, Robert (ed.), *Emet Ve-Emunah: Statement of Principles of Conservative Judaism* (The Jewish Theological Seminary, New York, 1988);

Green, Arthur, *Seek My Face, Speak My Name* (Jason Aronson, Northvale, 1992);

Green, Arthur, "Judaism for the Post-Modern Era." The Samuel H. Goldenson Lecture (Hebrew Union College–Jewish Institute of Religion, 1994. Reprinted with permission of Hebrew Union College Press);

Green, William Scott. Review of *Encyclopaedia of Religion*, from *Critical Review of Books and Religion 1989* (Scholars Press, Atlanta for the Journal of the American Academy of Religion and Journal of Biblical Literature, 1989);

Greenberg, Irving, "Voluntary Covenant" from *Perspective: A CLAL Thesis* (CLAL, New York, The National Center for learning and Leadership, 1982);

Guttman, Julius, *The Philosophy of Judaism: The History of Jewish Philosophy from Biblical Times to Franz Rosenzweig* (trans. David W Silverman) (Northvale, 1988);

Hallo, William W., David B. Ruderman and Michael Stanislawski (eds.), *Heritage: Civilization and the Jews: Source Reader* (Praeger Publishers, an imprint of Greenwood Publishing Group, Inc., Westport, CT, 1984); pp. 110, 144–45, 148–50. Reprinted with permission;

Halevi, Judah, *The Kuzari (Kitab Al Khazar): An Argument for the Faith of Israel* (trans. Hartwig Hirschfeld) (New York, 1954);

Halpern, Ben, "Apologia Contra Rabbines" from *Midstream*, Spring, 1956. The Theodor Herzl Foundation, New York;

Heschel, Abraham Joshua, *God in Search of Man* (The Jewish Publication Society, Philadelphia, 1956);

Hirsch, Samson Raphael, *The Nineteen Letters on Judaism* (Feldheim Publishers, New York, 1969);

Jacob, Walter, "Standards Now" from *Reform Judaism*, Fall, 1992;

Jacobs, Louis, "Judaism" from *Encyclopaedia Judaica* (Keter Publishing Co., Jerusalem 1972);

Jaffee, Martin, *Mishnah's Theology of Tithing: A Study of Tractate Ma'aserot* (Scholars Press, 1981);

Kaplan, Mordecai, *Questions Jews Ask: Reconstructionist Answers* (Reconstructionist Press, Elkins Park, PA, 1956);

Kobler, Franz (ed.), *Letters of Jews through the Ages* (East and West Library, New York, 1978);

Kook, Rabbi Abraham Isaac, *OROT* (Jason Aronson, Northvale);

Kook, Rabbi Abraham Isaac, *Classics of Western Spirituality*. Copyright ©1978 Ben Zion Boksen. Used by permision of Paulist Press;

Leibowitz, Yesha'ayahu, "Science and Jewish Religion" (trans. Benjamin Brown) from *Yehadut. Am Yehudi u-Medinat Israel* (Mosad Bialik, Jerusalem and Tel Aviv, 1979);

Levinas, Emmanuel, *The Levinas Reader* (Blackwell Publishers, Oxford, 1992);

Mackler, Aaron L., "Cases and Principles in Jewish Bioethics: Toward a Holistic Model" from Elliot N. Dorff and Louis E. Newman (eds.), *Contemporary Jewish Ethics and Morality: A Reader* (Oxford University Press, Oxford and New York, 1995, reprinted with permission of Oxford University Press);

Malkin, Yaakov, "The Faith of Secular Jews" from *What Do Secular Jews Believe* (Free Judaism, Jerusalem, 1998);

Marcus, Jacob R. (ed.), *The Jews in the Medieval World* (Greenwood Press, Westport, 1975);

Maimonides, Moses, *The Guide of the Perplexed* (trans. Shlomo Pines) (University of Chicago Press, Chicago and London, 1963);

Maimonides, Moses, *Ethical Writings of Maimonides* (ed. R. L. Weiss and C. E. Butterworth) (Dover, New York, 1983);

Martinez, F. Garcia, *The Dead Sea Scrolls Translated* (2nd edn.) (Brill, Leiden/William Eerdmans, Grand Rapids, 1996);

Moline, Jack, "Is Jewish Renewal Good for the Jews?" This article is reprinted with permission from *Sh'ma: A Journal of Jewish Responsibility*, vol. 27, no. 525, January 10, 1997;

Moore, George Foot, *Judaism in the First Centuries of the Christian Era*. Reprinted by permission of the publishers from *Judaism in the First Centuries of the Christian Era*, volume 2 by George Foot Moore, Cambridge, MA: Harvard University Press, Copyright © 1927, 1955 by Alfred H. Moore;

Neusner, Jacob, *The Mishnah* (Yale University Press, New Haven, 1988);

Plaskow, Judith, *Standing Again at Sinai: Judaism from a Feminist Perspective* Copyright © 1990 by Judith Plaskow. Reprinted by permission of HarperCollins Publishers, Inc;

Roth, Joel, "On the Ordination of Women as Rabbis" from Simon Greenberg (ed.), *The Ordination of Women as Rabbis* (The Jewish Theological Seminary, New York, 1988);

Salkin, Jeffrey K., *Being God's Partner: How to Find the Hidden Link between Spirituality and Your Work* (Jewish Lights Publishing, Woodstock, 1994);

Schulweis, Harold M., *Evil and the Morality of God*. Reprinted with permission of Hebrew Union College Press, 1984);

Siegel, Seymour, "A Jewish View of Economic Justice" from Donald G. Jones (ed.), *Business, Religion and Ethics* (Oelgeschlager, Gunn and Hain, Cambridge, MA, 1982);

Soloveitchik, Rabbi, J. B., "The Common Sense Rebellion Against Torah Authonity," from Rabbi Abraham R. Besdin (ed.), *Reflections of the Rav* (Ktav Publishing, 1989);

Umansky, Ellen M., and Dianne Ashton (eds.), *Four Centuries of Jewish Women's Spirituality: A Sourcebook* (Boston, 1992);

Vital, David, reprinted by permission of the publishers from *The Future of the Jews: A People at the Crossroads* by David Vital, Cambridge, MA: Harvard University Press, Copyright © 1990 by David Vital;

Yetsirah, Sefer, "Sefer Yetsirah: Text and Commentary" from David R. Blumenthal, *Understanding Jewish Mysticism: A Source Reader* (KTAV Publishing House, New York, 1978);

Yoffie, Eric, "Moses, Too, Was Once a Marginal Jew" from *Reform Judaism*, Winter 1995;

The Zionist Idea: A Historical Analysis and Reader (Atheneum, New York, 1973).

The publishers apologize for any errors or omissions in the above list and would be grateful to be notified of any corrections that should be incorporated in the next edition or reprint of this book.

PART I
The History of Judaism

1   Defining Judaism
Jacob Neusner

2   The Religious World of Ancient Israel to 586
Marvin A. Sweeney

3   Judaism and the Hebrew Scriptures
Philip R. Davies

4   Second Temple Judaism
Frederick J. Murphy

5   The Formation of Rabbinic Judaism, 70–640 CE
Günter Stemberger

6   The Canon of Rabbinic Judaism: The Mishnah and the Midrash
Jacob Neusner

7   Judaism and Christianity in the Formative Age
Bruce D. Chilton

8   Judaism in the Muslim World
Sara Reguer

9   Judaism in Christendom
David R. Carr

10   Philosophy in Judaism: Two Stances
S. Daniel Breslauer

11   Jewish Piety
Tzvee Zahavy

Chapter 1

Defining Judaism

Jacob Neusner

Writing in the Encyclopaedia Judaica, *the British theologian, Rabbi Louis Jacobs of London, undertakes a definition of Judaism that stresses matters of belief, appealing to an "essence of Judaism" as the medium of definition. His survey of statements of the "essence," as well as the concept "normative Judaism," and "recognition of constant ideas," forms a complement to the approach taken in the* Companion. *It also embodies the problems that a definition of "essence" or "mood" faces.*

A different approach altogether, that of William Scott Green, American historian of Judaism at the University of Rochester, underscores the error in confusing Judaism, the religion, with the ethnic group, the Jews. His review of how Judaism is treated in the Encyclopaedia of Religion *shows what is at stake in treating the history of the Jews as equivalent to the history of Judaism. He recognizes the relationship of the two: "like every religion, Judaism developed within concrete social and political conditions and cannot be fully understood independent of the circumstances of the people who practiced it." But Green's survey of the* Encyclopaedia of Religion *shows the confusion of sociology and theology that takes place when Jewishness and Judaism are made to intersect.*

A. Louis Jacobs, "Judaism: The Religion, Philosophy, and Way of Life of The Jews"

Definition

The term Judaism is first found among the Greek-speaking Jews of the first century CE (*Judaismes*, see 2 Macc. 2:21; 8:1; 14:38; Gal. 1:13–14). Its Hebrew equivalent, *Yahadut*, found only occasionally in medieval literature (e.g., Ibn Ezra to Deut.

Source for Reading A.: Jerusalem, 1972: Keter Publishing Co., vol. 10, pp. 383–97.

21:13), but used frequently in modern times, has parallels neither in the Bible (but see Esth. 8:17, *mityahadim*, "became Jews") nor in the rabbinic literature. (The term *Dat Yehudit*, found in Ket. 7:6, means no more than the Jewish law, custom, or practice in a particular instance, e.g., that a married woman should not spin or have her head uncovered in the street.)

The term "Torah"

The term generally used in the classical sources for the whole body of Jewish teaching is Torah, "doctrine," "teaching." Thus the Talmud (Shab. 31a) tells the story of a heathen who wished to be converted to the Jewish faith but only on the understanding that he would be taught the whole of the Torah while standing on one leg. Hillel accepted him, and in response to his request replied: "That which is hateful unto thee do not do unto thy neighbor. This is the whole of the Torah. The rest is commentary. Go and study." Presumable if the Greek-speaking Jews had told the story they would have made the prospective convert demand to be taught Judaism while standing on one leg.

Modern distinctions between "Judaism" and "Torah"

In modern usage the terms "Judaism" and "Torah" are virtually interchangeable, but the former has on the whole a more humanistic nuance while "Torah" calls attention to the divine, revelatory aspects. The term "secular Judaism" – used to describe the philosophy of Jews who accept specific Jewish values but who reject the Jewish religion – is not, therefore, self-contradictory as the term "secular Torah" would be. (In modern Hebrew, however, the word *torah* is also used for "doctrine" or "theory," e.g., "the Marxist theory", and in this sense it would also be logically possible to speak of a secular *torah*. In English transliteration the two meanings might be distinguished by using a capital *T* for the one and a small *t* for the other, but this is not possible in Hebrew which knows of no distinction between small and capital letters.)

A further difference in nuance, stemming from the first, is that "Torah" refers to the eternal, static elements in Jewish life and thought while "Judaism" refers to the more creative, dynamic elements as manifested in the varied civilizations and cultures of the Jews at the different stages of their history, such as Hellenistic Judaism, rabbinic Judaism, medieval Judaism, and, from the nineteenth century, Orthodox, Conservative, and Reform Judaism. (The term *Yidishkeyt* is the Yiddish equivalent of "Judaism" but has a less universalistic connotation and refers more specifically to the folk elements of the faith.)

It is usually considered to be anachronistic to refer to the biblical religion (the "religion of Israel") as "Judaism" both because there were no Jews (i.e., "those belonging to the tribe of Judah") in the formative period of the Bible, and because there are distinctive features which mark off later Judaism from the earlier forms, ideas, and worship. For all that, most Jews would recognize sufficient continuity to reject as unwarranted the description of Judaism as a completely different religion from the biblical.

The Essence of Judaism

The Hebrew writer Ahad Ha-Am (*Al Parashat Derakhim*, 4 [Berlin ed. 1924], 42) observed that if Hillel's convert had come to him demanding to be taught the whole of the Torah while standing on one leg, he would have replied: "Thou shalt not make unto thee a graven image, nor any manner of likeness' (Exod. 20:4). This is the whole of the Torah. The rest is commentary," that is, that the essence of Judaism consists in the elevation of the ideal above all material or physical forms or conceptions.

Ahad Ha-Am's was only one of the latest attempts at discovering the essence of Judaism, its main idea or ideas, its particular viewpoint wherein it differs from other religions and philosophies. This is an extremely difficult – some would say impossible – task, since the differing civilizations, Egyptian, Canaanite, Babylonian, Persian, Greek, Roman, Christian, Muslim, with which Jews came into contact, have made their influence felt on Jews and through them on Judaism itself. It is precarious to think of Judaism in monolithic terms. Developed and adapted to changing circumstances throughout its long history, it naturally contains varying emphases as well as outright contradictions. Belief in the transmigration of souls, for example, was strongly upheld by some Jewish teachers and vehemently rejected by others. Yet the quest has rarely ceased for certain distinctive viewpoints which make Judaism what it is. Some of these must here be mentioned.

Talmudic attempts to state essence

In a talmudic passage (Mak. 23b–24a) it is said that God gave to Moses 613 precepts, but that later seers and prophets reduced these to certain basic principles: David to eleven (Ps. 15); Isaiah to six (Isa. 33:15–16); Micah to three (Micah 6:8); Isaiah, again, to two (Isa. 56:1); and, finally, Habakkuk to one: "The righteous shall live by his faith" (Hab. 2:4). This would make trust in God Judaism's guiding principle.

In another passage the second-century rabbis ruled at the council of Lydda that although the other precepts of the Torah can be set aside in order to save life, martyrdom is demanded when life can only be saved by committing murder, by worshiping idols, or by offending against the laws governing forbidden sexual relations (e.g., those against adultery and incest). The historian Heinrich Graetz (in *Jewish Quarterly Review*, 1 (1889), 4–13) deduces from this ruling that there are two elements in the essence of Judaism: the ethical and the religious. The ethical includes in its positive side, love of mankind, benevolence, humility, justice, holiness in thought and deed, and in its negative aspects, care against unchastity, subdual of selfishness and the beast in man. The religious element includes the prohibition of worshiping a transient being as God and insists that all idolatry is vain and must be rejected entirely. The positive side is to regard the highest Being as one and unique, to worship it as the Godhead and as the essence of all ethical perfections.

Maimonides' Thirteen Principles

In the twelfth century, Maimonides (commentary to the Mishnah, on Sanh., ch. Helek [10]) drew up thirteen principles of the Jewish faith. These are: (1) belief in the existence of God; (2) belief in God's unity; (3) belief that God is incorporeal; (4) belief that God is eternal; (5) belief that God alone is to be worshiped; (6) belief in prophecy; (7) belief that Moses is the greatest of the prophets; (8) belief that the Torah is divine; (9) belief that the Torah is unchanging; (10) belief that God knows the thoughts and deeds of men; (11) belief that God rewards the righteous and punishes the wicked; (12) belief in the coming of the Messiah; (13) belief in the resurrection of the dead.

A close examination of Maimonides' thought reveals that his principles are far more in the nature of direct response to the particular challenges that Judaism had to face in his day than conclusions arrived at by abstract investigation into the main ideas of Judaism. The third principle, for instance, is clearly directed against cruder notions of deity which were popular among some talmudists in Maimonides' day. (Maimonides' contemporary critic, Abraham b. David of Posquières, while believing with Maimonides that God is incorporeal, refuses to treat a belief in God's corporeality as heretical since, he says, many great and good Jews do entertain such a notion because they are misled by a literal understanding of the anthropomorphic passages in Scripture and the rabbinic literature; see Maimonides, Yad, Teshuvah, 3:7). The seventh principle seems to be aimed against the Christian claims for Jesus and the Muslim claims for Muhammad. The ninth principle similarly serves as a rejection of the Christian and Muslim claim that Judaism had been superseded (see S. Schechter, *Studies in Judaism*, 1 (1896), 147–81).

Reactions to Maimonides

Joseph Albo (*Sefer ha-Ikkarim*, 1:26) reduces Maimonides' principles to three basic ones: (1) belief in God; (2) belief that the Torah is divine; (3) belief in reward and punishment; while Isaac Arama (*Akedat Yizhak*, Gate 55) reduces them to: (1) belief in *creatio ex nihilo*; (2) belief that the Torah is divine; (3) belief in the hereafter. On the other hand Isaac Abrabanel (*Rosh Amanah*, 23) is out of sympathy with the whole enterprise of trying to discover the basic principles of Judaism in that it implies that some parts of the Torah are less significant than others. Similarly, the sixteenth-century teacher David b. Solomon ibn Abi Zimra writes: "I do not agree that it is right to make any part of the perfect Torah into a 'principle' since the whole Torah is a principle from the mouth of the Almighty.

Our sages say that whoever states that the whole of the Torah is from heaven with the exception of one verse is a heretic. Consequently, each precept is a principle and a basic idea. Even a light precept has a secret reason beyond our understanding. How, then, dare we suggest that this is inessential and that fundamental?" (Radbaz, Resp. no. 344).

Modern trends

In modern times two new factors have been operative in the search for the essence of Judaism, one making the task more difficult, the other more urgent. The first is the rise of the *Wissenschaft des Judentums* movement in the nineteenth century. This had as its aim the objective historical investigation into the sources and history of Judaism. Its practitioners succeeded in demonstrating the complexity of Jewish thought and the fact that it developed in response to outside stimuli, so that there could no longer be any question of seeing Judaism as a self-contained unchanging entity consistent in all its parts. The second new factor was the emancipation of the Jew and his emergence into Western society, calling for a fresh adaptation of Judaism so as to make it viable and relevant in the new situation. The historical movement had demonstrated the developing nature of Judaism and seemed, there-fore, to offer encouragement to those thinkers who wished to develop the faith further in accord with the new ideals and challenges. Yet this very demonstration made it far more difficult to detect that which is permanent in Judaism when so much is seen to be fluid and subject to change. Among modern thinkers, Leo Baeck was so convinced that the quest was not futile that his book carries the revealing title, *The Essence of Judaism* (1948). Acknowledging the rich variety of forms and differing phenomena in Judaism's history, Baeck still feels able to declare: "The essence is characterized by what has been gained and preserved. And such *constancy*, such *essence*, Judaism possesses despite its many varieties and the shifting phases of its long career. In virtue of that essence they all have something in common, a unity of thought and feeling, and an inward bond."

The concept of "Normative Judaism"

Jewish thinkers who hold that an essence of Judaism can be perceived tend to speak of "normative Judaism," with the implication that at the heart of the Jewish faith there is a hard, imperishable core, to be externally preserved, together with numerous peripheral ideas, expressed to be sure by great Jewish thinkers in different ages but not really essential to the faith, which could be dismissed if necessary as deviations.

Unfortunately for this line of thinking no criteria are available for distinguishing the essential from the ephemeral, so that a strong element of subjectivity is present in this whole approach. Almost invariably the process ends in a particular thinker's embracing ideas he holds to be true and valuable, discovering these reflected in the tradition and hence belonging to the "normative," while rejecting ideas he holds to be harmful or valueless as peripheral to Judaism, even though they are found in the tradition. Nor is the statistical approach helpful. An idea occurring very frequently in the traditional sources may be rejected by some thinkers on the grounds that it is untrue or irrelevant, while one hardly mentioned in the sources may assume fresh significance in a new situation, to say nothing of the difficulties in deciding which sources are to be considered the more authoritative. The absurdities which can result from the "normative Judaism" approach can be seen when, for example, contemporary thinkers with a dislike for asceticism, who wish at the same time to speak in the name of Judaism, virtually read out of the faith ascetics such as Bahya ibn Paquda and Moses Hayyim Luzzatto (see, for instance, Abba Hillel Silver, *Where Judaism Differed* (1957), 182–223).

Recognition of constant ideas

However, if due caution is exercised and no exaggerated claims made, the idea of a normative Judaism is not without value in that it calls attention to the undeniable fact that for all the variety of moods in Judaism's history there does emerge among the faithful a kind of consensus on the main issues. It has always been recognized, for instance, after the rise of Christianity and Islam, that these two religions are incompatible with Judaism and that no Jew can consistently embrace them while remaining an adherent of Judaism. The same applies to the Far Eastern religions. This, of course, is very different from affirming that there are no points of contact between Judaism and other faiths, or no common concerns. Nor has the idea of a Judaism divorced from the peoplehood of Israel ever made much headway, even in circles in which the doctrine of Israel's chosenness is a source of embarrassment. Nor does Jewish history know of a Torah-less Judaism, even though the interpretations of what is meant by Torah differ widely. The most important work of Jewish mysticism, the Zohar, speaks of three grades or stages bound one to the other – God, the Torah, and Israel (Zohar, Lev. 73a–b). Historically considered it is true that Judaism is an amalgam of three ideas – belief in God, God's revelation of the Torah to Israel, and Israel as the people which lives by the Torah in obedience to God. The interpretation of these ideas has varied from age to age, but the ideas themselves have remained constant.

B.   William Scott Green, "Old Habits Die Hard: Judaism in the Encyclopaedia of Religion"

Two bad habits plague the study of Judaism. The first is the inveterate reduction of Jewish religion to the Hebrew Scriptures. The second is the assimilation of Jewish

Source for Reading B.:   Critical Review of Books and Religion, 1989 (Atlanta, 1989: Scholars Press for the Journal of the American Academy of Religion and Journal of Biblical Literature), pp. 23–40.

religion to Jewish peoplehood and Jewish history. Both habits of mind fundamentally misrepresent Judaism, though in different ways, and both frustrate the integration of Judaic data into the study of religion. Astonishingly, both of them pervade the treatment of Judaism in *The Encyclopedia of Religion*.

The first habit equates Judaism with the Hebrew Scriptures. It has two variations, one Christian, the other Jewish. Since both are prevalent in *The Encyclopedia of Religion*, it will help to survey them briefly. At its most vulgar, the Christian form relegates Judaism to an ancient, pre-Christian text and denies Jewish religion any vitality beyond it. At its most refined, the Christian form acknowledges a Jewish religion beyond the Bible but assumes that Jewish Scripture embodies Judaism's characteristics. Either way, Judaism emerges as tantamount to the "Old Testament," at best secondary in importance to the religion that allegedly supplanted it in the New. On the other side, the Jewish version of this habit depicts biblical religion not as the precursor but as the earliest form of Judaism and posits a direct continuity between them. On this view, Judaism alone correctly understands the Hebrew Scriptures and is the authentic heir to the legacy of Israel. Common to both variations of this habit are the categories "biblical Judaism" and "post-biblical Judaism," which are alleged to differ from one another in degree, but not in kind.

To identify the Hebrew Bible as Judaism is a confusion of categories that mistakes Scripture for religion. The Hebrew Scriptures are indeed Judaism's Scripture, and no one denies that some parts constitute a kind of template for some aspects of Judaic theology and practice. But Jewish religion is historically, morphologically, mythically, and ritually different from – and in some crucial respects even discontinuous with – the religion of ancient Israel mandated in Scripture. The texts that give Judaism its distinctive cast and shape are the rabbinic documents all of which are postbiblical and none of which has the status of Scripture within Judaism. They represent, define, and determine the character of Jewish religion more than does anything written in the Hebrew Scriptures. The conflation of Judaism and Jewish Scripture may validate basic and legitimate Judaic and Christian theological positions, but it obscures the contours, and hence the integrity, of Judaism as a religion.

The second habit fuses the study of Judaism with the study of Jewish institutional and communal life and thereby confounds the history of Judaism with the history of the Jews. It reflects the ideological conviction – especially appealing in modern times – that all Jews can and should understand themselves as a single people bound together by a common political and social history that extends backwards, unbroken, from the present to ancient Israel. No one denies that nearly everywhere Jews have constituted a distinct social group. No one denies that, like every religion, Judaism developed within concrete social and political conditions and cannot be fully understood independent of the circumstances of the people who practiced it. But these factors do not justify equating Jewish religion with whatever Jews did or do together to preserve their collective identity. Although all who practice and affirm Judaism are Jews, not all Jews affirm(ed) and practice(d) Judaism. This habit of mind subsumes Judaism under Jewish social identity and mistakes ethnicity for religion.

Because these two habits depict Judaism as epiphenomenal – as the offshoot of Scripture or ethnicity – they thwart the use of Judaic materials as routine components in the study of religion. They make the issue of religion secondary and thus are incongruous to the stated goals of *The Encyclopedia of Religion*.

Principal Articles

The principal articles consist of "an overview," seven articles on the history of Judaism in what an editor's note (8:127) calls "major regions of the Diaspora" (inexplicably, Judaism in the State of Israel is ignored in this section), two entries on Jewish studies (one covering the years 1818–1919, the other 1919 to the present), four entries on the modern forms of Judaism (Conservative, Orthodox, Reconstructionist, and Reform), and an article on Jewish people.

The entry entitled "An Overview" is impressive for its scope, erudition, and occasional eloquence, and it exhibits an admirable sensitivity to the varied positions of contemporary Jewish religious denominations. But its usefulness is severely diminished because it eschews the categories of the study of religion in favor of a different approach. Instead of supplying a critical definition or morphology of Judaism, which would have helped readers distinguish Jewish religion both from other religions and from other Jewish activities, the entry offers the following agenda:

> This article describes postbiblical Judaism in terms of the evolving expression of the Jewish people's covenant with God, understood in liberal religious terms. (8:129)

The entry does not define the key term "covenant" or explain the placement of it as a distinguishing variable of Jewish religion. (The *Encyclopedia's* entry on "Covenant" is no help. Ironically – but typically for the *Encyclopedia* – it discusses covenant in the "Old Testament," at Qumran and in the New Testament, and in Christian theology and church history, but ignores Judaism.) More important, the last clause of this programmatic sentence should have disqualified this entry from an encyclopedia of religion because "liberal religious terms" are normative rather than descriptive. They are terms of apology rather than analysis. Describing Judaism in "liberal religious terms" – which is like describing Christianity in Unitarian-Universalist terms – undermines the study of Judaism as a religion in two ways. First, it imposes on Judaism – especially ancient Judaism – anachronistic categories that highlight the religion's least distinctive traits and suppress its most distinctive ones. Second, particularly when discussing modern Judaism, it blurs the distinction between what is religion and what is not.

Before briefly illustrating these problems, it will help to establish a proper historical framework. At the outset of its inaugural section ("From the Bible to

Rabbinic Judaism"), the entry claims that "we have little hard data by which to trace the progress from biblical to rabbinic Judaism, despite some help from the biblical Book of Daniel" (8:129). Actually, we have lots. The Apocrypha, Pseud-epigrapha, the Qumran Scrolls, the writings of Josephus, rabbinic traditions about Pharisees and Sadducees, the New Testament, inscriptional records, and recent archeological finds – none of which the entry mentions, and all of which are more relevant than Daniel – supply "hard data" about the different Judaisms that flourished in the Land of Israel during the so-called Second Temple period. Although none of these testifies explicitly about the origins of rabbinic Judaism, they display the Judaic options available in antiquity and thereby establish a reasonably certain historical and religious context for rabbinism's formation and emergence.

In a section entitled "Way of the Rabbis," the entry divides rabbinic Judaism into three categories: responsibility of the individual; family in rabbinic Judaism; and Jewish community and Jewish people. These may reflect the interests of contemporary liberal Judaism, but they seriously misrepresent the emphases of the rabbinic texts themselves. As a consequence, the entry ignores these prom-inent characteristics of rabbinic Judaism: purity/impurity, the transfer of women, the holiness of the Land of Israel, the Torah-scroll as a sacred object, the super-natural abilities of rabbis, the sage as "living Torah," the collectivity of rabbinic literature, the conflict between the authority of Scripture and that of reason, and the union of sanctification and salvation.

Instead of highlighting these, the entry begins its description of rabbinic Juda-ism with a discussion of androcentrism, which concludes:

> The rabbis did assign women a comparatively high personal and communal status. Nonetheless, by egalitarian standards, the differentiation of women's duties from those of men, which are viewed as the norm, imposes on women a loss of dignity and worth. (8:130)

By egalitarian standards, nearly every religion "imposes on women a loss of dignity and worth," so this observation, though correct, reveals nothing particu-lar about rabbinism. More important, the facile condemnation of rabbinic sexism obscures a distinctive trait of rabbinic religion. The third Order of the Mishnah is entitled "Women" (Nashim), and in the Babylonian Talmud – rabbinism's most authoritative document – it occupies nearly one-fifth of the whole. The transfer of women is a self-declared preoccupation of rabbinic religion, but the rabbinic construction of gender and conception of gender relations – beyond a cursory nod to the conventional realms of home and family (8:131–32) – are overlooked in this entry. Surely the issue of women reveals more about Judaism than the distinction between the "promise and problem" of liberal Judaism and the "prom-ise and problems" of Orthodoxy (8:142, 143). (Given the prominence of this issue here, it is ironic that the *Encyclopedia's* entry "Androcentrism" neglects Judaism, save for a reference to the Shekinah.)

The entry's second point about rabbinism is that it was democratic:

> The troubling issue of sexism aside, rabbinic Judaism is remarkably democratic. It calls all Jews to the same attainable virtues: righteousness in deed, piety of heart, and education of the mind. . . . The sacred elite, the rabbinate, remains open to any man and recognizes no substantial barriers between rabbis and other Jews. (8:130)

Again the imposition of "liberal religious terms" yields an unilluminating description. Which religion calls its followers to unrighteousness, impiety, and ignorance? This depiction misses the ritual totalization – in action, speech, and thought – that defines rabbinic halakhah. Moreover, it mistakes the absence of a religious hierarchy and central authority for democracy. Although in principle any Jewish male could join rabbinism's religious elite (as is the case in any religion without a caste system or dynastic priesthood), rabbis sharply differentiated themselves from the ordinary Jews among whom they lived – and thus objectified their claims to authority and leadership – by distinctive speech and dress, by supererogatory piety, and by assertions that their knowledge of Torah gave them supernatural powers. Finally, rabbis in no way constituted a "sacred" class. If they had, the barrier between them and other Jews would have been more than "substantial"; it would have been, as in the case of the Israelite priest-hood, absolute.

From the perspective of liberal religion it may appear that rabbinic Judaism was mainly a matter of "an ethnic group's unique covenant with God and its consequences for the lives of the individuals who constitute the group" (8:131) and that "the rabbis exhibited a clear-cut sense of the unity and identity of the Jewish people, who were the sole recipients of God's law and thus bore unique witness to God" (8:133), but rabbinic literature shows these assessments to be oversimplifications. "The Jewish people" is a modern conception. Rabbinic literature speaks of "Israel," a social metaphor that rabbis themselves defined and circumscribed. Thus, rabbinic Judaism excluded from membership in "Israel," either in this world or the next, categories of people – from Samaritans to sectarians – who were not Gentiles and whom we would regard, ethnically, to be Jews. It also included Gentile proselytes in the category "Israel" and compared to the high priest those Gentiles who fulfilled Torah. Indeed, as the entry itself notes (8:135), some sages granted "righteous" Gentiles a place in the "world to come" (a view made normative by Maimonides – the very redemption rabbinism denied to impious Jews. Religion and ethnicity were not coessential, and conformity to the sages' Torah was the ultimate arbiter.

The imposition of "liberal religious terms" also affects the entry's description of time and theology in rabbinism. The entry interprets what it calls "Jewish time" as consisting of "three interrelated dimensions": the "personal" (rites of passage), the "annual-historical" (Sabbath and yearly festivals), and the "eschatological" (the time of the Messiah). It notes that rabbinic Judaism infused new meanings into the Israelite agricultural festivals of Passover, Shavu'ot, and Sukkot, but deems these meanings "historical": "Thus, the undeviating cycle of the year becomes a reminder and renewal of the Jewish people's unique historical experience" (8:133). Attention to the *Encyclopedia's* stated purpose would have helped here. The history of religion demonstrates that the themes and events evoked by these rites and festivals – creation, paradise, and exodus from Egypt, the revelation to Moses at Sinai – are neither personal nor historical, but paradigmatic and, therefore, mythic. These Judaic rituals and holy days exhibit a pattern common to many religions. They confer sense and meaning on contingent autobiography and history by connecting them to the perduring realm Eliade called "sacred time." None of this is discussed in the entry.

To the liberal eye, Israelite religion and rabbinic Judaism appear equally unliberal, so critical distinctions between them are difficult to discern. Although this entry speaks of rabbinism's "mix of continuity and creativity" (8:120) and acknowledges its "creative development" and its "reverent continuity with the past," the section titled "Beliefs of the Rabbis" emphasizes "the primacy of continuity in rabbinic belief" (8:134), which yields the following judgment:

> the rabbis did not see the loss of the Temple as a disaster requiring major theological reconstruction; rather, they found it a confirmation of the Bible's teaching.... Continuing the faith of the Bible as they understood it, the rabbis indomitably transcended profane history. (8:134)

It is correct that rabbinic Judaism saw the hand of God in the Temple's second destruction, which it could not regard as a gratuitous caprice. But after the debacle of the Bar Kokhba rebellion – which signalled precisely the enduring loss, not merely the temporary absence, of the Temple and its cult – rabbis generated the "major theological reconstruction" this statement denies. To take one obvious example, the Mishnah developed an unprecedented theology of sanctification, which located the power to effect holiness in the motivations and intentions of the ordinary Israelite – defined, of course, in rabbinic terms – to which God himself responded. Moreover, the claim that rabbis follow the Bible "as they understood it" is no argument for continuity. Church fathers did the same thing, with dramatically different results. At issue is *how* rabbis read Scripture, *how* they understood it, and *how* they made it speak with a rabbinic voice – all of which the entry neglects.

The entry's treatment of the pietistic, mystical, and philosophic developments in medieval and early modern Judaism is more disciplined than its handling of the rabbinic period, as are its discussions of modern Jewish philosophy. But in its description of the impact of modernity on Judaism, the normativity and advocacy of its "liberal religious terms" are all too evident. If, in the entry's own terms, readers are to understand Judaism as the "evolving expression of the Jewish people's covenant *with* God" (italics added), how are they to comprehend secular Jewish activities – which by definition do not involve God – as manifestations of Jewish religion? How are they to make sense of the following claim?

> The interplay between Judaism and modernity can best be illustrated by the devotion of Jews to interpersonal relationships. American Jews today express the long-standing rabbinic commitment to family and community by their disproportionate involvement in the helping professions (such as teaching, social work, and psychotherapy) and their intense concern for family relationships. In these areas they demonstrate a dedication lacking in their observance of the halakic dietary law and laws governing sexual relations between spouses. They seem now to believe that sanctifying life, their covenant goal, now requires giving these general human activities priority in Jewish duty. (8:141–2)

This argument seems to suggest that the career choices of modern Jews are somehow religiously determined. If so, shall we also see the hand of God in the disproportionate involvement of Jews in the American entertainment and movie industry, in the international diamond trade, and among the cabbies of London? Alternatively, the argument may mean to say that some values that earlier developed in Judaism persist in the modern secular Jewish community. Even if that be so – and it is notoriously difficult to demonstrate convincingly – by which analytic criterion do we classify the current expression of those values as religion? If, as the entry later suggests, "high culture" is the "'Torah' of secular Jews" (8:143), if "being politically informed and involved" is for Jews "the modern equivalent of a commandment" (8:144), what would count as not Torah, as not commandment? If secularity is evidence of religion, what can these terms mean?

The overarching difficulty with this principal article on Judaism is that it commits the bad habit of confusing religion with ethnicity. As a consequence, it vitiates religion, the very phenomenon the encyclopedia was constructed to explain.

The seven historical/geographical entries cover the following topics: Judaism in the Middle East and North Africa to 1492, Judaism in the Middle East and North Africa since 1492, Judaism in Asia and Northeast Africa, Judaism in Southern Europe since 1500, and Judaism in the Western Hemisphere. As a group, these entries do not formally distinguish Jewish religion from the Jewish institutional and social histories of the periods and regions they cover, so the degree of explicit attention to religion varies from entry to entry.

The most disciplined in the focus on religion is the article on Asia and Northeast Africa, which is especially useful for its discussion of the religious rituals of the Falashas and the Jews of Cochin, and the entry on Northern and Eastern Europe to 1500. The latter neatly describes the emergence of the *hasid* (pietist) and Talmud scholar as representatives of new Judaic ideals, and it offers a concise and insightful description of the shift from the eleventh century to the twelfth:

> The righteous self-image, the reverence for the dead martyrs, German Hasidism, and the scholasticism of the tosafists were part of a twelfth-century transformation of classical Judaism into a "traditional" Ashkenazic Judaism. (8:183)

Regrettably, this observation, which would have made a fine focus for the entry as a whole, is not developed.

The entry on the Middle East and North Africa to 1492 limns important developments in post-talmudic Judaism and offers a nicely detailed discussion of Judaic philosophy. Interested readers will regret that it does not say more about what the responsa literature reveals of the Judaism(s) of lay communities or about how the commentaries to the Mishnah and Talmud influenced the reception and understanding of these documents.

The four remaining entries in this category are exercises in Jewish history rather than the history of Judaism. The entry on Judaism in Southern Europe draws a helpful distinction between popular religious practices and the "idealized religion of the intellectual leadership" (8:172). Focusing on the latter, it provides a short and solid cultural history of Jewish intellectual and literary life that stresses the emergence of new forms of literature and the impact of non-Jewish culture on the cultural life of Jews. The article on the Middle East and North Africa since 1492 deals primarily with historical questions of Jewish political and legal status, demography, and community organization. It offers brief treatments of Joseph Karo, Isaac Luria, and Shabbetai Zevi. The entry on Judaism in Northern and Eastern Europe since 1500 combines the social and political history of the Jews in Europe with a summary treatment of major religious developments: Hasidism, *musar*, Reform, and Neo-Orthodoxy. The last entry in the set, on Judaism in the Western Hemisphere, focuses heavily on cultural history and treats Jewish religion organizationally rather than morphologically. Surprisingly, it has little to say about the peculiarity of the American context. Curiously, it pays excessive attention to American rabbinical seminaries, as if the history of American Judaism took place in them. A difficulty of these four in particular is the absence of a theory that correlates Jewish history and Jewish religion.... The entry "Jewish People" discusses "the nature of Jewish corporate identity, from the biblical period to the present" (8:30). For the reasons specified above, this monolithic conception is both anachronistic and misleading, particularly as a principal article on Judaism. The authentic religious categories "Torah" or "Israel" – both of which, by contrast, are native to Judaic literature and liturgy of all regions, periods, and groups – would have been far superior choices. (Amazingly, the *Encyclopedia* has no article on "Israel" at all.) Because the entry fails to distinguish Judaic reflection on "Israel" from the social and political circumstances of the Jews, it lacks a consistent perspective. Thus, the qualified observation that "medieval Judaism did not become a multinational *religion* in the sense that Christianity or Islam did" (8:36) (italics added) becomes, one paragraph later, a claim for the "mononational character of the Jewish people" and, still later, for "the national unity of the Jews" (8:38) – a very different matter which the entry's own listing of the "wide diversity of Jewish subcultures" in the Middle Ages renders doubtful. The confusion of ethnicity with religion robs this entry of analytical coherence.

General Articles

If the habit of confusing religion with ethnicity mars some major articles classified under "Judaism," the habit of reducing Judaism to the Hebrew Scriptures dominates the treatment of Judaism in the rest of the *Encyclopedia*. Indeed, the assumption that these two fields are continuous appears basic to the *Encyclopedia's* very conception. Primary responsibility for both subjects was assigned to a single editor.

When the entries in the categories of "Religious Phenomena," "Art, Science, and Society," and "Scholarly Terms" do not equate Jewish religion with the Bible, they exercise two other alternatives with respect to it. They either inappropriately ignore Judaism or grossly misrepresent it.

Again, it is impossible to deal with all of these individually, so some representative examples – listed, for convenience, alphabetically – will have to suffice.

The entry "Apostasy," in a section titled "Apostasy in Jewish Ritual Law," observes as follows:

> Apostasy needed to be legally regulated. "Whole Israel has a share in the world to come.... And these don't have a share in the world to come: whoever says 'There is no resurrection of the dead in the Torah' and 'There is no Torah from heaven,' and the Epicurean" (San. 10:1). About 100 CE the twelfth prayer of the so-called eighteen benedictions has been expanded by the *birkat ha-minim* ("the blessing over the heretics"): "For apostates let there be no hope. The dominion of arrogance do thou speedily root out in our days. And let Christians and the sectarians be blotted out of the book of the living." This amplification implies that apostates had earlier been cursed in Jewish divine service. Christian literature corroborates that after the fall of the temple Jews cursed Christians. (1:354)

There is not space here to correct all the mischief done by this paragraph. Perhaps it is enough to note that the rendering of Mishnah Sanhedrin 10:1 is both vulgar and inaccurate, *birkat ha-minim* does not mean "blessing over the heretics," the benediction cited is from the fourth century not the first, and the word in it translated here as "Christians" means something else. Jewish liturgical cursing of Christians in antiquity is something John Chrysostom might have wished for, but there is scant evidence for it.

The entry "Authority" discusses Buddhism, Christianity, and Islam as "founded religions," treats "primitive" and "archaic" religions, but ignores Judaism (and Hinduism). Although rabbinic Judaism made benedictions into a virtual art form, and although the first tractate of the Mishnah and both Talmuds is entitled "Blessings," the entry "Blessing" discusses only the Hebrew Scriptures, Islam, and Christianity. Despite the extensive development of halakhic codes in Judaism – all of which are listed in the entry "Halakhah: History of" – the entry "Codes and Codification," under a section amazingly entitled "Jewish Codes," discusses only the Book of the Covenant and the "legal parts of Deuteronomy."

The entry "Charity" gives an incomplete account of Maimonides on charity and then observes:

> Notwithstanding occasional references to liberality toward the gentiles, in Jewish tradition "charity begins at home," and for many centuries the object of charity was the fellow Jew – the individual, the family circle, and the community. (3:222)

What this entry invidiously labels "occasional references to liberality toward the gentiles" is in fact an explicit talmudic injunction to give charity to the Gentile poor as to the Jewish poor (Babylonian Talmud, Gittin 61a). The article "Confession of Sins" bypasses Judaism, as does the long entry on the "Crusades," which has separate sections on Christian and Muslim "perspectives." The entry "Eschatology" discusses only the Bible and the Pseudepigrapha, and then moves on to Christianity. The entry "Faith" mentions Judaism in a section called "Faith-as-Obedience," but refers only to 1 Sam. 15:22. It supplies detailed examples from Confucianism, Christianity, Buddhism, and Islam. (Ironically, the entry "Obedience" barely mentions Judaism.)

Remarkably, Judaism finds no place in the entries on "Migration and Religion" and "Oral Tradition." This occurs despite the fact that migration, both forced and voluntary, accounts for many developments – and is a fundamental mythic theme – in Judaism; and the extensive literature about oral tradition in Judaism. Likewise, the major entry "Poetry and Religion," which has separate subentries on Indian, Chinese, Japanese, Christian, and Islamic religions, makes no mention of Judaism. Surely a few pages could have been given over to a discussion at least of the Psalms in Judaic liturgy, the medieval *piyyutim*, Judah HaLevi, and the Nobel Prize winner Nelly Sachs.

One final example will conclude this sampling. The entry "Revelation" observes:

> The Judaism of the scribes (beginning with Ezra, fourth cent. BCE) shows a tendency to regard revelation as closed and to see the prophetic movement as now past. The Jewish tradition generally accepted these positions. Only Jewish mysticism ... regarded not only the once-for-all historical act of divine revelation but also the repeated mystical expressions of God as revelatory; the function of the latter is to bring out the implications of the historical revelation and make it intelligible. (12:360)

Even the slightest familiarity with some reliable secondary work on the theory of "oral Torah" in rabbinic Judaism would show how misleading this judgment is.

Although there are exceptions to these ignorant and neglectful entries – the article "Canon," for instance – and although there may be some not examined here that do a better job than these, the examples listed above should encourage readers to be very cautious about believing anything they read about Judaism in the general articles of *The Encyclopedia of Religion*.

This survey of the treatment of Judaism in *The Encyclopedia of Religion* provides no occasion to rejoice. It shows, grimly, that longpracticed habits of mind – within both Jewish studies and the study of religion – continue to exert a powerful and sinister influence on scholarship. With respect to the study of religion, Judaism remains largely a ghettoized subject. With respect to Judaism, the study of religion exhibits a field-wide and virtually systemic ignorance.

Chapter 2

The Religious World of Ancient Israel to 586

Marvin A. Sweeney

A.   Genesis 15:1–21

Genesis 15 presents the initial narrative concerning the covenant between YHWH and Abraham, in which YHWH promises Abraham that he will become a great nation and will possess the land of Israel. Davidic imagery and concepts, such as YHWH's promise of a son and heir and the boundaries of the land that correspond to the Davidic empire (cf., 2 Sam. 8), play an important role in this chapter. It is to be read together with Genesis 17, in which Abram's name is changed to Abraham, which inaugurates circumcision as a sign of Abraham's adherence to YHWH.

1. Some time later, the word of YHWH came to Abram in a vision. He said, "Fear not, Abram, I am a shield to you; Your reward shall be very great." 2. But Abram said, "O YHWH God, what can You give me, seeing that I shall die childless, and the one in charge of my household is Dammesek Eliezer!" 3. Abram said further, "Since You have granted me no offspring, my steward will be my heir." 4. The word of YHWH came to him in reply, "That one shall not be your heir; none but your very own issue shall be your heir." 5. He took him outside and said, "Look toward heaven and count the stars, if you are able to count them." And He added, "So shall your offspring be." 6. And because he put his trust in YHWH, He reckoned it to his merit. 7. Then He said to him, "I am YHWH who brought you out from Ur of the Chaldeans to assign this land to you as a possession." 8. And he said, "YHWH God, how shall I know that I am to possess it?" 9. He answered, "Bring Me a three-year-old heifer, a three-year-old she-goat, a three-year-old ram, a turtledove, and a young bird." 10. He brought Him all these and cut them in two, placing each half opposite the other; but he did not cut up the bird. 11. Birds of prey came down upon the carcasses, and Abram drove them away. 12. As the sun was about to set, a deep sleep fell upon Abram, and a great

dark dread descended upon him. 13. And He said to Abram, "Know well that your offspring shall be strangers in a land not theirs, and they shall be enslaved and oppressed four hundred years; 14. but I will execute judgment on the nation they shall serve, and in the end they shall go free with great wealth. 15. As for you, You shall go to your fathers in peace; You shall be buried at a ripe old age. 16. And they shall return here in the fourth generation, for the iniquity of the Amorites is not yet complete." 17. When the sun set and it was very dark, there appeared a smoking oven, and a flaming torch which passed between those pieces. 18. On that day YHWH made a covenant with Abram saying, "To your offspring I assign this land, from the river of Egypt to the great river, the river Euphrates: 19. the Kenites, the Kenizzites, the Kadmonites, 20. the Hittites, the Perizzites, the Rephaim, 21. the Amorites, the Canaanites, the Girgashites, and the Jebusites."

B.   Exodus 13:1–16

Exodus 13 points to the interrelationship between the Exodus narrative and worship of YHWH in the Temple. In calling for the consecration of the first-born to YHWH, the chapter draws upon the requirement that all men in Israel are obligated to present the first-fruits of their crops and the first-born of their flocks and herds to YHWH as a sacrifice at the Temple (see Ex. 22:28–29; 23:10–19; 34:18–26; Deut. 16:1–17). It apparently presupposes that all first-born males in Israel are obligated for sacred service to YHWH (see Num. 3:11–13 and 8:13–19, which designate the tribe of Levi as priests in place of the first-born), and it underlies the notion that Israel is the first-born of YHWH and thus a kingdom of priests and a holy nation (see Ex. 4:22–23; 19:5–6).

1. YHWH spoke further to Moses saying, 2. "Consecrate to Me every first-born; man and beast, the first issue of every womb among the Israelites is Mine." 3. And Moses said to the people, "Remember this day, on which you went free from Egypt, the house of bondage, how YHWH freed you from it with a mighty hand: no leavened bread shall be eaten. 4. You go free on this day, in the month of Abib. 5. So when YHWH has brought you into the land of the Canaanites, the Hittites, the Amorites, the Hivites, and the Jebusites, which He swore to your fathers to give you, a land flowing with milk and honey, you shall observe in this month the following practice: 6. Seven days you shall eat unleavened bread, and on the seventh day there shall be a festival to YHWH. 7. Throughout the seven days unleavened bread shall be eaten; no leavened bread shall be found with you, and no leaven shall be found in all your territory. 8. And you shall explain to your son on that day, "It is because of what YHWH did for me when I went free from Egypt." 9. "And this shall serve you as a sign on your hand and as a reminder on

your forehead – in order that the Teaching of YHWH may be in your mouth – that with a mighty hand YHWH freed you from Egypt." 10. You shall keep this institution at its set time from year to year. 11. And when YHWH has brought you into the land of the Canaanites, as He swore to you and to your fathers, and has given it to you, 12. you shall set apart for YHWH every first issue of the womb: every male firstling that your cattle drop shall be YHWH's. 13. But every firstling ass you shall redeem with a sheep; if you do not redeem it, you must break its neck. And you must redeem every first-born male among your children. 14. And when, in time to come, your son asks you saying, "What does this mean?" you shall say to him, "It was with a mighty hand that YHWH brought us out from Egypt, the house of bondage. 15. When Pharaoh stubbornly refused to let us go, YHWH slew every first-born in the land of Egypt, the first-born of both man and beast. Therefore I sacrifice to YHWH every first male issue of the womb, but redeem every first-born among my sons." 16. And so it shall be as a sign upon your hand and as a symbol on your forehead that with a might hand YHWH freed us from Egypt.

C.   Exodus 15:1–21

The Song of Moses in Exodus 15 celebrates YHWH's victory over the Pharaoh of Egypt at the time of the Exodus. It is a liturgical composition that apparently was performed in the Temple much like the Psalms (see 1 Chr. 16). Note that it portrays the dividing of the Red Sea as a new act of creation in which dry land emerges from the waters, and it points to YHWH's sanctuary as the goal of the people's journey.

1. Then Moses and the Israelites sang this song to YHWH. They said, I will sing to YHWH, for He has triumphed gloriously; Horse and driver He has hurled into the sea. 2. YHWH is my strength and might; He is become my deliverance. This is my God and I will enshrine Him' The God of my father, and I will exalt Him. 3. YHWH, the Warrior – YHWH is His name! 4. Pharaoh's chariots and his army He has cast into the sea; and the pick of his officers are drowned in the Sea of Reeds. 5. The deeps covered them; They went down into the depths like a stone. 6. Your right hand, O YHWH, glorious in power, Your right hand, O YHWH, shatters the foe! 7. In Your great triumph You break Your opponents; You send forth Your fury, it consumes them like straw. 8. At the blast of Your nostrils the waters piled up, The deeps froze in the heart of the sea. 9. The foe said, "I will pursue, I will overtake, I will divide the spoil; My desire shall have its fill of them. I will bare my sword – My hand shall subdue them." 10. You made Your wind blow, the sea covered them; They sank like lead in the majestic waters. 11. Who is like You, O YHWH, among the celestials; Who is like You, majestic in holiness, Awesome in

splendor, working wonders! 12. You put out Your right hand, The earth swallowed them. 13. In Your love You lead the people You redeemed; In your strength You guide them to Your holy abode. 14. The people hear, they tremble; Agony grips them the dwellers in Philistia. 15. Now are the clans of Edom dismayed; The tribes of Moab – trembling grips them; All the dwellers in Canaan are aghast. 16. Terror and dread descend upon them; Through the might of Your arm they are still as stone – Till Your people cross over, O YHWH, Till Your people cross whom You have ransomed. 17. You will bring them and plant in Your own mountain, The place You made to dwell in, O YHWH, The sanctuary, O YHWH, which Your hands established. 18. YHWH will reign forever and ever! 19. For the horses of Pharaoh, with his chariots and horsemen, went into the sea; and YHWH turned back on them the waters of the sea; but the Israelites marched on dry ground in the midst of the sea. 20. Then Miriam the prophetess, Aaron's sister, took a timbrel in her hand, and all the women went out after her in dance with timbrels. 21. And Miriam chanted for them, Sing to YHWH, for He has triumphed gloriously; Horse and driver He has hurled into the sea.

D.   Exodus 20:1–14

Exodus 20 presents one version of the Ten Commandments; the other appears in Deuteronomy 5. The Ten Commandments constitute a basic summation of the principles of YHWH's Torah or "Instruction" to the people of Israel revealed at Mt. Sinai. The present version points to the observance of Shabbat as an act of YHWH's creation; the version in Deuteronomy 5 differs in that it points to YHWH's deliverance of Israel from Egypt as the basis for Shabbat observance.

1. God spoke all these words, saying: 2. I YHWH am your God who brought you out of the land of Egypt, the house of bondage: 3. You shall have no other gods besides Me. 4. You shall not make for yourself a sculptured image, or any likeness of what is in the heavens above, or on the earth below, or in the waters under the earth. 5. You shall not bow down to them or serve them. For I YHWH your God am an impassioned God, visiting the guilt of the parents upon the children, upon the third and upon the fourth generations of those who reject Me, 6. but showing kindness to the thousandth generation of those who love Me and keep My commandments. 7. You shall not swear falsely by the name of YHWH your God; for YHWH will not clear one who swears falsely by His name. 8. Remember the sabbath day and keep it holy. 9. Six days you shall labor and do all your work, 10 but the seventh day is a sabbath of YHWH your God: you shall not do any work – you, your son or daughter, your male or female slave, or your cattle, or the stranger who is within your settlements. 11. For in six days YHWH made

heaven and earth and sea, and all that is in them, and He rested on the seventh day; therefore YHWH blessed the sabbath day and hallowed it. 12. Honor your father and your mother, that you may long endure on the land YHWH your God is assigning to you. 13. You shall not murder. You shall not commit adultery. You shall not steal. You shall not bear false witness against your neighbor. 14. You shall not covet your neighbor's house: you shall not covet your neighbor's wife, or his male or female slave, or his ox of his ass, or anything that is your neighbor's.

E. Deuteronomy 15:1–18

Ancient Israelite law is designed to promote justice in society at large. The following laws take up the issue of slavery, in which a man or woman might undertake service to a creditor in payment for a debt. The term of service and the conditions for release are carefully laid out. Some maintain that this is a revision of an earlier law in Exodus 21:1–11 that was designed to give greater rights to the debtor.

1. Every seventh year you shall practice remission of debts. 2. This shall be the nature of the remission: every creditor shall remit the due that he claims from his fellow; he shall not dun his fellow or kinsman for the remission proclaimed is of YHWH. 3. You may dun a foreigner; but you must remit whatever is due from your kinsmen. 4. There shall be no needy among you – since YHWH your God will bless you in the land that YHWH your God is giving you as a hereditary portion – 5. if only you heed YHWH your God and take to keep all this Instruction that I enjoin upon you this day. 6. For YHWH your God will bless you as He has promised you: you will extend loans to many nations, but require none yourself; you will dominate many nations, the will not dominate you. 7. If, however, there is a needy person among you, one of your kinsmen in any of your settlements in the land that YHWH your God is giving you, do not harden your heart and shut your hand against your needy kinsman. 8. Rather, you must open your hand and lend him sufficient for whatever he needs. 9. Beware lest you harbor the base thought, "The seventh year, the year of remission, is approaching," so that you are mean to your needy kinsman and give him nothing. He will cry out YHWH against you, and you will incur guilt. 10. Give to him readily and have no regrets when you do so, for in return YHWH your God will bless you in all your efforts and in all your undertakings. 11. For there will never cease to be needy ones in your land, which is why I command you: open your hand to the poor and needy kinsman in your land. 12. If a fellow Hebrew, man or woman, is sold to you, he shall serve you six years, and in the seventh year you shall set him free. 13. When you set him free, do not let him go empty-handed: Furnish him out of the flock, threshing floor, and vat, with which YHWH your God has blessed you. 15. Bear in

mind that you were slaves in the land of Egypt and YHWH your God redeemed you; therefore I enjoin this commandment upon you today. 16. But should he say to you, "I do not want to leave you" – for he loves you and your household and is happy with you – 17. you shall take an awl and put it through his ear into the door, and he shall become your slave in perpetuity. Do the same with your female slave. 18. When you do set him free, do not feel aggrieved; for in six years he has given you double the service of a hired man. Moreover, YHWH your God will bless you in all you do.

F.   Deuteronomy 16:1–17

Deuteronomy 16:1–17 relates the major festivals of the Israelite calendar, Pesach or Passover at the beginning of the grain harvest in the spring, Shavuot or Weeks at the conclusion of the grain harvest in the late spring or early summer, and Sukkot or Tabernacles at the time of the grape and olive harvest immediately prior to the rainy season in the fall. Note Deuteronomy 26, in which the Israelite farmer relates the sacred history of Israel at the time that he presents his offering at the Temple, thereby thanking YHWH for the benefits bestowed upon him.

1. Observe the month of Abib and offer a passover sacrifice to YHWH your God, for it was in the month of Abib, at night, that YHWH your God freed you from Egypt. 2. You shall slaughter the passover sacrifice for YHWH your God, from the flock and the heard, in the place where YHWH will choose to establish His name. 3. You shall not eat anything leavened with it; for seven days thereafter you shall eat unleavened bread, bread of distress – for you departed from the land of Egypt hurriedly – so that you may remember the day of your departure from the land of Egypt as long as you live. 4. For seven days no leaven shall be found with you in all your territory, and none of the flesh of what you slaughter on the evening of the first day shall be left until morning. 5. You are not permitted to slaughter the passover sacrifice in any of the settlements that YHWH your God is giving you; 6. but at the place where YHWH your God will choose to establish His name, there alone shall you slaughter the passover sacrifice, in the evening, at sundown, the time of day when you departed from Egypt. 7. You shall cook and eat it at the place that YHWH your God will choose; and in the morning you may start back on your journey home. 8. After eating unleavened bread six days, you shall hold a solemn gathering for YHWH your God on the seventh day; you shall do no work. 9. You shall count off seven weeks; start to count the seven weeks when the sickle is first put to the standing grain. 10. Then you shall observe the Feast of Weeks for YHWH your God, offering your freewill contribution according as YHWH your God has blessed you. 11. You shall rejoice before YHWH your God with your son

and daughter, your male and female slave, the Levite in your communities, and the stranger, the fatherless, and the widow in your midst, at the place where YHWH your God will choose to establish His name. 12. Bear in mind that you were slaves in Egypt, and take care to obey these laws. 13. After the ingathering from your threshing floor and your vat, you shall hold the Feast of Booths for seven days. 14. You shall rejoice in your festival, with your son and daughter, your male and female slave, the Levite, the stranger, the fatherless, and the widow in your communities. 15. You shall hold festival for YHWH your God seven days, in the place that YHWH your God will choose; for YHWH your God will bless all your crops and all your undertakings, and you shall have nothing but joy. 16. Three times a year – on the Feast of Unleavened Bread, on the Feast of Weeks, and on the Feast of Booths – all your males shall appear before YHWH your God in the place that He will choose. They shall not appear before YHWH empty-handed, 17 but each with his own gift, according to the blessing that YHWH your God has bestowed upon you.

G.   2 Samuel 6:1–19

David's selection of Jerusalem as his political and religious capital ensured his rule over all Israel. By bringing the Ark of YHWH to Jerusalem, David signaled his adherence to YHWH and laid the basis by which the House of David and Jerusalem would be regarded as YHWH's chosen monarch and city.

1. David again assembled all the picked men of Israel, thirty thousand strong. 2. Then David and all the troops that were with him set out from Baalim of Judah to bring up from there the Ark of God to which the Name was attached, the name YHWH of Hosts Enthroned on the Cherubim. 3. They loaded the Ark of God onto a new cart and conveyed it from the house of Abinadab, which was on the hill; and Abinadab's sons, Uzza and Ahio, guided the new cart. 4. They conveyed it from the house of Abinadab, which was on the hill, Uzzah walking alongside the Ark of God and Ahio walking in front of the Ark. 5. Meanwhile, David and all the House of Israel danced before YHWH to the sound of all kinds of cypress wood instruments, with lyres, harps, timbrels, sistrums, and cymbals. 6. But when they came to the threshing floor of Nacon, Uzzah reached out for the Ark of God and grasped it, for the oxen had stumbled. 7. YHWH was incensed at Uzzah, and God struck him down on the spot for his indiscretion, and he died there beside the Ark of God. 8. David was distressed because YHWH had inflicted a breach upon Uzzah; and that place was named Perez-uzzah as it is still called. 9. David was afraid of YHWH that day; he said, "How can I let the Ark of YHWH come to me?" 10. So David would not bring the Ark to his place in the City of David; instead, he diverted it to the house of Obed-edom the Gittite. 11. The Ark of YHWH remained in the house

of Obed-edom the Gittite three months, and YHWH blessed Obed-edom and his whole household. 12. It was reported to King David: "YHWH has blessed Obed-edom's house and all that belongs to him because of the Ark of God." Thereupon David went and brought up the Ark of God from the house of Obed-edom to the City of David, amid rejoicing. 13. When the bearers of the Ark of YHWH had moved forward six paces, he sacrificed an ox and a fatling. 14. David whirled with all his might before YHWH; David was girt with a linen ephod. 15. Thus David and all the House of Israel brought up the Ark of YHWH with shouts and with blasts of the horn. 16. As the Ark of YHWH entered the City of David, Michal daughter of Saul looked out of the window and saw King David leaping and whirling before YHWH; and she despised him for it. 17. They brought in the Ark of YHWH and set it up in its place inside the tent which David had pitched for it, and David sacrificed burnt offerings and offerings of well-being before YHWH. 18. When David finished sacrificing the burnt offerings and the offerings of well-being, he blessed the people in the name of YHWH of Hosts. 19. And he distributed among all the people – the entire multitude of Israel, man and woman alike – to each a loaf of bread, a cake made in a pan, and a raisin cake. Then all the people left for their homes.

H.   2 Samuel 7:1–16

Nathan's prophecy in 2 Samuel 7 articulates the basic theological outlook of the Davidic dynasty, i.e., that YHWH had chosen David as king and that the House of David would rule eternally in Jerusalem. Note the pun concerning the word "house," i.e., David proposes to build a "house" or "Temple" for YHWH, but YHWH proposes instead to build a "house" or "dynasty" for David. Note also that the prophecy allows for the punishment of Davidic monarchs when they do wrong, but the oracle assures David of YHWH's continuous support for his heirs.

1. When the king was settled in his palace and YHWH had granted him safety from all the enemies around him, 2. the king said to the prophet Nathan: "Here I am dwelling in a house of cedar, while the Ark of YHWH abides in a tent!" 3. Nathan said to the king, "Go and do whatever you have in mind, for YHWH is with you." 4. But that same night the word of YHWH came to Nathan: 5. "Go and say to My servant David: Thus said YHWH: Are you the one to build a house for Me to dwell in? 6. From the day that I brought the people of Israel out of Egypt to this day I have not dwelt in a house, but have moved about in Tent and Tabernacle. 7. As I moved about wherever the Israelites went, did I ever reproach any of the tribal leaders whom I appointed to care for My people Israel: Why have you built Me a house of cedar? 8. Further, say thus to My servant David: Thus said

YHWH of Hosts: I took you from the pasture, from following the flock, to be ruler of My people Israel, 9. and I have been with you wherever you went, and have cut down all your enemies before you. Moreover, I will give you great renown like that of the greatest men on earth. 10. I will establish a home for My people Israel and will plant them firm, so that they shall dwell secure and shall tremble no more. Evil men shall not oppress them any more as in the past, 11. ever since I appointed chieftains over My people Israel. I will give you safety from all you enemies. YHWH declares to you that He, YHWH, will establish a house for you. 12. When your days are done and you lie with your fathers, I will raise up your offspring after you, one of your own issue, and I will establish his kingship. 13. He shall build a house for My name, and I will establish his royal throne forever. 14. I will be a father to him, and he shall be a son to Me. When he does wrong, I will chastise him with the rod of men and the affliction of mortals; 15. but I will never withdraw My favor from him as I withdrew it from Saul, whom I removed to make room for you. 16. Your house and your kingship shall ever be secure before you; your throne shall be established forever."

I.   Isaiah 11:1–16

The prophet Isaiah was active in Jerusalem during the late eighth century B C E when the Assyrian empire destroyed Israel and subjugated Judah. He was firmly based in the Davidic tradition that YHWH would protect Jerusalem and the dynasty, but bring punishment if the king did wrong. When Ahaz declined to rely on YHWH during the Syro-Ephraimitic War, Isaiah maintained that Assyria would punish Judah for the king's lack of faith. Isaiah 11 points to the time when righteous Davidic rule would be restored over all Israel and the former Davidic empire, and the exiles from Assyria and Egypt would return home. Note the analogy between the Assyrian exile and the exodus from Egypt.

1. But a shoot shall grow out of the stump of Jesse, a twig shall sprout from his stock. 2. The spirit of YHWH shall alight upon him: a spirit of wisdom and insight, a spirit of counsel and valor, a spirit of devotion and reverence for YHWH. 3. He shall sense the truth by his reverence for YHWH: He shall not judge by what his eyes behold, nor decide by what his ears perceive. 4. Thus he shall judge the poor with equity and decide with justice for the lowly of the land. He shall strike down a land with the rod of his mouth and slay the wicked with the breath of his lips. 5. Justice shall be the girdle of his loins, and faithfulness the girdle of his waist. 6. The wolf shall dwell with the lamb, the leopard lie down with the kid; the calf, the beast of prey, and the fatling together, with a little boy to herd them. 7. The cow and the bear shall graze, their young shall lie down together; and the lion, like the ox, shall eat straw. 8. A babe shall play over a viper's hole, and an infant pass his

hand over an adder's den. 9. In all of My sacred mount nothing evil or vile shall be done; for the land shall be filled with devotion to YHWH as water covers the sea. 10. In that day, the stock of Jesse that has remained standing shall become a standard to peoples – nations shall seek his counsel and his abode shall be honored. 11. In that day, My Lord shall apply His hand again to redeeming the other part of His people from Assyria – as also from Egypt, Pathros, Nubia, Elam, Shinar, Hamath, and the coastlands. 12. He will hold up a signal to the nations and assemble the banished of Israel, and gather the dispersed of Judah from the four corners of the earth. 13. Then Ephraim's envy shall cease and Judah's harassment shall end; Ephraim shall not envy Judah, and Judah shall not harass Ephraim. 14. They shall pounce on the back of Philistia to the west, and together plunder the peoples of the east; Edom and Moab shall be subject to them and the children of Ammon shall obey them. 15. YHWH will dry up the tongue of the Egyptian sea. – He will raise His hand over the Euphrates with the might of His wind and break it into seven wadis, so that it can be trodden dry-shod. 16. Thus, there shall be a highway for the other part of His people out of Assyria, such as there was for Israel when it left the land of Egypt.

J.   Jeremiah 7:1–20

Jeremiah was a Levitical priest, apparently descended from the Elide line from the Temple at Shiloh (see 1 Sam. 1–4). His viewpoint reflects that of the Mosaic tradition in which YHWH's Torah or Instruction serves as the guiding principle for Israel's life. Although he was likely an early supporter of Josiah's Torah-based reform (see 2 Kgs. 22–23), Josiah's early death convinced him that Judah would suffer punishment like Israel. His Temple sermon in Jeremiah 7 points to the futility of relying solely on the Temple as a source of security, and calls upon the people to observe YHWH's Torah. Note his references to the destruction of the Shiloh sanctuary and to the ten commandments.

1. The word which came to Jeremiah from YHWH: 2. Stand at the gate of the House of YHWH, and there proclaim this word: Hear the word of YHWH, all you of Judah who enter these gates to worship YHWH! 3. Thus said YHWH of Hosts, the God of Israel: Mend your ways and your actions, and I will let you dwell in this place. 4. Don't put your trust in illusions and say, "The Temple of YHWH, the Temple of YHWH, the Temple of YHWH are these buildings." 5. No, if you really mend your ways and your actions; if you execute justice between one man and another; 6. if you do not oppress the stranger, the orphan, and the widow; if you do not shed the blood of the innocent in this place; if you do not follow other gods, to your own hurt – 7. then only will I let you dwell in this place, in the land that gave to your fathers for all time. 8. See, you are relying on illusions that are of no

avail. 9. Will you steal and murder and commit adultery and sear falsely, and sacrifice to Baal, and follow other gods whom you have not experienced, 10, and then come and stand before Me in this House which bears My name and say, "We are safe"? – Safe to do all these abhorrent things! 11. Do you consider this House, which bears My name, to be a den of thieves? As for Me, I have been watching – declares YHWH. 12. Just go to My place at Shiloh, where I had established My name formerly, and see what I did to it because of the wickedness of My people Israel. 13. And now, because you do all these things – declares YHWH – and though I spoke to you persistently, you would not listen; and though I called to you, you would not respond – 14. Therefore I will do to the House which bears My name, on which you rely, and to the place which I gave you and your fathers, just what I did to Shiloh. 15. And I will cast you out of My presence as I cast out your brothers, the whole brood of Ephraim. 16. As for you, do not pray for this people, do not raise a cry of prayer on their behalf, do not plead with Me; for I will not listen to you. 17. Don't you see what they are doing in the towns of Judah and in the streets of Jerusalem? 18. The children gather sticks, the fathers build the fire, and the mothers knead dough, to make cakes for the Queen of Heaven, and they pour libations to other gods, to vex Me. 19. Is it Me they are vexing? – says YHWH. It is rather themselves, to their own disgrace. 20. Assuredly, thus said YHWH God: My wrath and My fury will be poured out upon this place, on man and on beast, on the trees of the field and the fruit of the soil. It shall burn, with none to quench it."

K.   Psalm 19

Psalm 19 extols YHWH as the creator of the universe and as the giver of Torah. Insofar as the Temple is the source for instruction in YHWH's Torah in ancient Israel, this liturgical hymn apparently was employed during the course of Temple worship to reinforce the teaching of Torah to the people (see Deut. 31:10–13, which calls for the Torah to be read publicly every seven years).

1. For the leader. A psalm of David. 2. The heavens declare the glory of God, the sky proclaims His handiwork. 3. Day to day makes utterance, night to night speaks out. 4. There is no utterance, there are no words, whose sound goes unheard. 5. Their voice carries throughout the earth, their words to the end of the world. He places in them a tent for the sun, who is like a groom coming forth from the chamber, like a hero, eager to run his course. 7. His rising-place is at one end of heaven, and his circuit reaches the other; nothing escapes his heat. 8. The teaching of YHWH is perfect, renewing life; the decrees of YHWH are enduring, making the simple wise; 9. The precepts of YHWH are just, rejoicing the heart; the instruction of YHWH is lucid, making the eyes light up. 10. The fear of YHWH is

pure, abiding forever; the judgments of YHWH are true, righteous altogether, 11. more desirable than gold, than much fine gold; sweeter than honey, than drippings of the comb. 12. Your servant pays them heed; in obeying them there is much reward. 13. Who can be aware of errors? Clear me of unperceived guilt, and from willful sins keep Your servant; let them not dominate me; then shall I be blameless and clear of grave offense. 15. May the words of my mouth and the prayer of my heart be acceptable to You, O YHWH, my rock and my redeemer.

L.   Psalm 132

Psalm 132 points to the close interrelationship between the House of David and the Jerusalem Temple. Just as David had gone to great effort to find a home for YHWH and the Ark of the Covenant, so YHWH would swear to David that his dynasty would endure forever. Note that the Ark symbolically represents YHWH's kingship, as it serves as a footstool for YHWH's heavenly throne in the Holy of Holies of the Temple.

1. A song of ascents. O YHWH, remember in David's favor his extreme self-denial, 2 how he swore to YHWH, vowed to the Mighty One of Jacob, 3. "I will not enter my house, nor will I mount my bed, 4. I will not give sleep to my eyes or slumber to my eyelids 5. until I find a place for YHWH, an abode for the Mighty One of Jacob." 6. We heard it was in Ephrath; we came upon it in the region of Jaar. 7. Let us enter His abode, bow at His footstool. 8. Advance, O YHWH, to Your resting-place, You and Your mighty Ark! 9. Your priests are clothed in triumph; Your loyal ones sing for joy. 10. For the sake of Your servant David do not reject Your anointed one. 11. YHWH swore to David a firm oath that He will not renounce, "One of your own issue I will set upon your throne. 12. If your sons keep My covenant and My decrees that I teach them, then their sons also, to the end of time, shall sit upon your throne." 13. For YHWH has chosen Zion; He has desired it for His seat. 14. "This is my resting place for all time; here I will dwell, for I desire it. 15. I will amply bless its store of food, give its needy their fill of bread. 16. I will clothe its priests in victory, its loyal ones shall sing for joy. 17. There I will make a horn sprout for David; I have prepared a lamp for My anointed one. 18. I will clothe his enemies in disgrace, while on him his crown shall sparkle."

Chapter 3

Judaism and the Hebrew Scriptures

Philip R. Davies

A. The Habakkuk *Pesher* from Qumran (1QpHab), cols. 7–9

The name *"pesher"* is given to a particular kind of scriptural commentary of which several examples were found at Qumran. The name comes from the Hebrew word for "interpretation" and is frequently used to introduced the commentary that follows the citation of the scriptural verse. The *pesharim* are mostly devoted to prophetic texts, including Psalms (for David was regarded as a prophet), and they presuppose that prophetic words refer to the end-time and that the end-time is now. The *meaning* of the prophecy was not known to the prophets themselves, so that its time of fulfillment is a secret (Hebrew: *raz*). To unlock the secret requires divine inspiration, just as did the original prophecy, and such knowledge was given to the "Teacher of Righteousness," who is generally believed to have been the founder of the Qumran sect. The meaning of each verse, then, is dependent on neither the historical context of the original prophecy nor any literary context.

In a *pesher* exegesis, each statement (usually a verse or part of a verse) is viewed as an autonomous prediction and interpreted accordingly, without reference to the passage as a whole. Because the interpretation is inspired, there need be no logical connection between the "secret" (the text) and the "interpretation," but, in fact, individual words and phrases are given consistent equivalents, so that, for example, "wicked" always refers to the "wicked priest" and "righteous" to the Teacher of Righteousness. This kind of commentary fulfills several purposes. It sets out to show that everything is pre-ordained by God and that the events happening in the time of the readers point to an imminent "end." Another important purpose, however, is to demonstrate that

Source for reading A.: F. Garcia Martinez, *The Dead Sea Scrolls Translated* (Leiden: Brill/Grand Rapids: Eerdmans, second edition, 1996), pp. 200–1.

since the ancient prophets alluded to events in the history of the Teacher's followers, this group obviously constitutes the true Israel and is central in the divine plan.

The events alluded to in this *pesher* remain largely obscure to the modern reader, but the references to the Romans (under the name of "Kittim") place them in the middle of the first century B C E. Presumably those who first read this commentary were familiar with the history of their own group, to which the contents largely refer.

Col. VII   *1* And God told Habakkuk to write what was going to happen *2* to the last generation, but he did not let him know the end of the age. *3 Blank* And as for what he says: *Hab 2:2*] «So that the one who reads it/may run/». *4* Its interpretation concerns the Teacher of Righteousness, to whom God has disclosed *5* all the mysteries of the words of his servants, the prophets. *Hab 2:3* For the vision has an appointed time, it will have an end and not fail. *Blank 7* Its interpretation: the final age will be extended and go beyond all that *8* the prophets say, because the mysteries of God are wonderful. *9 Hab 2:3b* Though it might delay, wait for it; it definitely has to come and will not *10* delay. *Blank* Its interpretation concerns the men of truth, *11* those who observe the Law, whose hands will not desert the service *12* of truth when the final age is extended beyond them, because *13* all the ages of God will come at the right time, as he established *14* for them in the mysteries of his prudence. *Hab 2:4* See, *15* [his soul within him] is conceited and does not give way. *Blank* Its interpretation: they will double *16* [persecution] upon them [and find no mercy] at being judged. *Blank*

Col. VIII   *1* Its interpretation concerns all observing the Law in the House of Judah, whom *2* God will free from punishment on account of their deeds and of their loyalty *3* to the Teacher of Righteousness. *Hab 2:5–6* Surely wealth will corrupt the boaster *4* and one who distends his jaws like the abyss and is as greedy as death will not be restrained. *5* All the nations ally against him, all the peoples collaborate against him. *6* Are they not all, perhaps, going to chant verses against him, explaining riddles at his expense? *7* They shall say: Ah, one who amasses the wealth of others! How long will he load himself *8* with debts? *Blank* Its interpretation concerns the Wicked Priest, who *9* is called by the name of loyalty at the start of his office. However, when he ruled *10* over Israel his heart became conceited, he deserted God and betrayed the laws for the sake of *11* riches. And he stole and hoarded wealth from the brutal men who had rebelled against God. *12* And he seized public money, incurring additional serious sin. *13* And he performed repulsive acts of every type of filthy licentiousness. *Hab 2:7–8* Will *14* your creditors not suddenly get up, and those who shake you wake up? You will be their prey. *15* Since you pillaged many countries the rest of the peoples will pillage you. *16 Blank* The interpretation of the word concerns the Priest who rebelled *17* [...] the precepts of [God...]

Col. IX   *1* being distressed by the punishments of sin; the horrors of *2* terrifying maladies acted upon him, as well as vengeful acts on his fleshly body. And what *3* it says: *Hab 2:8a* «Since you pillaged many countries the rest of the peoples will pillage you». *Blank* Its interpretation concerns the last priests of Jerusalem, 5 who will accumulate riches and loot from plundering the peoples. 6 However, in the last days their riches and their loot will fall into the hands 7 of the army of the Kittim. *Blank* For they are *Hab 2:8a* «the greatest of the peoples». 8 *Hab 2:8b* For the human blood [split] and the violence done to the country, the city and all its/occupants/. *Blank* 9 Its interpretation concerns the Wicked Priest, since for the wickedness against the Teacher of 10 Righteousness and the members of his council God delivered him into the hands of his enemies to disgrace him 11 with a punishment, to destroy him with bitterness of soul for having acted wickedly 12 against his elect. *Hab 2:9–11* Woe to anyone putting ill-gotten gains in his house, placing 13 his nest high up to escape the power of evil! You have planned the insult 14 to your house, exterminating many countries and sinning against your soul. For 15 the stones will shout from the walls, and the wooden beams will answer.

B.   Josephus, *Antiquities* I:13 (222–236)

The well-known story of the binding of Isaac (Gen. 22) is retold by Josephus, writing at the end of the first century CE, with several interesting amendments and additions. The scriptural account is notoriously reticent about details and especially about the feelings of those involved, and Josephus, writing for a Greek-reading audience that expected its emotions to be engaged, supplies these in abundance. He also presents both Isaac and Abraham as models of virtue who would appeal to Jewish, Greek, and Roman readers because they show obedience, courage, and suppression of personal desire in the face of a divine imperative. The freedom with which Josephus treats the biblical story is in no way unusual; rather it is quite typical of the license taken by writers who wished to have scriptural stories dressed in the fashion of their own times, illustrating the lessons and virtues that were appropriate.

Particularly important here is Isaac's age: in Genesis he is a "lad" (Heb.: *na'ar*) and an almost silent victim. The Isaac of Josephus is a man eligible for military service (25 years) and prepared to be offered as a martyr and to meet Abraham's own father, God – the reward of the martyr being resurrection. This development of Isaac as a main character is in line with a wider trend among Jewish interpreters by which he changed from an innocent victim into a willing one and then, finally, into one whose act can bring atonement for Israel through a sacrifice that anticipates (and so replaces) the daily Temple sacrifice. This is how the Rabbinic doctrine known as the "Akedah," "Binding," came about, paralleling the Christian celebration of Isaac's sacrifice as a premonition of the death of Christ.

Source for reading B.:   Thackeray, in the Loeb edition (London: Heinemann/New York: Putnam, 1930), pp. 109–17; without footnotes.

(xiii. 1) Now Isaac was passionately beloved of his father Abraham, being his only son and born to him "on the threshold of old age" through the bounty of God. On his side, the child called out the affection of his parents and endeared himself to them yet more by the practice of every virtue, showing a devoted filial obedience and a zeal for the worship of God. Abraham thus reposed all his own happiness on the hope of leaving his son unscathed when he departed this life. This object he indeed attained by the will of God, who, however, desiring to make trial of his piety towards Himself, appeared to him and after enumerating all the benefits that He had bestowed upon him – how He had made him stronger than his enemies, and how it was His benevolence to which he owed his present felicity and his son Isaac – required him to offer up that son by his own hand as a sacrifice and victim to Himself. He bade him take the child up to the Morian Mount, erect an altar and make a holocaust of him: thus would he manifest his piety towards Himself, if he put the doing of God's good pleasure even above the life of his child.

(2) Abraham, deeming that nothing would justify disobedience to God and that in everything he must submit to His will, since all that befell His favoured ones was ordained by His providence, concealed from his wife God's commandment and his own resolve concerning the immolation of the child; nay, revealing it not even to any of his household, lest haply he should have been hindered from doing God's service, he took Isaac with two servants and having laden an ass with the requisites for the sacrifice departed for the mountain. For two days the servants accompanied him, but on the third, when the mountain was in view, he left his companions in the plain and proceeded with his son alone to that mount whereon king David afterwards erected the temple. They brought with them all else needed for the sacrifice except a victim. Isaac, therefore, who was now twenty-five years of age, while constructing the altar, asked what sacrifice they were about to offer, having no victim; to which his father replied that God would provide for them, seeing that He had power alike to give men abundance of what they had not and to deprive of what they had those who felt assured of their possessions: He would therefore grant him too a victim, should He vouchsafe to grace his sacrifice with His presence.

(3) But when the altar had been prepared and he had laid the cleft wood upon it and all was ready, he said to his son: "My child, myriad were the prayers in which I besought God for thy birth, and when thou camedst into the world, no pains were there that I did not lavish upon thine upbringing, no thought had I of higher happiness than to see thee grown to man's estate and to leave thee at my death heir to my dominion. But, since it was by God's will that I became thy sire and now again as pleases Him I am resigning thee, bear thou this consecration valiantly; for it is to God I yield thee, to God who now claims from us this homage in return for the gracious favour He has shown me as my supporter and ally. Aye, since thou wast born (out of the course of nature, so) quit thou now this life not by the common road, but sped by thine own father on thy way to God, the Father of all, through the rites of sacrifice. He, I ween, accounts it not meet for thee to depart this life by sickness or war or by any of the calamities that commonly befall mankind, but amid prayers and sacrificial ceremonies would receive thy soul and keep it near to Himself; and for me thou shalt be a protector and stay of my old age – to which end above all I nurtured thee – by giving me God in the stead of thyself."

(4) The son of such a father could not but be bravehearted, and Isaac received these words with joy. He exclaimed that he deserved never to have been born at all, were he to reject the decision of God and of his father and not readily resign himself to what was the will of both, seeing that, were this the resolution of his father alone, it would have been impious to disobey; and with that he rushed to the altar and his doom. And the deed would have been accomplished, had not God stood in the way, for He called upon Abraham by name, forbidding him to slay the lad. It was, He said, from no craving for human blood that He had given command for the slaughter of his son, nor had He made him a father only to rob him in such impious fashion of his offspring; no, He wished but to test his soul and see whether even such orders would find him obedient. Now that He knew the ardour and depth of his piety, He took pleasure in what He had given him and would never fail to regard with the tenderest care both him and his race; his son should attain to extreme old age and, after a life of felicity, bequeath to a virtuous and lawfully begotten offspring a great dominion. He moreover foretold that their race would swell into a multitude of nations, with increasing wealth, nations whose founders would be had in everlasting remembrance, that they would subdue Canaan by their arms and be envied of all men. Having spoken thus God brought from obscurity into their view a ram for the sacrifice. And they, restored to each other beyond all hope and having heard promises of such great felicity, embraced one another and, the sacrifice ended, returned home to Sarra and lived in bliss, God assisting them in all that they desired.

C.   Philo, *On the Migration of Abraham*, 1–5 (1–25)

Philo lived ca. 20 BCE–ca. 50 CE in Alexandria, the home of the largest Jewish population outside Palestine and a site of Greek learning. His works greatly influenced the Alexandrian Christian scholars Clement and Origen, and his continued influence on Christianity explains why so much of his work has been preserved. In his writings, he seeks to interpret the Torah in terms of a mixture of Stoic and Platonic (and other) philosophical ideas, and his principal contribution to Jewish exegesis was an allegorical interpretation of Scripture. In marrying Jewish and Greek ideas, he belongs with a number of Jewish historians, philosophers, writers, and even dramatists of the Hellenistic period who sought to reconcile the basic principles of Greek life and thought with what many Greeks sometimes viewed as a rather barbaric cult. Like many of these writers, Philo argued that the Jewish scriptures are as good (and older!) than the writings of the Greek philosophers.

While Philo did not deny the importance of literal adherence to the commands of the Torah, his hermeneutical key is allegory, a means of transforming statements (whether laws or stories) apparently about the material world into

Source for reading C.:   Colson and Whitaker, in the Loeb edition (London: Heinemann/New York: Putnam, 1932), pp. 132–47.

truths about the eternal world. This technique he borrowed from the Stoics, though it was used by Plato too. For Philo, Torah expresses the highest philosophical truth through which the wise liberate their eternal souls from the material world and unite them with the *logos*.

In the passage before us, the story of God's call of Abraham (Gen. 12) is interpreted as an allegory of the summons to the soul, represented by Abraham, to leave the world of senses. Land, kindred, and father's house all represent elements of the material world that must be escaped: body, sense, speech. The guide of the wise in accomplishing this is none other than Moses, the "Law-giving Word" (*logos*). The Gospel of John, and Christian doctrine, identified God's "word" with the divine Christ, but Philo assigns this role to Moses; and indeed he elsewhere (and perhaps here too) uses language that verges on making Moses himself divine, as the means by which, though example and by lawgiving, he expresses the mind of God (compare §4).

I. "And the Lord said unto Abraham, Depart out of thy land, and out of thy kindred, and out of thy father's house, into the land which I shall shew thee; and I will make thee a great nation and will bless thee and will make thy name great, and thou shalt be blessed. And I will bless them that bless thee, and them that curse thee I will curse, and in thee shall all the tribes of the earth be blessed" (Gen. 12:1–3).

God begins the carrying out of His will to cleanse man's soul by giving it a starting-point for full salvation in its removal out of three localities, namely, body, sense-perception, and speech. "Land" or "country" is a symbol of body, "kindred" of sense-perception, "father's house" of speech. How so? Because the body took its substance out of earth (or land) and is again resolved into earth. Moses is a witness to this, when he says, "Earth thou art and into earth shalt thou return" (Gen. 3:19); indeed he also says that the body was clay formed into human shape by God's moulding hand, and what suffers solution must needs be resolved into the elements which were united to form it. Sense-perception, again, is of one kin and family with understanding, the irrational with the rational, for both these are parts of one soul. And speech is our "father's house," "father's" because Mind is our father, sowing in each of the parts of the body the faculties that issue from itself, and assigning to them their workings, being in control and charge of them all; house – because mind has speech for its house or living-room, secluded from the rest of the homestead. It is Mind's living-place, just as the hearthside is man's. It is there that Mind displays in orderly from itself and all the conceptions to which it gives birth, treating it as a man treats a house.

And marvel not at Moses having given to speech the title of Mind's house in man; for indeed he says that God, the Mind of the universe, has for His house His own Word. It was the vision of this Word that the Self-trainer received when he emphatically declares "This is assuredly not the House of God" (Gen. 28:17), as much as to say "The House of God is not this that is all round me, consisting of things at which we can point or that fall under sense-perception generally, no, not such is God's House, but invisible, withdrawn from sight, and apprehended only by soul as soul. Who, then, can that House be, save the Word who is antecedent to all that has come into existence? the Word, which the Helmsman of the Universe grasps as a rudder to guide all things on their course? Even as, when He was fashioning the world, He employed it as His instrument, that the fabric of His handiwork might be without reproach.

II. We have now shewn how Moses uses "earth" to represent the body, "kindred" to represent sense-perception, "thy father's house" to represent speech. The words "Depart out of these" are not equivalent to "Sever thyself from them absolutely," since to issue such a command as that would be to prescribe death. No, the words import "Make thyself a stranger to them in judgement and purpose; let none of them cling to thee; rise superior to them all; they are thy subjects, never treat them as sovereign lords; thou art a king, school thyself once and for all to rule, not to be ruled; evermore be coming to know thyself, as Moses teaches thee in many places, saying "Give heed to thyself" (Ex. 24:12), for in this way shalt thou perceive those to whom it befits thee to shew obedience and those to whom it befits thee to give commands.

Depart, therefore, out of the earthly matter that encompasses thee: escape, man, from the foul prison-house, thy body, with all thy might and main, and from the pleasures and lusts that act as its jailers; every terror that can vex and hurt them, leave none of them unused; menace the enemy with them all united and combined.

Depart also out of sense-perception thy kin. For at present thou hast made a loan of thyself to each sense, and art become the property of others, a portion of the goods of those who have borrowed thee, and hast thrown away the good thing that was thine own. Yes, thou knowest, even though all men should hold their peace, how eyes draw thee, and ears, and the whole crowd of thine other kinsfolk, towards what they themselves love. But if thou desire to recover the self that thou hast lent and to have thine own possessions about thee, letting no portion of them be alienated and fall into other hands, thou shalt claim instead a happy life, enjoying in perpetuity the benefit and pleasure derived from good things not foreign to thee but thine own.

Again, quit speech also, "thy father's house," as Moses calls it, for fear thou shouldst be beguiled by beauties of mere phrasing, and be cut off from the real beauty, which lies in the matter expressed. Monstrous it is that shadow should be preferred to substance or a copy to originals. And verbal expression is like a shadow or copy, while the essential bearing of the matters conveyed by words resembles substance and originals; and it behoves the man, whose aim it is to be rather than to seem, to dissociate himself from the former and hold fast to the latter.

III. So we find that when the Mind begins to know itself and to hold converse with the things of mind, it will thrust away from it that part of the soul which inclines to the province of sense-perception, the inclining which among the Hebrews is entitled "Lot." Hence the wise man is represented as saying outright, "Separate thyself from me" (Gen. 13:9). For it is impossible for one who is possessed by love for all that is incorporeal and incorruptible to dwell together with one who leans towards the objects of sense-perception doomed to die. Right well, then, did the Sacred Guide inscribe one entire sacred book of the Law-giving "Exagoge" or "Leading out," for the name thus found was appropriate to the oracles contained in it. For being well qualified to train men and fully furnished for the admonition and correction of those who were capable of admonition and correction, he contemplates the task of taking out all the population of the soul right away from Egypt, the body, and away from its inhabitants; deeming it a most sore and heavy burden that an understanding endowed with vision should be under the pressure of the pleasures of the flesh, and should submit to such injunctions as its merciless cravings may lay upon it.

These, indeed, groaned over and greatly bewailed their bodily well-being, and the lavish abundance of things outside the body, which was theirs, for we read that "the children of Israel groaned by reason of their works" (Ex. 2:23). When they do this, the gracious God instructs His prophet regarding their coming out, and His prophet delivers them.

But some make a truce with the body and maintain it till their death, and are buried in it as in a coffin or shell or whatever else you like to call it. All the body-loving and passion-loving portions of these are laid in the grave and consigned to oblivion. But if anywhere by the side of these there grows up a virtue-loving tendency, it is saved from extinction by memories, which are a means of keeping alive the flame of noble qualities.

IV. So the Holy Word, deeming it unfitting that pure things should have impure things associated with them, provides for the safe-keeping of Joseph's bones, by which I mean the only relics of such a soul as were left behind untouched by corruption and worthy of perpetual memory (Gen. 50:25).

Those of the latter kind were these; Joseph's confidence that "God will visit" the race that has vision (Gen. 50:24), and will not utterly hand it over to Ignorance, that blind task-mistress; his discernment between the mortal and the incorruptible portions of the soul and his leaving behind to Egypt those which had to do with bodily pleasures and other forms of unrestrained passion, while concerning the incorruptible parts he made an agreement, that they should accompany those who went up to the cities of virtue, and should be conveyed thither, and had the agreement secured by an oath.

What, then, are the uncorrupted parts? His having nothing to do with Pleasure when she says, "Let us lie together" (Gen. 39:7) and enjoy the good things of mankind: the shrewdness coupled with the resoluteness which enabled him to recognize the products of empty fancies which many accounted to be good, and to distinguish them as mere dreams from those which are really so; and to confess that the true and certain interpretations of things are given under God's guidance (Gen. 40:8), while the doubtful imaginations that have no certainty follow the rule and line of the erring and deluded life of men who have not undergone purification, a life that finds its joy in the delights provided by bakers and cooks and butlers. Other traits of incorruption were these: he was proclaimed not the subject, but the ruler of all Egypt, the domain of the body (Gen. 41:41): he was proud to own himself a member of the Hebrew race (Gen. 40:15), whose wont it is, as the name "Hebrew" or "Migrant" indicates, to quit the objects of sense-perception and go after those of Mind: he gloried in the fact that "here he had done nothing" (ibid.), for to have performed no single act such as the worthless people there admired, but to have utterly hated and eschewed them all, was conduct that called for no slight praise: he derided lusts and all passions and their gross excesses (Gen. 39:14, 17): he feared God (Gen. 42:18) even though he was not yet ready to love Him: when in Egypt he claimed as his own the life that is real life, (V.) a claim which caused Israel to marvel in just amazement, and to cry, "It is a great matter in my eyes if my son Joseph still lives" (Gen. 45:28), and has not shared the death of vain opinions, and of the body the corpse he carries with him: he confesses that he is God's (Gen. 50:19), not the property of any created being: when making himself known to his brethren he thrust perforce from his presence, shaken and tottering, all those frames of mind that make the body their delight and think that their own doctrines afford them a firm standing (Gen. 45:1f): he declared that he had not received his commission at the hands of men, but had been appointed by God (Gen. 45:7p) to be duly constituted controller of the body and of things outside the body.

And these are but a few of the traits indicative of the better and holier standing, which utterly refuse to dwell in Egypt the bodily tenement, are never buried in a coffin at all, but, having passed out of all that is mortal, follow the guiding steps of Moses, the Law-giving Word. For Moses is the nursing- father who rears with fostering care noble deeds, words, designs, which, albeit often mingled with their opposites owing to the chaos and confusion which besets mortality, he none the less comes forward and separates from the rest, that the germs and shoots of moral excellence may not permanently be obliterated and lost.

Moses also urges the Israelites to quit right stoutly her who bears the name of mother of every monstrous thing, with no slow or lingering steps, but with exceeding speed; for he bids them with haste to sacrifice the Passover (Ex. 12:11), which means "a passing over," to the intent that the Mind with resolute purpose and unfailing eagerness may carry out both its passing away from the passions without turning back, and its thanksgiving to God its Saviour, Who brought it forth into liberty when it looked not for it.

D. Targum Pseudo-Jonathan on Genesis 4

Targums are Aramaic translations, sometime literal, sometimes free, of the Hebrew text. There are several of these for the Pentateuch, including the one known as the Pseudo-Jonathan Targum (also as the Jerusalem Targum or Yerushalmi). These written targums developed from synagogal practice but were subsequently edited in order to control the tendency to excessive freedom in rendering.

It is very important to bear in mind that most Jews in the ancient world knew Scripture either in Greek or Aramaic translation, and while the Greek translation stayed close to the original, the original targums, with their explanations and digressions, would have constituted the "bible knowledge" of most Aramaic-speaking Jews, who would not have known what exactly was in the Hebrew Scriptures and what not. A good deal of additional explanation is still found in the targums, allowing us to see where the scriptures were felt to need amplification and clarification.

While the targumic renderings deal with a number of problematic issues, it often requires some investigation to discover what the problem may have been and how the solution was reached. In some cases, these problems would no doubt have troubled those who went to the synagogue had they indeed heard a

Source for reading D.: John Bowker, *The Targums and Rabbinic Literature* (Cambridge: Cambridge University Press, 1969), pp. 132–4, without footnotes. Words in italics represent what is in the Hebrew.

literal translation. In other cases, problems are being discovered in the process of scholarly Rabbinic discussion. In any event, targum, as we see in the following selection, is no mere translation but serves as a hedge between literal statements of scripture and the meanings they *ought* to have.

1   *And* Adam was aware that *Eve his wife* had *conceived* from Sammael the angel, and she became pregnant *and bare Cain*, and he was like those on high, not like those below; and she *said, "I have* acquired *a man*, the angel of *the Lord."*

2   *And* she went on to bear from Adam, her husband, his twin sister and *Abel. And Abel was a keeper of sheep, but Cain was* a man working in the earth.

3   *And* it was at the end of the days on the fourteenth of Nisan *that Cain brought of the fruit of the ground*, the seed of flax, *an offering* of first things before *the Lord.*

4   *And Abel, he also brought of the firstlings of his flock and of the fat thereof. And* it was pleasing before the Lord, and the Lord showed favor *unto Abel and to his offering:*

5   *but unto Cain and to his offering he* did not show favor. *And Cain was very wroth, and* the image of his face *fell.*

6   *And the Lord said unto Cain, "Why art thou wroth? and why is* the image of your face *fallen?*

7   Is it not the case that if you have done your work *well* your guilt will be forgiven you? But if you have not done your work *well* in this world your sin will be kept for the day of the great judgment, and at the doors of your heart sin lies waiting. And into your hand I have given the power of the inclination to evil, and toward you will be its *desire*, and you will have authority over it for righteousness or for sin."

8   *And Cain* said to Abel his brother: "Come, and let us both go into the field." So it was that when they had both gone out into the field Cain answered and said to Abel: "I can see that the world was created in love, but it is not ordered by the issue of good works, because there is partiality in judgment; thus it is that your offering was accepted with favour, but my offering was not accepted with favour." Abel answered and said: "Certainly the world was created in love, and by the issue of good works it is ordered, and there is no partiality in judgment. But because the issue of my works was better than yours, so my offering has been accepted before yours with favor." Cain answered and said to Abel: "There is no judgment and no judge and no world hereafter; there is no good reward to be given to the righteous, nor any account to be taken of the wicked." Abel answered and said: "Certainly there is judgment and a judge and a world hereafter; there is a good reward to be given to the righteous, and the wicked will be called to account." And because of these words they fell into a dispute in the open field, and *Cain rose up against Abel his brother*, and drove a stone into his forehead, *and slew him.*

9   *And the Lord said unto Cain, "Where is Abel thy brother?" And he said, "I know not: am I my brother's keeper?"*

PHILIP R. DAVIES   41

10   *And he said, "What hast thou done? The voice* of the bloods of the killing of your brother which were swallowed into the clay cry before *me from the ground.*

11   *And now* because of your killing him *cursed art thou from the ground which hath opened her mouth to receive* the bloods *of thy brother from thy*

12   *hand: when thou tillest the ground it shall not* increase to give *unto thee strength* of her fruits. *"A fugitive and a wanderer shalt thou be in the earth."*

13   *And Cain said* before *the Lord:* "Severe indeed is my rebellion, more than to be borne, and yet it is possible with you to forgive it."

14   *Behold, thou hast* cast me forth *this day* on *the face of the ground; and from* before you can I ever *be hid?* But since I am a *fugitive and a wanderer in the earth,* any just person who *findeth me shall slay me.*

15   *And the Lord said unto him, "Therefore whosoever slayeth Cain* for seven generations it will be exacted from him." *And the Lord* marked on the face of Cain a letter from the great and glorious name, that *any finding him* should not kill him when they saw it on him.

16   *And Cain went out from* before *the Lord and dwelt in the land* of the wandering of his exile which was made on account of him from of old, like the garden of *Eden.*

17   *And Cain knew his wife; and she conceived, and bare Enoch: and he builded a city, and called the name of the city, after the name of his son, Enoch.*

18   *And unto Enoch was born Irad: and Irad begat Mehujael: and Mehujael begat Methushael: and Methushael begat Lamech.*

19   *And Lamech took unto him two wives: the name of the one was Adah, and the name of the other Zillah.*

20   *And Adah bare Jabal: he was* the lord *of such as dwell in tents and* are masters of cattle.

21   *And his brother's name was Jabal: he was* the lord *of all such as* take part in the song with *the harp and pipe.*

22   *And Zillah, she also bare Tubal-cain,* the lord of all workers who know the making of *brass and iron: and the sister of Tubal-cain was Naamah;* she was supreme in laments and songs.

23   *And Lamech said unto his wives:* "Adah and Zillah, hear *my voice: ye wives of Lamech, hearken unto my speech: for I have not slain a man* that we should be killed on his account, nor have I injured *a young man* that my offspring should be destroyed on his account.

24   Now *Cain* who had sinned and turned in repentance had seven generations extended to him; so is it not just that *Lamech,* the son of his son, who has not sinned, should be extended for seven and seventy?"

25   *And Adam knew his wife again* at the end of 130 years after the killing of Abel, *and she bare a son, and called his name Seth: for* she said: "The Lord has given me another *instead of Abel* whom *Cain slew."*

26   *And to Seth, to him also there was born a son; and he called his name Enosh.* That was the generation in whose days they began to err and make idols for themselves, and *to call* their idols by *the name of* the word of *the Lord.*

Chapter 4

Second Temple Judaism

Frederick J. Murphy

A.   Ezra and Nehemiah

The books of Ezra and Nehemiah tell of the return of the Jews from the
Babylonian exile and their restoring of Jerusalem, its Temple, and Jewish
society in Judah under the patronage of the Persian emperor. Ezra and Nehemiah, two prominent Jews in the Persian court, each made trips to Judah
during the early Second Temple period to reform Jewish society there according
to the law of Torah. The picture of the ideal Israel contained in these books is of
a community restored to the holy land, living there according to the written
Torah, brought by Ezra from the Babylonian Jewish community, and separating itself from all who do not obey this law, so as to maintain itself in purity as
God's holy people.

Ezra 1:2–3

The Persian king Cyrus allows the exiles to return to Judah and rebuild Jerusalem
and its Temple:

> Thus says King Cyrus of Persia: The LORD, the God of heaven, has given me all
> the kingdoms of the earth, and he has charged me to build him a house at
> Jerusalem in Judah. Any of those among you who are of his people – may their
> God be with them! – are now permitted to go up to Jerusalem in Judah, and
> rebuild the house of the LORD, the God of Israel – he is the God who is in Jerusalem.

Source for Readings A–E, H.:   All biblical translations, including 4 Ezra and 1 and 2 Maccabees: New
Revised Standard Version.

Ezra 4:1–5

The returned exiles refuse the help of the people of the land who also claim to worship God. Only the returned exiles and those who decide to join them in their interpretation and living out of the Torah are the true Israel.

> When the adversaries of Judah and Benjamin heard that the returned exiles were building a temple to the LORD, the God of Israel, they approached Zerubbabel and the heads of families and said to them, "Let us build with you, for we worship your God as you do, and we have been sacrificing to him ever since the days of King Esarhaddon of Assyria who brought us here." But Zerubbabel, Jeshua, and the rest of the heads of families in Israel said to them, "You shall have no part with us in building a house to our God; but we alone will build to the LORD, the God of Israel, as King Cyrus of Persia has commanded us." Then the people of the land discouraged the people of Judah, and made them afraid to build, and they bribed officials to frustrate their plan throughout the reign of King Cyrus of Persia and until the reign of King Darius of Persia.

Ezra 6:20b–21

The first Passover celebration by the returned exiles reveals the contours of the restored community. Only the returned exiles and those who separate themselves from "pollutions," that is, circumstances, people, practices, beliefs, and objects unacceptable according to the interpretation of Torah advocated by the returned exiles, are the true Israel.

> They killed the passover lamb for all the returned exiles, for their fellow priests, and for themselves. It was eaten by the people of Israel who had returned from exile, and also by all who had joined them and separated themselves from the pollutions of the nations of the land to worship the LORD, the God of Israel.

Ezra 7:6, 10–12, 14–15, 25–26

Ezra comes to Judah with a commission from the Persian king to enforce Torah as the law of the land. The king also supports the Jewish cult financially. Ezra's success is attributed to his knowledge and faithfulness to Torah.

> This Ezra went up from Babylonia. He was a scribe skilled in the law of Moses that the LORD the God of Israel had given; and the king granted him all that he asked, for the hand of the LORD his God was upon him. . . . For Ezra had set his heart to study the law of the LORD, and to do it, and to teach the statutes and ordinances in Israel. This is a copy of the letter that King Artaxerxes gave to the priest Ezra, the scribe, a

scholar of the text of the commandments of the LORD and his statutes for Israel: "Artaxerxes, king of kings, to the priest Ezra, the scribe of the law of the God of heaven: Peace.... You are sent by the king and his seven counselors to make inquiries about Judah and Jerusalem according to the law of your God, which is in your hand, and also to convey the silver and gold that the king and his counselors have freely offered to the God of Israel, whose dwelling is in Jerusalem.... And you, Ezra, according to the God-given wisdom you possess, appoint magistrates and judges who may judge all the people in the province Beyond the River who know the laws of your God; and you shall teach those who do not know them. All who will not obey the law of your God and the law of the king, let judgment be strictly executed on them, whether for death or for banishment or for confiscation of their goods or for imprisonment."

Nehemiah 8:1–4a, 5–6, 7b–8

Ezra promulgates the Torah in Jerusalem.

All the people gathered together into the square before the Water Gate. They told the scribe Ezra to bring the book of the law of Moses, which the LORD had given to Israel. Accordingly, the priest Ezra brought the law before the assembly, both men and women and all who could hear with understanding. This was on the first day of the seventh month. He read from it facing the square before the Water Gate from early morning until midday, in the presence of the men and the women and those who could understand; and the ears of all the people were attentive to the book of the law. The scribe Ezra stood on a wooden platform that had been made for the purpose. ... And Ezra opened the book in the sight of all the people, for he was standing above all the people; and when he opened it, all the people stood up. Then Ezra blessed the LORD, the great God, and all the people answered, "Amen, Amen," lifting up their hands. Then they bowed their heads and worshiped the LORD with their faces to the ground.... the Levites, helped the people to understand the law, while the people remained in their places. So they read from the book, from the law of God, with interpretation. They gave the sense, so that the people understood the reading.

Nehemiah 2:3–6, 8b

Nehemiah, Jewish cupbearer to the Persian king, receives the king's commission to come to Jerusalem and rebuild its walls.

I said to the king, "May the king live forever! Why should my face not be sad, when the city, the place of my ancestors' graves, lies waste, and its gates have been destroyed by fire?" Then the king said to me, "What do you request?" So I prayed to the God of heaven. Then I said to the king, "If it pleases the king, and if your servant has found favor with you, I ask that you send me to Judah, to the city of my ancestors' graves, so that I may rebuild it." The king said to me (the queen also was sitting beside him), "How long will you be gone, and when will you return?" So it pleased the king to send me, and I set him a date.... And the king granted me what I asked, for the gracious hand of my God was upon me.

Nehemiah 5:3–4, 7–12

Judahite peasants complain that the wealthy are taking their land when they cannot repay loans. Nehemiah, in accord with covenantal law, successfully appeals to the wealthy to return the land and to stop charging interest to their fellow Jews.

> There were also those who said, "We are having to pledge our fields, our vineyards, and our houses in order to get grain during the famine." And there were those who said, "We are having to borrow money on our fields and vineyards to pay the king's tax." ... After thinking it over, I brought charges against the nobles and the officials; I said to them, "You are all taking interest from your own people." And I called a great assembly to deal with them, and said to them, "As far as we were able, we have bought back our Jewish kindred who had been sold to other nations; but now you are selling your own kin, who must then be bought back by us!" They were silent, and could not find a word to say. So I said, "The thing that you are doing is not good. Should you not walk in the fear of our God, to prevent the taunts of the nations our enemies? Moreover I and my brothers and my servants are lending them money and grain. Let us stop this taking of interest. Restore to them, this very day, their fields, their vineyards, their olive orchards, and their houses, and the interest on money, grain, wine, and oil that you have been exacting from them." Then they said, "We will restore everything and demand nothing more from them. We will do as you say." And I called the priests, and made them take an oath to do as they had promised.

B.   Haggai and Zechariah

Haggai and Zechariah were prophets who urged the returned exiles to rebuild the Temple, seen as essential to ensuring God's presence among the people.

Haggai 1:2–11, 14

Through Haggai, God insists on the rebuilding of the Temple. Israel's prosperity depends on God's presence in the Temple.

> Thus says the LORD of hosts: These people say the time has not yet come to rebuild the Lord's house. Then the word of the LORD came by the prophet Haggai, saying: Is it a time for you yourselves to live in your paneled houses, while this house lies in ruins?

Now therefore thus says the LORD of hosts: Consider how you have fared. You have sown much, and harvested little; you eat, but you never have enough; you drink, but you never have your fill; you clothe yourselves, but no one is warm; and you that earn wages earn wages to put them into a bag with holes.

Thus says the LORD of hosts: Consider how you have fared. Go up to the hills and bring wood and build the house, so that I may take pleasure in it and be honored, says the LORD. You have looked for much, and, lo, it came to little; and when you brought it home, I blew it away. Why? says the LORD of hosts. Because my house lies in ruins, while all of you hurry off to your own houses. Therefore the heavens above you have withheld the dew, and the earth has withheld its produce. And I have called for a drought on the land and the hills, on the grain, the new wine, the oil, on what the soil produces, on human beings and animals, and on all their labors. . . .

And the LORD stirred up the spirit of Zerubbabel son of Shealtiel, governor of Judah, and the spirit of Joshua son of Jehozadak, the high priest, and the spirit of all the remnant of the people; and they came and worked on the house of the LORD of hosts, their God.

Haggai 2:6–7

Haggai predicts the glorification of the Temple and its recognition by the nations.

Thus says the LORD of hosts: Once again, in a little while, I will shake the heavens and the earth and the sea and the dry land; and I will shake all the nations, so that the treasure of all nations shall come, and I will fill this house with splendor, says the LORD of hosts.

Haggai 2:21–23

Haggai predicts the coming of a messianic kingdom that will overthrow the power of the nations. As God's signet ring, Zerubbabel will represent God's authority on earth. Haggai's messianic fervor did not find fulfillment in historical events.

Speak to Zerubbabel, governor of Judah, saying, I am about to shake the heavens and the earth, and to overthrow the throne of kingdoms; I am about to destroy the strength of the kingdoms of the nations, and overthrow the chariots and their riders; and the horses and their riders shall fall, every one by the sword of a comrade. On that day, says the LORD of hosts, I will take you, O Zerubbabel my servant, son of Shealtiel, says the LORD, and make you like a signet ring; for I have chosen you, says the LORD of hosts.

Zechariah 3:1–7

Zechariah sees the high priest of the restoration, Joshua, standing before God and being accused by the accusing angel (Heb.: *satan*). God defends Joshua and grants him access to Temple and heavenly courts, provided he is faithful to God's law. The passage legitimates the Second Temple priesthood and depicts it as the intermediary between God and Israel.

> Then he showed me the high priest Joshua standing before the angel of the LORD, and Satan standing at his right hand to accuse him. And the LORD said to Satan, ''The LORD rebuke you, O Satan! The LORD who has chosen Jerusalem rebuke you! Is not this man a brand plucked from the fire?'' Now Joshua was dressed with filthy clothes as he stood before the angel. The angel said to those who were standing before him, ''Take off his filthy clothes.'' And to him he said, ''See, I have taken your guilt away from you, and I will clothe you with festal apparel.'' And I said, ''Let them put a clean turban on his head.'' So they put a clean turban on his head and clothed him with the apparel; and the angel of the LORD was standing by.
>
> Then the angel of the LORD assured Joshua, saying, ''Thus says the LORD of hosts: If you will walk in my ways and keep my requirements, then you shall rule my house and have charge of my courts, and I will give you the right of access among those who are standing here.''

Zechariah 4:2–3, 8–9a, 12, 14

The prophet sees a symbolic vision in which Joshua and Zerubbabel, the two leaders of the restoration, are represented by two olive trees, interpreted as messiahs. They feed a lamp with seven flames, symbolizing their support of the Jerusalem cult.

> He said to me, ''What do you see?'' And I said, ''I see a lampstand all of gold, with a bowl on the top of it; there are seven lamps on it, with seven lips on each of the lamps that are on the top of it. And by it there are two olive trees, one on the right of the bowl and the other on its left.'' . . . The word of the LORD came to me, saying, ''The hands of Zerubbabel have laid the foundation of this house; his hands shall also complete it.''. . . I said to him, ''What are these two branches of the olive trees, which pour out the oil through the two golden pipes?'' . . . Then he said, ''These are the two anointed ones who stand by the Lord of the whole earth.''

C.   Daniel

Daniel is the only apocalypse in the Hebrew Bible. It was written in response to the persecution of Antiochus, probably around 165 BCE. Antiochus's attack on the Temple and on Judaism is seen as an attack by supernatural forces on God and his angels. It is typical of apocalypses to see human conflicts in the context of cosmic struggles, and to attribute understanding of these struggles to esoteric wisdom imparted by a supernatural figure to a human seer.

Daniel 7:2–3, 9–14, 23–27

Daniel's vision reveals the meaning of history. This chapter represents successive empires oppressing Israel as supernatural beasts arising out of the sea, a symbol of the primordial chaos opposing God's creative powers. Daniel witnesses a judgment scene in the heavenly court that results in defeat of Israel's enemies on earth. The one like a son of man is most likely the angelic patron of Israel, Michael. As Michael receives dominion in heaven, Israel receives the kingdom on earth.

I, Daniel, saw in my vision by night the four winds of heaven stirring up the great sea, and four great beasts came up out of the sea, different from one another....

> As I watched,
> thrones were set in place,
> and an Ancient One took his throne,
> his clothing was white as snow,
> and the hair of his head like pure wool;
> his throne was fiery flames,
> and its wheels were burning fire.
> A stream of fire issued
> and flowed out from his presence.
> A thousand thousands served him,
> and ten thousand times ten thousand stood attending him.
> The court sat in judgment,
> and the books were opened.

I watched then because of the noise of the arrogant words that the horn was speaking. And as I watched, the beast was put to death, and its body destroyed and given over to be burned with fire. As for the rest of the beasts, their dominion was taken away, but their lives were prolonged for a season and a time. As I watched in the night visions,

> I saw one like a human being
> coming with the clouds of heaven.
> And he came to the Ancient One
> and was presented before him.
> To him was given dominion
> and glory and kingship,
> that all peoples, nations, and languages
> should serve him.
> His dominion is an everlasting dominion
> that shall not pass away,
> and his kingship is one
> that shall never be destroyed....

This is what he (the interpreting angel) said: "As for the fourth beast,

there shall be a fourth kingdom on earth
  that shall be different from all the other kingdoms (the Seleucid kingdom);
it shall devour the whole earth,
   and trample it down, and break it to pieces.
As for the ten horns,
out of this kingdom ten kings shall arise,
   and another (Antiochus IV) shall arise after them.
This one shall be different from the former ones,
   and shall put down three kings.
He shall speak words against the Most High,
   shall wear out the holy ones of the Most High,
   and shall attempt to change the sacred seasons and the law;
and they shall be given into his power
   for a time, two times, and half a time.
Then the court shall sit in judgment,
   and his dominion shall be taken away,
  to be consumed and totally destroyed.
The kingship and dominion
   and the greatness of the kingdoms under the whole heaven
   shall be given to the people of the holy ones of the Most High;
their kingdom shall be an everlasting kingdom,
and all dominions shall serve and obey them."

Dan. 12:1–2

This is the earliest clear statement of belief in the resurrection. At the end of times, Michael will arise, there will be unprecedented suffering, and finally many of the good and the bad will arise for their eternal reward or punishment. Postmortem rewards and punishments are typical of apocalypses, and it is probably through apocalypticism that belief in the resurrection first enters Judaism.

At that time Michael, the great prince, the protector of your people, shall arise. There shall be a time of anguish, such as has never occurred since nations first came into existence. But at that time your people shall be delivered, everyone who is found written in the book. Many of those who sleep in the dust of the earth shall awake, some to everlasting life, and some to shame and everlasting contempt.

D.   1 Maccabees

Written around the end of the second century BCE, this book glorifies the Maccabees as the ones whom God chose to liberate Israel and its Torah and temple from the persecution of Antiochus IV. Using holy war motifs, it tells of how God defeated the Seleucids through the Maccabees. The book serves to legitimate Hasmonean rule.

1 Macc. 1:41–50, 54–64

Antiochus's persecution of Judaism is attributed to his desire for unity in his empire. The persecution is described in lurid detail.

> Then the king wrote to his whole kingdom that all should be one people, and that all should give up their particular customs. All the Gentiles accepted the command of the king. Many even from Israel gladly adopted his religion; they sacrificed to idols and profaned the sabbath. And the king sent letters by messengers to Jerusalem and the towns of Judah; he directed them to follow customs strange to the land, to forbid burnt offerings and sacrifices and drink offerings in the sanctuary, to profane sabbaths and festivals, to defile the sanctuary and the priests, to build altars and sacred precincts and shrines for idols, to sacrifice swine and other unclean animals, and to leave their sons uncircumcised. They were to make themselves abominable by everything unclean and profane, so that they would forget the law and change all the ordinances. He added, "And whoever does not obey the command of the king shall die." ...
>
> Now on the fifteenth day of Chislev, in the one hundred forty-fifth year, they erected a desolating sacrilege on the altar of burnt offering. They also built altars in the surrounding towns of Judah, and offered incense at the doors of the houses and in the streets. The books of the law that they found they tore to pieces and burned with fire. Anyone found possessing the book of the covenant, or anyone who adhered to the law, was condemned to death by decree of the king. They kept using violence against Israel, against those who were found month after month in the towns. On the twenty-fifth day of the month they offered sacrifice on the altar that was on top of the altar of burnt offering. According to the decree, they put to death the women who had their children circumcised, and their families and those who circumcised them; and they hung the infants from their mothers' necks.
>
> But many in Israel stood firm and were resolved in their hearts not to eat unclean food. They chose to die rather than to be defiled by food or to profane the holy covenant; and they did die. Very great wrath came upon Israel.

1 Macc. 2:19–22

The priest Mattathias, father of five sons, declares loyalty to Torah and vows to resist Antiochus.

> Mattathias answered and said in a loud voice: "Even if all the nations that live under the rule of the king obey him, and have chosen to obey his commandments, every-one of them abandoning the religion of their ancestors, I and my sons and my brothers will continue to live by the covenant of our ancestors. Far be it from us to

desert the law and the ordinances. We will not obey the king's words by turning aside from our religion to the right hand or to the left."

1 Macc. 4:42–59

Judah Maccabee cleanses and rededicates the sanctuary and institutes the feast of Hanukkah to commemorate the event.

> He chose blameless priests devoted to the law, and they cleansed the sanctuary and removed the defiled stones to an unclean place. They deliberated what to do about that altar of burnt offering, which had been profaned. And they thought it best to tear it down, so that it would not be a lasting shame to them that the Gentiles had defiled it. So they tore down the altar, and stored the stones in a convenient place on the temple hill until a prophet should come to tell what to do with them. Then they took unhewn stones, as the law directs, and built a new altar like the former one. They also rebuilt the sanctuary and the interior of the temple, and consecrated the courts. They made new holy vessels, and brought the lampstand, the altar of incense, and the table into the temple. Then they offered incense on the altar and lit the lamps on the lampstand, and these gave light in the temple. They placed the bread on the table and hung up the curtains. Thus they finished all the work they had undertaken.
>
> Early in the morning on the twenty-fifth day of the ninth month, which is the month of Chislev, in the one hundred and forty-eighth year, they rose and offered sacrifice, as the law directs, on the new altar of burnt offering that they had built. At the very season and on the very day that the Gentiles had profaned it, it was dedicated with songs and harps and lutes and cymbals. All the people fell on their faces and worshiped and blessed Heaven, who had prospered them. So they celebrated the dedication of the altar for eight days, and joyfully offered burnt offerings; they offered a sacrifice of well-being and a thanksgiving offering. They decorated the front of the temple with golden crowns and small shields; they restored the gates and the chambers for the priests, and fitted them with doors. There was very great joy among the people, and the disgrace brought by the Gentiles was removed.
>
> Then Judas and his brothers and all the assembly of Israel determined that every year at that season the days of dedication of the altar should be observed with joy and gladness for eight days, beginning with the twenty-fifth day of the month of Chislev.

1 Macc. 14:25–29, 35, 41–43

Israel proclaims Simon leader and high priest because of his defense of Torah and sanctuary.

> When the people heard these things they said, "How shall we thank Simon and his sons? For he and his brothers and the house of his father have stood firm; they have fought and repulsed Israel's enemies and established its freedom." So they made a record on bronze tablets and put it on pillars on Mount Zion.

This is a copy of what they wrote: "On the eighteenth day of Elul, in the one hundred and seventy-second year, which is the third year of the great high priest Simon, in Asaramel, in the great assembly of the priests and the people and the rulers of the nation and the elders of the country, the following was proclaimed to us:

"Since wars often occurred in the country, Simon son of Mattathias, a priest of the sons of Joarib, and his brothers, exposed themselves to danger and resisted the enemies of their nation, in order that their sanctuary and the law might be preserved; and they brought great glory to their nation.... The people saw Simon's faithfulness and the glory that he had resolved to win for his nation, and they made him their leader and high priest, because he had done all these things and because of the justice and loyalty that he had maintained toward his nation. He sought in every way to exalt his people.... The Jews and their priests have resolved that Simon should be their leader and high priest forever, until a trustworthy prophet should arise, and that he should be governor over them and that he should take charge of the sanctuary and appoint officials over its tasks and over the country and the weapons and the strongholds, and that he should take charge of the sanctuary, and that he should be obeyed by all, and that all contracts in the country should be written in his name, and that he should be clothed in purple and wear gold."

E.   2 Maccabees

This book recounts many of the same events as 1 Maccabees, but its emphases are different. It gives a more complete account of the events leading up to Antiochus's persecution. Although it gives credit to the Maccabees, it focuses more on God's action, and so it includes more miraculous episodes. The general theme of the book is that disaster befalls those who transgress God's law and postmortem vindication awaits those who die for the Torah.

2 Maccabees 4:7–17

This is the fullest description extant of the Hellenistic Reform, the attempt of some members of the Jerusalem ruling class to turn it into a Greek city. The author of 2 Maccabees sees this as apostasy which received its due punishment in Antiochus's persecution.

When Seleucus died and Antiochus, who was called Epiphanes, succeeded to the kingdom, Jason the brother of Onias obtained the high priesthood by corruption, promising the king at an interview three hundred sixty talents of silver, and from another source of revenue eighty talents. In addition to this he promised to pay one hundred and fifty more if permission were given to establish by his authority a gymnasium and a body of youth for it, and to enroll the people of Jerusalem as citizens of Antioch. When the king assented and Jason came to office, he at once shifted his compatriots over to the Greek way of life.

He set aside the existing royal concessions to the Jews, secured through John the father of Eupolemus, who went on the mission to establish friendship and alliance with the Romans; and he destroyed the lawful ways of living and introduced new customs contrary to the law. He took delight in establishing a gymnasium right under the citadel, and he induced the noblest of the young men to wear the Greek hat. There was such an extreme of Hellenization and increase in the adoption of foreign ways because of the surpassing wickedness of Jason, who was ungodly and no true high priest, that the priests were no longer intent upon their service at the altar. Despising the sanctuary and neglecting the sacrifices, they hurried to take part in the unlawful proceedings in the wrestling arena after the signal for the discus-throwing, disdaining the honors prized by their ancestors and putting the highest value upon Greek forms of prestige. For this reason heavy disaster overtook them, and those whose ways of living they admired and wished to imitate completely became their enemies and punished them. It is no light thing to show irreverence to the divine laws – a fact that later events will make clear.

2 Macc. 3:24–28

God protects the Temple when a representative of Antiochus, Heliodorus, attempts to confiscate its funds. Angels in the form of young men beat him severely.

When he (Heliodorus) arrived at the treasury with his bodyguard, then and there the Sovereign of spirits and of all authority caused so great a manifestation that all who had been so bold as to accompany him were astounded by the power of God, and became faint with terror. For there appeared to them a magnificently caparisoned horse, with a rider of frightening mien; it rushed furiously at Heliodorus and struck at him with its front hoofs. Its rider was seen to have armor and weapons of gold. Two young men also appeared to him, remarkably strong, gloriously beautiful and splendidly dressed, who stood on either side of him and flogged him continuously, inflicting many blows on him. [3:24–28] When he suddenly fell to the ground and deep darkness came over him, his men took him up, put him on a stretcher, and carried him away – this man who had just entered the aforesaid treasury with a great retinue and all his bodyguard but was now unable to help himself. They recognized clearly the sovereign power of God.

2 Macc. 5:17–20

Antiochus later despoils the Temple. The author explains his ability to do this by saying that the fates of Temple and people are linked. If the people sin, God will not protect the Temple.

Antiochus was elated in spirit, and did not perceive that the Lord was angered for a little while because of the sins of those who lived in the city, and that this was the reason he was disregarding the holy place. But if it had not happened that they were involved in many sins, this man would have been flogged and turned back from his rash act as soon as he came forward, just as Heliodorus had been, whom Seleucus the king sent to inspect the treasury. But the Lord did not choose the nation for the sake of the holy place, but the place for the sake of the nation. Therefore the place itself shared in the misfortunes that befell the nation and afterward participated in its benefits; and what was forsaken in the wrath of the Almighty was restored again in all its glory when the great Lord became reconciled.

F.   The Psalms of Solomon

This is a collection of psalms written during the first century BCE. Its primary interest is in the invasion of Jewish Palestine by the Romans, which it sees as a punishment of the inhabitants of Jerusalem who were not faithful to God's law. It expects a resurrection of the dead and the coming of a Davidic messiah who will drive both gentiles and unrighteous Jews from Jerusalem, the establishment of a holy community organized along original tribal lines, called children of God, who would obey God's will in every respect and bring success and blessing back to Israel.

PssSol 17:21–34

This passage expresses messianic hopes.

> See, Lord, and raise up for them their king,
> the son of David, to rule over your servant Israel
> in the time known to you, O God.
> Undergird him with the strength to destroy the unrighteous rulers,
> to purge Jerusalem from gentiles
> who trample her to destruction;
> in wisdom and righteousness to drive out
> the sinners from the inheritance;
> to smash the arrogance of sinners
> like a potter's jar;
> To shatter all their substance with an iron rod;
> to destroy the unlawful nations with the word of his mouth;
> At his warning the nations will flee from his presence;
> and he will condemn the sinners by the thoughts of their hearts.
> He will gather a holy people
> whom he will lead in righteousness;

Source for Reading F.:   James Charlesworth, *The Old Testament Pseudepigrapha* (New York: Doubleday, 1985), vol. 21, pp. 639–70.

and he will judge the tribes of the people
that have been made holy by the Lord their God.
He will not tolerate unrighteousness (even) to pause among them,
and any person who knows wickedness shall not live with them.
For he shall know them
that they are all children of their God.
He will distribute them upon the land
according to their tribes;
the alien and the foreigner will no longer live with them.
He will judge peoples and nations in the wisdom of his righteousness.
And he will have gentile nations serving him under his yoke,
and he will glorify the Lord in (a place) prominent (above) the whole earth.
And he will purge Jerusalem
(and make it) holy as it was even from the beginning,
(for) nations to come from the ends of the earth to see his glory,
to bring as gifts her children who had been driven out,
and to see the glory of the Lord
with which God has glorified her.
And he will be a righteous king over them, taught by God.
There will be no unrighteousness among them in his days,
for all shall be holy,
and their king shall be the Lord Messiah.
(For) he will not rely on horse and rider and bow,
nor will he collect gold and silver for war.
Nor will he build up hope in a multitude for a day of war.
The Lord himself is his king,
the hope of the one who has a strong hope in God.

G.   Josephus

Josephus was a priest from Jerusalem who was born in 37 CE and died around 100 CE. At the beginning of the war against the Romans, he was appointed commander of Galilee. His forces were quickly defeated and he became a translator and guide for the Romans. After the war he went to Rome and wrote several works that are the most important sources for events in the first century BCE and the first century CE. His *War* justifies Roman rule as being in accord with God's will and tries to demonstrate that the war was due to a few hotheads of whom God disapproved. In his works he also chronicles the insensitivity of Roman administrators to Jews and Jewish religion. Josephus defends Judaism against criticisms and shows that it is a religion and a people worthy of the utmost respect.

Source for Reading G.:   Loeb Classical Library (London: Heinemann/New York: Putnam, 1930).

Ant. 18 §§ 29–30

The hostility between Jews and Samaritans is seen when some Samaritans defile the Jerusalem Temple at Passover by strewing bones in the sacred precincts (6–8 CE).

> When the Festival of Unleavened Bread, which we call Passover, was going on, the priests were accustomed to throw open the gates of the temple after midnight. This time, when the gates were first opened, some Samaritans, who had secretly entered Jerusalem, began to scatter human bones in the porticoes and throughout the temple.

Ant. 15 §§ 365–66

Herod the Great maintains his rule through repression of his subjects and their religion.

> They (the people) resented his (Herod's) carrying out of such arrangements as seemed to them to mean the dissolution of their religion and the disappearance of their customs. And these matters were discussed by all of them, for they were always being provoked and disturbed. Herod, however, gave the most careful attention to this situation, taking away any opportunities they might have (for agitation) and instructing them to apply themselves at all times to their work. No meeting of citizens was permitted, nor were walking together or being together permitted, and all their movements were observed. Those who were caught were punished severely, and many were taken, either openly or secretly, to the fortress of Hyrcania and there put to death. Both in the city and on the open roads there were men who spied on those who met together.

Ant. 18 §§ 4–8

Josephus attributes all of the misfortunes of the first century BCE to Jewish desires for independence, whose first public expression was a tax revolt in 6 CE. The rebels hope for divine assistance, but Josephus says that they act contrary to God's will.

> But a certain Judas, a Gaulanite from a city named Gamala, who had enlisted the aid of Saddok, a Pharisee, threw himself into the cause of rebellion. They said that the assessment carried with it a status amounting to downright slavery, no less, and appealed to the nation to make a bid for independence. They urged that in case of success the Jews would have laid the foundation of prosperity, while if they failed to obtain any such boon, they would win honour and renown for their lofty aim; and that Heaven would be their zealous helper to no lesser end than the furthering of their enterprise until it succeeded – all the more if with high devotion in their hearts

they stood firm and did not shrink from the bloodshed that might be necessary. Since the populace, when they heard their appeals, responded gladly, the plot to strike boldly made serious progress; and so these men sowed the seed of every kind of misery, which so afflicted the nation that words are inadequate. When wars are set afoot that are bound to rage beyond control, and when friends are done away with who might have alleviated the suffering, when raids are made by great hordes of brigands (bandits) and men of the highest standing are assassinated, it is supposed to be the common welfare that is upheld, but the truth is that in such cases the motive is private gain. They sowed the seed from which sprang strife between factions and the slaughter of fellow citizens. Some were slain in civil strife, for these men madly had recourse to butchery of each other and of themselves from a longing not to be outdone by their opponents; others were slain by the enemy in war. Then came famine, reserved to exhibit the last degree of shamelessness, followed by the storming and razing of cities until at last the very temple of God was ravaged by the enemy's fire through this revolt.

War 2 §§ 224–27

This incident under the Roman prefect Cumanus (48–52 CE) shows volatility during Passover and the potential for clashes between Jews and their occupiers, and it illustrates Roman insensitivity to Jewish religion.

The usual crowd had assembled at Jerusalem for the feast of unleavened bread, and the Roman cohort had taken up its position on the roof of the portico of the temple; for a body of men in arms invariably mounts guard at the feasts, to prevent disorders arising from such a concourse of people. Thereupon one of the soldiers, raising his robe, stooped in an indecent attitude, so as to turn his backside to the Jews, and made a noise in keeping with his posture. Enraged at this insult, the whole multitude with loud cries called upon Cumanus to punish the soldier; some of the more hot-headed young men and seditious persons in the crowd started a fight, and, picking up stones, hurled them at the troops. Cumanus, fearing a general attack upon himself, sent for reinforcements. These troops pouring into the porticoes, the Jews were seized with irresistible panic and turned to fly from the temple and make their escape into the town. But such violence was used as they pressed round the exists that they were trodden under foot and crushed to death by one another; upwards of thirty thousand perished, and the feast was turned into mourning for the whole nation and for every household lamentation.

Ant. 20 §§ 97–98

Eschatological prophets who expected God to liberate Israel were a feature of the first century CE. Their expectations were given shape by stories of God's great deeds on behalf of Israel in the past, especially at the exodus and in the conquest of the land under Joshua.

During the period when Fadus was procurator of Judaea, a certain impostor named Theudas persuaded the majority of the masses to take up their possessions and to follow him to the Jordan River. He stated that he was a prophet and that at his command the river would be parted and would provide them an easy passage. With this talk he deceived many. Fadus, however, did not permit them to reap the fruit of their folly, but sent against them a squadron of cavalry. These fell upon them unexpectedly, slew many of them and took many prisoners. Theudas himself was captured, whereupon they cut off his head and brought it to Jerusalem.

Ant. 13 §§ 297–98

Josephus interprets the Pharisees and Sadducees in terms that a Hellenistic audience could understand – their views of the afterlife and of the tension between fate and freewill. Perhaps most important from a Jewish point of view, however, was that they disagreed on interpretation of Torah. The Pharisees were developing a substantial body of interpretation that would eventually feed into the Rabbinic literature, whereas the Sadducees took the more limited view of Torah that may have been typical of the ruling priests in Jerusalem.

The Pharisees had passed on to the people certain regulations handed down by former generations and not recorded in the Laws of Moses, for which reason they are rejected by the Sadducaean group, who hold that only those regulations should be considered valid which were written down (in Scripture), and that those which had been handed down by former generations need not be observed. And concerning these matters the two parties came to have controversies and serious differences, the Sadducees having the confidence of the wealthy alone but no following among the populace, while the Pharisees have the support of the masses.

H.   4 Ezra

This apocalypse was written about a generation after the destruction of the Temple. For three of its seven visions, the seer Ezra questions God's justice, since he has punished the only nation on earth that attempts to live by his laws. An angel presents God as the just one who punishes the wicked and rewards the good and who has prepared a future world for the sake of the righteous, a view that Ezra ultimately accepts.

4 Ezra 10:21–23

The following excerpt shows the depth of suffering caused by the loss of the Temple.

You see how our sanctuary has been laid waste, our altar thrown down, our temple destroyed; our harp has been laid low, our song has been silenced, and our rejoicing has been ended; the light of our lampstand has been put out, the ark of our covenant has been plundered, our holy things have been polluted, and the name by which we are called has been almost profaned; our children have suffered abuse, our priests have been burned to death, our Levites have gone into exile, our virgins have been defiled, and our wives have been ravished; our righteous men have been carried off, our little ones have been cast out, our young men have been enslaved and our strong men made powerless. And, worst of all, the seal of Zion has been deprived of its glory, and given over into the hands of those that hate us.

Chapter 5

The Formation of Rabbinic Judaism, 70–640 CE

Günter Stemberger

A.   B. Git. 56a–b: Yohanan ben Zakkai's Escape from Jerusalem

The foundational legend of Rabbinic Judaism is presented in a style that makes clear that it does not pretend to give an exact report of a historical fact. It reduces known facts to their essentials – as seen by the rabbis – and tells them in a popular, anecdotal style. The stratagem that a fugitive feigns death in order to be smuggled out of a beleaguered city is found in other texts from late antiquity, too, and may be regarded as a conventional topos; that Yohanan is led before the Roman general, predicts that he will become emperor, and, when this prediction becomes true, is granted a wish, has a direct parallel in what Josephus Flavius recounts as his own experience. For the rabbis, it is the explanation how, out of the ashes of Jerusalem, their own movement could grow, be tolerated and later even protected by the very same Romans who had destroyed the Temple. The biblical verses that are so central to the story demonstrate that this all came about according to God's will and plan.

Abba Siqara was the chief of the zealots in Jerusalem. He was the son of Rabban Yohanan b. Zakkai's sister. He sent word to him, "Come to me in secret."

He came.

He said to him, "How long are you going to act in this way and kill everybody through famine?"

He said to him, "What should I do? If I say anything to them, they'll kill me, too."

He said to him, "Find some sort of remedy for me to get out of here, maybe there will be the possibility of saving something."

Source for readings in chapter 5 – Unless otherwise indicated, all translations: Jacob Neusner.

He said to him, "Pretend to be sick and have everybody come and ask about you; have something bad smelling and put it by you, so people will think you're dead. Then let your disciples carry you but nobody else – so that no one will feel that you're still light, since people know that a living being is lighter than a corpse."

They did so. R. Eliezer came in at one side, and R. Joshua at the other. When they got to the gate, they wanted to stab him. He said to them, "People will say they stabbed their master." They wanted to shove him over the wall. He said to them, "People will say they shoved their master [over the wall]." They opened the gate for him, and he got out.

When he got there, he said, "Peace be unto you, O king, peace be unto you, O king."

He said to him, "You are subject to the death penalty on two counts; first of all, I'm not a king, and you called me king; second, if I really am king, then how come you didn't come to me up till now?"

He said to him, "As to your statement, 'I'm not king,' the truth is you really are king, because if you weren't king, then Jerusalem wouldn't have been handed over to you, for it has been written, 'Lebanon shall fall by a mighty one' (Is. 10:34), and 'mighty one' refers only to a king, in line with the verse, 'And their mighty one shall be of themselves' (Jer. 30:21). Not only so, but Lebanon speaks of the Temple, 'This goodly mountain and Lebanon' (Deut. 3:25). And as to what you have said, 'If I really am king, then how come you didn't come to me up till now?,' up to now, the zealots among us wouldn't let me come."

He said to him, "So if there's a jar of honey with a lizard wrapped around it, wouldn't you break the honey to get rid of the lizard?"

He shut up.

R. Joseph, and some say R. Aqiba, recited in his regard: " 'God turns wise men backward and makes their knowledge foolish' (Is. 44:25). He ought to have said to him, 'We would take a pair of tongs and grab the lizard and kill it but leave the jar whole.' "

In the meantime, an agent came to him from Rome. He said to him, "Arise, for the Caesar is dead, and the citizens of Rome propose to enthrone you at the head."

At that moment he had finished putting on one boot. He wanted to put on the other, but it wouldn't go on. He wanted to take off that one, but it wouldn't go off. He said, "What's going on?" He said to him, "Don't be distressed. Good news has come to you, for it is written, 'Good news makes the bone fat' (Prov. 15:30). So what's the solution? Bring someone you despise and let him walk before you: 'A broken spirit dries up the bones' (Prov. 17:22)." He did so and the boot went on . . . .

He said to him, "Now I'm going away, and I'm sending someone else. So ask something from me, which I'll give you."

He said to him, "Give me Yavneh and its sages, and the chain of Rabban Gamaliel, and a physician to heal R. Sadoq."

R. Joseph, and some say, R. Aqiba, recited in his regard the verse, " 'God turns wise men backward and makes their knowledge foolish' (Is. 44:25). He ought to have said to him to leave the place alone this time." But he thought that maybe that much he won't do, and there would not be the possibility of saving anything at all.

B. M. Abot 1:1–18: The Chain of Tradition

The second text is the most popular and best known passage from Rabbinic literature. The whole tractate Abot was added to the Mishnah much later; it justifies the Mishnaic enterprise as part of the Torah and offers a series of wisdom sayings and moral apophthegms in the name of the masters of the Mishnah as expression of the spirituality that underlies the Mishnaic halakhah. The chapter quoted demonstrates the direct connection between the revelation on Sinai and the teaching of the rabbis down to Simeon, the father of Rabbi Judah the Prince, the redactor of the Mishnah – although for the members of the dynasty of the patriarchs, it no longer uses the terminology of receiving and handing on the Torah. The encompassing message of all the moral sayings is the centrality of the study of Torah. The biblical verse that concludes the chapter is probably a later addition.

1:1 Moses received Torah at Sinai and handed it on to Joshua, Joshua to elders, and elders to prophets. And prophets handed it on to the men of the great assembly. They said three things: Be prudent in judgment. Raise up many disciples. Make a fence for the Torah.

1:2 Simeon the Righteous was one of the last survivors of the great assembly. He would say: "On three things does the world stand: On the Torah, and on the Temple service, and on deeds of loving-kindness."

1:3 Antigonus of Sokho received [the Torah] from Simeon the Righteous. He would say: "Do not be like servants who serve the master on condition of receiving a reward, but [be] like servants who serve the master not on condition of receiving a reward. And let the fear of Heaven be upon you."

1:4 Yose ben Yoezer of Zeredah and Yose ben Yohanan of Jerusalem received [the Torah] from them. Yose ben Yoezer says: "Let your house be a gathering place for sages. And wallow in the dust of their feet, and drink in their words with gusto."

1:5 Yose ben Yohanan of Jerusalem says: "Let your house be open wide. And seat the poor at your table. And don't talk too much with women." (He referred to a man's wife, all the more so is the rule to be applied to the wife of one's fellow. In this regard did sages say: "So long as a man talks too much with a woman, he brings trouble on himself, wastes time better spent on studying the Torah, and ends up an heir of Gehenna.")

1:6 Joshua ben Perahyah and Nittai the Arbelite received [the Torah] from them. Joshua ben Perahyah says: "Set up a master for yourself. And get yourself a companion-disciple. And give everybody the benefit of the doubt."

1:7 Nittai the Arbelite says: "Keep away from a bad neighbor. And don't get involved with a bad person. And don't give up hope of retribution."

1:8   Judah ben Tabbai and Simeon ben Shetah received [the Torah] from them. Judah ben Tabbai says: "Don't make yourself like one of those who advocate before judges [while you yourself are judging a case]. And when the litigants stand before you, regard them as guilty. But when they leave you, regard them as acquitted (when they have accepted your judgment)."

1:9   Simeon ben Shetah says: "Examine the witnesses with great care. And watch what you say, lest they learn from what you say how to lie."

1:10   Shemaiah and Avtalyon received [the Torah] from them. Shemaiah says: "Love work. Hate authority. Don't get friendly with the government."

1:11   Avtalyon says: "Sages, watch what you say, lest you become liable to the punishment of exile, and go into exile to a place of bad water, and disciples who follow you drink bad water and die, and the name of Heaven be thereby profaned."

1:12   Hillel and Shammai received [the Torah] from them. Hillel says: "Be disciples of Aaron, loving peace and pursuing grace, loving people and drawing them near to the Torah."

1:13   He would say [in Aramaic]: "A name made great is a name destroyed and one who does not add, subtracts. And who does not learn is liable to death. And the one who uses the crown, passes away."

1:14   He would say: "If I am not for myself, who is for me? And when I am for myself, what am I? And if not now, when?"

1:15   Shammai says: "Make your learning of the Torah a fixed obligation. Say little and do much. Greet everybody cheerfully."

1:16   Rabban Gamaliel says: "Set up a master for yourself. Avoid doubt. Don't tithe by too much guesswork."

1:17   Simeon his son says: "All my life I grew up among the sages and found nothing better for a person than silence. And the learning is not the thing, but the doing. And whoever talks too much causes sin."

1:18   Rabban Simeon ben Gamaliel says: "On three things does the world stand: On justice, on truth, and on peace. As it is said, 'Execute the judgment of truth and peace in your gates' (Zech 8:16)."

C.   Y. Peah 2:6, 17a: Written and Oral Torah

Closely connected is the third text from the Yerushalmi. To solve a legal problem, Nahum the Scribe invokes nearly the same chain of tradition back to Sinai. It is even claimed that, wherever the origin of a law is unknown, one may assume that it was transmitted to Moses on Sinai. This leads to a general

Source for Reading C.:   Roger Brooks, *The Talmud of the Land of Israel. Peah* (Chicago: University of Chicago Press, 1990), pp. 123–8.

discussion of the relationship between written and oral Torah; the oral Torah is more important – it alone distinguishes Israel from the nations. Other rabbis, basing themselves on the interpretation of the precise formulation of Ex. 34:27 and Deut. 9:10, try to demonstrate that the complete oral Torah, including the sayings of a learned student, is to be regarded as law transmitted to Moses on Sinai. What is implied in the chain of tradition of Abot is here made explicit.

Once R. Simeon of Mispah sowed [his field with two varieties of wheat].

[The matter came] before Rabban Gamaliel. So they went up to the Chamber of Hewn Stone, and asked about the law [regarding sowing two varieties of wheat in one field].

Said Nahum the Scribe, "I have received [the following ruling] from R. Miasha, who received it from his father, who received it from the Pairs, who received it from the Prophets, [who received] the law [given] to Moses on Sinai regarding one who sows his field with two varieties of wheat:

"If he brings [the two varieties of wheat] to the threshing floor in only one lot, [he] sets aside one [portion of produce as] *peah* [required to be left for the poor from the corner of the field].

"If he brings [the wheat] to the threshing floor in two lots, [he] sets aside two [portions of produce as] *peah*."

Said R. Zeira in the name of R. Yohanan, "If a ruling [on a matter of law] is transmitted to you and you do not know its rationale, do not reject it in favor of another. For many matters of law were transmitted to Moses on Sinai, and all of them are embodied in the Mishnah!"

Said R. Avin, "[This advice] is proper. [For consider the ruling regarding] two varieties of wheat – were it not for the fact that Nahum [the Scribe] came along and explained [the law] to us, would we know [its rationale]?

R. Zeira in the name of R. Eleazar: " 'The many teachings I wrote for him [have been treated as something alien]' (Hos. 8: 12). Now, do the Torah's many teachings consist of written laws? [No!] Rather, [the verse means that] those laws expounded on [the explicit authority of] written verses [i.e., those with prooftexts] are more numerous [and so more unfamiliar and alien] than those expounded on [the mere authority of] oral tradition [and without prooftexts]."

And is this the proper [interpretation of Hos. 8:12]? [Are there really more laws expounded with prooftexts than without? No!]

Rather this verse means that those matters expounded on [the authority of] written sources are weightier than those expounded merely on [the authority of] oral tradition. . . .

[Providing another interpretation of the verse] said R. Avin, " 'Had I written for you the bulk of my [orally transmitted] Torah, you would be considered like a foreigner.' [For] what [is the difference] between us and the gentiles? They bring forth their books, and we bring forth our books; they bring forth their national records, and we bring forth our national records." [The only difference between Israel and the gentile nations is that a portion of the Torah remains oral, and has a special claim upon the nation of Israel.]

R. Haggai said in the name of R. Samuel bar Nahman, "Some matters of law were transmitted orally, and some matters of law were transmitted in writing, but we do not know which of these are deemed more weighty. But [we can derive an answer] on the basis of that which is written [in Scripture], 'For in accordance with these commandments I make a covenant with you and with Israel' (Ex. 34:27). This proves that those [commandments] transmitted orally are more weighty."

R. Yohanan and R. Yudan b. R. Simeon [had a dispute over the interpretation of Ex. 34:27]:

One of them said, "If you observe [laws that are transmitted] orally and if you observe [laws that are transmitted] in writing, I shall establish a covenant with you. But if not, I shall not establish a covenant with you."

The other said, "If you not only observe that which is transmitted orally but also uphold that which is transmitted in writing, [then in addition to the covenant,] you will receive a reward. But if not, you will receive no reward."

R. Joshua b. Levi said, "[The precise wording with which Scripture describes Sinaitic revelation is crucial, for Deut. 9:10 states, 'Then the Lord gave me two stone tablets, written with the finger of God; and upon them was written according to all these words that the Lord spoke with you in the mountain, out of the midst of the fire on the day of assembly.'] [Note that for] 'upon them [was written],' [Scripture reads] 'and upon them [was written];' [for] 'all [the words],' [Scripture reads] 'according to all [the words];' [for] 'words,' [Scripture reads] 'these words.'

"[These special formulations are meant to teach that the Torah given at Sinai included more than just the words written upon the tablets, but also] Scripture, the Mishnah, the Talmud, and Aggadah. [All these types of law are deemed to have the authority of Sinaitic revelation.]"

[In fact, the verse implies that] even that which a learned student someday in the future will recite before his master has the status of a law transmitted to Moses on Sinai.

D.   Y. Sanhedrin 1:2, 19a: The Ordination of Rabbis

This short excerpt embodies all our historical problems with regard to Rabbinic ordination. What exactly is meant by this term? Is it the laying on of hands (implying the handing on of authoritative tradition) or appointment to a concrete task? The text also hints at changes in the method of appointments, representing a shift of power from individual rabbis to the court (any court or the court of the patriarch?) and to the patriarch.

It was taught: Ordination (SMYKWT) requires three judges.

Is not laying on of hands the same as ordination? There [in Babylon] they call appointment to a court "ordination."

Said R. Ba, "At first each one would appoint his own disciples [to the court]. For example, R. Yohanan b. Zakkai appointed R. Eliezer and R. Joshua; R. Joshua appointed R. Aqiba; and R. Aqiba, R. Meir, and R. Simeon."

He said, "Let R. Meir take his seat first." R. Simeon's face turned pale.

R. Aqiba said to him, "Let it be enough for you that I and your Creator recognize your powers." . . . .

They made the rule, "A court that made an appointment without the knowledge and consent of the patriarch – the act of appointment is null.

"And a patriarch who made an appointment without the knowledge and consent of the court – his appointment is valid."

They reverted and made the rule that the court should make an appointment only with the knowledge and consent of the patriarch, and that the patriarch should make an appointment only with the knowledge and consent of the court.

E.   Y. Yebamot 12:6, 13a: Rabbis in the Service of the Community

This excerpt from the Yerushalmi illustrates the problems of a rabbi's attempt to enter the service of a local community. The townspeople themselves had asked for a rabbi who could help them, and they received him with great honors, but he was not up to the stress of the situation. The simple questions they asked him left him dumbfounded, even though he subsequently could answer them without problems before the patriarch. The text may use a historical precedent but transforms it into an ideal situation – would the local people of Simonias have really been interested in the questions they asked? how would they have known the answers? – in order to warn Rabbinic students of the problems they might face and to teach them the right attitudes when entering community service.

The people of Simonia came before Rabbi [Judah the Prince]. They said to him, "We want you to give us a man to serve as preacher, judge, reader [of Scripture], teacher [of tradition], and to do all the things we need." He gave them Levi bar Sisi.

They set up a great stage and seated him on it. They came and asked him, "A woman without arms – with what does she remove the shoe [in the rite of *halitzah*; Deut. 25:5–10]?" And he did not answer.

If she spit blood . . . ?

And he did not answer.

They said, "Perhaps he is not a master of the law. Let us ask him something about lore."

They came and asked him, "What is the meaning of the following verse, as it is written, 'But I will tell you what is inscribed in the book, in truth' (Dan. 10:21). If it is truth, why is it described as inscribed? And if it is inscribed, why is it described as truth?" He did not answer them.

They came back to Rabbi and said to him, "Is this a mason of your mason's guild [a pupil of your school]?" He said to them, "By your lives! I gave you someone who is as good as I am."

He sent and summoned him and asked him. He said to him, "If the woman spit blood, what is the law?" He answered him, "If there is a drop of spit in it, it is valid."

"A woman without arms – how does she remove the shoe?" He said to him, "She removes the shoe with her teeth."

He said to him, "What is the meaning of the following verse, as it is written, 'But I will tell you what is inscribed in the book, in truth' (Dan. 10: 21). If it is truth, why is it described as inscribed, and if it is inscribed, why is it described as truth?"

He said to him, "Before a decree is sealed, it is described as inscribed. Once it is sealed, it is described as truth."

He said to him, "And why did you not answer the people when they asked you these same questions?"

He said to him, "They made a great stage and seated me on it, and my spirit became exalted."

He recited concerning him the following verse of Scripture: " 'If you have been foolish, exalting yourself, or if you have been devising evil, put your hand on your mouth' (Prov. 30: 32). What caused you to make a fool of yourself in regard to teachings of Torah? It was because you exalted yourself through them."

F.   Leviticus Rabbah 13:5: The Four Kingdoms

This text is typical of the renewed interest in history in the second stage of Rabbinic thought, mainly in the Yerushalmi, Genesis Rabbah, and Leviticus Rabbah. The normal approach is the apocalyptic periodization of history, based mainly on Daniel and its idea of the four kingdoms hostile towards Israel. Knowing that his own period is that of the fourth empire, the midrashist can assure his readers and listeners that the end of a negative history is close; after the fourth empire, i.e., Rome, pagan or Christian, there will be the hoped for messianic reign and the glorious future of Israel. Although this approach to history might be regarded as ahistorical and applicable to any biblical text mentioning groups of four, the effort of the midrashist to find his own position within the course of history causes him to refer to many historical facts and figures that otherwise would not have been of any interest to the rabbis. The same effort also brings them to consider many aspects of contemporary experiences with the oppressing world power of Rome in order to identify it more clearly with the fourth kingdom.

Said R. Ishmael b. R. Nehemiah, "All the prophets foresaw what the pagan kingdoms would do [to Israel].

"The first man foresaw what the pagan kingdoms would do [to Israel].

"That is in line with the following verse of Scripture: 'A river flowed out of Eden [to water the garden, and there it divided and became four rivers]' [Gen. 2:10]"...

"[There it divided] and became four rivers" (Gen. 2:10) – this refers to the four kingdoms.

"The name of the first is Pishon (PSWN)" (Gen. 2:11).

This refers to Babylonia, on account [of the reference to Babylonia in the following verse:] "And their [the Babylonians'] horsemen spread themselves (PSW)" (Hab. 1:8).

[It is further] on account of [Nebuchadnezzar's] being a dwarf, shorter than ordinary men by a handbreadth.

"It is the one which flows around the whole land of Havilah" (Gen. 2:11).

This [reference to the river's flowing around the whole land] speaks of Nebuchadnezzar, the wicked man, who came up and surrounded the entire land of Israel, which places its hope in the holy one, blessed be he....

"The name of the second river is Gihon; [it is the one which flows around the whole land of Cush]" (Gen. 2:13).

This refers to Media, which produced Haman, that wicked man, who spit out venom like a serpent.

It is on account of the verse: "On your belly will you go" (Gen. 3:14).

"It is the one which flows around the whole land of Cush" (Gen. 2:13).

[We know that this refers to Media, because it is said:] "Who rules from India to Cush" (Est. 1:1).

"And the name of the third river is Tigris (HDQL), [which flows east of Assyria]" (Gen. 2:14).

This refers to Greece [Syria], which was sharp (HD) and frivolous (QL) in making its decrees, saying to Israel, "Write on the horn of an ox [= announce publicly] that you have no portion in the God of Israel."

"Which flows east (QDMT) of Assyria" (Gen. 2:14).

Said R. Huna, "In three aspects the kingdom of Greece was in advance (QDMH) of the present evil kingdom [Rome]: in respect to shipbuilding, the arrangement of camp vigils, and language."...

"And the fourth river is the Euphrates (PRT)" (Gen. 2:14).

This refers to Edom [Rome], since it was fruitful (PRT), and multiplied through the prayer of the elder [Isaac at Gen. 27:39]....

Another explanation: "Parat" – because in the end, "I am going to exact a penalty (PR) from it."

That is in line with the following verse of Scripture: "I have trodden (PWRH) the winepress alone" (Is. 63:3).

Abraham foresaw what the evil kingdoms would do [to Israel].

"[As the sun was going down] a deep sleep fell on Abraham; [and, lo, a dread and great darkness fell upon him]" (Gen. 15:12).

"Dread" (YMH) refers to Babylonia, on account of the statement, "Then Nebuchadnezzar was full of fury (HMH)" (Dan. 3:19).

"Darkness" refers to Media, which brought darkness to Israel through its decrees: "to destroy, to slay, and to wipe out all the Jews" (Esth. 7:4).

"Great" refers to Greece.

Said R. Judah b. R. Simon, "The verse teaches that the kingdom of Greece set up one hundred twenty-seven governors, one hundred and twenty-seven hyparchs, and one hundred twenty-seven commanders." . . .

"Fell on him" (Gen. 15:12). This refers to Edom, on account of the following verse: "The earth quakes at the noise of their [Edom's] fall" (Jer. 49:21).

There are those who reverse matters.

"Fear" refers to Edom, on account of the following verse: "And this I saw, a fourth beast, fearful, and terrible" (Dan. 7:7).

"Darkness" refers to Greece, which brought gloom through its decrees. For they said to Israel, "Write on the horn of an ox that you have no portion in the God of Israel."

"Great" refers to Media, on account of the verse: "King Ahasuerus made Haman [the Median] great" (Est. 3:1).

"Fell on him" refers to Babylonia, on account of the following verse: "Fallen, fallen is Babylonia" (Is. 21:9). . . .

Moses foresaw what the evil kingdoms would do [to Israel].

"The camel, rock badger, and hare" (Deut. 14:7).

The camel (GML) refers to Babylonia, "Happy will be he who requites (GML) you, with what you have done to us" (Ps. 147:8).

"The rock badger" (Deut. 14:7) – this refers to Media.

Rabbis and R. Judah b. R. Simon.

Rabbis say, "Just as the rock badger exhibits traits of uncleanness and traits of cleanness, so the kingdom of Media produced both a righteous man and a wicked one."

Said R. Judah b. R. Simon, "The last Darius was Esther's son. He was clean on his mother's side and unclean on his father's side."

"The hare" (Deut 14:7) – this refers to Greece. The mother of King Ptolemy was named "Hare" [in Greek: *lagos*].

"The pig" (Deut. 14:7) – this refers to Edom [Rome].

Moses made mention of the first three in a single verse and the final one in a verse by itself (Deut. 14:7, 8). Why so?

R. Yohanan and R. Simeon b. Laqish.

R. Yohanan said, "It is because [the pig] is equivalent to the other three."

And R. Simeon b. Laqish said, "It is because it outweighs them."

R. Yohanan objected to R. Simeon b. Laqish, " 'Prophesy, therefore, son of man, clap your hands [and let the sword come down twice, yea thrice]' " (Ezek. 21:14).

And how does R. Simeon b. Laqish interpret the same passage? He notes that [the threefold sword] is doubled (Ezek. 21:14).

R. Phineas and R. Hilqiah in the name of R. Simon: "Among all the prophets, only two of them revealed [the true evil of Rome], Assaf and Moses.

"Assaf said, 'The pig out of the wood ravages it' (Ps. 80:14).

"Moses said, 'And the pig, [because it parts the hoof and is cloven-footed but does not chew the cud]' [Lev. 11:7].

"Why is [Rome] compared to a pig?

"It is to teach you the following: Just as, when a pig crouches and produces its hooves, it is as if to say, 'See how I am clean [since I have a cloven hoof],' so this evil kingdom acts arrogantly, seizes by violence, and steals, and then gives the appearance of establishing a tribunal for justice."

There was the case of a ruler in Caesarea who put thieves, adulterers, and sorcerers to death, while at the same time telling his counselor "That same man [I] did all these three [crimes] on a single night."...

Another interpretation [now treating "bring the cud" (GR) as "bring along in its train" (GRR)]:

"The camel" (Lev. 11:4) – this refers to Babylonia.

"Which brings along in its train" – for it brought along another kingdom after it.

"The rock badger" (Lev. 11:5) – this refers to Media.

"Which brings along in its train" – for it brought along another kingdom after it.

"The hare" (Lev. 11:6) – this refers to Greece.

"Which brings along in its train" – for it brought along another kingdom after it.

"The pig" (Lev 11:7) – this refers to Rome.

"Which does not bring along in its train," for it did not bring along another kingdom after it.

And why is it then called "pig" (HZYR)? For it restores (MHZRT) the crown to the one who truly should have it [namely, Israel, whose dominion will begin when the rule of Rome ends].

That is in line with the following verse of Scripture: "And saviors will come up on Mount Zion to judge the Mountain of Esau [Rome], and the kingdom will then belong to the Lord" (Ob. 1:21).

G.   B. Baba Qamma 83b–84b: Biblical Foundation of the Mishnah

The last text illustrates how the Babylonian Talmud unites the philosophical way of reasoning typical of the Mishnah with the open dependence on the revealed text of Scripture so prominent in Rabbinic writings of the second period – Yerushalmi and contemporary midrashim. The M. B.Q. 8:1 states, contrary to the plain meaning of Ex. 21:24, that somebody who blinded his fellow's eye shall not be blinded but has to pay monetary compensation. The text – only a very small excerpt from a lengthy discussion in the Babli – now tries to demonstrate that this ruling of the Mishnah corresponds exactly to the meaning of the biblical text. The question is taken up time and again in order to prove that a literal understanding of the biblical text would be in conflict with the overall system of biblical law and that for this reason the ruling of the Mishnah, which never refers to the biblical text, is the only correct understanding of the Bible.

M. B.Q. 8:1: He who injures his fellow is liable to [compensate] him on five counts: (1) injury, (2) pain, (3) medical costs, (4) loss of income [lit.: loss of time], and (5) indignity. For injury: How so? [If] one has blinded his eye, cut off his hand, broken his leg, they regard him as a slave up for sale in the market and make an estimate of how much he was worth beforehand [when whole], and how much he is now worth....

Talmudic Commentary: Why [should there be monetary compensation]? Scripture states, "An eye for an eye" (Ex. 21:24), so might I not say that it means an eye literally?

Perish the thought! For it has been taught on Tannaite authority: Might one suppose that if someone blinded a person's eye, the court should blind his eye? Or if he cut off his hand, then the court should cut off his hand, or if he broke his leg, the court should break his leg? Scripture states, "He who hits any man...and he who hits any beast" – just as if someone hits a beast, he is assigned to pay monetary compensation, so if he hits a man, he is required to pay monetary compensation.

And if you prefer, then note the following: "Moreover you shall take no ransom for the life of a murderer, who is guilty of death" (Num. 35:31) – for the life of a murderer you shall take no ransom, but you shall take a ransom for the major limbs, which will not grow back.

To what verse in regard to smiting does the cited passage "He who hits any man...and he who hits any beast" refer? If we say, to "And he who kills a beast shall make it good, and he who kills a man shall be put to death" (Lev. 24:21), that verse refers to not personal damages but death. Rather, it is the following: "And he who smites a beast mortally shall make it good: life for life" (Lev. 24:18), and, nearby, "and if a man maim his neighbor as he has done so shall it be done to him" (Lev. 24:19).

But that verse speaks not at all of smiting!

We are speaking of what happens when one hits, that is at the foundation of this verse, and what happens when one hits, that is at the foundation of the other: just as hitting mentioned in the case of the beast speaks of payment of monetary damages, so also here smiting in the case of man speaks of payment of reparations in money.

Yeah, well, what about, "And he who hits any man mortally shall surely be put to death" (Lev. 24:17)?

That speaks of monetary compensation.

How do you know it speaks of monetary compensation? Maybe it speaks of the death penalty?

Perish the thought! First of all, it is linked with the stated case, "He who hits a beast mortally shall make it good," and, furthermore, it is written in context, "as he has done, so shall be done to him" (Lev. 24:19) – meaning, then, monetary compensation!

What is the meaning of, And if you prefer...?

This is what troubled the Tannaite author of the passage: How come you derive the lesson on the law covering a human being who injures a human being from the law that covers the case of a human being that hits an animal, and not from the law governing a case in which a human being kills another human being? In that case,

I would answer: we derive the law covering injury, from the law covering injury, and do not derive the law covering injury from the law covering murder. But then, someone could well argue, derive the law of injury dealing with man from another case of a tort done to man, but do not derive the law of injury on man from the case of a beast. And that explains the resort to a further proof, namely, And if you prefer, then note the following: "Moreover you shall take no ransom for the life of a murderer, who is guilty of death" (Num. 35:31) – for the life of a murderer you shall take no ransom, but you shall take ransom for the major limbs, which will not grow back.

But does the verse, "Moreover you shall take no ransom for the life of a murderer, who is guilty of death" (Num. 35:31), serve that purpose in particular, namely, to exclude not taking ransom for the major limbs? Is it not required so that the All-Merciful might make the statement that you should not impose upon such a criminal two penalties, that is, do not take money from him and then put him to death?

Not at all, for that proposition derives from "According to his crime" (Deut. 25:2), meaning, for one crime you hold him liable, but you do not hold him liable for two crimes.

Still, maybe the sense of the All-Merciful is that you should not take money from him and then release him?

If that were the case, Scripture should have said, "You shall not take a ransom for the one who is guilty of death." Why specify "for the life of the murderer in particular," unless it is to show that "for the life of the murderer" you shall take no ransom, but you shall take a ransom for the major limbs, which will not grow back?

Then since it is written, "Moreover you shall take no ransom," why do I have to draw an analogy in the matter of hitting a beast and a human being?

Say: If I had to derive the rule only from that passage, I might have supposed, if he wants, let him give the actual eye, and if he wants, let him give the price of the eye. So we are informed: just as if someone hits a beast, he is assigned to pay monetary compensation, so if he hits a man, he is required to pay monetary compensation.

Chapter 6

The Canon of Rabbinic Judaism: The Mishnah and the Midrash

Jacob Neusner

A.   The Mishnah

To make sense of the Mishnah we have to pay close attention to how the document formulates its ideas, to what the document says, and to the issues that lie beneath the surface of the Mishnah's statement. To show what is required, let us take up the final paragraph of Mishnah-tractate Uqsin (3:11):

A.   Honeycombs: from what point are they susceptible to uncleanness in the status of liquid?

B.   The House of Shammai say, "When one smokes out [the bees from the combs, so that one can potentially get at the honey]."

C.   The House of Hillel say, "When one will actually have broken up [the honeycombs to remove the honey]."

Let us look, first of all, at the way in which the passage spells out its main point and then turn to the proposition before us. The authors begin with an announcement of the topic at hand, honeycombs, and then ask their question, A. We have a single sentence by way of an answer:

> *Honeycombs: from what point are they susceptible to uncleanness in the status of liquid?*
> *When ["it is from the point at which"] one smokes out [the bees from the combs, so that one can get at the honey].*

or:

> *Honeycombs: from what point are they susceptible to uncleanness in the status of liquid?*
> *"When one will actually have broken up [the honeycombs to remove the honey]."*

So we have a question followed by a selection of answers, and each answer can stand on its own to respond to the question. Not only so, but the simple analysis involving identifying successive sentences shows us how the sentences are broken up and brought together into a single coherent statement. This is done by creating a dispute out of several autonomous statements. We assign a statement to an authority, the Houses of Shammai and Hillel. Then we make all the statements bearing attributions into a sequence of responses to a simple problem, thus a dispute. The formulation of the passage is very tight, a kind of poetry. The original Hebrew shows even closer balance than does the English, since, at M. Uqs. 3:11, the statements of the two Houses are made up of precisely the same number of syllables. So the match is precise.

We need hardly notice that it is very easy to memorize such highly patterned language. In point of fact, most of the Mishnah is written not in narrative prose, flowing declarative sentences for instance, but in these brief thought units with a question (normally implicit) and an answer, set forth in a disciplined way. There will be a set of thought-units following a single syntactic and grammatical pattern. Put together, they set forth three or five cases that allow one readily to recover the principle that explains all of them. Accordingly, we deal with a piece of writing quite different from simple narrative, in that the author wants us to learn the point by putting together things that are given to us to draw a conclusion that is not spelled out for us – a very warm compliment to us as readers.

What is at stake in this rather odd dispute? At issue is the status, uncleanness or clean – of liquid, which is susceptible to the uncleanness deriving from sources of uncleanness specified by Leviticus Chapters Eleven through Fifteen. The premise of the question, "from what point does liquid become susceptible," is that liquid may or may not be susceptible to uncleanness at all.

Let us work our way back from the answer to the question, beginning with the principle the question allows us to derive as shared by both parties. One party maintains that the liquid of honeycombs is susceptible to uncleanness when one has smoked out the bees, the other, when one has broken the honeycombs. Clearly, therefore, when I have access to the honey, so that I may make use of it, the honey is susceptible; hence all agree that liquid that is not accessible to human use (in this context) is deemed insusceptible; Lev. 11:34, 37 are read to make that point. So much for the concrete issue.

But what is the principle at hand? I have interpolated some words to make clear in context the issue of whether what is potential is real. That is to say, do I take account of what potentially may happen, or do I treat as fact only what has happened? The House of Shammai say that once you have smoked out the bees, you have access to the honey. What is potential is treated as equivalent to what is actual. Since you can get at the honey, it can be useful to you and so is susceptible. The House of Hillel say that only when you actually have broken the honeycombs by a concrete deed is the honey susceptible. What is potential is not taken into account, only what is actual.

So at stake in this odd passage is a very familiar debate. It specifically concerns the old philosophical problem of the acorn and the oak, the egg and the chicken, the potential and the actual. Clearly we are in the hands of a very odd author, who mounts discourse at three dimensions all at once: (1) through *how* things are said, (2) through *what* is said, and (3) through *what lies beneath the surface* of things as well. That author has enormous respect for us, the readers, assuming that we read and hear with so astute and sentient an interiority as to gain the message even in the subtle media through which the message is conveyed. With such a compliment paid to us, how can we decline the invitation to study all sixty-three Mishnaic tractates, five hundred thirty-one chapters in all! With this in mind, let us ask how the Mishnah puts forward a theological statement through the discussion of legal problems. What follows is Professor Martin Jaffee's exposition of how the Mishnah states that Israel and God form partners in the possession of the Holy Land.

B.   Martin Jaffee, How the Mishnah Makes a Theological Statement: Mishnah Ma'aserot Chapter One

Tractate Maaserot (Tithes) defines the class of produce which is subject to Scripture's diverse agricultural tithes, and determines when payment of these taxes is due. It thus amplifies, in rather predictable ways, those aspects of Scripture which are likely to interest Israelites concerned with the proper tithing of their food. That is, the tractate tells its audience what to tithe, and stipulates when they must remove the offerings from food they wish to eat. Where Scripture is clear on these matters, Mishnah is content to repeat and highlight the obvious. Thus in regard to the kinds of produce which must be tithed, Maaserot simply affirms Scripture's view that these gifts, the priestly dues and tithes, are to be offered from all produce grown in the fields of the Land of Israel (cf. Deut. 14:22): [The tractate's questions are:] When, in the course of a crop's growth, may it be used to satisfy the obligation to tithe? When, further, in the course of the harvest of the crop, must the tithes actually be paid? . . .

Mishnah's answer to this twofold question is generated by Scripture's assumption that the agricultural offerings of the Land of Israel are a sacred tax which Israelites owe to God for the property they take from his Land (Lev. 27:30). Accordingly, the tractate points out that produce *may* be tithed as soon as it ripens, for at this point the crop becomes valuable as property. Payment of the tithes is not due, however, until the farmer or householder actually claims his harvested produce as personal property. This occurs, in Maaserot's view, whenever a person brings untithed produce from his field into his home, or when he prepares untithed produce for sale in the market. Produce appropriated in this fashion is forbidden for consumption until it is tithed. Having claimed the produce

Source for Reading B.:   Martin Jaffee, Mishnah's Theology of Tithing: A Study of Tractate Ma'aserot (Scholars Press, 1981), pp. 1–2, 4–6, 28–30, 40.

for his own personal use, the farmer must remove those portions which belong to God before he may use it himself. . . .

[The tractate thus addresses a theological problem.] That is to determine, and then to adjudicate, the respective claims of man and God to the produce of the Land of Israel. At stake, in other words, is the relationship of Israel to the Lord of its ancestral land. The theological agendum emerges most clearly if, from our present standpoint, we return to the key points which interest Mishnah as produce passes from the field of the Israelite farmer to his table. We recall that produce first becomes subject to the law of tithes when it ripens in the field. God's claim to the tithes of the produce, is made only when the produce itself becomes of value to the farmer. Only after produce has ripened may we expect the farmer to use it in his own meals, or sell it to others for use in theirs. Thus God's claim to it is first provoked, and must therefore be protected, from that point onward. As we have seen, the produce is permitted as food only if the farmer acknowledges God's prior claim, e.g., by refraining from eating it as he would his own produce. Should the farmer overreach his privilege, however, either by preparing to make a meal of the produce in his field or by claiming to be its sole owner, he loses his privilege to eat altogether, until he tithes. Once God's claim against the produce is satisfied by the removal of the tithes, the produce is released for use in all daily meals. It is now common food. . . .

The fundamental theological datum of Maaserot, then, is that God acts and wills in Mishnah-tractate Ma'aserot in response to human intentions, God's invisible action can be discerned by carefully studying the actions of human beings. . . . Nowhere do the framers of Maaserot expect – or allow for – unilateral or uncontrollable actions proceeding from the initiative of God. As in the time of the Temple, then, God remains Lord of the Land of Israel, and owner of its fruits. But when his Temple no longer stands and his Land has been defiled, his status as Lord depends upon the action of his remaining people. That is the whole point of linking God's claim upon the tithes to the social rhythms of the agricultural enterprise. Those who impose upon themselves the task of reconstructing the human and social fabric of Israelite life make effective the holiness of the Land and make real the claims of its God. This reciprocity between Israel and its God, the near parity between two partners in the task of re-creation, is what distinguishes the vision of Mishnah-tractate Ma'aserot's thinkers from that of the priestly theoreticians of Scripture, from whom Mishnah inherits and transforms the law of tithes.

1:1

A.   A general principle they stated concerning tithes:

B.   anything that is

    (1)   food,

    (2)   cultivated,

    (3)   and which grows from the earth is subject to [the law of] tithes.

C. And yet another general principle they stated:
D. anything which at its first [stage of development] is food and which at its ultimate [stage of development] is food –
E. even though [the farmer] maintains [its growth] in order to increase the food [it will yield] –
F. is subject [to the law of tithes whether it is] small or large (i.e., at all points in its development).
G. But (w-) anything (lk s-) which at its first [stage of development] is not food, yet which at its ultimate [stage of development] is food (e.g., the fruit of trees: T. 1:1b)
H. is not subject [to the laws of tithes] until it becomes edible.

M. Ma'aserot 1:1

The three criteria enumerated at B point out that all plants cultivated by man as food are subject to the law of tithes. When such agricultural produce is harvested, the householder must designate a fixed percentage of it as heave-offering and tithes. These offerings are deemed sanctified and are therefore set aside from the rest of the harvest for the use of priests and others to whom such offerings are due (M. Ter. 3:5–8). Only after the removal of these offerings is the remaining produce deemed "unconsecrated," and permitted for general consumption.

The subject of this process of sanctification and deconsecration is food (B1) that exhibits two distinguishing characteristics. As agricultural produce, it is the focus of the Israelite farmer's labor on his own land (B2), and, as plant-life, it grows from land given to Israel by God (B3). According to B, then, the law of tithes applies only to food which man labors to produce from land leased from God. Sanctification, in other words, pertains only to produce which issues from land over which both God and man have legitimate claims. Man's claim is justified by his need and his labor, God's by his ultimate ownership of the land and all its fruits. Claims on both sides are satisfied by the separation of a portion of the produce for God. With God's portion removed, the remainder is deemed fit for human consumption. In Mishnah's technical language, it is now *hulin metuqanin*, food which has been made suitable for common use by the removal of offerings. . . .

[O]nce produce is edible it is subject to the law even if the farmer does not deem it worthy of harvest until the yield is greater. At issue is the criterion for determining when a crop is deemed to be food. Such a criterion can be based upon either the actual condition of the produce, i.e., its edibility, or the actions of the farmer, i.e., his harvest of the crop for food. E rules that the edibility of the produce is the normative criterion, for its edible condition permits us to assume that the farmer deems the produce useful as food. The alternative criterion is that we deem the crop to be food only when it is harvested as such. This would permit the farmer to use the produce prior to the harvest without removing tithes. By rejecting this alternative, E stresses the fact that food is food whether man intends to harvest it as such or not. It is subject to the law when it is edible, regardless of human intentions. As we shall see, the problem of establishing when the objective condition of produce imposes upon it the strictures of the law, and when, on the other hand, the subjective intentions of the owner are determinative, proves to be recurrent concern of the tractate (cf. M. 4:5–6)....

1:4

A.   And among green vegetables –
B.   cucumbers, and gourds, and chatemelons, and muskmelons.
C.   Apples and citrons
D.   are subject [to the law of tithes whether they are] large or small.
E.   R. Simeon exempts citrons which are immature.
F.   That which is subject [to the law] among bitter almonds [i.e., the small ones] is exempt among sweet [almonds].
G.   That which is subject [to the law] among sweet almonds [i.e., the large ones] is exempt among bitter [almonds].

M. Ma'aserot 1:4

What is striking in all this is that the entire mechanism of restrictions and privileges, from the field to home or market, is set in motion solely by the intentions of the common farmer. Priests cannot claim their dues whenever they choose, and God himself plays no active role in establishing when the produce must be tithed. Indeed, the framers of Maaserot assume a profound passivity on the part of God. For them, it is human actions and intentions which move God to affect the world. God's claims against the Land's produce, that is to say, are only reflexes of those very claims on the part of Israelite farmers. God's interest in his share of the harvest, as I said, is first provoked by the desire of the farmer for the ripened fruit of his labor. His claim to that fruit, furthermore, becomes binding only when the farmer makes ready to claim his own rights to its use, whether in the field or at home or market.

The fundamental theological datum of Maaserot, then, is that God acts and wills in response to human intentions, God's invisible action can be discerned by carefully studying the actions of human beings. This datum must now be assessed in the context of the time and place in which Tractate Mishnah-tractate Ma'aserot is constructed. With the Mishnah as a whole, Maaserot comes into being in second-century Palestine, at a time in which Israel's hopes for God's victory over his enemies have been abandoned, and in a place in which his Temple, the visible symbol of his presence, no longer stands. In such a time and place, both Maaserot's loyalty to Scripture's ancient tithing law, and its distinctive innovations upon that law, are equally suggestive. Fundamentally, Maaserot affirms an essential continuity of God's Lordship over the Land of Israel. It presents Scripture's command to tithe all the fruit of the field as an obligation which extends even to the present. God's ancient tax on the Land must still be offered in its proper season, as it was when the Temple still stood and its priestly officiants brought God's blessing from heaven into the Land. At a time in which God's inability to protect his Land or its inhabitants has long been clear, this is a bold claim indeed. Maaserot asserts that historical catastrophe has left the sacred economy of Israel undisturbed. While Temple is gone, the Land remains holy and its fruit is still under the claim of God. Those remaining in the Land, it follows, remain bound by the ancient system of obligations which their ancestors accepted in covenant with God.

C.   The Midrash: Genesis Rabbah – The Rules of History Set Forth by Revelation

The framers of Genesis Rabbah intended to find those principles of society and of history that would permit them to make sense of the ongoing history of Israel. These principles they found in Scripture, and that is how the sages formed Midrash as prophecy. They took for granted that Scripture speaks to the life and condition of Israel, the Jewish people. And that address, they understood as fact, was not to Israel in olden times alone or mainly, but to Israel in the here and now: this morning's newspaper, as God would publish it in heaven!

In view of the framers of Midrash as prophecy, the entire narrative of Genesis is so formed as to point toward the sacred history of Israel, the Jewish people: its slavery and redemption; its coming Temple in Jerusalem; its exile and salvation at the end of time. In the reading of the authors at hand, therefore, the powerful message of Genesis proclaims that the world's creation commenced a single, straight line of events, leading in the end to the salvation of Israel and through Israel all humanity. That message – that history heads toward Israel's salvation – sages derived from the book of Genesis and contributed to their own day. Therefore in their reading of Scripture, a given story will bear a deeper truth about what it means to be Israel, on the one side, and what in the end of days will happen to Israel, on the other. True, their reading makes no explicit reference to what, if anything, had changed in the age of Constantine. But we do find repeated references to the four kingdoms, Babylonia, Media, Greece, Rome – and beyond the fourth will come Israel, fifth and last. So the sages' message, in their theology of history, was that the present anguish prefigured the coming vindication of God's people.

It follows that sages read Genesis as the history of the world with emphasis on Israel. So the lives portrayed, the domestic quarrels and petty conflicts with the neighbors, all serve to yield insight into what was to be. Why so? Because the deeds of the patriarchs taught lessons on how the children were to act, and, it further followed, the lives of the patriarchs signaled the history of Israel. Israel constituted one extended family, and the metaphor of the family, serving the nation as it did, imparted to the stories of Genesis the character of a family record. History become genealogy conveyed the message of salvation. These propositions really laid down the same judgment, one for the individual and the family, the other for the community and the nation, since there was no differentiating. Every detail of the narrative therefore served to prefigure what was to be, and Israel found itself, time and again, in the revealed facts of the history of the creation of the world, the decline of humanity down to the time of Noah, and, finally, its ascent to Abraham, Isaac, and Israel.

In Genesis Rabbah, the entire narrative of Genesis is so formed as to point toward the sacred history of Israel, the Jewish people: its slavery and redemption; its coming Temple in Jerusalem; its exile and salvation at the end of time. The powerful prophetic message of Genesis in the rereading of the authorship of Genesis Rabbah proclaims that the world's creation commenced a single, straight line of significant events, that is to say, a history, leading in the end to the salvation of Israel and through Israel all humanity. In the story of the beginnings of creation, humanity, and Israel, we find the message of the meaning and end of the life of the Jewish people. The deeds of the founders supply signals for the children about what is going to come in the future. So the biography of Abraham, Isaac, and Jacob also constitutes a protracted account of the history of Israel later on. If the sages of Judaism could announce a single syllogism and argue it systematically, that is the proposition upon which they would insist.

We may now generalize on the theory of history in Genesis Rabbah. The sages who produced that book understood that stories about the progenitors, presented in the book of Genesis, define the human condition and proper conduct for their children, Israel, in time to come. Accordingly, they systematically asked Scripture to tell them how they were supposed to conduct themselves at the critical turnings of life. The first thing to notice is how a variety of events is made to prove a syllogism. The stories of Genesis therefore join stories of other times and persons in Israel's history. All of them equally, and timelessly, point to prevailing rules. Syllogistic argument, resting on lists of facts of the same classification, wrests the narrative out of its one-time and time-bound setting and turns it into a statement of rules that prevail everywhere and all the time for Israel. Here is a good example of the mode of argument of the document.

Genesis Rabbah 96

XCVI:III

1.A.   "And when the time drew near that Israel must die, [he called his son Joseph and said to him, 'If now I have found favor in your sight, put your hand under my thigh and promise to deal loyally and truly with me. Do not bury me in Egypt, but let me lie with my fathers; carry me out of Egypt and bury me in their burying place.' He answered, 'I will do as you have said.'

And he said, 'Swear to me.' And he swore to him. Then Israel bowed himself upon the head of his bed]" (Gen. 47:29–31):

B. "There is no man that has power of the spirit ... neither is there dominion in the day of death" (Eccl. 8:8).

C. Said R. Joshua of Sikhnin in the name of R. Levi, "As to the trumpets that Moses made in the wilderness, when Moses lay on the point of death, the Holy One, blessed be he, hid them away, so that he would not blow on them and summon the people to him.

D. "This was meant to fulfill this verse: ' ... neither is there dominion in the day of death' (Eccl. 8:8).

E. "When Zimri did his deed, what is written? 'And Phineas went after the man of Israel into the chamber' (Num. 25:8). So where was Moses, that Phineas should speak before he did?

F. ' ... neither is there dominion in the day of death' (Eccl. 8:8).

G. "But the formulation expresses humiliation. Salvation was handed over to Phineas, [and Moses] abased himself.

H. "So too with David: 'How king David was old' (1 Kgs. 1:1). What is stated about him when he lay dying? 'Now the days of David drew near, that he should die' (1 Kgs. 21:1).

I. "What is said is not '*King* David,' but merely 'David.'

J. "The same applies to Jacob, when he was on the point of death, he humbled himself to Joseph, saying to him, 'If now I have found favor in your sight.' [So he abased himself, since there is no dominion on the day of death.]

K. "When did this take place? As he drew near the end: 'And when the time drew near that Israel must die.' "

What strikes the exegete is the unprepossessing language used by Jacob in speaking to Joseph. The intersecting verse makes clear that, on the day of one's death, one no longer rules. Several examples of that fact are given, Moses, David, finally Jacob. So the syllogism about the loss of power on the occasion of death derives proof from a number of sources, and the passage has not been worked out to provide the exegesis of our base verse in particular. The exposition is all the more moving because the exegete focuses upon his proposition, rather than on the great personalities at hand. His message obviously is that even the greatest lose all dominion when they are going to die. In this way the deeds of the founders define the rule for the descendants.

As a corollary to the view that the biography of the fathers prefigures the history of the descendants, sages maintained that the deeds of the children – the holy way of life of Israel – follow the model established by the founders long ago. So they looked in Genesis for the basis for the things they held to be God's will for Israel. And they found ample proof. Sages invariably searched the stories of Genesis for evidence of the origins not only of creation and of Israel but also of Israel's cosmic way of life, its understanding of how, in the passage of nature and the seasons, humanity worked out its relationship with God. The holy way of life that Israel lived through the seasons of nature therefore would make its mark upon the stories of the creation of the world and the beginning of Israel

Part of the reason sages pursued the interest at hand derived from polemic. From the first Christian century theologians of Christianity maintained that salvation did not depend upon keeping the laws of the Torah. Abraham, after all, had been justified and he did not keep the Torah, which, in his day, had not yet been given. So sages time and again would maintain that Abraham indeed kept the entire Torah even before it had been revealed. They further attributed to Abraham, Isaac, and Jacob rules of the Torah enunciated only later on, for example, the institution of prayer three times a day. But the passage before us bears a different charge. It is to Israel to see how deeply embedded in the rules of reality were the patterns governing God's relationship to Israel. That relationship, one of human sin and atonement, divine punishment and forgiveness, expresses the most fundamental laws of human existence. Here is yet another rule that tells sages what to find in Scripture.

Genesis Rabbah 98

XCVIII:I
1.A. "Then Jacob called his sons [and said, 'Gather yourselves together, that I may tell you what shall befall you in days to come. Assemble and hear, O sons of Jacob, and hearken to Israel, your father. Reuben, you are my first-born, my might and the first fruits of my strength, pre-eminent in pride and pre-eminent in power. Unstable as water, you shall not have pre-eminence, because you went up to your father's bed, then you defiled it, you went up to my couch!']" (Gen. 49:1–4):
  B. "I will cry to God Most High, [unto God who completes it for me]" (Ps. 57:3):
  C. "I will cry to God Most High": on the New Year.
  D. "...unto God who completes it for me": on the Day of Atonement.
  E. To find out which [goat] is for the Lord and which one is for an evil decree.
2.A. Another matter: "I will cry to God Most High, [unto God who completes it for me]" (Ps. 57:3):
  B. "I will cry to God Most High": refers to our father, Jacob.
  C. "...unto God who completes it for me": for the Holy One, blessed be he, concurred with him to give each of the sons a blessing in accord with his character.
  D. "Then Jacob called his sons [and said, 'Gather yourselves together, that I may tell you what shall befall you in days to come]."

The intersecting verse invites the comparison of the judgment of the Days of Awe to the blessing of Jacob, and that presents a dimension of meaning that the narrative would not otherwise reveal. Just as God decides which goat serves what purpose, so God concurs in Jacob's judgment of which son/tribe deserves what sort of blessing. So Jacob stands in the stead of God in this stunning comparison of Jacob's blessing to the day of judgment. The link between Jacob's biography and the holy life of Israel is fresh.

Sages read the narrative of creation and the fall of Adam to testify to the redemption and the salvation of Israel. The following passage provides a stunning example of the basic theory of sages on how the stories of creation are to be read:

Genesis Rabbah 29

XXIX:III

1.A.   "And Noah found grace" (Gen. 6:8):

   B.   Said R. Simon, "There were three acts of finding on the part of the Holy One, blessed be he:

   C.   " 'And you found [Abraham's] heart faithful before you' (Neh. 9:8).

   D.   " 'I have found David my servant' (Ps. 89:21).

   E.   " 'I found Israel like grapes in the wilderness' (Hos. 9:10)."

   F.   His fellows said to R. Simon, "And is it not written, 'Noah found grace in the eyes of the Lord' (Gen. 6:8)?"

   G.   He said them, "He found it, but the Holy One, blessed be he, did not find it."

   H.   Said R. Simon, " 'He found grace in the wilderness' (Jer. 31:1) on account of the merit of the generation of the Wilderness."

The proposition draws on the verse at hand, but makes its own point. It is that the grace shown to Noah derived from Israel. Noah on his own – that is, humanity – enjoyed salvation only because of Israel's merit. The proposition is striking and daring. God "found," that is, made an accidental discovery, of a treasure, consisting only of three: Abraham, David, and Israel. These stand for the beginning, the end, and the holy people that started with Abraham and found redemption through David. As if to underline this point, we refer, H, to the generation of the wilderness and its faith, which merited gaining the Land.

A cogent and uniform worldview accompanied the sages at hand when they approached the text of Genesis. This worldview they systematically joined to that text, fusing the tale at hand with that larger context of imagination in which the tale was received and read. Accordingly, when we follow the sages' mode of interpreting the text, we find our way deep into their imaginative life. Scripture becomes the set of facts that demonstrate the truth of the syllogisms that encompassed and described the world, as sages saw it. The next stage in my demonstration of the systematic and deeply polemical reading at hand will take the simple form of successive illustration of the basic thesis. That thesis is that Israel's salvific history informs and infuses the creation of the world. That story takes on its true meaning from what happened to Israel, and it follows that Israel's future history accounts for the creation of the world.

Genesis Rabbah 20

XX:I

1.A.   "Then the Lord God said to the serpent, 'Because you have done this, cursed are you above all cattle and above all wild animals'" (Gen. 3:14):

  B.   "A slanderer shall not be established in the earth; the violent and wicked man shall be hunted with thrust upon thrust" (Ps. 140:12).

  C.   Said R. Levi, "In the world to come the Holy One, blessed be he, will take the nations of the world and bring them down to Gehenna. He will say to them, 'Why did you impose fines upon my children.' They will say to him, 'Some of them slandered others among them. The Holy One, blessed be he, will then take these [Israelite slanderers] and those and bring them down to Gehenna."

2.A.   Another interpretation: "A slanderer" refers to the snake, who slandered his creator.

  B.   "Will not be established [standing upright] on earth:" "Upon your belly you shall go" (Gen. 3:14).

  C.   "The violent and wicked man shall be hunted:" What is written is not "with a thrust" but "with thrust after thrust," [since not only the serpent was cursed]. What is written is "thrust after thrust," for man was cursed, woman was cursed, and the snake was cursed.

  D.   "And the Lord God said to the serpent . . ."

We have an exegesis of a base verse and intersecting verse in the "classic" form in which the intersecting verse is fully worked out and only then drawn to meet the base verse. No. 1 treats the intersecting verse as a statement on its own, and then No. 2 reads the verse in line with Gen. 3:14. But the intersecting verse is hardly chosen at random, since it speaks of slander in general, and then at No. 2 the act of slander of the snake is explicitly read into the intersecting verse. So the intersection is not only thematic, not by any means. The upshot of the exercise links Israel's history to the history of humanity in the garden of Eden. No. 1 focuses upon the sacred history of Israel, making the point that slanderers in Israel cause the nation's downfall, just as the snake caused the downfall of humanity.

Genesis Rabbah 19

XIX:VII

1.A.   "And they heard the sound of the Lord God walking in the garden in the cool of the day" (Gen. 3:8):

2.A.   Said R. Abba bar Kahana, "The word is not written, 'move,' but rather, 'walk,' bearing the sense that [the Presence of God] leapt about and jumped upward.

B.   "[The point is that God's presence leapt upward from the earth on account of the events in the garden, as will now be explained:] The principal location of the Presence of God was [meant to be] among the creatures down here. When the first man sinned, the Presence of God moved up to the first firmament. When Cain sinned, it went up to the second firmament. When the generation of Enosh sinned, it went up to the third firmament. When the generation of the Flood sinned, it went up to the fourth firmament. When the generation of the dispersion [at the tower of Babel] sinned, it went up to the fifth. On account of the Sodomites it went up to the sixth, and on account of the Egyptians in the time of Abraham it went up to the seventh.

C.   "But, as a counterpart, there were seven righteous men who rose up: Abraham, Isaac, Jacob, Levi, Kahath, Amram, and Moses. They brought the Presence of God [by stages] down to earth.

D.   "Abraham brought it from the seventh to the sixth, Isaac brought it from the sixth to the fifth, Jacob brought it from the fifth to the fourth, Levi brought it down from the forth to the third, Kahath brought it down from the third to the second, Amram brought it down from the second to the first. Moses brought it down to earth."

E.   Said R. Isaac, "It is written, 'The righteous will inherit the land and dwell therein forever' (Ps. 37:29). Now what will the wicked do? Are they going to fly in the air? But that the wicked did not make it possible for the Presence of God to take up residence on earth [is what the verse wishes to say]."

What is striking is the claim that while the wicked (gentiles) drove God out of the world, the righteous (Israelites) brought God back into the world. This theme, linking the story of the Fall of man to the history of Israel, with Israel serving as the counterpart and fulfillment of the fall at creation. The next composition still more strikingly shows that the creation and fall of man finds its counterpart in the formation and sanctification of Israel. So Israel serves, as did the first man, as the embodiment of humanity. But while Adam sinned and was driven from paradise, Israel through atonement will bring humanity salvation. In this way the book of Genesis serves a purpose quite pertinent to the theological program of the compilers of Genesis Rabbah.

Chapter 7

Judaism and Christianity in the Formative Age

Bruce Chilton

A. Matthew 12

The Gospel according to Matthew was written around 80 CE in Damascus, while Luke was written around 90 CE in Antioch. Both reflect an earlier tradition of Jesus' sayings (routinely called "Q"), which circulated from around the year 35. The saying that especially concerns us is embedded in both Gospels; the differences between them show that it should not be assumed that the Gospels are verbatim records of Jesus' words and that "Q" was not the stable, written source it is sometimes supposed to have been. At the same time, this selection shows how tensions with Israel as usually identified grew as "Q" evolved.

22 Then was brought forward to him a demon-possessed man, blind and deaf; and he healed him, so that the deaf man spoke and saw.
23 And all the crowds were beside themselves, and were saying,
    Is *he* David's son?
24 The Pharasayahs heard and said,
    He does not put out demons except by Baalzebul, ruler of the demons!
25 He knew their thoughts and said to them,
    Every kingdom divided against itself is wasted, and every city or house divided against itself will not stand.
26 And if Satan puts out Satan, he is divided against himself! So how will his kingdom stand?
27 And if I by Baalzebul put out demons, by whom do your sons put them out? For this, they themselves will be your judges.
28 But if I put out demons by God's spirit, then the sovereignty of God has arrived upon you!

Source for readings in chapter 7 – All translations in this chapter are by the author.

29 Or: how is someone able to enter into the house of the strong man and to seize his vessels, unless he binds the strong man first? And then he will rob his house!

30 One who is not with me is against me, and one who does not gather with me scatters!

31 For this I say to you, Every sin and curse will be released for men, but the curse of the spirit will not be released.

32 And whoever says a word against the one like the person, it will be released for one; but whoever says a word against the holy spirit, it will not be released for one, neither in this age nor in the coming age!

33 Either make the tree fine and its fruit fine, or make the tree rotten and its fruit rotten! Because the tree is known from the fruit.

34 Offspring of vipers! How will you speak good things, being evil yourselves? Because from the overflow of the heart the mouth speaks.

35 The good man puts good things out from the good store, and the evil man from the evil store puts out evil things.

36 But I say to you that every idle saying which people speak, they will pay back an account concerning it in judgment day.

37 Because from your words you will be made righteous, and from your words you will be found guilty.

38 Then some of the letterers and Pharasayahs replied to him, saying,
    Teacher, we wish to see a sign from you.

39 He replied and said to them,
    An evil and adulterous generation seeks a sign, and a sign shall not be given to it, except the sign of the prophet Yona.

40 Because exactly as Yonah was in the belly of the monster three days and three nights, so the one like the person will be in the heart of the earth three days and three nights.

41 Ninevite men will arise in the judgment with this generation and will condemn it, because they repented at Yona's proclamation, and look: greater than Yona is here!

42 South's queen will be raised in the judgment with this generation, and will condemn it, because she came from the limits of the earth to hear the wisdom of Solomon, and look: greater than Solomon is here!

43 But when the unclean spirit goes out from the person, it passes through waterless places seeking repose, and does not find it.

44 Then it says, I will turn back to my house, whence I went out. It goes and finds it free, swept and adorned.

45 Then it proceeds and takes along with itself seven other spirits more evil than itself, and entering dwells there. And the endings of that person become worse than the beginnings. So it will be also in the evil generation.

B.   Thomas (sayings 79–85)

The Gospel according to Thomas was composed during the second century. Often, however, it splices independent, earlier traditions within materials that seem to come from the Synoptic Gospels. A comparison of the passage from Luke 11:27–36 and this section of Thomas will suggest that. Instead of being integrated within the narrative framework of the Synoptic Gospels (which ultimately derived from Peter), Thomas develops a thematic structure in which Jesus' sayings are ordered in response to questions and interjections of his followers. The association of sayings in the present section shows how crucial the issue of saving knowledge (*gnosis*) is within the presentation of Thomas.

79   A woman in the crowd said to him, Favored the belly that bore you and the breasts that gave you suck! He said, Favored those who have heard the word of the Father and have kept it in truth. For there will be days when you will say, Favored the belly that has not conceived and the breasts that have not given milk.
80   Jesus said, Whoever has come to know the world has discovered the body, and whoever has discovered the body, of him the world is not worthy.
81   Jesus said, Let him who has become wealthy reign, and let him who has power renounce.
82   Jesus said, Who is near to me is near to the fire, and who is far from me is far from the kingdom.
83   Jesus said, Images appear to people, but the light within them is hidden in the image of the Father's light. He will be revealed, but his image is hidden by the light.
84   Jesus said, When you see your likeness, you are happy, But when you see your images that came into being before you and that neither die nor appear, how much you will bear!
85   Jesus said, Adam came from great power and great wealth, but he was not worthy of you. For had he been worthy, he would not have tasted death.

C.   Galatians 2

In his letter to the Galatians, written around the year 53 CE, Paul refers both to the occasion that provoked his creative theology and to the arguments that produced his theology. The episodic, direct character of his communication and his thought is reflected in the style of the letter. He refers to the major disciple

Peter, for example, both as "Keypha," the Aramaic term for "rock," and as Rock (*Petros* in Greek).

1   Then after fourteen years again I went up to Jerusalem, with Barnabas – taking Titus along, too.

2   Yet I went up by apocalypse, and I laid out to them the message which I was preaching among the gentiles. But privately, to those prominent: otherwise, I would somehow have been running (or having run) for nothing.

3   However, not even Titus, who was with me, being a Greek, was compelled to be circumcised.

4   Yet as for the sneaky, false brothers – who came in to inspect our freedom, which we have in Jesus Christ, so they might enslave us:

5   to them not for an hour did we yield in submission, so the truth of the message might remain for you.

6   Yet concerning those who were indeed prominent in some way: of whatever sort they were means nothing to me, because God does not consider a person's face. Because to me those who were prominent added nothing.

7   Rather, however, having seen that I had been entrusted with the message of foreskin, just as Rock of the circumcision,

8   because the one who empowered Rock for an apostolate of circumcision empowered me also for the gentiles,

9   and having known the grace given to me, Yaqob and Keypha and Yochanan, who were prominent (indeed, pillars), gave to me and Barnabas right hands of fellowship, so that we were for the gentiles, and they for the circumcision.

10 Except only that we remember the poor, which was the very thing I was also eager to do.

11 Yet when Keypha came to Antioch, I withstood him face to face, because he was condemned.

12 Because before some from Yaqob came, he was eating with the gentiles. But when they came, he drew back and separated himself, fearing those of circumcision.

13 And the rest of the Jews were hypocritical with him, with the result that even Barnabas was take up in their hypocrisy.

14 But when I saw that they did not walk straight to the truth of the message, I said to Keypha before all, If you, being a Jew, live gentilely and not Jewishly, how can you compel the gentiles to Judaize?

15 We are Jews by nature and not sinners from gentiles,

16 but knowing that man is not made righteous from works of law, except through Christ Jesus' faith, we also believe in Jesus Christ, so that we are made righteous from Christ's faith and not from law's works, because all flesh will not be made righteous from law's works.

17   But if in seeking to be made righteous by Christ we ourselves are found to be sinners, is Christ therefore sin's servant? Of course not!

18   But if I build again what I tore down, I show myself to be a transgressor.

19   Because through law I died to law, so I might live to God. With Christ I have been crucified.

20   I live, yet no longer I: but Christ lives in me. But what now I live in flesh, I live by faith in the son of God who loved me and delivered himself over for me.

21   I do not invalidate the grace of God: for if righteousness is through law, therefore Christ died gratuitously.

D.   Hebrews 9

Owing to the importance of the Epistle to the Hebrews for our theme, virtually the entire letter might have been included here. But its climax is easily discerned in Chapter 9. The more stately, well fashioned character of the prose marks a change from the style of Paul himself.

1   The first covenant had both rules of service and earthly sanctuary.

2   For the first tabernacle was prepared, in which were both the lampstand and the table, and the presentation of bread, that is called Sanctuaries.

3   And after the second curtain, a tabernacle called, Sanctuaries of Sanctuaries,

4   having a gold censer and the ark of the covenant covered all over with gold, in which was a gold urn having the *manna* and the rod of Aaron which sprouted and the tables of the covenant,

5   and above it Cherubim of glory overshadowing the place of appeasement, concerning which it is not now to speak in detail.

6   These having been so prepared, the priests completing the services enter continually into the first tabernacle,

7   but into the second only the high priest, once a year, not without blood – which he offers for himself and the inadvertences of the people.

8   By this the holy spirit makes clear that the way of the Sanctuaries has not yet been manifested, while the first tabernacle has existence.

9   This is a parable for the present age, according to which both gifts and sacrifices offered are not able to perfect the one who serves in conscience,

10   but deal only with foods and drinks and different immersions, rules of flesh until correction's time.

11   But Christ has become high priest of good things that have come, through the better and more perfect tabernacle not made with hands, that is, not of this creation.

12   Neither through goats and cows' blood, but through his own blood, he entered once for all into the Sanctuaries, having found eternal redemption.

13   Because if the blood of goats and bulls and heifer's ashes sprinkled on those defiled sanctifies for the purification of the flesh,

14   by how much more will the blood of the Christ, who offered himself through the eternal spirit, unblemished to God, purify our conscience from dead works, to serve the living God?

E.   Justin, *The First Apology* 1–3

Justin addressed his *First Apology* to the Emperor Antoninus Pius (138–161 CE). The work is remarkable for its philosophical confidence and its attempt to influence imperial policy by means of rational argument. Justin marks the shift of the second century, which saw Christianity emerge from its roots as a Judaic movement to become a religion that claimed universal relevance.

To the Emperor, Titus Aelius Hadrian Antoninus Pius Augustus Caesar, and to his son Verissimus the philosopher, and to Lucius the philosopher, natural son of a Caesar and adopted son of Pius, lover of learning, and to the sacred Senate, and all the Roman people, I, Justin, son of Priscus and grandson of Baccheius, natives of Flavia Neapolis in Palestine, present this address and petition on behalf of persons of every nation who are unjustly hated and flagrantly abused, myself being one of them.

Men truly pious and philosophical are led by their reasons to honor and love only what is true, and refuse to follow traditional opinions, when they are false. Nor does sound reason call on us merely to reject the guidance of those who have done or taught anything wrong, but the lover of truth himself must always, even under threat of death, and regardless of his own life, choose to do and say what is right. I ask you then, who are called pious and philosophers, guardians of justice and lovers of learning, to give good heed and attention to my address. If you are such indeed, it will be made evident. For we have come, not to flatter you by our words or to entertain you by our discourse, but to beg that after accurate and thorough investigation you pass judgment, refusing to be swayed – by prejudice or by desire to please the superstitious, or to be influenced by irrational fears, or the evil rumors that have long been circulated – to give a decision that will prove to be an injury to ourselves. As for us, we are sure no harm can be done to us, unless we are proved evildoers or wicked men. For you can kill us, but you can not harm us.

Now in case anyone think this statement unreasonable and rash, we demand that the charges against the Christians be investigated, and if they are substantiated, that the Christians be punished as they deserve; or rather, we ourselves will punish them. But if no one can prove anything against us, true reason forbids you for the sake of malicious rumor to wrong blameless men, and you yourselves as well, who would be willing to govern not by judgment but by passion. Any right-minded person would pronounce this the only fair and just method, namely, that subjects render an honest account of their lives and doctrine; and that rulers, in their turn, give their decision not with tyrannical violence, but piously, by the dictates of philosophy. For both rulers and ruled will then prosper. One of the ancients somewhere said, Unless both rulers and ruled are philosophers, states can not be happy. It is our duty, accordingly, to allow everyone an opportunity to inspect our life and teachings; otherwise, by keeping people ignorant of our ways, we would share the penalty with them for mental blindness. It is your duty, when you hear us, to be – as reason demands – just judges. For if, after learning the truth, you fail to do what is just, you will be without excuse before God.

F.   Clement of Alexandria, *Paidagogos* 6.32–6.35

During the last decade of the second century, Clement of Alexandria offered instruction to Christians in that great city and intellectual center. He was active there until the persecution which broke out in 202 under Septimus Severus. Clement developed a brilliant philosophy of Christian faith, which he produced in conscious opposition to Gnostic teachings. His greatest works constitute a trilogy. The first is an introduction to Christianity as a superior philosophical teaching (the *Protrepticos*); the second, the *Paidagogos* or "Tutor" (from which our excerpt is taken), is an account of how Christ serves as our moral guide in the quest for true knowledge and perfection. Finally, his "Miscellanies," the *Stromateis* (literally, "Carpet Bags"), is a wide-ranging and complex work. Initially, it was intended as a defense of Clement's thesis that Christian revelation surpasses the achievements of human reason, but its structure and expression are obscure. For that reason, the *Paidagogos* is the best introduction to Clement's innovative philosophy of Christianity.

It will not be improper to adopt the words of those who teach that the remembrance of higher things is a refinement of the spirit and who hold that the process of refinement is a withdrawal from inferior things by recalling higher things. Recalling higher things necessarily leads to repentance for the lower. That is to say, these people maintain that the spirit retraces its steps when it repents. In the same way, after we have repented of our sins, renounced our wickedness and been purified by baptism, we turn back to the eternal light, as children to their Father. Rejoicing in the spirit, Jesus said: "I praise you, Father, God of heaven and earth, that you hid these things from the wise and prudent, and revealed them to infants." The Paedagogue and Teacher is there naming us infants, meaning that we are more ready for salvation that the worldly wise who, believing themselves wise, have blinded their own eyes. And he cries out in joy and in great delight, as if attuning himself to the spirit of the infants: "Yes, Father, for such was your good pleasure." That is why he has revealed to infants what has been hid from the wise and prudent of this world.

It is with good reason, then, that we consider ourselves as the children of God, who, having put off the old man and the cloak of wickedness, have put on the incorruption of Christ, so that, being renewed, a holy people, reborn, we might keep the man unstained, and he might be an infant in the sense of a new-born child of God, purified of uncleanness and vice. The blessed Paul, at any rate, settles the matter for us in unmistakable words, when he writes in the First Epistle to the Corinthians: "Brethren, do not become children in mind, but in malice be children and in mind mature."

That other passage of his: "When I was a child, I thought as a child, I spoke as a child," is a figure of speech for his manner of living under the law, when he persecuted the Word, not as one become simple, but as one still senseless, because he thought childish things, and spoke childish things, blaspheming him. The word "childish" can signify these two different things, one good and one bad.

"Now that I have become a man," Paul continues, "I have put away childish things." He is not referring to the growing stature that comes with age, nor yet to any definite period of time, nor even to any secret teaching reserved only for men and the more mature when he claims that he left and put away all childishness. Rather, he means to say that those who live by the law are childish in the sense that they are subject to fear, like children afraid of monsters, while those who are obedient to the Word and are completely free are in his opinion, men: we who have believed, who are saved by our own voluntary choice and who are not subject to unreasonable fear, but only sensible concern. We will find proof of this in the Apostle himself, for he says that the Jews were heirs according to the first covenant, but according to the promise, we are: "Now I say, as long as the heir is a child, he differs in no way from a slave, though he is the master of all; but he is under guardians and stewards until the time set by his father. So we, too, when we were children, were enslaved under the elements of the world. But when the fullness of time came, God sent his son, born of a woman, born under the law, that he might redeem those who were under the law, that we might receive the sonship," through him. Notice that he admits that those who are subject to fear and to sin are infants, but considers those who are subject to faith mature, and calls them sons, in contrast with those infants who live by the law. "For you are no longer a slave," he says, "but a son; and if a son, an heir also through God." But what is lacking to the son after he has obtained the inheritance?

But it is well to expound that first passage. "When I was a child," that is, when I was a Jew (he was a Hebrew from the first), "I thought as a child," since I followed the law; "Now that I have become a man," no longer thinking the things of a child – that is, of the law – but those of a man – that is, of Christ who is, as I remarked before, the only one Scripture considers a man – "I put away the things of a child." Yet there is a childhood in Christ, which is perfection, in contrast to that of the law.

Now that we have reached this point, let us defend this childlikeness of ours by interpreting the passage from the Apostle in which he says: "I fed you with milk, as infants in Christ, not solid food, for you were not yet ready for it. Nor are you now ready for it." Now, it does not seem to me that these words should be taken in the Jewish sense. I will set beside it another passage from Scripture: "I will bring you forth to a good land that flows with milk and honey." A considerable difficulty arises from the figure used in these passages; what do they mean to convey? If the childhood implied by the reference to milk is only the beginning of faith in Christ, and is minimized as puerile and imperfect, then how can the repose enjoyed by the perfect and the knowledgeable (*gnostic*), implied by the expression "strong meat," be spoken of in any favorable way as the milk of children? Can it not be that the particle "as," which shows that a metaphor is being used, really indicates some such thing as this: "I have fed you milk in Christ," and then, after a short pause, adding "as infants"? If we break up the reading in this way, we shall convey this meaning: "I have instructed you in Christ, who is the simple and true and real spiritual nourishment." That is what life-giving milk really is by nature, flowing from breasts of tender love. Therefore, understand the whole passage in this way: "Just as nurses nourish new-born children with milk, so also I have nourished you with Christ the Word who is milk, feeding you, bit by bit, a spiritual nourishment."

G.   Origen, *On First Principles* 2.11.2–4

Born in 185 CE, Origen knew the consequences which faith could have in the Roman world: his father died in the persecution of Septimus Severus in 202. Origen accepted the sort of renunciation demanded of apostles in the Gospels, putting aside his possessions to develop what Eusebius calls the philosophical life demanded by Jesus (see Eusebius, *History of the Church* 6.3). His learning resulted in his appointment to the catechetical school in Alexandria, following the great examples of Pantaenus and Clement. Origen later moved to Caesarea in Palestine, as a result of a bitter dispute with Demetrius, the bishop of Alexandria. During the Decian persecution (250 CE), Origen was tortured, and he died of ill health in 254. Origen was the most powerful Christian thinker of his time. His *Hexapla* pioneered the comparative study of texts of the Old Testament, while his commentaries and sermons illustrate the development of a conscious method of interpretation. His most characteristic work, *On First Principles*, is the first comprehensive Christian philosophy. It offers a systematic account of God, the world, free will, and Scripture. His *Against Celsus* is a classic work of apologetics, and his contribution to the theory and practice of prayer is unparalleled.

Throughout, Origen remains a creative and challenging thinker. Condemned by councils of the Church for his daring assertion that even the devil could one day repent and be saved, Origen is perhaps the most fascinating theologian in the Christian tradition.

Now some men, who reject the labor of thinking and seek after the outward and literal meaning of the law, or rather give way to their own desires and lusts, disciples of the mere letter, consider that the promises of the future are to be looked for in the form of pleasure and bodily luxury. And chiefly on this account they desire after the resurrection to have flesh of such a sort that they will never lack the power to eat and drink and to do all things that pertain to flesh and blood, not following the teaching of the apostle Paul about the resurrection of a "spiritual body." Consequently they go on to say that even after the resurrection there will be engagements to marry and the procreation of children, for they picture to themselves the earthly city of Jerusalem about to be rebuilt with precious stones laid down for its foundations and its walls erected of jasper and its battlements adorned with crystal; it is also to have an outer wall composed of different precious stones, namely, jasper, sapphire, chalcedony, emerald, sardius, onyx, chrysolite, chrysoprase, hyacinth and amethyst. Then, too, they suppose that "aliens" are to be given them to minister to their pleasures, and that they will have these for "plowmen" or "vinedressers" or "wall-builders," so that by them their ruined and fallen city may be raised up again; and they consider that they are to receive the "wealth of nations" to live on and that they will have control over their riches, so that even the camels of Midian and Ephah will come and bring them "gold, incense and precious stones."

All this they try to prove on prophetic authority from those passages which describe the promises made to Jerusalem; where it is also said that "they who serve God shall eat and drink, but sinners shall hunger and thirst," and that "the righteous shall enjoy gladness, but confusion shall possess the wicked." From the New Testament, too, they quote the Savior's saying, in which he makes a promise to his disciples of the gladness that wine brings; "I will not drink of this cup until the day that I drink it new with you in my Father's kingdom." They add also the following, that the Savior calls those blessed who now hunger and thirst, and promises them that they shall be filled; and they quote from the Scriptures many other illustrations, the force of which they do not perceive must be figurative. Then, too, after the fashion of what happens in this life, and of this world's gradations of dignity or rank or supreme power, they consider that they will be kings and princes, just like the corresponding earthly rulers, relying on the saying in the Gospel, "You shall have authority over five cities." And, to speak briefly, they desire that all things which they look for in the promises should correspond in every detail with the course of this life, that is, that what exists now should exist again. Such are the thoughts of men who believe indeed in Christ, but because they understand the divine Scriptures in a Jewish sense, they extract from them nothing that is worthy of the divine promises.

Those, however, who accept the theory of the Scriptures which accords with the meaning of the apostles do indeed hope that the saints will eat; but that they will eat the "bread of life," which is to nourish the soul with the food of truth and wisdom, and enlighten the mind and to cause it to drink from the cup of divine wisdom, as the divine Scripture says: "Wisdom has prepared her table, she has slain her victims, she has mingled her wine in the bowl and cries with a loud voice, Turn in to me and eat the bread which I have prepared for you, and drink the wine which I have mingled for you." The mind, when nourished by this food of wisdom to a whole and perfect state, as man was made in the beginning, will be restored to the "image and likeness" of God; so that, even though a man may have departed out of this life insufficiently instructed, but with a record of acceptable works, he can be instructed in that Jerusalem, the city of the saints, that is, he can be taught and informed and fashioned into a "living stone," a "stone precious and elect," because he has borne with courage and endurance the trials of life and the struggles after piety. There, too, he will come to a truer and clearer knowledge of what is already proclaimed here, that "man does not live by bread alone, but by every word that proceeds out of the mouth of God." So, the princes and rulers must be understood to be those who both rule over those of lower condition and instruct and teach them and initiate them into things divine.

But if these considerations seem to fall short to minds which hope for what is worthy of desire, let us back up a little, and although an immature longing for the reality of things is natural to us and implanted in our soul, let us inquire so that we may at last be able, by a consistent theory, to describe the true forms of the "bread of life" and the quality of that "wine" and the property of the "principalities." As, then, in those arts, which are accomplished by hand, the design, the why or how or for what uses a thing is made, is a matter of judgment, but its practical efficacy is unfolded through the help of the work of the hands, so in the case of God's works, which have been made by him, we see them, but their design and meaning must remain a secret. Now when our eye sees the works of the craftsman, if an article which has been made with unusual skill, immediately the heart burns to discover of what sort it is and how and for what uses it was made. Much more, and beyond all comparison, does the heart burn with unspeakable longing to learn the reason of those things which we perceive to have been done by God. This longing, this love has, we believe, undoubtedly been implanted in us by God; and as the eye naturally demands light and vision and our body by its nature desires food and drink, so our mind cherishes a natural and appropriate longing to know God's truth and to learn the causes of things.

H.   Eusebius, *History of the Church* 8.8.1–8.9.6

Eusebius (260–340), bishop of Caesarea (from 314 C E), was deeply influenced by the martyr Pamphilus, his teacher and model. Eusebius was imprisoned in

309 at the same time Pamphilus was, although Eusebius himself was released. After Constantine embraced Christianity, Eusebius was prominent in the ecumenical Church at various councils from Nicea onward, as well as a friend of the Emperor. His *History of the Church* is the starting point of ecclesiastical history. He expresses better than anyone both the pitiless quality of the persecution under Diocletian, and the inexpressible relief which followed. As he explains at the end of the excerpt, by the time of Diocletian's withdrawal in 305 CE, the Empire was divided (among four rulers, known as the tetrarchy, two in the east and two in the west). The mention of Constantine heralds the new day which Eusebius saw dawning in his own lifetime.

One must admire those of them also that were martyred in their own land, where countless numbers – men, women, and children – despising this passing life, endured various forms of death for the sake of our Savior's teaching. Some of them were committed to the flames after being scraped and racked and grievously scourged, and suffering other manifold torments terrible to hear, while some were submerged in the sea; others with a good courage stretched forth their heads to them that cut them off, or died in the midst of their tortures, or perished of hunger; and others again were crucified, some as malefactors usually are, and some, even more brutally, were nailed in the opposite manner, head-downwards, and kept alive until they should perish of hunger on the cross.

But it surpasses all description what the martyrs in the Thebais endured as regards both outrages and agonies. They had the entire body torn to pieces with sharp sherds instead of claws, even until life was extinct. Women were fastened by one foot and swung through the air to a height by devices, head-downwards, their bodies completely naked without even a covering; and thus they presented this most disgraceful, cruel and inhuman of all spectacles to the whole company of onlookers. Others, again, were fastened to trees and trunks, and so died. For they drew together by machinery the very strongest of the branches, to each of which they fastened one of the martyr's legs, and then released the branches to take up their natural position: thus they contrived to tear apart all at once the limbs of those who were the objects of this device. And indeed all these things were done, not for a few days or for some brief space, but for a long period extending over whole years. Sometimes more than ten, at other times above twenty persons were put to death; and at other times not less than thirty, now nearer sixty, and again at other times a hundred men would be slain in a single day, along with quite young children and women, being condemned to manifold punishments which followed one on the other.

And we ourselves also beheld, when we were at these places, many executed all at once in a single day, some of whom suffered decapitation, others the punishment of fire. So many were killed that the murderous ax was dulled and, worn out, was broken in pieces, while the executioners themselves grew utterly weary and took it in turns to succeed one another. It was then that we observed a most marvelous eagerness and a truly divine power and zeal in those who had placed their faith in the Christ of God. As soon as sentence was given against one group, some from one quarter and others from another would leap up to the tribunal before the judge and confess themselves Christians. They paid no heed when faced with terrors and the varied forms of tortures, but undaunted spoke boldly of piety towards the God of the universe, and with joy and laughter and gladness received the final sentence of death. They sang and sent up hymns and thanksgivings to the God of the universe even to the very last breath.

I.   Augustine, *The City of God* 22.14–22.15

Augustine was born in 354 CE in Tagaste in North Africa, the son of a petty administrator and his Christian wife. A benefactor from Tagaste enabled him to continue his studies in rhetoric in Carthage, where he was deeply influenced by his reading of Cicero and then embraced the popular philosophy of Manicheanism. Its conception of the struggle between good and evil as two masses opposed to one another appealed to him deeply.

Further study in Rome and Milan led to Augustine's conversion to Christianity. Rome brought him into contact with thinkers who showed him that Manicheanism was based upon unproved dogma, while in Milan he heard the sermons of Bishop Ambrose. Ambrose demonstrated to Augustine that the authority of faith did not contradict reason. At the same time, a reading of Neo-Platonism enabled Augustine to conceive of God as immaterial, beyond time and space.

Philosophy was the first expression of Augustine's faith. Even while he was preparing for baptism, he wrote treatises, and he continued doing so in Rome afterwards. Then he returned to Tagaste, living and writing with a few friends. A visit to Hippo Regius proved fateful, however. He was made a priest, and later became bishop of the small town. He continued to write extensively, but in a more pointed way against those who attacked the Church. He particularly concerned himself with Manicheanism. But in addition, he criticized two viewpoints which demanded perfection of Christians. The Donatists attempted to force from the Church those who had cooperated with Roman authorities during the period of persecution, while the Pelagians argued that human effort was sufficient to attain redemption. In those controversies, Augustine's mastery of the concept of grace was brilliantly articulated.

In addition, Augustine wrote on how to instruct new members of the Church, and homilies which were the basis of his popular fame. Three profoundly innovative works have influenced the world of letters and Christian doctrine ever since. His *Confessions* (finished in 400) are the epitome of his introspective method: the analysis of his own life enables him to lay out the forces at work in the human soul. *The City of God* (413–425), occasioned by the sack of Rome in 410, sets out the pattern of redemption within the patterns of global history. *On the Trinity* – his great synthetic work begun in 400 – is a meditation on the imprint of God's image within us and around us. He died in 430, while Hippo was under siege by the Vandals. The following selection, from the conclusion of *The City of God*, demonstrates in a dramatic way that the history of which Augustine spoke was fundamentally metaphysical, and not a simple account of the events of the world.

What are we to say about infants, except that they will not be raised with the small body in which they died, but by a miracle of God will receive in a moment what would have accrued to them at a later time? For in the saying of the Lord: "A hair of your head will not perish," it is stated that nothing which once was will be lacking, but it is not denied that there may be something more which once was lacking. But the dead infant lacked the full size of his body. Though a perfect infant he certainly lacks the perfection of bodily extent, beyond which, when it has accrued, his stature could not increase. All men have this limit of perfection; they are conceived and born with it, but they have it in principle, not in actual mass, just as all the members already exist latently in the seed, and even after birth some things are still lacking, such as teeth and the like. In this principle which is impressed on the corporeal substance of each one the parts which as yet do not exist, or rather (if I may say so), are not seen, are already latent and with the passage of time they will come into being, or better, into view. So by this principle the infant who is going to be short or tall is already short or tall. In accordance with this principle we assuredly do not fear any diminution of the body in the resurrection. For even if the equality of all required all to reach gigantic extent, so that those who were largest need lose nothing in stature and thus belie the saying of Christ that not even a hair of the head would perish, how could the creator who created all things from nothing lack material to add whatever as marvelous designer he knows should be added?

But since Christ rose with the same bodily extent as that with which he died, it is wrong to say that when the time of the general resurrection comes his bodily size will increase, so that he will be equal to the tallest, though he had no such size in the body when he appeared to his disciples with the size in which he was known to them. But if we say that all larger bodies must be reduced to the standard of the Lord's body, much will waste away from the bodies of many, though he promised that not a hair would perish. Hence it follows that each one is to receive his own measure, whether the actual size that he had at death (in youth or when old) or if he died beforehand, the size that he would have reached. And we must understand that what the Apostle says about "the measure of the age of the fullness of Christ" was spoken for another purpose, that is, that the measure of his age will be completed when to him as head all among Christian people are

added to perfect his members. Or, if this had reference to the resurrection of bodies, we should understand that the bodies of the dead do not rise with shape either older or younger than the state of youth, but have bodies of the age and strength that we know Christ reached here. For even the learned of this world have defined youth as reaching to thirty years, stating that when that limit is reached, then man begins to decline into the worse conditions of a burdensome and senile age. Hence it was not said "into the measure of the body," or "into the measure of the height," but "into the measure of the age of the fullness of Christ."

Chapter 8

Judaism in the Muslim World

Sara Reguer

A. A Late Twelfth Century Curriculum of Advanced Study: Joseph b. Judah ibn 'Aqnin, *Tibb al-Nufus*

The Jewish people have always been synonymous with education. The expression "People of the Book" came to be applied to them early, and the "Book" was more than the Bible – it was the portable oral interpretation as well. Thus, on the eve of the rise of Islam, a Jewish education involved the Bible, Mishnah, and Talmud.

The influence of the world of Islam, both religious and secular, on the Jews is clearly reflected in the curriculum reproduced below. Written in Arabic by Joseph b. Judah ibn 'Aqnin (ca. 1160–1226) in *Tibb al-Nufus* ("Cure of Sick Souls"), it describes what a person ought to study to secure a solid Jewish and general education. The curriculum is geared toward both the brilliant student, who could cover it by age twenty, and the slower student who might never complete it. It is a graded curriculum, starting from "aleph-bet" and ending in philosophy. It also contains bibliographies and instructions for teachers. Much of the curriculum is based on that of Muslim scholars such as Al-Farabi (d. 950), who relied on the ancient Greeks.

Reading and writing

The method of instruction must be so arranged that the teacher will begin first with the script, in order that the children may learn their letters, and this is to be kept up until there is no longer any uncertainty among them. This script, is of course, the "Assyrian,"[1] the use of which has been agreed upon by our ancestors.

Source for reading A.:   Jacob R. Marcus, *The Jew in the Medieval World* (New York, 1974), pp. 374–7.

Then he is to teach them to write until their script is clear and can be read easily. He should not however keep them too long at work striving for beauty, decorativeness, and special elegance of penmanship. On the contrary, that which we have already mentioned will be sufficient.

Torah, Mishnah, and Hebrew grammar

Then he is to teach them the Pentateuch, Prophets, and Hagiographa, that is the Bible, with an eye to the vocalization and modulation in order that they may be able to pronounce the accents correctly. Then he is to have them learn the Mishnah until they have acquired a fluency in it. "Teach though it to the children of Israel; put it in their mouths" (Deut. 31:19). The teacher is to continue this until they are ten years of age, for the sages said, "At five years the age is reached for the study of the Scriptures, at ten for the study of the Mishna" (M. Abot 5:21). The children are then taught the inflections, declensions, and conjugations, the regular verbs . . . and other rules of grammar.

Poetry

Then the teacher is to instruct his pupils in poetry. He should, for the most part, have them recite religious poems and whatever else of beauty is found in the different types of poetry, and is fit to develop in them all good qualities.

Talmud

Then say the wise: "At fifteen the age is reached for the study of Talmud" (Abot 5:21). Accordingly when the pupils are fifteen years of age the teacher should give them much practice in Talmud reading until they have acquired fluency in it. Later, when they are eighteen years of age, he should give them the type of instruction in it which lays emphasis on deeper understanding, independent thinking, and investigation.

Philosophic observations on religion

When the students have spent considerable time in study which is directed toward deeper comprehension and thoroughness, so that their mental powers have been strengthened; when the Talmud has become so much a part of them that there is hardly any chance of its being lost, and they are firmly entrenched in the Torach and the practice of its commands; then the teacher is to impart to them the third necessary subject. This is the refutation of the errors of apostates and heretics and the justification of those views and practices which the religion prescribes.

Philosophic studies

These studies are divided into three groups. The first group is normally dependent on matter, but can, however, be separated from matter through concept and imagination. This class comprises the mathematical sciences. In the second group speculation cannot be conceived of apart from the material, either through imagination or conception. To this section belong the natural sciences. The third group has nothing to do with matter and has no material attributes, this group includes in itself metaphysics as such.

Logic

But these sciences are preceded by logic which serves as a help and instrument. It is through logic that the speculative activities, which the three groups above mentioned include, are made clear. Logic presents the rules which keep the mental powers in order, and lead man on the path of clarity and truth in all things wherein he may err.

Mathematics, arithmetic

The teacher will then lecture to his students on mathematics, beginning with arithmetic or geometry, or instruct them in both sciences at the same time.

Optics

Then the students are introduced into the third of the mathematical sciences, namely optics.

Astronomy

Then they pass on to astronomy. This includes two sciences. First, astrology, that is, the science wherein the stars point to future events as well as to many things that once were or now are existent. Astrology is no longer numbered among the real sciences. It belongs only to the forces and secret arts by means of which man can prophesy what will come to pass, like the interpretation of dreams, fortune-telling, auguries, and similar arts. This science, however, is forbidden by God. . . . The second field of astronomy is mathematical. This field is be included among mathematics and the real sciences. This science concerns itself with the heavenly bodies and the earth.

Music

After studying the science of astronomy the teacher will lecture on music to his students. Music embraces instruction in the elements of the melodies and that which is connected with them, how melodies are linked together, and what condition is required to make the influence of music most pervasive and effective.

Mechanics

This includes two different things. For one thing it aims at the consideration of heavy bodies insofar as they are used for measurements.... The second part includes the consideration of heavy bodies insofar as they may be moved or insofar as they are used for moving. It treats, therefore, of the principles concerning instruments whereby heavy objects are raised and whereby they are moved from one place to another.

Natural sciences, medicine

Let us now speak of the second section of the philosophic disciplines, that is, the natural sciences. After the students have assimilated the sciences already mentioned the teachers should instruct them in the natural sciences. The first of this group that one ought to learn is medicine, that is, the art which keeps the human constitution in its normal condition, and which brings back to its proper condition the constitution which has departed from the normal. This latter type of activity is called the healing and cure of sickness, while the former is called the care of the healthy. This art falls into two parts, science and practice.

After the students have learned this art the teacher should lecture to them on the natural sciences as such. This discipline investigates natural bodies and all things whose existence is incidentally dependent on these bodies. This science also makes known those things out of which, by which, and because of which these bodies and their attendant phenomena come into being.

Metaphysics

After this one should concern oneself with the study of metaphysics, that which Aristotle has laid down in his work, Metaphysics. This science is divided into three parts. The first part investigates "being" and whatever happens to it insofar as it is "being." The second part investigates the principles with respect to proofs which are applied to the special speculative sciences. These are those sciences, each one of which elucidates, along speculative lines, a definite discipline, as for instance, logic, geometry, arithmetic, and the other special sciences which are similar to those just mentioned.

Furthermore, this part investigates the principles of logic, of the mathematical sciences, and of natural science, and seeks to make them clear, to state their peculiarities, and to enumerate the false views which have existed with respect to the principles of these sciences. In the third part there is an investigation of those entities which are not bodies nor a force in bodies.

This is the first among sciences. All the other sciences, which are but the groundwork of philosophy, have this discipline in mind.

Note

1   What is meant is the Aramaic square script that has been standard for Hebrew for the past two millennia.

B.   Maimonides' Philosophy: Introduction to *The Guide of the Perplexed*

Rabbi Moses ben Maimon (known as RaMBaM; 1135–1204) was the most renowned Jewish philosopher of the Islamic world. His most famous halakhic works are the Arabic *Commentary to the Mishnah* and his Hebrew law code, the *Mishneh Torah* ("Repetition of the Law"). His philosophical work, written in Arabic, is *The Guide of the Perplexed (Moreh Nevukhim)*. Born in Cordoba, Spain, Maimonides had to flee because of the persecutions of the invading Almohades who, against the tenets of Islam, were forcibly converting non-believers. He wandered through North Africa and the land of Israel before finally settling in Fustat/Cairo in 1165, where he became a court physician.

Medieval philosophy had many staple concerns and addressed a wide range of problems that cut across religious frontiers. It also had a range of applied problems such as faith and reason, revelation, creation, and the nature of God, miracles, law, and ethics. This led to a reexamination of religious practices and beliefs.

In keeping with the writing style of his time, Maimonides wrote a dedication and introduction to *The Guide of the Perplexed* that state the method and purposes of the book. The student must prepare properly before addressing this book and must progress from logic, mathematics, science, and the liberal arts, to metaphysics.

Source for reading B.: Moses Maimonides, *The Guide of the Perplexed*, translated by Shlomo Pines (Chicago and London: University of Chicago Press, 1963), vol. 1, pp. 5–20.

Introduction to Part One

The first purpose of this treatise is to explain the meanings of certain terms occurring in books of prophecy. . . . It is not the purpose of this treatise to make its totality understandable to the vulgar or to beginners in speculation, nor to teach those who have not engaged in any study other than the science of the Law – I mean the legalistic study of the Law. For the purpose of this treatise and of all those like it is the science of Law in its true sense. Or rather its purpose is to give indications to a religious man for whom the validity of our Law has become established in his soul and has become actual in his belief – such a man being perfect in his religion and character, and having studied the sciences of the philosophers and come to know what they signify. The human intellect having drawn him on and led him to dwell within its province, he must have felt distressed by the externals of the Law and by the meanings of the above-mentioned equivocal, derivative, or amphibolous terms, as he continued to understand them by himself or was made to understand them by others. Hence he would remain in a state of perplexity and confusion as to whether he should follow his intellect, renounce what he knew concerning the terms in question, and consequently consider that he has renounced the foundations of the Law. Or he should hold fast to his understanding of these terms and not let himself be drawn on together with his intellect, rather turning his back on it and moving away from it, while at the same time perceiving that he had brought loss to himself and harm to his religion. He would be left with those imaginary beliefs to which he owes his fear and difficulty and would not cease to suffer from heartache and great perplexity.

This treatise also has a second purpose: namely, the explanation of very obscure parables occurring in the books of the prophets, but not explicitly identified there as such. Hence an ignorant or heedless individual might think that they possess only an external sense, but no internal one. However, even when one who truly possesses knowledge considers these parables and interprets them according to their external meaning, he too is overtaken by great perplexity. But if we explain these parables to him or if we draw his attention to their being parables, he will take the right road and be delivered from this perplexity. That is why I have called this treatise the Guide of the Perplexed.

I do not say that this treatise will remove all difficulties for those who understand it. I do, however, say that it will remove most of the difficulties, and those of the greatest moment. A sensible man thus should not demand of me or hope that when we mention a subject, we shall make a complete exposition of it, or that when we engage in the explanation of the meaning of one of the parables, we shall set forth exhaustively all that is expressed in that parable. An intelligent man would be unable to do so even by speaking directly to an interocutor. How then could he put it down in writing without becoming butt for every ignoramus who, thinking that he has the necessary knowledge, would let fly at him the shafts of his ignorance? We have already explained in our legal compilations some general propositions concerning this subject and have drawn attention to many themes. Thus we have mentioned there that the "Account of the Beginning" identical with natural science, and the "Account of the Divine Chariot" with divine science; and have explained the rabbinic saying: The 'Account of the Divine Chariot' ought not to be taught even by one man, except if he be wise and able to understand by himself, in which case only the chapter headings may be transmitted to him" (Hagigah 11b, 13a). Hence you should not ask of me here anything and the chapter headings. And even those are not set down in order or arranged in coherent fashion in this treatise, but rather are scattered and entangled with other subjects that are to be clarified. For my purpose is that the truths be glimpsed and then again be concealed, so as not to oppose that divine purpose which one cannot possibly oppose and which has concealed from the vulgar among the people those truths especially requisite for His apprehension. As He has said: "The secret of the Lord is with them that fear Him" (Ps. 25:14). Know that with regard to natural matters as well, it is impossible to give a clear exposition when teaching some of their principles as they are. For you know the saying of the sages, may their memory be blessed: "The 'Account of the Beginning' ought not to be taught in the presence of two men" (Hagigah 11b). Now if someone explained all those matters in a book, he in effect would be teaching them to thousands of men. Hence these matters too occur in parables in the books of prophecy. The sages, may their memory be blessed, following the trail of these books, likewise have spoken of them in riddles and parables, for there is a close connection between these matters and the divine science, and they too are secrets of that divine science.

You should not think that these great secrets are fully and completely known to anyone among us. They are not. But sometimes truth flashes out to us so that we think that it is day, and then matter and habit in their various forms conceal it so that we find ourselves again in an obscure night, almost as we were at first. We are like someone in a very dark night over whom lightning flashes time and time again. Among us there is one for whom the lightning flashes time and time again, so that he is always, as it were, in unceasing light. Thus night appears to him as day. That is the degree of the great one among the prophets, to whom it was said: "But as for you, stand here by Me" (Deut. 5:28), and of whom it was said: "that the skin of his face sent forth beams" (Ex. 34:29), and so on. Among them there is one to whom the lightning flashes only once in the whole of his night; that is the rank of those of whom it is said: "They prophesied, but they did so no more" (Num. 11:25). There are others between whose lightning flashes there are greater or shorter intervals. Thereafter comes he who does not attain a degree in which his darkness is illumined by any lightning flash. It is illumined, however, by a polished body or something of that kind, stones or something else that give light in the darkness of the night. And even this small light that shines over us is not always there, but flashes and is hidden again, as if it were the "flaming sword which turned every way" (Gen. 3:24). It is in accord with these states that the degrees of the perfect vary. As for those who never even once see a light, but grope about in their night, of them it is said: "They know not, neither do they understand; they go about in the darkness" (Ps. 82:5). The truth, in spite of the strength of its manifestation, is entirely hidden from them, as is said of them: "And now men see not the light which is bright in the skies" (Job 37:21). They are the vulgar among the people. There is then no occasion to mention them here in this treatise.

Know that whenever one of the perfect wishes to mention, either orally or in writing, something that he understands of these secrets, according to the degree of his perfection, he is unable to explain with complete clarity and coherence even the portion that he has apprehended, as he could do with the other sciences whose teaching is generally recognized. Rather there will befall him when teaching another that which he had undergone when learning himself. I mean to say that the subject matter will appear, flash, and then be hidden again, as though this were the nature of this subject matter, be there much or little of it. For this reason, all the sages possessing knowledge of God the Lord, knowers of the truth, when they aimed at teaching something of this subject matter, spoke of it only in parables and riddles. They even multiplied the parables and made them different in species and even in genus. In most cases the subject to be explained was placed in the beginning or in the middle or at the end of the parable; this happened where a parable appropriate for the intended subject from start to finish could not be found. Sometimes the subject intended to be taught to him who was to be instructed was divided – although it was one and the same subject – among many parables remote from one another. Even more obscure is the case of one and the same parable corresponding to several subjects, its beginning fitting one subject and its ending another. Sometimes the whole is a parable referring to two cognate subjects within the particular species of science in question. The situation is such that the exposition of one who wishes to teach without recourse to parables and riddles is so obscure and brief as to make obscurity and brevity serve in place of parables and riddles. The men of knowledge and the sages are drawn, as it were, toward this purpose by the divine will first as they are drawn by their natural circumstances. Do you not see the following fact? God, may His mention be exalted, wished us to be perfected and the state of our societies to be improved by His laws regarding actions. Now this can come about only after the adoption of intellectual beliefs, the first of which being His apprehension, may He be exalted, according to our capacity. This, in its turn, cannot come about except through divine science, and this divine science cannot become actual except after a study of natural science. This is so since natural science borders on divine science, and its study precedes that of divine science in time as has been made clear to whoever has engaged in speculation on these matters. Hence God, may He be exalted, caused His book to open with the "Account of the Beginning," which, as we have made clear, is natural science. And because of the greatness and importance of the subject and because our capacity falls short of apprehending the greatest of subjects as it really is, we are told about those profound matters – which divine wisdom has deemed necessary to convey to us – in parables and riddles and in very obscure words. As (the sages) have said: "It is impossible to tell mortals of the power of the 'Account of the Beginning.' For this reason Scripture tells you obscurely: In the beginning God created (Gen. 1:1)," and so on.[1] They thus have drawn your attention to the fact that the above-mentioned subjects are obscure. You likewise know Solomon's saying: "That which was is far off, and exceeding deep; who can find it out?" (Eccles. 7:24). That which is said about all this is in equivocal terms so that the multitude might comprehend them in accord with the capacity of their understanding and the weakness of their representation, whereas the perfect man, who is already informed, will comprehend them otherwise.

We had promised in the *Commentary on the Mishnah* that we would explain strange subjects in the "Book of Prophecy" and in the "Book of Correspondence" – the latter being a book in which we promised to explain all the difficult passages in the Midrashim[2] where the external sense manifestly contradicts the truth and departs from the intelligible. They are all parables. However, when, many years ago, we began these books and composed a part of them, our beginning to explain matters in this way did not commend itself to us. For we saw that if we should adhere to parables and to concealment of what ought to be concealed, we would not be deviating from the primary purpose. We would, as it were, have replaced one individual by another of the same species. If, on the other hand, we explained what ought to be explained, it would be unsuitable for the vulgar among the people. Now it was to the vulgar that we wanted to explain the import of the Midrashim and the external meanings of prophecy. We also saw that if an ignoramus among the multitude of rabbanites should engage in speculation on these Midrashim, he would find nothing difficult in them, inasmuch as a rash fool, devoid of any knowledge of the nature of being, does not find impossibilities hard to accept. If, however, a perfect man of virtue should engage in speculation on them, he cannot escape one of two courses: either he can take the speeches in question in their external sense and, in so doing, think ill of their author and regard him as an ignoramus – in this there is nothing that would upset the foundations of belief; or he can attribute to them an inner meaning, thereby extricating himself from his predicament and being able to think well of the author whether or not the inner meaning of the saying is clear to him. With regard to the meaning of prophecy, the exposition of its various degrees, and the elucidation of the parables occurring in the prophetic books, another manner of explanation is used in this treatise. In view of these considerations, we have given up composing these two books in the way in which they were begun. We have confined ourselves to mentioning briefly the foundations of belief and general truths, while dropping hints that approach a clear exposition, just as we have set them forth in the great legal compilation, the *Mishneh Torah*.

My speech in the present treatise is directed, as I have mentioned, to one who has philosophized and has knowledge of the true sciences, but believes at the same time in the matters pertaining to the Law and is perplexed as to their meaning because of the uncertain terms and the parables. We shall include in this treatise some chapters in which there will be no mention of an equivocal term. Such a chapter will be preparatory for another, or it will hint at one of the meanings of an equivocal term that I might not wish to mention explicitly in that place, or it will explain one of the parables or hint at the fact that a certain story is a parable. Such a chapter may contain strange matters regarding which the contrary of the truth sometimes is believed, either because of the equivocality of the terms or because a parable is taken from the thing being represented or vice versa. . . .

Instruction with Respect to this Treatise

If you wish to grasp the totality of what this treatise contains, so that nothing of it will escape you, then you must connect its chapters one with another; and when reading a given chapter, your intention must be not only to understand the totality of the subject of that chapter, but also to grasp each word that occurs in it in the course of the speech, even if that word does not belong to the intention of the chapter. For the diction of this treatise has not been chosen at haphazard, but with great exactness and exceeding precision, and with care to avoid failing to explain any obscure point. And nothing has been mentioned out of its place, save with a view to explaining some matter in its proper place. You therefore should not let your fantasies elaborate on what is said here, for that would hurt me and be of no use to yourself. You ought rather to learn everything that ought to be learned and constantly study this treatise. For it then will elucidate for you most of the obscurities of the Law that appear as difficult to every intelligent man. I adjure – by God, may He be exalted! – every reader of this treatise of mine not to comment upon a single word of it and not to explain to another anything in it save that which has been explained and commented upon in the words of the famous sages of our Law who preceded me. But whatever he understands from this treatise of those things that have not been said by any of our famous sages other than myself should not be explained to another; nor should he hasten to refute me, for that which he understood me to say might be contrary to my intention. He thus would harm me in return for my having wanted to benefit him and would "repay evil for good" (Ps. 38:21). All into whose hands it falls should consider it well; and if it slakes his thirst, though it be on only one point from among the many that are obscure, he should thank God and be content with what he has understood. If, on the other hand, he finds nothing in this treatise that might be of use to him in any respect, he should think of it as not having been composed at all. If anything in it, according to his way of thinking, appears to be in some way harmful, he should interpret it, even if in a far-fetched way, in order to "pass a favorable judgment" (Ethics of the Fathers 1:6). For as we are enjoined to act in this way toward our vulgar ones, all the more should this be so with respect to our erudite ones and sages of our Law who are trying to help us to the truth as they apprehend it. I know that, among men generally, every beginner will derive benefit from some of the chapters of this treatise, though he lacks even an inkling of what is involved in speculation. A perfect man, on the other hand, devoted to Law and, as I have mentioned, perplexed, will benefit from all its chapters. How greatly will he rejoice in them and how pleasant will it be to hear them! But those who are confused and whose brains have been polluted by false opinions and misleading ways deemed by them to be true sciences, and who hold themselves to be men of speculation without having any knowledge of anything that can truly be called science, those will flee from many of its chapters. Indeed, these chapters will be very difficult for them to bear because they cannot apprehend their meaning and also because they would be led to recognize the falseness of the counterfeit money in their hands – their treasure and fortune held ready for future calamities. God, may He be exalted, knows that I have never ceased to be exceedingly apprehensive about setting down those things that I wish to set down in this treatise. For they are concealed things; none of them has been set down in any book – written in the religious community in these times of Exile – the books composed in these times being in our hands. How then can I now innovate and set them down? However, I have relied on two premises, the one being (the sages') saying in a similar case, "It is time to do something for the Lord" (Ps. 119:126), and so on; the second being their saying, "Let all your acts be for the sake of heaven" (Ethics of the Fathers 2:7). Upon these two premises have I relied when setting down what I have composed in some of the chapters of this treatise.

To sum up: I am the man who when the concern pressed him and his way was straitened and he could find no other device by which to teach a demonstrated truth other than by giving satisfaction to a single virtuous man while displeasing ten thousand ignoramuses – I am he who prefers to address that single man by himself, and I do not heed the blame of those many creatures. For I claim to liberate that virtuous one from that into which he has sunk, and I shall guide him in his perplexity until he becomes perfect and he finds rest.

Introduction

One of seven causes should account for the contradictory or contrary statements to be found in any book or compilation.

The first cause: The author has collected the remarks of various people with differing opinions, but has omitted citing his authorities and has not attributed each remark to the one who said it. Contradictory or contrary statements can be found in such compilations because one of the two propositions is the opinion of one individual while the other proposition is the opinion of another individual.

The second cause: The author of a particular book has adopted a certain opinion that he later rejects; both his original and later statements are retained in the book.

The third cause: Not all the statements in question are to be taken in their external sense; some are to be taken in their external sense, while some others are parables and hence have an inner content. Alternatively, two apparently contradictory propositions may both be parables and when taken in their external sense may contradict, or be contrary to, one another.

The fourth cause: There is a proviso that, because of a certain necessity, has not been explicitly stated in its proper place; or the two subjects may differ, but one of them has not been explained in its proper place, so that a contradiction appears to have been said, whereas there is no contradiction.

The fifth cause: arises from the necessity of teaching and making someone under-stand. For there may be a certain obscure matter that is difficult to conceive. One has to mention it or to take it as a premise in explaining something that is easy to conceive and that by rights ought to be taught before the former, since one always begins with what is easier. The teacher, accordingly, will have to be lax and, using any means that occur to him or gross speculation, will try to make that first matter somehow understood. He will not undertake to state the matter as it truly is in exact terms, but rather will leave it so in accord with the listener's imagina-tion that the latter will understand only what he now wants him to understand. Afterward, in the appropriate place, that obscure matter is stated in exact terms and explained as it truly is.

The sixth cause: The contradiction is concealed and becomes evident only after many premises. The greater the number of premises needed to make the contra-diction evident, the more concealed it is. It thus may escape the author, who thinks there is no contradiction between his two original propositions. But if each proposition is considered separately, a true premise being joined to it and the necessary conclusion drawn – and this is done to every conclusion: a true premise being joined to it and the necessary conclusion drawn – after many syllogisms the outcome of the matter will be that the two final conclusions are contradictory or contrary to each other. That is the kind of thing that escapes the attention of scholars who write books. If, however, the two original propositions are evidently contradictory, but the author has simply forgotten the first when writing down the second in another part of his compilation, this is a very great weakness, and that man should not be reckoned among those whose speeches deserve considera-tion.

The seventh cause: In speaking about very obscure matters it is necessary to conceal some parts and to disclose others. Sometimes in the case of certain dicta this necessity requires that the discussion proceed on the basis of a certain premise, whereas in another place necessity requires that the discussion proceed on the basis of another premise contradicting the first one. In such cases the vulgar must in no way be aware of the contradiction; the author accordingly uses some device to conceal it by all means....

...Divergences that are to be found in this treatise are due to the fifth cause and the seventh. Know this, grasp its true meaning, and remember it very well so as not to become perplexed by some of its chapters.

And after these introductory remarks, I shall begin to mention the terms whose true meaning, as intended in every passage according to its context, must be indicated. This, then, will be a key permitting one to enter places the gates to which were locked. And when these gates are opened and these places are entered into, the souls will find rest therein, the eyes will be delighted, and the bodies will be eased of their toil and of their labor.

Notes

1   Cf. *Midrash Sheni, Ketuvim, Batei Midrashot*, IV.
2   Maimonides uses here and subsequently the term *derashot*.
3   The verse continues as follows: "for they have infringed Your Law" (cf. Berakhot 63).

Chapter 9
Judaism in Christendom

David R. Carr

A. Solomon ben Isaac on Forced Conversion

Certain medieval Jewish scholars loomed as dominant authorities. In the late eleventh century, one of the greatest among them, Solomon ben Isaac of Troyes (1040–1105), known by the acronym Rashi, produced Talmudic and Biblical glosses widely-known by both Jewish scholars and, later, by the thirteenth-century, Christian Hebraists. Through his legal commentaries and responsa, he also was an important figure in the shaping of medieval Jewish self-identity and communal life.

Rashi's responsum on forced conversion during the First Crusade, 1096–1105, exemplifies the problems caused Jewish communities by Christian zealotry. His opinion, grounded in both Scripture and earlier decisions, reveals his legal reasoning. Here, in the face of militant hostility, he affirms Jewish identity despite individual weakness and shows his desire to preserve both the social and cultural identity of Jewish communities.

Herewith do I, the undersigned, answer him who has questioned me concerning the marriage of a certain girl who was married at a time when she and the groom, as well as the witnesses to the ceremony, had already been forced by Gentiles to disavow the Jewish religion.

I am of the opinion that this woman requires a bill of divorcement before she can marry another man. The marriage of a Jew who has even voluntarily become an apostate and then marries is legal [according to Jewish law]. For it is said [Joshua 7:11]: "Israel has sinned," meaning [B. San. 44a] that even though he

Source for reading A.:   Jacob R. Marcus, ed., *The Jew in the Medieval World: A Source Book, 315–1791* (Westport: Greenwood, 1975; orig. pub. 1938), pp. 301–3. [Original text: Judah Rosenberg, ed., *Zikron Yehudah* (Berlin, 1846), p. 52b.]

has sinned he is still an Israelite. How much the more is this true in the case of all these forced converts who are still loyal to God. Notice in this particular case how their final conduct reflects their original attitude, for as soon as they were able to find some form of escape they returned to Judaism. And even though the witnesses may have led a loose life while living among the non-Jews and may be suspected of the iniquities of the Gentiles, nevertheless their testimony to the marriage does not thereby become invalid. . . .

Peace! Solomon the son of Rabbi Isaac.

B.   Judah ha-Levi: Poem on Return to Zion

The greatest of the medieval Hebrew poets, Judah ha-Levi (ca. 1075–1141) was also a philosopher and practiced medicine at Toledo until 1108 and the murder of his patron. He produced secular and religious poems, his "Songs of Zion," and a philosophical work, *The Kuzari*, before his religious ideals led him to abandon Spain for Palestine in 1140. Judah's poem on return to Zion gives poetic voice to the romantic impulse of those Jews scattered in the medieval diaspora to return to the land of Israel. While he appreciates the material benefits of Iberia, they mean little compared with the spiritual rewards of the Promised Land.

My heart is in the east, and I in the uttermost west –
How can I find savour in food? How shall it be sweet to me?
How shall I render my vows and my bonds, while yet
Zion lieth beneath the fetter of Edom, and I in Arab chains?
A light thing would it seem to me to leave all the good things of Spain –
Seeing how precious in mine eyes to behold the dust of the desolate sanctuary.

C.   Moses ibn Ezra: Poem on Worldliness

With the Almoravid conquest at the end of the eleventh century, Andalusian Jewish intellectuals such as the poet Moses ibn Ezra (1070–1139) began migrating to Christian territories. In this poem on worldliness, Moses, as did many contemporary Christians, advises the rejection of secular rewards for

Source for reading B.:   William W. Hallo, David B. Ruderman, and Michael Stanislawski, eds., *Heritage: Civilization and the Jews, Source Reader* (New York: Praeger, 1984), p. 112.
Source for reading C.:   William W. Hallo, David B. Ruderman, and Michael Stanislawski, eds., *Heritage: Civilization and the Jews, Source Reader* (New York: Praeger, 1984), p. 110.

spiritual and intellectual ones. The "brother of wisdom" might be either prudence or reason. Note the depiction of the world as a corrupting wife. The bill of divorcement, mentioned by Rashi in source A, was secured by women as well as by men.

> The world is like a woman of folly,
> Vain are her pomp and glory;
> She speaks sweet words, but verily
> Under her tongue is a snare.
> O brother of wisdom, frustrate her cunning;
> Turn thou her glory into shame.
> Hasten, and send her from thee forever –
> Her bill of divorcement in her hand!

D.   Moses ben Nahman: The Disputation at Barcelona

Nahmanides (1194–1270), a Spanish talmudist, philosopher, poet, and communal leader, lived in Gerona and was the chief Jewish spokesman at the disputation at Barcelona (1263), the most famous of several such confrontations between Christian and Jewish intellectuals. Here he addresses the fundamental divide between Jews and Christians – the soterial nature of Jesus of Nazareth. His argument centers on the rejection of the miraculous as contrary to nature and reason.

... [T]hus we all agreed to speak first on the subject of the Messiah, whether he has already come as Christians believe, or whether he is yet to come as Jews believe. And after that we would speak on whether the Messiah was truly divine, or entirely human, born from a man and a woman. And after that we would discuss whether the Jews still possess the true law, or whether the Christians practice it.

... The Messiah is not fundamental to our religion.... [T]he real point of difference between Jews and Christians lies in what you say about the fundamental matter of the deity; a doctrine which is distasteful indeed.... But the doctrine in which you believe, and which is the foundation of your faith, cannot be accepted by the reason, and nature affords no ground for it, nor have the prophets ever expressed it. Nor can even the miraculous stretch as far as this as I shall explain with full proofs in the right time and place, that the Creator of Heaven and earth resorted to the womb of a certain Jewess and grew there

Source for reading D.:   Norman F. Cantor, ed., *The Medieval Reader* (New York: HarperCollins, 1994), pp. 244–5.

for nine months and was born as an infant, and afterwards grew up and way betrayed into the hands of his enemies who sentenced him to death and executed him, and that afterwards, as you say, he came to life and returned to his original place. The mind of a Jew, or any other person, cannot tolerate this; and you speak your words entirely in vain, for this is the root of our controversy.

E.   Solomon bar Simson on the Mainz Martyrs

Crusading fervor sometimes resulted in anti-semitic violence. Jewish chroniclers provided accurate descriptions of the fate of those who resisted forced conversion to Christianity, here at the beginning of the First Crusade in 1096. This account of the fate of the Mainz martyrs from Solomon bar Simson's *Chronicles* reveals their expectation of an eternal afterlife. The ritualistic concern for the condition of the knife blade shows that the deaths transcended mere suicides and were seen as sacrifices.

When the people of the Sacred Covenant saw that the Heavenly decree had been issued and that the enemy had defeated them and were entering the courtyard, they all cried out together – old and young, maidens and children, menservants and maids – to their Father in Heaven....

All of them declared willingly and wholeheartedly, "After all things, there is no questioning the ways of the Holy One, blessed by He and blessed be His Name, Who has given His Torah and has commanded us to allow ourselves to be killed and slain in witness to the Oneness of His Holy Name. Happy are we if we fulfill His will, and happy is he who is slain or slaughtered and who dies attesting the Oneness of his Name. Such a one is destined for the World-to-Come, where he will sit in the realm of the saints.... Moreover – for such a one a world of darkness is exchanged for a world of light, a world of sorrow for one of joy, a transitory world for an eternal world."

Then in a great voice they all cried out as one: "We need tarry no longer, for the enemy is already upon us. Let us hasten and offer ourselves as a sacrifice before God. Anyone possessing a knife should examine it to see that it is not defective, and let him then proceed to slaughter us in sanctification of the Unique and Eternal One, then slaying himself – either cutting his throat or thrusting the knife into his stomach."

Source for reading E.:   Shlomo Eidelberg, ed., *The Jews and the Crusaders: The Hebrew Chronicles of the First and Second Crusades* (Madison: University of Wisconsin Press, 1977), pp. 30–1.

F.   Abraham ibn Daud of Toledo on Samuel ha-Nagid

Abraham's chronicle recorded the accomplishments of the courtier rabbi, Samuel ha-Nagid, author of *Sefer Seder ha-Kabbalah*. Such leaders and patrons played a crucial role in maintaining Judaism in the west. Samuel's accomplishments were made possible by his administrative service to Muslim rulers in Spain. The geographic spread and religious significance of his influence merited great praise.

Rabbi Samuel ha-Levi was appointed Prince in the year 4787 [1027], and he conferred great benefits on Israel in Spain, in north-western and north-central Africa, in the land of Egypt, in Sicily, even as far as the Babylonian academy, and the Holy City, Jerusalem. All the students who lived in those lands benefited by his generosity, for he bought numerous copies of the Holy Scriptures, the Mishnah, and the Talmud – these, too, being holy writings. . . .

To every one – in all the land of Spain and in all the lands that we have mentioned – who wanted to make the study of the Torah his profession, he would give of his money. He had scribes who used to copy Mishnahs and Talmuds, and he would give them as a gift to students, in the academies of Spain or in the lands we have mentioned, who were not able to buy them with their own means. . . . Besides this, he furnished olive oil every year for the lamps of the synagogues in Jerusalem. He spread the knowledge of the Torah very widely and died an old man, at a ripe age, after having acquired the four crowns: the crown of the Torah, the crown of high station, the crown of Levitical descent, and what is more than all these, the crown of a good name merited by good deeds.

G.   Maimonides regarding a Hebrew Translation of *Guide of the Perplexed*

Maimonides' reply to the French rabbis of Lunel (1199 or 1200) acknowledges the respect accorded him by distant scholars. Maimonides begs off translating his own work and points to the existence of both translators and commerce in apparently expensive texts. While he wrote the *Guide* in Arabic and other vernaculars were employed for religious texts, Hebrew remained the universal language of Jewish scholarship.

Source for reading F.:   Jacob R. Marcus, ed., *The Jew in the Medieval World: A Source Book, 315–1791* (Westport: Greenwood, 1975; orig. pub. 1938), pp. 299–300. [Original text: A. Neubauer, *Mediaeval Jewish Chronicles* (Oxford, 1887), vol. 1, pp. 71–3.]
Source for reading G.:   Franz Kobler, ed., *Letters of Jews through the Ages* (New York: East and West Library, 1978), vol. 1, pp. 215–17.

I received your previous and present letters, signed by men of great distinction, and I send my greetings to all of you and to each of you. Your words and verses as well as your questions reveal your great love of the Torah, your zeal for learning and your desire of knowledge.

I have already apologized for the delay of my answer. I have dealt with your doubts, and am forwarding to you now the third part of the "Guide of the Perplexed" in the Arabic language. However, with regard to your request that I may translate the text into the holy tongue for you – I myself could wish that I were young enough to be able to fulfil your wish concerning this and the other works which I have composed in the language of Ishmael. . . . I have not even time to work out and to improve my commentaries and other works composed in the rabbinic language . . . to say nothing of making translations from one language into another.

. . . But you have in your midst the learned and well instructed R. Samuel ben Judah [ibn Tibbon], on whom the Lord has bestowed the necessary insight and excellent penmanship for performing the translation you have asked for. I have already written to him about this subject.

. . . You stand alone in raising the banner of Moses. You apply yourselves to the study of the Talmud, and also cherish wisdom. The study of the Torah in our communities has ceased . . .

. . . Only lately some well-to-do men came forward and purchased three copies of my code [*Mishneh Torah*] which they distributed through messengers. . . . Thus it remains for you alone to be a strong support to our religion.

Therefore be firm and courageous for the sake of our people and our God; make up your minds to remain brave men. Everything depends on you; the decision is in your hands. Do not rely upon my support, because I am an old man with grey hair.

H.   Judah ibn Tibbon on Education

Judah's admonition in the second half of the twelfth century, prompted by his disappointment in his son, shows the primacy of religious over professional education, his expectation that education contributes to moral development, and his willingness to invest in texts. Contrary to Judah's concern expressed here, his son, Samuel ben Judah, would later translate Maimonides' *Guide of the Perplexed*.

My son, listen to my precepts, neglect none of my injunctions. Set my admonition before thine eyes, thus shalt thou prosper and prolong thy days in pleasantness. . . .

Source for reading H.:   Franz Kabler, ed., *Letters of Jews through the Ages* (New York: East and West Library, 1978), vol. 1, pp. 156–65.

Thou knowest, my son, how I swaddled thee and brought thee up, how I led thee in the paths of wisdom and virtue. I fed and clothed thee; I spent myself in educating and protecting thee, I sacrificed my sleep to make thee wise beyond thy fellows, and to raise thee to the highest degree of science and morals. These twelve years I have denied myself the usual pleasures and relaxations of men for thy sake, and I still toil for thine inheritance.

I have assisted thee by providing an extensive library for thy use and have thus relieved thee of the necessity of borrowing books. Most students must wander about to seek books, often without finding them. But thou, thanks be to God, lendest and borrowest not. Of many books, indeed, thou ownest two or three copies. I have besides procured for thee books on all the sciences, hoping that thy hand might "find them all as a nest." Seeing that thy creator had graced thee with a wise and understanding heart, I journeyed to the ends of the earth and fetched for thee a teacher in secular sciences. I neither heeded the expense nor the danger of the ways....

But thou, my son, didst deceive my hopes! Thou didst not choose to employ thy abilities, hiding thyself from all the books, not caring to know them or even their titles...

...Seven years and more have passed since thou didst begin to learn Arabic writing but, despite my entreaties, thou hast refused to obey...

...Nor hast thou acquired sufficient skill in Hebrew writing, though I paid, as thou must remember, thirty golden pieces annually to thy master...

Therefore, my son! stay not thy hand when I have left thee, but devote thyself to the study of the Torah and to the science of medicine. But chiefly occupy thyself with the Torah...

...Awake, my son! from thy sleep; devote thyself to science and religion; habituate thyself to moral living, for "habit is master over all thing". As the Arabian philosopher holds, there are two sciences, ethics and physics. Strive to excel in both!

...My son! If thou writest aught, read it through a second time, for no man can avoid slips....A man's mistakes in writing bring him into disrepute; they are remembered against him all his days.

...See to it that thy penmanship and handwriting are as beautiful as thy style. The beauty of a composition depends on the writing, and the beauty of the writing, on pen, paper and ink; and all these excellencies are an index to the author's work.

...Examine thy Hebrew books at every new moon, the Arabic volumes once in two months, and the bound codices once every quarter. Arrange thy library in fair order...

Never refuse to lend books to anyone who has not means to purchase books for himself....If thou lendest a volume make a note of it....Every Passover and Tabernacles call in all books out on loan.

Make it a fixed rule in thy house to read the Scriptures and to peruse grammatical works on Sabbaths and festivals, also to read Proverbs and the Ben Mishle...

I. Joseph ibn Caspi on Education and Philosophy (1332)

The controversies revolving around the compatibility of religion and philosophy permeated Jewish communities from the thirteenth century. Joseph here steers a middle course between those who reject traditional authority and those who denounce Aristotelian philosophy, but firmly supports the study of the latter.

There are, my son! two dispositions among contemporary Jews which must be firmly avoided by thee.

The first class consists of sciolists, whose studies have not gone far enough. They are destroyers and rebels, scoff at the words of Rabbis of blessed memory, treat the practical precepts as of little account, and accept unseemly interpretations of biblical narratives. They betray unmistakably their inadequate acquaintance with the philosophical writings of Aristotle and his disciples....

The second class referred to above includes those of our people who hold in contempt genuine philosophy as presented in the works of Aristotle and his like.... Now, my son, I do not blame this class because they devote all their time to the Talmudic argumentation.... But I do blame them because they despise science and those engaged in its study.

My son! When thou meetest such men, address them thus: My masters! What sin did your father detect in the study of logic and philosophy?... Is it a terrible crime to use words with accuracy?... And then, what say ye of the work of Aristotle and Maimonides? Have you examined the inside of their books?

J. Solomon ben Isaac's Exegesis of Torah (1105)

Rashi's exegetical techniques provide a parallel to those of contemporary and subsequent Christian scholastics. Exegesis was crucial to establishing authoritative halakhic statements and Talmudic studies. The discussion of the text includes the logical categorizing of various qualities as well as reference to respected authorities.

Leviticus 19:18: "Thou shalt not take vengeance, nor bear any grudge against the children of thy people, but thou shalt love thy neighbor as thyself: I am the Lord."

Source for reading I.: Franz Kabler, ed., *Letters of Jews through the Ages* (New York: East and West Library, 1978), vol. 1, pp. 267–8.
Source for reading J.: Jacob R. Marcus, ed., *The Jew in the Medieval World: A Source Book, 315–1791* (Westport: Greenwood, 1975; orig. pub. 1938), p. 361.

Thou shalt not take vengeance: A person says: "Lend me your sickle," and the other fellow answers, "No." On the following day the other fellow says: "Lend me your axe," and the person answers: "I won't lend you, just as you didn't lend me." This is vengeance. But how then would you define a grudge? A person says: "Lend me your axe." The other fellow answers, "No." But the very next day the other fellow says: "Lend me your sickle" and the man answers: "Surely, here it is. I'm not like you who wouldn't lend me your axe." Now this is a grudge, because this man was treasuring up hatred in his heart, even though he didn't take vengeance.

Thou shalt love thy neighbor as thyself: Rabbi Akiba said this is a basic principle of the Torah.

K.   Testament of Eleazar of Mayence on Piety and Charity (ca. 1357)

The wills of medieval Jews provide interesting demonstrations of cultural values. Eleazar's will attests to the esteem he held for moral righteousness, charity, and education. Clearly, he finds communal life necessary to the preservation of Judaism among the young, both male and female. Here hygiene accompanies hospitality, the former perhaps emphasized because of the recent plagues.

These are the things that my sons and daughters shall do at my request. They shall go to the house of prayer morning and evening, and shall pay special regard to the *tefillah* and the *shema*. So soon as the service is over, they shall occupy themselves a little with the Torah, the Psalms, or with works of charity. Their business must be conducted honestly, in their dealings both with Jew and Gentile. They must be gentle in their manners and prompt to accede to every honorable request. They must not talk more than is necessary; by this will they be saved from slander, falsehood, and frivolity. They shall give an exact tithe of all their possessions; they shall never turn away a poor man empty-handed, but must give him what they can, be it much or little. If he beg lodging over night, and they know him not, let them provide him with the wherewithal to pay an innkeeper. Thus shall they satisfy the needs of the poor in every possible way...

...[M]y sons and daughters should live in communities, and not isolated from other Jews, so that their sons and daughters may learn the ways of

Source for reading K.:   Jacob R. Marcus, ed., *The Jew in the Medieval World: A Source Book, 315–1791* (Westport: Greenwood, 1975; orig. pub. 1938), pp. 314–15. [Israel Abrahams, ed., *Hebrew Ethical Wills* (Philadelphia, 1926), pp. 208–18.]

Judaism.... [T]hey must not let the young of both sexes go without instruction in the Torah...

... Be very particular to keep your houses clean and tidy.... [F]or every injurious condition and sickness and poverty are to be found in foul dwellings. Be careful over the benedictions; accept no divine gift without paying back the Giver's part....

On holidays and festivals and Sabbaths seek to make happy the poor, the unfortunate, widows and orphans, who should always be guests at your tables; their joyous entertainment is a religious duty...

L.   Maimonides on Law

Maimonides' massively popular work ranged over a broad spectrum of issues. Here his legal philosophy remarkably synthesizes seemingly disparate notions of law: law as valid because it is divinely commanded and law as valid because of its utility.

... [T]here are people who do not seek for them [laws] any cause at all, saying that all the laws are consequent upon the will [of God] alone. There are also people who say that every commandment and prohibition in these laws is consequent upon wisdom and aims at some end, and that all the laws have causes and were given in view of some utility. It is, however, the doctrine of all of us – both of the multitude and of the elite – that all the laws have a cause, though we are ignorant of the causes of some of them and we do not know the manner in which they conform to wisdom...

... Those commandments whose utility is clear to the multitude are called *mishpatim* [judgments], and those whose utility is not clear to the multitude are called *huqqim* [statutes]...

... [T]he Law does not pay attention to the isolated. The Law was not given with a view to things that are rare. For in everything that it wishes to bring about, be it an opinion or a moral habit or a useful work, it is directed only toward the things that occur in the majority of cases and pays no attention to what happens rarely or to the damage occurring to the unique human being because of this way of determination and because of the legal character of the governance. For the Law is a divine thing; and it is your business to reflect on the natural things in which the general utility... necessarily produces damages to individuals.... [F]or if it were made to fit individuals, the whole would be corrupted and you would make out of it something that varies.

Source for reading L.:   Maimonides, *Ethical Writings of Maimonides*, R. L. Weiss and C. E. Butterworth, eds. (New York: Dover, 1983), pp. 138–9, 141–2. [*Guide of the Perplexed*, chap. 26, 34.]

M.   Maimonides on Art and Idolatry

Maimonides' code broke from its predecessors by abandoning the order of the Babylonian Talmud and creating a new system of classification. Note also that specific references were not supplied by Maimonides but have been added. Here he classes three-dimensional human representation as idolatrous (and hence prohibited) and two-dimensional ones as art (and therefore permitted). The fineness of his distinction was not accepted by Christian and Muslim iconoclasts who rejected all representation of human forms.

It is forbidden to make images to serve as ornaments even though they are not to be used for idolatry, because it is said in the Bible [Exod. 20:20]: "Ye shall not make with Me – gods of silver, or gods of gold, ye shall not make unto you." This includes even images of silver and gold which are only made for ornament, lest fools be misled by them and think they are for purposes of idolatry. However, this prohibition against fashioning ornaments applies only to the form of the human being, and hence one is not allowed to fashion any human form either in wood or plaster or in stone. This holds when the form is raised like a design or a mural relief found in a reception hall and the like. When one fashions these he is to be punished. However, if the form were to be engraved or painted like sketches on panels or boards, or be like the figures woven into a rug, behold these are permitted.

N.   Solomon ben Adret on Faith and Reason (Second Half of the Thirteenth Century)

The controversy over the eternity of matter, also present in Christianity, prompted this attack on Maimonides and Aristotelianism that affirms the superiority of faith and tradition to science and reason. The acceptance of miracles conflicts, at least superficially, with the defense of Judaism offered by Nahmanides at Barcelona in the same period.

You ask about my attitude to that Aggadah according to which the world will come to an end after a certain time; you have found in the writings of R. Moses ben Maimon statements which are opposed to this.

Source for reading M.:   Jacob R. Marcus, ed., *The Jew in the Medieval World: A Source Book, 315–1791* (Westport: Greenwood, 1975; orig. pub. 1938), pp. 364–6. [*Mishneh Torah*, X, 7–15; III, 10–11.]
Source for reading N.:   Franz Kobler, ed., *Letters of Jews through the Ages* (New York: East and West Library, 1978), vol. 1, pp. 248–50.

Know that in all these and similar matters, when we try to examine them with the help of pure science, the latter view must prevail; we are then indeed forced to conclude that the world will never cease to exist, since science rests upon perceptions and observations of nature, and we see that all planets as well as the earth move continually without change. He who believes, however, in the end of the world does this not on the ground of any perception but on the ground of the traditions of the sages, his belief in which cannot be shattered. What has been founded on tradition or prophetic inspiration cannot be overthrown by any science in the world, for science ranks far below prophetic inspiration. This is a principle agreed upon by the confessors of all positive religions and most of all by the confessors of our own true faith. We believe in the whole tradition as we believe in the supernatural miracles....

.... [T]he divine wisdom is of greater value to us than human wisdom and... we must give unconditional preference to a tradition preserved by our forefathers, which is deeply rooted and takes its origin from the prophets, rather than to the results of our limited human knowledge....

O.   Solomon ben Adret's Ban on Study of Philosophy by Youths (1305)

As seen in previous selection, religious conservatives, fearful of the perceived corruption of the faith by Aristotelianism, sought to exclude the study of philosophy by those insufficiently armored by religious study. The dominance of Aristotelian texts in the study of medicine clearly raised problems for the numerous Jewish physicians. This text appears after a poetic condemnation of those studying Greek philosophy.

Therefore have we decreed and accepted for ourselves and our children, and for all those joining us, that for the next fifty years, under the threat of the ban, no man in our community, unless he be twenty-five years old, shall study, either in the original language or in translation, the books which the Greeks have written on religious philosophy and the natural sciences....

It is also forbidden for any member of our community to teach any Jew under twenty-five years of age any of these sciences lest they drag him away from the law of Israel which is superior to all these teachings. How can a human being not be afraid to judge between the wisdom of man, who builds only on analogy, argument, and guess, and... the wisdom of the Superior Being, between whom and us there is

Source for reading O.:   Jacob R. Marcus, ed., *The Jew in the Medieval World: A Source Book, 315–1791* (Westport: Greenwood, 1975; orig. pub. 1938), pp. 190–91. [Abraham Kahana, *Sifrut ha-Historiyya ha-Yisreelit* (Warsaw, 1922), vol. 1, pp. 252–3.]

hardly any comparison? . . . This, certainly, would lead one to complete heresy and from this, indeed, may every student of the Torah be delivered!

We have, however, excluded from this our general prohibition the science of medicine, even though it is one of the natural sciences, because the Torah permits the physician to heal . . . .

P.   The Book of Splendor (The Zohar) (1286)

One reaction against Aristotelianism was devout Jews' acceptance of mystical, Neoplatonic beliefs. Increased devotion to ritualistic practices accompanied the rise of Hasidism and the spread of Kabbalism among the mystically inclined (Ma'aseh Merkavah 8.2.1; Heikhalot Rabbati 16:3–5).

3.   Then came Rabban Simeon ben Gamaliel, Rabbi Eliezer the Great [et al.] . . . We came and sat before him [Nehunyah ben Ha-Qanah]. The mass of members of the fellowship [*haverim*] remained standing, for they saw sparks of fire and torches of blazing fire separating them from us. Rabbi Nehunyah ben Ha-Qanah sat and expounded in order all the matters of the Merkavah, both the descent and ascent, how he who descends should descend, and how he who ascends should ascend.
4.   When anyone wishes to descend to the Merkavah, he should invoke Suryah, Prince of the Divine Presence, and conjure him one hundred and twelve times by TVTRVSY'S who is called TVTRVSYY ZVRTQ TVRTQ TVRTBY'EL TVPGR AShR-VYLY'Y ZBVDY'EL VZHDRY'EL TNR'EL VShQRHVZY'Y RHBYRVN "DYRYRVN V'DYRYRYRVN YHVH the God of Israel.
5.   He should take care not to recite in invocation more or less than one hundred and twelve times (if he adds or subtracts – his blood is on his own head!), but as his mouth pronounces the names he counts one hundred and twelve on his fingers. At once he descends and achieves mastery over the Merkavah.

Q.   Wisdom of the Chaldeans

Kabbalism incorporated magical rituals directed at controlling mundane events as well as spiritual matters. Kabbalistic and hermetic texts such as this one from

Source for reading P.:   Philip S. Alexander, ed. and trans., *Textual Sources for the Study of Judaism* (Ottawa: Barnes & Noble, 1984), pp. 117, 120–1.
Source for reading Q.:   Jacob R. Marcus, ed., *The Jew in the Medieval World: A Source Book, 315–1791* (Westport, Conn.: Greenwood, 1975; orig. pub. 1938), pp. 245–6 [Moses Gaster, "The Wisdom of the Chaldeans: An Old Hebrew Astrological Text," *Proceedings of the Society of Biblical Archaeology*, 22 (1900), 344.]

the fourteenth century intrigued both Jews and Christians during the fifteenth century.

How to make Someone Fall in Love with you:

On the sixth day Anael functions. He is the ruler appointed on all manner of love...

If thou wishest to employ him, make a tablet of fine silver, draw upon it the likeness of a woman in accordance with the woman thou likest; then write on her shoulder her name and the name of her mother, and the name of the one who loves her, and that of his mother, and draw her hands outstretched. Draw then under her right arm the figure of a nice young man, and write on his shoulder Arbiel; under her left arm draw the image of another young man and write on his forehead Niniel; behind her draw the image of a man with red ink and write on his shoulder Lahabiel.

Chapter 10

Philosophy in Judaism: Two Stances

S. Daniel Breslauer

I. Is There Jewish Philosophy or Jewish Philosophers?

This first section states the problem facing students of Judaism and philosophy. Ancient thinkers, represented here by the Greek author Josephus, thought that Judaism and philosophy were not only compatible but identical. Modern scholars, with contrasting views, are represented by Julius Guttmann, a disciple of Franz Rosenzweig, and by Isaac Husik, a historian of Jewish philosophy.

A. Flavius Josephus: Philosophy Is Judaism; Judaism Is Philosophy

This first passage comes from Flavius Josephus (38–100 BCE) in his spirited defense of the Jews against their defamers. Josephus was a Palestinian Jewish aristocrat who claims to have studied with all the major sectarian groups of the time, to have favored the Pharisees, and to have taken part in the great war against Rome (66–73 CE). Some Jews regard him as a traitor for having capitulated to the Romans. On the other hand, in works such as this, he defends the Jews against those who calumniate against them. He is arguing that the Greek historians have misrepresented the Jews and claims that Jews are inherently philosophical, as even the earliest philosophers, such as Aristotle, recognized. His polemic suggests that either Jews are inherently philosophical or that philosophy derives from Judaism.

Source for Reading A.:   The Complete Works of Josephus, William Whiston, tr. (Grand Rapids, 1960), *Against Apion* Book I: 22, p. 615.

Pythagoras, therefore, of Samos, lived in very ancient times, and was esteemed as a person superior to all philosophers, in wisdom and piety towards God. Now it is plain that he did not only know our doctrines, but was in very great measure a follower and admirer of them.... For it is very truly affirmed of this Pythagoras, that he took a great many of the laws of the Jews into his own philosophy.... Aristotle related what follows of a Jew.... This man was by birth a Jew and came from Celesyria; these Jews are derived from the Indian philosophers; they are named by the Indians *Calami* and by the Syrians *Judaei*, and took their name from the country they inhabit, which is called Judea; but for the name of their city it is a very awkward one, for they call it Jerusalem. Now, this man, when he was hospitably treated by a great many, came down from the upper country to the places near the sea, and became a Grecian, not only in his language, but in his soul also; insomuch that when we ourselves happened to be in Asia about the same places whither he came, he conversed with us and with all other philosophical persons, and made a trial of our skill in philosophy; and as he had lived with many learned men, he communicated to us more information than he received from us.

B.   Julius Guttmann: Philosophy Is Alien to Judaism

Julius Guttmann (1880–1950), ordained a rabbi in Germany, scholar in sociology, philosophy, and the history of Jewish philosophy, taught at the University of Breslau, the Hochshule für die Wissenschaft des Judentums, and, after his emigration in 1934 to what was then Palestine, in the Hebrew University in Jerusalem. He published a major work that covers the history of Jewish philosophy from the Bible to Franz Rosenzweig as well as several studies on the philosophy of religion generally influenced by the works of Rudolf Otto. His orientation clearly reflects the ideas of Franz Rosenzweig. Guttmann sees religion as the framework within which Jewish culture and thought developed, first within the land of Israel and then, in a limited way, during the medieval period. He suggests that the modern period represents a dramatic change insofar as it has made possible a secular Judaism, a Judaism outside of the framework of religion. The most dramatic alteration of Judaism, however, in his view, was the separation of the people from the land in which its thought developed organically with the culture. As early as 1922, in a work on the land of Israel and Judaism, published even before he emigrated to Palestine, Guttmann expressed his view that Jewish thinking requires the context of the Jewish land.

This selection is part of Guttmann's introduction to his history of Jewish philosophy. It suggests that philosophy, as a product of Jewish diaspora

Source for Reading B.:   Julius Guttmann, *The Philosophy of Judaism: The History of Jewish Philosophy from Biblical Times to Franz Rosenzweig*, David W. Silverman, tr. (Northvale, 1988), pp. 3–4.

experience, is not inherently Judaic but represents an intrusion into Judaism. While Guttmann holds that there is an intrinsic and natural Jewish religion, he denies an equally inherent Jewish philosophy.

The Jewish people did not begin to philosophize because of an irresistible urge to do so. They received philosophy from outside sources, and the history of Jewish philosophy is a history of the successive absorptions of foreign ideas which were then transformed and adapted according to specific Jewish points of view.

Such a process first took place during the Hellenistic period. Judaeo-Hellenistic philosophy is so thoroughly imbued with the Greek spirit, however, that it may be regarded, historically speaking, as merely a chapter in the development of Greek thought as a whole. It disappeared quickly without leaving behind any permanent impact upon Judaism.

Philosophy penetrated Jewish intellectual life a second time in the Middle Ages. It was Greek philosophy at second hand, for the philosophic revival took place within the orbit of Islamic culture and was heavily indebted to Islamic philosophy, which, in its turn, derived from Greek systems of thought. This time, however, the vitality of Jewish philosophy proved stronger than during the Hellenistic period. It persisted from the ninth century to the end of the Middle Ages, and some traces of it are still discernible as late as the middle of the seventeenth century. Nonetheless, it is true to say that throughout this time, Jewish philosophy remained closely bound to the non-Jewish sources from which it originated.

After Judaism had entered the intellectual world of modern Europe, modern Jewish thought remained indebted to contemporary trends of European philosophy. This applies not only to the contribution of Jewish thinkers to the philosophic labors of the European nations, but also to those systems of thought specifically concerned with the interpretation and justification of the Jewish religion. The former has its place in the general history of modern philosophy; its dependence on contemporary thought is consequently a truism. But even Jewish philosophy in the specific and narrow sense of the term, like its Christian counterpart, operated within the framework, the methods, and the conceptual apparatus of modern European philosophy.

The peculiar character of Jewish existence in the Diaspora prevented the emergence of a Jewish philosophy in the sense in which we can speak of Greek, Roman, French, or German philosophy. Since the days of antiquity, Jewish philosophy was essentially a philosophy of Judaism. Even during the Middle Ages which knew something like a total, all-embracing culture based on religion philosophy rarely transcended its religious center. This religious orientation constitutes the distinctive character of Jewish philosophy, whether it was concerned with using philosophic ideas to establish or justify Jewish doctrines, or with reconciling the contradictions between religious truth and scientific truth. It is religious philosophy in a sense peculiar to the monotheistic revealed religions which, because of their claim to truth and by virtue of their spiritual depth, could confront philosophy as an autonomous spiritual power.

Armed with the authority of a supernatural revelation, religion lays claim to an unconditioned truth of its own, and thereby becomes a problem for philosophy. In order to determine the relationships between these two types of truth, philosophers have tried to clarify, from a methodological point of view, the distinctiveness of religion. This is a modern development; earlier periods did not attempt to differentiate between the methods of philosophy and religion, but sought to reconcile the contents of their teachings. Philosophy was thus made subservient to religion; and philosophical material borrowed from the outside was treated accordingly. In this respect the philosophy of Judaism, whatever the differences in content deriving from the specific doctrines and the concepts of authority of the religions concerned, is formally similar to that of Christianity and of Islam. Appearing for the first time in Jewish Hellenism, this type of philosophy, though not productive of original ideas, nevertheless proved of far-reaching significance and influence. From Jewish Hellenism it passed to Christianity, was transmitted to Islam, from whence it returned, in the Middle Ages, to Judaism.

C.   Isaac Husik: Jewish Philosophy in the Past but Not the Present

Isaac Husik (1876–1939), unlike Guttmann, abandoned his pursuit of a rabbinical degree. He came from Lithuania, near Kiev, to Philadelphia in the United States in 1888 and spent the rest of his life there. He taught at Gratz College and then joined the faculty of the University of Pennsylvania as a professor of philosophy. He is best known as a scholar of medieval Jewish philosophy and translator of such works as Joseph Albo's *Book of Principles of Jewish Faith*. His type of study of medieval Jewish thinkers occasioned some criticism by those who claimed that a professor of Jewish philosophy should be promoting such philosophy rather than merely excavating the thought of the past. In the conclusion to his historical survey, however, Husik makes it clear why no such modern philosophy is possible. He discovers that the symbiosis of philosophy and religion in the middle ages cannot be repeated after the experience of Enlightenment and Emancipation. While such religious philosophy was natural for Jews, Christians, and Muslims during one historical period, with the passing of those historically specific conditions, such religious philosophy was no longer possible. For Husik this is an inescapable conclusion from his studies, not, as for Guttmann, a presupposition on which he builds his survey.

Source for Reading C.:   Isaac Husik, *Medieval Jewish Philosophy* (Philadelphia, 1940), pp. 431–2.

Thus the stream of philosophical thought which rose among the Jews in Babylonia and flowed on through the ages, ever widening and deepening its channel, passing into Spain and reaching its high watermark in the latter half of the twelfth century in Maimonides, began to narrow and thin out while spreading into France and Italy, until at last it dried up entirely in that very land which opened up a new world of thought, beauty and feeling in the fifteenth century, the land of the Renaissance. Jewish philosophy never passed beyond the scholasticist age, and the freedom and light which came to the rest of the world in the revival of ancient learning and the inventions and discoveries of the modern era found the Jews incapable of benefiting by the blessings they afforded. Oppression and gloom caused the Jews to retire within their shell and they sought consolation for the freedom denied them without in concentrating their interests, ideals and hopes upon the Rabbinic writings, legal as well as mystical. There have appeared philosophers among the Jews in succeeding centuries, but they either philosophized without regard to Judaism and in opposition to fundamental dogmas, thus incurring the wrath and exclusion of the synagogue, or they sought to dissociate Judaism from theoretical speculation on the ground that the Jewish religion is not a philosophy but a rule of conduct. In more recent times Jewry has divided itself into sects and under the influence of modern individualism has lost its central authority making every group the arbiter of its own belief and practice and narrowing the religious influence to matters of ceremony and communal activity of a practical character. There are Jews now and there are philosophers, but there are no Jewish philosophers and there is no Jewish philosophy.

II. Judaism and Philosophy in the Hellenistic Age

Philosophy in the Hellenistic age meant the teachings of Aristotle and Plato and their later followers and imitators. This "Greek" thought provided categories by which to understand reality and to interpret the variety of experiences as part of a single unified system. The following presents an example from the Alexandrian Jew Philo Judeaus (20 BCE–50 CE).

D.   Philo of Alexandria: Jewish Scripture as Philosophy

Philo lived in a Hellenistic setting, and his writings reveal his desire to show the compatibility between Judaism and Greek thought. He wrote commentaries on the legal aspects of the Bible, on allegorical interpretations of the Bible, and exegetical explanations of biblical passages. He also wrote treatises focusing on

Source for Reading D.:   Philo of Alexandria, *On the Creation of the World*, 77–8, in Hans Lewy, ed., "Philo: Selections," in *Three Jewish Philosophers* (New York, 1965), pp. 54–6.

philosophical themes that are only tangentially associated with Judaism. He also chronicled Jewish life in Alexandria in works on the pogroms in Alexandria and his embassy to the emperor Gaius. His work *On the Contemplative Life* depicts a Jewish ascetical community.

The selection below is part of his biblical exegesis that seeks to demonstrate the high intellectual quality of the Jewish scriptures. Philo's approach is allegorical and philosophical. He suggests that there is a hidden philosophical message in the apparently historical narrative about the creation of the world. This way of approaching the Bible influenced Christian writers more than later Jewish thinkers, perhaps because Philo wrote in Greek. That decision reveals an important aspect of Philo's self-appointed task. He sought to show both Hellenized Jews and the sophisticated non-Jews of Alexandria that the Bible was a philosophical work that could stand comparison to the best in Greek writing. Here he uses the biblical narrative as a point of departure for philosophical speculation. The literal meaning of the biblical text is only the pretext for a discussion of basic philosophical concerns, especially those concerning the nature of the divine being and of human nature. While the Bible only implies the importance of such questions, Philo seeks to show that these philosophical concerns are central to Jewish religion.

On Man's Creation after the Image of God

Moses tells us that man was created after the image of God after His likeness (Gen. i. 26). Right well does he say this, nothing earth-born is more like God than man. Let no represent the likeness as one to a bodily form; for neither God in human form, nor is the human body God-like. No, it is in respect of the Mind, the sovereign element of the soul, that the word "image" is used; for after the pattern of a single Mind, even the Mind of the Universe as an archetype mind in each of those who successively came into molded. It is in a fashion a god to him who carries enshrines it as an object of reverence; for the human evidently occupies a position in men precisely answer in that which the great Ruler occupies in all the world. invisible while itself seeing all things, and while comprehending the substance of others, it is as to its own substance perceived; and while it opens by arts and sciences roads branching in many directions, all of them great highways, it comes through land and sea investigating what either element contains. Again, when on soaring wing it has contemplated the atmosphere and all its phases, it is borne yet higher to the ether and the circuit of heaven, and is whirled round with the dances of planets and fixed stars, in accordance with the laws of perfect music, following that love of wisdom which guides its steps. And so, carrying its gaze beyond the confines of all substance discernible by sense, it comes to a point at which it reaches out after the intelligible world, and on descrying in that world sights of surpassing loveliness, even the patterns and the originals of the things of sense which it saw here, it is seized by a sober intoxication, like those filled with Corybantic frenzy, and is inspired, possessed by a longing far other than theirs and a nobler desire. Wafted by this to the topmost arch of the things perceptible to mind, it seems to be on its way to the Great King Himself; but, amid its longings to see Him, pure and untempered rays of concentrated light stream forth like a torrent, so that by its gleams the eye of the understanding is dazzled.

Why Man Came Last in the World's Creation

It is obvious to inquire why man comes last in the world's creation; for, as the sacred writings show, he was the last whom the Father and Maker fashioned. Those, then, who have studied more deeply than others the laws of Moses and who examine their contents with all possible minuteness, maintain that God, when He made man partaker of kinship with Himself in mind and reason best of all gifts, did not begrudge him the other gifts either, but made ready for him beforehand all things in the world, as for a living being dearest and closest to Himself, since it was His will that when man came into existence he should be at a loss for none of the means of living and of living well. The means of living are provided by the lavish supplies of all that makes for enjoyment; the means of living well by the contemplation of the heavenly existences, for, smitten by their contemplation, the mind conceives a love and longing for the knowledge of them. And this philosophy took its rise, by which man, mortal though he be, is rendered immortal. Just as givers of a banquet do not send out the summonses to supper till they have everything in readiness for the feast; and those who provide gymnastic and scenic contests, before they gather the spectators into the theatre or the stadium, have in readiness a number of combatants and performers to charm both eye and ear; exactly in the same way the Ruler of all things, like some provider of contests or of a banquet, when about to invite man to the enjoyment of a feast and a great spectacle, made ready beforehand the material for both. He desired coming into the world man might at once find both a banquet and a most sacred display, the one full of all things that earth and rivers and sea and air bring forth for use and for enjoyment, the other of all sorts of spectacles, most impressive in their substance, most impressive in their qualities, and circling with most wondrous movements, in an order to fitly determined always in accordance with proportion of numbers and harmony or evolutions. In all these one might rightly say that there was the real music, the original and model of all other from which the men of subsequent ages, when they had painted the images in their own souls, handed down an art most vital and beneficial to human life.

III.   The Medieval Period

While Jewish philosophers in the medieval period referred to Plato and Aristotle as did the earlier ones in Hellenistic times, they philosophized in a different context. A wide consensus united Jewish, Muslim, and Christian thinkers, creating a "religious philosophy" common to all three traditions. Jewish philosophers sought to show how Judaism and its teachings fit into that general agreement. The three thinkers representing this period are Saadia ben Josef al-Fayyumi, Gaon of Sura (892–942), the Spanish Jewish philosopher, Judah Halevi (1075–1141), and the most famous and influential of medieval Jewish Sephardic philosophers, Moses Maimonides (1135–1204).

E.   Saadia Gaon: Defending Tradition

Saadia ben Josef al-Fayyumi, Gaon of Sura (892–942), was an active religious leader, polemicist, biblical commentator and philosopher. Born and educated in Egypt, he first attained recognition by defending the Babylonian Jewish communities against attacks from scholars in the land of Israel. He eventually came to Babylonia as head of the Yeshivah at Pumbedita and later became involved in disputes with both Karaites and some Jewish leaders. He wrote works of Jewish law in Arabic as well as several Arabic translations and paraphrases of biblical books. What follows comes from his introduction to his philosophical work, called in Arabic *Kitab al-Amanar wa-al-I'tiqadat*, and in Hebrew *Sefer ha-Emunot ve-ha-Deot*, usually translated as *The Book of Doctrines and Beliefs*. The book explores issues such as anthropomorphism in the Bible, the creation of the world, the meaning of revelation, the nature of the divine and the human, immortality, and the virtuous life. The introduction, however, provides a defense of revealed religion and its congruence with rational truth. Before beginning his philosophical exegesis of Judaism, Saadia seeks to show that philosophy and reason are indeed valid ways to approach religious thought generally and Judaism in particular.

(...) it is desirable that we should now mention the sources of truth and certainty, which are the origin of all knowledge and the fountain of all cognition. We shall discuss the matter so far as it has a bearing on the subject of this book. We affirm then that there exist three sources of knowledge: (1) The knowledge given by sense perception, (2) the knowledge given by Reason; (3) inferential

Source for Reading E.:   Saadia Gaon, "Book of Doctrines and Beliefs," in Alexander Altmann, tr., *Three Jewish Philosophers* (New York, 1965), pp. 36, 37.

knowledge. . . . But we, the Congregation of the Believers in the Unity of God, accept the truth of all the three sources of knowledge, and we add a fourth source, which we derive from the three preceding ones, and which has become a Root of Knowledge for us, namely, the truth of reliable Tradition. For it is based on the knowledge of sense perception and the knowledge of Reason. . . . It may be asked: If the doctrines of religion can be discovered by rational inquiry and speculation, as God has told us, how can it be reconciled with His wisdom that He announced them to us by way of prophetic revelation and verified them by proofs and signs of a visible character and not by rational arguments? To this we will give a complete answer with the help of God. We say: God knew in His wisdom that the final propositions which result from the labour of speculation can only be attained in a certain measure of time. Had he, therefore, made us depend on speculation for religious knowledge, we should have existed without religion for some time until the work of speculation was completed and our labour had come to an end. Perhaps many of us would never have completed the work because of their inability and never have finished their labour because of their lack of patience; or doubts may have come upon them, and confused and bewildered their finds. From all these troubles God (be He exalted and glorified) saved us quickly by sending us His Messenger, announcing through him the Tradition, and allowing us to see without own eyes signs in support of it and proofs which cannot be assailed by doubts . . . In the case of some of us it may take a very long time until our speculation is completed, but we shall be none the worse for that, and if another one is held up in his studies on account of some hindrance, he will nevertheless not remain without religion. Even women and children and people incapable of speculation will possess a complete religion and be aware of its truths, for all human beings are equal so far as the knowledge of the senses is concerned.

F.   Judah Halevi: The Special Function of the Jews

Judah Halevi (1075–1141) attained fame as a philosopher and poet. Born in Muslim Spain, he wandered throughout the Iberian Peninsula and frequented Christian principalities during the period of the Reconquest. This indigent life led to a disillusionment with Jewish life in exile, and he wrote often and eloquently about his longing to return to the land of Israel. His major philosophical work, portions of which follow here, emphasizes the primacy of religious experience over philosophical theory. As originally conceived, and as its name implies, this work, *The Kuzari*, is a defense of the Jewish people and

Source for Reading F.:   Judah Halevi, *The Kuzari (Kitab Al Khazari): An Argument for the Faith of Israel,* Hartwig Hirschfeld, tr. (New York, 1954), pp. 44–5, 141–2.

its religion. It seems to have been stimulated by questions raised by a Karaite critic, but its real focus is on the superiority of faith to philosophical reason. The work is divided into five parts that touch upon the justification of Jewish religion, Jewish ideas of the deity, an exposition of Jewish law and tradition, a discussion of biblical prophecy, and a critique of philosophy. The dramatic framework of the polemic is the case of a king who has a vision telling him that while his intentions are good, his actions are not. Determined to discover the true religion the king asks representatives of philosophy, Christianity, and Islam to argue their case before him. Unsatisfied with these arguments, the king reluctantly calls upon a Jew. The rest of the book consists of the Jew's exposition of Judaic religion. These selections come from the first book, demonstrating Halevi's justification of faith and the basis of religion, and from the third book, showing Halevi's understanding of Jewish law and practice.

The Kuzari (Book I)

10.   Al Khazari: Indeed, I see myself compelled to ask the Jews, because they are the relic of the Children of Israel. For I see that they constitute in themselves the evidence for the divine law on earth.

He then invited a Jewish Rabbi, and asked him about his belief.

11.   The Rabbi replied: I believe in the God of Abraham, Isaac and Israel, who led the children of Israel out of Egypt with signs and miracles; who led them in the desert and gave them the land, after having made them traverse the sea and the Jordan in a miraculous way; who sent Moses with His law, and subsequently thousands of prophets, who confirmed His law by promises to the observant, and threats to the disobedient. Our belief is comprised in the Torah – a very large domain.

12.   Al Khazari: I had not intended to ask any Jew, because I am aware of their reduced condition and narrow-minded views, as their misery left them nothing commendable. Now shouldst thou, O Jew, not have said that thou believest in the Creator of the world, its Governor and Guide, and in Him, who created and keeps thee, and such attributes which serve as evidence for every believer, and for the sake of which He pursues justice in order to resemble the Creator in His wisdom and justice?

13.   The Rabbi: That which thou dost express is religion based on speculation and system, the research of thought, but open to many doubts. Now ask the philosophers, and thou wilt find that they do not agree on once action or one principle, since some doctrines can be established by arguments, which are only partially satisfactory, and still much less capable of being proved.

14.   Al Khazari: That which thou sayest now, O Jew, seems to be more to the point than the beginning, and I should like to hear more.

15.   The Rabbi: Surely the beginning of my speech was just the proof, and so evident that it requires no other argument.

The Kuzari Part III

7.   The Rabbi: The social and rational laws are those generally known. The divine ones, however, which were added in order that they should exist in the people of the "Living God" who guides them, were not know until they were explained in detail by Him. Even those social and rational laws are not quite known, and though one might know the gist of them, their scope remains unknown. We know that the giving and comfort and the feeling of gratitude are as incumbent on us as is chastising of the soul by means of fasting and meekness; we also know that deceit, immoderate intercourse with women, and cohabitation with relatives are abominable; that honoring parents is a duty, etc. The limitation of all these things to the amount of general usefulness is God's. Human reason is out of place in matters of divine action, on account of its incapacity to grasp them. Reason must rather obey, just as a sick person must obey the physician in applying his medicines and advice.

G.   Maimonides: The Philosophical Function of Judaism

Moses ben Maimon (1135–1270), known also as RAMBAM or Maimonides, perhaps the most renowned of Jewish philosophers, was born and educated in Cordoba, Spain. Because of the invasion of the Almohads in 1148, he and his family began a life of wandering. During this time, he began writing his impressive corpus, which includes a commentary on the Mishnah, letters to oppressed Jews counseling them on forced conversion and messianism, an influential compendium of Jewish law, the *Mishneh Torah*, and his philosophical masterpiece, *The Guide of the Perplexed*. By the end of his life, Maimonides had a position of power in Egypt under the rule of Saladin. He was recognized as the head of the Fostat Jewish community, and his son eventually inherited from him the mantle of Jewish leadership in Egypt. Unlike Saadia or Halevi, Maimonides's philosophical orientation is Aristotelian. He readily criticizes his predecessors and hints that he must conceal some of his more revolutionary ideas. The *Guide*, a selection from which follows, is divided into three parts. The first introduces the justification for philosophizing about religion and guidance in ways of understanding the apparently irrational terms used in the Bible applied to the deity. The second part discusses philosophical issues, such as

Source for Reading G.:   Moses Maimonides, *The Guide of the Perplexed*, Shlomo Pines, tr. (Chicago, 1963), pp. 532–3.

proof for the existence, incorporeality, and unity of God, theories of creation, and the meaning of miracles and prophecy. The third part provides an exposition of esoteric biblical passages, an interpretation of providence, and a justification for Jewish law. The following selection, III:33, is from the third part, providing a philosophical defense of Jewish law.

To the totality of purposes of the perfect Law there belong the abandonment, depreciation, and restraint of desires in so far as possible, so that these should be satisfied only in so far as this is necessary. You know already that most of the lusts and licentiousness of the multitude consist in an appetite for eating, drinking, and sexual intercourse. This is what destroys man's last perfection, what harms him also in his first perfection, and what corrupts most of the circumstances of the citizens and of the people engaged in domestic governance. For when only the desires are followed, as is done by the ignorant, the longing for speculation is abolished, the body is corrupted, and the man to whom this happens perishes before this is required by his natural term of life; thus cares and sorrows multiply, mutual envy, hatred, and strife aiming at taking away what the other has, multiply. All this is brought about by the fact that the ignoramus regards pleasure alone as the end to be sought for its own sake. Therefore God, may His name be held sublime, employed a gracious ruse through giving us certain laws that destroy this end and turn thought away from it in every way. He forbids everything that leads to lusts and to mere pleasure.

IV.   The Modern Period

Modern Jewish experience is challenged by the antagonism of antisemitism and the Jewish embrace of emancipation. In this setting, Jews must defend their sacred texts, rationalize their continued existence as a parochial and self-differentiated people, and justify their traditional lifestyle. As a result, two movements of modern Jewish philosophy have emerged, one critical and one defensive of tradition. The former is represented here by Baruch Spinoza (1632–1677), the latter by Hermann Cohen (1842–1918) and Emmanuel Levinas (1906–1995).

H.   Baruch Spinoza: A Modern Critique of Judaism

Baruch Spinoza (1632–1677) spent his entire life in Amsterdam but was more truly a citizen of the world. Born of former Marranos, he approached Jewish

Source for Reading H.:   Baruch Spinoza, *Tractatus Theologico-Politicus*, Samuel Shirley, tr. (Gebhardt Edition, 1925) (Leiden, 1989), pp. 54–5, 89, 91, 100.

tradition and texts from a radically modern point of view. The critical moment of his biography is his excommunication from the synagogue in 1656, which reveals that, even though most of his works were published after his death, his thought was well known in his own time. As a philosopher, his writings such as *On the Correction of the Understanding* and *The Ethics* reveal a translation of medieval categories into a modern mode. From the Jewish standpoint, the most important of his works is his *Theologico-Political Treatise* (published in 1670), which takes a rationalistic view of the Hebrew Bible. Spinoza seeks to liberate philosophy from religion by confining religion to political ideology and contending that the Bible offers evidence of this. The selections from the *Treatise* given below show the major critical thrust of Spinoza's approach, a thrust that all later Jewish thinkers had to take into consideration.

Now I found nothing expressly taught in Scripture that was not in agreement with the intellect or that contradicted it.... So I was completely convinced that Scripture does not in any way inhibit reason and has nothing to do with philosophy, each standing on its own footing.... I show in what way Scripture must be interpreted, and how all our understanding of Scripture and of maters spiritual must be sought from Scripture alone, and not from the sort of knowledge that derives from the natural light of reason ... the object of knowledge by revelation is nothing other than obedience, and so it is completely distinct from natural knowledge in its purpose, its basis and its method, that these two have nothing in common, that they each have a separate province that does not intrude on the other, and that neither should be regarded as ancillary to the other.

Everyone's true happiness and blessedness consists solely in the enjoyment of good, not in priding himself that he alone is enjoying that good to the exclusion of others.... The Hebrews surpassed other nations not in knowledge nor in piety, but in quite a different respect; or (to adopt the language of Scripture directed to their understanding) that the Hebrews were chosen by God above all others not for the true life nor any higher understanding – though often admonished thereto – but for a quite different purpose.... Thus the Hebrew nation was chosen by God before all others not by reason of its understanding nor of its spiritual qualities, but by reason of its social organisation (sic) and the good fortune whereby it achieved supremacy and retained it for so many years.

The mark of circumcision, too, I consider to be such an important factor in this matter that I am convinced that this by itself will preserve their nation for ever. Indeed, were it not that the fundamental principles of their religion discourage manliness, I would not hesitate to believe that they will one day, given the opportunity – such is the mutability of human affairs – establish once more their independent state, and that God will again choose them.

Source for Reading I.: Hermann Cohen, *Reason and Hope: Selections from the Jewish Writings of Hermann Cohen.* Eva Jospe, tr. (New York, 1971), pp. 45, 48, 89.

I.   Hermann Cohen: Modern Religion out of the Sources of Judaism

Hermann Cohen (1842–1918) reflects the German-Jewish culture of his time. He excelled as an academic scholar, teaching at Marburg University from 1876–1912 and establishing the "Marburg School" of Neo-Kantian philosophy. While never divorcing himself entirely from Jewish life, Judaic concerns were secondary in his career until 1880, when he responded to an attack on Judaism by the German historian Heinrich von Treitschke, who had lamented the "invasion" of Germany by Jewish youth. Thereafter he wrote often and passionately on Jewish subjects. When he retired from Marburg at the age of seventy, Cohen taught in the *Lehranstalt für die Wissenschaft des Judentums* in Berlin. The lectures from that period became the basis for his most important work, *The Religion of Reason, From the Sources of Judaism* (published posthumously). That volume studies Judaism as the ideal philosophical religion, based on several key issues in Cohen's own thinking.

The selections here are from a more generally accessible source, Cohen's popularizing of his ideas, published as *Jewish Writings* by Bruno Strauss in 1924. These selections clarify Cohen's conception of religion, and Judaism in particular, as ethics. They also reflect his enthusiastic vision of a symbiosis between Germanism and Judaism that will usher a messianic universalism into the modern period. This symbiosis has both political and intellectual aspects, binding Jews in loyalty to their German nation and uncovering the basic similarities between Jewish thought and German thought as exemplified in Immanuel Kant.

A religion's right to exist is derived from its concept of God. And this concept must be constantly reaffirmed and perfected.

This is particularly true of Judaism which, as a matter of principle, makes no distinction between religion and ethics. For the God of Judaism is the God or morality. That means that His significance lies wholly in His disclosure as well as His guarantee of ethics. He is the Author and Guarantor of the moral universe. This significance of God as the ground of the moral universe is the meaning of the fundamental principle of God's unity.

Love of our country is a necessary corollary of the idea of the Messianic God, as is our striving for a fatherland where we can be at home and where general culture and intellectual pursuits can flourish. For Messianic mankind by no means implies a disintegration of all nations, but rather their unification in a spirit of morality. Even a league of nations would not mean the disappearance of different states but merely their alliance for the establishment of a genuinely international law. The Messianic God does not represent merely a future image of world history, however, He demands – by virtue of the eternal ideas conjoined in Him – political action [in the present] and continuous, tireless participation in various concrete national tasks. It is the duty of any Jew to help bring about the Messianic age by involving himself in the national life of his country.

The close resemblance between Judaism and Kant's religious thought is also evidenced by the fact that Kant, when writing about the Trinity – a concept for which he had to make allowances owing to the political tendency of his religious essay – recognizes the Son only and then equates him with the idea of mankind. Scholasticism had already interpreted the Trinity in moral and psychological terms, which points up a certain liberating trend in the reasoning of the Middle Ages. The pantheistic structure of romanticism, however, rests on the dogma of God's incarnation. God is man, for God is nature as such – a dogma which here becomes the guiding principle of all metaphysics and certainly not of ethics alone. But ethics is thereby actually eliminated as a separate discipline, for it is absorbed into the general process of natural becoming.

J.   Emmanuel Levinas: Translating Judaism into Modern Philosophy

Emmanuel Levinas (1906–1995) was born in Lithuania and died in Paris. This not only created a discrepancy in his birth date (January 12 according to the Russian calendar and December 30 according to the western calendar) but also indicates the duality of his self-presentation. He offers his thinking first as a contribution to general philosophy; only in more popular works does the Jewish agenda of his writing become clear. This sense of bridging several worlds reflects Levinas's personal history. His family was displaced by the Russian government in 1915, the Russian Civil War made them move again, and, in 1923, he moved to the University of Strasbourg in France. In 1928, he traveled to Germany and studied phenomenology under Edmund Husserl and Martin Heidegger. Returning to France, World War II displaced him again, this time as he served in the French army and his family hid from the Nazis. All this travel suggests both the fluidity of his life and of his thought. His major works, *Totality and Infinity* (1961) and *Otherwise Than Being or Beyond Existence* (1974), established his philosophical reputation by offering a comprehensive view of reality based on moral priorities, on the ethical obligations, and on duties arising from awareness of the Other. These "Greek" writings, however, find an echo in Levinas's specifically Judaic writings. In lectures given after

Sources for Readings J.:   Emmanuel Levinas, *The Levinas Reader*, Seàn Hand, ed. (Oxford, 1992), pp. 172–3, 185, 186; Emmanuel Levinas, *Beyond the Verse: Talmudic Readings and Lectures*, Gard D. Mole, tr. (Bloomington, 1994), pp. 200–1. [For the text "We Jews who wish to remain…"]

1957 at the annual colloquia of French-Speaking Jewish Intellectuals, Levinas offered commentaries on the Talmud that reflected his philosophy intertwined with Judaic sources. He also wrote about contemporary Jewish interests, such as the Holocaust, Bible, and Israel. The following selections show Levinas as both a philosopher and a commentator on Judaic matters.

A religious thought which appeals to religious experiences allegedly independent of philosophy already, inasmuch as it is founded on experience, refers to the "I think," and is wholly connected on to philosophy. The "narration" of religious experience does not shake philosophy and cannot break with presence and immanence, of which philosophy is the emphatic completion. It is possible that the word God has come to philosophy out of religious discourse. But even if philosophy refuses this discourse, it understands it as a language made of propositions bearing on a theme, that is, as having a meaning which refers to a disclosure, a manifestation of presence.

The bearers of religious experience do not conceive of any other signification of meaning. Religious "revelation" is therewith already assimilated to philosophical disclosure; even dialectical theology maintains this assimilation. That a discourse can speak otherwise than to say what has been seen or heard on the outside, or previously experienced, remains unsuspected. From the start then a religious being interprets what he lived through as an experience. In spite of himself he already interprets God, of whom he claims to have an experience, in terms of being, presence and immanence. . . .

The intelligibility of transcendence is not something ontological. The transcendence of God cannot be stated or conceived in terms of being, the element of philosophy, behind which philosophy sees only night. But the break between philosophical intelligibility and the beyond being, or the contradiction there would be in com-prehending infinity, does not exclude God from signifyingness, which, if it is not ontological, does not simply amount to thoughts bearing on being in decline, to views lacking necessity and word-plays. . . .

Transcendence as signification, and signification as the signification of an order given to subjectivity before any statement, is the pure one-for-the-other. Poor ethical subjectivity deprived of freedom! Unless this would be the trauma of a fission of the self that occurs in an adventure undergone with God or through God. But in fact this ambiguity also is necessary to transcendence. Transcendence owes it to itself to interrupt its own demonstration and monstration, its phenomenality. It requires the blinking and dia-chrony of enigma, which is not simply a precarious certainty, but breaks up the unity of transcendental apperception, in which immanence always triumphs over transcendence.

Here Levinas reflects on the conditions, and meaning, of continuing Jewish self-identity.

We Jews who wish to remain so know that our heritage is no less human than that of the West, and is capable of integrating all that our Western past has awoken among our own possibilities. We have assimilation to thank for this. If we are contesting it at the same time, it is because this "withdrawal into the self" which is so essential to us, and so often decried, is not the symptom of an outmoded stage of existence but reveals a beyond of universalism, which is what completes or perfects human fraternity. In Israel's peculiarity a peak is reached which justifies the very durability of Judaism. It is not a permanent relapse into an antiquated provincialism.

But it is a peculiarity that the long history from which we are emerging has left in a state of sentiment and faith. It needs to be made explicit to thought. It cannot here and now provide educational rules. It still needs to be translated into the Greek language which, thanks to assimilation, we have learnt in the West. Our great task is to express in Greek those principles about which Greece knew nothing. Jewish peculiarity awaits its philosophy. The servile imitation of European models is no longer enough. The search for references to universality in our Scriptures and texts of the oral Law still comes from the process of assimilation. These texts, through their two thousand-year-old commentaries, still have something else to say.

Chapter 11

Jewish Piety

Tzvee Zahavy

While piety and devotion fill all facets of the life of the traditional Jew, this piety is most moving at times of personal passage, such as coming of age, passing away, or marrying. The selections that follow illustrate these aspects of the pious life and others: the coming of age ceremony (Bar Mitzvah), the dedication of a new home, rules for visiting the sick, the procedures for preparing the dead for burial, the ritual for dedicating a tombstone, and, at the end, the marriage ceremony.

The passages come from a Rabbinical handbook called Hamadrikh: The Rabbi's Guide. A Manual of Jewish Religious Rituals, Ceremonials and Customs *(Hebrew Publishing Co., 1939). This guide appropriately serves our purpose because it so vividly illustrates the real-life pious practice of Judaism in the life-events of contemporary Jews. Indeed, since its publication, this definitive guide has been used by Orthodox rabbis at the major life-cycle events in Judaism. Besides presenting the actual texts and describing the actions to be taken in the rituals, the guide provides a summary of the laws and customs for each event. The reader thus will find here the blessings, Psalms, and other texts that are chanted and recited and several code-like summaries of the customs surrounding the pious practice of Judaism in the life of the observant Jew.*

The author of the guide, Rabbi Hyman Goldin, was born near Vilna in 1882 and emigrated to the United States in 1900. He was an attorney as well as a rabbi and wrote some fifty books. He is best known for his translation of the Kitzur Shulchan Aruch (The Digest of the Code of Jewish Law). *He also wrote a controversial work,* The Case of the Nazarene Reopened, *published in 1948, and translated several tractates of the Mishnah. He died in 1972.*

A. Rules for a Bar Mitzvah

The rules set forth so explicitly for the celebration of a young man's coming of age (Bar Mitzvah) reflect the strong tendency to regulate all times of life, including moments of celebration. The rules shape the festive celebration in light of the responsibilities faced by one who now enters the community of the pious.

1.   On the day a male youth enters his fourteenth year, that is, he is thirteen years and one day old, he becomes *Bar Mitzvah* (i.e., subject to punishment) (*Abot* V, 21), and is for the first time called up to pronounce a benediction over the Torah. According to the opinion of Rabbenu Asher, this rule of law, that a youth of thirteen becomes subject to punishment, was handed down by Moses on Sinai (*Teshubat Rabbenu Asher*, rule 17; *Rashi* ad Abot V, 21)

2.   After the Bar Mitzvah has pronounced the second benediction over the Torah, the father pronounces a benediction, without mentioning the name of God or His kingship, thus:

Praised be He who hath released me from the responsibility of this one (*Orah Hayyim* CCXXV, 2, gloss).

For, before his son has become Bar Mitzvah, the father was held responsible for the actions of his son (*Beer Heteb* ad *Orah Hayyim* 1. c., note 4).

3.   It is the duty of every father to prepare a feast on the day his son becomes Bar Mitzvah (*Beer Heteb* 1. c.).

Special Prayer for a Bar Mitzvah

May He who blessed our ancestors Abraham, Isaac and Jacob, bless this youth who was called up today in honor of God and in honor of the Torah, and to give thanks for all the good that God has done for him. As a reward for this, may the Holy One, praised be He keep him and grant him life. May He incline his ear to be perfect with Him, to study His Law, to walk in His ways, to observe His commandments, statutes and judgments. May he be successful and prosperous in all his ways, and may he find grace and mercy in the eye of God and man. May his parents deserve to raise him up to the study of the Law, to the nuptial canopy and to good deeds. Let us say, amen.

B. Dedication of a House

Creating a household in Israel enables the transmission of the pious culture. No moment more encapsulates this idea than the celebration of the dedication of a new house. The rules and Psalms designated for the occasion place the acquisition of material into the context of the spiritual and historical destiny of all Israel.

1.   If one builds or buys a house, even if he previously possessed another house, he must pronounce the benediction, "Who hast granted us life," etc. (*Berakhot* 54a, 59b; *Maim. Berakhot* X, 1; *Orah Hayyim* CCXXIII, 3).

2.   The benediction should be pronounced at the time the purchase is made or upon the completion of the building, although he had not yet made use of the same, as the benediction is pronounced on account of his joy of acquiring the house (*Orah Hayyim* 1. c. 4).

3.   It is the custom to prepare a feast and be joyful at celebrating the dedication of a house, and to give charity to the poor. This custom is based on Midrashic dictum (*Tanhuma, Bereshit*):

The Holy One, praised be He, blessed and sanctified the Sabbath upon completing the world, like a human being who builds a house and makes a feast.

4.   The owner of the house should recite these chapters from the Psalms. [Recitation of Psalms 15, 106, 121, and 30 follows.]

C.   Laws for Visiting the Sick

Visitation of the sick is another example of an act of pure communal devotion that normally would be a subjective encounter undertaken out of the goodness of one's heart. As the texts below show, Judaism distills an objective phenomenology from this pious act and concretizes a set of rules and procedures for the visitation.

1.   It is the duty of every man to visit a person who has fallen sick (*Baba Mesia* 30b; *Maim. Abel* XIV, 1; *Yoreh Deah* CCCXXXV, 1).

2.   The near of kin and friends who are accustomed to visit the sick person's home often should visit him as soon as they are informed of his sickness. Acquaintances, who were not frequent visitors of his house, should not call immediately, but should wait until at least three days have elapsed, in order not to spoil his chance of recovery by casting upon him the designation of an invalid. If, however, one is stricken ill suddenly, even acquaintances should visit him immediately (*Yerushalmi Peah* III, 17d; *Maim. Abel* XIV, 5; *Yoreh Deah* CCCXXXV, 1).

3.   He who visits the sick frequently is praiseworthy, providing he does not become troublesome to the invalid (*Nedarim* 39b; *Maim.* 1. c., 4; *Yoreh Deah* 1. c., 2).

4.   The essential feature in the religious duty of visiting the sick is to pay attention to the needs of the invalid, to see what is necessary to be done for his benefit, and to give him the pleasure of one's company; also to consider his condition and to pray for mercy on his behalf. If one visits the sick, but fails to pray for mercy, he does not fulfill his religious duty (*Yoreh Deah* 1. c., 4, gloss; *Kitzur Shulhan Arukh* CXCIII, 3).

5.   When the visitor prays for mercy, he should include the invalid he visits amongst all the sick of Israel, and say thus: "May the Omnipresent have mercy upon thee and send thee a perfect cure among all the sick of Israel." On the Sabbath and Festivals, he should add: "This is Sabbath (Festival), we are forbidden to complain, but a cure is near, because His mercy is abundant; celebrate the day of rest in peace" (*Shabbat* 12b; *Maim. Shabbat* XXIV, 2).

6.   They who visit the sick should speak with him with judgment and tact; they should speak in such manner so as neither to encourage him with false hopes, nor to depress him by words of despair (*Kitzur Shulhan Arukh* CXCIII, 5).

7.   One should visit neither a person suffering from abdominal troubles so as not to put him to disgrace, nor one who is troubled with his eye-sight, nor one who suffers with headaches. A person who is very ill and to whom conversation is difficult should not be visited personally (*Nedarim* 48a; *Maim. Abel* XIV, 5; *Yoreh Deah* CCCXXXV, 8), but one should call at the door of the house to make inquiries regarding his condition, and to ascertain if he is in need of anything; he should pay heed to his distress and pray for mercy on his behalf (*Yoreh Deah* 1. c.).

8.   If a sick person desires to confirm his last will by means of symbolical ceremony of transferring possession (*kinyan*), it may be done even on the Sabbath (*Baba Batra* 156b; *Hoshen ha-Mishpat* CCLIV, 1). If he desires to send for his next of kin, a non-Jew may be hired and sent for them even on the Sabbath (*Orah Hayyim* CCCVI, 9).

9.   If a member of the family of the invalid dies, the latter should not be informed thereof so that it may not worry him. If however he does hear about it he should not be told to tear a rent in his garments, so that his distress be not increased (*Yoreh Deah* CCCXXXVII).

10.   Immediately upon coming in to visit the sick, one should recite:

And the Lord will take away from thee all sickness: and He will put none of the evil diseases of Egypt which thou knowest, upon thee, but He will lay them upon all them that hate thee.

And He said: "If thou wilt diligently hearken to the voice of the Lord thy God, and wilt do that which is right in His eyes, and wilt give ear to His commandments, and keep all His statutes, I will put none of the diseases upon thee, which I have put upon the Egyptians; for I am the Lord that healeth thee.

Peace, peace to him that is far off and to him that is near, saith the Lord that createth the fruit of the lips; and I will heal him.

Upon going out, one should say:

May the Omnipresent have mercy upon thee and send thee a perfect cure among all the sick of Israel.

On the Sabbath and Festivals, one should add:

This is Sabbath (Festival), we are forbidden to complain, but a cure is near, because His mercy is abundant; celebrate the day of rest in peace.

D.   Laws of Purification (Taharah) and Shrouds

Devoted care for the remains of the dead is strongly emphasized in Judaism. The texts below spell out the exacting ways that piety must be invoked in the sacred activity of purification of the body prior to burial. Though piety and devotion are again objectified, this heightens the feelings of involvement in the period of grief that a community undergoes when one of its members passes away.

1.   The rite of washing the corpse before burial should not be commenced before the shrouds are ready (*Derekh ha-Hayyim*)

2.   It is the custom to make the shrouds of fine white linen, but they must not be too costly (*Moed Katan* 27b; *Maim. Abel* IV, 1; *Yoreh Deah* CCCLII, 1, 2).

3.   Neither a hem nor a knot of any sort may be made while sewing the shrouds, or when dressing the dead (*Minhage Yeshurun* CCX; *Hokhmat Adam*).

4.   The shrouds should consist of no less than three garments: The shirt, the breeches, and the overgarment with the girdle. White stockings should be put on the legs of the corpse and a white cap on his head (*Sefer ha-Hayyim*).

5.   A dead male should be wrapped in a *tallith* with fringes, and one of the fringes should be rendered unfit for religious use, to indicate that the dead are exempt from fulfilling the Law. The better procedure, however, is, instead of rendering one fringe unfit, to put one fringe in the corner pocket of the *tallith* when the body is already in the grave. If the deceased leaves a costly *tallith* in which he prayed during his lifetime, it is not proper to wrap him in an inferior *tallith*, for a person is anxious to be buried in the *tallith* in which he prayed during his lifetime (*Yoreh Deah* CCCLI, 2; *Hokhmat Adam*; *Kitzur Shulhan Arukh* CXCVII, 1).

6.   The body of a dead female must be attended to only by females. In the place of the *tallith*, an additional overgarment is placed on her shoulders (*Semahot* XII; *Yoreh Deah* CCCLII, 3; *Derekh ha-Hayyim*).

7.   When beginning the washing of the body, respect must be shown to the dead as though he were alive. No idle conversation should be indulged in in the presence of the dead, but it is permissible to speak of the necessary preparations for the funeral. The body must not be moved from place to place by a single person, but it must be performed by two or more persons, to prevent the corpse's legs and hands from being suspended (*Derekh ha-Hayyim; Sefer ha-Hayyim*).

8.   Those engaged in attending the dead shall say the following prayer before commencing their duties (*Ma'abar Yabbok*).

O God of kindness and mercy, whose ways are merciful and truthful, Thou hast commanded us to practice righteousness and truth with the dead and engage in properly burying them, as it is written (*Deut.* XXI, 23): "But thou shalt surely bury him." May it therefore, be Thy will, O Lord our God, to give us fortitude and strength to properly perform our undertaking of this holy task of cleaning and washing the body, and putting on the shroud, and burying the deceased. O keep us Thou from any harm or fault, that we fail not in the work of our hand, and grant that the verse be fulfilled regarding us: "He who observes the commandments shall never know aught of evil." May our merit, in the performance of this work of loving-kindness, prolong our lives in happiness, and may the mercy of God rest on us forever.

9.   Purification of the body: The entire body, including the head, should be washed with warm water. The fingers and toes, and well as all other parts of the body, should be thoroughly cleansed, the hair of the dead should be combed (*Yoreh Deah* CCCLII, 4 *Hokhmat Adam*).

10.   The corpse must be entirely enveloped in a white sheet while being cleansed, and the body should be washed, while half covered, by holding up the ends of the sheet. The washing must be started from the head, and then downward to the feet (*Sefer ha-Hayyim*).

11.   Care should be taken not to place the body with its face downward, as that is a degrading position, but it should he inclined, first on one side and then on the other (*Yoreh Deah* CCCLII, 4: *Kitzur Shulhan Arukh* CXCVII, 2).

12.   After the body has been thoroughly cleansed, it is placed in a standing position on the ground or upon straw, and nine *kabbim* of water should be poured over the head so that it runs down over the entire body. This last operation constitutes the real purification (*taharah*) (*Kitzur Shulhan Arukh* CXCVII, 2). While the water is poured over the corpse, the mouth should be covered by hand or otherwise, to prevent the water from running into it. The body is then thoroughly dried (*Derekh ha-Hayyim*).

When pouring the water on the corpse, the following is recited:
  And I will pour upon you pure water, and ye shall be cleansed; from all your uncleanness and abomination will I purify you.

13.   Concerning the measure of nine *kabbim* there is a diversity of opinion. To comply with the law, it is therefore best to take about twenty-four quarts of water. It is not necessary that the water be poured out of one vessel, as the contents of two or even three vessels may be combined to make up the required quantity. It is, however, necessary to commence pouring out the contents of the second vessel before the first is finished, and from the third before the second is finished. Even when pouring the water out of one vessel, the flow must not be interrupted. Four vessels cannot be combined to be counted as one, even if the water is poured out

from all four simultaneously (*Magen Abraham* ad *Orah Hayyim* DCVI, note 9; *Kitzur Shulhan Arukh* CXCVII, 3).

14. Then an egg is beaten with a little wine (the beating should be done in the shell of the egg), and the head of the dead washed therewith (*Yoreh Deah* CCCLII, 4, gloss; *Kitzur Shulhan Arukh* 1. c.. 4).

15. Care should be taken not to allow the fingers of the dead man's hands to remain closed (*Kitzur Shulhan Arukh* 1. c., 5).

16. After having been cleansed, the corpse should not be allowed to remain in the place where the rites of purification had taken place, but it must be placed inside the house towards the door (*Kitzur Shulhan Arukh* 1. c., 6; *Ma'abar Yabok*).

17. The board upon which the corpse was washed must not be turned over (*Kitzur Shulhan Arukh* 1. c.).

18. One must not kiss his dead children, because it is dangerous (*Kitzur Shulhan Arukh* 1. c., 7).

19. If one falls and dies instantly from wounds from which blood issued forth, and there is apprehension that the blood that sustains life was absorbed in his clothes, his body should not be ritually cleansed; he should be interred with his garments and shoes, but above the garments he should be wrapped in a sheet which is called *sobeb*. It is customary to dig up the earth at the spot where he fell, and if blood happens to be there, all that earth upon which blood was found should be buried with him. Only the garments which he wore when he fell are to be interred, but if there were blood-stains on other garments which he did not wear at the time, or if he was placed upon pillows and sheets whilst the blood was flowing, all these need not be buried with him, but they must be thoroughly washed until no trace of blood remains, and the water should be poured into his grave. If, however, the one who fell and died did not bleed at all, his garments must be removed, and his body must be cleansed and dressed in shrouds, as is done in the case of all other dead persons (*Beer Heteb* ad *Yoreh Deah* CCCLXIV, note 7; *Hokhmat Adam* CLVII, 10; *Kitzur Shulhan Arukh* CXCVII, 9).

20. If blood has flown from the injured body and his clothes were removed, and thereafter he recovered and lived for a few days and then died, he must be cleansed and dressed in shrouds. Even if his body is stained with the blood which issued forth from him, he should be cleansed, for the blood lost during his life-time is not to be regarded; we are only concerned with the blood which one loses while dying, for it is likely that this was the blood that sustains life, or it is possible that the blood sustaining life has become mixed therewith (*Beer Heteb l.c.; Hokhmat Adam* 1. c.; *Kitzur Shulhan Arukh* 1. c., 10).

21. The body of a person that was drowned should be stripped of its clothes, and be treated as required by law in the case of ordinary death. In some communities it is the custom to bury drowned persons in the clothes in which they are found; such custom should be observed without interference (*Beer Heteb* 1. c.; *Hokhmat Adam* 1. c.; *Kitzur Shulhan Arukh* 1. c., 9).

22. If a woman dies while giving birth, the laws applying to a slain person apply also to her, and if it is known that she has lost much blood, she must not be

cleansed. If the blood had already ceased flowing and then she died, she should be treated as required by law in the case of all other dead persons. In many communities it is customary to cleanse the body of any woman that dies at childbirth; and there are also many other customs prevailing in such cases; such customs should be observed without interference (*Beer Heteb* 1. c.; *Kitzur Shulhan Arukh* 1. c., 11).

23.   It is forbidden to derive any benefit from either the dead body or the shrouds, whether it be of a Jew or a non-Jew. Likewise ornamental objects which are attached to the corpse, as for instance a wig tied to, or woven into the hair, or artificial teeth, must be interred with the body, and no one is permitted to derive any benefit therefrom. Such ornamental objects that are not attached to the body, one is permitted to use. In any event, use may be made of articles which are not reckoned as a part of the body, such as jewelry and clothes (*Sanhedrin* 47b – 48a; *Arakhin* 47b; *Maim. Abel* XIV, 11; *Yoreh Deah* CCCXLIX, 1, 2).

E.   Order of the Wedding Ceremony

Finally, the wedding ceremony shows how cultural rituals can intermix. The new status of the couple who marry reflects a complex combination of material issues, social changes, and spiritual dimensions. The ceremony includes the reading of an Aramaic legal document (the *Ketubah*), the recitation of Hebrew blessings, and symbolic gestures that meld together the concrete and the imagined in a transition to a newly sanctioned condition for bride and groom within the pious community of Israel.

It is the custom that, when the bride is a virgin, the Rabbi and the bridegroom visit the bride before the performance of the *hupah* ceremony. The bridegroom covers the bride's head and face with a veil, while the Rabbi pronounces the following blessing:

> Our sister, be thou the mother of thousands of myriads. God make thee as Sarah, Rebekah, Rachel and Leah.

> May the Lord bless thee and keep thee. May the Lord let His countenance shine upon thee, and be gracious unto thee. May the Lord lift up His countenance upon thee, and give thee peace.

The *Ketubah* (marriage contract) is now written as required by law. The witnesses attesting to the *Ketubah* must not be related either to the bridegroom or to the bride. Thereafter it is necessary to make a *Kinyan* (the legal formality of symbolic delivery, the Rabbi handing over a kerchief to the bridegroom), and inform the bridegroom that in doing this he obligates himself to fulfill all the terms and conditions embodied in the *Ketubah* and to pay the additional sum mentioned therein.

Entrance march: The Rabbi takes his place under the *Hupah*, facing the entrance.

The bridegroom is led by his father and mother, or their representatives, to the *hupah*. The Rabbi, upon seeing the groom enter, says:

> *Barukh haba* (may he who cometh be blessed).

Under the *hupah*, the bridegroom is placed facing the Rabbi's right (eastward, if possible), and the Rabbi either recites or chants:

> He who is supremely mighty;
> He who is supremely praised;
> He who is supremely great;
> May He bless this bridegroom and bride.

Now the bride is led by her parents, or their representatives, to the *hupah*. The Rabbi, upon seeing the bride enter, says:

> *Berukhah habaah* (may she who cometh be blessed).

Then the Rabbi either chants or recites the following:

Mighty is our God.

Auspicious signs, and good fortune. Praiseworthy is the bridegroom. Praiseworthy and handsome is the bride.

In some localities, it is customary to march with the bride around the bridegroom seven times; while in others, they march around three times. Now the bride is placed at the right of the bridegroom, facing the Rabbi's left.

An address may be delivered by the Rabbi at this point.

Betrothal benedictions:

The Rabbi fills a goblet with wine, and recites the following two benedictions over it:

Praised be Thou, O Lord our God, King of the universe, who hast created the fruit of the vine.

Praised be Thou, O Lord our God, King of the universe, who hast sanctified us with Thy commandments, and hast commanded us concerning forbidden connections, and hast forbidden us those who are merely betrothed, but hast allowed to us those lawfully married to us through *hupah* and betrothal. Praised be Thou, O Lord, who sanctifiest Thy people Israel through *hupah* and betrothal.

The bridegroom and the bride are given to taste from the goblet of wine.

RABBI TO GROOM:

> N. N. (*naming the groom*): do you of your own free will and consent, take... (*naming the bride*) to be your wife; and do you promise to love, honor and cherish her throughout life? If so, answer, Yes.

RABBI TO BRIDE:

> N. N. (*naming the bride*): do you of your own free will and consent, take... (*naming the groom*) to be your husband, and do you promise to love, honor and cherish him throughout life? If so, answer, Yes.

The Rabbi then appoints two witnesses, who must not be related to either the groom or the bride, to witness the betrothal.
RABBI TO GROOM:

> You will now betrothe the bride, in the presence of these two witnesses, by placing this ring upon the forefinger of her right hand, and say to her in Hebrew:

> *HARE AT MEKUDESHET LI BETABAAT ZU, KEDAT MOSHE VEYISRAEL.*
> Behold, thou art betrothed to me with this ring, in accordance with the
> Law of Moses and Israel.

After this the *ketubah* (nuptial agreement) is read.

FORM OF KETUBAH
On the (first) day of the week, the... day of the month..., in the year five thousand, seven hundred and... since the creation of the world, the era according to which we are accustomed to reckon here in the city of (name of city, state and country), how (name of bridegroom), son of (name of father), surnamed (family name), said to this virgin ("Widow", or "Divorce", as the case may be and so on throughout) (name of bride), daughter of (name of father), surnamed (family name): "Be thou my wife according to the law of Moses and Israel, and I will cherish, honor, support and maintain thee in accordance with the custom of Jewish husbands who cherish, honor, support and maintain their wives in truth. And I herewith make for thee the settlement of virgins, two hundred silver zuzim, which belongs to thee, according to the law of Moses and Israel; and (I will also give thee) thy food, clothing and necessaries, and live with thee as husband and wife according to universal custom." And Miss (name of bride), this virgin, consented and became his wife. The wedding outfit that she brought unto him from her father's house, in silver, gold, valuables, wearing apparel, house furniture, and bedclothes, all this (name of bridegroom), the said bridegroom, accepted in the sum of one hundred silver pieces, and (name of bridegroom), the bridegroom consented to increase this amount from his own property with the sum of

one hundred silver pieces, making in all two hundred silver pieces. And thus said (name of bridegroom), the bridegroom: "The responsibility of this marriage contract, of this wedding outfit, and of this additional sum, I take upon myself and my heirs after me, so that they shall be paid from the best part of my property and possession that I have beneath the whole heaven, that which I now possess or may hereafter acquire. All my property, real and personal, even the mantle on my shoulders, shall be mortgaged to secure the payment of this marriage contract, of the wedding outfit, and of the addition made thereto, during my lifetime and after my death, from the present day and forever." (Name of bridegroom), the bridegroom, has taken upon himself the responsibility of this marriage contract, of the wedding outfit and the addition made thereto, according to the restrictive usages of all marriage contracts and the additions thereto made for the daughters of Israel, in accordance with the institution of our sages of blessed memory. It is not to be regarded as a mere forfeiture without consideration or as a mere formula of a document. We have followed the legal formality of symbolical delivery (*kinyan*) between (name of bridegroom), the son of . . ., the bridegroom and (name of bride), the daughter of . . ., this virgin, and we have used a garment legally fit for the purpose, to strengthen all that is stated above,

And everything is valid and confirmed.

Attested to.. (Witness)

Attested to.. (Witness)

A second goblet of wine is now filled, over which the Rabbi recites or chants the following seven marriage benedictions:

Praised be Thou, O Lord our God, King of the universe, who hast created the fruit of the vine.

Praised be Thou, O Lord our God, King of the universe, who hast created all things to Thy glory.

Praised be Thou, O Lord our God, King of the universe who hast created man.

Praised be Thou, O Lord our God, King of the universe, who hast made man in Thine image, after Thy likeness, and out of his very self, Thou hast prepared unto him a perpetual fabric. Praised be Thou, O Lord, who hast created man. May she who is childless (Zion) be exceedingly glad and rejoice when her children shall be reunited in her midst in joy. Praised be Thou, O Lord, who gladdenest Zion through (restoring) her children.

Mayest Thou gladden the beloved friends (the newly married couple), as Thou didst gladden Thy creature (Adam) in the Garden of Eden in time of yore. Praised be Thou, O Lord our God, who gladdenest the bridegroom and the bride.

Praised be Thou, O Lord our God, King of the universe, who hast created joy and gladness, bridegroom and bride, rejoicing, song, pleasure and delight, love and brotherhood, peace and fellowship. Soon may there be heard in the cities of Judah, and in the streets of Jerusalem, the voice of joy and gladness, the voice of the bridegroom and the voice of the bride, the jubilant voice of bridegrooms from their nuptial canopies, and of youths from their feasts of song. Praised be Thou, O Lord, who gladdenest the bridegroom and the bride.

The bridegroom and the bride are given to taste from the goblet of wine.

A glass is now broken by the bridegroom, and those present proclaim: "*Mazal tov*" (good fortune).

The guests wash their hands for the repast, and upon breaking bread say:

Praised be Thou, O Lord our God, King of the universe, who causest the earth to yield bread.

Before Grace after the Meal, the Rabbi recites or chants the following blessing:

May He who blessed our ancestors Abraham, Isaac and Jacob, bless the bridegroom and the bride and henceforth prosper their ways upon which they walk. May they always find grace and favor in the eyes of those who meet them. May they deserve to build a famous and a praiseworthy house in Israel. May peace reign in their home, and may contentment and happiness be in their hearts all the days of their lives. May He bless with all good the best man and the bride's maid, and all those that are assembled here, and prolong their lives in happiness. May He send blessing and prosperity upon all the work of their hands, as well as upon all Israel, their brethren; and let us say, Amen.

PART II

The Principal Doctrines of Judaism

12 The Doctrine of Torah
    Jacob Neusner

13 The Doctrine of God
    Alan J. Avery-Peck

14 The Doctrine of Israel
    Jacob Neusner

15 The Doctrine of Hebrew Language Usage
    David H. Aaron

Chapter 12

The Doctrine of Torah

Jacob Neusner

The doctrine of Torah extended beyond the theological boundaries of Rabbinic Judaism in its classical age and permeated the Judaic philosophical writings of the Middle Ages and modern Judaic thought as well. The Torah was now held to have preexisted the creation of the world, and a variety of philosophers took up that proposition. The relationship between the contents of the Torah and the capacities of human reason to attain the same convictions interested the medieval philosophers as well, as the rationalist tradition asked why revelation was needed to accord access to what rationality on its own can have accomplished. In modern times, philosophers located the Torah within historical time. Historicistic philosophy treated the Torah as the result of the Jews' own history, and, in the Hegelian framework, treated the Oral Torah as "the history of the evolution of the Jewish spirit . . . inseparable from the written Torah." Others, in the Kantian mode, underscored the moral side of the Torah. Zionism, for its part, treated the Torah as "the religious civilization of the Jewish People." In the following article Warren (Zev) Harvey surveys the way in which the symbol of the Torah made its way through various chapters in the history of Judaism. At each point we see how the successive intellectual systems made their systemic statement through what they said about the Torah.

A. Warren (Zev) Harvey, "Torah"

Torah (Heb. תּוֹרָה).

The term

Torah is derived from the root ירה which in the *hifil* conjugation means "to teach" (cf. Lev. 10:11). The meaning of the word is therefore "teaching," "doctrine," or "instruction"; the commonly accepted "law" gives a wrong impression. The word is used in different ways but the underlying idea of "teaching" is common to all.

In the Pentateuch it is used for all the body of laws referring to a specific subject e.g., "the *torah* of the meal offering" (Lev. 6:7), of the guilt offering (7:1), and of the Nazirite (Num. 6:21), and especially as a summation of all the separate *torot* (cf. Lev. 7:37–38; 14:54–56). In verses, however, such as Deuteronomy 4:44, "and this is the Torah which Moses set before the children of Israel" and ibid., 33:4, "Moses commanded us a Torah, an inheritance of the congregation of Jacob" and the references in the Bible to "the Torah of Moses" (cf. Josh. 1:7; Ezra 3:2; 7:6; 8:1, 8; Mal. 3:22), it refers particularly to the Pentateuch as distinct from the rest of the Bible. In later literature the whole Bible was referred to as *Tanakh*, the initial letters of Torah (Pentateuch), *Nevi'm* (Prophets), and *Ketuvim* (Hagiographia), a meaning it retained in halakhic literature to differentiate between the laws which are of biblical origin (in its Aramaic form, *de-Oraita* "from the Torah") and those of rabbinic provenance (*de-rabbanan*). The term is, however, also used loosely to designate the Bible as a whole.

A further extension of the term came with the distinction made between the Written Torah (Torah *she-bi-khetav*) and the Oral Torah (Torah *she be-al peh*). The use of the plural *Torot* (e.g., Gen. 26:5) was taken to refer to those two branches of divine revelation which were traditionally regarded as having been given to Moses on Mount Sinai (Yoma 28b). Justification was found in the verse of Exodus 34:27, which can be translated literally as "Write thou these words for by the mouth of these words I have made a covenant." The word "write" (*ketav*) was regarded as the authority for the Written Law (hence Torah *she-bi-khetav*, i.e., the Torah included in the word *ketav*) while "by the mouth" (*al pi*) was taken to refer to the Torah *she-be-al peh* (i.e., the Torah referred to in the phrase *al pi*; cf. Git. 60b.) Lastly, the word is used for the whole corpus of Jewish traditional law from the Bible to the latest development of the *halakhah*. In modern Hebrew the word is used to designate the system of a thinker or scholar, e.g., "the *torah* of Spinoza."

Source for reading A.: Encyclopedia Judaica, vol. 15, cols. 1236–46.

Origin and preexistence

"Moses received the Torah from Sinai" (Avot 1:1). Yet there is an ancient tradition that the Torah existed in heaven not only before God revealed it to Moses, but even before the world was created. The apocryphal book of The Wisdom of Ben Sira identified the Torah with preexistent personified wisdom (1:1–5, 26; 15:1; 24:1 ff.; 34:8; cf. Prov. 8:22–31). In rabbinic literature, it was taught that the Torah was one of the six or seven things created prior to the creation of the world (Gen. R. 1:4; Pes. 54a, et al.). Of these preexistent things, it was said that only the Torah and the throne of glory were actually created, while the others were only conceived, and that the Torah preceded the throne of glory (Gen. R. 1:4). According to Eliezer ben Yose the Galilean, for 974 generations before the creation of the world, the Torah lay in God's bosom and joined the ministering angels in song (ARN 31, p. 91, cf. Gen. R. 28:4, et al.). Simeon ben Lakish taught that the Torah preceded the world by 2,000 years (Lev. R. 19:1, et al.) and was written in black fire upon white fire (TJ, Shek. 6:1, 49d, et al.). Akiva called the Torah, "the precious instrument by which the world was created" (Avot 3:14). Rav Hoshaiah, explicitly identifying the Torah with the preexistent wisdom of Proverbs, said that God created the world by looking into the Torah as an architect builds a palace by looking into blueprints. He also took the first word of Genesis not in the sense of "In the beginning," but in that of "By means of the beginning," and he taught that "beginning" (probably in the philosophic sense of the Greek *arche*) designates Torah, since it is written of wisdom (= Torah), "The Lord made me the beginning of His way" (Prov. 8:22; Gen. R. 1:1). It was also taught that God took council with the Torah before He created the world (Tanh. B. 2, et al.). The concept of the preexistence of the Torah is perhaps implicit in the philosophy of Philo, who wrote of the preexistence and role in creation of the Word of God (*logos;* e.g., Op. 20, 25, 36; Cher. 127) and identified the Word of God with the Torah (Mig. 130; cf. Op. and II Mos.).

Saadiah Gaon rejected the literal belief in preexistent things on the grounds that it contradicts the principle of creation ex nihilo. In his view, Proverbs 8:22, the verse cited by Rav Hoshaiah, means no more than that God created the world in a wise manner (*Beliefs and Opinions* 1:3; cf. Saadiah's commentary on Proverbs, ad loc.).

Judah b. Barzillai of Barcelona raised the problem of place. Where could God have kept a preexistent Torah? While allowing that God could conceivably have provided an ante-mundane place for a corporeal Torah, he preferred the interpretation that the Torah preexisted only as a thought in the divine mind. Ultimately, however, he expressed the opinion that the Torah's preexistence is a rabbinic metaphor, spoken out of love for the Torah and those who study it, and teaching that the Torah is worthy to have been created before the world (commentary on *Sefer Yetzirah, pp. 88–9; cf. Solomon b. Abraham Adret, Perushei Aggadot*).

Abraham ibn Ezra raised the problem of time. He wrote that it is impossible for the Torah to have preceded the world by 2,000 years or even by one moment, since time is an accident of motion, and there was no motion before God created the celestial spheres; rather, he concluded, the teaching about the Torah's pre-existence must be a metaphoric riddle (cf. Commentary on the Torah, introd., "the fourth method" (both versions); cf. also Judah Hadassi, *Eshkol ha-Kofer*, 25b–26a; and cf. Abraham Shalom, *Neveh Shalom*, 10:8).

Judah Halevi explained that the Torah precedes the world in terms of teleology; God created the world for the purpose of revealing the Torah; therefore, since, as the philosophers say, "the first of thought is the end of the work," the Torah is said to have existed before the world (*Kuzari* 3:73).

Maimonides discussed the origin of the Torah from the standpoint of the epistemology of the unique prophecy of Moses (*Guide of the Perplexed* 2:35; 3:51; et al.; cf. Yad, introd.). The tradition of the preexistence of the Torah was not discussed in the *Guide of the Perplexed*; however, the closely related tradition of the preexistence of the throne of glory was (2:26, 30, et al.). The discussions of Moses' prophecy and of the throne of glory are esoteric and controversial, and each reader will interpret them according to his own views, perhaps inferring Maimonides' position concerning the origin of the Torah.

Within the framework of his Neoplatonic ontology, Isaac ibn Latif suggested that the Torah precedes the world not in time, but in rank. He cited the aggadic statements that the Torah and the throne of glory preceded the world, and that the Torah preceded the throne of glory, and he intimated that the Torah is the is the upper world (wisdom or intellect) which ontologically precedes the middle world (the celestial spheres, the throne of glory) which, in turn, ontologically precedes the lower world (our world of changing elements; *Sha'ar ha-Shamayim*).

While the tradition of the preexistence of the Torah was being ignored or explained away by most philosophers, it became fundamental in the Kabbalah. Like Ibn Latif, the kabbalists of Spain held that the Torah precedes the world ontologically. Some kabbalists identified the primordial Torah with *Hokhmah* (God's wisdom), the second of the ten Sefirot in emanation. Others identified the Written Torah with the sixth *Sefirah, Tiferet* (God's beauty), and the Oral Torah with the tenth *Sefirah, Malkhut* (God's kingdom). Emanational precedence signifies creative power; and it was with the Torah that God created the angels and the worlds, and with the Torah He sustains all (Zohar 3, 152a; Num. 9:1).

Hasdai Crescas, who in the course of his revolutionary critique of Aristotelian physics had rejected the dependence of time on motion, was able to take pre-existence literally as chronological. He interpreted the proposition about the preexistence of the Torah as a metonymy, referring actually to the purpose of the Torah. Since, according to him, the purpose of the Torah and the purpose of the world are the same, namely, love, and since the purpose or final cause of an object chronologically precedes it, it follows that the purpose of the Torah (i.e., love) chronologically preceded the world. As its final cause, love (= the purpose of the Torah) is a necessary condition of the world; and this is the meaning of the talmudic statement, "Were it not for the Torah [i.e., the purpose of the Torah, or love], heaven and earth would not have come into existence" (Pes. 68b; *Or Adonai* 2:6, 4; cf. Nissim b. Reuben Gerondi, Commentary on Ned. 39b).

Joseph Albo also interpreted the preexistence of the Torah in terms of final causality, but his position was essentially that of Judah Halevi, and not that of his teacher, Crescas. He reasoned that man exists for the sake of the Torah; everything in the world of generation and corruption exists for the sake of man; therefore, the Torah preceded the world in the Aristotelian sense that the final cause in (the mind of) the agent necessarily precedes the other three causes (*Sefer ha-Ikkarim* 3:12; cf. Jacob b. Solomon ibn Habib, *Ein Ya'akov*, introd.; Joseph Solomon Delmedigo, *Novelot Hokhmah*, 1).

The theory, based on the statement of Rav Hoshaiah, that the Torah was the preexistent blueprint of creation was elaborated by Isaac Arama. Isaac Abrabanel, Moses Alshekh, Judah Loew b. Bezalel, and others.

In modern Jewish philosophical literature, Nachman Krochmal analyzed the interpretation of the author of *Sha'ar ha-Shamayim* (Ibn Latif and not, as Krochmal supposed, Ibn Ezra) of the Torah's preexistence, and his analysis bears implications for his own idealistic concept of the metaphysical and epistemological precedence of the spiritual (*Moreh Nevukhei ha-Zeman*, 17; cf. 12, 16).

Franz Rosenzweig, in his existentalist reaction to the intellectualist interpretation of the Torah by German rabbis, appealed to the *aggadah* of the preexistence of the Torah in an attempt to show the absurdity of trying to base the claim of the Torah merely on a juridical or historical reason: "No doubt the Torah, both Written and Oral, was given Moses on Sinai, but was it not created before the creation of the world? Written against a background of shining fire in letters of somber flame? And was not the world created for its sake?" ("The Builders," in: N. Glatzer (ed.), *On Jewish Learning* (1955), 78).

Nature and purpose

In the Bible, the Torah is referred to as the Torah of the Lord (Ex. 13:9, et al.) and of Moses (Josh. 8:31, et al.), and said to be given as an inheritance to the congregation of Jacob (Deut. 33:4). Its purpose seems to be to make Israel "a kingdom of priests and a holy nation" (Ex. 19:6). It was said that "the commandment is a lamp and the Torah is light" (Prov. 6:23). The Torah was called "perfect," its ordinances "sweeter than honey and the flow of honeycombs" (Ps. 19:8, 11; cf. 119: 103; Prov. 16:24). Psalm 119, containing 176 verses, is a song of love for the Torah whose percepts give peace and understanding.

In the apocryphal book The Wisdom of Ben Sira, the Torah is identified with wisdom (see above). In another apocryphal work, the laws of the Torah are said to be drawn up "with a view to truth and the indication of right reason" (Arist. 161). The Septuagint rendered the Hebrew *torah* by the Greek *nomos* ("law") probably in the sense of a living network of traditions and customs of a people. The designation of the Torah by *nomos*, and by its Latin successor *lex* (whence, "the Law"), has historically given rise to the sad misunderstanding that Torah means legalism.

It was one of the very few real dogmas of rabbinic theology that the Torah is from heaven (Heb. *Torah min ha-shamayim*; Sanh. 10:1, et al.; cf. Ex. 20:22 [19]; Deut. 4:36); i.e., the Torah in its entirely was revealed by God. According to the *aggadah*, Moses ascended into heaven to capture the Torah from the angels (Shab. 89a, et al.). In one of the oldest mishnaic statements, Simeon the Just taught that (the study of the) Torah is one of the three things by which the world is sustained (Avot 1:2). Eleazar ben Shammua said: "Were it not for the Torah, heaven and earth would not continue to exist" (Pes. 68b; Ned. 32a; cf. Crescas' interpretation above). It was calculated that "the whole world in its entirety is only 1/3200 of the Torah" (Er. 21a; cf. TJ, Pe'ah 1:1, 15d). God Himself was said to study the Torah daily (Av. Zar. 3b, et al.).

The Torah was often compared to fire, water, wine, oil, milk, honey, drugs, manna, the tree of life, and many other things; it was considered the source of freedom, goodness, and life (e.g., Avot 6:2, 3, 7); it was identified both with wisdom and with love (e.g., Mid. Ps. to 1:18). Hillel summarized the entire Torah in one sentence: "What is hateful to you, do not to your fellow" (Shab. 31a). Akiva said: "The fundamental principle of the Torah is the commandment, 'Love thy neighbor as thyself'" (Lev. 19:18). His disciple Simeon ben Azzai said that its fundamental principle is the verse (Gen. 5:1) which teaches that all human beings are descended from the same man, and created by God in His image (Sifra, Kedoshim 4:12; TJ, Ned. 9:3, 41c; Gen. R. 24:7).

Often the Torah was personified. Not only did God take council with the Torah before He created the world (see above), but according to one interpretation, the plural in "Let us make man" (Gen. 1:26) refers to God and the Torah (Tanh. Pekudei, 3). The Torah appears as the daughter of God and the bride of Israel (PR 20; 95a, et al.). On occasion, the Torah is obliged to plead the case of Israel before God (e.g., Ex. R. 29:4).

The message of the Torah is for all mankind. Before giving the Torah to Israel, God offered it to the other nations, but they refused it; and when He did give the Torah to Israel, He revealed it in the extraterritorial desert and simultaneously in all the 70 languages, so that men of all nations would have a right to it (Mekh., Yitro, 5; Sif. Deut. 343; Shab. 88b; Ex. R. 5:9; 27:9; cf. Av. Zar. 3a: "a pagan who studies the Torah is like a high priest"). Alongside this universalism, the rabbis taught the inseparability of Israel and the Torah. One rabbi held that the concept of Israel existed in God's mind even before He created the Torah (Gen. R. 1:4). Yet, were it not for its accepting the Torah, Israel would not be "chosen," nor would it be different from all the idolatrous nations (Num. 14:10; Ex. R. 47:3 et al.).

In the Hellenistic literature contemporaneous with the early rabbinic teachings, Philo considered the Torah the ideal law of the philosophers, and Moses the perfect lawgiver and prophet and the philosopher-ruler of Plato's *Republic* (II Mos. 2). His concept of the relationship of the Torah to nature and man was Stoic: "The world is in harmony with the Torah and the Torah with the world, and the man who observes the Torah is constituted thereby a loyal citizen of the world" (Op. 3). He wrote that the laws of the Torah are "stamped with the seals of nature," and are "the most perfect picture of the cosmic polity" (II Mos. 14, 51). Josephus, in his *Against Apion*, discoursed on the moral and universalistic nature of the Torah, emphasizing that it promotes piety, friendship, humanity toward the world at large, justice, charity, and endurance under persecution. Both Philo and Josephus wrote that principles of the Torah, e.g., the Sabbath, have been imitated by all nations.

Saadiah Gaon expounded a rationalist theory according to which the ethical and religious-intellectual beliefs imparted by the Torah are all attainable by human reason. He held that the Torah is divisible into (1) commandments which, in addition to being revealed, are demanded by reason (e.g., prohibitions of murder, fornication, theft, lying); and (2) commandments whose authority is revelation alone (e.g., Sabbath and dietary laws), but which generally are understandable in terms of some personal or social benefit attained by their performance. Revelation of the Torah was needed because while reason makes general demands, it does not dictate particular laws; and while the matters of religious belief revealed in the Torah are attainable by philosophy, they are only attained by it after some time or, in the case of many, not at all. He taught that the purpose of the Torah is the bestowal of eternal bliss (*Beliefs and Opinions*, introd. 6, ch. 3). He held that Israel is a nation only by virtue of the Torah (see below).

In the period between Saadiah and Maimonides, most Jewish writers who speculated on the nature of the Torah continued in the rationalist tradition established by Saadiah. These included Bahya ibn Paquda, Joseph ibn Ẓaddik, Abraham ibn Ezra, and Abraham ibn Daud. Judah Halevi, however, opposed the rationalist interpretation. He allowed that the Torah contains rational and political laws, but considered them preliminary to the specifically divine laws and teachings which cannot be comprehended by reason, e.g., the laws of the Sabbath which teach the omnipotence of God and the creation of the world (*Kuzari* 2:48, 50). The Torah makes it possible to approach God by awe, love, and joy (2:50). It is the essence of wisdom, and the outcome of the will of God to reveal His kingdom on earth as it is in heaven (3:17). While Judah Halevi held that Israel was created to fulfill the Torah, he wrote that there would be no Torah were there no Israel (2:56; 3:73).

Maimonides emphasized that the Torah is the product of the unique prophecy of Moses. He maintained that the Torah has two purposes; first, the welfare of the body and, ultimately, the welfare of the soul (intellect). The first purpose, which is a prerequisite of the ultimate purpose, is political, and "consists in the governance of the city and the well-being of the state of all its people according to their capacity." The ultimate purpose consists in the true perfection of man, his acquisition of immortality through intellection of the highest things. The Torah is similar to other laws in its concern with the welfare of the body; but its divine nature is reflected in its concern for the welfare of the soul (*Guide of the Perplexed*, 3:27). Maimonides saw the Torah as a rationalizing force, warring against superstition, imagination, appetite, and idolatry. He cited the rabbinic dictum, "Everyone who disbelieves in idolatry professes the Torah in its entirety" (Sif. Num. 110; Guide 3:29; Yad, Ovedei Kokhavim, 2:4), and taught that the foundation of the Torah and the pivot around which it turns consists in the effacement of idolatry. He held that the Torah must be interpreted in the light of reason.

Of the Jewish philosophers who flourished in the 13th and early 14th centuries, most endorsed Maimonides' position that the Torah has as its purpose both political and spiritual welfare. Some, like Samuel ibn Tibbon and Isaac Albalag, argued that its purpose consists only or chiefly in political welfare. Others emphasized its spiritual purpose, like Levi b. Gershom, who taught that the purpose of the Torah is to guide man – the masses as well as the intellectual elite – toward human perfection, that is, the acquisition of true knowledge and, thereby, an immortal intellect.

While Maimonides and the Maimonideans generally restricted their analyses of the nature of the Torah to questions of its educational, moral, or political value, the Spanish kabbalists engaged in bold metaphysical speculation concerning its essence. The kabbalists taught that the Torah is a living organism. Some said the entire Torah consists of the names of God set in succession (cf. Nahmanides, *Perushei ha-Torah*, Preface) or interwoven into a fabric (cf. Joseph Gikatilla, *Sha'arei Orah*). Others said that the Torah is itself the name of God. The Torah was identified with various *Sefirot* in the divine body (see above). Ultimately, it was said that the Torah is God (Menahem Recanati, *Ta'amei ha-Mitzvot*, 3a; Zohar 2, 60a [Ex. 15:22]). This identification of the Torah and God was understood to refer to the Torah in its true primordial essence, and not to its manifestation in the world of creation.

The first Jewish philosopher to construct a metaphysics in which the Torah plays an integral role was Hasdai Crescas, who, notwithstanding his distinguished work in natural science, was more sympathetic to the Kabbalah than to Aristotle. He taught that the purpose of the Torah is to effect the purpose of the universe. By guiding man toward corporeal happiness, moral and intellectual excellence, and felicity of soul, the Torah leads him to the love of neighbor and, finally, the eternal love of God (*devekut*), which is the purpose of all creation (*Or Adonai*, 2:6). Like Judah Halevi, he took an ultimately anti-intellectualist position, and maintained, in opposition to the Maimonideans, that the very definition of the Torah as the communication of God to man implies beliefs about the nature of God and His relation to man which cannot, and need not, be proved by philosophy.

Joseph Albo, developing some Maimonidean ideas, taught that the Torah, as divine law, is superior to natural law and conventional-positive law in that it not only promotes political security and good behavior, but also guides man toward eternal spiritual happiness (*Sefer ha-Ikkarim*, 1:7).

In the writings of Isaac Arama, Isaac Abrabanel, Moses Alshekh, Judah Loew b. Bezalel, and other late medievals, the conflicting approaches to the Torah of Maimonideanism and the Kabbalah converged to give expression to the theme, already adumbrated in Philo, that the Torah exists in the mind of God as the plan and order of the universe (Arama, *Akedat Yiẓḥak*; 1 Abrabanel, *Mifalot Elohim*, 1:2; Alshekh, *Torat Moshe* to Genesis 1:1; Judah Loew, *Netivot Olam*, 1:1; *Tiferet Yisrael*, 25; cf. above). In Italy, Judah b. Jehiel (Messer Leon), influenced by the Renaissance emphasis on the art of rhetoric, composed the *Nofet Ẓufim*, in which he analyzed the language of the Bible and, in effect, presented the first aesthetic interpretation of the Torah (cf. Judah Abrabanel, *Dialoghi di Amore*).

Influenced by Maimonides, Baruch Spinoza took the position taken by some early Maimonideans that the Torah is an exclusively political law. However, he broke radically with those Maimonideans and with all rabbinic tradition by denying its divine nature, by making it an object of historical-critical investigation, and by maintaining that it was not written by Moses alone but by various authors living at different times. Moreover, he considered the Torah primitive, unscientific, and particularistic, and thus subversive to progress, reason, and universal morality. By portraying the Torah as a product of the Jewish people, he reversed the traditional opinion (but cf. Judah Halevi) according to which the Jewish people are a product of the Torah.

Like Spinoza, Moses Mendelssohn considered the Torah a political law, but he affirmed its divine nature. Taking a position similar to Saadiah's, he explained that the Torah does not intend to reveal new ideas about deism and morality, but rather, through its laws and institutions, to arouse men to be mindful of the true ideas attainable by all men through reason. By identifying the beliefs of the Torah with the truths of reason, Mendelssohn affirmed both its scientific respectability and its universalistic nature. By defining the Torah as a political law given to Israel by God, he preserved the traditional view that Israel is a product of the Torah, and not, as Spinoza claimed, vice versa.

With the rise of the science of Judaism *(Wissenschaft des Judentums)* in the nineteenth century, and the advance of the historical-critical approach to the Torah, many Jewish intellectuals, including ideologists of Reform like Abraham Geiger, followed Spinoza in seeing the Torah, at least in part, as a product of the primitive history of the Jewish nation. Nachman Krochmal, in his rationalist-idealist philosophy, attempted to synthesize the historical-critical thesis that the Torah is a product of Jewish history, with the traditional thesis that the entire Torah is divinely revealed. He maintained that, from the days of Abraham and Isaac, the Hebrew nation has contained the Absolute Spiritual, and this Absolute Spiritual was the source of the laws given to Moses on Mt. Sinai, whose purpose is to perfect the individual and the group, and to prevent the nation's extinction. The Oral Torah, which is, in effect, the history of the evolution of the Jewish spirit, is inseparable from the Written Torah, and is its clarification and conceptual refinement; which is to say, the true science of the Torah, which is the vocation of the Jewish spirit, is the conceptualization of the Absolute Spiritual (*Moreh Nevu-khei ha-Zeman*, esp. 6–8, 13).

The increasing intellectualization of the Torah was opposed by Samuel David Luzzatto and Salomon Ludwig Steinheim, two men who had little in common but their fideism. They contended – as Crescas had against the Maimonideans – that the belief that God revealed the Torah is the starting point of Judaism, and that this belief, with its momentous implications concerning the nature of God and His relation to man, cannot be attained by philosophy. Luzzatto held that the foundation of the whole Torah is compassion. Steinheim, profoundly opposing Mendelssohn, held that the Torah comes to reveal truths about God and His work.

While Spinoza and Mendelssohn had emphasized the political nature of the Torah, many rationalists of the late nineteenth and early twentieth centuries emphasized its moral nature. Moritz Lazarus identified the Torah with the moral law, and interpreted the rabbinical statement, "Were it not for the Torah, heaven and earth would not continue to exist" (see above), as corresponding to the Kantian teaching that it is the moral law that gives value to existence. Hermann Cohen condemned Spinoza as a willful falsifier and a traitor to the Jewish people for his claim that the Torah is subversive to universalistic morality. He held that the Torah, with its monotheistic ethics, far from being subversive to universalism, prepares a Jew to participate fully and excellently in general culture (in this connection, he opposed Zionism and developed his controversial theory of "Germanism and Judaism"). He maintained that in its promulgation of commandments affecting all realms of human action, the Torah moves toward overcoming the distinction between holy and profane through teaching all men to become holy by always performing holy actions, i.e., by always acting in accordance with the moral law.

In their German translation of the Bible, Martin Buber and Franz Rosenzweig translated *torah* as *Weisung* or *Unterweisung* ("Instruction") and not as *Gesetz* ("Law"). In general, they agreed on the purpose of the Torah: to convert the universe and God from It to Thou. Yet they differed on several points concerning its nature. Buber saw the Torah as the past dialogue between Israel and God, and the present dialogue between the individual reader, the I, and God, the Thou. He concluded that while one must open himself to the entire teaching of the Torah, he need only accept a particular law of the Torah if he feels that it is being spoken now to him. Rosenzweig objected to this personalist and antinomian position of Buber's. Taking an existentialist position, he maintained that the laws of the Torah are commandments to do, and as such become comprehensible only in the experience of doing, and, therefore, a Jew must not, as Buber did, reject a law of the Torah that "does not speak to me," but must always open himself to the new experience which may make it comprehensible. Like Cohen – and also like the Hasidim – he marveled that the law of the Torah is universal in range. He contended that it erases the barrier between this world and the world to come by encompassing, vitalizing, and thereby redeeming everything in this world.

The secular Zionism of the late nineteenth and early twentieth centuries gave religious thinkers new cause to define the relationship between the Torah and the Jewish nation. Some defined the Torah in terms of the nation. Thus, Mordecai Kaplan translated Aḥad Ha-Am's sociological theory of the evolution of Jewish civilization into a religious, though naturalistic, theory of the Torah as the "religious civilization of the Jews." Others, like Buber and Rosenzweig, considering secular nationalism dangerous, tried to "interdefine" the Torah and the nation. Whereas Buber saw the Torah as the product of a dialogue between the nation and God, he held that the spirit of the nation was transfigured by that dialogue. Rosenzweig, whose position here resembles Judah Halevi's, stated both that the nation's chosenness is prior to the Torah, and that the acceptance of the Torah is an experiential precondition of its chosenness. Other thinkers defined the nation in terms of the Torah. Thus, Abraham Isaac Kook, whose thought was influenced by the Kabbalah, taught that the purpose of the Torah is to reveal the living light of the universe, the suprarational spiritual, to Israel and, through Israel, to all mankind. While the Written Torah, which reveals the light in the highest channel of our soul, is the product of God alone, the Oral Torah, which is inseparable from the Written Torah, and which reveals the light in a second channel of our soul, proximate to the life of deeds, derives its personality from the spirit of the nation. The Oral Torah can live in its fullness only when Israel lives in its fullness – in peace and independence in the Land of Israel. Thus, according to Kook, modern Zionism, whatever the intent of its secular ideologists, has universalistic religious significance, for it is acting in service of the Torah (see esp. *Orot ha-Torah*).

In the State of Israel, most writers and educators have maintained the secularist position of the early Zionists, namely, that the Torah was not revealed by God, in the traditional sense, but is the product of the national life of ancient Israel. Those who have discussed the Torah and its relation to the state from a religious point of view have mostly followed Kook or Buber and Rosenzweig. However, a radically rationalist approach to the nature of the Torah has been taught by Yeshayahu Leibowitz who, in the Maimonidean tradition, emphasizes that the Torah is a law for the worship of God and for the consequent obliteration of the worship of men and things; in this connection, he condemns the subordination of the Torah to nationalism or to religious sentimentalism or to any ideology or institution. Outside the State of Israel, a similarly iconoclastic position has been taken by the French phenomenologist Emmanuel Levinas, who has gone further and written that the love for the Torah should take precedence even over the love for God Himself, for only through the Torah – that knowledge of the Other which is the condition of all ethics – can man relate to a personal God against Whom he can rebel and for Whom he can die.

ETERNITY (or NONABROGABILITY). In the Bible there is no text unanimously understood to affirm explicitly the eternity or non-abrogability of the Torah; however, many laws of the Torah are accompanied by phrases such as, "an everlasting injunction through your generations" (Lev.3:17, et al.).

The doctrine that the Torah is eternal appears several times in the pre-tannaitic apocryphal literature; e.g., Ben Sira 24:9 ("the memorial of me shall never cease") and Jubilees 33:16 ("an everlasting law for everlasting generations").

Whereas the rabbis understood the preexistence of the Torah in terms of its pre-revelation existence in heaven, they understood the eternity or non-abrogability of the Torah in terms of its post-revelation existence not in heaven; i.e., the whole

Torah was given to Moses and no part of it remained in heaven (Deut. 8:6, et al.). When Eliezer ben Hyrcanus and Joshua ben Hananiah were debating a point of Torah and a voice from heaven dramatically announced that Eliezer's position was correct, Joshua refused to recognize its testimony, for the Torah "is not in heaven" (Deut. 30:12), and must be interpreted by men, unaided by the supernatural (BM 59b). It was a principle that "A prophet is henceforth not permitted to innovate a thing" (Sifra, Be-Ḥukkotai 13:7; Tem. 16a; but he was permitted to suspend a law temporarily (Sif. Deut. 175)). The rabbis taught that the Torah would continue to exist in the world to come (e.g., Eccles. R. 2:1), although some of them were of the opinion that innovations would be made in the messianic era (e.g., Gen. R. 98:9; Lev. R. 9:7).

Philo saw the eternity of the Torah as a metaphysical principle, following from the Torah's accord with nature. He believed that the laws and enactments of the Torah "will remain for all future ages as though immortal, so long as the sun and the moon and the whole heaven and universe exist" (II Mos. 14; cf. Jer. 31:32–35). The belief in the eternity of the Torah appears also in the later apocryphal works (e.g., I Bar. 4:1; Ps. of Sol. 10:5) and in Josephus (Apion 2:277).

With the rise to political power of Christianity and Islam, two religions which sought to convert Jews and which argued that particular injunctions of the Torah had been abrogated, the question of the eternity or "non-abrogatability" of the Torah became urgent.

Saadiah Gaon stated that the children of Israel have a clear tradition from the prophets that the laws of the Torah are not subject to abrogation. Presenting scriptural corroboration for this tradition, he appealed to phrases appended to certain commandments, e.g., "throughout their generations, for a perpetual covenant" (Ex. 31:16). According to one novel argument of his: the Jewish nation is a nation only by virtue of its laws, namely, the Torah; God has stated that the Jewish nation will endure as long as the heaven and earth (Jer. 31:35–36); therefore, the Torah will last as long as heaven and earth (cf. Philo, above). He interpreted the verses, "Remember ye the Torah of Moses...Behold, I will send you Elijah..." (Mal. 3:22–23), as teaching that the Torah will hold valid until the prophet Elijah returns to herald the resurrection (*Beliefs and Opinions* 3:7).

Maimonides listed the belief in the eternity of the Torah as the ninth of his 13 principles of Judaism, and connected it with the belief that no prophet will surpass Moses, the only man to give people laws through prophecy. He contended that the eternity of the Torah is stated clearly in the Bible, particularly in Deuteronomy 13:1 ("thou shalt not add thereto, nor diminish from it") and Deuteronomy 29:28 ("the things that are revealed belong unto us and to our children for ever, that we may do all the words of this Torah"). He also cited the rabbinic principle: "a prophet is henceforth not permitted to innovate a thing" (see above). He offered the following explanation of the Torah's eternity, based on its perfection and on the theory of the mean: "The Torah of the Lord is perfect" (Ps. 19:8) in that its statutes are just, i.e., that they are equibalanced between the burdensome and the indulgent; and "when a thing is perfect as it is possible to be within its species, it is impossible that within that species there should found another thing that does not fall short of the perfection either because of excess or deficiency." Also, he mentioned the argument that the prophesied eternity of the name of Israel ("For as the new heavens and the new earth, which I will make, shall remain before Me . . . so shall your seed and your name"; Isa. 66:22) entails the eternity of the Torah (cf. Saadiah above). He held that there will be no change in the Torah after the coming of the Messiah (commentary on Mishnah, Sanh. 10; Yad, Yesodei ha-Torah, 9; cf. *Sefer ha-Mitzvot; Guide of the Perplexed* 2:29, 39; Abraham ibn Daud, *Emunah Ramah*).

Hasdai Crescas listed the eternity of the Torah as a nonfundamental true belief; i.e., required by Judaism, but not essential to the concept of Torah. Unlike Saadiah and Maimonides, he did not try to found this belief directly on a biblical text (but cf. his *Bittul Ikkarei ha-Noẓerim*, 9), but solely on the rabbinic dictum: "A prophet is henceforth not permitted to innovate a thing" (see above). To elucidate the belief from the point of view of speculation, he presented an argument from the perfection of the Torah, which differed markedly from its Maimonidean precursor. The argument proceeds as follows: The Torah is perfect for it perfectly guides men toward the ultimate human happiness, love. If God were to abrogate the Torah, He would surely replace it, for it is impossible that He would forsake His purpose to maximize love. Since the Torah is perfect, it could be replaced only by an equal or an inferior; but if inferior, God would not be achieving His purpose of maximizing love; and if equal, He would be acting futilely. Therefore, He will not abrogate the Torah. Against the argument that replacement of the Torah by an equal but different law would make sense if there was an appreciable change—for better or worse—in the people who received it, he retorted characteristically that the Torah is the excellent guide for all, including both the intellectuals and the backward (*Or Adonai*, 3, pt. 1, 5:1–2).

Joseph Albo criticized Maimonides for listing the belief in the eternity of the Torah as an independent fundamental belief of Judaism. In a long discussion, which in many places constitutes an elaboration of arguments found in Crescas, he contended that non-abrogation is not a fundamental principle of the Torah, and that moreover, no text can be found in the Bible to establish it. Ironically, his ultimate position turned out to be closer to Maimonides' than to Crescas'; for he concluded that the belief in the non-abrogation of the Torah is a branch of the doctrine that no prophet will surpass the excellence of Moses (*Sefer ha-Ikkarim*, 3:13–23).

After Albo, the question of the eternity of the Torah became routine in Jewish philosophical literature (e.g., Abraham Shalom, *Neveh Shalom* 10:3–4; Isaac Abrabanel, *Rosh Amanah*, 13). However, in the Kabbalah it was never routine. In the 13th century *Sefer ha-Temunah* a doctrine of cosmic cycles or shemittot (cf. Deut. 15) was expounded according to which creation is renewed every 7,000 years, at which times the letters of the Torah reassemble, and the Torah enters the new cycle bearing different words and meanings. Thus, while eternal in its unrevealed state, the Torah, in its manifestation in creation, is destined to be abrogated. This doctrine became popular in later kabbalistic and hasidic literature, and was exploited by the heretic Shabbetai Zevi and his followers, who claimed that a new cycle had begun, and in consequence he was able to teach that, "the abrogation of the Torah is its fulfillment!"

Like his contemporary Shabbetai Zevi, but for much different reasons (see above), Spinoza committed the heresy of advocating the abrogation of the Torah. Subsequently, in the 19th century, Reform ideologists held that the abrogation of parts of the traditional Torah was not a heresy at all but was necessary for the progress of the Jewish religion. Similarly, many intellectuals and nationalists held that it was necessary for the progress of the Jewish nation. Ahad Ha-Am called for the Torah in the Heart to replace the Torah of Moses and of the rabbis, which having been written down, had, in his opinion, become rigid and ossified in the process of time.

Jewish philosophers of modern times have not concentrated on the question of the eternity or non-abrogability of the Torah. Nevertheless, it is not entirely untenable that the main distinction between Orthodox Judaism and non-Orthodox Judaism is that the latter rejects the literal interpretation of the ninth principle of Maimonides' Creed that there will be no change in the Torah.

Chapter 13

The Doctrine of God

Alan J. Avery-Peck

A.   George Foot Moore, "God and the World"

In the face of the events of the first centuries CE – the destruction of the Jerusalem Temple in 70, the failed Bar Kokhba revolt of 133–135, and the ascent of Christianity in the fourth through sixth centuries – the rabbis of the Talmud and Midrash presented new and distinctive conceptualizations of God's role in history. Without denying God's power over and knowledge of all human events, Rabbinic ideology increasingly refocused people's concerns, from the events of political history, over which individuals have little control, to events within the life and authority of each person and family, to the recurring actions that define who we are and demarcate what is truly important to us. These concerns for family and community, for business and social ethics, and for modes of acknowledging our debt to God for immediate blessings – the food we eat and the wonders of the universe evidenced in the daily rising and setting of the sun – were developed alongside an entirely new conception of God. This distinctively Rabbinic conception held that God's miracles could not and should not be anticipated immediately to restore the nation's past glory and that people must, rather, through their own actions, create and perfect a world of holiness such as God intended there to exist. Indeed, Talmudic rabbis asserted, God's actions in history are largely beyond human comprehension. This meant that, rather than the biblical notion of faith's emerging from an examination of what God has done for the people Israel, allegiance to God and the covenant was to be developed through the people's own philosophical and theological inquiry, through a recognition and acceptance of God's power and might even though those divine attributes are not visible on the stage of contemporary history.

Source for reading A.:   George Foot Moore, *Judaism in the First Centuries of the Christian Era* (Cambridge, MA: Harvard University Press, 1954), vol. 2, pp. 359–80.

Yet even as they developed these new and distinctive modes of thinking about God, Talmudic masters continued to proclaim God's absolute power as creator and ruler of all. This aspect of the Rabbinic assertion of the truth of Scripture is delineated in the following selection from George Foot Moore's classic study of Judaism in late antiquity. While Moore's presentation, which homogenizes sources from a wide range of historical periods and social settings, cannot be viewed as historical, its collation of diverse sayings creates a comprehensive picture of the central ideas expressed about God by Jews in late antiquity.

In accordance with the principle of revelation, the existence of God is not a subject for question or argument; he has revealed himself in Scripture, and Scripture teaches men to recognize the manifestations of his power, his wisdom, his goodness, in nature and history and providence. Dogmatic atheism and theoretical skepticism are the outcome of philosophical thinking, to which the Jews had no inclination. They knew the man who thought there was no God and conducted himself accordingly; but what such men really meant was that no higher power concerned itself about men's doings – there was no providence and no retribution.[1] Even the radical disbelief of the man who "denies the root" (namely, God), comes to this end by the practical, not the theoretical road; it begins with not hearkening to the word of the Lord as defined and expounded by scholars, and not doing all His commandments (Lev. 26: 14).[2] Philo, living in a centre where all the conflicting currents of Hellenistic philosophy met and strove together, had to debate this question from philosophical premises and with philosophical arguments, and to confute both skepticism and materialistic atheism.[2]

The first great question of religious philosophy, as Philo puts it, is Whether the Deity exists?; the second, What is it in its essential nature? The former he thinks it easy to prove; the latter question is not only difficult but perhaps unanswerable. In the ontological sense in which Philo means it, Palestinian Judaism, to which all metaphysic was alien, never speculated on the nature of God at all.[3]

Monotheism also, the corner-stone of Judaism, remains, as in the Bible, the religious doctrine that there is one God and no other, or, if it must be expressed abstractly, the doctrine of the soleness of God, in contradiction to polytheism, the multiplicity of gods. There is no assertion or implication of the unity of God in the metaphysical sense such as Philo means when he says, "God is sole, and one ($\overset{\prime}{\epsilon}\nu$), not composite, a simple nature,[4] while everyone of us, and of all other created things, is many" ($\pi o\lambda\lambda\acute{a}$), etc. Wholly remote from Jewish thought is the idea of God as pure and simple being ($\tau\grave{o}$ $\overset{\prime}{o}\nu$), in his proper nature an unknowable and unnamable Absolute, as Philo conceives it when he develops his fundamental philosophy. Jewish monotheism was reached through the belief that the will of God for righteousness is supreme in the history of the world; one will rules it all to one end – the world as it ought to be. In this way a national god became the universal God. Its origin was thus, to put it in a word, moral, rather than physical or metaphysical; and it was therefore essentially personal.

Monotheisms of diverse characters and tendencies have arisen in other ways. The sovereign god in a monarchically organized pantheon may be exalted so far above all others that they become only the ministers of his sole supreme will. Not infrequently their godhead is saved by the discovery that they are names, forms, manifestations, of the god who is the whole pantheon in one (*pantheus*). A physical philosophy may call the whole of nature god, and more particularly the all-pervading energetic mind; while religious feeling, aided by the mere necessities of language, may give a measure of personality to this immanent reason of the universe in nature and in man. Or, again, the one reality of an idealistic monism, the Absolute, may be similarly personified, and become a god to worship. In none of these is the moral character of God predominant; and therefore in none of them was personality essential to the very idea of God, as it is in Judaism. Jewish monotheism had no tendency toward monism, whether ontological or cosmic, or to the religious counterpart of monism, pantheism.

The assertion of the soleness of God and argument against the many gods have naturally a larger room in the apologetic of Hellenistic Jews than in the Palestinian schools and synagogues. The authors of the former lived in the midst of polytheism; they wrote to exhibit the superiority of Judaism, whether it be considered philosophically, religiously, or morally, and in the endeavor to convert Gentile readers from their vain idols to serve the living God. They were conscious of having, so far as the unity of the godhead is concerned, the best Greek thought on their side. They made florilegia of the monotheistic, or monotheistic-sounding, utterances of Greek poets, and to make the volume of testimony more impressive fabricated many more. The venerable Sibyl became a prophetess of the one God:

αὐτὸς γὰρ μόνος ἐστὶ θεὸς κοὐκ ἔστιν ἔτ' ἄλλος[5]

or, with more doctrine:

εἷς θεός ἐστι μόναρχος ἀθέσφατος αἰθέρι ναίων
αὐτοφυὴς ἀόρατος ὁρώμενος αὐτὸς ἅπαντα.[6]

Polytheism did not confront them, however, as a theoretical pluralism of gods – in *theory*, most educated Greeks in that age were not pluralists – but practically as the worship of a multiplicity of gods represented by images or, as among the Egyptians, by living animals. Idolatry was the universal concomitant of polytheism, and the Jews made no difference between them. The satire on idolatry which begins in the prophets is a commonplace of Hellenistic polemic; by its side are denunciations of it as the most heinous of sins, giving to the work of men's hands the honor that belongs to the God that made heaven and earth.[7] So monstrous is this aberration that the author of the Wisdom of Solomon endeavors to explain it as a progressive declension from natural and comparatively harmless beginnings till the depth of degradation is reached in Egyptian theriolatry.[8]

In Judaea the hostility of the Jews to everything resembling idols or idolatry forced regard upon contemptuous governors, little wont to respect the prejudices of their subjects. They would not even suffer Roman ensigns to be brought into the city of Jerusalem because they had images on them, and when Pilate introduced them nevertheless, constrained him to withdraw them.[9] It was not necessary to go far from Jerusalem, however, to find the obnoxious cults flourishing. Herod, who rebuilt the Jewish temple with such magnificence, erected in Samaria – renamed Sebaste – a great temple to the emperor Augustus. Caesarea, Herod's new seaport, and later the usual residence of the procurators, was predominantly a heathen city, as were the cities of the Decapolis.

But however familiar the spectacle of heathenism may have been, the teachers of Palestine, addressing themselves to men of their own religion, did not feel it necessary to polemize against polytheism and idolatry as the Hellenistic literature does.[10] Under the head of "heathenism" ('abodah zarah) in the Mishnah and elsewhere they are concerned to ordain precautions, first, against acts which might seem by inference to recognize the objects and places the Gentiles regard as divine or sacred, as well as against becoming in even the most remote way accessory to idolatrous worship; and, in the second place, to warn Jews against the vices which they regarded as the offspring of heathenism, and to avoid situations and associations which might invite suspicion that they were contaminated by such vices.

If the leaders of Palestinian Jewry had little fear of actual lapse into polytheism and idolatry, they had greater concern about a defection from the strict monotheistic principle of a different kind, the currency of the belief that there are "two authorities." The references to this error do not define it. A theory of "two authorities" might be entertained by thinkers who held that God is the author of good only, and that for the evil in the world another cause must be assumed;[11] or by such as in their thinking so exalted God above the finite as to find it necessary to interpose between God and the world an inferior intermediate power as demiurge;[12] or – as frequently happened – both these motives might concur. It is evident also that Gentile Christianity, with its Supreme God, the Father, and its Son of God, creator and saviour, was founded on a doctrine of two powers. Judged by the standard of the numerically exclusive and uncompromisingly personal monotheism of Jewish orthodoxy, all these were dualistic heresies, and in the condemnation of them the orthodox probably made no superfluous discriminations. This is no reason, however, why we should be equally indiscriminate and introduce a new confusion into a perplexed matter by labelling the Jews who held such theories "Jewish Gnostics." ...

How easily the pious desire to associate God with good only might glide into constructive heresy is illustrated by the interdiction of certain turns of phrase in prayer. Thus, to say "Good men shall bless Thee" is a "heretical form of expression."[13] If the leader in prayer says, "Thy mercy extends even to the sparrow's nest, and because of good (i.e. benefits bestowed) be Thy name remembered," he is to be silenced.[14] Even a bare liturgical repetition such as "(We) thank, thank," is, with some excess of scruple, suspected of acknowledging "two powers."[15]

One of the earliest mentions of two powers is in Sifrè on Deut. 32, 29, which verse is shown to be an arsenal of weapons against diverse heretics – those who say that there is *no* ruling power in heaven, and those who say that there are *two* – "there is no God beside me"; or such as hold that whatever power there is cannot bring to life nor cause death, cannot inflict injury or confer benefits.[16] On what grounds the assertion of two powers rested is not indicated. Nothing much more definite is to be got out of another relatively old passage in the Mekilta on Exod. 20, 2 ("I am the Lord thy God"). These words guard against the inference of a plurality of gods from different ways in which God is described in Scripture – at the Red Sea as a man of war (Exod. 15, 3), or when the elders of Israel saw him, as a venerable man, full of compassion (Exod. 24, 10; Dan. 7, 9). Here the dualists are supposed to be Gentiles (אומות העולם). R. Nathan, however, finds in the words (and in such parallels as Isa. 44, 6; 41, 4b, etc.) an answer for the heretics (*minim*) who assert that there are two powers; but gives no intimation who the heretics were or why they made the assertion.[17]

That two powers gave the Law and two powers created the world was argued by some from the *elohim* in Exod. 20, 1 and Gen. I, I, taken as a numerical plural; to which the answer is given that in both cases the *verbs* of which *elohim* is the subject are in the singular number.[18] The first chapter of Genesis offered other opportunities for heretical argument, especially, "Let *us* make man in *our* image, after *our* likeness" (Gen. 1, 26; cf. 3, 22).[19]

The difficulty of reconciling the evils in the world with the goodness of God was so strongly felt in the early centuries of our era in the East and the West, and a dualistic solution of one kind or another was so widely accepted in philosophy and religion, that it is idle to attempt to identify the Jewish circles which adopted this solution. It must suffice us to know that there were such circles; that they tried to fortify their position with texts of Scripture; and that the rabbis refuted them with their own weapons. It is certain also that, whatever leanings there may have been in this direction, Judaism, with its inveterate monotheism, was not rent by dualistic heresies as Christianity was for centuries.

As in the Bible, heaven – the celestial spaces above the sky – is the place of God's abode.[20] In later books and in the uncanonical literature the name "God of heaven" is frequently both in the mouth of foreigners[21] and of Jews.[22] In the next stage Heaven became a common metonymy for God, as in 1 Maccabees,[23] and in the language of the Palestinian schools and synagogues,[24] e.g. "the kingdom of Heaven." That the heavens were the seat of the highest god was the universal belief of the age, and various Syrian gods of heaven were seeking their fortunes in the Roman world under the name of the sky-god Jupiter – Jupiter Heliopolitanus of Baalbek, Jupiter Dolichenus of Commagene, and the rest; while conversely the Zeus whom Antiochus IV installed in the temple in Jerusalem was in Syrian speech a "Lord of heaven." ...

But although God is thus supramundane, throned high above the world, he is not extramundane, aloof and inaccessible in his remote exaltation. The subject of the passage in the Talmud in which R. Levi's astronomical wisdom about celestial distances is introduced without dissent is the nearness of God, taking as its text Deut. 4, 7: "What great nation is there that has a god as near to it as the Lord our God is whenever we call to him?" Near, with every kind of nearness, as is intimated by the plural of the predicate. A false god (idol) seems to be near, but is really remote (Isa. 46, 7); a man has such a god with him in his house, but if the man cry to it for help until he dies, it will not hear him nor save him from his straits. The Holy One (the true God) seems to be far off, but there is nothing nearer than He. For the seeming distance R. Levi is here cited, and a further calculation of the room occupied by the holy beasts,[25] all showing how high the abode of God is above the world. "But let a man go into the synagogue and take his place behind the pulpit and pray in an undertone, and God will give ear to his prayer, as it is said: 'Hannah was speaking within herself, only her lips moved, but her voice was not audible,'[26] and God gave ear to her prayer; and so he does to all his creatures, as it is said, 'A prayer of the afflicted when he covers his face and pours out his thought before the Lord.'[27] It is as when a man utters his thought in the ear of his fellow, and he hears him. Can you have a God nearer than this who is as near to his creatures as mouth to ear?"[28]

God's earthly dwelling place was the tabernacle and afterwards the temple. His great love to Israel is manifest in that, from his throne above the seven heavens, so far away, leaving them all, he came to dwell near his people in the goat-skin tent he bade them set up for him.[29] At the dedication of Solomon's temple, the cloud that hid God's glory filled the sanctuary (1 Kings 8, 10 f.). Even after the destruction of the temple, it was maintained by Eleazar ben Pedat that God's Presence (*shekinah*) still abode on the ruined site in accordance with his promise, "My eyes and my mind will be there perpetually" (1 Kings 9, 3).[30] In Solomon's dedication prayer, however, there is clear distinction made between God's abode in heaven and his manifestation in the temple: "The heaven and the heaven of heavens cannot contain thee, much less this house which I have built" (1 Kings 8, 27). Solomon prays that when men present their offerings or their petitions in the temple, or turn toward it in prayer even though in exile, God in heaven, his dwelling place, will hear their prayer, and grant their supplication. If God has a tabernacle or temple on earth, it is not that he needs a place to dwell in, for his holy house on high was there before the world was created,[30] but, we might put it, because men need some visible thing by which to realize his loving presence.

In reality God is everywhere present. The whole vast universe is his house, as the author of the Book of Baruch, in an eloquent passage, sets forth.[31] Because he is in one place he is no less elsewhere. In R. Levi's comparison: "The tabernacle was like a cave that adjoined the sea. The sea came rushing in and flooded the cave; the cave was filled, but the sea was not in the least diminished. So the tabernacle was filled with the radiance of the divine presence, but the world lost nothing of that presence."[32] Another comparison for this all-pervading presence of God in the world is the soul of man. As the soul fills the body, so God fills his world, as it is written, "Do not I fill heaven and earth? saith the Lord." The likeness of the soul to God is carried out in particulars: The soul sustains the body – God sustains the world (Isa. 46, 4); the soul outlasts the decrepit body – God outlasts the world (Psalm 102, 26); the soul is one only in the body – God is one only in the world (Deut. 6, 4); like God, the soul sees but is not seen; it is pure; it never sleeps, etc.[33]

This comparison must not be taken to imply that God was conceived as a kind of *anima mundi*, or as the all-permeating directing mind in the universe like the Stoic Logos. Its meaning is that God is everywhere present. He appeared to Moses in a despised thorn-bush, not in a carob tree or a fig (trees that men value), it is explained, to teach that there is no place on earth void of the divine presence (*shekinah*).[34] The ubiquity of God is affirmed in many other places, with diverse proofs. Thus from Job. 38, 35, "Canst thou despatch lightnings, and they go, and say unto thee, Here we are?" it is deduced: "God's messengers are not like men's. Men's messengers have to return to him that sent them; but with Thee it is not so. Thou sendest lightnings and they go. It does not say 'and they return,' but 'they go, and they say' etc. Wherever they go, they are constantly in Thy presence, and say, We have accomplished Thy commission, confirming what is written, 'Do not I fill heaven and earth?'" (Jer. 23, 24).[35] On Exod. 17, 6, "Behold I stand before thee there," the Mekilta has: "In every place where thou findest the prints of a man's foot, there am I before thee."[36]

The interest of the Jews in affirming that God is in every place was not philosophical nor primarily theological, but immediately religious. The great text was Jer. 23, 23 f.: "Am I a god at hand, saith the Lord, and not a god afar off? Can any hide himself in secret places that I shall not see him? Do not I fill earth and heaven, saith the Lord?" No sin, however done in secrecy and in darkness, can escape the eye of him who fills heaven and earth.[37] On the other hand, that wherever we are, and in whatever estate, God is present with us, gives a realizing sense of his providence.

Hellenistic Jewish literature exhibits similar conceptions. "The spirit of the Lord fills the world, and the spirit that embraces the universe takes knowledge of every word; wherefore no one who gives utterance to unjust speech can escape notice, nor will reproving justice pass him by."[38] So also the Letter of Aristeas: "Our lawgiver (Moses) ... showed first of all that there is only one God, and his power is manifest throughout all things, every place being full of his dominion; and that nothing of all that men do secretly on earth escapes him, but whatever any one does stands open to his sight, and even what is not yet done.... Even if a man purposes in his mind to do an evil, he does not escape God's knowledge, to say nothing of the evil he has already done."[39]

Philo's religious doctrine is the same.[40] God does not go anywhither, since he fills all things. On Gen. 3, 8, he comments: It is impossible to hide from God, "for God fills all things and pervades all things, and has left nothing, no matter how solitary, void of himself. What kind of place can a man occupy in which God is not? As the Scripture testifies elsewhere: 'God is in the heaven above and on the earth beneath, and there is no other but He.' (Deut. 4, 39). And again: 'Here I stand, before thou dost' (Exod. 17, 6). For God exists prior to every creature and is found everywhere; wherefore no one can hide from him."[41] Similarly, on Cain's words, "If thou dost drive me out today from the face of the earth, and from thy face I shall be hidden" (Gen. 4, 14): "What do you say, my dear sir? If you were cast out from the whole earth, would you then be hidden? How?...Would it be possible for a man, or any creature, to be hidden from God, who is before him everywhere, whose sight reaches to the ends of the earth, who fills the whole, of whom not the smallest of existing things is devoid?"

The interest in the universal presence of God is in the universality and immediacy of his knowledge and of his providential activity. That God knows everything that is, and all that goes on in the world, is so often reiterated in the Bible and is illustrated and emphasized in so many ways, it is of such fundamental importance in a religion which sees the history of the nations and the life of individuals ordered by the moral will of a personal God, that the all-embracing and immediate knowledge of God is necessarily one of the pillars of Jewish faith. God knows all the secrets of nature as only the author of nature can know them, from the movements of the stars in the heavens to the habits of the shyest creatures of the desert (Job. 38 f.). To the ends of the earth he sees everything under the whole heaven (Job 28, 24); the abyss beneath, the abode of the shades, lies uncovered before him (Job. 26, 6). He knows the past from the beginning of the world, and the future to its end, for he has ordained, and he brings to pass; what he reveals of his plan by his prophets infallibly comes true.[42]

For personal religion it is of even greater moment that he knows *men* with an all-embracing, an inescapable, knowledge – their fortunes and their character, their most secret deeds, their unarticulated words, their thoughts before they have taken shape in their own minds; no concealment and no deception avails aught with him.[43] The theme is a favorite one with the moralists. Sirach frequently reverts to it: "He explores the great abyss and the mind of man, and sees through all their subtleties; he reveals bygone things and things yet to be, and uncovers the trace of secrets. He lacks no kind of intelligence, and nothing escapes him."[44]

That God knows the thoughts of all the multitude and variety of mankind is especially dwelt on in the Palestinian literature. "If a man sees crowds of men, he should repeat the eulogy: 'Blessed is He who is wise in mysterious things,' for as the features of no two are alike so the thoughts of no two are alike."[45] From I Chron. 28, 9, "For the Lord searches all hearts (minds), and understands all the formation of thoughts," R. Isaac teaches: "Before a thought is formed in a man's mind, it is already manifest to Thee," or, according to another reporter, "Before an embryo is formed, its thoughts are already manifest to Thee."[46] ...

The almighty power of God was not in Judaism a theological attribute of omnipotence which belongs in idea to the perfection of God; it was, as in the prophets, the assurance that nothing can withstand his judgment or thwart his purpose.[47] The omnipotence of God is thus interlocked with the teleology of history. The creator and ruler of the world comprehends all things in one great plan, glimpses of which he has given to his prophets. This plan includes a golden age for his people, the visions of which merge into a golden age for all mankind, when in the universality of the true religion, and of conformity to his righteous and gracious will, peace and prosperity shall also be universal, while nature itself shall be transformed to make the earth a fit dwelling place for such transfigured inhabitants.

The obstacles to the realization of this plan were to human view insuperable; but to God insuperable obstacles were nothing. When His time came, the proud empire that bestrode the world like the colossus in Nebuchadnezzar's dream should collapse at a stroke and utterly vanish away.[48] In that *dies irae* the superhuman powers of evil share the doom of the human: "The Lord will punish the host of high heaven on high and the kings of the earth upon the earth."[49]

Faith in the fulfilment of God's promised purpose dwelt upon the mighty deeds of God in olden times, in Egypt and at the Red Sea, in the conquest of Canaan. The so-called historical Psalms which recite – sometimes in prosaic enumeration – such *magnalia dei* frequently have this for one of their motives.[50] Omnipotence, which, like finite force, has in itself no religious character, acquires profound religious significance through its relation to God's end in the world; it is a cornerstone of faith.

God's power has no limit but his own will; he can do anything that he wills to do. In general, the power of God in nature is conceived as exercised directly; forces of nature acting as "second causes," and laws of nature according to which these forces operate, have no place in the native religious thought of the Jews.[51] The regularity of nature, so far as it is an observed fact, if it be reflected on at all, is merely the ordinary way of God's working. Of the uniformity of nature, the postulate of modern science – "a question begged at the outset" – no anticipation entered their minds. God was as free to act in an extraordinary way, if he saw occasion for it, as in his ordinary way; with this view of nature the one was as natural as the other. The contrast we make between natural and supernatural events did not exist; all events were equally the immediate work of God.

To understand the Jewish conception of miracle, we must enter into their way of thinking about God and nature. A miracle, from this point of view, is an extraordinary phenomenon or occurrence wrought by God, presumably for some special purpose. It cannot be described as something at variance with the laws of nature, transcending or suspending them, for, as has been said, there was no idea of laws of nature in the modern sense. Nor is it the mere wonder of it that makes such an event a miracle; it is the religious interpretation of the occurrence, the belief that in this phenomenon or event God in a peculiar way manifests his presence, reveals his will, or intervenes for the deliverance of his worshippers and the discomfiture of their enemies, to provide for their needs in distressful times, to avert calamities, to heal mortal diseases, and to save from a thousand evils where human help is vain. The greatness, the power, of God is abundantly manifest in the ordinary course of nature; it is his goodness that is peculiarly revealed in the miracle as faith interprets and appropriates it.

It could not be conceived, therefore, that the age of miracle was past. Signal interventions in history such as stood out on the pages of the ancient Scriptures there were not; but greater even than the deliverance from Egypt would be the wonders God would work in the greater deliverance that was to come. Meanwhile miracles on the individual scale continued; and if the question sometimes arose why they had become less frequent than formerly, it was a sufficient answer that their contemporaries were less worthy that God should work a miracle for them or by their hands.[52] The coming of rain in a season of drought in answer to the prayers of individuals is a kind of miracle about which there are many stories, and some such rain-making saints are the subject of what may aptly be called a professional legend.[53] Others wrought a greater variety of miracles. Among these Hanina ben Dosa, a disciple of Johanan ben Zakkai at the end of the first century of our era, is particularly remembered. By his prayers a son of his master Johanan ben Zakkai was healed of a grave illness.[54] Again when a son of Gamaliel II was very ill, the father sent two of his disciples to Hanina ben Dosa that he might beseech God's mercy upon the son. Hanina at once went up to the chamber on the roof and prayed for him; when he came down he said to the messengers, Go, for the fever has left him. They asked, Are you a prophet? He replied, I am neither a prophet nor the son of a prophet, but I have learned that if I have freedom in prayer, I know that it is accepted; if not, I know that it is rejected.[55] They noted down in writing the hour at which he said this, and when they arrived at Gamaliel's house and reported the matter, he said: By the divine service![56] At that exact hour, no more and no less, the fever left him and he asked for a drink of water. Hanina's prayers once caused a shower of rain to hold up for his own convenience, and then to fall again. His prayer on that occasion seemed to countervail that of the high priest.[57] So great was his reputation that it is said, in an apocryphal Mishnah, "When Hanina ben Dosa died there were no workers of miracles left."[58] Besides such saints in answer to whose prayers God wrought wonders, there were healers and exorcists who effected their cures by the use of charms and the power of names, as the disciples of Jesus are said to have done by his name.[59]

That what we should call the ordinary operations of God's providence are no less wonderful than miracles is observed by more than one teacher. Mention of rain is made in connection with the resurrection of the dead in the second of the Eighteen Prayers (M. Berakot 5, 2), because in the Scripture the miracle of rain is made equal to the miracle of resurrection. Both are wrought by the hand of God; of both it is said "God opens" (Deut. 28, 12; Ezek. 37, 12)....Nay, greater than the resurrection of the dead, for resurrection is only for men, rain for animals too; resurrection only for Israelites, rain for the other nations as well; or resurrection is for the righteous alone, while rain comes upon the righteous and the wicked.[60]

R. Eleazar (ben Pedat) said, The Scripture puts provision for man's needs in the same category with deliverance; as this provision is of every day, so deliverance is of every day. R. Samuel ben Naḥman said, It is greater than deliverance, for deliverance comes by the hand of an angel – "the angel who delivers me from every evil" (Gen. 48, 16) – but provision for man's need's by the hand of God himself, who "opens his hand and satisfies the desire of every living being" (Psalm 145, 16). R. Joshua ben Levi declared that this constant provision was no less a wonder than the cleaving of the Red Sea (Psalm 136, 13 and 25).[61] God is continually working miracles without men's knowing it, in protecting them from unknown evils (Job 37, 5).[62] But a man should not needlessly expose himself to peril in the expectation that God will miraculously deliver him; God may not do so; and even if a miracle is wrought for him, the man earns demerit by his presumption.[63]

God has the power to do in his world whatever he wills,[64] and he has the right of the creator to deal as he wills with his creatures.[65] But nothing is more firmly established in the Jewish thought of God than that he does not use this power wilfully like some almighty tyrant, but with wisdom and justice and for a supremely good end. A certain Pappos paraphrased Job 23, 13 ("He is one,[66] and who shall gainsay him; he wishes a thing and does it"): God is sole judge over all the inhabitants of the world, who can contradict his sentence? Against this implication of an arbitrary and irresponsible God Akiba protested energetically. There is indeed no gainsaying him who created the world by a word, but his judgment is always according to truth and justice.[67] The words of God in Isa. 27, 4 ("I would stride upon it") are interpreted as a reflection: If by one step I overstepped and transgressed justice, "I should set it all on fire" – at once the world would be consumed.[68]

That God is almighty makes it possible for him to be lenient. "Thou hast compassion upon all men because thou canst do all things, and dost overlook the sins of men unto repentance." "Thy might is the basis of justice, and that thou art sovereign over all makes thee spare all."[69] The author implies that only conscious weakness in a government makes unsparing and indiscriminate severity necessary even in the administration of justice, lest evil doing or rebellion get beyond control. A similar thought is expressed by R. Joshua ben Levi: Moses called God "the great and mighty and terrible."[70] But when foreigners danced in his temple he seemed no longer terrible; when foreigners reduced his people to servitude he seemed no longer almighty. Then came the men of the Great Assembly and restored the crown (of the divine attributes) to its ancient completeness, by teaching that the very culmination of his almightiness is that he represses his wrath and is longsuffering with the wicked.[71]

Notes

1   The denial of these was frequent. See Eccles. 7, 15; 8, 14; 9, 2, et passim. So the ungodly (ἀσεβεῖς) in Wisdom of Solomon, 1, 16–2, 20. The wicked man contemns

God, saying to himself, "Thou wilt not require" (Psalm 10, 13): לית דין ולית דיין, that is, "there is no judgement and no judge," Gen. R. 26, 6.

2   De opificio mundi c. 61 § 170 (ed. Mangey I, 41). For a synopsis of Philo's arguments see Drummond, Philo Judaeus, II, 1 ff.

3   There is no reason to think that the theosophy which counted among its adepts some of the leading schoolmen at the beginning of the second century had any philosophy in its composition.

4   Philo's philosophy concurs with his religion in the proposition that there is but *one* God. See e.g. De opificio mundi c. 61 § 171 (ed. Mangey I, 41). In De confusione linguarum c. 33 § 170 (ed. Mangey I, 431) he quotes to this effect, Homer, Iliad ii, 204 f., just as Aristotle does at the end of Metaphysics xi. On the unity and simplicity of the divine nature, see Legg. allegor. ii. 1 § 1 f.

5   Oracula Sibyllina, iii, 629.

6   Ibid. iii, 11 f.; cf. Frag. 1, 7 ff. (ed. Geffcken, p. 227 f.).

7   Wisdom of Solomon, 13–15; Ep. of Aristeas § 134 ff. (ed. Wendland); Orac. Sibyll. iii, 29–31; 586–590; v, 75 ff.; Frag. 3, 21–31, and in many other places; Philo, De decalogo c. 2 § 6–9 (ed. Mangey II, 181); De monarchia c. 2 § 21 (II, 214), and elsewhere.

8   Wisdom of Solomon, 15, 18 f.; cf. 11, 15; 12, 24; Ep. of Aristeas § 138; Philo, De decalogo c. 16 § 76–80 (II, 193 f.); Josephus, Contra Apionem, i. 28 init. etc.; Sibyllines, see the preceding note.

9   Josephus, Antt. xviii. 3, 1. Cf. also the tearing down of the golden eagle which Herod had set over the main entrance to the temple, ibid. xvii. 6, 2–4.

10   As Schechter says, the laws against idolatry were not a practical issue. (Some Aspects of Rabbinic Theology, p. 141.) Such passages as Enoch 99, 7–9; Jubilees 11, 4–7; 12, 2–8; 22, 18–22; Test. of the Twelve Patriarchs, Naphtali, 3, 3 f., have a historical appropriateness in the mouth of the supposed speakers rather than an actual interest.

11   Philo attributes this doctrine to the Essenes. It is with them one of the evidences of godliness (τοῦ φιλοθέου) τὸ πάντων μὲν ἀγαθῶν αἴτιον, κακοῦ δὲμηδενὸς νομίζειν εἶναι τὸ θεῖον. Quod omnis probus liber c. 12 § 84 (ed. Mangey II, 458). The doctrine is Platonic, De republica ii. 379c: God is good, and therefore cannot be the cause of any kind of evils; cf. ibid. 380c. Philo himself often affirms it: e.g. De confusione lingg. c. 36 § 180 (ed. Mangey I, 432).

12   Philo's own transcendent conception of the Deity requires such mediation, which he finds in the Logos, δι' οὖ σύμπας ὁ κόσμος ἐδημιουργεῖτο (De sacerdotibus c. 5, § 81 ed. Mangey II, 225).

13   M. Megillah 4, 9. The nature of the heresy is not defined. Jer. Megillah 75c finds it in an implication of "two powers"; see also Tosafot on Megillah 25a, top. A different explanation is given by Rashi.

14   See the passages cited in the preceding note; also M. Berakot 5, 3; Berakot 33b.

15   M. Megillah, M. Berakot ll. cc.

16   Sifrè Deut. § 329.

17   Mekilta, Baḥodesh 5 (ed. Friedmann f. 66b; ed. Weiss f. 74a).

18   Gen. R. 8, 9.

19   See e.g. Gen. R. 8, 8. The heretics here were probably Christians; cf. Justin Martyr, Trypho, 62, 1 ff. See Sanhedrin 38a, where a number of such contentious plurals are adduced, including Dan. 7, 9 (cf. Justin, l.c. 31).

20   1 Kings 8, 30–49, and parallel in 2 Chron. 6; Psalm 2, 4; 11, 4, etc. Cf. also Isa. 57, 15; Psalm 103, 19; 2 Macc. 3, 39.

21   Ezra 1, 2 (Jehovah, God of heaven); 6, 9, 10; 7, 12, 21, 23.

22   Ezra 5, 11, 12; Neh. 1, 4, 5; 2, 4; Dan. 2, 18, 19, 37, 44; Psalm 136, 26; 1 Macc. 3, 18; Judith 5, 8; 6, 19; Tobit 10, 11, 12. Enoch 13, 4; 106, 11; Jubilees 12, 4; 20, 7; 22, 19; Testaments, Reuben, 1, 6, etc. In the Sibyllines, Ἑκὸς ἐπουράντος, οὐράντος.

23   I Macc. 3, 50; 4, 10, 24, 40; 12, 15; 16, 3; cf. Dan. 4, 23. Not, however, it should be observed, in the nominative as subject.

24   See Vol. II, 98.

25   Ezek. 1, 5 ff.

26   1 Sam. 1, 13.

27   Psalm 102 (title).

28   Jer. Berakot 13a. The passage is not older than the fourth century, but the doctrine was good in any century. The lesson from the Prophets at the principal service on the Day of Atonement begins with Isa. 57, 15: "Thus saith the lofty and exalted One, abiding for ever, Holy is his name; I dwell in the high and holy place (heaven), and with the contrite and lowly in spirit." Megillah 31a.

29   Tanḥuma ed. Buber, Terumah § 8; cf. ibid. Bemidbar § 14; Naso § 19.

30   Ibid. Shemot § 10. Contrary to the opinion that at the destruction of the temple the Shekinah ascended to heaven (Samuel ben Naḥman, ibid.), Eleazar ben Pedat quotes also Psalm 3, 5; Ezra 1, 3.

30   Tanḥuma ed. Buber, Naso § 19.

31   Baruch 3, 24 ff.

32   Cant. R. on Cant. 3, 10, and with slight verbal variations Pesiḳta ed. Buber f. 2b; Num. R. 12, 4. Cf. Augustine's figure of the boundless sea and the sponge (Confessions vii. 5, 1). God, who fills heaven and earth (Jer. 23, 24), spoke with Moses between the staves of the ark. R. Meir, Gen. R 4, 4.

33   Lev. R. 4, 8; Berakot 10a.

34   Exod. R. on Exod. 3, 3 (c. 2, 5).

35   Mekilta, Bo 1 (ed. Friedmann f. 2a; ed. Weiss f. 2a, below); Baba Batra 25a.

36   Mekilta, Beshallaḥ 6 (ed. Friedmann f. 52b; ed. Weiss f. 60b); cf. Mekilta de R. Simeon ben Yoḥai ed. Hoffmann, p. 81.

37   Tanḥuma ed. Buber, Naso § 6 (f. 14b–15a).

38   Wisdom of Solomon 1, 7 f.; see also what follows.

39   Aristeas, ed. Wendland § 132 f. With the inclination of these writers to avoid the semblance of anthropomorphism by speaking of the ubiquity of the spirit or the power of God, cf. pp. 434 ff.

40   With his metaphysical doctrine we are not here concerned.

41   Legg. allegor. iii. 2 § 4 (ed. Mangey I, 88).

42   See e.g. Isa. 41, 22–24; 43, 10–13; 44, 6–8, etc.

43   See e.g. Amos 9, 2–4; Jer. 23, 23 f.; Prov. 5, 21; 15, 3; Job 34, 21; Psalm 139, etc.

44   Ecclus. 42, 18–20; cf. 16, 17–23; 17, 15–20; Wisdom of Solomon 1, 6 ff.; Baruch 3, 32; Psalms of Solomon 14, 8, etc.

45   Jer. Berakot 13c; Tos. Berakot 7, 2; cf. Tanḥuma ed. Buber, Phineas § 1.

46   Gen. R. 9, 3. The idea is developed at length in Agadat Bereshit 2 (ed. Buber, p. 4).

47   See especially Isa. 40 ff.

48   Dan. 2, 31 ff.

49   Isa. 24, 21–23.

50   E.g. Psalm 106.

51   God has imposed on the elements bounds and measures; for the movements of the stars, and in the instincts of animals, he has established norms which they may not transgress and bring disorder into the cosmos. These ordinances are laws which God has imposed upon his creatures, as he has imposed laws upon men.

52   Berakot 20a.

53   The Talmuds on Ta'anit iii. have various legends of this kind. The most famous name is Ḥoni ha-Me'aggel in the first century B C.

54   Berakot 34b.

55   Berakot 1. c.; Jer. Berakot 9d; cf. M. Berakot 5, 5. This sign is attributed in Tos. Berakot 3, 4 to Akiba.

56   Berakot 34b. Compare the similar story of Jesus at Cana and the courtier's son at Capernaum, John 4, 46–53.

57   Ta'anit 24b.

58   M. Soṭah 9, 15 (a late appendix).

59   Particularly one Jacob of Kefar Sekanya (or Samma) in Galilee. 'Abodah Zarah 27b; Tos. Ḥullin 2, 22 f. Cf. Acts 3, 6; 4, 10, etc.

60   Gen. R. 13, 6; Berakot 33a; Jer. Berakot 9a, below; Ta'anit 7a, top; cf. Matt. 5, 45.

61   Gen. R. 20, 9; cf. Pesaḥim 118a; Pesiḳta R. ed. Friedmann f. 152a. (This bit of bread that a man puts into his mouth is a more difficult thing than the deliverance of Israel). See Bacher, Pal. Amoräer, I, 178, 487; II, 21.

62   Midrash Shemuel 9, 2; Midrash Tehillim on Psalm 106, init. Bacher l. c. II, 85.

63   Shabbat 32a; Ta'anit 20b.

64   Jer. 32, 17 ff.

65   Jer. 18, 2–6; Isa. 45, 9; cf. Paul, Rom. 9, 14 ff.

66   So the text was understood.

67   Mekilta, Beshallaḥ 6 (ed. Friedmann f. 33a: ed. Weiss f. 40a, top). Somewhat expanded, Tanḥuma ed. Buber, Shemot § 14; ibid. Wayyera § 21; cf. Akiba, Abot, 3, 15.

68   Tanḥuma ed. Buber, Mishpaḥim § 4. (Cf. Heraclitus, Frag. 29, Bywater.)

69   Wisdom of Solomon 11, 23; 12, 16–18. See the whole fine passage.

70   Deut. 10, 17.

71   Yoma 69b. Cf. Jer. Berakot 11c; Jer. Megillah 74c. Bacher, Pal Amoräer, I, 182 f.

Chapter 14
The Doctrine of Israel

Jacob Neusner

A.   Israel as *Sui Generis* in the Mishnah

When we ask the authorship of the Mishnah to tell us in explicit terms how they define (an) "Israel," they direct our attention to the one passage in which they systematically answer that question. It is framed, as a question of social definition must be, in terms of who is "in" and who is "out." (An) "Israel" thus is defined within the categories of inclusion and exclusion, which implicitly yields the definition that all who are out are out and all who are in are in, and, all together, the ones that are in (implicitly) constitute the social entity or social group at hand. When the Mishnah's authorship wishes to define "Israel" by itself and on its own terms, rather than as a classification among other classifications in an enormous system of taxonomy, "Israel" may be set forth as an entity not only in its own terms but also *sui generis*. Here is an "Israel" that, at first glance, is defined not in relationships but intransitively and intrinsically (M. San. 11:1):

A.   All Israelites have a share in the world to come,

B.   as it is said, "your people also shall be all righteous, they shall inherit the land forever; the branch of my planting, the work of my hands, that I may be glorified" (Is. 60:21).

C.   And these are the ones who have no portion in the world to come:

D.   He who says, the resurrection of the dead is a teaching which does not derive from the Torah, and the Torah does not come from Heaven; and an Epicurean.

E.   R. Aqiba says, "Also: He who reads in heretical books,

F.   "and he who whispers over a wound and says, 'I will put none of the diseases upon you which I have put on the Egyptians, for I am the Lord who heals you' (Exod. 15:26)."

G.   Abba Saul says, "Also: He who pronounces the divine Name as it is spelled out."

Israel is defined inclusively: to be "Israel" is to have a share in the world to come. "Israel" then is a social entity made up of those who share a common conviction, and that "Israel" therefore bears an other-worldly destiny. Other social entities are not so defined within the Mishnah – and that by definition! – and it must follow that (an) "Israel" in the conception of the authorship of the Mishnah is *sui generis* in that other social entities do not find their definition within the range of supernatural facts pertinent to "Israel" an "Israel" is a social group that endows its individual members with life in the world to come; an "Israel"[ite] is one who enjoys the world to come. Excluded from this "Israel" are "Israel"[ite]s who within the established criteria of social identification exclude themselves. The power to define by relationships does not run out, however, since in this supernatural context of an Israel that is *sui generis*, we still know who is "Israel" because we are told who is "not-Israel," now, specific non-believers or sinners. These are, as we should expect, persons who reject the stated belief (M. San. 1:2):

A.   Three kings and four ordinary folk have no portion in the world to come.
B.   Three kings: Jeroboam, Ahab, and Manasseh.
C.   R. Judah says, "Manasseh has a portion in the world to come,
D.   "since it is said, 'And he prayed to him and he was entreated of him and heard his supplication and brought him again to Jerusalem into his kingdom' (2 Chr. 33:13)."
E.   They said to him, "To his kingdom he brought him back, but to the life of the world to come he did not bring him back."
F.   Four ordinary folk: Balaam, Doeg, Ahitophel, and Gehazi.

Not only persons but also classes of Israelites are specified, in all cases contributing to the definition of (an) Israel. The excluded classes of Israelites bear in common a supernatural fault, which is that they have sinned against God. We begin with those excluded from the world to come who are not Israel, namely, the generation of the flood and the generation of the dispersion. This somewhat complicates matters, since we should have thought that at issue in enjoying the world to come would be only (an) "Israel." It should follow that gentiles of whatever sort hardly require specification; they all are alike. But the focus of what follows – classes of excluded Israelites, who have sinned against God – leads to the supposition that the specified gentiles are included because of their place in the biblical narrative. The implication is not that all other gentiles enjoy the world to come except for these, and the focus of definition remains on Israel, pure and simple (M. San. 11:3–4):

11:3

A.   The generation of the flood has no share in the world to come,
B.   and they shall not stand in the judgement,

C. since it is written, "My spirit shall not judge with man forever" (Gen. 6:3)

D. neither judgment nor spirit.

E. The generation of the dispersion has no share in the world to come,

F. since it is said, "So the Lord scattered them abroad from there upon the face of the whole earth" (Gen. 11:8).

G. "So the Lord scattered them abroad" – in this world,

H. "and the Lord scattered them from there" – in the world to come.

I. The men of Sodom have no portion in the world to come,

J. since it is said, "Now the men of Sodom were wicked and sinners against the Lord exceedingly" (Gen. 13:13)

K. "Wicked" – in this world,

L. "And sinners" – in the world to come.

M. But they will stand in judgment.

N. R. Nehemiah says, "Both these and those will not stand in judgment,

O. "for it is said, 'Therefore the wicked shall not stand in judgment [108A], nor sinners in the congregation of the righteous' (Ps. 1:5)

P. "'Therefore the wicked shall not stand in judgment' – this refers to the generation of the flood.

Q. "'Nor sinners in the congregation of the righteous' – this refers to the men of Sodom."

R. They said to him, "They will not stand in the congregation of the righteous, but they will stand in the congregation of the sinners."

S. The spies have no portion in the world to come,

T. as it is said, "Even those men who brought up an evil report of the land died by the plague before the Lord" (Num. 14:37)

U. "Died" – in this world.

V. "By the plague" – in the world to come.

W. "The generation of the wilderness has no portion in the world to come and will not stand in judgment,

X. "for it is written, 'In this wilderness they shall be consumed and there they shall die' (Num. 14:35)," the words of R. Aqiba.

Y. R. Eliezer says, "Concerning them it says, 'Gather my saints together to me, those that have made a covenant with me by sacrifice' (Ps. 50:5)."

Z. "The party of Korah is not destined to rise up,

AA. "for it is written, 'And the earth closed upon them' – in this world.

BB. "'And they perished from among the assembly' – in the world to come," the words of R. Aqiba.

CC. And R. Eliezer says, "Concerning them it says, 'The Lord kills and resurrects, brings down to Sheol and brings up again' (1 Sam. 2:6)."

DD. "The ten tribes are not destined to return,

EE. "since it is said, 'And he cast them into another land, as on this day' (Deut. 29:28). Just as the day passes and does not return, so they have gone their way and will not return," the words of R. Aqiba.

FF.   R. Eliezer says, "Just as this day is dark and then grows light, so the ten tribes for whom it now is dark – thus in the future it is destined to grow light for them."

11:4

A.   The townsfolk of an apostate town have no portion in the world to come,
B.   as it is said, "Certain base fellows [sons of Belial] have gone out from the midst of thee and have drawn away the inhabitants of their city" (Deut. 13:14).
C.   And they are not put to death unless those who misled the [town] come from that same town and from that same tribe,
D.   and unless the majority is misled,
E.   and unless men did the misleading.
F.   [If] women or children misled them,
G.   of if a minority of the town was misled,
H.   or if those who misled the town came from outside of it,
I.   lo, they are treated as individuals [and not as a whole town],
J.   and they [thus] require [testimony against them] by two witnesses, and a statement of warning, for each and every one of them.
K.   This rule is more strict for individuals than for the community:
L.   for individuals are out to death by stoning.
M.   Therefore their property is saved.
N.   But the community is put to death by the sword,
O.   Therefore their property is lost.

The catalogue leaves us no doubt that the candidates for inclusion or exclusion are presented by the biblical narrative. Hence I see no implicit assumption that all *gentiles* except those specified have a share in the world to come. That seems to me a proposition altogether beyond the imagination of this authorship.

B.   Genesis Rabbah: The Metaphor of the Family, "Israel"

When sages wished to know what (an) "Israel" was, in the fourth century, in response to the triumph of Christianity and its denial that "Israel after the flesh" constituted Israel at all, they reread the story of Scripture's "Israel"'s origins. To begin with, as Scripture told them the story, "Israel" was a man, Jacob, and his children are "the children of Jacob." That man's name was also "Israel," and, it followed, "the children of Israel" comprised the extended family of that man. By extension, "Israel" formed the family of Abraham and Sarah, Isaac and Rebecca,

Jacob and Leah and Rachel. "Israel" therefore invoked the metaphor of genealogy to explain the bonds that linked persons unseen into a single social entity; the shared traits were imputed, not empirical. That social metaphor of "Israel" – a simple one, really, and easily grasped – bore consequences in two ways. First, children in general are admonished to follow the good example of their parents. The deeds of the patriarchs and matriarchs therefore taught lessons on how the children were to act. Of greater interest in an account of "Israel" as a social metaphor, "Israel" lived twice, once in the patriarchs and matriarchs, a second time in the life of the heirs as the descendants relived those earlier lives. The stories of the family were carefully reread to provide a picture of the meaning of the latter-day events of the descendants of that same family. Accordingly, the lives of the patriarchs signaled the history of Israel.

The polemical purpose of the claim that that abstraction, "Israel," was to be compared to the family of the mythic ancestor lies right at the surface. With another "Israel," the Christian Church, now claiming to constitute the true one, Jews found it possible to confront that claim and to turn it against the other side. "You claim to form 'Israel after the spirit.' Fine, and we are Israel after the flesh – and genealogy forms the link, that alone." (Converts did not present an anomaly, of course, since they were held to be children of Abraham and Sarah, who had "made souls," that is, converts, in Haran, a point repeated in the documents of the period.) That fleshly continuity formed of all of "us" a single family, rendering spurious the notion that "Israel" could be other than genealogically defined. But that polemic seems to me adventitious and not primary. At the same time the metaphor provided a quite separate component to sages' larger system.

Genesis Rabbah 61

LXI:VII

1.A.   "But to the sons of his concubines, Abraham gave gifts, and while he was still living, he sent them away from his son Isaac, eastward to the east country" (Gen. 25:6):

  B.   In the time of Alexander of Macedonia the sons of Ishmael came to dispute with Israel about the birthright, and with them came two wicked families, the Canaanites and the Egyptians.

  C.   They said, "Who will go and engage in a disputation with them."

  D.   Gebiah b. Qosem [the enchanter] said, "I shall go and engage in a disputation with them."

  E.   They said to him, "Be careful not to let the Land of Israel fall into their possession."

  F.   He said to them, "I shall go and engage in a disputation with them. If I win over them, well and good. And if not, you may say, 'Who is this hunchback to represent us?'"

G.   He went and engaged in a disputation with them. Said to them Alexander of Macedonia, "Who lays claim against whom?"

H.   The Ishmaelites said, "We lay claim, and we bring our evidence from their own Torah: 'But he shall acknowledge the firstborn, the son of the hated' (Deut. 21:17). Now Ishmael was the firstborn. [We therefore claim the land as heirs of the first-born of Abraham.]"

I.   Said to him Gebiah b. Qosem, "My royal lord, does a man not do whatever he likes with his sons?"

J.   He said to him, "Indeed so.

K.   "And lo, it is written, 'Abraham gave all that he had to Isaac' (Gen. 25:2)."

L.   [Alexander asked,] "Then where is the deed of gift to the other sons?"

M.   He said to him, " 'But to the sons of his concubines, Abraham gave gifts, [and while he was still living, he sent them away from his son Isaac, eastward to the east country]' (Gen. 25:6)."

N.   [The Ishmaelites had no claim on the land.] They abandoned the field in shame.

The metaphor now shifts, with the notion of Israel today as the family of Abraham, as against the Ishmaelites, also of the same family, gives way. But the theme of family records persists. Canaan has no claim, for Canaan was also a family, comparable to Israel – but descended from a slave. The power of the metaphor of family is that it can explain not only the social entity formed by Jews, but the social entities confronted by them. All fell into the same genus, making up diverse species. The theory of society before us – that is, the theory of "Israel" – thus accounts for the existence, also, of all societies, and, as we shall see when we deal with Rome, the theory of "Israel" does so with extraordinary force.

O.   The Canaanites said, "We lay claim, and we bring our evidence from their own Torah. Throughout their Torah it is written, 'the land of Canaan.' So let them give us back our land."

P.   Said to him Gebiah b. Qosem, "My royal lord, does a man not do whatever he likes with his slave?"

Q.   He said to him, "Indeed so."

R.   He said to him, "And lo, it is written, 'A slave of slaves shall Canaan be to his brothers' (Gen. 9:25). So they are really our slaves."

S.   [The Canaanites had no claim to the land and in fact should be serving Israel.] They abandoned the field in shame.

The same metaphor serves both "Israel" and "Canaan." Each formed the latter-day heir of the earliest family, and both lived out the original paradigm. The mode of thought at hand imputes the same genus to both social entities, and then makes its possible to distinguish among the two species at hand. The final claim in the passage before us moves away from the metaphor of family. But the notion of a continuous, physical descent is implicit here as well. "Israel" has inherited the wealth of Egypt. Since the notion of inheritance forms a component of the metaphor of family (a conception critical, as we shall see in the next section, in the supernatural patrimony of the "children of Israel" in the merit of the ancestors), we survey the conclusion of the passage.

T. The Egyptians said, "We lay claim, and we bring our evidence from their own Torah. Six hundred thousand of them left us, taking away our silver and gold utensils: 'They despoiled the Egyptians' (Exod. 12:36). Let them give them back to us."

U. Gebiah b. Qosem said, "My royal lord, six hundred thousand men worked for them for two hundred and ten years, some as silversmiths and some as goldsmiths. Let them pay us our salary at the rate of a *denar* a day."

V. The mathematicians went and added up what was owing, and they had not reached the sum covering a century before the Egyptians had to forfeit what they had claimed. They abandoned the field in shame.

V. [Alexander] wanted to go up to Jerusalem. The Samaritans said to him, "Be careful. They will not permit you to enter their most holy sanctuary."

W. When Gebiah b. Qosem found out about this, he went and made for himself two felt shoes, with two precious stones worth twenty-thousand pieces of silver set in them. When he got to the mountain of the house [of the Temple], he said to him, "My royal lord, take off your shoes and put on these two felt slippers, for the floor is slippery, and you should not slip and fall."

X. When they came to the most holy sanctuary, he said to him, "Up to this point, we have the right to enter. From this point onward, we do not have the right to enter."

Y. He said to him, "When we get out of here, I'm going to even out your hump."

Z. He said to him, "You will be called a great surgeon and get a big fee."

The Ishmaelites, Abraham's children, deprived as they were of their inheritance, fall into the same genus as does Israel. So too, as I said, did Canaan. As to the Egyptians, that is a different matter. Now "Israel" is that same "Israel" of which Scripture spoke. The social metaphor shifts within the story, though, of course, the story is not affected.

Families have histories, and "Israel" as family found in the record of its family-history those points of coherence that transformed events into meaningful patterns, that is, the history of the social unit, the nation-family, as a whole. This matter is simply expressed by the common wisdom, like parent, like child, the apple does not fall far from the tree, and the like. Whether true or false, that folk wisdom surely accounts for the commonsense quality of sages' search, in the deeds of the patriarchs and matriarchs, for messages concerning the future history of the children. But sages assuredly were not common folk. They were philosophers, and their inquiry constituted a chapter in the history of what used to be called natural philosophy, and what today we know as social science. Specifically, sages looked in the facts of history for the laws of history. They proposed to generalize, and, out of generalization, to explain their own particular circumstance. That is why, as I said, we may compare them to social scientists or social philosophers, trying to turn anecdotes into insight and to demonstrate how we may know the difference between impressions and truths. Genesis provided facts concerning the family. Careful sifting of those facts will yield the laws that dictated why to that family things happened one way, rather than some other.

Among these social laws of the family history, one took priority, the laws that explained the movement of empires upward and downward and pointed toward the ultimate end of it all. Scripture provided the model for the ages of empires, yielding a picture of four monarchies, to be followed by Israel as the fifth. Sages repeated this familiar viewpoint. In reading Genesis, in particular, they found that time and again events in the lives of the patriarchs prefigured the four monarchies, among which, of course, the fourth, last, and most intolerable was Rome. Israel's history falls under God's dominion. Whatever will happen carries out God's plan, and that plan for the future has been laid out in the account of the origins supplied by Genesis. The fourth kingdom, Rome, is part of that plan, which we can discover by carefully studying Abraham's life and God's word to him.

Genesis Rabbah 44

XLIV:XVIII

1.A. "Then the Lord said to Abram, 'Know of a surety [that your descendants will be sojourners in a land that is not theirs, and they will be slaves there, and they will be oppressed for four hundred years; but I will bring judgment on the nation which they serve, and afterward they shall come out with great possessions']" (Gen. 15:13–14):

B. "Know" that I shall scatter them.

C. "Of a certainty" that I shall bring them back together again.

D. "Know" that I shall put them out as a pledge [in expiation of their sins].

E. "Of a certainty" that I shall redeem them.

F. "Know" that I shall make them slaves.

G. "Of a certainty" that I shall free them.

The passage parses the cited verse and joins within its simple formula the entire history of Israel, punishment and forgiveness alike. Not only the patriarchs, but also the matriarchs, so acted as to shape the future life of the family, Israel. One extended statement of the matter suffices. Here is how sages take up the detail of Abraham's provision of a bit of water, showing what that act had to do with the history of Israel later on. The intricate working out of the whole, involving the merit of the patriarchs, the way in which the deeds of the patriarchs provide a sign for proper conduct for their children, the history and salvation of Israel – the whole shows how, within a single metaphor, the entire system of the Judaism of the dual Torah could reach concrete expression.

Genesis Rabbah 48

XLVIII:X

2.A. "Let a little water be brought" (Gen. 18:4):

  B. Said to him the Holy One, blessed be he, "You have said, 'Let a little water be brought' (Gen. 18:4). By your life, I shall pay your descendants back for this: 'Then sang Israel this song,' "Spring up O well, sing you to it"' (Num. 21:7)."

  C. That recompense took place in the wilderness. Where do we find that it took place in the Land of Israel as well?

  D. "A land of brooks of water" (Deut. 8:7).

  E. And where do we find that it will take place in the age to come?

  F. "And it shall come to pass in that day that living waters shall go out of Jerusalem" (Zech. 14:8).

  G. ["And wash your feet" (Gen. 18:4)]: [Said to him the Holy One, blessed be he,] "You have said, 'And wash your feet.' By your life, I shall pay your descendants back for this: 'Then I washed you in water' (Ezek. 16:9)."

  H. That recompense took place in the wilderness. Where do we find that it took place in the Land of Israel as well?

  I. "Wash you, make you clean" (Is. 1:16).

  J. And where do we find that it will take place in the age to come?

  K. "When the Lord will have washed away the filth of the daughters of Zion" (Is. 4:4).

  L. [Said to him the Holy One, blessed be he,] "You have said, 'And rest yourselves under the tree' (Gen. 18:4). By your life, I shall pay your descendants back for this: 'He spread a cloud for a screen' (Ps. 105:39)."

  M. That recompense took place in the wilderness. Where do we find that it took place in the Land of Israel as well?

  N. "You shall dwell in booths for seven days" (Lev. 23:42).

  O. And where do we find that it will take place in the age to come?

  P. "And there shall be a pavilion for a shadow in the day-time from the heat" (Is. 4:6).

  Q. [Said to him the Holy One, blessed be he,] "You have said, 'While I fetch a morsel of bread that you may refresh yourself' (Gen. 18:5). By your life, I shall pay your descendants back for this: 'Behold I will cause to rain bread from heaven for you' (Exod. 16:45)"

  R. That recompense took place in the wilderness. Where do we find that it took place in the Land of Israel as well?

  S. "A land of wheat and barley" (Deut. 8:8).

   T.   And where do we find that it will take place in the age to come?
   U.   "He will be as a rich grain-field in the land" (Ps. 82:16).
   V.   [Said to him the Holy One, blessed be he,] "You ran after the herd ['And
        Abraham ran to the herd' (Gen. 18:7)]. By your life, I shall pay your
        descendants back for this: 'And there went forth a wind from the Lord and
        brought across quails from the sea' (Num. 11:27)."
   W.   That recompense took place in the wilderness. Where do we find that it
        took place in the Land of Israel as well?
   X.   "Now the children of Reuben and the children of Gad had a very great
        multitude of cattle" (Num. 32:1).
   Y.   And where do we find that it will take place in the age to come?
   Z.   "And it will come to pass in that day that a man shall rear a young cow
        and two sheep" (Is. 7:21).
  AA.   [Said to him the Holy One, blessed be he,] "You stood by them: 'And he
        stood by them under the tree while they ate' (Gen. 18:8). By your life, I
        shall pay your descendants back for this: 'And the Lord went before them'
        (Exod. 13:21)."
  BB.   That recompense took place in the wilderness. Where do we find that it
        took place in the Land of Israel as well?
  CC.   "God stands in the congregation of God" (Ps. 82:1).
  DD.   And where do we find that it will take place in the age to come?
  EE.   "The breaker is gone up before them . . . and the Lord at the head of them"
        (Mic. 2:13).

Everything that Abraham did brought a reward to his descendants. The enormous emphasis on the way in which Abraham's deeds prefigured the history
of Israel, both in the wilderness and in the Land and, finally, in the age to come,
provokes us to wonder who held that there were other children of Abraham,
beside this "Israel." The answer – the triumphant Christians in particular, who
right from the beginning, with Paul and the evangelists, imputed it to the earliest
generations and said it in so many words – then is clear. We note that there are
five statements of the same proposition, each drawing upon a clause in the base
verse. The extended statement moreover serves as a sustained introduction to the
treatment of the individual clauses that now follow, item by item. Obviously, it is
the merit of the ancestors that connects the living Israel to the lives of the
patriarchs and matriarchs of old.

   While Abraham founded Israel, Isaac and Jacob carried forth the birthright and
the blessing. This they did through the process of selection, ending in the assignment of the birthright to Jacob alone. The importance of that fact for the definition
of "Israel" hardly requires explication. The lives of all three patriarchs flowed
together, each being identified with the other as a single long life. This immediately produced the proposition that the historical life of Israel, the nation, continued the individual lives of the patriarchs. The theory of who is Israel, therefore,
is seen once more to have rested on genealogy: Israel is one extended family, all

being children of the same fathers and mothers, the patriarchs and matriarchs of Genesis. This theory of Israelite society, and of the Jewish people in the time of the sages of Genesis Rabbah, made of the people a family, and of genealogy, a kind of ecclesiology. The importance of that proposition in countering the Christian claim to be a new Israel cannot escape notice. Israel, sages maintained, is Israel after the flesh, and that in a most literal sense. But the basic claim, for its part, depended upon the facts of Scripture, not upon the logical requirements of theological dispute. Here is how those facts emerged in the case of Isaac (Genesis Rabbah LXIII:III):

1.A. "These are the descendants of Isaac, Abraham's son: Abraham was the father of Isaac" (Gen. 25:19):

B. Abram was called Abraham: "Abram, the same is Abraham" (1 Chr. 1:27).

C. Isaac was called Abraham: "These are the descendants of Isaac, Abraham's son, Abraham."

D. Jacob was called Israel, as it is written, "Your name shall be called more Jacob but Israel" (Gen. 32:29).

E. Isaac also was called Israel: "And these are the names of the children of Israel, who came into Egypt, Jacob and his" (Gen. 46:8).

F. Abraham was called Israel as well.

G. R. Nathan said, "This matter is deep: 'Now the time that the children of Israel dwelt in Egypt' (Exod. 12:40), and in the land of Canaan and in the land of Goshen 'was four hundred and thirty years' (Exod. 12:40)." [Freedman, p. 557, n. 6: They were in Egypt for only 210 years. Hence their sojourn in Canaan and Goshen must be added, which means, from the birth of Isaac, Hence the children of Israel commence with Isaac. And since he was Abraham's son, it follows that Abraham was called Israel.]

The polemic at hand, linking the patriarchs to the history of Israel, claiming that all of the patriarchs bear the same names, derives proof, in part, from the base verse. But the composition in no way rests upon the exegesis of the base verse. Its syllogism transcends the case at hand. The importance of Isaac in particular derived from his relationship to the two nations that would engage in struggle, Jacob, who was and is Israel, and Esau, who stood for Rome. By himself, as a symbol for Israel's history Isaac remained a shadowy figure. Still, Isaac plays his role in setting forth the laws of Israel's history. To understand what is to follow, we recall that Esau, in sages' typology, always stands for Rome. Later we shall see that the representation of Esau as sibling, brother, and enemy, distinguishes Esau/ Rome from all other nations. Esau is not an outsider, not a gentile, but also not Israel, legitimate heir. We once more recall the power of the social theory to hold all together all of the middle-range components of society: all nations within a single theory. The genealogical metaphor here displays that remarkable capacity (Genesis Rabbah LXV:XIII):

1.A.   "[He said, 'Behold I am old; I do not know the day of my death.] Now then take your weapons, [your quiver and your bow, and go out to the field and hunt game for me, and prepare for me savory food, such as I love, and bring it to me that I may eat; that I may bless you before I die']" (Gen. 27:2–4):

   B.   "Sharpen your hunting gear, so that you will not feed me carrion or an animal that was improperly slaughtered.

   C.   "Take your *own* hunting gear, so that you will not feed me meat that has been stolen or grabbed."

Isaac's first point is that Esau does not ordinarily observe the food laws, e.g., concerning humane slaughter of animals. He furthermore steals, while, by inference, Jacob takes only what he has lawfully acquired. This prepares the way for the main point:

2.A.   "Your quiver:"

   B.   [Since the word for "quiver" and the word for "held in suspense" share the same consonants, we interpret the statement as follows:] he said to him, "Lo, the blessings [that I am about to give] are held in suspense. For the one who is worthy of a blessing, there will be a blessing."

3.A.   Another matter: "Now then take your weapons, your quiver and your bow and go out to the field:"

   B.   "Weapons" refers to Babylonia, as it is said, "And the weapons he brought to the treasure house of his god" (Gen. 2:2).

   C.   "Your quiver" speaks of Media, as it says, "So they suspended Haman on the gallows" (Esth. 7:10). [The play on the words is the same as at No. 2.]

   D.   "And your bow" addresses Greece: "For I bend Judah for me, I fill the bow with Ephraim and I will story up your sons, O Zion, against your sons, O Javan [Greece]" (Zech. (9:13).

   E.   "and go out to the field" means Edom: "Unto the land of Seir, the field of Edom" (Gen. 32:4).

Once more the patriarchs lay out the future history of their family, and, in dealing with their own affairs, prefigure what is to come. The power of the metaphor of family is not exhausted in its capacity to link household to household; quite to the contrary, as with any really successful metaphor, it draws everything into one thing and makes sense of the whole all together and all at once.

   To conclude, let us survey a systematic statement of the power of merit to redeem Israel. This statement appeals to the binding of Isaac as the source of the merit, deriving from the patriarchs and matriarchs, which will in the end lead to the salvation of Israel (Genesis Rabbah LVI:II):

4.A.   "... and we will worship [through an act of prostration] and come again to you" (Gen. 22:5):

B. He thereby told him that he would come back from Mount Moriah whole and in peace [for he said that *we* shall come back].

5.A. Said R. Isaac, "And all was on account of the merit attained by the act of prostration.

B. "Abraham returned in peace from Mount Moriah only on account of the merit owing to the act of prostration: '... and we will worship [through an act of prostration] and come [then, on that account] again to you' (Gen. 22:5).

C. "The Israelites were redeemed only on account of the merit owing to the act of prostration: 'And the people believed ... then they bowed their heads and prostrated themselves' " (Exod. 4:31).

D. "The Torah was given only on account of the merit owing to the act of prostration: 'And worship [prostrate themselves] you afar off' (Exod. 24:1).

E. "Hannah was remembered only on account of the merit owing to the act of prostration: 'And they worshipped before the Lord' (1 Sam. 1:19).

F. "The exiles will be brought back only on account of the merit owing to the act of prostration: 'And it shall come to pass in that day that a great horn shall be blown and they shall come that were lost ... and that were dispersed ... and they shall worship the Lord in the holy mountain at Jerusalem' (Is. 27:13).

G. "The Temple was built only on account of the merit owing to the act of prostration: 'Exalt you the Lord our God and worship at his holy hill' (Ps. 99:9).

H. "The dead will live only on account of the merit owing to the act of prostration: 'Come let us worship and bend the knee, let us kneel before the Lord our maker' (Ps. 95:6)."

The entire history of Israel flows from its acts of worship ("prostration") and is unified by a single law. Every sort of advantage Israel has ever gained came about through that act of worship. Hence what is besought, in the elegant survey, is the law of history. The Scripture then supplies those facts from which the governing law is derived. The governing law is that Israel constitutes a family and inherits the merit laid up as a treasure for the descendants by the ancestors.

C.   Israel as *Sui Generis* in the Yerushalmi's Theory of Salvation

The clearest picture of the Yerushalmi's theory of Israel's salvation – therefore of Israel's status as a social entity that is *sui generis* – is to be found in the sages' reading of Scripture. Specifically, the world view projected by them upon the heroes of ancient Israel most clearly reveals the Yerushalmi's sages' view of themselves and their world. Sages naturally took for granted that the world they knew in the fourth century had flourished a thousand and more years earlier. The values they embodied and the supernatural powers they fantasized for themselves were projected backward onto biblical figures. Seeing Scripture in their own model, sages took the position that the Torah of old, its supernatural power and salvific promise, in their own day continued to endure – among themselves. In consequence, the promise of salvation contained in every line of Scripture was to be kept in every deed of learning and obedience to the law effected under their auspices. So while they projected backward the things they cherished in an act of (to us) extraordinary anachronism, in their eyes they carried forward, to their own time, the promise of salvation for Israel contained within the written Torah of old.

If David, King of Israel, was like a rabbi today, then a rabbi today would be the figure of the son of David who was to come as King of Israel. It is not surprising, therefore, that among the many biblical heroes whom the Talmudic rabbis treated as sages, principal and foremost was David himself, now made into a messianic rabbi or a rabbinical Messiah. He was the sage of the Torah, the avatar and model for the sages of their own time. That view was made explicit, both specifically and in general terms. I give one striking expression of the proposition at hand. If a rabbi was jealous to have his traditions cited in his own name, it was because that was David's explicit view as well. In more general terms, both David and Moses are represented as students of Torah, just like the disciples and sages of the current time (Y. San. 2:6.IV):

A.   It is written, "And David said longingly, 'O that someone would give me water to drink from the well of Bethlehem [which is by the gate]'" (1 Chr. 11:17).
B.   R. Hiyya bar Ba said, "He required a teaching of law."
C.   "Then the three mighty men broke through [the camp of the Philistines]" (1 Chr. 11:18).
D.   Why three? Because the law is not decisively laid down by fewer than three.
E.   "But David would not drink of it; [he poured it out to the Lord, and said, 'Far be it from me before my God that I should do this. Shall I drink the lifeblood of these men? For at the risk of their lives they brought it']" (1 Chr. 11:18–19).
F.   David did not want the law to be laid down in his own name.
G.   "He poured it out to the Lord" – establishing [the decision] as [an unattributed] teaching for the generations, [so that the law should be authoritative and so be cited anonymously].

Y. Sheqalim 2:4.V

0.   David himself prayed for mercy for himself, as it is said, "Let me dwell in thy tent for ever! Oh to be safe under the shelter of thy wings, selah" (Ps. 61:4).

P.   And did it enter David's mind that he would live for ever?

Q.   But this is what David said before the Holy One, blessed be he, "Lord of the world, may I have the merit that my words will be stated in synagogues and schoolhouses."

R.   Simeon b. Nazira in the name of R. Isaac said, "Every disciple in whose name people cite a teaching of law in this world – his lips murmur with him in the grave, as it is said, 'Your kisses are like the best wine that goes down smoothly, gliding over lips of those that sleep' (Song 7:9).

S.   "Just as in the case of a mass of grapes, once a person puts his finger in it, forthwith even his lips begin to smack, so the lips of the righteous, when someone cites a teaching of law in their names – their lips murmur with them in the grave."

These extracts reveal how the Talmud's authorities readily saw their concerns in biblical statements attributed to David. "Water" meant "a teaching of Torah." "Three mighty men" were of course judges. At issue was whether or not the decision was to be stated in David's own name – and so removed from the authoritative consensus of sages. David exhibits precisely those concerns for the preservation of his views in his name that, in earlier sections, we saw attributed to rabbis.

All of this scarcely conceals sages' deeper convictions, for, we remember, David the rabbi also was in everyone's mind David the Messiah. The principal development attested by the Yerushalmi is the figure of the sage, honored with the title of rabbi, his centrality in the social and salvific world of the Jewish nation. Sages so defined the national historical life of Israel that it was matched by and joined to the local and private life of the village. The whole social entity, "Israel," thereby served as a paradigm of ultimate perfection, sanctification – hence – salvation. "Israel" constituted a social entity that was in genus, not solely in species, absolutely unique on the face of the earth. The closer the sages came to the everyday realities of "Israel"'s life, the more concrete the abstraction, "Israel," became, and the more sages represented the abstraction – beginning with themselves and their most concrete social group (not merely "entity") – as an "Israel" that was not merely particular but unique.

Chapter 15

The Doctrine of Hebrew Language Usage

David H. Aaron

A. The Mishnah and Tosefta: Translations Are Appropriate

The following passages from the Mishnah and Tosefta reflect some of the central attitudes of early rabbinic Judaism to the use of translation for liturgy within the synagogue as well as in a few other contexts (oaths, Tefillin, etc.). While conflicting opinions appear regarding some details, these texts convey the overarching principle that translations are appropriate in ritual contexts. This early rabbinic leniency on the issue of translation is, of course, to be contrasted with what later became the dominant practice, an almost exclusively Hebrew liturgy.

Mishnah Sotah 7:1–4

These are said in any language: (1) the pericope of the accused wife [Num. 5:19–22], and (2) the confession of the tithe [Dt. 26:13–15], and (3) the recital of the *Shema* [Dt. 6:4–9], and (4) the Prayer, (5) the oath of testimony, and (6) the oath concerning a bailment.

And these are said [only] in the Holy Language: (1) the verses of the firstfruits [Dt. 26:3–10], (2) the rite *of halisah* [Dt. 25:7,9], (3) blessings and curses [Dt. 27:15–26], (4) the blessing of the priests [Num. 6:24–26], (5) the blessing of a high priest [on the Day of Atonement], (6) the pericope of the king [Dt.

Source for Reading A.: Translation details are given for each individual reading.
Mishnah sotah – Jacob Neusner, *The Mishnah* (New Haven: Yale University Press, 1988).

17:14–20]; the pericope of the heifer whose neck is to be broken [Dt. 21:7f.], and (8) [the message of] the anointed for battle when he speaks to the people [Dt. 20:2–7].

THE VERSES OF THE FIRSTFRUITS [Mishnah Sotah 7:2] how so? *And you will answer and say before the Lord thy God* (Dt. 26:5). And later on it says, *And the priests will answer and say* (Dt. 27:14). Just as *answering* which is said in that later passage is in the Holy Language, so *answering* which is said here [in reference to the first fruits] is in the Holy Language.

The rite of halisah [Mishnah Sotah 7:2] – how so? *And she will answer and say* (Dt. 25:9). And later on it says, *And the Levites will answer and say* (Dt. 27:14). Just as later on *answering* is to be in the Holy Language, so here *answering* is to be said in the Holy Language. R. Judah says, "*And she will answer and say, Thus* – [*so* it is not valid] unless she says precisely these words."

Blessings and curses – how so? When Israel came across the Jordan and arrived before Mount Gerizim and before Mount Ebal in Samaria, near Shechem, beside the oak of Moreh, as it is written, *Are they not beyond the Jordan*...(Dt. 11:30) and elsewhere it says, *And Abram passed through the land to the place of Shechem to the oak of Moreh* (Gen. 12:6) – just as the oak of Moreh spoken of there is at Shechem, so the oak of Moreh spoken of here is at Shechem – six tribes went up to the top of Mount Gerizim, and six tribes went up to the top of Mount Ebal. And the priests and Levites and ark of the covenant stood at the bottom, in the middle [between two mountains]. The priests surround the ark, and the Levites [surround] the priests, and all Israel are round about, since it says, *And all Israel and their elders and officers and judges stood on this side of the ark and on that*...(Josh. 8:33). They turned their faces toward Mount Gerizim and began with the bless – "Blessed is the man who does not make a graven or molten image." And these and those answer, "Amen." They turned their faces toward Mount Ebal and began with the curse: *Cursed is the man who makes a graven or molten image* (Dt. 27:15). And these and those answer, "Amen." [And this procedure they follow] until they complete the blessings and the curses. And afterward they brought stones and built an altar and plastered it with plaster. And they wrote on it all the words of the Torah in seventy languages, as it is written *very plainly* (Dt. 27:8). And they took the stones and came and spent the night in their own place (Josh. 4:8).

The blessing of the priests – how so? In the provinces they say it as three blessings, and in the sanctuary, as one blessing. In the sanctuary one says the Name as it is written but in the provinces, with a euphemism. . . .

Tosefta Sotah 7:7

Blessings, Hallel, the Shema [and] the Prayer are said in any language. Rabbi says, "I say that the Shema is said only in the Holy Language, as it is said, *And these words* (Dt. 6:6)." The blessing of the priests – this refers to the blessing which is said when the priests stand on the steps of the *ulam*.

Mishnah Megillah 1:8

There is no difference between sacred scrolls and phylacteries and *mezuzot* except that sacred scrolls may be written in any alphabet ["language"], while phylacteries and *mezuzot* are written only in square ["Assyrian"] letters. Rabban Simeon b. Gamaliel says, "Also, in the case of sacred scrolls they have been permitted to be written only in Greek."

B.   The Talmud: The Language of Liturgy

The *Shema* and *Amidah* are the two most significant rubrics within a Jewish prayer service. The *Hallel*, an anthology of Pslams (configured in a short and long version), is recited on the three Festivals (Pesah, Shavuot, Sukkot), Hanukkah, and on New Moons. The following passage from Tractate Megillah also discusses further the use of Scriptural translations. The central concern here is the question of comprehension. What are the implications of hearing a prayer or Scriptures read in a language that one does not understand?

B.   Megillah 17a–18a (selections)

IF ONE READS THE MEGILLAH BACKWARDS HE HAS NOT PERFORMED HIS OBLIGATION. IF HE READS IT BY HEART, IF HE READS IT IN A TRANSLATION [TARGUM] IN ANY LANGUAGE, HE HAS NOT PERFORMED HIS OBLIGATION. IT MAY, HOWEVER, BE READ TO THOSE WHO DO NOT UNDERSTAND HEBREW IN A LANGUAGE OTHER THAN HEBREW. IF ONE WHO DOES

Tosefta Sotah – Jacob Neusner, *The Tosefta: Nashim* (New York: Ktav Publishing House, 1979).
Mishnah Megillah – Jacob Neusner, *The Mishnah*.
Megillah – *The Soncino Talmud*, edited by I. Epstein (London: The Soncino Press, 1938); the Mishnah is represented in upper-case letters.

NOT UNDERSTAND HEBREW HEARS IT READ IN HEBREW, HE HAS PERFORMED HIS OBLIGA-
TION.

Whence is this rule [not to read backward] derived? Raba said: The text says, *according to the writing thereof and according to the appointed time thereof* (Esther 9:27): just as the appointed time cannot be backward, so the [reading from the] writing must not be backward. But does the text speak here of *reading?* It speaks of *keeping*, as it is written, *that they would keep these two days! –* The truth is that we derive the rule from here, as it is written: *And that these days should be remembered and kept."* "Remembering" is here put on the same footing as "keeping": just as keeping cannot be in the wrong order, so remembering also.

A Tanna stated: The same rule applies to *Hallel*, to the recital of the *Shema*, and to the *Amidah* prayer. Whence do we derive the rule as regards *Hallel? –* Rabbah said: Because it is written, *From the rising of the sun unto the going down thereof* [*the Lord's name is to be praised*] (Ps. 113:3). R. Joseph said, [from here]: *This is the day which the Lord hath made* (Ps. 118:24).

"To the recital of the *Shema*," as it has been taught: The *Shema* must be recited as it is written. So Rabbi. The Sages, however, say: It may be recited in any language. What is Rabbi's reason? Scripture says [17b] [*And these words*] *shall be* (Dt. 6:6), which implies, they shall be kept as they are. And what is the reason of the Rabbis? – Because Scripture says, *Hear [O Israel]* (Dt. 6:4), which implies, in any language which you understand. How then can Rabbi [hold otherwise], seeing that it is written, *Hear?* – He requires that word for the injunction, "Let thine ear hear what thou utterest with thy mouth." The Rabbis, however, concurred with the authority who said that if one recites the *Shema* without making it audible, he has performed his obligation.

May we say that Rabbi was of the opinion that the whole of the Torah has been ordained [to be recited] in any language? For should you assume that it has been ordained [to be recited] only in the holy tongue, why should the words "*and they shall be*" be inserted [in reference to the *Shema*]? – These were necessary. For it might have occurred to me to understand "*hear*" in the same sense as the Rabbis [in terms of any language] therefore the All-Merciful wrote "*and they shall be.*"

May we then say that the Rabbis were of the opinion that the whole of the Torah was ordained [to be recited] only in the holy tongue, since, should you assume that it was ordained to be recited in any language, [I might ask], why should "*hear*" be inserted [in reference to the *Shema*]? – This word is necessary. For it might occur to me to understand "*and they shall* be" in the same sense as Rabbi. Therefore the All-Merciful wrote, "*hear.*"

IF ONE READS IT IN A TRANSLATION HE HAS NOT PERFORMED HIS OBLIGATION. How are we to understand this? Are we to suppose that it is written in Hebrew and he reads it in a translation and he reads it in a translation.

IT MAY, HOWEVER, BE READ TO THOSE WHO DO NOT SPEAK HEBREW IN A LANGUAGE OTHER THAN HEBREW. But you have just said, IF ONE READS IT IN ANY [OTHER] LANGUAGE HE HAS NOT PERFORMED HIS OBLIGATION? Rab and Samuel both answered that what is referred to here is the Greek vernacular. How are we to understand this? Shall we say that it is written in Hebrew and he reads it in Greek? This is the same as saying by heart? R. Aha said in the name of R. Eleazar: What is referred to is where it is written in the Greek vernacular.

An objection was brought [against the dictum of Rab and Samuel] from the following: "If one reads it in Coptic, in Hebraic, in Elamean, in Median, in Greek, he has not performed his obligation"! – This [statement] means only in the same sense as the following: "If one reads it in Coptic to the Copts, in Hebrew to the Hebrews, in Elamean to the Elameans, in Greek to the Greeks, he has performed his obligation." If that is the case, why do Rab and Samuel explain the Mishnah to refer to the Greek vernacular? Let them make it refer to any vernacular? – The fact is that the Mishnah agrees with the Baraitha, and the statement of Rab and Samuel was meant to be a general one [thus]: Rab and Samuel both say that the Greek vernacular is good for all peoples. But it is stated, "[He may read] in Greek for the Greeks – for the Greeks, that is, he may, but for others not? – They [Rab and Samuel] concurred with Rabban Simeon b. Gamaliel, as we have learnt: "Rabban Simeon b. Gamaliel says: Scrolls of the Scripture also were allowed to be written only in Greek." Let them then say. The *halackah* is as stated by Rabban Simeon b. Gamaliel? Had they said, The *halackah* is as stated by Rabban Simeon b. Gamaliel, I should have understood them to mean that this is the case with other books of the Scriptures but not with the Megillah, of which it is written, *according to the writing thereof*. Therefore we are told [that this is not so].

IF ONE WHO DOES NOT UNDERSTAND HEBREW HEARD IT READ IN HEBREW, HE HAS PERFORMED HIS OBLIGATION. But he does not know what they are saying? He is on the same footing as women and ignorant people. Rabina strongly demurred to this saying; And do we know the meaning of *ha-abashteranim bene ha-ramakim* (Esther 8:10)? But all the same we perform the precept of reading the Megillah and proclaiming the miracle. So they too perform the precept of reading the Megillah and proclaiming the miracle.

C.   The Talmud: Torah Language and Colloquial Speech

This passage in Tractate Qiddushin bears witness to how sensitive the sages were with regard to the various strands and dialects of Hebrew as it developed over the many centuries since the giving of Torah. There are many discussions in the Talmud that reflect this awareness, often playful in character. Such passages reiterate the principle expressed in rabbinic literature that "the Torah uses its own language and the sages their own" (e.g., B. Hul. 137b, B. A.Z. 58b).

B. Qiddushin 70a–b

He came and found him making a parapet. He said to him, "Doesn't the master concur with what R. Huna bar Idi said Samuel said, Once a man is appointed administrator of the community, it is forbidden for him to do servile labor before three persons?" He said to him, "I'm just making a little piece of the balustrade." He said to him, "So what's so bad about the word, parapet, that the Torah uses, or the word partition, that rabbis use?" He said to him, "Will the master sit down on a seat?" He said to him, "So what's so bad about chair, which rabbis use, or the word stool, which people generally use?" He said to him, "Will the master eat a piece of citron-fruit?" He said to him, "This is what Samuel said, Whoever uses the word 'citron-fruit' is a third puffed up with pride. It should be called either etrog, as the rabbis do, or lemony-thing, as people do." He said to him, "Would the master like to drink a goblet of wine?" He said to him, "So what's so bad about the word wineglass, as rabbis say, or a drink, as people say?" He said to him, "Let my daughter Dunag bring something to drink?" He said to him, "This is what Samuel said, People are not to make use of a woman." "But she's only a minor!" "In so many words said Samuel, People are not to make use of a woman in any manner, whether adult or minor."

D.   The Midrashic Literature: The Preference for Hebrew

Among others, two passages from Sifre Deuteronomy (333, 46) reflect a strong preference for the use of Hebrew over other languages. Despite this, the old myth that Torah was revealed in multiple languages was also included in this anthology (343). The selections from Genesis Rabbah all relate aspects of the "metasemantics" developed by the rabbis. The brief passage from Midrash

Qiddushin – Jacob Neusner, The Talmud of Babylonia, Tractate Qiddushin (Atlanta: Scholars Press, 1992).

Leviticus Rabbah reflects how the preservation of Hebrew became a central religious value. Such a passage would have been written at a moment of transition in history, when the loss of Hebrew as a vernacular made its preservation dependent upon a religious value.

Sifre Deuteronomy 333

It is taught in the name of R. Meir: All who dwell in the Land of Israel, recite the Shema morning and evening, and speak the holy language are assured to dwell in the world-to-come.

Sifre Deuteronomy 46

Teach them to your children, and recite them (Dt. 11:19). From this verse it is learned: When a child beings to speak, his father should speak to him in the holy tongue and teach him Torah; if he does not speak to him in the holy tongue and does not teach him Torah, it is as thought he were burying him, for Scripture says, *Teach them to your children, and recite them . . . so that you and your children may endure* (Dt. 11:19, 21). If you teach them to your children, your days and the days of your children will be multiplied; if you do not, your days and the days of your children will be made fewer.

Sifre Deuteronomy 343

He said: The Lord came from Sinai (Dt. 33:2). When the Holy One revealed Himself to give Torah to Israel, He revealed Himself not in one language, but in four. He said *The Lord came from Sinai*, in Hebrew; *and shone upon them from Seir* in the language of Rome; *He appeared from Mount Paran* in the Arab language; *and approached from Ribeboth-kodesh* in the Aramaic language.

Midrash Genesis Rabbah 1.10

R. Yonah in the name of R. Levi: Why was the world created by means of the letter *bet?* Just as a *bet* is closed on its sides, but pen toward its front, so it is that

Translations of Sifre Deuteronomy materials are drawn, in part, from William G. Braude's translation of H. N. Blalik and Y. H. Ravnitzky, *The Book of Legends* (New York: Schocken Books, 1992), although I have emended them, especially with regard to biblical verses. This volume contains other passages relevant to Hebrew as the holy language and to language usage in general (pp. 374–6).

you have no authority to expound concerning that which is above, below, before and after. [...]

Why [was the world created] by means of the letter *bet?* In order to inform you that there are two worlds. Another approach: Why [was the world] created by means of a letter *bet?* Because the letter connotes blessing [*b'rakhah*]. And why [was the world] not [created] by means of a letter *alef?* Because the letter connotes a curse [*arirah*].

Another approach: Why wasn't [the world created] by means of an *alef?* So as not to give the heretics the opportunity to say: How can the world possibly endure, for it was created by means of a curse [*arirah*]. [To avoid this] the Holy One, blessed be He, said, Behold I am creating it with the connotation of blessing, oh that it should only endure!

Another approach: Why by means of a *bet?* Just as this *bet* has two projecting points, one upward and one behind it, when people say to it: Who is your creator, he shows them by means of its points which is upward saying: He who is above created me. And what is his name: And he shows them by means of its point which is behind: *YHVH* is his name.

R. Eleazar b. Abinah in the name of R. Aha: For 26 generations the letter *alef* complained before the Holy One, blessed be He, saying: Master of the universe, I am the first of the letters but you did not create your world with me. The Holy One, blessed be He, said to him: The world and all contained therein was only created through the merit of Torah. Tomorrow, I will be giving my Torah on Sinai and I will begin [speaking] with you: *I* [Anokhi] *am the Lord your God* (Ex. 20:1). Bar Hutah said: Why is its name *alef?* Because it denotes the sum of a thousand. *The world which he commanded for a thousand* [elef] *generations* (Ps. 105:8).

Midrash Genesis Rabbah 1.11

R. Simon in the name of R. Yehoshua b. Levi. The rule was given to Moses at Sinai that the letters *m, n, tz, p, k* [should take a different form at the end of words]. R. Yirmiya in the name of R. Hiyya bar Aba: This is what Seers instituted. It once happened on a stormy day, that the sages did not enter the House of Assembly. Some youngsters were there and [seeing that the sages weren't coming] they said, Come let us deal in *tzofim.* They said, What is the reason that there are two forms of *m,* two forms of *n,* two forms of *tz,* two *p,* two *k?* This teaches [that Torah was transmitted] from Utterance to utterance, from Faithful to faithful, from Righteous to righteous, from Mouth to mouth, from Hand to hand, i.e., from the Hand of the Holy One, blessed be He, to the hand of Moses. [The Sages] took note of them and they developed into great learned men in Israel. And there are those who say that these children were R. Eleazar, R. Yehoshua and R. Akiva. To them they applied the verse: *Even a child is known by his doings* (Prov. 20:11).[1]

Midrash Genesis Rabbah 12.10

When they were created [b'hibbaram].[2] R. Abbahu said in R. Yohanan's name: He created them with the letter *hey*. All letters demand an effort to pronounce them, whereas the *hey* demands no effort; similarly, not with labour nor wearying toil did the Holy One, blessed be He, create His world, but *By the* word *of the Lord*, and *The heavens were* already *made* (Ps. 33:6). R. Judah the Nasi (asked R. Samuel b. Nahman: As I have heard that you are a master of *haggadah*, tell me the meaning of, *Extol Him who rides the clouds*, b'Yah *is His name* (Ps. 68:5)?' Said he to him: There is not a single place which has not someone appointed to rule over it: thus a commissioner in a province is appointed to its governorship; a magistrate in a province is appointed to its governorship. Similarly, who is appointed to the governorship of His world? The Holy One, blessed be He: "*B'Yah is His name*" means *biyah* (governorship) is His name. Alas for those who are gone and will not return! he exclaimed. I asked R. Eleazar, and he did not explain it thus. But the verse, *Trust in the Lord for ever and ever, for in Yah* [b'Yah], *the Lord, you have an everlasting Rock* (Is. 26:4) means: By these two letters did the Lord create His world.

Now we do not know whether this world was created with a *hey* or the next world with a *yod*, but from what R. Abbahu said in R. Yohanan's name regarding what *b'hibbaram* means, *by means of a* hey *He created them*, it follows that this world was created by means of a *hey*. Now the *hey* is closed on all sides and open underneath: that is an indication that all the dead descend into *she'ol*; its upper hook is an indication that they are destined to ascend thence; the opening at the side is a hint to penitents. The next world was created with a *yod*: as the *yod* has a bent [curved] back, so are the wicked: their erectness shall be bent and their faces blackened [with shame] in the Messianic future, as it *is* written, *Then man's haughtiness shall be humbled* (Is. 2:17). What will [the wicked] say? *As for idols they shall vanish completely* (Is. 2:18).

R. Berekiah said in the name of R. Judah b. R. Simon: Not with labour nor wearying toil did the Holy One, blessed be He, create His world, but "*By the word of the Lord, and the heavens were* already *made.*" *B'hibbaram* with a *hey* created He them. It was like a king who rebuked his servant, so that he stood still in bewilderment; even so, *The pillars of heaven tremble, astonished at His blast* (Job 26:11).

Midrash Genesis Rabbah 18.4

She shall be called isha, *because she was taken out of* ish (Gen. 2:23). From this you learn that the Torah was given in the Holy Tongue. R. Phinehas and R. Helkiah in

R. Simon's name said: Just as it was given in the holy Tongue, so was the world created with the Holy Tongue.

Midrash Genesis Rabbah 74.14

R. Samuel bar Nahman said in the name of Yohanan: Do not think lightly of the Syriac language, for we find that the Holy One pays honor to it in the Torah, in the Prophets, and in the Writings. In the Torah: *yegar-sahaduta* (Gen. 31:47); in the Prophets: *Thus shall you say to them: Let the gods, who did not make heaven and earth, perish from the earth and from under these heavens* (Jer. 10:11, written in Aramaic); in the Writings: *the Chaldeans spoke to the king in Aramaic, "O king, live forever!"* (Dan 2:4).

Midrash Leviticus Rabbah 32.5

R. Huna taught in the name of Bar Kappara: On account of four things Israel was redeemed from Egypt. Because they did not change their [Hebrew] names nor their language; they did not gossip, nor did any of them commit sexual immoralities.

Notes

1   For other adaptations of this theme, see B. Shab. 104a, and the Y. Meg. 71d.
2   Reading the Hebrew word, *b'hibbaram*, as *bhe-baram*, "by means of the letter *he* he created them."

E.   Mysticism: The Power of Individual Letters

Little is known about the origins of the Hekhalot literature. Sefer Yetzirah is an even greater mystery. While the Hekhalot literature shares much in common with other rabbinic sources in terms of style, mythology and, in some instances, even genre, Sefer Yetzirah has no structural or thematic relationship with any other early rabbinic document. There are many passages in the Hekhalot literature that read similarly to some of the selections we have brought from Midrash Genesis Rabbah. This is because both documents share a common conceptualization of semantics (or metasemantics). In the selection here, the focus is on the power of the individual letters in bringing one wisdom. The Sefer Yetzirah passages may constitute a variation on the meta-semantics established within the midrashic corpus, but there is no denying that they move well beyond the concepts explicitly found in those contexts. Here it is not only that the letters have meaning, but through various combinations of letters the universe was created and is sustained. Obvious dependence upon Hellenistic ideas about the physical universe appear throughout the book. Ironically, the ascendancy of Hebrew's role in the cosmogony emerges only as a result of syncretism between Jewish and Greek learning.

Hekhalot Literature

In the hour when you pray, pronounce [the] three names that the angels of glory pronounce.... And when you pray, pronounce at the end [the] three letters that the *hayyot* pronounce in the hour when they behold and see '*rks*, the Lord, the God of Israel.... And when you recite another prayer, pronounce [the] three letters that the *galgalim* [angels] of the Merkavah pronounce, which sing a praise before the throne of glory.... This is the acquisition of wisdom, because everyone who pronounces these [letters] acquires eternal wisdom.

Selections from *Sefer Yetzirah*, chapter 1

1   By means of thirty-two wonderful paths of wisdom, *yh, yhvh* Hosts, *Elohim* of Israel, Living *Elohim*, and Eternal King, *El Shaddai*, Merciful and Gracious, High and Uplifted, Who inhabits Eternity, exalted and holy is His Name, engraved. And He created His universe by three principles: by border and letter and number.

2   There are ten intangible sefirot and twenty-two letters as a foundation: three are Mothers, and seven double, and twelve simple.

10   Two: Spiritual Air from Spirit. He engraved and hewed out in it twenty-two letters as a foundation: three Mothers, and seven double, and twelve simple, and they are of One Spirit.

11   Three: Spiritual Water from Spiritual Air. He engraved and hewed out in it chaos and disorder, mud and mire. He engraved it like a kind of furrow. He raised it like a kind of wall. He surrounded it like a kind of ceiling. He poured snow over them and it became earth, as it is said, *For He said to the snow, "Be earth"* (Job 37:6).

12   Four: Spiritual Fire from Spiritual Water. He engraved and hewed out in it the Throne of Glory, Seraphim, and Ophanim, and Hayot, and Ministering

Hekhalot Literature – From Peter Schäfer, *The Hidden and Manifest God: Some Major Themes in Early Jewish Mysticism*, translated by Aubrey Pomerance (Albany: SUNY Press, 1992), p. 92. The passage can be found in Peter Schäfer, *Synopse zur Hekhalot-Literatur* (Tübingen: Mohr, 1981), § 564.
Sefer Yetzirah – Drawn from David R. Blumenthal, *Understanding Jewish Mysticism: A Source Reader* (NY: Ktav Publishing House, 1978).

Angels. And from the three of them He established his Dwelling-Place, as it is said: *Who makes winds His messengers, the flaming fire His ministers* (Ps. 104:4).

13   He chose three of the simple letters, sealed them with Spirit and set them into His great Name, *yhv*, and sealed through them six extremities. Five: He sealed Height; He turned upward and sealed it with *yhv*. Six: He sealed Abyss; He turned downward and sealed it with *yvh*. Seven: He sealed East; He turned forward and sealed it with *hyv*. Eight: He sealed West; He turned backward and sealed it with *hvy*. Nine: He sealed South; He turned right and sealed it with *vyh*. Ten: He sealed North; He turned left and sealed it with *vhy*.

14   These ten intangible sefirot are One-Spirit of Living *Elohim*, Spiritual Air from Spirit, Spiritual Water from Spiritual Air, Spiritual Fire from Spiritual Water, Height, Abyss, East. West. North. and South.

Sefer Yetzirah, chapter 3

1   Three Mothers: Aleph. Mem. Shin – their foundation is the scale of merit and the scale of guilt. with the tongue being that which tips the balance between them.

2   Three Mothers: Aleph. Mem. Shin – a great secret. wonderful and concealed. and He seals with six rings. And from them go out Air, Fire, and Water. From them the Fathers are born, and from the Fathers, the Progeny. Know, count, and form, for the fire bears the water.

3   Three Mothers: Aleph, Mem, Shin: He engraved them. He hewed them out. He combined them. He weighed them. and He set them at opposites. and He formed through them: Three Mothers: Aleph, Mem, Shin in the universe, and Three Mothers: Aleph, Mem, Shin in the year, and Three Mothers: Aleph, Mem, Shin in the body of male and female.

4   Three Mothers: Aleph, Mem, Shin: The product of [elemental] Fire is the Heavens; the product of [elemental] Air is Air; and the product of [elemental] Water is Earth. Fire is above. Water is below; and Air tips the balance between them. From them the Fathers are generated, and from them, everything is created.

5   Three Mothers: Aleph, Mem, Shin are in the universe: Air, Water and Fire: Heavens were created first from [elemental] Fire. Earth was created from [elemental] Water. Air was created from [elemental] Air and it tips the balance between them.

6   Three Mothers: Aleph, Mem, Shin are in the year: Cold, Heat, and Temperate-state: Heat was created from [elemental] Fire. Cold was created from [elemental] Water. Temperate-state was created from [elemental] Air and it tips the balance between them.

7   Three Mothers: Aleph, Mem, Shin are in the body of male and female: Head, Belly, and Chest: Head was created from Fire. Belly was created from Water. Chest was created from Air and it tips the balance between them.

8   He caused the letter Aleph to reign over Air, and

> He tied a crown to it, and
> He combined them with one another, and
> He formed through them:
>> Air in the universe, and the
>> Temperate-state in the year, and the
>> Chest in the body of male with Aleph, Mem, Shin,
>>> and female with Aleph, Shin, Mem.

9   He caused the letter Mem to reign over Water, and

> He tied a crown to it, and
> He combined them with one another, and
> He formed through them:
>> Earth in the universe, and
>> Cold in the year, and the
>> Belly in the body of male with Mem, Aleph, Shin,
>>> and female with Mem, Shin, Aleph.

10   He caused the letter Shin to reign over Fire, and

> He tied a crown to it, and
> He combined them with one another, and
> He formed through them:
>> Heavens in the universe, and
>> Heat in the year, and
>> Head in the body of male with Shin, Aleph, Mem,
>>> and female with Shin, Mem, Aleph.

PART III

Modern and Contemporary Judaisms

16   Reform Judaism
Dana Evan Kaplan

17   Orthodox Judaism
Benjamin Brown

18   Conservative Judaism: The Struggle between Ideology and Popularity
Daniel Gordis

19   New Age Judaism
Jeffrey K. Salkin

Chapter 16

Reform Judaism

Dana Evan Kaplan

A.   Eugene B. Borowitz, "A Liberal Jewish Approach to Ritual"

Eugene Borowitz is regarded as the most important religious thinker in the Reform Movement today. Borowitz has tried to build a modern theology in a postmodern world that will enable Jews to re-establish both an emotional and an intellectual bond to their religious heritage. In the selection below, Borowitz conceives a Reform approach to Jewish ritual, arguing that ritual can deepen our spiritual lives and can be a critical factor in transforming our view of existence. The role of ritual is a central issue in the Reform movement today, as many serious Reform Jews consider re-embracing aspects of the tradition that were once considered inappropriate within Reform Judaism. This excerpt is from a book entitled *Liberal Judaism*, published by the Reform movement's Union of American Hebrew Congregations and intended for the educated Reform Jew as well as any others who might be interested.

I find that when I try talking to liberal Jews about the importance of ritual they often become quite uncomfortable.

They do not mind some Hebrew and ceremonialism when at temple. Perhaps they include the lighting of Shabbat candles as part of their lifestyle. But that is about as far as they are willing to go personally, so their attitude in these discussions indicates. I am not certain why my positive appeal for more ritual makes them anxious. Perhaps they fear that opening their lives in this way may soon lead to their being swamped with religious demands. Consider the traditional blessing before performing a major rite. We thank God "who has sanctified us by divine commandments and commanded us to. . . ." If we took these words literally – and did not choose to rebel – we would indeed have to undertake the entire

Source for reading A.:   Eugene Borowitz, *Liberal Judaism*, pp. 410–18.

repertoire of Jewish ceremonial. Our first step, then, in talking together about ritual must be a quick reminder: liberal Jews emphasize personal freedom in Judaism.

We believe that religion is as much humankind's creation as God's inspiration. Most of our thinkers say that ethics is as close as we can come to what God "wants" of us. When it comes to ritual, they admit we are dealing largely with what people have wanted to do for God. In this view, ceremonialism discloses more of human need and imagination than it does of God's commands. So when liberals use the classic words of Jewish blessing (translated above), "*asher kide-shanu bemitsvotav vetsivanu le ...,*" we are pausing to acknowledge God's part in our human religious creativity. The God-given authority of the commandments our Jewish forebears took literally has become figurative for us.

Understanding the essential humanity of Jewish ritual endows us with the right to decide which traditional acts we shall still do or not do. More excitingly, it empowers us to create the new rites needed to express better our present-day Jewishness. The strongly positive attitude to ritual I reflect in these pages is not intended to infringe on your personal freedom to choose for yourself. I am not writing to tell you what you must do but only to help you make your own informed, conscientious choice.

For many years liberal Judaism proclaimed itself to be a rational religion, though it included a strong esthetic component. Its thinkers spoke more often of the idea of God or the God-concept than directly of God. They also saw universal ethics as the primary way of living one's religion. Ritual therefore became a relatively unimportant part of their conception of Jewish obligation. If anything, their new sense of liberal freedom operated negatively in relation to Jewish tradition. Personal responsibility now meant they were now free not to do most of the classic Jewish rites.

Many liberal Jews today still contend that they are too rational to need a ritual component in their lives. I detect an emotional undertone in many such protestations. It comes out most clearly when one suggests that they use their liberal Jewish freedom to take on ritual practices as well as to dispense with them. Suggest, say, that perhaps we ought to rethink our old attitudes toward keeping kosher or to praying bareheaded and people who claim to be thoroughly rational can become quite heated. I find that quite appropriate for, as we shall see, rituals involve the affective as well as the cognitive aspects of being human.

Another factor needs to be considered. People who have grown up with a Judaism relatively empty of rite have an emotional stake in a restrained, coolly dignified, liberal pattern of practice. They may be embarrassed by not knowing the words or acts or songs involved in a richer Jewish ceremonial life. They may simply never have learned how to let themselves feel the special mood ritual seeks to create. At the extreme are those poor people who shudder at the possibility of doing an act which will clearly identify them as Jews. In such cases, the insistence on "rationality" is only a rationalization for their Jewish self-hate. . . .

Once we acknowledge that we are less exclusively cerebral and more happily Jewish than we once may have thought, we can share in the new contemporary openness to ritual....

All of the features we have found in human ritual generally are also found in religion. Its distinguishing characteristics arise from religion's unique view of reality. Secular rites mark special moments. Religion does this as well, but, because of its transcendent view of things, it goes much further. It seeks to turn much of everyday life into special moments. It aims to have us share its seers' insight that every instant is a precious gift, not anything we could by right demand. It therefore provides us with rituals by which we may interrupt the apparent profanity of commonplace activity and, by reaching for the holy, sanct-ify our lives.

This transforming view of existence begins with individual lives. All religions have ceremonies to herald the great moments of the life-cycle: birth, maturation, marriage, death, and whatever else they value highly. Such rites can reach so deep into our souls that even skeptics often temporarily suspend their questioning and rejoice that, among the infinite possibilities of existence, this blessing has been vouchsafed them – or, in mourning, acknowledge that life has deeper meaning than what they normally have seen in it.

Religion also seeks to refresh our usual sense of time. This begins with each day. Is awakening in the morning not worth an instant of celebrating? Then we can say the *Modeh Ani*, "I acknowledge before You, O enduring ruler, that you have graciously restored my soul to me." Is having another meal not worth an expression of gratitude? Then we can pronounce the Motsi and give thanks to the ultimate source of our sustenance. And, of course, Judaism has been most successful in changing people's views of time by its notion of a Sabbath.

These rites and the many others which might punctuate our daily lives im-mediately connect us with our Jewish people. Our sages identified many moments when we should try to bring a touch of the sacred into our lives. They provided us with words to say on such occasions; in some cases, they described acts to do. Utilizing their Hebrew words links us with them, with all the Jewish generations before us, and with all those today who carry on the Covenant. If, as well, we share their sense of the Sacred, performing these rituals strengthens our dedica-tion to Judaism's high ideals....

The difference between religious and all other human rituals arises from religion's unique focus: its rites direct us to God. By words, acts, tunes, attitudes, silences, perhaps with the use of special or ordinary artifacts, we human beings pause and reach out to God. Through religious ritual we seek to transcend the ordinary and open ourselves up to the sacred dimension of reality, what Rudolf Otto termed "the numinous." We often use quite prosaic means – bread and wine, for example. Through earthly words or things, utilized in the special way we call ritual, we renew our relationship, even for an instant, with the Extraordinary....

In many rituals the approach to God is quite direct. Jewish blessings – often themselves the ritual – begin, "Baruch Atah Adoni,..." – "Blessed are You,

Adonai...." Our tradition directs each of us to turn to God often in gratitude and thanks. Thus, before we munch a carrot we are told to say, "Blessed are You, Adonai, Ruler of the universe, who creates the fruit of the ground." Through nine Hebrew words we relate another routine act of eating to the essential ground of all existence, the ultimate reality on which we base our lives.

In other cases the relation with God is indirect. We leave our home and our eyes fall on or our fingers reach out to our mezuzah. If we allow its significance to register, a quick consciousness of our Jewish identity dawns in us. We remember that our home has been built on Jewish values and that we ought now to apply them in the world. If we are more spiritually sensitive we may also recall the texts of the mezuzah. They not only proclaim God's unity – the same one God outside our home as in it – but the corollary duty to love God with all our heart, soul, and might. In that fleeting instant we are reminded of the standard of our lives and the Covenant partnership which endows us with inalienable personal dignity.

Pausing for a second before our mezuzah and letting all this sink in will not necessarily keep us from behaving like scoundrels. Rituals have no magic power. They may not change us and they cannot coerce God. Doing them does not excuse abusing our freedom by doing evil, and they do not win us God's favor despite how badly we have behaved. But they can provide us with a means of trying to maintain a personal, Jewish contact with the Holy. In a world where so many other influences work to demean us, religious ritual must be considered a therapeutic necessity and a life-affirming activity.

B.   Walter Jacob, "Standards Now"

The question of standards – the demand that, as a requirement of membership, individuals perform specific ritual actions or ascribe to particular beliefs – in a liberal religious movement is deeply problematic. Yet, as sociologists have demonstrated, the lack of standards has weakened nonfundamentalist congregational movements of all types, setting in motion a dynamic in which the church or synagogue is regarded as no more than a place to come for life cycle events and major holidays. In this reading, Walter Jacob argues that Reform Judaism presents Jews with a theoretically sound methodology for reinterpreting traditional Jewish belief and making informed decisions on how to practice a modern form of the religion. But, Jacob recognizes, this theoretical model is generally completely ignored in modern American society, and most Reform congregations are filled with people who are either unable or unwilling to take Reform Judaism seriously. He therefore argues that, in contrast to the current sense of absolute autonomy that exists in the Reform movement, religious

Source for reading B.:   Reform Judaism, Fall 1992, p. 64.

standards are needed. While certainly not a position that most Reform Jews would be willing to implement, Jacob's critique is a sound, if devastating, attack on the present state of Reform Judaism as it is practiced by most Reform Jews in America today. Jacob offers an alternative to the apathy so prevalent.

Reform Judaism is a noble expression of Judaism, presenting us with lofty ideals. As generally practiced, however, it does not respond adequately to our daily lives. To remedy this unfortunate state of affairs, we need to formulate clear standards for Reform Jewish practice. We can begin this process of reforming Reform by coupling Judaism's prophetic message with its legal moorings – the halachah. We do so each Shabbat when we read Torah and Haftarah; why not do it at home and on the job? There should be a Reform Jewish ethical standard for each of us, whether we are a chemist, a homemaker, a lawyer, or a stockbroker.

Too often the specifies of our religious life have been lost through inertia and an unwillingness to take Reform Judaism seriously. We have used autonomy as an excuse for neglect. It is now time to move in a totally different direction.

When our founders rebelled against a stagnant Orthodoxy, they chose the high road of individual autonomy, selecting the best from our past to give Jewish content and meaning to our present-day lives. No one can fault this ideal, but it has not worked. We need direction, standards – a system of mitzvot (ethical observances) – and halachah as we go beyond guidance to governance.

The autonomous decision-making process to which our forebears entrusted the specific expression of Reform Judaism had been too ambitious, leading to outcomes they had not foreseen. Instead of making thoughtful Jewish choices based on careful examination of the sources, many Reform Jews have simply abandoned or neglected vast areas of Jewish practice. They feel that Reform Judaism makes no demands upon them and has no requirements. Perhaps even more unfortunate, the underlying sense of mitzvot has ceased to be a factor in our religious life.

To correct this imbalance, a greater degree of our individual autonomy must be surrendered to the legitimate demands of our Jewish community. As Reform Jews, we have forfeited only a minimum of autonomy, and therefore have received only a minimum of communal commitment in return. For the sake of the future of the Reform Movement, we must now be willing to yield some of the autonomy we have come to take for granted. Does a physician or lawyer simply follow his or her own conscience in deciding when to perform an organ transplant or to end a life? Is there not a Reform position? Regarding sexual ethics, do we permit anything which the general society considers all right?

Historically, individual congregations had forsaken a considerable amount of independence. At the turn of the century, for example, many abandoned their local liturgies in favor of the Union Prayerbook. Congregations were free to use their own siddurum, but the vast majority adopted a common prayer book, and have continued to use successive editions as the CCAR has updated them. There are many other areas of observance, such as bar/bat mitzvah, funerals, and conversions, in which congregations voluntarily have taken a similar path, sometimes doing so as a result of gentle persuasion, sometimes as a matter of solidarity.

Placing greater emphasis on community does not mean that the rights of individuals to differ and chart new paths ought to be curtailed. The Reform Movement will always be open to new ideas, but if we must choose between a Reform Judaism that provides guidance or one that provides governance, the latter must be our path. Such a path requires that we adopt measurable religious standards for our leaders, board members, and all our congregants. Family as well as professional life should meet the standards we set. Those who wish to remain outside this system will need to work out their own rationale for their actions.

As we embark on the path of more governance, we should remember that change comes slowly in Judaism. The Talmud, Alfasi, Maimonides, and Caro all were met with considerable opposition. Each set standards by which Jews could measure ourselves – standards modified continuously through the centuries. Let us sound a clarion call for standards now and make mitzvot and halachah a reality in the life of every Reform Jew.

C. Eric Yoffie, "Moses, Too, Was Once a Marginal Jew"

In the past twenty years, one of the most important policy issues facing the organized Jewish community has been how to respond to the fact that large numbers of Jews were loosening or cutting their ties with the organized Jewish community. Some, such as Dr. Steven Bayme of the American Jewish Committee, argue that the bulk of the Jewish community's financial and communal resources should be used to reinforce the Jewish identity and commitment of those who remain at least moderately affiliated with the Jewish community. Others argue that outreach to the totally assimilated, including those who have intermarried, is a task of critical importance. In this excerpt, Rabbi Eric Yoffie, president of the Union of American Hebrew Congregations, explains why he believes that outreach is so important.

North American Jewish leaders are engaged in an argument in which the stakes are so high, the issues so complex, and the public reaction so uncertain that both sides have sometimes been less than forthright in stating their case. The issue in question is this: In the struggle to preserve "continuity," should we expend precious resources to bring those on the fringes of Jewish life – the unaffiliated, the uninvolved, the marginally connected – into the communal fold?

Source for reading C.: *Reform Judaism*, Winter 1995, pp. 1–13.

In the past, Jewish communal institutions have concentrated on providing social services, fighting anti-Semitism, and defending Israel and other embattled Jewish communities. In the past few years, however, as concerns about external threats have receded, fears of an internal collapse have intensified. Assimilation, intermarriage, and disaffiliation have reach pandemic proportions in the United States. Under these circumstances it is impossible to continue with communal business as usual. Shoring up the internal bonds that tie us to Knesset Yisrael – the indivisible collectivity of the Jewish people – is now a matter of the highest priority....

Essentially two schools have emerged, each with a radically different view of our community's religious mission and future. The first points to the overwhelming difficulty of maintaining Jewish belief, observance, and commitment in North America's open and pluralistic environment. Advocates of this school argue that our community is wealthy and its institutions strong, but still a substantial percentage of Jews have chosen to forsake their Judaism. "Is this not inevitable?" they ask. After all, in a liberal democracy, private morality is decidedly a private concern. How then can we hope to influence the spiritual fate of individuals who prefer the freedoms and pleasures of the general culture to the demands of our Jewish tradition? Why waste our energy running after those who know where we are and what we offer but consistently turn their backs on us? And are not those on the periphery of our community – the assimilated, the intermarried, the indifferent – often looking for a watered-down, syncretistic, no-commitment Judaism, assuming that they are looking for anything at all?

It is quality that counts, they argue, not quantity. Strengthening our shared religious heritage is our only hope for Jewish continuity, but this will only be possible for the select few. Increasing the number of Jews is desirable, they say, but less important than depth of commitment and maintenance of standards. And for those who embrace this position, the practical implications are clear: the community should concentrate its resources on programs and institutions which serve the deeply committed and highly motivated, such as day schools and yeshivot....

But there is another school of thought, based on very different assumptions and leading to radically different conclusions. It is the school with which Reform Judaism has always identified, and it is a rejection, root and branch, of Jewish Darwinism. It holds that numbers are important and affirms the importance of every Jew – and his or her partner – in keeping the Jewish people alive and in maintaining Israel's covenant with God.

Our position does not dismiss the importance of Jewish day schools and other intensive educational experiences; on the contrary, it views with pride the recent flowering of the day school movement among Reform ranks. But we acknowledge the simple reality that more than half of American Jews are currently unaffiliated with a synagogue, and half of all Jewish children in America receive no Jewish education whatsoever. We refuse to forsake these children and their parents, or to assume that they cannot reenter the sanctity and symbolism of Jewish existence.

In our insistence on collective Jewish survival, the Reform movement believes that it is being neither mindlessly optimistic nor foolishly credulous. Our broad, inclusive, and embracing view of the Jewish future flows from religious and sociological assumptions about the dynamics of Jewish life, beginning with a theological mandate: the nature of the covenant between God and the Jewish people forbids the exclusion of any Jew, however wayward, from our people's collective destiny. We must commit ourselves to reclaiming the estranged in our midst.

Since the revelation at Sinai, and even before, all Jews carry within themselves a fragment of the Schechinah, the Divine presence, and are linked in a bond of shared responsibility to the people Israel. As Jewish mystics have taught, in every Jew there dwells a pintele yid – the eternal spark of "Yiddishkeit" that can rekindle the spirit of faith and teshuvah – return.

The sociological reality of teshuvah is an objective and documentable phenomenon. Jews on the margins often maintain an emotional identification with their roots and an amorphous but very real sense of belonging. It is true for Eastern European Jews cut off from Jewish life for two generations, for alienated Jews, for intermarried Jews, for Jews who have not belonged to a synagogue since childhood, and even for Jews who have never participated in a Jewish event. Virtually every rabbi has a story to tell about a synagogue leader or activist who was previously detached form the community and then unexpectedly found his or her way back . . . .

The issue of return takes on special urgency in today's Jewish world for both moral and practical reasons. The Shoah has irrevocably shaped our thinking; it leaves no place for notions of selective survival, or for the compromises and excuses upon which such ideas are built. A people that has been devastated by the Holocaust can find no morally acceptable rationale for focusing on one group of Jews while turning its back on another.

The practical argument for drawing in Jews is equally compelling . . . numbers matter, and the dynamism of a Jewish community is almost always directly related to its critical mass.

If any branch of Judaism can succeed in reclaiming estranged Jews, it is Reform. We offer a serious religious message rooted in values which resonate with the sensibilities and intellectual passions of modern Jews. Reform's devotion to tikkun olam has strong appeal to young religious seekers who regard issues of justice as integral to their lives. Reform's commitment to the absolute equality of men and women offers hope to a generation of women that takes gender equality for granted and views sexist language as a major obstacle to serious religious involvement. And Reform's welcoming philosophy of outreach to interfaith families is an important asset to Jews of all ages who hold respect for others as a basic value.

Still, a word of caution. Attracting the unaffiliated to our synagogues is only a first step. To touch Jewish souls, congregations must practice a Judaism of substance and religious depth, rooted in a liberal view of Torah. They should be warm, welcoming, and all-embracing, taking Jews out of the solitude of their homes and providing them with places to study, celebrate, and observe the rituals of our tradition that give meaning and purpose to people's lives.

Ultimately, our synagogues must be so vibrant and joyful that it will never occur to born Jews not to affiliate or ask "why be Jewish?" The richness of Jewish living, the grandeur of Jewish ethics, and the majesty of Jewish faith will speak for themselves.

We must commit ourselves to collective, not selective survival. Let's urge federations and foundations to invest in the Jewish future by funding worthy programs designed to reach marginal, inactive, and unaffiliated Jews; encourage such efforts by synagogue movements across the religious spectrum; and see to it that the Reform movement, uniquely suited to respond to the religious needs of this population, launches a major new initiative, building on the successful efforts of our "Taste of Judaism" program and innovative congregational initiatives to transmit our message throughout the land.

Will such a baal teshuvah campaign work? We cannot be certain, and we need not be. If we draw only 20 percent of those on the periphery into synagogue life, we will have added upwards of half a million Jews to the ranks of the Jewishly committed! But our ultimate motivation runs deeper, relating not to numbers but to faith: we will bring our message to the community, unaffiliated and affiliated alike, because we are confident that being a Reform Jew deepens one's love of God, promotes the practice of Torah, and strengthens our shared destiny as a holy people.

D. Henry Cohen, "Rabbinic Officiation and Mixed Marriage Revisited"

The most serious threat facing American Judaism is not anti-Semitism but intermarriage. Irving Kristol wrote, "The danger facing American Jews today is not that Christians want to persecute them, but that Christians want to marry them."[1] Of the three major denominations in American Judaism, the Reform movement has the highest rate of intermarriage; it is also the most attractive to intermarried Jews of all denominations who are considering affiliating with a synagogue. The Reform rabbinate has had to face the question of how to respond to these couples. Statistics seem to indicate that, although the Central Conference of American Rabbis (CCAR) is on record as opposing officiation at intermarriages, approximately forty percent of the Reform clergy do so anyway. This is possible because of the nonbinding nature of all CCAR resolutions, unlike in the case of the Conservative and Orthodox rabbinate, where denominational decisions of this nature are regarding as binding on all rabbis of that

Source for reading D.: CCAR Journal, Winter 1996, pp. 47–54.

movement. In this excerpt, Rabbi Henry Cohen outlines his views on officiating at intermarriages. He wrote in the aftermath of the 1996 CCAR convention in Philadelphia, which focused on this issue.

It is tempting to greet the 1996 debate over rabbinic officiating at mixed marriages with a sigh. How often have we heard the arguments pro and con! Officiators warn that their refusal would be perceived as rejection, as slamming the door of Judaism in the face of couples, even couples who are committed to sending their children to a Jewish religious school. They may cite instances of couples with whom they developed a relationship through the premarital process and were able to facilitate their affiliation with a synagogue.

Opponents of officiation, the majority of CCAR members, warn that the very public act of officiating is perceived as giving sanction to mixed marriage and so sends a signal to all Jewish singles: not to worry. You can marry a Christian and still find a rabbi to conduct the ceremony and make your parents if not happy, at least less unhappy.

Rabbinic officiating at mixed marriage is part of the problem, not part of the solution. Officiators are often being conned when couples promise to "rear their children as Jews." Even if their intentions are sincere, they cannot really give their children an effective Jewish education so long as one parent is not Jewish. Given the importance of parental role models, these children will not be able to develop a strong Jewish identity. Surely the children's children will not marry Jews.

Opponents of officiation may find support in Egon Mayer's study, "Intermarriage and Rabbinic Officiation," which concludes that no connection was found "between rabbinic officiation or nonofficiation and the subsequent Jewish expressions of the couple . . . Rabbis who had justified their decisions to officiate . . . on the assumption that they were helping 'save' the couple for Judaism may wish to reconsider their position." Proponents of officiating may quote the very same study and arrive at a different conclusion: "Those whose requests for officiation were rebuffed are significantly less interested in their children being Jewish than those who were married by a rabbi. Thus, the willingness of rabbis to officiate at mixed-religion marriages seems to be related to the prospects of such parents raising their children as Jews." It should also be noted that the Mayer study was based on questions posed to those spouses who were not born Jewish.

Since my emeritization, I have been engaged in research based on eighty-eight questionnaires received from couples still together at whose mixed marriages I officiated between 1965 and 1981 and who made a commitment to send their children to a Jewish religious school. At none of these weddings did I co-officiate with Christian clergy. I compared the responses of these mixed marrieds with those of thirty nine intraJewish couples at whose weddings I officiated during the same years. Responses were received from 88 percent of those who were sent questionnaires and most of the remaining 12 percent were contacted by phone.

After conducting selected interviews, a Beliefs and Values Survey was sent to those mixed married couples at whose weddings I officiated between 1965 and 1981 and those mixed marrieds at whose weddings I officiated between 1990 and 1994. Finally, there was a small but significant response to a Beliefs and Values Survey sent to sons and daughters of both intermarried and intramarried couples who had completed at least seven years of Jewish education. . . .

I am convinced that officiating has given me, as the rabbi, a much greater opportunity than my nonofficiating colleagues have, to develop a positive relation with the couple and through that relation to encourage their connection with the Jewish faith and people. I am aware that some of my nonofficiating colleagues also take the time to extend a warm welcome to mixed married couples. However, I firmly believe that the premarital discussions and the wedding, itself, make it much easier for the rabbi to have an impact. . . .

Rabbinic officiating, if part of a process of counseling, will usually encourage the movement toward the Jewish faith and people. Rabbis who refuse to officiate will often be perceived as rejecting the couple and may, despite their best efforts, find it more difficult to establish a positive relationship. I have often had to explain the reasons for the refusal of a colleague to officiate, so that the couple would not be so resentful. I do recognize that officiating, in and of itself, may not be a decisive or even a significant factor. However, I have found that officiating greatly facilitates the process of counseling that can lead a couple to provide a meaningful Jewish education for their children. If the bride and groom recognize that the Jewish dimension of the wedding is appropriate only if they follow through on their commitment to preserve Judaism in their home and to rear their children as Jews, then officiating will have the effect of opening the door and saying: welcome!

Note

1   Christopher C. DeMuth and Irving Kristol, eds., *The Neo-Conservative Imagination* (Washington, 1995), p. 203.

E.   A Statement of Principles for Reform Judaism

After about a year of considerable controversy, a statement of principles for Reform Judaism was developed and proposed for adoption at the CCAR conference at Pittsburgh in May, 1999. This statement of principles was a pale imitation of Rabbi Richard Levy's original draft, which had been watered down in order to avoid an acrimonious and potentially destructive split in

Source for reading E.:   Adopted at the May 1999 Pittsburgh Convention of the Central Conference of American Rabbis

the movement between the increasing numbers of neo-traditionalists and the diminishing but still significant Classical Reformers. The final draft eliminated all the references to specific *mitzvot*, references that had so infuriated and alienated those for whom Reform Judaism was not compatible with putting on *tefillin* (phylacteries) or going to a *mikveh* (ritual bath). It was passed with the promise that there will be extensive future commentary and discussion.

Preamble

On three occasions during the last century and a half, the Reform rabbinate has adopted comprehensive statements to help guide the thought and practice of our movement. In 1885, fifteen rabbis issued the *Pittsburgh Platform*, a set of guidelines that defined Reform Judaism for the next fifty years. A revised statement of principles, the *Columbus Platform*, was adopted by the Central Conference of American Rabbis in 1937. A third set of rabbinic guidelines, the *Centenary Perspective*, appeared in 1976 on the occasion of the centenary of the Union of American Hebrew Congregations and the Hebrew Union College–Jewish Institute of Religion. Today, when so many individuals are striving for religious meaning, moral purpose and a sense of community, we believe it is our obligation as rabbis once again to state a set of principles that define Reform Judaism in our own time.

Throughout our history, we Jews have remained firmly rooted in Jewish tradition, even as we have learned much from our encounters with other cultures. The great contribution of Reform Judaism is that it has enabled the Jewish people to introduce innovation while preserving tradition, to embrace diversity while asserting commonality, to affirm beliefs without rejecting those who doubt, and to bring faith to sacred texts without sacrificing critical scholarship.

This "Statement of Principles" affirms the central tenets of Judaism – God, Torah, and Israel – even as it acknowledges the diversity of Reform Jewish beliefs and practices. It also invites all Reform Jews to engage in a dialogue with the sources of our tradition, responding out of our knowledge, our experience and our faith. Thus we hope to transform our lives through *kedushah*, holiness.

God

We affirm the reality and oneness of God, even as we may differ in our understanding of the Divine presence.

We affirm that the Jewish people is bound to God by an eternal *b'rit*, covenant, as reflected in our varied understandings of Creation, Revelation and Redemption.

We affirm that every human being is created *b'tzelem Elohim*, in the image of God, and that therefore every human life is sacred.

We regard with reverence all of God's creation and recognize our human responsibility for its preservation and protection.

We encounter God's presence in moments of awe and wonder, in acts of justice and compassion, in loving relationships and in the experiences of everyday life.

We respond to God daily through public and private prayer, through study and through the performance of other *mitzvot*, sacred *bein adam la Makom*, to God, and *bein adam la-chaveiro*, to other human beings.

We strive for a faith that fortifies us through the vicissitudes of our lives – illness and healing, transgression and repentance, bereavement and consultation, despair and hope.

We continue to have faith that, in spite of the unspeakable evils committed against our people and the sufferings endured by others, the partnership of God and humanity will ultimately prevail.

We trust in our tradition's promise that, although God created us as finite beings, the spirit within us is eternal.

In all these ways and more, God gives meaning and purpose to our lives.

Torah

We affirm that Torah is the foundation of Jewish life.

We cherish the truths revealed in Torah, God's ongoing revelation to our people and the record of our people's ongoing relationship with God.

We affirm that Torah is a manifestation of *ahavat olam*, God's eternal love for the Jewish people and for all of humanity.

We affirm the importance of studying Hebrew, the language of Torah and Jewish liturgy, that we may draw closer to our people's sacred texts.

We are called by Torah to lifelong study in the home, in the synagogue and in every place where Jews gather to learn and teach. Through Torah study we are called to *mitzvot*, the means by which we make our lives holy.

We are committed to the ongoing study of the whole array of *mitzvot* and to the fulfillment of those that address us as individuals and as a community. Some of these *mitzvot*, sacred obligations, have long been observed by Reform Jews; others, both ancient and modern, demand renewed attention as the result of the unique context of our own times.

We bring Torah into the world when we seek to sanctify the times and places of our lives through regular home and congregational observance. Shabbat calls us to bring the highest moral values to our daily labor and to culminate the work-week with *kedushah*, holiness, *menuchah*, rest and *oneg*, joy. The High Holy Days call us to account for our deeds. The Festivals enable us to celebrate with joy our people's religious journey in the context of the changing seasons. The days of remembrance remind us of the tragedies and the triumphs that have shaped our people's historical experience both in ancient and modern times. And we mark the milestones of our personal journeys with traditional and creative rites that reveal the holiness in each stage of life.

We bring Torah into the world when we strive to fulfill the highest ethical mandates in our relationships with others and with all of God's creation. Partners with God in *tikkun olam*, repairing the world, we are called to help bring about the messianic age. We seek dialogue and joint action with people of other faiths in the hope that together we can bring peace, freedom and justice to our world. We are obligated to pursue *tzedek*, justice and righteousness, and to narrow the gap between the affluent and the poor, to act against discrimination and oppression, to pursue peace, to welcome the stranger, to protect the earth's biodiversity and natural resources, and to redeem those in physical, economic and spiritual bondage. In so doing, we reaffirm social action and social justice as a central prophetic focus of traditional Reform Jewish belief and practice. We affirm the *mitzvah* of *tzedakah*, setting aside portions of our earnings and our time to provide for those in need. These acts bring us closer to fulfilling the prophetic call to translate the words of Torah into the works of our hands.

In all these ways and more, Torah gives meaning and purpose to our lives.

Israel

We are Israel, a people aspiring to holiness, singled out through our ancient covenant and our unique history among the nations to be witnesses to God's presence. We are linked by that covenant and that history to all Jews in every age and place.

We are committed to the *mitzvah* of *ahavat Yisrael*, love for the Jewish people, and to *k'lal Yisrael*, the entirety of the community of Israel. Recognizing that *kol Yisrael arevim zeh ba-zeh*, all Jews are responsible for one another, we reach out to all Jews across ideological and geographical boundaries.

We embrace religious and cultural pluralism as an expression of the vitality of Jewish communal life in Israel and the Diaspora.

We pledge to fulfill Reform Judaism's historic commitment to the complete equality of women and men in Jewish life.

We are an inclusive community, opening the doors of Jewish life to people of all ages, to varied kinds of families, to all regardless of their sexual orientation, to *gerim*, those who have converted to Judaism, and to all individuals and families, including the intermarried, who strive to create a Jewish home.

We believe that we must not only open doors for those ready to enter our faith, but also to actively encourage those who are seeking a spiritual home to find it in Judaism.

We are committed to strengthening the people Israel by supporting individuals and families in the creation of homes rich in Jewish learning and observance.

We are committed to strengthening the people Israel by making the synagogue central to Jewish communal life, so that it may elevate the spiritual, intellectual and cultural quality of our lives.

We are committed to Medinat Yisrael, the State of Israel, and rejoice in its accomplishments. We affirm the unique qualities of living in *Eretz Yisrael*, the land of Israel, and encourage *aliyah*, immigration to Israel.

We are committed to a vision of the State of Israel that promotes full civil, human and religious rights for all its inhabitants and that strives for a lasting peace between Israel and its neighbors.

We are committed to promoting and strengthening Progressive Judaism in Israel, which will enrich the spiritual life of the Jewish state and its people.

We affirm that both Israeli and Diaspora Jewry should remain vibrant and interdependent communities. As we urge Jews who reside outside Israel to learn Hebrew as a living language and to make periodic visits to Israel in order to study and to deepen their relationship to the Land and its people, so do we affirm that Israeli Jews have much to learn from the religious life of Diaspora Jewish communities.

We are committed to furthering Progressive Judaism throughout the world as a meaningful religious way of life for the Jewish people.

In all these ways and more, Israel gives meaning and purpose to our lives.

Baruch she-amar ve-haya ha-olam.
Praised be the One through whose word all things came to be.
May our words find expression in holy actions.
May they raise us up to a life of meaning devoted to God's service
And to the redemption of our world.

Chapter 17

Orthodox Judaism

Benjamin Brown

A.   Rabbi Moshe Sofer (*The Hatam Sofer*): A Testament

Hungarian Jewry's most prominent rabbinical leader, Rabbi Moshe Sofer, better known as the Hatam Sofer (1762–1839) led the first clear-cut Orthodox response to the challenges of modernity, coining the motto that later became the banner of radical Orthodoxy: "*Haddash Asur min ha-Torah*" ("the new is forbidden by the Torah"). Originally addressed to his family, the Hatam Sofer's testament has become, since his death in 1839, the manifesto of hardline Orthodoxy, especially in Hungary. The original Hebrew text is full of puns and biblical allusions that cannot be captured in translation.

With the help of God, Thursday, 15th of Kislev 5597 [1837].

For man knows not his time . . . It is a time to do for the Lord's sake, to increase [the observance of] thy Law,[1] to elevate the house of our God and to rebuild its wrecks. You, my sons, daughters, sons-in-law, grandsons, and their offsprings, hear me and you shall live.[2]

Do not let your hearts open to the words of the evil-doers who have emerged of late and gone far from God and his Torah. Do not dwell in their neighborhood and do not join with them in any way.

And do not ever touch the books of Moses Mendelssohn, and thus shall you never stumble. Rather, learn and teach your children *Tanakh* [= the Old Testament] with Rashi's commentary and Torah with Ramban's, for they are the foremost sources of stern faith, and from them you shall win the greatest wisdom.

Source for reading A.:   Most of the translation appears in Y. D. Shulman, *The Chasam Sofer – The Story of Rabbi Moshe Sofer* (New York, London, and Jerusalem, 1992), pp. 253–4.

And if, God forbid, you will have to go through hunger and thirst – may the Lord assist you to overcome his test. Stand firm and do not turn to the idols, namely, to your own judgement.

The women should read books in Yiddish, printed in our traditional font and based on our sages' *Aggadah* [= the Talmud's non-halakhic texts], and nothing else.

I strictly warn you to keep away from theatres, God forbid, and wish you rather to attend the Holy Temple to be rebuilt, where you shall see the pleasantness of God[3] and the joy of his children.

And if, as I hope, the Lord blesses you with plenty, do not grow proud or treat any decent person disrespectfully. Remember that we are the children of Abraham, Isaac, and Jacob, the disciples of our master Moses, the servants of King David. Our father [= Abraham] said: "I am dust and ashes" (Gen. 18:27); our Master [= Moses] said: "What are we?" (Exod. 16:7–8); our King [= David] said: "I am worm, not man" (Ps. 22:7). And the messiah will come in the guise of a pauper riding a donkey (Zech. 9:9). In the light of this, where is there room for haughtiness or pride?

Collect strength to learn the Divine Torah dilligently and thoroughly. Organize public learning, and if you have only little resources, use them to teach the public as much as you can. Do it for His Name's sake alone, not for any other purpose. Be sure your heart is pure in this, for He repels the hypocrites.

Do not change your name, language, or clothing[4] to imitate the ways of the gentiles.

Do not worry that I have not left you wealth. The father of orphans[5] will have mercy on orphans, and He shall not abandon you. His power to help is unlimited.

Do not make the divine Torah a crown to decorate with, nor a spade to dig with.[6] Certainly shall you not become travelling preachers for pay. For what you deserve shall find you in your own place.

Do not say that times have changed, for "we have an old Father,"[7] blessed be He, who has not changed and never will change. May no evil occur, and we all be blessed from the Lord's dwellings.

The insignificant Moshe Sofer of Frankfort On The Main.

Notes

1   Based on Pss. 119 and 126.
2   Based on Amos 5:4.
3   Based on Ps. 27:4.
4   Based on Exod. Rabbah 20:21.
5   See Ps. 68:6.
6   See M. Ab. 4:5.
7   See Gen. 44:20.

B.   Rabbi Samson Raphael Hirsch, "Emancipation"

Rabbi Samson Raphael Hirsch (1808–88), leader of the Frankfurt Orthodox congregation, represents the response to modernity known as Neo-Orthodoxy, defined by the belief that observant Judaism is basically consistent with humanistic values. His *Nineteen Letters*, also known as *"Iggrot Tzafun"* (not *"Tzafon,"* as some read), was his first published work. The first letter is written by Benjamin, a young Jewish man who abandoned religious observance, to his friend, Naphtali, an Orthodox rabbi. The next letters, Naphtali's responses, convince Benjamin, step by step, to return to Orthodoxy. The last letters deal with Orthodoxy's due response to the challenges of the time. The following text, Letter Sixteen, focuses on Emancipation.

YOU ASK ME FOR MY OPINION on the question which at present so greatly agitates the minds of men; namely emancipation. You wish to know whether I consider it feasible and desirable according to the spirit of Judaism. The new conception of Judaism which you have acquired, dear Benjamin, has rendered you so uncertain as to whether such ideals could be reconciled with the eternal ideals of our faith. You have begun to doubt whether the acceptance of these new relations is in harmony with the spirit of Judaism, inasmuch as it approximates to a close union with that which is different and alien, and a severance of the ties which bind us all to Israel's lot. You doubt its desirability, because, through too much intimacy with the non-Jew, Israel's own special characteristics might easily be obliterated. I respect your scruples, and will communicate to you my own opinion. Let us first examine whether it is in harmony with the spirit of Judaism.

When Israel began its great wandering through the ages and among the nations, Jeremiah proclaimed it as Israel's duty to:

> Build houses and dwell therein; plant gardens and eat the fruit thereof; take wives unto yourselves, and beget sons and daughters, and take wives for your sons and give your daughters in marriage that they bear sons and daughters, and that you multiply *there*, and diminish not. *And seek the peace of the city whither I have exiled you, and pray for it to the Lord, for in its peace there will be unto you peace.* (Jeremiah 29:5–7)

To be pushed back and limited upon the path of life is, therefore, not an essential condition of the *Galuth*, Israel's exile among the nations. On the contrary, it is our duty to join ourselves as closely as possible to the state which receives us into its midst, to promote its welfare and not to consider our own well-being as in any way separate from that of the state to which we belong.

Source for reading B.:   Samson Raphael Hirsch, *The Nineteen Letters on Judaism* (New York: Feldheim Publishers, 1969), pp. 106–11.

This close connection with states everywhere is not at all in contradiction to the spirit of Judaism, for the independent national life of Israel was never the essence or purpose of our existence as a nation, but only a means of fulfilling our spiritual mission.

Land and soil were never Israel's bond of union. That function was always fulfilled solely by the common task set by the Torah. Therefore the people of Israel still forms a united body, though it is separated from a national soil. Nor does this unity lose any of its reality though Israel accept everywhere the citizenship of the nations among which it is dispersed. This spiritual unity (which may be designated by the Hebrew terms *am* and *goy*, but not by the term "nation," unless we are able to separate from that word the inherent concept of common territory and political power) is the only communal bond we possess, or ever expect to possess, until that great day shall arrive when the Almighty shall see fit in His inscrutable wisdom to unite again His scattered servants in one land, and the Torah shall be the guiding principle of a state, a model of the meaning of Divine Revelation and the mission of humanity.

For this future, which is promised us in the glorious predictions of the inspired prophets as a goal of the *Galuth*, we hope and pray, but actively to accelerate its coming is prohibited to us. The entire purpose of the Messianic age is that we may, in prosperity, exhibit to mankind a better example of "Israel" than did our ancestors the first time, while, hand in hand with us, the entire race will be joined in universal brotherhood through the recognition of God, the All-One.

It is on account of this the purely spiritual nature of its national character that Israel is capable of the most intimate union with states, with, perhaps, this difference. While others seek in the state only the material benefits which it secures, considering possessions and pleasures as the highest good, Israel can regard it only as a means of fulfilling the mission of mankind.

Summon up before your mental vision the picture of such an Israel, dwelling in freedom among the nations, and striving to attain to its ideal. Picture every son of Israel a respected and influential priest of righteousness and love, disseminating among the nations not specific Judaism – for proselytism is forbidden – but pure humanity. What a mighty impulse to progress, what a luminary and staff in the gloomy days of the Middle Ages would Israel have beer then, if its own sin and the insanity of the nations had not rendered such a *Galuth* impossible. How impressive, how sublime it would have been if, in the midst of a race that adored only power, possessions and enjoyment, there had lived quietly and publicly human beings of a different sort, who beheld in material possessions only the means for practicing justice and love towards all, a people whose minds, imbued with the wisdom and truth of the Law, maintained simple, straightforward views, and emphasized them for themselves and others in expressive, vivid symbolic acts.

But it would seem as though Israel first had to be fitted, through the endurance of the harsh and cruel aspects of exile, for proper appreciation and utilization of the milder and gentler aspects of dispersion.

When *Galuth* will be understood and accepted as it should be, when, in suffering, the service of God and His Torah will be understood as the only task of life, when, even in misery, God will be served, and material abundance esteemed only as a means for this service, then, perhaps, Israel will be ready for the far greater temptations of prosperity and happiness in dispersion. Thus the answer to our question is quite obvious. Just as it is our duty to endeavour to obtain those material possessions which are the fundamental condition of life, so also is it the duty of every one to take advantage of every alleviation and improvement of his condition open to him in an honest way. For, the more means, the more opportunity is given to him to fulfill his mission in its broadest sense; and it is the duty of the community no less than that of the individual to obtain for all its members the opportunities and privileges of citizenship and liberty. Do I consider this desirable? I bless emancipation when I see how the excess of oppression drove Israel away from a normal life, limited the free development of its noble character, and compelled many individuals to enter, for the sake of self-preservation, upon paths which they were too weak to refuse to enter.

I bless emancipation when I notice that no spiritual principle, not even one of foolish fanaticism, stands in its way, but that it is opposed only by those passions which are degrading to humanity, namely, greed for gain and narrow selfishness. I rejoice when I perceive that in this concession of emancipation, regard for the natural rights of men to live as equals among equals is freely extended without force or compulsion, but purely through the power of their own inner truth. I welcome the sacrifice of the base passions wherever it is offered, as the dawn of reviving humanity in mankind, and as a preliminary step to the universal recognition of God as the sole Lord and Father, and of all human beings as the children of the All-One.

But for Israel I only bless it if, at the same time, there will awaken in Israel the true spirit which strives to fulfill the mission of Israel regardless of whether or not there is to be emancipation, to elevate and ennoble ourselves, to implant the spirit of Judaism in our souls, in order that it may generate a life in which that spirit shall be reflected and realized. I bless it, if Israel will regard emancipation not as the goal of its vocation, but only as a new condition of its mission, and as a new test, much severer than the trial of oppression. But I should grieve if Israel understood itself so little, and had so little comprehension of its own spirit that it would welcome emancipation as the end of the *Galuth*, and as the highest goal of its historic mission. If Israel should regard this glorious concession merely as a means of securing a greater degree of comfort in life, and greater opportunities for the acquisition of wealth and enjoyment, it would show that Israel had not comprehended the spirit of its own Law, nor learned anything from exile. And sorrowfully indeed would I mourn if Israel were so far to forget itself as to deem emancipation not too dearly purchased through capricious curtailment of the Torah, capricious abandonment of the chief element of our very being. We must become Jews, Jews in the true sense of the word, imbued with the spirit of the Law, accepting it as the fountain of spiritual and ethical life. Then Judaism will

gladly welcome emancipation as affording a greater opportunity for the fulfillment of its task, the realization of a noble and ideal life.

C.   Rabbi Avraham Isaac ha-Cohen Kook on the Unity of Contradiction

Rabbi A.Y. Kook (1865–1935) is the most prominent thinker of the Zionist
Religious Movement. He was born in Lithuania but was exposed to both Litvish
and Hasidic influences. In 1904 he was appointed rabbi of the New *Yishuv* [=
the proto-Zionist and Zionist settlers]. In this post he came to appreciate the
idealism of the new immigrants, most of whom were secular. His monistic
theology is based on Kabbalah and Hasidism but is influenced by various
philosophers, Jewish and non-Jewish. The following texts are typical of his
writing, reflecting his grand, quasi-poetic style. The first of them is an example
for his dialectical metaphysics. As a part of this philosophy he believes in the
ultimate unity of contradictions, including those that raise problems for the
modern Jew: faith and science, heteronomous halakhah and autonomous
morality, etc. As on many other occasions, Rabbi Kook writes here on two
levels of significance: the overt, that can be understood literally, and the
alluded, which refers to Kabbalistic concepts (here interpreted in the footnotes).

The Inner Peace

Man's capacities being limited, [it appears that] one notion contradicts[1] the other,
one feeling contradicts the other, one image contradicts the other. But the truth
is, that one notion strengthens the other, one feeling nourishes the other, one
image completes the other. And the more a person's spirit ascends, the more his
mental vessels grow broad, until he finds himself filled with a grand content,
namely Inner Peace,[2] and sees the compliance of the different notions, feelings
and images with one another.

And his spirit grows broader and broader, until it reaches the depth of depths,
where contradiction is sharp and bitter and evokes a tremendous wrath of
Holiness. But there, as Inner Knowledge broadens and expands throughout all
of Man's spiritual stature,[3] a penetrating, piercing Peace turns to prevail, and
descends as deep as the Abyss.[4]

There is a path that one has to go through in order to reach this sublime level.
At the first stage, one stands in the lower level where one is still susceptible to the
affliction of contradictions. At that stage, too, there are two paths, the one higher

Source for reading C.:   Rabbi A. Y. Kook, *Orot ha-Kodesh* (Jerusalem, 1992), part I, sec. 10, pp. 13–14.

than the other. On the first path, a notion contradicts the other and negates it altogether, so that the notion newly-obtained appears to annihilate the notion negated and empty it of content. Yet on the other path, the notion newly-obtained draws the essence from the notion negated, so that the latter is absorbed into the former. Now if one judges according to the outside of the vessel, one may believe that Man destroys and negates the contradicted notion, while actually, if one looks at the Inner Light [that is within it], one can understand that this way Man constructs and internalizes it. And so this course proceeds on and on, with the help of feelings and images, until eventually . . . it comes to the highest sublimity, which is the depth of Peace in its developed form, where all the notions, feelings and images are integrated into one organic unit, where each part completes the other and brings it to perfection, and no dissonance is heard.

Blessed is the people that this is his fate, blessed be the people whose God is the Lord.[5] *Blessed is the people that is able to know the Master of the Universe, the King who owns Peace,*[6] *a king who sings, out of love and contentment, a song of agreeable love, the Song of Songs by Solomon.*[7]

Notes

1   The Hebrew word for "contradict" also stands for "destroy" or "abrogate."
2   The Hebrew for Peace (*shalom*) is linked with wholeness and perfection. Here and below, Rabbi Kook alludes to the Kabbalistic conception that God acts in the world through ten "Vessels" (*kelim*, better known as *Sephirot*), which may seem distinct to human eyes but are united in their divine source. According to Kabbalah, this structure is reflected in various fields of reality and particularly in the human soul. Man's role is to ascertain that the Vessels function in harmony ("peace"). This goal is advanced by every Mitzvah, especially if accompanied by mystical understanding (which is often referred to as the "inner" view).
3   "Knowledge" (*Da'at*) is the name of the third "vessel." In the divine realm it is responsible for concentrating the Divine Emanation (or Divine Light, in the Kabbalists' metaphor) which flows from the upper Vessels and spreading it down to the lower Vessels. The equivalent force in the human soul is responsible of uniting the various intellectual notions, internalizing them and attaching them to the lower, emotional capacities.
4   In the Kabbalah, the Abyss (*Tehom*) is the dwelling place of the Evil forces. Rabbi Kook means here that the Peace attained in the realm of the Holy is so powerful that it penetrates even into the realm of Evil.
5   Ps. 144:15. Rabbi Kook means here that the unification of all the contradictions is in God, which is the uppermost level of reality (later referred to as "the Supernal Holy").
6   After Shir ha-Shirim Rabbah, 3:11. The Midrash interprets the name "Solomon" in the Song of Songs (3: 7) as referring to God, "a king who owns Peace." The name Solomon (*Shelomo*) is derived from the same linguistic root as the word Peace.
7   Singing is conceived in Kabbalah as a higher form expression than words, since words confine thought, while music, like mystical insight, leaves it without boundaries. According to this conception, the Kabbalists interpreted the sages' saying: "All

Scriptures are holy, the Song of Songs is the holy of holies" (M. Yad. 3:5). In Rabbi Kook's terminology, "the Holy of Holies" (or the "Supernal Holiness") signifies the uppermost level of reality, the Perfect Good, in which all good is unified, and the seeming contradictions dissolve. See also previous notes.

D.   Rabbi A. Y. Kook on Ideological Diversity and Unity

Here Rabbi Kook applies the position stated above in the metaphysical sphere to conflicts in the social and political arena. Note his belief that all three forces in conflict have a share in the Supernal Holiness, though only a limited and partial share. Everything that expresses aspiration to the Good and sublime is a partial reflection of the Perfect Good, which is the Supernal Holiness. In this sense, secular idealists have religious aspirations, even though they denounce this fact and define their ideals in radically irreligious, and sometimes anti-religious, terms. On the other hand, Orthodoxy, too, even if presumed to represent the ideals of Holiness, is only a partial and limited reflection of the Supernal Holiness.

XVIII

Three forces are wrestling now in our camp. The battle between them is especially discernible in Erets Israel, but their effect draws from the life of the nation at large, and their roots are set within the consciousness penetrating the expanses of human spirit. We should be unfortunate if we allowed these three forces – which must necessarily unite amongst us, to strengthen one the other and perfect it, that each might check the extremism of the other – to remain scattered, mutually antagonistic, and schismatic. The Holy, the Nation, and Humanity – these are the three major demands of which all life, our own and every man's, is composed. However the distribution, whether one element occupies a major or minor portion, it is impossible to find a permanent form of human life that is not composed of these three elements. The desired mixture of these three great demands must arise in every group that aspires to future life. When we observe our lives and see that these forces, despite their potential for synthesis, are increasingly divided, we are called to come to the rescue. The foundation of the schism are the negative aspects that each force views in its counterpart. The "negative aspects" in and of themselves are really not deserving of this title, for in every isolated faculty, especially psychic, there are bound to be drawbacks, specifically when it expands at the expense of other faculties. In this, there is no

Source for reading D.:   Rabbi Abraham Isaac Kook, *Orot*, translated and with an introduction by Bezalel Naor (Northvale: Jason Aronson, 1993), sec. 18, pp. 176–8.

discrimination between the holy and the secular: all must enter under the "line of measure" and all require proportion. "Even the holy spirit which rests on the prophets, rests in proportion." But divisiveness where there should have been unity brings about the gradual emptying of spirit. Positive awareness gradually dissipates because of the intensifying shrinking of that particular faculty, which stubbornly resists the nature of spirit to unite with complementary elements. Instead, a negative awareness comes to nurture life. Then each master of some specific faculty is filled with fiery energy vis-à-vis his negation of the other faculty or faculties that he refuses to recognize. In such a life-style, the situation is terrible, the spirit broken, the position of truth, its inner awareness together with its love, falters and disappears, by virtue of the fact that it (truth) has been parceled.

The three official parties in the life of our nation: one, the Orthodox party, as we are accustomed to call it, which carries the banner of the holy, pitches stridently, jealously, bitterly for Torah and commandments, faith, and all that is holy in Israel; the second, the new Nationalist party, campaigns for all the aspirations of the nationalist tendency, which comprises much of the pure naturalism of the nation, which desires to renew its national life, after it was so long hidden within due to the violence of the bitter exile, and much of that which it absorbed from other nations, which it desires to recognize as positive inasmuch as it deems it fitting for itself (the Jewish People) as well; the third is the Liberal party, which not so long ago carried the banner of Enlightenment, whose influence is still great in wide circles, does not fit into the nationalist scheme and seeks the universal human content of the Enlightenment, culture, ethics, and so forth. It is understood that in a healthy state there is a need for these three forces together, and we must always aspire to come to this healthy state, in which these three forces together will reign in all of their plenitude and goodness, in a whole, harmonious state in which there is neither lack nor superfluity, for the Holy, the Nation and Man, will cleave together in a love lofty and practical. The individuals and also the parties, each of whom finds his talents best suited for one of these three elements, will congregate together in worthy friendship to recognize each the positive mission of his companion. Then this consciousness will be increasingly perfected, until not only will each recognize the positive aspect of each faculty as something worthy to be employed for the general welfare of the synthetic spirit and also for the individual benefit of the establishment of that particular faculty under whose banner he finds himself – but beyond this, the positive content of the negative aspect of each faculty, in proportion, he will recognize as good, and know that for the good of the particular faculty, which he tends to, he must be influenced to a degree by the negating aspect, whereby the other faculty negates this force so dear to him. By negating, it puts in perspective and saves him from the dangerous liability of superfluity and exaggeration. This is that most difficult of rituals in the Temple, kemizah (taking a precise handful of flour), "that he neither add nor detract." Thus when we look intelligently at the eruptions from which we suffer so in our generation, we will know that there is but one way before us: that everyone, whether individual or group, take to heart this lesson, and together with the defensiveness that everyone feels toward that element to which he is attached, by natural temperament and by habit and training, he will know how to use faculties that reside in other persons and parties, in order to round himself and his party, whether through the ratifying aspect of those other faculties or through the good portion of their negating qualities, which truly fortify his particular strength by preserving him from the undoing of exaggeration, which causes weakening and flabbiness. In this manner we can hope to arrive at a state of living worthy of one nation in the land.

It is understood that our lumping of the holy as one of three elements, each of which must sometimes restrain itself in order to leave space for the other, applies only to the technical and practical side of the holy and to the intellectual and emotional sides that relate thereto. However, the essence of supernal holiness is the general subject; this very restraint is part of its task, just as all the tasks that come to perfect the world and life, carry their blessing from the Holy. Therefore the exalted ideal thought, the divine thought, is truly free of all restrictions. Closeness to God is filled always with an expansiveness beyond all borders. *To all I have spied an end – Your commandment is very broad.* When man and nation will stride in the practical and intellectual paths of righteousness, which are hemmed in, they will (eventually) reach the expansive transcendence. *From the strait I called God; God answered me with an expanse.*

E.   Rabbi A. Y. Kook on Secular Zionist Idealism

Rabbi Kook's views regarding the secular Zionists' role in history drove him to an exceedingly tolerant position towards them, often harshly criticized by many Haredim. Even a moderate Haredi leader like the third Rebbe of Gur, Rabbi A.M. Alter, said after he met him that indeed he is "a man of all virtues" but "his love for Zion knows no limits, and [therefore] he says that the impure is pure, and welcomes it." Here, Rabbi Kook explains in what sense the secular idealists' soul is more sublime than that of the Orthodox, and why even their very attack on religion is cherishable and has, paradoxically, a religious value.

Note that "the world of chaos" and "the world of order" are figurative translations for two key-concepts in Lurianic Kabbalah: *Olam ha-Tohu* (approximately: "The World of Primeval Void") and *Olam ha-Tikkun* (approximately: "The World of Mending" or "The World of Restitution"). This Kabbalist

Source for reading E.:   "Souls of Chaos," in Abraham Isaac Kook, *The Lights of Penitance, the Moral Principles, Lights of Holiness, Essays, Letters and Poems*, translation and introduction by Ben-Zion Bokser (New York: Paulist Press, 1978), pp. 256–8.

doctrine maintains that when God created the world, he first emanated his light in all its intensity, creating the *Olam ha-Tohu*. However, this creation failed: The Divine Light was too strong and the Vessels destined to receive it could not resist it and were broken. Sparks of the Light were caught within the broken Vessels, and elements of Good were captured by Evil. In a second attempt to create the world, God emanated the Light in a more limited manner, and this time the Vessels functioned properly, creating our world, *Olam ha-Tikkun*. Here the perfection of the world is not given but needs to be achieved through a long historical process of *Tikkun* (mending, or restitution), in which people have to work for the harmony among the Divine Vessels and to rescue the Divine Sparks. Some later *thinkers* interpreted this doctrine as a metaphor conveying that a readily perfect world is impossible, and the best possible world is a world in which the Divine Good is revealed only in partial, limited appearances. Rabbi Kook asserts that the Souls of *Olam ha-Tohu* are those who wish the Perfect Good in its whole, uncompromising appearance, and that is why they reject any imperfect good in our world. He is aware that their insistence on attaining the impossible Perfect here and now may be harmful and cause a "breaking of the Vessels," but he sees it as a high spiritual level, especially needed in a messianic period.

Souls of Chaos

The conventional pattern of living, based on propriety, on the requisites of good character and conformity to law – this corresponds to the way of the world of order. Every rebellion against this, whether inspired by levity or by the stirring of a higher spirit, reflects the world of chaos. But there is a vast difference in the particular expressions of the world of chaos, whether they incline to the right or the left [positive or negative in motivation]. The great idealists seek an order so noble, so firm and pure, beyond what may be found in the world of reality, and thus they destroy what has been fashioned in conformity to the norms of the world. The best among them also know how to rebuild the world that has thus been destroyed, but those of lesser stature, who have been touched only slightly by the inclination to idealism – they are only destroyers, and they are rooted in the realm of chaos, on its lowest level.

The souls inspired by the realm of chaos are greater than the souls whose affinity is with the established order. They are very great; they seek too much from existence, what is beyond their own faculties to assimilate. They seek a very great light. They cannot bear what is limited, whatever is confined within a prescribed measure. They descended from their divine abode in accordance with the nature of existence to generate new life; they soared on high like a flame and were thrust down. Their endless striving knows no bounds; they robe themselves in various forms, aspiring constantly to what is beyond the measure of the possible. They aspire and they fall, realizing that they are confined in rules, in limiting conditions that forbid expansion toward the unlimited horizons, and they fall in sorrow, in despair, in anger, and anger leads to – wickedness, defiance, destruction and every other evil. Their unrest does not cease – they are represented by the impudent in our generation, wicked men who are dedicated to high principles, those who transgress conventional norms defiantly rather than because of some lust. Their souls are of very high stature; they are illumined by the light that shines from the realm of chaos. They chose destruction and they are engaged in destroying, the world is undermined by them, and they with it. But the essence of their aspiration is a dimension of holiness, that which in souls content with measured progress would yield the vigor of life.

The souls inspired by a destructive zeal reveal themselves especially at the end of days, before the great cataclysm that precedes the emergence of a new and more wondrous level of existence, when the old boundaries expand, just prior to the birth of a norm above the existing norms. In times of redemption insolence is on the increase. A fierce storm rages, more breaches appear, acts of insolence mount continually because they can find no satisfaction in the beneficence offered by the limited light. It does not satisfy all their yearnings, nor does it unravel for them the mystery of existence. They rebel against everything, including also the dimension of the good that could lead them to a great peace and help them rise to great heights. They rebel and they are indignant, they break and they discard; they seek their nourishment in alien pastures, embracing alien ideals and desecrating everything hallowed, but without finding peace.

These passionate souls reveal their strength so that no fence can hold them back; and the weaklings of the established order, who are guided by balance and propriety, are too terrified to tolerate them. Their mood is expressed in Isaiah (33:14): "Who among us can dwell with the devouring fire? Who among us can dwell with those who destroy the world?" But in truth there is no need to be terrified. Only sinners, those weak in spirit and hypocrites, are frightened and seized by terror. Truly heroic spirits know that this force is one of the phenomena needed for the perfection of the world, for strengthening the power of the nation, of man and of the world. Initially this force represents the realm of the chaotic, but in the end it will be taken from the wicked and turned over to the hands of the righteous who will show the truth about perfection and construction, in a great resoluteness, inspired by clear perception and a steady and undimmed sense of the practical.

These storms will bring fructifying rain, these dark clouds will pave the way for great light, as the prophet envisioned it: "And the eyes of the blind shall see out of obscurity and out of darkness" (Isa. 29:18).

F.   Rabbi Avraham Yesha'ayahu Karelitz on Israel as a New Torah Center

By contrast to moderate voices, such as Rabbi Avraham Yitzhak Kook (1865–1935), Yesha'ayahu Karelitz, known as the Hazon Ish (1878–1954), found dialogue with the secular society useless. According to him and his doctrinal partners, the Torah alone had preserved the Jewish people during two thousand years in exile, and the Torah alone could guarantee survival in the future. Putting one's confidence in a fragile and perilous human experiment, like the state of Israel, is a terrible mistake. The Hazon Ish thus is, in many respects, the father of Israeli haredi society. He wrote several volumes of talmudic and Halakhic interpretations under the title *Hazon Ish* (literally: "The Vision of a Man," in which the Hebrew letters ISH form an acronym for Avraham Yesha'ayahu), which gave him his nickname. He also wrote a short, unaccomplished work on faith and trust, disputing the Musar movement's ideas, which was published posthumously. Almost unknown in his Lithuanian fatherland, the Hazon Ish won his fame only after the age of sixty, in Palestine, where he became the most influential Orthodox leader.

The Hazon Ish aspired to build the land of Israel as a new Torah center and instructed the Haredim to focus all efforts on this goal. The following letter shows the great importance he attributed to this enterprise.

Greetings and blessings for the new year.

Your honorable letter has reached me, and I was pleased to read that you are all well. As for the [foundation of the] ——— Yeshivah in ———: I am always very happy about every yeshivah founded in our Holy Land, for we have no other remnant but the Torah, and Yeshivahs are Torah-fortresses. The a.m. yeshivah is, like her fellow yeshivahs, a fortified stronghold for raising disciples and *talmidei hakhamim* [Halakhah-learned men] to become future sages, Torah masters of their generation. Blessed be he who was privileged to take part in building the a.m. yeshivah, for his merit shall last forever.

I repeat my blessings for the new year, a good year as pleased by you and by myself, who always wish you good –

Source for reading F.: Kovetz Igrot [= Collected letters] (Bnei Brak, 1990), vol. III, no. 65, p. 91.

G.   Rabbi Avraham Yesha'ayahu Karelitz on Extremism

The Hazon Ish's policy detached the Haredi society not only from secular Jews but also from their fellow-Orthodox, the Zionist-Religious Jews. He saw them as a "middle-way" ideology, and he used this word in a purely pejorative sense.

The same way that simplicity and truth are synonymous, thus extremity and greatness are. Extremity is the perfection of the subject. He who partisans Middle-Way and mediocrity, and despises extremity, should find his place among falsifiers or reasonless people.

If there is no extremity – there is no perfection, and if there is no perfection – there is no beginning. Beginning is always disturbed with relentless questions and doubts. Naive faith is the sharp response, that clarifies the truth and settles that which is in doubt.

We are accustomed to hear certain circles[1] boasting of not being extremists, and nevertheless do they leave themselves the title of a faithful Jews, loyal to the Torah and its laws. We permit ourselves to remark, from our own point of view, that the same way the lovers of wisdom do not love it only in small amounts and hate it in large ones, thus also the lovers of the Torah and its precepts cannot love the Middle Way and hate extremity.

All the fundamentals of faith, the Thirteen Essentials [of Maimonides] and what entails thereof, are always in a sharp contrast with the easily-accepted ideas and the current-life conventions. The condition of clearly and unquestionably recognizing the truth of the former, which also renders steadfast adherence to them, is the agreeable Extremity, and those who admit to have never tasted the sweetness of Extremity, admit with it that their belief in the fundamentals of our religion is not wholehearted, either because of intellectual or emotional lack, and that they are but slightly bound thereto. Adversely, the extremists, in spite of their deep desire to feel sorry for those who fail to reach the extreme line, do not honor nor cherish their opponents. When the differences come to practical issues, which inevitably cause fights and quarrels, the abyss that separates the two parties grows further large, and the tear-apart is unrecoverable.

The case where the Middle-Way approach has a right of existence is where the Middle-Way men love extremity with all their soul, wish to attain it and bring up their children to aspire to reach this peak. But what a miserable thing is the Middle-Way approach that despises the Extremity.

The duty of our education is to teach Extremity! – The weapon on our armor is the contempt and abhorrence toward those who scorn Extremity. Indeed, the

Source for reading G.:   *Kovetz Igrot*, Bnei Brak, 1990, vol. III, no. 61, pp. 85–7. The translation is partly inspired by: Shimon Finkelman, *The Chazon Ish* (New York, 1989), pp. 218–19.

youths, with their hot temper, do not deter from personally attacking the scorners, often excessively, but their development toward becoming true Torah lovers, which demands spiritual elevation, cannot let any hindrance stand on their way to Heavenly degrees. Those who have established Middle-Way schools were nor successful, because of the forgery inherent to this approach. An intelligent mind shuns this forgery. Their education supplies justifications to the student who turns his back on the laws imposed upon him against his will and to the beliefs that trouble him for being contested to current-life conventions. Such a student had been deprived of the secret weapon of Extremity, his parents and teachers being scornful towards it.

Note

1   I.e., the Zionist religious.

H.   Rabbi Yoel Teitlbaum of Satmar on the Holocaust as Divine Punishment

Rabbi Yoel Teitlbaum of Satmar (1886–1979) fled from the Holocaust to Jerusalem and then to New York. There he rebuilt his Hasidic community, which soon became the greatest Hasidic movement and the leading force of extremist Haredism. In response to the foundation of the State of Israel, he published his anti-Zionist book, *Va-Yoel Moshe* (literally: "And Moses was content," based on Exod. 2:21; the title alludes to the author's first name, Yoel, and to his ancestor, Rabbi Moshe Teitlbaum, the founder of the hasidic dynasty from which the Satmar emerged). The book, conceiving the Holocaust as a divine punishment for the sins of Zionism, became the essential work of radical Haredi anti-Zionism.

During the recent years we have gone through many hardships and sufferings as bitter as wormwood,[1] of measure never known since Israel has become a nation, and "unless the Lord had left us a remnant [behold, we would have been as Sodom, and resembled Gomorrah]."[2]

   ... Now it has always been the Jewish custom, that at every trouble that came up they tried to find out the cause thereof, namely, what sin was it that had brought it forth, so they could come to repent and return to the Lord, as we find in the Bible and the Talmud....

Source for reading H.:   Va-Yoel Moshe (New York, 1961), introduction, pp. 5–6.

...Now in our generation, one doesn't have to dig very far to find out what was the sin that brought this horror upon us, for it is explicitly written in the words of our Sages, based on Scripture. They taught [that the Lord adjured the Children of Israel], that if they breach the oaths – not to surmount the Walls[3] and not to push on the Redemption – "I shall abandon you to be slaughtered as the gazelles and the hinds of the field."[4] And, due to our sins, thus it was. For the heretics and nonbelievers [= the Zionists] made all sorts of endeavors to breach these oaths, to surmount the Walls and to take themselves freedom and sovereignty before time has come, which is the essence of "pushing on the Redemption." And they drew the majority of the Jews to this impure idea.

...And it is explicated in the Talmud, *Shevuot* 39, that in all sins the sinner alone is punished, but in the sin of breach of oath – the punishment is upon the sinner, his family and the entire world. From this saying, that the whole world suffers due to the individual sinner's action, we can learn how severe is the sin of breach of oath. *A fortiori* in this breach of oath, which was made in many actions and in great multitude, for in the last several years it seemed that nearly most of the Jews assisted their actions in various ways, and did it openly and publicly, while but few had the merit of proper protest. This is why this suffering came upon us, which the Sages described as being abandoned to slaughter, God forbid. And [it is said that] "every calamity comes down to the world because of the Wicked, but begins its affliction with the Righteous."[5]

Notes

1 See Prov. 5:4ff.
2 Is. 1:9.
3 I.e., not to carry out a mass immigration.
4 B. Ket. 111a, based on Song 2:7, 3:5, 8:4.
5 See B. B.Q. 60a.

I. Rabbi Joseph Baer Soloveitchik on the Objectivity of Halakha

Rabbi J. B. Soloveitchik (1903–93) was born to a family of renowned Talmudic scholars but received university education in Germany. His philosophy integrates his Lithuanian-Yeshiva sources together with neo-Kantian and existentialist elements. During the 1950s he became the most prominent leader of

Source for reading I.: Rabbi J. B. Soloveitchik, "The Common Sense Rebellion against Torah Authority," in Rabbi Abraham R. Besdin, ed., *Reflections of the Rav*, pp. 143–8.

American Modern Orthodox Judaism. One of his major contributions to modern Jewish thought is his philosophy of halakhah. In contrast to Buber and other modern Jewish thinkers, he maintains that man's aspiration to feel closer to God cannot be exhausted by subjective religious experience. It needs a system of rules that enables him to attach the sublime, but elusive, meeting with his maker to his tangible everyday life. This aim is attained through the halakhah, which Rabbi Soloveitchik perceives as an a priori, objective, quasi-scientific system of categories, through which humanity can apply divine revelation to the world.

The following excerpt was adapted from one of Rabbi Soloveitchik's lectures. As he often does, he explains his point by portraying ideal types. In the previous pages of the lecture, he described the figure of Moses and that of Korah, who rebelled against him (Num. 16), and, as the sages added, challenged him with questions about the rationale of some precepts. In Rabbi Soloveitchik's eyes, Korah represents the personality that sees God's precepts as based on *Daa't*, common-sense rationale, and wishes to fulfill them according to that rationale. Moses, on the other hand, perceives God's Word as "the specialized knowledge ... acquired by extensive and detailed study." Korah's approach represents "religious subjectivism," giving primacy to the "psychological and emotional aspect in the practice of Halakhah" and willing to perform a Mitzvah only insofar as it serves these values. Moses, in contrast, is identified with the Talmudic scholar who sees the value of the Mitzvah in the Mitzvah itself and, through its performance, seeks to evoke religious emotion. The former alludes to non-Orthodox tendencies, while the latter to the type of Orthodox analytical halakhist whom Rabbi Soloveitchik views as a religious ideal.

In response to Korah, we feel it necessary to reaffirm the traditional Jewish position that there are two levels in religious observance, the objective outer *mitzvah* and the subjective inner experience that accompanies it. Both the deed and the feeling constitute the total religious experience; the former without the latter is an incomplete act, an imperfect gesture. We can easily demonstrate that the *Halakhah* values both. In the observance of *keri'at Shema*, of *tefillah*, of *avelut*, of *simhat Yom Tov*, we recite fixed and standardized texts and we perform precise ritual acts. Yet, the real consummation, the *kiyyum*, is realized in the experience, *belev*. The objective *Halakhah* recognizes the emotional response as an essential part of the religious experience.

However, we do not regard the qualitative and subjective experience as primary. Rather, the objective act of performing the *mitzvah* is our starting point. The *mitzvah* does not depend on the emotion; rather, it induces the emotion. One's religious inspiration and fervor are generated and guided by the *mitzvah*, not the reverse. The goal is proper *kavvanah* and genuine *devekut*, but these can be religiously authentic only if they follow the properly performed *mitzvah*. The emotion generated by the *mitzvah* is circumscribed and disciplined by the

Halakhah and its character is not left open to possible distortion by human desires and fantasies. The halakhically defined *mitzvah* has quantitative dimensions and precise perimeters, and these establish the authenticity of the genuinely Jewish religious experience.

This is a *ḥiddush*, an insight which is not commonly understood. The only solid reality is the *mitzvah*, the integrity of which the *Halakhah* can define and control. It is the *mitzvah* act which has been Divinely prescribed and halakhically formulated; emotional responses cannot be so mandated, because, by their very nature, they are not subject to precise definition.

In teaching the *Halakhah* and its proper application, the ḥokhmah dimension of knowledge is decisive; *da'at*, common sense, is insufficient. This was Korah's error, for in the realm of the *Halakhah* only the Torah scholar is the authority and common sense can be misleading.

Why Cannot the Emotions Be Trusted?

Why does the *Halakhah* refuse to give primacy to the emotions, to the inner feelings? Why does it not consider *devekut*, religious fervor, a more genuine and authentic experience than the outward act of performing a *mitzvah*? It is because there are three serious shortcomings in making the religious act dependent on human emotion and sentiment.

First, the religious emotion is volatile, ever-changing, and unstable, even within one individual. To correlate the outward act to the inner emotion would require regular adjustments. The *mitzvah* would continually have to be modified and, at times, nullified in favor of new symbolic acts that would correspond to the person's emotional state. The format and identity of the *mitzvah* would be destroyed and no continuity of identifiable performance would be possible.

Second, each person feels an experience differently. Rituals would continually have to be reformulated to correspond to the feelings of different individuals at different times. What was inspiring to one person might not affect another at all. No community (*Kehillah*) service of God would be possible, since group worship presupposes a unifying constancy. What would be appropriate today would be obsolete tomorrow, and what is appreciated in one community may be unintelligible in another.

This kind of ever-changing worship, which responds to varying sensations, is basically idolatrous. That this was a major point of contention in the argument between Moses and Korah is indicated in the *Tanḥuma* quoted by Rashi (*ibid.* v. 16): "[Moses] said to them: 'According to the custom of the heathens, there are numerous forms of Divine worship and, consequently, numerous priests, for they cannot assemble for worship in one temple. We, however, have one God, one ark, one Law, one altar, all constituting one form of worship'." Communal worship should be constant and not buffeted by the winds of fashion and subject to varying moods of diverse individuals. Moses contended that Korah's emphasis on the primacy of the emotions would destroy the religious identity of the people and result in fragmented sects. The fact that Jews of all times and from different parts of the world are able to worship together – even allowing for minor variations of liturgical custom – is directly due to the constancy of form which is controlled by the *Halakhah*.

Third, we have no reliable gauge to differentiate secular types of response from the genuinely religious experience. There are many non-religious reactions which claim transcendental qualities of holiness. The love impulse, the aesthetic quest of the artist, and, nowadays, the indulgence in potent mind-transforming drugs, can easily be confused with the religious experience. But in fact they are inherently secular and do not reach out beyond the stimulated sense to God. They never transcend man's finite limitations. Pagans in ancient times abandoned themselves to hypnotic trances and orgiastic ceremonies, and mistakenly identified these as religious experiences. The self was never transcended; man starts with himself and does not communicate beyond himself. The Torah, therefore, emphasizes the *mitzvah*, which reflects God's will; it has the stamp of immutability and universality. The great religious romance of man with God, the emotional transport, follows one's observance of the *mitzvah*, not the reverse....

Halakhah as Hokhmah

In Judaism, it is the *mitzvah* which initiates the religious experience. The halakhic legal system, as a *hokhmah*, has its own methodology, mode of analysis, conceptualized rationale, even as do mathematics and physics. An analogy with science would be helpful here. Aristotelean physics, which dominated the ancient and medieval world, was in some instances faulty precisely because it relied on common-sense experiences. It maintained that an object falls because it has weight, which seems outwardly reasonable but which Galileo and Newton showed to be wrong. They replaced common-sense, surface judgments by scientific laws, a picture of reality which differs from surface appearances. What are heat, sound and matter but creations of the human mind in mathematical terms? These are qualities which we perceive with our senses, but their real identity is defined in conceptual, not empirical terms.

Similarly, the Oral Law has its own epistemological approach, which can be understood only by a *lamdan* who has mastered its methodology and its abundant material. Just as mathematics is more than a group of equations, and physics is more than a collection of natural laws, so, too, the *Halakhah* is more than a compilation of religious laws. It has its own *logos* and method of thinking and is an autonomous self-integrated system. The *Halakhah* need not make common sense any more than mathematics and scientific conceptualized systems need to accommodate themselves to common sense.

When people talk of a meaningful *Halakhah*, of unfreezing the *Halakhah* or of an empirical *Halakhah*, they are basically proposing Korah's approach. Lacking a knowledge of halakhic methodology, which can only be achieved through extensive study, they instead apply common-sense reasoning which is replete with platitudes and clichés. As in Aristotelean physics, they judge phenomena solely from surface appearances and note only the subjective sensations of worshippers. This *da'at* approach is not tolerated in science, and it should not receive serious credence in *Halakhah*. Such judgments are pseudo-statements, lacking sophistication about depth relationships and meanings.

The approach of Moses prevailed. The survivors of the catastrophe which befell Korah's group later conceded that, in the words of our Sages, "Moses is truth and his interpretation of Torah is truth – and we are liars" (B. B.B. 74a). This judgment is still valid. In our day, we are witnessing a resurgence of strength among those religious groups that are committed to the Oral Law as a *ḥokhmah*, and who therefore recognize Torah scholars, *Gedole Yisrael*, as the legitimate teachers of Israel. Common sense can only spread confusion and havoc when applied to the *Halakhah*, as it does with all specialized disciplines.

J. Rabbi Menahem Mendl Schneerssohn of Lubavitch

The Rebbe of Lubavitch (1902–94) was born in Russia, studied in Germany and France, and then arrived at the United States. Married to his predecessor's second daughter, Rabbi Menahem Mendl became a rebbe after a short heredity struggle with his brother-in-law. Under his leadership, the Habad (Lubavitch) movement gained an unprecedented worldwide audience. His collected discourses and letters were published in voluminous series. The following discourse is from his last year of activity and presents some of his typical motifs: His acute anticipation of "Moshiach [= messiah] Now," his hasidic optimism, his belief in relative progress, and his care for the spiritual advancement of the gentiles besides that of Jews. It also exemplifies the Habad way of interpreting worldly phenomena as reflecting higher, spiritual processes, through the use of kabbalistic concepts.

Recently it has often been spoken[1] about the fact that according to all signs our generation is the last generation of Exile, and consequently the first generation of Redemption, for we have completed all the process of discernment [of Good from Evil][2] and are prepared for the true and whole Salvation by our Messiah, indeed right away.

Source for reading J.: A discourse from the 23rd of Kislev 5752 [= 1992], published in *D'var Malkhut* [= King's Word], for Vayeshev–Hanukkah, 5758 [=1997], by Otzar ha-Hasidim, KEHAT publication, 770 Eastern Parkway, New York.

Some ask: the Redemption necessitates that the whole world is prepared for it, not only one person or one group of people in one part of the world; for Redemption includes the gathering of desolate Jews from the four fringes of earth, as well as [the accomplishment of] the process of discernment among the gentiles, too. Where, then, do we see such a change in the world, that may show more preparedness than in generations before?

This can be understood if we first clarify the reason for the Jews' wandering from place to place.

The dispersion of Jews in various countries worldwide (the Jewish people is characterized as "scattered and dispersed among the peoples"[3]) is in external view a descent, and as much as the dispersion is greater, the descent is lower. Yet, we read the Sages' words: "It was God's grace that the Jews were dispersed among the nations."[4] The inner [= mystical] interpretation of this is well known: Wherever Jews arrive, they adopt the manners of the place (those which are halakhically permitted), use the country language in secular matters etc. ... But these customs later are used to serve religious purposes, and thus are elevated to become a part of the worship of God.

In Hasidic terms ... the fact that God exiled Israel in various places in the world, was in order to have them discern, purify and elevate the captive Sparks of Divine Light that are in each and every place. This is why "It was God's grace that the Jews were dispersed among the nations;" because through this dispersion they gained a higher degree of the Worship of God, the merit of redeeming the Sparks that dwell in the customs of *all* countries and *all* places.

... According to this we can now understand the ascent of our generation compared to generations before. In previous generations there was no such large dispersion of the Jews in all fringes of the world as it is today. Certainly this wasn't the situation when the Temple existed and the Children of Israel were in and around the Land of Israel, but also in the first generations of exile, when Jews resided only in certain countries, and anyhow only in the Northern hemisphere; In later generations, though, they dispersed in many more countries, and reached even the Southern hemisphere (in America, etc.). In each generation we see a further advancement of this process until in our time we see its peak, as Jews can be found indeed in all parts of the globe, keeping the Torah and its precepts while acting in the customs of the place, including the establishment of Torah institutions everywhere.

When we observe this – even momentarily – we can see the ascent of our generation compared to previous generations, which notes the [advancement of the] process of discernment and the elevation of all the countries of the world.

Now according to the signs mentioned above (and several times before), the process of discernment has been completed, and hence it is clear why we are already facing Redemption in our day.

Notes

1   By the rebbe himself.
2   According to many views in Kabbalah and Hasidism, Evil has no existence of its own, and the only way it can exist is by parasitically attaching to the Good. At present, the world is in a state of Good and Evil mixed together, and this is why Evil still exists. The task laid upon humans is to discern Good from Evil and thus to free Good from the attachment of Evil and have Evil fade out. This process of *Beirur* [= "discernment"] is gradually achieved in history, and its accomplishment is the expected Redemption. In kabbalistic symbolism, the units of Good are described as Sparks of the Divine Light scattered in the world, and those of Evil, as Peels that cover them. The Sparks are, then, captured by the Peels, and our role is to discern them from one another and elevate the Sparks back to their divine source. Holy Sparks might be laid not only in the hands of Evil but in all parts of the world.
3   Esther 3:8.
4   See B. Pes. 87b.

K.   Yesha'ayahu Leibowitz on Science and Jewish Religion

Professor Leibowitz (1903–94) was born in Riga, Latvia, and obtained a scientific education in Germany. After his immigration to Palestine, he was involved in political discussions and became widely known for his provocative statements. He published books on scientific and philosophical issues, but the best known are his collected essays on theological, social, and political questions. The following text is taken from his lecture at the Eleventh Annual Convention of Jewish Thought, which was dedicated to the subject of "science and Jewish religion."

We should use a typology that distinguishes the anthropocentric religion[1] from the theocentric religion,[2] and the question at stake [of science versus religion] can only be posed from the viewpoint of anthropocentric religion.

We can find the common denominator of all religions in their determination of Man's stance before God. The anthropocentric religion conceives this stance in view of human needs or values, and here the distinction between needs and values becomes vague. Its motto, as well as its purpose, is "Salvation," the salvation of Man – and God is a means for this end. Adversely, the motto of theocentric religion is "Worship," the Worship of God by Man, and its purpose is

Source for reading K.: "Science and Jewish Religion," in *Yehadut, Am Yehudi u-Medinat Israel* [= Judaism, Jewish People and the State of Israel] (Jerusalem and Tel Aviv: Mosad Bialik, 1979), pp. 337–46.

phrased in the first article of the Shulhan Arukh: "One must collect strength and stand up in the morning to serve his Creator." Against the religion that is perceived in view of what it endows Man, there is the religion which is perceived in view of what it demands from Man. And there is no greater contrast than this.

Since many generations, it is customary in Judaism to regard as the foremost symbol of faith the act of the only man about whom Scripture says that he "believed in the Lord:"[3] "Now do I know that you are a God-fearing man, seeing that you did not withhold your son, your only son, from me."[4] On the other hand, the foremost symbol of the other religion is the Cross – the sacrifice that God brought to Man, offering His own son for Man's sake.

The satisfaction of human need or human value can appear in many levels, starting with the stomach and sexuality and ending with the elevation of the soul or the amendation of Man. From a religious point of view, there is no difference between all these: whether religion is "needed" to man – ... for "life, sons, food"[5] or God is "needed" as a guarantee of Morality, as it is in the theory of the great Jew Hermann Cohen – in all these approaches, Man actually worships himself, and God is but a means for him. Only from this conception of religion there is an encounter between science and religion, where the question asked regarding religion is: What can it contribute to Man in the sphere of information, i.e. what information on the world and what explanations of it can religion provide? – what scientific benefit can Man draw from Faith? – hence they stem, the problems of confronting the information provided by religion with the information provided by scientific research.

Adversely, it is customary in Judaism to write over the ark in every synagogue the verse: "I have set the Lord always before me."[6] This means: not that I always set Man before me, not that I always set the world before me. A religion that satisfies a need, regardless what sort of need – whether of the stomach or the soul, whether physical or spiritual – is not the Worship of God but the worship of Man himself, or Man's society or Mankind as a whole. However, it is not the worship of God. Judaism's three thousand year history cannot be understood without this aspect of undertaking the Kingdom of God through undertaking the yoke of the Torah and its precepts.

... Judaism, being the religion of Torah and precepts as manifested in the Halakha, is a demand posited by man, not an information delivered to him. . . . Scientific knowledge of Nature or history is psychologically imposed upon anyone who understands it, and one is not free to accept or reject it. Religious consciousness, however, is Man's own free decision to undertake the subjection to the Kingdom of God and the yoke of the Torah and its precepts.

... From the point of view held by the Jewish religious person, who conceives Judaism as the submission to the Kingdom of God, and its manifestation as the endeavor to observe the laws of Halakha, the confrontation between science and religion does not exist. . . . in fact, no scientific knowledge has ever been actually drawn from religion, and moreover, a person who recognizes religion as the Worship of God must not expect religion to provide him scientific information.

All which is phrased in the Torah in the form of information on Man, on Nature, on history or on the world – are none but the various forms and manifestations of that which cannot be said at all: The stance of Man before God and his duty to serve Him.

Notes

1   Namely, a human-centered religion. We will now see that Leibowitz perceives Christianity as an example of such a religion.
2   Namely, a God-centered religion. Leibowitz clearly refers to what he perceives as the ideal of Judaism.
3   See Gen. 15:6. Reference is to Abraham.
4   Gen. 22:12.
5   See B. M.Q. 28a, an expression often quoted in Hasidism. Leibowitz is aware that what he calls the anthropocentric approach has appeared in historical Judaism. He often stresses that Judaism accepted this type of faith only as a compromise, while its ultimate ideal has been the worship of God *Lishma* [= for its own sake].
6   Ps. 16:8.

Chapter 18

Conservative Judaism: The Struggle between Ideology and Popularity

Daniel Gordis

The documents of the Conservative movement presented here reflect the recent struggles of Conservative Judaism for self-definition. While many fascinating documents from the late nineteenth and early twentieth century shed light on the movement as it exists today, our desire is to portray Conservative Judaism as a living entity and to understand the world of Conservative Judaism as it exists today, to illustrate, for instance, the tensions between "folk" and "elite," "tradition" and "change," "popularity" and "ideology" that are still so apparent in Consevative practice and thinking.

   Keep in mind that these are only excerpts. At times, an ellipsis indicates that only a few words were omitted, but, in other cases, the same symbol is used when several pages were skipped. To get the best possible sense of these documents, it is always best, of course, to seek out the originals and to read them carefully.

A. Emet Ve-Emunah – A Statement of Principles

Emet Ve-Emunah was composed in 1988 as an attempt to delineate the basic components of Conservative Jewish belief. In the years since its appearance, it has been both widely praised for its conciseness and sharply critiqued for its seeming inability to take one particular stance and to adhere to it. Nonetheless, it remains the single most commonly cited Statement of Principles of the Conservative movement. As you read the following sections, ask yourself: Does the statement on revelation appeal to the reader's "soul" or intellect? What is the impact of having a movement's central statement include

Source for Reading A.: Robert Gordis, ed., *Emet Ve-Emunah: Statement of Principles of Conservative Judaism* (New York: Jewish Theological Seminary of America, 1988).

phrases like "some of us" and "others of us"? Is the language here meantto explain or to motivate? What is the nature of the "religious" Conservative Jew as it emerges from this passage? As you survey the section on the "Ideal Conservative Jew," ask yourself: What are the major challenges, both internal and external, that the leadership of the Conservative movement believes its members face? How does Conservative Judaism propose to address those challenges? Would the other movements agree or disagree with the three major elements that comprise the "ideal Conservative Jew" as described here?

Revelation

The nature of revelation and its meaning for the Jewish people, have been understood in various ways within the Conservative community. We believe that the classical sources of Judaism provide ample precedents for these views of revelation....

Some of us conceive of revelation as the personal encounter between God and human beings. Among them there are those who believe that this personal encounter has propositional content, that God communicated with us in actual words. For them, revelation's content is immediately normative, as defined by rabbinic interpretation. The commandments of the Torah themselves issue directly from God. Others, however, believe that revelation consists of an ineffable human encounter with God. The experience of revelation inspires the verbal formulation by human beings of norms and ideas, thus continuing the historical influence of this revelational encounter.

Others among us conceive of revelation as the continuing discovery, through nature and history, of truths about God and the world. These truths, although always culturally conditioned, are nevertheless seen as God's ultimate purpose for creation. Proponents of this view tend to see revelation as an ongoing process rather than as a specific event.

Halakhah

Halakhah consists of the norms taught by the Jewish tradition, how one is to live as a Jew.... Since each age requires new interpretations and applications of the received norms, Halakhah is an ongoing process. It is thus both an ancient tradition, rooted in the experience and texts of our ancestors, and a contemporary way of life, giving value, shape, and direction to our lives.

For many Conservative Jews, Halakhah is indispensable first and foremost because it is what the Jewish community understands God's will to be. Moreover, it is a concrete expression of our ongoing encounter with God. This divine element of Jewish law is understood in varying ways within the Conservative community, but, however it is understood, it is for many the primary rationale for obeying Halakhah, the reason that undergirds all the rest. . . .

We in the Conservative community are committed to carrying on the rabbinic tradition of preserving and enhancing Halakhah by making appropriate changes in it through rabbinic decision. This flows from our conviction that Halakhah is indispensable for each age. As in the past, the nature and number of adjustments of the law will vary with the degree of change in the environment in which Jews live. The rapid technological and social change of our time, as well as new ethical insights and goals, have required new interpretations and applications of Halakhah to keep it vital for our lives; more adjustments will undoubtedly be necessary in the future. These include additions to the received tradition to deal with new circumstances and, in some cases, modifications of the corpus of Halakhah.

While change is both a traditional and a necessary part of Halakhah, we, like our ancestors, are not committed to change for its own sake. Hence, the thrust of the Jewish tradition and the Conservative community is to maintain the law and practices of the past as much as possible, and the burden of proof is on the one who wants to alter them. Halakhah has responded and must continue to respond to changing conditions, sometimes through alteration of the law and sometimes by standing firm against passing fads and skewed values. Moreover, the necessity for change does not justify any particular proposal for revision. Each suggestion cannot be treated mechanically but must rather be judged in its own terms, a process which requires thorough knowledge of both Halakhah and the contemporary scene as well as carefully honed skills of judgment.

Following the example of our rabbinic predecessors over the ages, however, we consider instituting changes for a variety of reasons. Occasionally the integrity of the law must be maintained by adjusting it to conform to contemporary practice among observant Jews. Every legal system from time to time must adjust what is on the books to be in line with actual practice if the law is to be taken seriously as a guide to conduct. New technological, social, economic, or political realities sometimes require legal action. Some changes in law are designed to improve the material conditions of the Jewish people or society at large. The goal of others is to foster better relations among Jews or between Jews and the larger community. In some cases changes are necessary to prevent or remove injustice, while in others they constitute a positive program to enhance the quality of Jewish life by elevating its moral standards or deepening its piety.

The Ideal Conservative Jew

Throughout most of its history, Jewish life was an organic unity of home and community, synagogue and law. Since the Emancipation, however, Judaism has been marked by increasing fragmentation. Not only do we find Jewish groups pitted against one another, but the ways in which we apprehend Judaism itself have become separate and distinct. That unified platform upon which a holistic Jewish life was lived has been shattered. Participating in a majority culture whose patterns and rhythms often undermine our own, we are forced to live in two worlds, replacing whole and organic Judaism with fragments: ritual observance or Zionism, philanthropy or group defense; each necessary, none sufficient in itself.

Facing this reality, Conservative Judaism came into being to create a new synthesis in Jewish life. Rather than advocate assimilation, or yearn for the isolation of a new ghetto, Conservative Judaism is a creative force through which modernity and tradition inform and reshape each other....

Three characteristics mark the ideal Conservative Jew. First, he or she is a willing Jew, whose life echoes the dictum, "Nothing human or Jewish is alien to me." This willingness involves not only a commitment to observe the *mitzvot* and to advance Jewish concerns, but to refract all aspects of life through the prism of one's own Jewishness. That person's life pulsates with the rhythms of daily worship and Shabbat and *Yom Tov*. The moral imperatives of our tradition impel, that individual to universal concern and deeds of social justice. The content of that person's professional dealings and communal involvements is shaped by the values of our faith and conditioned by the observance of *kashrut*, of Shabbat and the holidays. That person's home is filled with Jewish books, art, music and ritual objects. Particularly in view of the increasing instability of the modern family, the Jewish home must be sustained and guided by the ethical insights of our heritage.

The second mark of the ideal Conservative Jew is that he or she is a learning Jew. One who cannot read Hebrew is denied the full exaltation of our Jewish worship and literary heritage. One who is ignorant of our classics cannot be affected by their message. One who is not acquainted with contemporary Jewish thought and events will be blind to the challenges and opportunities which lie before us. Jewish learning is a lifelong quest through which we integrate Jewish and general knowledge for the sake of personal enrichment, group creativity and world transformation. Finally, the ideal Conservative Jew is a *striving* Jew. No matter the level at which one starts, no matter the heights of piety and knowledge one attains, no one can perform all 613 *mitzvot* or acquire all Jewish knowledge. What is needed is an openness to those observances one has yet to perform and the desire to grapple with those issues and texts one has yet to confront. Complacency is the mother of stagnation and the antithesis of Conservative Judaism.

Given our changing world, finality and certainty are illusory at best, destructive at worst. Rather than claiming to have found a goal at the end of the road, the ideal Conservative Jew is a traveler walking purposefully towards "God's holy mountain."

B.   A Responsum on Sabbath Observance

Having now read a more theoretical exposition on the nature of Conservative Judaism, we can turn our attention to that area that most regularly reflects the tensions and commitments of Conservative Jewish life, the realm of change in Jewish law. We begin with the classic statement that advocated permitting Conservative Jews to drive in an automobile to Sabbath services, an issue. Read not only the answer, but the question as well. The way that the rabbi in question poses his dilemma speaks volumes about the world he serves, the world of the "folk" as opposed to that of the religious "elite."

The Question

As a rabbi in Israel, I turn to you, my Colleagues, for assistance in a question both theoretic and practical which has caused me concern and anxiety. One cannot serve a congregation for any time without being depressed and disheartened by the widespread disintegration of Sabbath observance among our people. This breakdown of one of the major institutions in Jewish life is too deep and too prevalent to be countered by preachment and exhortations. Sermons declaring the pre-eminence of the Sabbath in Jewish life, or extolling its spiritual beauty and social significance are politely received by our congregants but exert no influence on their practices or habits.

Yet the American Jew is not innately resistant to religious forms and values. I find among many in my congregation a fine receptivity to Jewish teaching and a marked interest in Jewish affairs. Some recognize the lack of spiritual satisfactions in their present mode of living and evince eagerness not alone for instruction in Jewish ideas but likewise for guidance in their practical conduct as Jews.

They are Jews who not only have been born into the modern, industrial world, but have also been educated in its institutions and have been mentally and psychologically shaped and moulded by its approaches, attitudes and activities. To ignore this fact and to speak to them as if they were the identical counterparts of their East European forbears is to engage in futile rhetoric. On the other hand, to overlook the spiritual alertness and interest as well as the healthy Jewish pride and desire for Jewish identification which motivate them, is to doom to atrophy those characteristics which hold forth greatest promise for the future of American Jewish life. To do nothing, or to mouth easy formulas that have a respectable past behind them, is to abandon to the haphazard forces of the pervasive secular environment much of the richest potential for Jewish living in this land.

Source for Reading B.:   Mordechai Waxman, *Tradition and Change* (New York: Rabbinical Assembly and United Synagogue of Conservative Judaism, 1958), pp. 351 ff.

I know, dear Colleagues, that the question of the Sabbath, as indeed of Jewish religious life, has agitated you as it has disturbed every earnest and thinking Jew. It cannot be met on a level of individual action since the problem is far too aggravated for such a necessarily fragmentary approach to it. In addition, were every rabbi to work in terms of his individual judgment, the confusion and disharmony in our midst would be greatly intensified.

Our Conservative movement must marshal its forces to meet the problem I have described. I therefore turn to you to ask for guidance in instructing my people as to our view as a movement on the Sabbath disciplines, our best thought as to its proper observance and a practical program by which its meaning may be better understood, its spirit more widely shared, its sanctities more greatly respected by the congregations that look to us, as Conservative rabbis, for guidance and instruction.

The Response

A program for the revitalization of Sabbath observance must seriously reckon with the realities of modern life. These realities as they relate to Sabbath observance possess a twofold character, economic and spiritual. It is the merest truism to state that the overwhelming majority of our people are not presently spiritually prepared to forego the opportunity for economic advancement in favor of Sabbath observance. It is equally true that in many instances the abandonment of work on the Sabbath would entail a complete disruption of a family's economic basis. Any program for Sabbath observance in our time that does not honestly reckon with these facts is doomed to futility. However, we should continue to hold out as our ultimate objective observance of the Sabbath by cessation from all gainful employment; an objective that a shift in circumstance, such as the universal adoption of the five-day working week, may permit an increasing number of our people to realize. In our efforts in behalf of the program that we propose, this ultimate goal must be made both vivid and explicit. But that goal will lose its contact with reality unless, in the meantime, we keep alive in the lives of our people, through a positive program, the sense of the sanctity and high spiritual value of the Sabbath. So, then, one must begin with our people in the situation, economic, social and spiritual, in which they presently find themselves. A journey around the world begins with a single step.

The program that we propose, then, is not to be regarded as the full and complete regimen of Sabbath observance, valid for all Jews for all times and for all places. On the contrary, it is aimed to meet the particular situation that confronts us, a situation without parallel in the long annals of Judaism. Our program seeks to reintroduce into the lives of our people as much Sabbath observance and spirit as we may reasonably hope our people will, with proper education, accept...

Refraining from the use of a motor vehicle is an important aid in the maintenance of the Sabbath spirit of repose. Such restraint aids, moreover, in keeping the members of the family together on the Sabbath. However, where a family resides beyond reasonable walking distance from the synagogue, the use of a motor vehicle for the purpose of synagogue attendance shall in no wise be construed as a violation of the Sabbath but, on the contrary, such attendance shall be deemed an expression of loyalty to our faith.

We are well aware in, the above connection, that in accordance with Jewish law one may worship at home as well as in the synagogue. We are equally aware, however, that the practice of private prayer has unfortunately fallen into such disuse that only the very minimal number of people engage in prayer unless it be at a synagogue service. Indeed, it is a well-grounded supposition that were it not for synagogue attendance on the Sabbath, there would be no prayer for most of our people from the end of one week to the other. Moreover, when almost every Jew had some measure of competence in understanding the Torah and our sacred literature, many Jews could and did spend some time in studying Torah. Today, however, this condition no longer obtains. The average Jew's knowledge of Torah and his Jewish information are gained through the synagogue and in great measure through the sermon which both instructs and inspires our people to live in accordance with our faith. Hence, in our time regular attendance at the synagogue has become a sine qua non for the maintenance of Judaism. We [therefore] state in our program for the revitalization of the Sabbath that the traditional interdiction of riding on the Sabbath for the purpose of attending the synagogue service may, in the discretion of the local rabbi, be modified under the conditions we have described above.

C.   Joel Roth: Faculty Paper Urging the Ordination of Women

Unlike Orthodoxy, which – because of its claim that Jewish law does not change – cannot seriously entertain the possibility of ordaining women, or Reform, which did not need to justify the move in halakhic terms, the Conservative movement felt both constrained by Jewish law *and* obliged to consider seriously the moral moment of this issue. When the Jewish Theological Seminary began to seriously consider the issue in the early 1980s, Seminary faculty were asked to author papers on the subject. Professor Joel Roth, a member of the Talmud department, wrote a paper that ultimately became the basis on which the Chancellor of the Seminary authorized the ordination of women.

Much of Roth's argument centers on the traditional exemption of women from what are called "positive time-bound commandments," that is, rituals that are "do's" as opposed to "do not's" and that must be performed at a fixed time. Women are traditionally exempted from this category of commandments,

Source for Reading C.:   In: Simon Greenberg, ed., *On the Ordination of Women as Rabbis* (New York: Jewish Theological Seminary of America, 1988), pp. 127 ff.

which includes prayer, and it is in light of this exclusion from the requirement for regular prayer that traditional arguments further hold that they cannot lead the community in prayer. Roth's paper is a rigorous attempt to deal with that objection. As you read this excerpt, ask yourself whether Roth's tone is similar to or different from that of the previous readings and in what ways. What animates Roth's interest in the issue, and does his language sound like the kind of discourse that would speak in a compelling fashion to lay people?

The exemption of women from positive time-bound commandments has been variously rationalized. Some have affirmed that the exemption is intended to emphasize the centrality of the woman's role in relation to her husband, the home, and the family. That function is so central that the observance of *mitzvot* which might conflict with it is suspended because of it. Others contend that women have been exempted from such *mitzvot* because they have an innate religious sensitivity which makes their observance unnecessary. Whether either of these rationalizations is correct is of little moment to our present inquiry. Suffice it to say, that whatever the reason for the traditional exemption of women the exemption itself has had the long-standing weight of precedent to support it. . . .

I am opposed to two alternatives which are often proposed. The first alternative recommends the adoption of a [rabbinic decree] obligating all women to observe all *mitzvot* from which they are exempt. The second alternative recommends a pronouncement affirming that women should refrain from the observance of those mitzvot from which they are exempt, even if they may have the legal right to observe them. I am opposed to the issuance of a [rabbinic decree] because the imposition of legal obligation [this decree] would make noncompliance with the dictates of that [decree] sinful. That would result in the creation of a large class of sinners where none now exists. I dread the thought that the Faculty of the Seminary, or any other segment of the Conservative Movement, should seek to impose a set of obligations not already recognized by the tradition upon any woman who is satisfied with the *status quo*.

On the other hand, there is an ever increasing number of Jewish women who see their roles differently, if not for their entire lives, then at least for significant segments of their lives. If such women view the traditional exemption as based upon the claim of the mother's familial centrality, they may yearn greatly to be more active participants in Jewish religious life during the years that they are not actively "mothering." Indeed, many may find it possible to remain equally religiously active even during peak periods of "mothering." If women are capable of holding full-time and responsible jobs without serious encroachment on their familial responsibilities, there is no reason to believe that the "onus" of the observance of positive time-bound commandments would become the "straw that broke the camel's back." If such women see the traditional exemption as based upon the innate female religious sensitivity, they may choose to abide by the traditional patterns. But many women do not perceive themselves as more sensitive religiously than their male counterparts. In the final analysis, it is their own perception of their need for *mitzvot* which is most important.

Women who wish to observe *mitzvot* should be given every encouragement to do so, since there is sufficient legal precedence. At present, regrettably, such women are subjected to the most virulent type of vilification by two very different groups. Observant men have looked so askance at women who have adopted the observance of *mitzvot* from which they are exempt, that they give the impression that their behavior must be forbidden. The very people to whom such women turn for assurance that their behavior falls within legal parameters, for that is a great concern of many of them, give the opposite impression by merely tolerating their behavior, even if they do not actively attempt to discourage it.

These women, too, are often castigated by women who accept their traditional exemption from *mitzvot*. They are told either that they are trying to be like men or that they are allowing men to dictate what women should be. To the best of my knowledge and observation, these women are motivated, by and large, by purely religious motives. That does not imply that they were not at all affected by the spirit that animates the various women's or feminist movements.

Women must be allowed to increase their patterns of religious observance without hindrance from men or other women. Indeed, since their observance of *mitzvot* is permissible, there is no reason why they should not be encouraged in their quest, if that is the path they have chosen.

To be sure, it must be made absolutely clear to all women who adopt the observance of *mitzvot* that there is often more involved than observance alone. That is particularly true either where a *minyan* is needed or where the issue of agency is involved. They must understand that only obligated individuals constitute a quorum and only one who is obligated can serve as the agent for others. Just because a woman comes to services, or dons *tallit* and *tefillin*, or receives an *aliyah* does not mean she has the right to be counted toward a *minyan* or to act as agent in behalf of one who is obligated to perform a *mitzvah*.

Women may be counted in a *minyan* or serve as *shatz* [prayer-leader] only when they have accepted upon themselves the voluntary obligation to pray as required by the law, and at the times required by law, and only when they recognize and affirm that failure to comply with the obligation is sin. Then they may be counted in the quorum and serve as the agents for others. This is the position which I would recommend to the Faculty for adoption.

I anticipate that objections of various sorts will be raised against this recommendation, and would like to respond in advance to those objections which I foresee.

How can I require women to accept a voluntary obligation and recognize the consequence of noncompliance as sin when the concepts of "obligation" and "sin" are rarely mentioned by men? How can I count men in a *minyan* if they show up at services sporadically, never praying otherwise, and surely not viewing their regular failure to pray as sin in any way, yet refuse to count toward a *minyan* any woman who comes every day in order to say *kaddish*, or even without saying *kaddish*, but refuses to recognize the sinful nature of her noncompliance if she ever fails to pray?

I answer that I am fully aware of these realities, but my concern is for the halakhic status of behaviors, not for the common misconceptions of the halakhic status of those behaviors. If we have failed to educate our constituents that, from our perspective, obedience to Jewish law is obligatory and not voluntary, that does not deny that it is, in fact, obligatory. A man is obligated to pray whether or not he recognizes that obligation. Any time he does pray he complies with the obligation and can be counted toward the quorum. When he does not pray at the required times he sins whether or not he recognizes that failure as sin.

The halakhic status of a woman's prayer is very different. She can be considered obligated, and count toward the *minyan*, only when she accepts the status of obligation upon herself. Her obligation is self-imposed, and not other-imposed. It requires *recognition* of the obligatory state, and that, in turn, demands conscious recognition of the consequences of failure to comply with the obligation. The consequences are called sin. Only when those elements are present can she be considered legally obligated. If a woman prays without considering herself obligated, she exercises a right of hers, but does not fulfill an obligation. A prayer quorum requires people who are obligated, not people who are exercising a right. Whenever men pray they are fulfilling an obligation; women, though, may pray as the exercise of a right, as opposed to the fulfillment of an obligation. Thus, men always count toward a *minyan*, but women may not....

Before offering a specific proposal for consideration, I would like to emphasize as strongly as I can that the issue of male–female equality plays no part in my thinking on the subject. I find no ethical objection to discrimination against an entire class, when the discrimination is justified and defensible. I have made it quite clear, I hope, that I would be opposed to any argument for women's ritual rights which was predicated on an *a priori* claim that men and women must be equal. Testimonial equality between men and women may be the *result* of grappling with the issue of women and testifying, but it is not its underlying motivation. I reiterate that for me the underlying motivation for the difficult struggle is the firm conviction that the grounds for the disqualification of women as witnesses, which grounds are, in my opinion, the only possible continuing justification of the proscriptive norm, are no longer applicable. It is simply inconceivable to me that anyone could cogently argue that modern women are generally unreliable as witnesses, that the entire class of women should be disqualified. If ever a claim of "times have changed" is appropriate, surely it is so regarding the rabbinic perception of the character of women...

We have demonstrated...that there are no insurmountable halakhic objections to the granting of ordination per se to women.

D.   Elliot Dorff: Position Paper on Homosexuality and Sexual Ethics

The next major halakhic issue the Conservative movement is likely to face is that of the status of gays and lesbians, including matters such as commitment ceremonies for gay and lesbian couples as well as admission of gays and lesbians into the movement's rabbinical schools. When this issue first came to the fore in a powerful way, leaders of the movement asked Rabbi Elliot Dorff, a Conservative thinker, to author a monograph on the subject of human sexuality. The following are excepts from his efforts. As you read, you will encounter references to the role of science in halakhah as well as an implicit approach to change in Jewish law. As we have seen, these are both central areas of interest in the formulation of the Conservative approach to Judaism.

Whatever the specific grounds which led people to this view, those who held it opposed instituting commitment ceremonies for homosexuals, or sexually active homosexuals as rabbis, or investing them as cantors. Some within this group also thought that sexually active homosexuals should not be granted honors in the synagogue or be allowed to serve as youth leaders or teachers.

Others within the Committee on Jewish Law and Standards took a different view. They recognized that not all those who have homoerotic feelings or engage in homosexual episodes in their teenage years are homosexual in orientation and that sexual orientation spans a spectrum from those who are totally heterosexual to those who are totally homosexual. Still, new scientific findings and, more importantly, the testimony of homosexuals themselves provide us with ample evidence that those who are clearly homosexual do not choose to be so. On the contrary, they generally have intimations of their orientation early in their lives and often do everything in their power to convince themselves otherwise so as to avoid the stigma and prejudice which society inflicts on homosexuals. This often includes heterosexual dating and behavior and sometimes even marriage and children.

Since legal demands or prohibitions only make logical sense if the people being commanded can fulfill them, and since the Torah and Jewish tradition clearly assumed the homosexual's ability to choose to be heterosexual, this group within the Law Committee declared that homosexuality should no longer be considered an abomination, for that implies that the person could choose to do otherwise. In addition, they argued, since all of the relevant professional organizations and

Source for Reading D.: *"This Is My Beloved, This Is My Friend": A Rabbinic Letter on Intimate Relations* (New York: Rabbinical Assembly, 1996).

most mental health professionals assert that sexual orientation is ingrained in a person from an early age and cannot be changed, homosexuals do not pose a threat to heterosexual, family life. Furthermore, recommending celibacy for homosexuals is, in the view of this group, cruel and, moreover, not in accord with classical Jewish views of the body and sexuality as God's gift whose legitimate pleasures it is a sin to deny.

In light of all these factors, this latter group maintained that our moral and legal assessment of homosexuality should change. Specifically, homosexuality should no longer be considered an abomination, and all halakhic disabilities should be removed. For those who accept this view, the same Jewish norms governing heterosexual relationships would govern homosexual sex, including all of the concepts, values, and norms [we delineated above regarding heterosexual relationships]. This would lead some in this group to advocate performing commitment ceremonies as a way of creating strong, monogamous, loving, and Jewishly committed relationships among homosexuals.

The Committee on Jewish Law and Standards passed four responsa on the issue of homosexual sex. Three rejected it either as a *toevah* (abomination) or as undermining family-centered Judaism or as requiring an or as an impermissible uprooting of a law of the Torah. One maintained that homosexual sex should not be seen as a *toevah* and recommended a commission to study the entire issue of human sexuality. The Committee on Jewish Law and Standards determined that commitment ceremonies should not be performed and that sexually active homosexuals should not be admitted to the Movement's rabbinical and cantorial schools. The fourth responsum qualified both of these last provisions as subject to further research and possible revision. It was left to each synagogue rabbi to determine the extent to which homosexuals could be teachers or youth leaders within the congregation and the extent to which homosexuals would be eligible for positions of synagogue leadership and honors within prayer services.

Chapter 19
New Age Judaism

Jeffrey K. Salkin

New Age Judaism, a style of Jewish thought and practice within American non-Orthodox Judaism, has brought spiritual renewal into the American Judaism of the last decades of the twentieth century. In these readings, we explore the various sources of and approaches to this renewal, from the search for a more vibrant prayer life to the use of Judaism in finding meaning in the world of work. In each case, the author responds to an implicit question concerning the value of Judaism in bringing meaning into the life of the individual. As is clear throughout, at the heart of this question is a recognition that the traditional American synagogue, seen as stilted and boring, no longer serves the needs of many young Jews.

A. Neil Gillman, "On the New Jewish Spirituality"

Professor Neil Gillman notes the popularity of the new Jewish spirituality, reflecting on the recent great gains in Jewish music, Jewish creative worship, and healing. But Gillman sees much to criticize in this new emphasis on Jewish spirituality. Among his complaints is the lack of intellectual rigor, and the essay thus sketches Gillman's own understanding of an authentic sense of Jewish piety.

Spirituality is now very much "in." Witness the multiplicity of new books on God, angels, meditation practices, and the nurturing of the soul; (a recent visit to a prominent university book store disclosed one shelf labelled "Religion" and six floor-to-ceiling shelves on "Spirituality"); the spread of Jewish healing centers and of healing services; the "B. J. phenomenon" (B'nai Jeshurun, a revived synagogue on Manhattan's Upper West Side where over a thousand congregants sing and

Source for reading A.: Sh'ma 27/522, 1996, pp. 3–5.

dance their way through the Friday evening *Kabbalat Shabbat* service); the renewed interest in Hasidism and Jewish mysticism; and the popularity of authors such as Arthur Green, David Wolpe, Lawrence Kushner and the late Aryeh Kaplan.

Three Models of Authenticity

Finally, note the presence across the country of a group of Jewish spiritual-seekers, all dissatisfied with the formality and impersonal nature of the worship service in their synagogues, all confessing to unmet religious needs, all searching elsewhere to find settings where these needs may be met, sometimes in *Chabad*, in *havurot*, or in the extreme, in New Age cults and ashrams. Some Reform and Conservative rabbis have hearkened to this message and have transformed the culture of their synagogues. In other settings, the dissident group meets inform-ally for study and worship in some other room in the building, and finds itself in tension with the Board of the synagogue and the style of the Sanctuary service, with the rabbi caught in an uneasy mediating role.

Some years ago, I published an article (*Conservative Judaism*, Winter, 1985–6) which anticipated this phenomenon. In retrospect, I am unhappy with the terminology I used then, though not at all with the inquiry itself or its conclu-sions. What I then proposed as three models of Jewish "spirituality," I would now call three models of Jewish "authenticity," reserving the term "spirituality" for what I then called the "pietistic" model.

I proposed then that Judaism provides three models of how to be an authentic religious Jew, three answers to the question: "What does God demand of me above all?" The three models are the behavioral (God demands that we do certain things), the intellectual (God demands study), and the spiritual (God demands passion). Each is rooted in our classical texts, each has had a long and noble history, each has its advocates, ancient and modern, each suggests a curriculum for Jewish religious education, and each produces its own institutional incarnations. I also argued that most serious religious Jews fit intuitively into one or the other of these models, but that our synagogues must provide settings for the expression of all three.

Models in Tension

What I then failed to emphasize sufficiently was the extent to which each of these is in tension with the other two, that adopting one of them involves genuine trade-offs in terms of other froms of authentic Jewish religious expression, and even more, that there are genuine dangers to the integrity of Judaism in adopting any of these to the exclusion of the other two. These are the issues I would like to address in this context.

On a personal note, my own intuitive model is the intellectual. I returned to Judaism in my college years on the wings of theology; I am an academician, involved full-time in studying, teaching and writing on Jewish texts and ideas. To be sure, I am an observant Jew (i.e. I "behave" according to Jewish law, as interpreted by Conservative Judaism), and from time to time, I find myself inflamed by a passionate religious reaction to certain experiences. But neither of these other models mobilizes my primary Jewish energy. To use my somewhat flip criterion, when am I least likely to look at my watch? When I study and teach Torah.

I would like to believe that I am thoroughly comfortable with my model of Jewish expression. But I am not. I have been drawn into the new Jewish spirituality, first by the need to communicate with my students, many of whom would never be serious Jews without that impulse, and also by my own intangible sense that something vitally important is to be found there – important not only for the Jewish community but also for me.

So within the past five years, I have begun to attend and teach at *Refaenu* Conferences, participate in healing services, read the literature of the movement, gingerly experiment with meditation exercises, and supplement my *Wissenschaft* (the reigning Western academic approach to the study of Torah which emphasizes detached, critical scholarship) writing and teaching with an attempt to extract the lasting religious meaning of the texts I teach.

But these new approaches continue to demand an extra effort on my part. I retain an intangible sense that they are not genuinely in tune with my own Jewish identity. At those moments I revert to the conviction that my personal tension reflects the tension inherent in the very availability of multiple models of Jewish authenticity.

The implicit dynamic involved in adopting one model over the other two is that this model tends to become a caricature of Judaism. Witness what happens when each of the other two models triumphs: Jewish behaviorism tends to become an unthinking, unfeeling, robot-like fidelity to Jewish practice for its own sake, and Jewish intellectualism tends to become a cerebral exercise, disconnected from the real lives and real feelings of real Jews.

The new Jewish spirituality is clearly a reaction to two centuries in which these other two models reigned supreme. From the start of the Enlightenment, Jewish expression has canonized either the intellectual or the behavioral model, the first in modern Jewish scholarship and in its offshoots, modern liberal Jewish religious movements, and the second in Orthodoxy.

Spirituality Has Its Trade-Offs

Reactionary movements have a salutary effect; they re-establish a balance that was lost. In the case of the new spirituality, the reaction has also been fueled by cultural trends in the world at large – for the new spirituality is clearly not only a Jewish phenomenon – and also by recent developments in American religious Jewry that can only be cheered. I can think of two such developments off-hand: Jewish feminism, the emergence of a significant number of talented women rabbis, and more important, of a group of Jewish women – Tikva Frymer-Kensky, Ellen Umansky, Rachel Adler, Deborah Orenstein and Nina Beth Cardin are just some of the more notable ones – who have attempted to define a distinctively feminist model of Jewish spirituality; and the new Reconstructionism, a significantly revisionist version of Mordecai Kaplan's own teachings. It should also be noted that under the impulse of the new spirituality, rabbinic education in the liberal movements has been drastically transformed within the past decade.

But all reactions also tend to become caricatures and the new Jewish spirituality is no exception. Its own inherent dangers are of course, anti-intellectualism and anti-nomianism, both abhorrent to Judaism. I detect the first in a generalized impatience with the hard work of text-study, with rigorous theological inquiry, and with the sharp, critical analysis of the central ideas in Jewish thought. I detect the second in the casual way some of our congregants dismiss those ritual practices which don't speak to their personal emotional needs.

The Broader Perspective

The impulse behind the new spirituality is the primacy of feeling, an emphasis on personal emotional fulfillment which dictates everything that is to be appropriated or discarded from Judaism. But what about Judaism's classical emphasis on structure, on *mitzvah*, on discipline, on communal norms, and on the study of Torah as the gateway to fathoming God's will for us?

What I plead for is a margin of self-awareness, a sense of history, an appreciation of the dynamics that have always governed Jewish religious expression, and a critical understanding of the tensions that contemporary culture exerts on the shape of our Judaism. I plead also that our rabbis and teachers understand that we are the heirs of the entire Jewish past, that we must serve as advocates of Judaism at its richest.

History will have its say, whatever we do. Generations from now, Jewish thinkers will bemoan the lack of spirituality in the Jewish community, and look nostalgically to the role models of our day. But we, at least should not be slaves to the culture of the contemporary.

B.   Arthur Green, "Judaism for the Post-Modern Era"

In this crucial essay, Arthur Green looks at the spiritual condition of the Jewish people as it enters the new millennium. Noting that, by and large, all modern Jews have entered modernity and have, to some extent, undergone a process of

Source for reading B.:   The Samuel H. Goldenson Lecture, Hebrew Union College–Jewish Institute of Religion, 1994.

secularization, Green wonders what kind of Judaism they will need for the next epoch of Jewish history. His whimsical answer emerges from a personal ad in which a woman describes herself as "spiritual, not religious." In imagining the life of this young woman, Green sees her as a spiritual dabbler in a number of New Age techniques and mysticisms. He notes the kind of spirituality she might seek and the kind of spirituality that might ultimately win hearts and minds to Judaism in the next era.

What shall we say of the Jewish people as it enters this third millenium of what we shall generously call the *Common Era?* ... We can begin by saying how divided Jewry is: between Orthodox and heterodox, between Israeli and diaspora, and along various lesser fault-lines as well. We can begin in good Jewish fashion by bemoaning our fate, by saying how the Jewish people, though indeed alive, is very nearly dying yet again, this time from assimilatory pressures rather than from persecution. Let us all rise and recite the intermarriage statistics, which we as rabbis know by heart the way our rabbinic forebears knew (mishniot).

But let us begin with a different sort of truth, leaving aside for a moment these all-too-familiar litanies. We begin the twenty-first century in a post-revolutionary situation. The period behind us was that of the modernization of the Jewish people. Over the course of some two hundred years, beginning in Germany in the mid-eighteenth century and extending to 1950 for Yemenites and 1990 for Ethiopians, the Jewish people was transformed by its encounter with modernity. Most of us descendants of Jews who emigrated from Eastern Europe have now had about a century of living with modernity. . . .

Our migration, then, whether to America or to the urbanity of Vienna, Lodz, or Moscow, was a migration of the mind as well as the body. The old faith quickly crumbled as we made our adjustments to the material and intellectual demands of that ongoing stream of modernity into whose cold waters we had been immersed so suddenly. Secular education became the great dream of the Jew who sought a true grasp of reality first through mastering the physical and then the social sciences. As we joined a Western post-Christian intellectual tradition that had fought long and hard to free itself from ecclesiastical control, the Jew's presence itself bore witness to the liberation of the university's mind and spirit from the last vestiges of Christian domination. The price for our acceptance into that new-found freedom – one that most Jews were entirely willing, even eager, to pay – was that we too cast off the remains of our "superstitious" shackles and join in the creation of not a Judeo-Christian but in fact a post-Jewish and post-Christian self-consciously secular, science-based world view. That demand was as clear at the City College of my father's generation as it was for those Jews who left the shtetl not for New York but for Moscow, and whose sadly de-Judaized grandchildren we meet today. . . .

Jewry of 2000 lives in a post-revolutionary situation. Some eighty-five percent of the Jewish people has voted with its feet, stepping outside the realm of committed halakhic practice and the traditional categories of Jewish religious faith. It is with the Judaism of these Jews that we are here concerned. We presume that a traditionalist minority will survive, even if deeply divided within itself. Our relations with that group are an ongoing concern, but not our topic on this occasion. We want to know what sort of Judaism will and should exist for liberal or heterodox – I intentionally refuse to employ the denominational terms – Jews in the coming century. What kind or kinds of Jewish expression will be important to them, almost all fourth-plus generation Americans, enjoying a comfortable material existence in a land of plenty, living with bits of residual alienation but no overt persecution or memory of discrimination, living in families with ties to Christian as well as Jewish Americans. What Judaism will such Jews want, need, and create for this new epoch of our collective history?

I take as my specific focus for this discussion a young woman who made her first public appearance as a subject of Jewish theological discussion in the personals column of New York's *Jewish Week* about a year ago. (I have a friend in New York – an otherwise happily married rabbi, insofar as I know – who follows those columns assiduously. "This one you've got to see," he told me.) She described herself as: *DJF, 34. Spiritual, not religious. Seeking like-minded JM*, etc.

This young woman should indeed be of interest to us. Allow me to treat her, if you will, as an icon of our age. I think she has a pretty clear idea of what she means by "spiritual, not religious." You could meet her, along with a great many other Jews, at a Kripalu Yoga Ashram retreat, where she goes for a weekend of Yoga, massage, a lecture on spiritual teachings, healthy vegetarian food, and conversations with like-minded people. You will not meet her at your synagogue, from which she continues to feel alienated. But she fasts and meditates on Yom Kippur, a day that has some "special meaning" for her. She reads both Sufi and Hasidic stories. She used to go to Shlomo Carlebach concerts and occasionally lapses into one of his tunes. Passover with her family is still an obnoxious and boisterous, "totally unspiritual," as she would say, affair. But one year her folks were away on a cruise, and she got to go to a women's seder. It was a little too verbal and too strident for her tastes, but she'd like to try more of that sort of thing, if it were conveniently available. She read part of *I and Thou* years ago and liked it, but most of her inspiring reading has been by Eastern authors or by Americans who have chosen an Eastern path. The fact is that she really doesn't read very much at all. Being of the video generation, she'd much rather watch tapes of lectures by the Dalai Lama, which she owns, than read his book....

Why is she turned off to the liberal synagogue where she grew up and was a בת מצוה (bat mitzvah)? Some of it, she knows, is still post-adolescent rebellion. Her parents and their friends seemed like such hypocrites the only times they went, on the high holidays and for family occasions, mouthing words that had nothing to do with their entirely secular and success-oriented lifestyles. Part of it was that the temple represented acceptance of everything she had disliked about suburbia: the big cars, the expensive clothes, the rigid conventionalism of it all. She knew they did some good things at the temple – the committee for the homeless, for example, where she'd helped out a few times. But there was nothing *spiritual* about that to her; it was just doing the right thing. She began discovering her own spiritual self after college, much of it in the course of the painful break-up of her first marriage. A guy she was seeing took her on her first Yoga retreat. By then the synagogue had been left far behind.

But there is more to it than that. *Spiritual, not religious.* She doesn't know whether she believes in God. Certainly the God-centered religion she encountered in the synagogue never spoke much to her. Some of it was the male language and the regal metaphors; worshiping "the King of the universe" is not something she is motivated to do. How can she walk into the synagogue or open the prayer-book if she thinks she "doesn't believe in God"? And yet this world does not seem like it is ruled by anyone, or else how could there be a Bosnia? "Or a Holocaust," she hastens to add. And how could we be destroying life on our planet by all this excess consumption and pollution, if we were the subjects of some universal King? The language seems at best hypocritical, but even more, just false to her experience of life in the world.

But this agnosticism is of a new sort. It emphatically is not about a denial of spirituality.... For her, spirituality is something that begins from within, has to do with a perception of the universe, with a perspective on existence itself. It begins with experience, not with a declaration of belief. It is a sense that all of being is One, that each of us is an expression of an inner core of Oneness, that the same One manifest in you is also present in me, and that our task is to find and be in touch with that One within ourselves and within one another....

What do we representatives of Judaism have to offer this young woman? I have spent this time introducing you to her because I believe that she bespeaks our post-modern situation. In associating her with post-modernity I mean to say three things:

1   The long, drawn-out struggle of the Western religious traditions against the process of secularization is gone and forgotten. The process has reached its completion; secularity is the beginning point. She and everyone she knows have always seen their lives as the result of combined biological, social, and economic forces. Even her "inner life," when it first began to impose itself on her, was something she saw as a probable result of biochemical imbalance, and her first instinct was to treat it pharmacologically. Her soul does not natively speak any spiritual language. There is no memory of a pre-modern past, no link to the "old country," no reservoir of Jewish memory, no sentimental return to the melodies of childhood. Our seeker finds herself adrift in secular, brash, competitive New York. The reasons for her spiritual search are themselves the realities of post-modern living: the anomie and rootlessness of modernity now aggravated by the tremendous increase in the pace at which humans are expected to live and the brain is expected to function....

2   She is a child of the global village. True, there was some bit of Jewish education in her childhood, but she was also writing Haiku already in the fourth

grade. Her school was "twinned" with a school on a Navajo reservation in Arizona, and she learned some of their chants at a meeting of the two groups, to which the suburban New York kids brought gifts ("donations") for the reservation from their material civilization. She has a close friend who is an Indonesian Muslim, who lived with her as an exchange student when they were both in high school. Her school class contained as many students who themselves came from China and Korea as there were Jews and half- or quarter-Jews of long forgotten immigrant background. In fact she was identified mostly as Caucasian and native-born American at school, rather than as anything more particular. She doesn't have much money for travel these days, but Asia will be her first destination when she does.

3   She knows as well as she knows herself that modernity has failed. Liberated from once-normative behavioral constraints, from traditional women's roles, from any subjugation to authority other than that of the minimalist state, she finds herself seeking out wisdom and truth from such figures and sources who might serve to reconstitute some center of authority in her life. As a health-conscious New Yorker of her generation, she feels herself confronted daily with the ever more compounded errors of thoughtless overconsumption, disregard for the environment even to the point of its bare livability, and the constant pressures that an endlessly soaring human population place upon our world. She can feel the growing crowdedness of the planet in the subway car around her. Her own quest has developed in the shadow of all these awarenesses, and is in part her way of responding to them.

In the face of what she experiences as a massive failure of modernity to provide meaning structures to guide her through the maze of interpersonal complexities in her adult single state, to inspire us collectively to do something to keep the physical world alive and nourishing of life, or that will lead her to an encounter with Truth on a deeper level, she has come to reject modernity as a source of values. She is therefore not much interested in hearing from rabbis, clerics, or other wisefolks who themselves seem corrupted by their compromise with modernity. Instead she finds herself seeking out the wisdom of the ancients, the true knowledge, in our language the תורת חיים (Torot haim – the knowledge of life), the Torah of עץ החיים (etz haha'im – the tree of life) rather than עץ הדעת (etz hada'at – tree of wisdom), that was there before modernity banished it. She is willing to hear this ancient teaching from yogis, lamas, female teachers who present it as wicca, or anyone else who seems to represent an authentic voice of pre-modern worldly wisdom. She would be quite happy to encounter this wisdom in Jewish form if she could find a rabbi/teacher who was neither liberal, and therefore compromised by modernity, nor Orthodox and therefore likely to "lay a trip on her" about observance and exclude her as a woman....

The person I have described in the preceding paragraphs is neither the most profound nor the most casual among today's Jewish seekers who turn to Eastern traditions. These include some highly trained and knowledgeable people, themselves now masters and teachers within specific schools of tradition, generally the more intellectual, including both Zen and Tibetan Buddhism as well as Vedanta and other forms of contemplative Hindu practice.... In depicting someone of "middlebrow" seriousness, I intend neither to glorify nor to demean her quest. What is most important is to ask how we will address such people, and to realize that such seeking can hardly be dismissed as a "cult" phenomenon or as a passing fad.

In considering what we have to offer our *yiddishe* Jane Doe, I challenge us to ask ourselves deep questions about where our own commitments lie. Many of us chose Jewish heterodoxy because our values were like hers, but in an earlier version. We liked Martin Buber's distinction between *religiosity* and *religion*, and shared his feeling that too much had been frozen in the old forms of Jewish observance. But as leaders of liberal Jewish institutions we too became defenders of another version of institutionalized religion, and perhaps lost some of our attunement to that religiosity. For us Jane's ad should be first a call to תשובה (teshuva), to return to the inner search that brought us here in the first place. This may mean a washing out of our mouths for some of the "answers" we have provided for the Jews we serve, when we should have just told them that we too are seekers. We too were attracted to the life of faith without being literal believers in the revealed authority of Judaism and its practices. We too may yearn more for a spiritual attitude toward life than we believe in the God-images we offer to Jews through the pages of the prayerbook we place before them. For a variety of reasons, including our greater closeness to immigrant memories, to the Holocaust, to the birth of Israel, to the influence of teachers and friends, we were able to find a place within Judaism, though not with complete theological comfort. Some of us have buried the questions for decades; others of us struggle with them every day of our lives as rabbis and teachers. The time has come for us to share our quest, including our unanswered questions, with some of the many thousands of young Jews who do not know that questing is possible within the Jewish tradition, and have come to see us as mere representatives of a closed and overdetermined religious establishment.

In the course of this new openness, we may need to reconsider just how committed we are to what I call the *vertical metaphor* that lies at the heart of Jewish religious language. The particular ancient Near Eastern culture out of which the Jewish people and its religion emerged was one that worshiped sky-gods.... Even our mystical thinking is much influenced by this deep-seated way of thinking: the visionary "ascends" through the seven heavens before seeing the throne of God's glory; the Kabbalist binds "rung to rung" in an attempt to reach ever greater heights of knowledge and closeness to God.

But suppose we allowed ourselves to be freed from this upper world/lower world way of thinking. Dare we imagine a Jewish faith less than fully wedded to this single root-metaphor? Some of our greatest philosophers and mystics in prior ages went quite far in trying to understand reality in terms of *inner* and *outer* rather than *higher* and *lower*. They would have us think of the quest for God as a journey inward, where the goal is an ultimately deep level within the self rather than the top of the mountain or the throne in heaven. The Torah tells us that our earliest ancestors were diggers of wells. Suppose we try, in seeking that Torah, to reach for the water that flows freely from the depths of Abraham's well rather than the Torah that came down carved in stone from the mountaintop that reached into heaven. The journey to Torah would then go inward, peeling off layer after layer of externals, rather than climbing higher and higher....

In turning to the well or spring rather than the mountain as our key metaphoric embodiment of the source of Torah, I am suggesting much more than a change of direction. I propose that we need to reconstitute Judaism as a religion friendly to the notion of quest, to a vision of life as an unending voyage in search of truth or God or Oneness, but one in which some measure of that goal is attained incidentally, בהיסח הדעת (b'hiseah hada'at), along the way. The Judaism of the foot of the mountain has not much room for seekers. Torah has already been given; we live in the afterglow of revelation. For purposes of praxis, there is a Set Table where we can look up how it is we are to live, what to do in any given situation. Our questing – which does go on in classical Judaism, to be sure – takes the form of commentary, but commentary to a text that is already given, already fixed in its primary meaning. And the event of revelation, the moment of encounter between the divine mind and the human is to be seen through the distant veil of generations, דור דור וסופריו דור דור וספריו (dor dor ve-sofrav, dor dor ve-sfarav), each writer and book adding another layer of distance....

If Western religion is going to speak to post-moderns, it will have to learn to do so in a new key. The transformations required will be deep-seated, and it is not entirely clear that they will work. I believe that the best guides we have in this search for a new and yet tradition-rooted religious language are the mystics of the West, if read selectively. I believe they are important partly because of the profundity of their symbolic language and imagination, but also because of the example they provide of a radical transformation of meaning within the history of a religious tradition, while maintaining and even deepening the symbols and sancta of that tradition. I believe that the Kabbalistic re-shaping of Judaism is the most profound change in the history of that tradition after the Prophets' revolutionary reshaping of the sacred as they encountered it in the religions of pre-Israelite antiquity. Indeed, it is probably to that first re-shaping that we should now first turn our attention....

C.   Jeffrey K. Salkin, "What Is Spirituality, Anyway?"

The author has invented a Jewish theology of the workplace, demonstrating how religious values can infuse one's work, how work can reflect a sense of

Source for reading C.: Jeffrey K. Salkin, *Being God's Partner: How to Find the Hidden Link between Spirituality and Your Work* (Woodstock: Jewish Lights Publishing, 1994), pp. 51–5.

divine obligation and spiritual uplift, and how one can achieve balance in life. Such models have earlier been found in Buddhism and Christianity, but had been lacking in Judaism. This chapter redefines spirituality and shows how work, once believed to be divorced from religion, may be seen as a spiritual path. The author makes a case for ending the artificial bifurcation of religion and "real life."

For many people, "work" and "spirituality" negate and contradict each other; they are polar opposites that come from two entirely different universes.

Such individuals may be well-versed in the concept of "work": They do it almost every day. But they do not properly understand the concept of "spirituality." To them, "work" is wholly practical, rooted in the necessities of this world and geared toward providing for self and family. "Spirituality," on the other hand, is otherworldly, ethereal and has little bearing on what seems to be one of the most mundane, demanding and unavoidable aspects of our lives: Our jobs and our professions.

For them, the concept of spirituality has to be reconstructed, almost from the ground up. These doubters have to reorient themselves to spirituality's surprising practicality, to its broad applications to every facet of our lives, and to the surprising symmetry it has with work.

But this is hard for many of us to believe. That difficulty arises because of our preconceived notions about the nature of spirituality, work, and "the real world."

As a rabbi, I have heard many misconceptions from lay people about spirituality. Below are some of the most frequently voiced opinions about spirituality – and how I respond to them.

Work is about being active. Isn't spirituality basically a passive stance towards the world?

Sometimes, but *only* sometimes.

By "passive" spirituality, I mean those moments when God's light and grace seem to flow almost on their own volition into our lives. Some of this is admittedly "foxhole" theology: A faith that comes upon you in the midst of a crisis or an emergency: "I was almost run over by a car, but God saved me" or "I was sure my baby would die of pneumonia, but something stronger than medicine saved her."

Such a moment of faith is very Jewish. It is the faith of Moses, who, upon asking God, "Let me see your glory [*kavod*]!" hears God responding, "I will let all my goodness pass before you." *Kavod* is usually translated as "divine glory," but a better translation is "a moment of divine, ineffable wonder."

This is also the faith of the Psalmist, who often speaks of God's miraculous redeeming presence. On a communal level, it is the events that we commemorate on a holiday such as Passover (and to a lesser extent on Purim) when the entire Jewish people felt God's power in history.

But spirituality is more than feeling that you have been temporarily lifted from the mundane world. Spirituality is *active* as well as *passive*. This means that we search for and intentionally *create* moments and possibilities in which our eyes open to a reality that is beyond us, yet very much part of us.

No wonder many of us have trouble relating spirituality to work. If we think that work is active, and that spirituality is passive, how can work be spiritual? But *if* we realize that we can be active agents of God in the world, then we can fulfill some of our Jewish duties even while we're on the job.

I've had spiritual experiences and feelings, but I only know about them after they've happened. You can't really plan for this to happen – certainly not in your work.

This is 20–20 hindsight spirituality. *Something* may have connected us to a higher and deeper reality, but the experience came, it went, and now it's gone. The next time it comes will be truly wonderful, but one can't really make it happen.

Yet, it is possible to create a mindset, an attitude, a posture that will help us experience the world anew – and not merely *ruminate* upon a past experience that was uplifting. It is also possible to *plan* to experience something, such as work, spiritually.

One thing we can do is to *re-frame* our experiences. This means that we choose to interpret our experiences so that we see them as pathways to God. I believe that Judaism wants it no other way. Hasidic masters inserted meditations (*kavannot*) throughout the texts of their prayer books. These were intended to focus worshippers' minds and souls on the essence of the immediate spiritual task. Everything we do is subject to contemporary *kavannot* that can help us focus on the higher implications of our actions.

Such focusing, of course, means being radically open to such experiences and having a vivid, creative imagination. Abraham H. Maslow, the pioneering humanistic psychologist, called mystical, illuminating, transcendent moments "peak experiences." Spirituality brings peak experiences to everyday life; it is the ability – and the desire – to find those junctures where our reality and God's reality intersect; it is learning how to feel God in every part and every moment of our life.

How can we talk about God being in our work if spirituality happens in the "other" world, not in this world?

"Spirituality" is not the opposite of "worldliness." We should not let our heads soar into the clouds if our feet are not anchored on the ground. To do so is to lose any sense of mundane reality – a reality that we need to survive in this world. We do not need to flee to other worlds to feel the presence of God: Holiness exists in *this* world and in the rhythms of daily existence.

Hasidism teaches the doctrine of *avodah be-gashmiyut*, of worshipping God through such physical acts as eating, drinking, sex, and even through the way we conduct business. Consciousness about such seemingly mundane acts lets us redeem the sparks of holiness that are present in the world; it prevents us from succumbing to the dangers of an overwrought spirituality that distances us from the realities of existence.

Perhaps the most potent lesson of Jewish spirituality is that redemption resides in *this* world. As the late Jewish theologian Abraham Joshua Heschel wrote, "God will return to us when we shall be willing to let Him in – into our lands and our factories, into our Congress and clubs, into our courts and investigating committees, into our homes and theaters." Heschel found spirituality in political action. Walking alongside Martin Luther King, Jr. in Selma, Alabama, he felt, for example, that "my feet were praying." Deuteronomy 30:12 also tries to keep our spiritual feet on the ground: "It [the Torah and God's teachings] is not in the heavens." *It* is in every moment of our lives, in our every action, in our work.

Isn't spirituality about emotion? And isn't work about the rational mind?

Some people define spirituality as "religion *plus* emotion." *Religion* in one's work is hard enough. But *emotion?* Many people believe that work can't be about emotion. As a doctor told me, "You'll lose your mind if you do nothing but *feel* all the time at work. Sometimes work just *has* to be routine." Moreover, in the compartmentalized way that we sometimes view the world, *work* is the rational arena and *religion* is the place where emotions take over. Mixing the two would be a categorical violation of the highest order.

Some people might argue that totally severing our emotions from our work would make us even more effective in our careers. But would it be worth it?

I don't think so. Such a severing of emotions from the work world would only further contribute to the mind/body split so common today. Jewish spirituality asks us to strive to be like God, to be *echad*, "one," just as God is One. By attempting to experience God in our work, we affirm that no sector of everyday experience is aloof from the divine.

D.   Jack Moline, "Is Jewish Renewal Good for the Jews?"

While there clearly is much to applaud in the Jewish Renewal movement, there is also much to criticize. Rabbi Jack Moline's essay does precisely that, noticing an over-emphasis on the new, a lack of reverence and awe, and posing the question of whether this is really Judaism at all.

Source for reading D.:   *Sh'ma*, 27/525, January 10, 1997, pp. 1–3.

If you were to ask me my basic criticism of the three American brands of liberal Judaism, I would offer this statement: the architects of Reform, Conservative and Reconstructionist Judaism all assumed that American Jews would make the effort to reform, conserve or reconstruct that which came before. But while Wise, Schechter and Kaplan themselves were steeped in tradition, the innovations they introduced to Judaism became the baseline for later adherents. That which was to bring the past into the future too often became an excuse to leave the past behind.

If you were to ask me what redeems all three American brands of Judaism, I would say this: mostly, there is a deep reverence for and awe of God, Torah and the community of Israel.

Jewish Renewal in Action

If you were to ask me my basic criticism of the Jewish Renewal (JR) movement, it would be the same. Seeking to "renew" both the disaffected of our people and the Judaism we have supposedly outgrown, the visionaries have repeated the mistakes of earlier reformers. As a result, there is far too often no "re-" in "renew."

However, Jewish Renewal does not seem to embrace the redeeming reverence and awe. And so, I believe that even though Jewish Renewal can lay solid claim to being Jewish, it cannot lay claim to being Judaism.

I am uninterested in the historical comparisons made by other critics of Jewish Renewal. The highly creative and articulate teachers who have envisioned Jewish Renewal can defend it for what it is intended to be. I look instead to the experience of "doing" Jewish Renewal and to those who participate in it, as I did during a week at Elat Chayyim. While I came back to my suburban synagogue with some remarkable techniques to enhance and deepen traditional practice, I found the orthodoxies which JR has adopted regarding God, Torah and Israel placed me behind a tie-dyed *mechitzah*.

Re-Visioning God

Most distressing to me is Jewish Renewal's attempt to define God in politically correct terms. Rabbi Jonathan Omer-man (no stranger to JR) teaches that we refer to God each morning as *el chai v'kayam*. *El chai*, the living God, implies a certain accessibility and flux. Life involves constant change, growth and (yes!) renewal. But a God who is *el kayam* is One who is established, unchanging and mostly inaccessible. Rabbi Omer-man warns that however much we would like God to be perpetually *el chai*, the warm and fuzzy aspects of God's nature are but a fraction of a percent of God's being. Only by standing in awe of *el kayam* do we begin to appreciate the totality of God's presence in our lives.

However, *el kayam* is in disfavor in Jewish Renewal. God is love and wants us to act with love, not to fear God or be obedient out of a sense of mere obligation.

Again and again, embracers of Jewish Renewal told me of the sense of liberation from law and expectation which they found in JR. They felt they did not need to really know anything traditional – merely be open to the loving experience of God, in a Jewish context. (There is something uncomfortably familiar in this God-of-love-who-requires-not-the-law approach.)

As a result "power images" are mostly expunged. The familiar euphemism for God's name, *Adonai*, is too male, too power-trippy, too anachronistic. God as commander, judge, king, ruler is virtually taboo, except as a reflection of ourselves (one exercise had us pretend to crown ourselves as we recited "the King who sits on a high and mighty throne"). Instead, God is spirit, source, breath, wellspring whose proper title is *Yah*.

Moving Too Far

Torah, our window to God, is also disparaged. A young intern at Elat Chayyim objected to the idolatry of Torah. "It's just a book that was written a long time ago," he said. Though some who were present were upset to tears, the young man received hearty accolades for his insight from the teachers and leaders who were present. Of course Torah has always been interpreted and applied. In the past, however, the purpose was always to preserve the sacred content and context of God's word.

Instead, JR looks to the innovations and commentaries of the mentors of the day who, no small matter, are exceptionally well-grounded in tradition, both academic and kabbalistic. However, what they offer to disaffected, undereducated Jews is considered the baseline. For the mentors, it is a point of arrival. For the students, it is a point of departure. Far from being a place of entry into the community of Jews in this world, students of JR return to the Jewish community only to find less common ground with educators, rabbis and God-bless-them laypeople in their local synagogues, organizations and public policy groups.

I get the uneasy sense that such disaffection is just fine with some of the leaders of JR. They have a messianic sense of mission, to transform Judaism and rescue it from the shackles of the rabbinic model and the prophetic call which typify Conservative and Reform Judaism. And thank God Mordecai Kaplan did not believe in life after death; he would be spinning in his grave to see how his Reconstructionism has been co-opted in Jewish Renewal circles.

Obsession with Sex

Jewish Renewal seems to have it backwards. I was always taught that the role Judaism was to play in society was to seek to transform injustice and separation from God through our values. Instead, JR is transforming Judaism by infusing it with values from other societies, most notably America.

Most lamentable among those values is the contemporary obsession with sex. Gender is a construct of grammar; sex is a construct of body and relationship. When the two are confused, as happens often in JR, sexuality assumes a highly exaggerated prominence. In Hebrew, every word has gender. In English, only personal pronouns have gender. Therefore, it is easy for an English speaker when reading or learning Hebrew to make the mistake of ascribing sexual nuances to gendered words.

Mistakes are not always bad, if they lead to new insights and greater holiness. Because the sexual metaphor is used (sparingly) in Torah to warn against infidelity to God, one might expect that the elevation of the sexual metaphor in Jewish Renewal would bring with it a renewed ethic of fidelity in intimacy.

I was encouraged to discover that Elat Chayyim has a strict policy which prohibits the *initiation* of a sexual relationship between faculty and students during the week of residence. (Rabbinic organizations need such a code of conduct!) But everything else about sex and Jewish Renewal seems to fall into the category of "consenting adults can do no wrong." With sexuality a central metaphor for theological interaction, the danger of a virtually unrestricted attitude toward sex is evident. There is a difference between a loving experience (or even a succession of loving experiences) and a life of loving commitment. As Rabbi Raphi Friedman has similarly observed, there is a difference between a spiritual experience (or even a succession of spiritual experiences) and a life of spirituality. In both cases, the former is an attempt to rise above the mundane. The latter – the goal which typifies Judaism in all its expressions – is an attempt to raise the mundane.

It is the conceit of every generation that they can better fulfill Micah's admonitions to do justice and love kindness than generations past. By casting off the yoke of the tradition so carelessly, Jewish Renewal compounds that conceit by ignoring Micah's ultimate requirement: to walk humbly with God.

PART IV

Special Topics in Understanding Judaism

20 Ethics of Judaism
Elliot N. Dorff

21 Women in Contemporary Judaism
Judith R. Baskin

22 Judaism as a Theopolitical Phenomenon
Daniel J. Elazar

23 Theology in Contemporary Judaism
Neil Gillman

24 Secular Forms of Jewishness
Paul Mendes-Flohr

25 Judaism and Zionism
Yosef Gorny

26 The "Return" to Traditional Judaism at the End of the Twentieth
Century: Cross Cultural Comparisons
M. Herbert Danzger

Chapter 20
Ethics of Judaism

Elliot N. Dorff

A.   Jewish Ethics: Aaron L. Mackler, "Cases and Principles in Jewish Bioethics: Toward a Holistic Model"

"Ethics" refers to the *theory* of morals. It is a level of abstraction higher than moral discussions, examining broad issues such as the processes through which we are to reach decisions of what is right and wrong. In the essay before us, Rabbi Aaron Mackler, Ph.D., Associate Professor of Theology at Duquesne University, responds to this question, arguing that to apply the Jewish heritage to contemporary moral problems, no part of Judaism should automatically take precedence over any other part. Rather, we should seek to embrace a holistic approach, in which Jewish law, theology, stories, and practice all play a role in coming to a decision.

In recent years a number of writers have argued for a greater focus on theory and principles in Jewish ethics, and in particular Jewish bioethics. Classical approaches of Halakhah (Jewish law), which are marked by attention to precedents and reliance on analogy, are portrayed as too limited to address problems found in such areas as biomedical ethics. They are criticized also as lacking the focus on theory and formal elegance that we have come to expect from ethics. One author argues that instead of looking to particular cases as precedents, we should focus our attention on fundamental beliefs and principles, and seek a broad theological view of what it is to be human.[1] Another asserts that contemporary approaches in Jewish ethics rise or fall on the basis of their methodological assumptions: "If interpretation is meant to be more than ad hoc decision-making,

Source for Reading A.:   Printed for the first time in Elliot N. Dorff and Louis E. Newman, eds., *Contemporary Jewish Ethics and Morality: A Reader* (New York: Oxford, 1995), pp. 177–93.

it must rest upon a theoretical foundation," which must be "stated explicitly and defended."[2]

The attractiveness of theory and foundation principles cuts across denominational lines. David Ellenson in the Reform movement argues that the case-based approach fails to give adequate weight to individual self-determination as a basic principle.[3] Some Orthodox thinkers instead portray the sanctity of life as a decisive fundamental principle that should trump competing considerations. While the substantive differences between these views are profound, both would agree that the enterprise of Jewish bioethics appropriately focuses on general theory and foundational principles.

At the same time that these Jewish ethicists have argued for a need to turn from cases to theory and general principles, many in philosophical bioethics and clinical ethics have argued for the need to move in the opposite direction. They have criticized foundationalism, an approach which seeks to establish with certainty one basic principle (or at most a few such principles), and to deduce rules and resolve particular cases on the basis of this foundation.[4] Critics have pointed to the difficulty of establishing broad principles that provide meaningful guidance in particular cases. "Applied ethics" models that focus on theory and foundationalist principles have been condemned as making inflated claims regarding their principles, and as producing simplistic and inequitable decisions or failing to provide guidance in actual cases. These concerns have led to arguments for a return to cases and casuistic approaches in bioethics, focusing on the details of cases and looking to analogical reasoning and case judgments.[5]

In this paper I will advance a holistic model for Jewish ethics and bioethics. My holistic model includes attention to both particular and general concerns. It holds that there need be no absolute and invariable order of priority among particular judgments, rules and laws, and general principles and values. Neither grand principles expressing the essence of Judaism nor rigid formal criteria need be foundational. In addressing a specific issue (a local level of justification), a particular claim may be supported by a more general norm, or vice versa. A variety of approaches to a problem can each shed light, serve as correctives to other approaches, and contribute to a resolution. At the global level, justification is (to use John Rawls's phrase) "a matter of the mutual support of many considerations, of everything fitting together into one coherent view."[6] The term *holistic* is meant to designate an approach to reasoning and deliberation, and not a metaphysical thesis. The holistic model is compatible with a variety of metaethical positions, including a view that assertions in Jewish ethics correspond to a higher reality or are objectively true.[7] By combining criteria of input and coherence, the holistic model allows for the testing, reshaping, and justification (or vindication) not only of particular beliefs but also of the system of Jewish ethical beliefs as a whole.

I first will present the outlines of the holistic model and suggest its affinities to classical approaches in Jewish ethics.[8] I then will argue that my holistic model best accounts for the significance of general principles and particular rules and precedents in Jewish bioethics. The model also offers an understanding of the contribution of insights of conscience or judgment relative to established norms and provides a basis for the interaction of elements identified as Jewish with other sources of ethical insight such as philosophical ethics. I will conclude by sketching briefly an example of how the model would operate in approaching a particular issue, that of access to health care.

Coherence Reasoning in the Holistic Model

My approach, with its reliance on back-and-forth reasoning and the accompanying rejection of foundationalism, corresponds with the model of reflective equilibrium, developed by John Rawls and others. Rawls describes the process of reflective equilibrium, crucial for the development and justification of moral theory, as beginning with a set of considered judgments, including case judgments as well as more general norms and theoretical concerns. We postulate those principles that would best account for such judgments, and revise principles and more particular judgments in a process of mutual adjustment, with the result (as well as the process) referred to as reflective equilibrium. Wide reflective equilibrium includes consideration of all available theoretical views and reasonable arguments.[9]

Coherence is central to a holistic understanding of the acquisition and justification of beliefs, as found in my model and that of Rawls. Following Laurence BonJour in his discussion of empirical knowledge, I understand coherence as a rich concept that includes more than mere consistency. As BonJour observes:

> Intuitively, coherence is a matter of how well a body of beliefs "hangs together": how well its component beliefs fit together, agree or dovetail with each other, so as to produce an organized, tightly structured system of beliefs, rather than either a helter-skelter collection or a set of conflicting subsystems. It is reasonably clear that this "hanging together" depends on the various sorts of inferential, evidential, and explanatory relations which obtain among the various members of a system of beliefs, and especially on the more holistic and systematic of these.[10]

A coherent system of beliefs must avoid logical inconsistencies, but positive connections between beliefs are also required. The coherence of a system is increased in proportion to the number and strength of inferential connections between component beliefs, with explanatory connections central but other inferential connections contributing as well.[11] Coherence is pursued step-by-step in a process of mutual adjustment, as connections of explanation, inference, and analogy are drawn and their implications explored.[12]

In the context of a particular case, a holistic approach to reasoning would investigate detailed circumstances, explore analogies with other known cases, and consider the implications of general rules, values, and principles. An example of this approach is provided by Martin Luther King Jr.'s "Letter from Birmingham City Jail." In this essay King weaves together considerations large and small, general norms and particular case judgments, in order to create a coherent and compelling argument for a particular course of action. He addresses broad issues, including general criteria of when a law is unjust, and articulates a grand vision of the United States and of the church (and religious institutions in general).[13] At a general level King's letter seeks to reconcile broad norms. King is committed to respecting the law, and acknowledges that simple defiance of the law unacceptably would lead to anarchy. At the same time his commitments to justice and human flourishing lead him to oppose laws mandating segregation. King seeks to respect both principles to the extent possible: he would break the law only when no other alternative is available that is consistent with compelling demands of justice, and when the law is broken so as to cause least harm to the principle of lawfulness.[14]

King's letter not only invokes general principles but also appeals to particular case judgments in arguing against segregation. He describes his daughter crying at being told that blacks are not admitted at the Funtown amusement park and a black man was sleeping in his automobile because no hotel would accept him. The judgment of these cases as wrong and intolerable corroborates the need to act against segregation.[15] Further, King does not only use cases to support the pursuit of justice and opposition to desegregation in general terms. He argues for a particular type of action in a particular place at a particular time.[16]

King's holistic deliberation illustrates the interplay of considerations of a variety of levels of generality in reshaping beliefs so as to strengthen coherence. In this process a rule of obedience to the law is revised. A broader principle of respect for the law is also tested, and emerges as vindicated. Even from his cell, King warns of the dangers of lawlessness and accepts the breaking of the law only by those who (among other qualifications) are willing to join him in jail, so as to remain faithful to the broader principle. The process of holistic deliberation not only leads to a decision for the case at hand but contributes to the testing and reshaping of more general norms, which emerge as strengthened in being more clearly articulated, substantively improved, and more fully vindicated.

Holism in Classical Jewish Ethics

I believe that a holistic model provides the best construction of much work in Jewish ethics in all areas, including those involving health and medicine. A holistic approach clearly characterizes ethical reasoning of a traditional Jew in everyday life, in the absence of dramatic conflict. One seeking to follow Jewish ethics would be aware of detailed norms of halakhah governing his or her interaction with other people. He or she also would be conscious of traditional sources and popular culture offering paradigmatic examples of ethical behavior, stories of saints and moral heroes, maxims, and admonitions to develop ethical virtues. For example, the Bible provides detailed laws governing ethical behavior, prudent maxims in the Book of Proverbs, narratives of heroes and villains, psalms describing the characteristics of the person of integrity worthy of standing in God's presence. Rabbinic literature as it developed over the centuries would provide a physician, for example, with laws concerning responsibilities toward patients, admonitions to humility and virtue, stories of Abba the therapeutic bleeder and other models to emulate, a prayer attributed to Maimonides expressing the physician's devotion to the patient and humility before God, and so forth. Out of these rich and varied sources one would weave the pattern of a Jewish ethical life.

The holistic model would be followed in the academy as well. The Talmud, for example, does not follow the abstract logical schema of a work of geometry. Rather, a talmudic tractate is a *masechet*, a webbing or weaving together of material. The sages of the Talmud found themselves in a sea of texts and beliefs, including the various books of the Bible, statements attributed to earlier sages, and their own reason and experience. They would construct arguments and utilize exegetical tools in order to reconcile earlier rabbinic statements or biblical verses. Small and large generalizations would be built, step-by-step, to provide guidance in new cases and construct a richer whole. These methods would serve to maximize coherence, using the rich sense of coherence noted earlier, while retaining as much as possible of the original input.

A holistic approach also characterizes the reasoning of later generations of rabbis addressing complex or dilemmatic problems in *teshuvot*, or halakhic responsa. Like Martin Luther King Jr. in his essay (ceteris paribus) they would pursue a holistic pattern of reasoning. Typically writers of responsa survey previous sources, analyze fact patterns, elucidate analogies and disanalogies with paradigmatic cases, formulate generalizations, and balance competing concerns. Their argument does not take the form of a foundationalist deduction from first principles, but rather a process of cumulative reasoning yields a judgment in the particular case vindicated relative to alternatives.

Principles and Cases

The classical Jewish approach to ethical issues, then, is similar to that found in case law. Attention focuses on the evaluation of particular cases and consideration of potential analogies to precedents. Daniel Gordis, among other thinkers, has urged greater attention to fundamental principles and broad generalizations. He argues that concentrating on particular cases often forces analogies, and at best distracts attention from the real issues under consideration. Thus, for example, attempts to define criteria for the determination of death should not focus on particular precedent cases or rules; rather, such issues should be explored at the level of our "implicit conceptions of the value of human life and personhood." Guidance for when life-sustaining treatment may be stopped should be sought through consideration of "the fundamental beliefs motivating us" rather than the details of paradigmatic cases or legal codes. In general, "If the Jewish community hopes to be able to articulate sophisticated analyses of these issues, the immediate challenge is to begin a philosophical/theological conversation which can lead to a Jewish conception of personhood or some other fundamental principle which can then be applied in a normative manner."[17]

I would grant Gordis that precedent cases and rules often seem distant from contemporary health care decision making, and their implications may be unclear. For example, the sixteenth-century Shulhan Arukh sets forth a set of rules for a *goses*, one who is imminently dying, with death likely within three days.[18] Basing itself on earlier sources, the Shulhan Arukh states that one cannot cause the patient to die more quickly, for example, by removing a pillow from under his head. On the other hand, if someone is chopping wood outside the patient's window, preventing peaceful acceptance of death, one can ask him to stop. If the patient's tongue is covered with salt, understood to delay the dying process, that too can be removed. These particular judgments have been taken to support a general norm that one cannot cause death, but one may remove an obstacle that is impeding death. Even so, differences between removing a pillow on the one hand and removing salt or silencing a woodchopper on the other are far from clear and have been construed in various ways by different writers. The implications of these precedents at best underdetermine the array of contemporary treatment decisions that may arise, such as those involving respirators, artificial nutrition and hydration, antibiotics, or vasopressors.[19]

One can readily understand why authors such as Gordis and others have wanted to turn to general principles for more definitive guidance. However, recent works in philosophical ethics and bioethics have noted limitations in reliance on fundamental principles as well. While many principles are attractive and strike us as plausible, none has the absolute certainty and exclusive authority to provide definitive foundations for our system of ethical beliefs. Broad theories tend to pursue an elegant simplicity at the expense of evading the complexities of morality, forcing various duties and sources of value into the Procrustean bed of a single (or few) ultimate principle(s). Even if foundationalist principles could somehow be established, they would provide too insubstantial a basis for ethical reasoning about particular issues and cases. An exclusive focus on broad and abstract norms fails to provide the sensitive and prudent guidance needed, and leads instead to speculative irrelevance or overly blunt imposition of generalizations.[20]

All of these considerations mandate caution in asserting fundamental principles in any system. Attempts to establish such principles in Jewish ethics face additional problems. The claim would need to be that one principle (or perhaps a hierarchically arranged set) represents the essence of Judaism in a definitive way. Attempts to define such as essence have produced multiple and differing plausible candidates. Such a claim, it would seem, would need to be based on sources such as the Bible, rabbinics, Jewish philosophy, or Jewish history. Each of these sources is complex and variegated, with values and perspectives that are incommensurable and coexist in tension with each other. Jewish texts and thought are too complex to allow for the establishment of one principle as fundamental to the exclusion of all others.[21]

For example, in deciding about care for a dying patient, many principles seem plausible. Principles might assert that one must seek to benefit the patient, or respect the patient who is created in God's image. It is less clear, though, exactly what these principles would imply for the formulation of rules or resolution of a case. What benefits the patient? Should the preservation of life in the midst of suffering be considered a benefit, or should certain measures be deemed optional and forgone in order to serve the patient's good? What are the implications of the patient being created in God's image? Some have argued that we therefore must sustain every moment of life, for each moment has infinite value. Or perhaps we are called on to have compassion for our fellow creature, whose suffering pains God and whose loss of dignity, as it were, lessens the divine image. Or perhaps the most crucial implication of being created in the divine image is that each person has free will, and so we must respect the autonomous choices of each person. On reflection, each of these claims seems plausible, each resonates with sources in the Bible, in rabbinic literature, in Jewish philosophy. If each is right, though, none can be right in a simple way. The basic beliefs in Judaism provide some general considerations, but these may conflict, and require careful interpretation and evaluation in particular cases.

No clear foundation is available. General principles may conflict and under-determine the result in particular cases. Precedents may be distant from the case at hand and themselves have implications that are unclear. Jewish ethical evaluation would need to look at both sorts of elements for guidance. I will sketch in the following an example illustrating how such a model might proceed.

Conscience and Particular Judgments

Some might suggest a different response to the lack of definitive guidance from particular precedents or general principles. They might assert that this limitation simply shows that the decision rests with the judgment of each individual, following his or her own conscience. Appeals to moral intuitions may be found in a variety of philosophical approaches, and reliance on individual conscience has played a respected role in classical liberal thought, including much of modern Jewish ethics. Developments in fields such as psychology, as well as philosophy, have made it difficult to believe in a faculty of conscience as infallible and foundational, or a Kantian anthropology of the pure noumenal self legislating universal law in a manner identical to any other self.[22] Other approaches in philosophical ethics that are based on particular judgments as foundational, and attempt to resolve all cases with such intuitions or to build unidirectionally from particular to general, have faced problems as well. Classical intuitionists have failed to establish the validity or even the plausibility of intuitive cognition, and especially to provide an account of a special cognitive faculty.[23] Further, as Henry Sidgwick argues, individuals who seek to rely solely on immediate intuitions do not always find themselves "conscious of clear immediate insight" when confronting a challenging case and face difficulties in making their judgments consistent.[24]

Moreover, even if an infallible cognitive or conscientious faculty could be established, this would tend to dissipate rather than provide a foundation for Jewish ethics. The findings of a Kantian noumenal self, or the perceptions of a special intuitive faculty, would seem to apply for all persons, abstracting from any religious commitment or any other characteristics. This is certainly how the process was understood by thinkers such as Kant and the British intuitionists. Most writers in contemporary Jewish bioethics, however, would acknowledge some central role for Jewish sources and beliefs. As such views reject the classical liberal understanding of conscience, they can no longer assume the power accorded to particular conscientious judgments in that model. They stand in need of a new account of conscience and its relationship to Jewish beliefs and experiences.

I would suggest that judgments play a crucial role in Jewish ethics, as they do in all systems of legal and ethical reasoning. Judgments are best understood not as infallible cognitive insights but as similar to trained judgments in other fields, such as science and medicine.

This approach follows Richard Boyd's suggestion that trained judgments and intuitions may play the same role in ethics as they do in science. Through theoretical study, professional training, and practical experience, an individual "acquires a 'feel' for the issues" of the field and gains proficiency in making informal judgments. These judgments are in part intuitive, in that they go beyond that which can be accounted for by explicit inferences; nevertheless, they are informed by experience and training, and generated as part of an epistemic package that includes theories and practices. The status of these trained judgments is not crucially different from that of judgments for which more explicit reasons are available.[25] Similarly, Boyd argues, "Moral intuitions, like physical intuitions, play a limited but legitimate role in empirical inquiry *precisely because* they are linked to theory *and* to observations in a generally reliable process."[26]

Many fields of deliberation have a role for such trained judgments which complement rather than replace general norms. These judgments provide guidance that may be helpful in some cases in which explicit justification is insufficient to specify a course of action. In medicine, for example, clinical judgment is often needed to formulate a diagnosis, prognosis, or treatment recommendation. The need for clinical judgment does not reduce the importance of physical findings and laboratory tests of the particular patient, or knowledge of general norms and familiarity with analogous cases. Moreover, the intuitive judgment is not a mystical insight but builds on the training of the physician in the general norms and methodologies of medicine, and experience with many cases.

This model explains how the judgments of a Jewish ethicist or other individual can be Jewish. Such judgment is not akin to perception in the sense of raw feels and sensations, but rather the perceptiveness of the trained and experienced person of wisdom. In Jewish ethics as in other fields, perceptive judgments are influenced by experience and reflect the total of one's training, commitments, and beliefs.

As a first and minimal claim, judgments in bioethics can fill in gaps and provide nuanced resolutions. Like the clinical judgments of a physician, they can offer guidance when explicit justification is insufficient to specify a course of action. This role corresponds to the significance of judgment acknowledged by Aharon Lichtenstein, for example. For Lichtenstein, an individual's "moral sense" may be relied on within the realm of *lifnim mishurat hadin*, or within the boundaries of the law. So long as an individual is acting in accord with all general norms, that person's ethical insight may further specify the contours of ethically appropriate action.[27]

My model allows for a more ambitious claim as well. Particular conscientious judgments may represent new input that challenges and enriches the system of beliefs, leading to its growth. The insights of conscience could at least play a heuristic role, like a lead for a journalist or the glimmer of an idea for a medical researcher. Even those who see the *halakhic* process as definitive will generally acknowledge that legal authorities will be concerned with ethical implications of positions, and will make some degree of effort to try to shape a *halakhic* decision in accord with their judgment regarding "the right and the good," the equities of the case at hand. When the insight of conscience disagrees with the established judgments of the system, there is at least reason to reconsider the situation. At the same time, conscientious judgments neither are infallible nor should they automatically trump other considerations. Like paradigmatic cases, rules, and values, they represent an important though fallible indicator of the correct judgment for Jewish bioethics.

Jewish and Universal Elements

The holistic model also provides a framework for incorporating insights gained from non-Jewish sources such as philosophical ethics, in addition to elements deriving from Jewish sources. The relationship of ethical reasoning within the Jewish tradition and intersocietal or universal standards has been a central issue for Jewish thought, especially throughout the modern period. As I argue elsewhere, Jewish thinkers such as Eugene Borowitz have wanted to rely on both types of sources.[28] Borowitz is committed to "a universal sense of ethics, one which every human being ought to acknowledge and obey." "Only if we affirm that there is a universal ethical order, one whose commands everyone can know, can we rightly demand...that people resist 'unjust orders' despite fearsome pressure." At the same time, Borowitz is committed to avoid losing all distinctive elements in Jewish ethics by reducing it to a universal standard. He depicts himself as one of those "who know that the universalistic path is unreliable without the corrective guide of Torah." "Asserting the dominance of human reason makes Judaism a hostage to whatever version of rationalism the thinker finds convincing."[29] Retaining commitments to particularly Jewish and universal elements is attractive but difficult. I believe that my holistic model can assist in the work needed to synthesize and adjust these competing elements of Jewish ethics.

Sophisticated liberal thinkers such as Borowitz may acknowledge that the Jewish tradition defines ethical duties within the boundaries of universal ethics. Conversely, as seen earlier, Orthodox thinkers such as Lichtenstein may acknowledge that ethical concerns define duties within the boundaries of *Halakhah*. Each thus would accord with my holistic model to a significant extent in acknowledging multiple sources of guidance. However, not only would these two approaches differ in emphasis, but each would insist that its chosen criterion should always be given priority. Greatest controversy ensues when conflict arises between elements within the Jewish ethical tradition and claims seen to represent universal ethics. Often deliberation about this complex issue takes on a polemical cast. Some would claim that *halakhah* (as they understand it) represents God's word, which is by definition decisive over any insight arising from human ethics. Borowitz, in contrast, acknowledges *halakhah* as representing duties to fellow Jews but claims that ethics (as he understands it) represents his duty to God, which must be decisive in case of conflict.[30]

I would argue that there is no gold standard in ethics that is accessible to us, no cognitive faculty or other pipeline to ethical truth. Similarly, God's will is not known infallibly, and the Talmud indicates that even a heavenly voice would not obviate the need for complex and fallible deliberation.[31] Jewish bioethics appropriately gains guidance from a variety of powerful but imperfect indicators of the way in which the enterprise should proceed. These include Jewish values and concepts as well as particular rules and cases in Jewish law, and also ethical claims found compelling on the basis of general ethical considerations. None of these is known with sufficient certainty and precision to enjoy absolute or lexical priority.[32] In the face of conflict among these factors, those engaged in Jewish bioethics should undertake a process of back-and-forth reasoning. They should reexamine and seek to readjust elements. The goal, consistent with input from the wealth of the Jewish tradition as well as other sources, is to maximize coherence of beliefs.

Perspectives from philosophical ethics, and even from other cultures and religions, represent a powerful if volatile source of input for the holistic model. Elements within the system of Jewish ethics could be legitimate even when they diverge from norms in other systems. As Stuart Hampshire argues, one cannot simply pick and choose elements of different cultures, for they may be incompatible with each other and fail to support a coherent way of life; Hampshire terms this claim the "no-shopping principle."[33] Still, conscious consideration of the insights of differing ethical traditions, including various approaches in philosophical ethics, can afford a perspective that leads to the tradition being challenged and enriched. In some cases this could include modification in the tradition, or at least in the way that the tradition is understood, articulated, and applied.[34]

The holistic model also provides a basis for considering the implications of Jewish bioethics for others, as I will discuss subsequently. Dialogue between Judaism and other approaches in ethics does not depend on the establishment of common foundations. Consensus at any level of generality strengthens the warrant of the beliefs in question.

Example: Access to Health Care

The issue of justice and access to health care illustrates some of the ways in which the holistic model functions.[35] This issue reflects revolutionary developments in medical technology and social structure, and finds little direct precedent in the source of Jewish bioethics. In developing a response to this issue, both broad values and principles, and particular cases and rules, would play a role. Biblical narrative and law affirm the value of each individual human life, the obligation to meet the requirements of justice, and God's concern for the weak and poor.[36] Rabbinic Judaism developed the Hebrew Bible's values of justice and support for the poor into an approach of *tzedakah*, literally meaning justice.[37]

These general concepts and values frame the broad contours of a Jewish ethical position but underdetermine such a view. These norms might be seen as compatible with radical egalitarianism, reliance on voluntary charity, or any of a spectrum of intermediate positions. They also fail to provide guidance about the level of health care that should be provided. Detailed rules found in Jewish sources add to the process. For example, *halakhic* sources indicate that "each individual is obligated to give *tzedakah* . . . If one gives less than is appropriate, the courts may administer lashes until he gives according to the assessment, and the courts may go to his property in his presence and take the amount that it is appropriate for him to give."[38] The obligation for *tzedakah* in Judaism is binding, analogous to the obligation to pay income taxes in the United States. More generally, rabbinic Judaism developed a detailed system of enforceable obligations and careful allocation to achieve foundational justice.[39]

Further guidance is provided by drawing analogies with related issues. Cases involving lifesaving action represent a category of acute needs that are traditionally seen to take precedence even over general obligations of *tzedakah*. Most prominent is the redemption of captives, those captured by slave traders or unjustly held prisoner. Maimonides, for example, states that "the redemption of captives takes precedence over the support of the poor, and there is no greater obligatory precept than the redemption of captives." He offers the explanation that "a captive falls in the category of the hungry and the thirsty and the naked, and stands in danger of his life."[40] Accordingly, funds collected or allocated for any other purpose may be diverted to securing the release of captives when necessary. The redemption of captives provides a precedent analogous to at least some types of medical care. Both concern individuals who are suffering and may be in immediate danger, with special needs that vary greatly among individuals. Jewish ethics understands society to have a fundamental obligation to save lives whenever possible, diverting funds from other projects as required.[41]

A crucial issue remains of specifying the level of health care to be provided, especially when threats to life are not direct. In general, Jewish sources understand society to be responsible to assure provision of the needs of persons. The Talmud sets parameters in its exegesis of the verse in Deut. (15:8): "You shall surely open your hand to him, and shall surely lend him sufficient for his need/lack [*dei mahsoro*], according as he needs/lacks." The Talmud cites an earlier rabbinic interpretation: " 'Sufficient for his lack' – you are commanded to support him, and you are not commanded to enrich him; 'according as he lacks' – even a horse on which to ride, and a servant to run in front of him."[42] Later sources provide a list of paradigmatic examples. "If it is appropriate to give him bread, they give him bread; if dough, they give him dough; ... if to feed him, they feed him. If he is not married and wants to take a wife, they enable him to marry; they rent a house for him, and provide a bed and furnishings...."[43] However, traditional Jewish sources devote little attention to specifying the levels of food, shelter, or medical care required by justice. The key to the understanding of need seems to be the idea of lack, or that which is missing.[44] While individualized cases of persons coming to lack that which they had previously possessed are considered in the codes, the general standard against which lacks are evaluated is largely implicit and difficult to formulate with precision. These precedents, in conjunction with the general values noted earlier, provide significant but incomplete guidance in defining a societal responsibility to provide for health care needs. Extrapolating from these cases to modern health care concerns remains uncertain at best.

Here I believe that philosophical insights can add to the deliberative process by contributing to a clearer and more complete articulation of a Jewish ethical position. Philosophical ethicists such as Norman Daniels have developed a concept of needs in terms of "species-typical functioning." For Daniels, basic or

> course-of-life needs, would include food, shelter, clothing, exercise, rest, companionship, a mate.... [A] deficiency with respect to them "endangers the normal functioning of the subject of need considered as a member of a natural species...."
> Health care needs will be those things we need in order to maintain, restore, or provide functional equivalents (where possible) to normal species functioning.[45]

Both Daniel's understanding of need in terms of lack, and his list of paradigmatic needs, correspond with the positions found in *halakhic* sources. This understanding contributes to a construction of Jewish sources that identifies a general principle, which in turn assists in discerning the implications of the traditional model for new cases.

More generally, ethical insights, deriving in part from philosophical ethics, subtly shape the deliberative process throughout. For example, I believe that drawing an analogy from redeeming captives to supplying health care for those in need is supported by a number of factors, which are not limited to but include ethical concerns. In contrast, I would be more reticent to draw analogies from some discussions in traditional sources about priorities of rescue. The Mishnah states that a Cohen (or priest) takes precedence over a Levite, who takes precedence over an Israelite, and so forth through lower castes.[46] Even if one is reluctant to condemn this passage, ethical concerns would be one factor counting against extending this ruling to contemporary cases. Throughout the process of deliberation, explicitly Jewish sources are central, but general ethical insights contribute to a process of reshaping and vindicating beliefs.

Conversely, Jewish sources in turn could lead to the reshaping and vindicating of general ethical positions on these matters. The Jewish model of *tzedakah* provides a set of understandings and practices, developed to be both principled and pragmatic, for the achievement of social justice over a fairly broad-based community. At the least, this model can be heuristically useful as a source of insights and guidelines which might be appropriately translated to the contemporary United States. For committed Jews the translation of Jewish views of justice to American society is supported by the traditional injunction to support poor non-Jews along with poor Jews, "for the sake of the paths of peace."[47] For the general reader the relevance of Jewish insights on justice and health care depends on their intuitive appeal, their resonance wiht accepted American values, and their coherence with the perspectives of other groups and individuals in United States society.

The values of Judaism represent one important perspective within the United States' pluralistic society, to be compared with the perspectives of other groups and individuals as part of a process of developing a consensus. Aside from any value this may have in terms of politics or feasibility,[48] the consensus may have a deeper philosophical significance, although the scope of this paper allows only a brief sketching of this possibility.

In surveying the philosophical studies prepared for the President's Commission on Biomedical Ethics, Daniel Wikler finds significance in an overlapping consensus of various philosophical approaches. He notes that rival theories agree that "[e]very person ought to be assured of access to some decent minimum of health care service," and argues:

> This conclusion cannot be said to have been "proved" by this collection of arguments, but the fact that a recommendation of universal access to (at least some) health care follows from such disparate sets of premises suggests that the recommendation is "insensitive" to choice of moral theory. Even if we do not know which moral theory is correct, then, and thus cannot provide a ground-level-up proof that all should have access to a minimum of health care, such a belief has been rendered reasonable and perhaps even compelling.

The inclusion of Judaism (and other religious traditions) in this consensus bolsters the claim that the recommendation is theory-insensitive and thus strengthens the warranted status of the belief that access to health care ought to be provided.[49]

Finally, judgment is needed throughout the process. My holistic model does not provide any simple formula for decision making but rather depends on consideration of a wealth of factors. Often the final resolution, and certainly its details, depend on the prudent judgment of the decision maker. As described previously, intuitive judgment is neither a mystical insight nor an arbitrary choice, but rather expert judgment reflects the system of Jewish ethics as a whole. The need for such judgment becomes especially apparent as one attempts to move from the considerations noted earlier to specific policy choices, the articulation of clinical guidelines, and decision making in particular cases.

Conclusion

In this essay I have sketched the outlines of a holistic model for Jewish ethics and bioethics and have offered considerations that I believe support this model. I have shown how my holistic model accounts for the significance of general principles and particular rules and precedents; for the role of particular insights of conscience or judgment; and for the interaction of elements identified as Jewish with other sources of ethical insight such as philosophical ethics. Each of these elements contributes to the enterprise of Jewish bioethics; conversely, no one factor is definitive of Jewish bioethics, or takes priority over all competing concerns. In the event of conflict or uncertainty, a process of careful deliberation is required.

My approach thus differs from those of some other thinkers both methodologically, in rejecting foundationalism, and substantively, in arguing that their favored element (whether precedent, principle, or conscientious insight) will not always be decisive. The holistic model for Jewish bioethics is an old-new approach, one that I believe both corresponds with approaches in the Jewish tradition and recommends itself for contemporary work in Jewish ethics, including bioethics. The model is compatible with realism, with certain actions being objectively required as God's will or rationally compelling, but does not require foundationalism. Rather, the combination of input and coherence serves to reshape and vindicate beliefs in Jewish bioethics.

The current state of knowledge is imperfect in this as in all fields. While the importance and profundity of the issues in Jewish bioethics make claims of certainty attractive, they also emphasize the importance of humility, intellectual honesty, and responsibility. Traditionally, the greatest of judges in difficult cases would use phrases such as *l'fi aniyut dati*, "according to the modesty of my understanding," and *tzarich iyyun*, "the matter requires further attention." Uncertainty would be acknowledged, and the process would be open to new considerations. A process of careful deliberation would yield guidance that is substantive and valuable but not absolute. The work of the holistic process of study, deliberation, and ethical action will not yield simple and definitive answers. The process, like Rawls' reflective equilibrium, is always ongoing.

Acknowledgments

I would like to thank Elliot Dorff and Neil Gillman for their insightful comments, and Tom Beauchamp, Henry Richardson, and LeRoy Walters for their help in an earlier work in which I developed the philosophical model on which I drew in preparing this paper. The remaining faults are, of course, my own.

Notes

1   Daniel Gordis, "Wanted – The Ethical in Jewish Bio-Ethics," *Judaism* 38 (1989): 28–40.
2   Louis E. Newman, "Woodchoppers and Respirators: The Problem of Interpretation in Contemporary Jewish Ethics," *Modern Judaism* 10 (1990): 17–42.
3   David H. Ellenson, "How to Draw Guidance from a Heritage: Jewish Approaches to Mortal Choices," in *A Time to Be Born and a Time to Die: The Ethics of Choice*, ed. Barry S. Kogan (New York: Aldine de Gruyter, 1991), 219–32.
4   An approach that relied on a definition or methodological criterion as absolutely definitive, or that attempted to base itself on infallible particular judgments and reason solely from the more specific to the more general, would also exhibit a foundationalist structure.
5   See, e.g., Baruch A. Brody, *Life and Death Decision Making* (New York: Oxford University Press, 1988); Albert R. Jonsen and Stephen Toulmin, *The Abuse of Casuistry: A History of Moral Reasoning* (Berkeley: University of California Press, 1988); and Aaron L. Mackler, "Cases and Judgments in Ethical Reasoning: An Appraisal of Contemporary Causistry and Holistic Model for the Mutual Support of Norms and Case Judgments," Ph.D. diss., Georgetown University, 1992, esp. 66–72.
6   John Rawls, *A Theory of Justice* (Cambridge, Mass.: Belknap Press, Harvard University Press, 1971), 21, 579.
7   The holistic model is akin to a coherence approach to justification, not a coherence understanding of truth. On this difference, see, e.g., Laurence BonJour, *The Structure of Empirical Knowledge* (Cambridge, Mass: Harvard University Press, 1985), 157–8. The model is compatible with a variety of metaethical views. I argue elsewhere for the compatibility of a holistic approach to justification with a correspondence understanding of truth, with our coherently justified beliefs providing evidence of moral validity or truth. The approach is one of indirect realism and draws on models developed for empirical knowledge and natural science as well as in ethics. See Mackler, "Cases."
8   I do not claim that my holistic model is unprecedented in Jewish thought. Rather, I take it as a merit of my approach that it accords with much of the most profound and compelling work in Jewish ethics, including consideration of ethical issues in Halakhah. My explicitly holistic model should clarify the approach implicit in such works. By explicitly raising the need for a variety of input, it also will serve to broaden the range of factors feeding into the deliberative process, enriching the process and

contributing to its vindication. Articulating a holistic methodology also will help to guard against oversimplification and impoverishment in Jewish ethical thought, whether motivated by religious ideology or a belief that narrow foundations must be accepted as the price of philosophical respectability.

I believe that the holistic model would apply for Jewish ethics, as informed by Halakhah, or for *halakhah* (construed broadly) as it addresses ethical issues. To the extent that these two areas can be distinguished, different elements within the model may be emphasized for one or the other. On the relationship of Jewish law and ethics, see, e.g., Elliot N. Dorff, "The Interaction of Jewish Law and Morality," *Judaism* 26 (1977): 455–66; Louis E. Newman, "Ethics as Law, Law as Religion: Reflections on the Problem of Law and Ethics in Judaism," *Shofar* 9 (1990): 13–31; and the sources cited on p. 13 of the latter article.

9   John Rawls, *A Theory of Justice*, 195–201, 19–22, 46–53, 577–87; John Rawls, "The Independence of Moral Theory," *Proceedings and Addresses of the American Philosophical Association* 48 (1974–75): 7–8; Norman Daniels, "Wide Reflective Equilibrium and Theory Acceptance in Ethics," *Journal of Philosophy* 76 (1979): 257 n. See also Rawls, "Outline of a Decision Procedure for Ethics," *Philosophicaal Review* 60 (1951): 178–82.

10   BonJour, *The Structure of Empirical Knowledge*, 93.

11   BonJour, *The Structure of Empirical Knowledge*, 91–100. BonJour's account of coherence fits well with Rawl's model of reflective equilibrium and approach to justification, and helps to tie together what may appear to be disparate elements of Rawls's discussion in *A Theory of Justice*. If reflective equilibrium is understood simply to seek a consistent set of judgments and principles, then theoretical concerns and inferential arguments (which are clearly important to Rawls) would play a separate and supplemental role in Rawls's holistic justification. With coherence understood in BonJour's strong sense, the pursuit of coherence in wide reflective equilibrium incorporates such concerns. Cf. the differing approach of Daniels, "Wide Reflective Equilibrium," 258–61.

12   As noted earlier, the holistic model allows reasoning to proceed from the general to the particular or the particular to the general in local contexts of justification. Global justification incorporates both sorts of arguments in the pursuit of coherence, properly understood. The pursuit of coherence may well lead not only to revisions of particular judgments but also to significant change in concepts and general principles. See Mackler, "Cases and Judgments in Ethical Reasoning," 253 n.

13   Martin Luther King Jr., *A Testament of Hope: The Essential Writings and Speeches of Martin Luther King, Jr.*, ed. James Melvin Washington (New York: HarperCollins, 1986), 289–302, esp. 293–4, 298–302, 217. Substantively, a law is unjust when it degrades human personality; formally, a law is unjust when it is not universal and binding on all; procedurally, a law is unjust when a minority is excluded from the process of its creation.

14   One recontruction of King's argument would pose obeying the law and opposing segregation as conflicting prima facie obligations. On prima facie duties, see W. D. Ross, *The Right and the Good* (Oxford: Clarendon Press, Oxford University Press, 1930); Tom L. Beauchamp and James F. Childress, *Principles of Biomedical Ethics*, (New York: Oxford University Press, 1989), 51–55. James D. Wallaces's (compatible) reconstruction focuses on an appeal to the values undergirding the conflicting principles, in particular to the basic value or point of lawfulness. In King's words:

"I submit that an individual who breaks a law that conscience tells him is unjust, and willingly accepts the penalty by staying in jail to arouse the conscience of the community over its injustice, is in reality expressing the very highest respect for the law" (King, *A Testament of Hope*, 294; James D. Wallace, *Moral Relevance and Moral Conflict* [Ithaca, N.Y.: Cornell University Press, 1988], 87–93.

15   King, *A Testament of Hope*, 290–8. King also invokes cultural paradigms, ranging from Amos to Thomas Jefferson, in arguing by analogy for the legitimacy of his "extremism" in pursuit of justice.

16   Consistent with the maxim that good ethics begins with good facts, King stresses the need for "collection of the facts" as the first step of a nonviolent campaign of civil disobedience. King describes the organizational structure of the Southern Christian Leadership Conference and summarizes a variety of economic and political considerations contributing to the choice of a particular day on which to begin demonstrations. He emphasizes as well that the proper ethical response in Birmingham in March 1963 cannot be reduced to a set of actions but requires specific intentions and the cultivation of qualities of character as well. "One who breaks an unjust law must do it openly, lovingly"; tone and intention are here integral parts of the action of civil disobedience (ibid., 294, 289–91).

King shows that detailed claims and arguments of the sort associated with casuistry are fully compatible with claims and arguments made at a general level, such as those concerning the criteria determining the justice of a law. His essay exemplifies the key elements of casuistry as presented by Jonsen and Toulmin, *The Abuse of Casuistry*, esp. 251–7. King relies on paradigms and analogies, and invokes maxims. He analyzes circumstances, giving attention to the traditional list of "who, what, where, when, why, how, and by what means." King also develops a cumulative set of arguments, leading to a resolution, a forceful statement of the proper action in the case at hand. King's essay shows both that commitment to a moral imperative is compatible with careful deliberation and attention to detail and that a casuistic method is compatible with certainty and forceful commitment. While King devotes little attention to issues of ethical theory in his essay, this does not reflect an incompatibility between theory and the ethical considerations he does addresses but rather a choice of focus and emphasis. Rawls (*A Theory of Justice*, 364 n) notes the compatibility and complementarity of his more theoretical approach and that of King.

17   Gordis, "Wanted – The Ethical in Jewish Bio-Ethics," 32, 34, 38.

18   Shulhan Arukh, Y.D. 339.

19   Varying interpretations of the *goses* precedent are surveyed by Newman, "Wood choppers and Respirators," 22–6; Immanuel Jakobovits, *Jewish Medical Ethics*, 2nd edn. (New York: Bloch, 1975), 121–5, 275–6; Avram Israel Reisner, "A Halakhic Ethic of Care for the Terminally Ill," *Conservative Judaism* 43, no. 3 (1991): 52–89; Fred Rosner, "Euthanasia," in his *Modern Medicine and Jewish Ethics*, (Hoboken, N.J.: KTAV, and New York: Yeshiva University Press, 1991), 197–215; Eliezer Yehudah Waldenberg, *Tzitz Eliezer* (Jerusalem: Mosad Harav Kook, 1985), 13, no. 89. An approach to this issue based on a differing set of precedents may be found in Elliot N. Dorff, "A Jewish Approach to End-Stage Medical Care," *Conservative Judaism* 43, no. 3 (1991): 3–51 and in his *Matters of Life and Death: A Jewish Approach to Modern Medical Ethics* (Philadelphia: Jewish Publication Society, 1998), ch. 8.

20   See, e.g., Annette Baier, *Postures of the Mind* (Minneapolis: University of Minnesota Press, 1985), 230; Rawls, *A Theory of Justice*, 51, 577–9. For further discussion of these concerns, see Mackler, "Cases and Judgments in Ethical Reasoning." Writers argue that we may have greater knowledge and confidence at the more specific than at the theoretically more fundamental level; the methodology of natural science suggests that justification and claims to knowledge begin with the more specific and slowly work through intermediate levels of generalization, rather than rush to first principles and grand theory (Ross, *The Right and the Good*, 19ff.; Stephen E. Toulmin, *The Place of Reason in Ethics* [Chicago: University of Chicago Press, 1986]; repr. of *An Examination of the Place of Reason in Ethics* [Cambridge: Cambridge University Press, 1950], 172–6; Rawls, *A Theory of Justice*, e.g., 19–21, 579–86; Brody, *Life and Death Decision Making*, 13–14).

21   Similarly, both Jewish ethics and Jewish thought in general have proven too complex to allow the statement of a definitive set of principles, despite the attempts of Maimonides and others in the Middle Ages, as well as thinkers in the modern era.

22   While Eugene Borowitz posits the individual's conscientious understanding as the ultimate touchstone of ethical decision making, he acknowledges the limitations of classical liberalism. "The vision of humankind as rational and rationality itself implying a Kant-like ethics lost its old compelling power ... What remained of Kantian ethics faded as psycho-analysis from within and anthropology and Marxism from without demonstrated that, realistically, 'conscience' mostly meant the introjected parent or group interest." Or as Boroowitz more bluntly quotes from the book of Jeremiah, "The heart is the most devious of all things – and desperately sick. Who can understand it?" Eugene B. Borowitz, *Exploring Jewish Ethics* (Detroit: Wayne State University Press, 1990), 182, 131, 85, citing Jer. 17:9.

23   See Bernard Williams, *Ethics and the Limits of Philosophy* (Cambridge, Mass.: Harvard University Press, 1985), 93–94. Baruch A. Brody attempts to revive such cognitive intuitionism in *Life and Death Decision Making* and in "Intuitions and Objective Moral Knowledge," *Monist* 62 (1977): 446–56.

24   Henry Sidgwick, *The Methods of Ethics*, 7th edn. (London: Macmillan, 1907; repr., Indianapolis: Hackett Publishing Company, 1981), 98–100 (bk. 1, chap. 8).

25   Richard N. Boyd, "How to Be a Moral Realist," in *Essays on Moral Realism*, ed. Geoffrey Sayre-McCord (Ithaca, N.Y.: Cornell University Press, 1988), 192–93, 200. Likewise in medicine, clinical judgment is often needed to formulate a diagnosis, prognosis, or treatment recommendation. The need for clinical judgment does not reduce the importance of physical findings and laboratory tests of the particular patient, or knowledge of general norms and familiarity with analogous cases. Moreover, the intuitive judgment is not a mystical insight but builds on the training of the physician in the general norms and methodologies of medicine, and experience with many cases. See also Mackler, "Cases and Judgments in Ethical Reasoning," esp. 282–5.

26   Ibid., 207–8. Boyd characterizes the process as one of reflective equilibrium.

27   Aharon Lichtenstein, "Does Jewish Tradition Recognize an Ethic Independent of Halakha?" in *Contemporary Jewish Ethics*, ed. Menachem Marc Kellner (New York: Sanhedrin Press, 1978), 114–17.

28   In my review of Eugene Borowitz's *Exploring Jewish Ethics*, *CCAR Journal* 40 (Spring 1993): 89–91.

29   Borowitz, *Exploring Jewish Ethics*, 34, 202; idem, *Renewing the Covenant* (Philadelphia: Jewish Publication Society, 1991), 64.

30   Borowitz, *Exploring Jewish Ethics*, 190.

31   Babylonian Talmud [B.] *Bava Metzia* 59b.

32   As Rawls (*A Theory of Justice*, 42–3) explains the concept, lexical ordering "is an order which requires us to satisfy the first principle in the ordering before we can move on to the second, the second before we consider the third, and so on. A principle does not come into play until those previous to it are either fully met or do not apply."

33   Stuart Hampshire, *Morality and Conflict* (Cambridge, Mass.: Harvard University Press, 1983), 148. Hampshire argues for the essential differentiation of various ways of life in choosing among not fully compatible values. He allows that some norms, such as justice and utility, represent ethical criteria that hold across societies.

34   A commitment to reasoning within the context of a tradition and belief in the primacy of one's own tradition are compatible with the modification of the tradition in response to outside input. See Alasdair MacIntyre, *After Virtue*, 2nd edn. (Notre Dame, Ind.: University of Notre Dame Press, 1984), 270, 276; David Novak, *Jewish Social Ethics* (New York: Oxford University Press, 1992), 3–4; Mackler, "Cases and Judgments in Ethical Reasoning," 294–304. My model would agree with David Hartman's view that a "religious culture has greater opportunities for inner purification and depth when it widens its range of perception through exposures to modes of thought and experiences that stem from other cultural frameworks." *A Living Covenant: The Innovative Spirit in Traditional Judaism* (New York: The Free Press, Macmillan, 1985), 103.

35   I consider this issue in greater depth in Aaron L. Mackler, "Judaism, Justice, and Access to Health Care," *Kennedy Institute of Ethics Journal* 1 (1991): 143–61.

36   See, e.g., Gen. 1–4, 2:15; Deut. 10:17–18.

37   The Talmud (B. *Bava Batra* 9a–10a) states that *tzedakah* is as important as all other commandments put together, that it redeems from death and hastens the redemption of the world, and makes one worthy of receiving the divine presence. Traditional sources mandate personal consideration and respect for the poor; see Shulhan Arukh, Y.D. 249:3.

38   Shulhan Arukh, Y.D. 248:1.

39   See Shulhan Arukh, Y.D. 249, 256–7.

40   *Mattenot Aniyyim* 8:10. See similarly Shulhan Arukh, Y.D. 252:1.

41   Shulhan Arukh, Y.D. 252:4; B. *Gittin* 45a. The Talmud and later codes consider the possibility of a limit on extraordinary expenditures in order to avoid onerous societal burdens. While legal authorities do not explicitly reject such a concern, they accord it relatively little weight. The responsibility to provide for the redemption of captives may also be limited when the captive is responsible for his own predicament, though only in the most extreme cases. The Shulhan Arukh considers the case of one who sells himself into captivity, or is held prisoner as a result of defaulting on a loan. The community must pay to free the captive if this is the first or second time that he has brought about his own captivity, but the community need not make such payments after the third such occurrence. In case of immediate threat to the captive's life, though, even the captive responsible for his own captivity must be rescued. (Shulhan Arukh, Y.D. 252:6). By analogy, those who make choices (in lifestyle or health care) that turn out to be unfortunate or irresponsible thereby attenuate their claims to societal support

but do not forfeit all such claims. Society must continue to provide some care even for those responsible for their own misfortune, especially in cases involving threats to life.

42   B. *Ketubbot* 67b.

43   Shulhan Arukh, Y.D. 250:1.

44   Thus the talmudic exegesis noted earlier. In his legal code Maimonides (*Mattenot Aniyyim* 7:3) paraphrases the guideline, "according to that which is lacking for the poor person, you are commanded to give him . . . You are commanded to fill in for his lack, and you are not commanded to enrich him."

45   Norman Daniels, *Just Health Care* (Cambridge: Cambridge University Press, 1985), 26–32.

46   *Horayot* 3:7–8.

47   Shulhan Arukh, Y.D. 251:1.

48   Cf. John Rawls, "The Domain of the Political and Overlapping Consensus," *New York University Law Review* 64 (May 1989): 233–50.

49   Daniel Wikler "Philosophical Perspectives on Access to Health Care: An Introduction," in *Securing Access to Health Care: President's Commission for the Study of Ethical Problems in Medicine and Biomedical and Behavioral Research*, vol. 2 (Washington, D.C.: U.S. Government Printing Office, 1983). Wikler's arguments fits well with my holistic model and with Norman Daniels's ("Wide Reflective Equilibrium" 275–8) account of wide reflective equilibrium, in particular with his discussion of intersubjective agreement and convergence as providing evidence of moral truth. When the widening of reflective equilibrium by including views of Judaism and other traditions results in convergence with results obtained on philosophical and secular grounds, it would seem that the evidence for moral truth is strengthened. On overlapping consensus, see also Rawls, "The Domain of the the Political." A yet more ambitious claim for the significance of Jewish views for United States policy is advanced in Elliot N. Dorff, "Jewish Tradition and National Policy," in *Commandment and Community: New Essays in Jewish Legal and Political Philosophy*, Daniel H. Frank, ed. (Albany: State University of New York Press, 1995), pp. 85–109.

B.   Jewish Morality: Seymour Siegel, "A Jewish View of Economic Justice"

"Morals" refers to the concrete norms of what is good or bad, right or wrong, in a given situation.

Rabbi Seymour Siegel, Ph.D., who was Professor of Theology and Ethics at the Jewish Theological Seminary of America until his death, maintains that Judaism views business from three fundamental perspectives: a *theology* of economics, according to which God does not object, but on the contrary, intends that we change the world through our efforts; an *anthropology* of economics, in

Source for Reading B.:   In: Donald G. Jones, ed., *Business, Religion, and Ethics* (Cambridge, MA: Oelgeschlager, Gunn, and Hain, 1982), pp. 89–98.

which human beings are seen as having both good and bad tendencies; and an *ethics* of economics, according to which competition is good, but at the same time we are to provide for the needy. These general moral principles serve as the foundation for specific Jewish moral norms concerning business.

When a person is brought before the Heavenly Court, they first ask him, "Were you honest in business?"

Talmud, Shabbat, 33b

In analyzing Jewish economic theory it is necessary to point out that throughout the more than three-thousand-year history of the Jewish people, national sovereignty was achieved only during a relatively short time. Most of the history of the Jews was lived under foreign rule and in the status of a minority. The major period of national independence was during biblical times when economic structures were relatively primitive. It is, therefore, difficult to make direct applications of biblical or talmudic principles to the complicated and intricate economies of our time. Yet it is instructive to analyze the principles of economic justice emerging from Jewish tradition, if for no other reason than that these principles, as frequently misunderstood, have so often been utilized to justify socialism and other noncapitalist systems.

In the biblical picture, the Garden of Eden story represents *original rightness*; that is, the state of things that *ought* to be. This is in contrast to historical time when things are obviously the way they are – which is different from the normative state depicted in the Garden. Only in the End of Days will the state of affairs return to its original rightness. Therefore consideration of the first chapters of Genesis yields a picture of the normative state of existence, according to the biblical mind.

Even when Adam was in the Garden of Eden he was admonished "to work it and guard it." The talmudic rabbis, noting this fact, taught that "Even Adam tasted nothing before he worked, as it is said, 'and He put him into the Garden of Eden to till it and to keep it'; only then is it written: 'Of every tree of the garden thou mayest eat freely.' " Rabbi Tarfon adds, "The Holy One, praised be He, likewise did not cause His Schechinah (divine presence) to rest upon Israel before they did work, as it is said, 'and let them make Me a sanctuary, then shall I dwell among them.' "

It is assumed, therefore, that the human being was to labor in the world. This was the divine intent. Creation is not perfect, finished, all ready for human consumption. Human effort, the creation of new resources and the guarding of those that already exist, is indispensable to make life livable. In the Garden of Eden there is, of course, no problem of justice, exploitation of workers, or a just wage. In the Garden there is perfect harmony. The human pair is in harmony with itself; both are in harmony with nature, which produces all that is necessary (with the aid of man's toil).

In the biblical story, this idyllic harmony is upset by human sin, which is the misuse of human freedom to defy the divine. Paradise is then lost. Historical time begins. The workplace is the place where the means of life are produced – now, however, the primordial harmony is lost. Work yields results. It also yields strife and discomfort: "By the sweat of thy brow shalt thou eat breat." There will be weeds and thistles. Nature will not always be cooperative. Sin – that is, greed and the drive for ego-enhancement at the expense of others – makes the whole economic life fraught with paradoxes and ambiguities. The realistic situation is that the notion of uncoerced harmony motivated by love is utopian – an imposs- ible dream. In reality, economic life is a struggle that includes the inevitable human drive for gain at the expense of others. This fact must be accepted as a tragic necessity of life. It also makes it mandatory that there be restraints and laws applied to economic activity.

Left to their own devices, men would, as the saying goes, "swallow each other up alive." We need some coercion – laws – to restrain and inhibit the inevitable sins that humans commit against each other, for pure love in human affairs is only rarely possible, if ever. Because there is sin, it is necessary to institute a system of *justice*, which is the institutionalization of love, and the best possible arrangement given the human condition. Justice approximates the ideal. Justice is not the ideal. It is the concretization of the ideal – the rule of love – within the ambiguities of existence. To demand the ideal or to think we have it is utopian. It is to pretend that we can regain paradise. It is an illusion because Paradise will be regained only in the End of Days – not now, in historical time.

In the entire history of Judaism, beginning with the Bible and continuing through the various epochs of Jewish history, it was taken for granted that the economic life of man would involve agriculture, manufacturing, and buying and selling for profit. There is no indication that the profit system is in any way evil or that it will yield to something "higher." Material wealth itself was seen as a blessing. The patriarchs blessed their children that they might possess economic goods. The Prophets of Israel, the most eloquent spokesmen for social justice, did not advocate revolution or the socialization of the means of production and distribution. They opposed and condemned in the name of the God of Justice the use of false weights and measures; the exploitation of the poor by the rich; and the buying off of judges and the cornering of markets so as to raise prices. Overturning of society was not demanded, but repentance – that is, a return to the moral law and the end of the perversion of the laws of justice and compassion that ought to govern the lives of men and women – was required. The rich are condemned not because they are rich but because they use their wealth to wield unjust power over those who are weaker, by bribing judges and raising prices through mono- polies. They are also admonished to be compassionate and help those who are in need by loans and gifts of charity.

God's Work on Earth

Thus we see a system that looks favorably on the creation of new wealth, and recognizes the need for coercion in human affairs to curb the tendency within man to exploit whatever he has to deprive others of their rights and freedoms. Yet to analyze the Jewish view on social justice more deeply, it is necessary to dwell on three aspects of the problem. First, what is the general view of the world that is proposed as undergirding the activity of buying, selling, producing, and inventing? This leads to what might be called the *theology* of economics. Second, what is the view of man reflected in the processes that are promoted to order the economic life? This might be called an *anthropology* of economics. Third, what ethical guidelines are imposed upon the economic life? This might be called the *ethics* of economics.

The theology of economics

In the normative Judeo-Christian viewpoint, creation is open, not limited, not yet completely finished. God has not created the world "ready-made," to remain the way it came forth from his hand. The human being – in the splendid rabbinic phrase – is a partner with God in the work of creation. The human being's place in creation is to preserve the world but also to transform it. *The greatest of all natural resources for the creation of economic goods is the mind and energy of man.* Manufacturing, inventing new things, thrusting into the unknown, and breaking with encrusted methods of distribution and production are not, as the Greeks thought of it, *hubris*. It is rather the fulfillment of the human estate; it is doing God's work on earth.

Indeed, the rabbis of the Talmud, knowing the Promethean myth, deliberately retell it to change its thrust. They teach that when Adam was expelled from the Garden of Eden, he spent his first night in fear – for it was dark and full of dread. God, seeing his plight, sent him two sticks and told him to rub them together that fire could be created. In the light and warmth generated by the flame, Adam and Eve found comfort and challenge. Fire, the symbol of civilization, industry, and modification of nature, is not, as in the Promethean myth, *stolen* from the gods; rather it is a gift given to Adam to make it possible for him to fulfill his mission in the world.

This leads to a positive approach to the goods of the world. The material things are not evil, filthy, to be shunned and disdained. Because creation belongs to God, the material is good. Furthermore, man's task is to so modify, use, and transform Creation so that it will yield more material goods: to increase food, shelter, clothing, and convenience. Man must not only guard Creation – but also make it yield more to increase the comfort of human beings. It is important to create wealth so that there can be more to be put at the disposal of humankind.

The anthropology of economics

Jewish teachers stress the necessity of seeing the human being as he is – with his faults and weaknesses, and his holy dimension. They were neither cynical about human possibilities, nor utopian about failings.

The rabbinic psychology is based on the idea that the human being is made up of two *yetsers* (coming from a root meaning to create) – that is, two drives that are part of the human makeup. One of these is called *yetser hatov*, the good inclination. This is the source of the power of human beings to transcend their own self-interest. It makes it possible for humans to obey God's laws, even when it means giving up their own freedom and desires. It makes it possible for men to perform deeds of loving kindness and compassion; to perform sacrificially for the sake of others. The other, much stronger, inclination is called the *yetser hara*, the evil inclination. It comprises the drive toward ego enhancement, selfishness, greed, and idolatry (that is, putting oneself in the center, instead of God). Life is a battle waged continually between the two *yetsers*. The *yetser hara* will be completely uprooted only in the End of Days when all things will be redeemed. Until that time, we must deal with it; try to modify it; and be on guard against it.

There is a striking rabbinic statement concerning the *yetser hara* that has a direct bearing on our discussion.

> The evil inclination is sometimes called good. How can this be? Were it not for the evil inclination a man would not marry, build a house, or engage in commerce.

It is true that business and economic ventures, toil, and labor are the outcome of the baser motives of human nature. The drive to create and accumulate wealth is pushed by the desire to have more and to be above others. From this point of view it is the result of the *yetser hara*. Yet when people channel this drive for ego enhancement into hard work, daring, invention, risk, and dedication, which are indispensable for successful outcomes, the sum total of the world's goods is increased. In this view, the evil inclination is entitled to be called good. The evil inclination is not good; but it can lead to good. Since we are dealing with ambiguous forces, we are in need of regulation, obedience to law – in other words, the influence of the good inclination. Left to itself, the drive for more material wealth will lead to much good, but it will also use the power thus created to seize illegitimate power.

It is important to point out again that the Judaic tradition is antiutopian. It does not foresee, except in the end of time, the total elimination of the *yetser hara*. Therefore, *all* human structures – political, social, and economic – are flawed. *None* produces perfect harmony. *All* can be transformed into instruments of evil. The tradition is likewise aware of the capacity of the human being to obey a transcendent source of value. We have the power to give up some of our own goods for the sake of others or for the sake of the whole. This is the outcome of the workings of the good inclination. The good inclination is the drive that makes possible hard work and self-sacrifice for the good of the community. It is also the source of the human capacity for *tsedaka*, philanthropy, which is the extension of a helping hand to those who are poor, unfortunate, sick, aged, or destitute.

Yet even in this there is a dialectical tension. Ideally from the moral point of view, philanthropy should be freely given, uncoerced – as men frequently do give. This provides philanthropy with its moral tone. However, Judaic thought is not that sanguine. It does not believe that those who are needy should depend *totally* on the *yetser hatov* of others. In the view of Judaism, the community can enforce philanthropy, or at least the minimum amount necessary. This makes *tsedaka* a combination of coercion and free will; forced compassion may not be morally laudable – however, it does increase the sum total of good to others. Thus the anthropology of economics characteristic of Judaism is very similar to the classical free-market outlook. Human desire for ego enhancement works to create more and more wealth. Adam Smith's "invisible hand" recognizes the same irony: that evil – perhaps against its own will – thus serves the good. And as Smith knew, this ambiguity requires laws and safeguards as well as a certain amount of "forced philanthropy."

The ethics of economics

From the Judaic viewpoint competition is good, for it lowers the price and increases the quality of the product. The community is, therefore, obliged to ensure, as much as possible, a situation where competition can be secured. This meant that rabbinic authorities were particularly concerned about monopolies because they can lead to price-fixing, thus making the lot of the poor more difficult. One example from rabbinic literature – which seems quaint to modern ears – illustrates the viewpoint of the rabbis.

Jewish women were required to offer two doves as a sacrifice after each birth, based on the Levitical legislation. Since many lived far from Jerusalem, they waited to offer the doves when they made the pilgrimage to the Temple on festivals. This sometimes meant that they could not bring their sacrifices for intervals of several years. When they did get to Jerusalem they therefore often had to offer several pairs of doves – a pair for each confinement. Thus the seasonal demand for doves was high. At one time they reached the very high price of two dinarii. Rabbi Simeon b. Gamaliel, the leader of the religious Council, proclaimed:

> By the Temple, I shall not sleep this night until they cost one silver dinar (one twenty-fifth of a golden dinar). He went to the House of Study and taught: If a woman has five miscarriages or five births she need bring but one offering . . . By the end of the day a pair of doves cost one-quarter of a silver dinar each.

Price-gouging by monopolists can be combated even by changing cherished ritual laws. But *profit* is justified. It serves as a motive for the creation of wealth, and therefore, helps to progress the affairs of the world.

The profit system inevitably results in differences of income. There are some who are rich, others who are poor. There are those who because of age, health, or circumstance cannot compete with those more fortunate. The community has a responsibility to maintain those individuals who cannot earn enough to maintain themselves. This was expressed in the great and important mitzvah (commandment) of philanthropy.

When I was a child, I was told over and over again that one either gives charity or receives it. But would it not be more equitable to equalize incomes? This is the subject of an interesting conversation that is recorded in rabbinic literature:

> It has been taught: Rabbi Meir used to say: The critic of Judaism may bring against you the argument, "If your God loves the poor, why does he not support them?" If so, answer him, "So that through them we may be merited for the rewards of the World to Come."

Turnus Rufus, who was a Roman and who frequently engaged in dialogues with the talmudic rabbis, upon hearing of this argument complained, citing a parable.

> Once a king was angry with his son. He put him in prison and ordered that he be given no food or drink. And a man went and gave him food and drink. If the king heard would he not be angry?

Rabbi Akiva (the most prominent of the rabbis) answered him:

> I will illustrate by another parable. Suppose an earthly king was angry with his son, and put him in prison, and ordered that no food or drink should be given to him, and someone went and gave him food and drink. If the king heard of it, would he not send him a present?

This strange conversation illustrates two basic approaches to the question of why there are poor and rich in the society. Turnus Rufus (perhaps representing the pagan approach) views those who are poor as being punished and cursed by the gods. Therefore, to alleviate the lot of the poor is to go against fate, the will of the gods. Rabbi Akiva (representing the Judaic view) seems to be saying that those who are poor lack some of the gifts given to the richer citizens. Inequality is the result of differences of luck, endowment, effort, talent (most of these are, after all, God's gift). Providence allows this situation as a reward for those who labor to achieve and also to present a challenge to the more prosperous to practice philanthropy. The rich and poor are both the children of God.

In this approach there is a polarity. There is a constant interplay between the individual and the community. On the one hand, the central figure is the individual. The commandments are addressed to him. He is commanded to help his fellow man. However, an indispensable and all-inclusive role is given to the community. The community supervises, enforces, and administers *tsedaka*. The individual gives his donation to the community. The community establishes the institutions for the sick, the poor, the disturbed, and the aged. But this leads to a high-powered, mechanized philanthropy, and that is not good. Therefore, coupled with the communal activity, there is a call for *personal* involvement in the assistance of those who need help. A person should himself assist the poor, especially the aged, in filling their personal needs. *The main thing is that the person who needs help gets it.* In the words of one of the great contemporary teachers of Judaism (A. J. Heschel), "...we insist on the deed and pray for the intention."

There is another aspect of philanthropy that is relevant to our discussion. Maimonides, the greatest of the Jewish teachers of the medieval period, designates eight degrees of charity. He writes: "The highest degree exceeded by none, is that of the person who assists a poor person by providing him a gift or a loan or by accepting him into a business partnership or by helping him find employment – in a word, by putting him where he can dispense with other people's aid." Philanthropy can demean the recipient. The ultimate aim is to make the recipient self-sufficient so that he does not require assistance from others. This raises his dignity and enhances his humanness.

In sum, the *theology* of economics underlying Judaic thought is based on a concept of the human responsibility to use creation to "complete" it, to create wealth and abundance.

The *anthropology* of economics in Judaism recognizes the dual nature of man. The drive for ego enhancement, though founded in "greed," leads to the creation of wealth and thus can be seen as "good."

The *ethics* of economics requires honesty and justice, a fully competitive system, and care for the poor and the needy through individual giving and "enforced philanthropy" administered by the community. Private property is a basic element. Ultimately, however, the world belongs to God. We are, therefore, obliged to use the world to further the divine purpose, and also to heed his command to make it possible for all his children to have their basic needs fulfilled.

Justice for All

All societies acknowledge the responsibility to establish justice. (Even totalitarian regimes have "ministries of justice.") In Jewish teachings, the duty to establish justice is one of the Seven Noahide Commandments – the duties of which are incumbent upon the whole human race. Justice, in this view, is rooted in the demands of God, Who is the God of Justice.

Justice can be understood in various ways. There are varying definitions. But underlying all the relativities in the understanding of justice is the conception that it involves, at the very least, the unbiased, impartial adjustment of conflicting claims in terms of some determined standard. Partiality or bias in judgment is by definition injustice. The true judge applies the rule according to the evidence. The Bible exhorts the judge not to favor *the rich or the poor* in judgment (Ex. 23:3). The law, in its majesty, applies to all regardless of their status in the society or the community. Of course, if after the judgment you wish to help the poor man pay his debt, it behooves you to do so – out of *philanthropic feelings.* But justice demands the application of the norms of morality to everyone.

Justice is the institutionalization of the law of love in concrete, real society. In love, all others are treated as "thou's." As Buber himself pointed out, in real life this "law" has to be translated into procedures, law, institutions, and legislation. This means that for society to function, a measure of love is sacrificed to make life possible.

Injustice, the perversion of fairness, is usually the result of the undue concentration of power in one source. Those who wield power – without any "check or balance" – are subject to corruption. There has to be constant vigilance and criticism of existing arrangements in order to prevent the injustices that come in the wake of unrestrained power.

This is particularly important in the realm of economic justice. The just economic order, as we have remarked, is a basic requirement of biblical religion. God is the God of justice. He wants his children to imitate him. He has given us the fruits of the earth. He has also given us minds to thrust into the unknown, and the energy to produce. The use of our power to increase the goods of the earth is a fulfillment of a divine command.

There seems to be a natural drive in argumentation and debate to try to seize the middle ground. This is true especially of the classical papal encyclicals. It is clear that unrestricted *liberalism*, as the papal documents use the phrase, is not adequate. It tends to produce too great concentrations of power, which can lead to injustice. This is why the creation of trade unions to make it possible for the worker to bargain on levels of rough equality with his employer is necessary. (It is also necessary to curb the powers of the unions when they become vehicles of injustice). Similarly, *socialism*, which requires centralization and collectivism, is guaranteed to produce tyranny. The reins of economic power cannot be held either by a monopolistic economic conglomerate or by an elitist party bureaucracy. Tyranny, in both cases, is almost inevitable.

What has emerged from the experience of the twentieth century is that the closest approximation of a just economic order is one in which there is freedom to engage in enterprise and the creation of wealth. This freedom has to be tempered by legislation and enforcement of reasonable measures to limit the formation of monopolies and to enforce honesty and fairness. There can be a difference of opinion as to how much regulation is necessary. But there is no debate that there should be *some* regulation. There also has to be some "enforced philanthropy" so that the community provides a floor under those who cannot fully participate in the economic life. Workers should be able to organize freely so as to bargain collectively with their employers, even as the public must remain vigilant against unbridled union power as against any other concentrated source of power.

If the twentieth century has taught us anything, it has taught that there is nothing as dangerous as a utopian power. Utopianism is the belief that in historical time the ideal society will be produced, an illusion that human beings frequently have been prone to adopt. But no existing or future social order will embody the ideal of love. We must try to improve our society so that it moves *closer to* the ideal. Only at the End of Time will the original rightness be restored.

Until then, we trust the Lord of creation to help us overcome the frustrations and challenges of our time. The free-market economy that leads to the production of wealth, the enlargement of freedom, and the stimulation of enterprise is, so far, the best system human beings have found to share in God's work of creation.

Chapter 21

Women in Contemporary Judaism

Judith R. Baskin

A wealth of recent literature illuminates the variety of ways in which Jewish women are reinterpreting their religious roles and practices at the same time as they redefine and enrich the diverse forms of Judaism that characterize the contemporary world Jewish community. Under the influence of the feminist movement of the late twentieth century, women, particularly in North America, have encouraged religious renewal in liberal forms of Jewish practice and institutional life, demanding access to a tradition that has rarely considered women as central figures in its history, thought, religious practice, or communal life. At the beginning of the twenty-first century, egalitarian worship and study options in which women have the same responsibilities and possibilities of communal worship, synagogue leadership, and Rabbinic and cantorial ordination as men are the norm in Reform and Reconstructionist Judaisms and are almost uniformly a feature of Conservative practice as well. Nor have the traditional forms of Jewish practice been immune from the influences of the outside world; new educational possibilities for women and redefined understandings of women's spiritual roles and options are frequently found in Orthodox contexts as well. The following readings highlight these changes.

A. Tamar Frankiel, *The Voice of Sarah: Feminine Spirituality and Traditional Judaism*

Tamar Frankiel writes of the spiritual benefits of women's roles in traditional forms of Judaism, which she believes support inherent gender-based

Source for reading A.: Tamar Frankiel, *The Voice of Sarah: Feminine Spirituality and Traditional Judaism* (New York: Biblio Press, 1990), pp. 82–3.

distinctions. For Frankiel, it is through the bearing and nurturing of children, the preparation and serving of food, the creation and preservation of *shalom bayit* (household harmony), and their special affinity to the Sabbath, New Moons, and other Jewish festivals, that women fulfil their distinctive roles in Jewish life. In the following reading Frankiel speaks of the various benefits of the rituals prescribed for the *niddah*, the menstruating woman.

At the time of niddah a woman does not come near her husband. This is our solitude, our darkness, our hiddeness – an opportunity to go inward, that can lead to a spiritual focus. When we take additional time out for spiritual pursuits during the days of niddah, it can sometimes relieve emotional distress – the anxiety, deflated energy, or depression that many of us experience at this time. Some women find it a fortuitous time for dreams or visualizations that give us insight or comfort.

The time of niddah is also a time of preparation. After finding our place of solitude, we move into the other rhythm, preparing to join again with our husbands. Jewish mysticism tells us that when husband and wife unite at permitted times, and especially on Shabbat or at the end of her period of niddah when it is a mitzvah to do so, their union reflects the union of masculine and feminine in the divine. This is a special kind of holy act: two people in their physical being and their natural energies reflect the culmination of the divine creative process, making a unity from what had been a duality. The two who had been separated, like Adam and Chava, now come together as God and the world.

This is the essential reason why Jews do not practice celibacy. Marriage is important – so important that the blessing on a newborn infant is that he or she will be raised to "Torah, *chupah* [marriage], and good deeds." More than in any other tradition, marriage is of the essence of Jewish work in the world. Only in the union between man and woman can we touch with our own natures the process that the whole world is about: to come together, to overcome our separation, to be at one. At-one-ness in Judaism comes in an act of pleasure and creativity, as though God made the world just for this.

In these rituals we can also hear the echo, in our own practice, of holiness: sexuality is to be guarded, preserved for the right times, as a powerful source of creativity. In marriage we develop the discipline that makes this possible. Romantic love is egotistical, seeking one round after another of pleasurable feelings, but with no further aim. Even extended "relationships" that go beyond mere romance are founded primarily on the desires of the partners for companionship and security – essentially self-centered aims. As Jewish women, as sexual beings, we aim at holiness, so our partnership is different, beginning with the sexual dimension. It is essential to set apart the time and place. We count the days, prepare ourselves for the monthly renewal that comes with immersion in a mikvah. Together with our husbands, we develop the discipline of abstinence and careful attention to the nature of our contact and speech.

Then our monthly immersion is truly an experience of renewal. Water, especially the gathering of waters in a pool, is part of a nearly universal feminine symbolism. "Mikvah" means the gathering of waters, and immersion is always in either a natural body such as a pond or sea or an indoor pool specially constructed so as to be connected to naturally gathered waters, like a pool of fresh rainwater. The waters of a mikvah are, as Rabbi Aryeh Kaplan pointed out, connected to the waters of Eden,[7] the original rivers that flowed from the garden. They make for us each month a rebirth of spiritual virginity.

The rhythm of this "woman's mitzvah" highlights a different dimension of her experience of herself in relationship – not this time through nourishing and nurturing, but through the dynamic of withdrawal and joining, separation and union. We move from inwardness to transformation and renewal, then to the willingness to give ourselves to another in a coming together that mirrors the union of the world with its source. Individuality and independence are balanced at a deep level with interdependence and mutual surrender. The rites and practices make for a demanding path in some ways, while in other respects nothing could seem more natural. The practices of *taharat hamishpocheh* ensure that the structure of intimacy in a family is founded on the woman's inner rhythms, an anchor to the inner psychic life of the family and the people, a ground of holiness in our relationships.

B.   Marcia Falk, "Introduction of New Blessings"

An important manifestation of the impact of feminism on Jewish religious life in North America is alterations in liturgical language and practice, including broadening references to the congregation of worshippers to include women as well as men, gender-neutral language about God, inclusion of references to Jewish foremothers together with forefathers in prayer language, alterations of the Hebrew as well as the vernacular liturgy, reflections of women's experiences in liturgical contexts, and the creation of biblical interpretations (*midrashim*) that imagine the experiences and feelings of female scriptural characters. To explore these developments, we begin with a discussion by the contemporary liturgist Marcia Falk, author of *The Book of Blessings: New Jewish Prayers for Daily Life, the Sabbath, and the New Moon Festival* (San Francisco: Harper San Francisco, 1996), on her efforts to craft meaningful prayer language for contemporary Jewish communities, especially those which embrace feminist values.

Source for reading B.:   Marcia Falk, "Introduction of New Blessings," in Ellen M. Umansky and Dianne Ashton, eds., *Four Centuries of Jewish Women's Spirituality: A Sourcebook* (Boston, 1992), pp. 241–2.

The following new *berakhot* (blessings) are examples of the new liturgy that I have been composing for the past several years. For a long time before I began to write my own blessings, I struggled with the traditional Hebrew prayers, attempting to make them work for me, wanting to have them articulate what I believe as a practicing feminist Jew. I finally had to acknowledge that, unlike Humpty Dumpty, I could not make words mean whatever I wanted them to. Although my private *kavvanot* (meditations) could help me focus to pray, they could not stretch the meanings of the liturgy beyond certain limits: I simply could not trick myself into believing that the traditional Hebrew prayers expressed the theology out of which I live. Nor did they express the values of the Jewish communities with which I identify, especially those of the Jewish feminist community.

Nonetheless, I feel (as I have always felt) strongly connected to my history as a Jew and, in particular, to the Hebrew poetic tradition – the tradition that produced the liturgy that appears in our prayer books today. But tradition implies process and change, the movement of the past into the future, the continual forging of links on an unending chain. The liturgy was not always "fixed"; the old prayers were once new creations of individuals living in particular cultures and times. Prayers changed as communities changed; they evolved as Judaism itself evolved. I believe that the challenge for heterodox Jewish communities today – and especially for those that embrace feminist values – is not just to study and preserve the classic texts but to create new ones, just as we create new practices and customs, to keep Jewish tradition moving forward into the future.

My *berakhot* do not bless a "Lord God King of the Universe" or, indeed, any "sovereign" at all. Instead, they point toward a divinity that is immanent, that inheres in all creation and nurtures all creativity. Because I believe in a monotheism that does not deny diversity but instead celebrates differences, I use a multiplicity of images to point toward an underlying unity – the unity that embraces all creation. Thus, no single formula replaces the "Lord God King" in my *berakhot*; rather, I vary my metaphors for divinity to reflect the particular moment being marked by the blessing. All my images have their roots in classical Jewish sources – Bible, *midrash*, *piyyut* – although, of course, most are turned and shaped to reflect my own poetic sensibility.

The first blessing below is a new *kiddush* (sanctification) over wine, to mark the festival of *Rosh Hodesh* (New Moon), which was traditionally designated as a women's holiday. Although in the past there have been no special blessings for women to say on *Rosh Hodesh*, today Jewish women are creating new rituals and celebrations for this monthly occasion. My blessing is intended for use in these rituals as well as in other new events and occasions that Jews wish to mark as a community. Following the *kiddush* is my *sheheheyanu* blessing, to be used for all new occasions as well as movements of renewal.

*Kiddush (Sanctification)
for New Holidays and
Occasions*

נְבָרֵךְ אֶת עֵין הַחַיִּים מַצְמִיחַת פְּרִי הַגֶּפֶן וְנִשְׁזֹר אֶת שָׂרִיגֵי חַיֵּינוּ
בְּמָסֹרֶת הָעָם.

*N'varekh et ein ha-hayyim matzmihat p'ri ha-gafen
V'nishzor et sarigei hayyeinu b'masoret ha-am.*

Let us bless the source of life that nurtures fruit on
the vine as we weave the branches of our lives into
the tradition.

*Sheheheyanu
(Blessing for Renewal)*

נְבָרֵךְ אֶת מַעְיַן חַיֵּינוּ שֶׁהֶחֱיָנוּ וְקִיְּמָנוּ וְהִגִּיעָנוּ לַזְּמַן הַזֶּה.

*N'varekh etma'yan hayyeinu, sheheheyanu, v'kiyy'manu,
v'higgianu, la-z'man ha-zeh.*

Let us bless the flow of life that revives us, sustains us,
and brings us to this time.

C.   Merle Feld, "Healing After a Miscarriage" and "We All Stood Together"

Developing our inquiry into the emergence of a contemporary liturgy shaped
by and responsive to women's lives, these two poems by Merle Feld indicate
how spiritual meditations on experiences distinctive to women can enrich the
liturgical tradition.

Healing after a Miscarriage

Nothing helps. I taste ashes
in my mouth. My eyes are flat,
dead. I want no platitudes,
no stupid shallow comfort.
I hate all pregnant women,
all new mothers, all soft babies.
The space I'd made inside myself
where I'd moved over
to give my beloved room to grow –
now there's a tight angry
bitter knot of hatred there instead.

Source for reading C.:   Merle Feld, "Healing After a Miscarriage" and "We All Stood Together," in
Merle Feld, *A Spiritual Life: A Jewish Feminist Journey* (Albany, 1999), pp. 58, 205.

What is my supplication?
Stupid people and new mothers,
leave me alone.
Deliver me, Lord,
of this bitter afterbirth.
Open my heart
to my husband-lover-friend
that we may comfort each other.
Open my womb
that it may yet bear
living fruit.

We All Stood Together

for Rachel Adler

My brother and I were at Sinai
He kept a journal
of what he saw
of what he heard
of what it all meant to him

I wish I had such a record
of what happened to me there

It seems like every time I want to write
I can't
I'm always holding a baby
one of my own
or one for a friend
always holding a baby
so my hands are never free
to write things down

And then
as time passes
the particulars
the hard data
the who what when where why
slip away from me
and all I'm left with is
the feeling

But feelings are just sounds
the vowel barking of a mute
My brother is so sure of what he heard
after all he's got a record of it
consonant after consonant after consonant

> If we remembered it together
> we could recreate holy time
> sparks flying

D.   Ellen M. Umansky, "Re-Visioning Sarah: A Midrash on Genesis 22"

Like many other contemporary Jewish feminists, Ellen Umansky encourages the creation of new midrashim as a way to revision traditional literature through the lens of female experience. In this way women are reinterpreted from "objectified Others" to "normative Jews whose experiences of God, Torah, and Israel can add to, challenge, and transform previously held theological convictions."[1] In this example, Umansky offers speculation about Sarah's perspective on the events of Genesis 22, the "Binding of Isaac."

It was morning. Sarah had just awakened and reached over to touch her husband, Abraham, to caress him, but Abraham wasn't there. Neither, she discovered, was Isaac, her only son, Isaac, whom she loved more than anyone or anything in the world. She quickly dressed and went outside, hoping they'd be nearby. But they were gone, and so was Abraham's ass and his two young servants. It wasn't unusual for Abraham to take Isaac somewhere, but never this early and never without saying good-bye. And so she waited, and wept, and screamed.

Hours passed. It was hot and Sarah thought about going inside to escape the heat of the sun. But what if I miss them, she thought. I want to make sure that I catch the first glimpse of them, even if they're far away. And so she stood and waited...and waited...and waited. She felt anxious, nervous, upset. "Where could they be?" "Where has Abraham taken my son?" The sun began to set. She started to shiver, partly from the cold, mostly from fear. Again she cried, and wailed, and moaned. Isaac had been God's gift to her, a sign of His love and a continuing bond between them. She had laughed when God told her she was pregnant. She was old and no longer able to bear a child. But God had given her Isaac and filled her breasts with milk and for the first time in her life Sarah was happy.

She looked around her and saw the fields, now empty, and in the distance saw the mountains, sloping upwards into the sky. And then she saw them...Abraham walking with his ass and his servants and Isaac far behind, walking slowly, his head turning from side to side, his hands oddly moving as though he were

Source for reading D.:   Ellen M. Umansky, "Re-Visioning Sarah: A Midrash on Genesis 22," in Ellen M. Umansky and Dianne Ashton, eds., *Four Centuries of Jewish Women's Spirituality: A Sourcebook* (Boston, 1992), p. 235.

trying to make sense of something, and Sarah knew in that instant where Abraham and Isaac had been and why they had gone. Though she could barely make out the features of Isaac's face, she could tell from his movements and his gestures that he was angry, that he wanted nothing to do with his father who had tried to kill him. Abraham was almost down the mountain by now and soon would be home. He'd try to explain, to make her understand *his* side of the story. But Sarah wanted no part of it. She was tired of hearing Abraham's excuses and even more tired of hearing what *he* thought God demanded. And so Sarah turned and went inside and prayed that if only for one night, Abraham would leave her alone.

Note

1   Ellen M. Umansky, "Jewish Feminist Theology," in Eugene B. Borowitz, *Choices in Modern Jewish Thought: A Partisan Guide* (West Orange, 1995), p. 338.

E.   Susan Grossman, "On *Tefillin*"

Side by side with changes in liturgical language have been adoption by some women of prayer accoutrements such as head covering (*kippah*) and prayer shawl (*tallit*) that generally are part of Jewish men's worship in traditional settings. In this selection, Rabbi Susan Grossman describes her decision to pray with *tefillin*, the prayer boxes containing parchment scrolls that have traditionally been wrapped on the forehead and the left arm by Jewish men during weekday morning prayers.

When I was interviewed for entrance into the Jewish Theological Seminary Rabbinical School, as part of the first class to accept women for ordination, the interviewers reminded me that acceptance into the program also meant acceptance of all *mitzvot* on my part; *all mitzvot*, even those I might previously have not felt obligated to observe as a woman. The morning after my interview, I took down my husband's *tefillin* and a book explaining how to put them on. I slipped the *yad* (the hand *tefillin*) over my arm once, twice... seven times.... I placed the *rosh* (the head *tefillin*) on my head.... Everything felt strange and constricting until I began wrapping my fingers with the straps of the *yad*. As I wound the straps around my second and ring fingers, I read from the prayer book this excerpt from the prophet Hosea:

Source for reading E.:   In Ellen M. Umansky and Dianne Ashton, eds., *Four Centuries of Jewish Women's Spirituality: A Sourcebook* (Boston, 1992), pp. 280–2.

I will betroth you to Myself forever,
I will betroth you to Myself in righteousness and in justice, in kindness and in mercy,
I will betroth you to Myself in faithfulness and you shall know the Lord.

It is with great wisdom that the Rabbis compared the relationship between God and Israel to that of a husband and wife. As someone who had not been raised religious but had become religious only after college, I had experienced the great joy and passion one feels in serving God during those first years of great growth in Judaism. I would do any *mitzvah* I learned about, and I would search to find more *mitzvot* to do. I felt like a bride who selflessly sought to discover and then fulfill any desire of my groom. This honeymoon period, with its intensity of feeling and selflessness, is hard to match. Between husband and wife this feeling is rekindled monthly at the end of the woman's menstruation when she returns from the *mikveh* and husband and wife resume relations anew. Wrapping myself in *tefillin* now provides a daily rekindling of my feelings for serving God, a rededication of the actions of my hands, the desires of my heart and the intentions of my mind to do God's will.

This idea, of course, is not new. It is explicit in the paragraph said before putting on the *yad*. Yet, until I began saying this paragraph as part of my observance of the *mitzvah* of *tefillin*, I could not understand it in a way that was meaningful to me. I learned a second very important lesson in accepting the *mitzvah* of *tefillin*: one cannot always wait to understand a *mitzvah* or even wait to be attracted to observe a *mitzvah* before actually observing it, for often the understanding comes only through the observance. By doing, I was able to appropriate the act, internalize it, and synthesize a relationship to the act that had meaning for me, a meaning certainly within the bounds of traditional interpretation but on which I added an extra, feminist, significance.

For all the rich meaning I found in the traditional liturgy, I still felt the need to add a particularly female aspect to this *mitzvah*, may be because of the overwhelming history of rabbis denying women the right to wear *tefillin*. One day, after completing the winding of the *yad* strap around my fingers and hand, I found myself winding the end of the *yad* strap four times across my palm around the rest of the strap wound around my hand so that the strap would not unravel while I recited the prayers. While doing this I spontaneously added this meditation, one line for each extra wrapping:

> May you imbue me with wisdom,
> and let me serve you with all my actions,
> all my intellect,
> and all my emotions.

Then I realized I had made four windings, which could represent each of the foremothers of Judaism. Since then I have continued to add the four securing windings on my plan to hold the wound *yad* strap in place, reciting the short meditation above but thinking about how each line relates to each of the matriarchs:

> "May you imbue me with wisdom," as you filled Sarah with wisdom, for she was your prophetess with whom you did speak; "and let me serve you with all my actions," as did Rivka, who ensured that your will was followed in determining who would next lead Israel; with "all my intellect," as did Leah, whose eyes, according to *midrash*, were weak, weak from studying so hard, and you assured that she was blessed according to the values of the society in which she lived; and with "all my emotions," as does Rachel who weeps and pleads before you for mercy on her children, us, the people of Israel.

I have since looked at the seven windings around the arm to find personal significance in them as well. To me, the seven windings reflect a unification of the heritage passed on to us by the three patriarchs, Abraham, Isaac, and Jacob, and the four matriarchs, Sarah, Rebecca, Leah, and Rachel. It is only when we combine the strengths and contributions of both our male and our female heritages, and only when we recognize and rejoice in all our individual strengths and talents – those defined traditionally as male or as female – that we are truly serving God as individuals and as a community.

The choice to observe is, in effect, a privilege for those in the process of becoming observant. Having grown up with little Jewish education, it is often wiser to do a little at a time and keep adding observance than to accept everything at once and become overwhelmed. This is an important process, for we must make each new observance our own, just as I have made laying *tefillin* my own. For women, even those raised religious, the question of whether to take on *mitzvot* that were not traditionally observed by women raises similar questions as well.

There is a line all *baalei teshuvah* (returnees to observance) cross, a point not marked by any rite of passage, yet an important watershed in the life of becoming observant. It is the point when one's Jewish lifestyle is essentially settled. One knows how to observe. One organizes one's life around the Jewish calendar. One knows where on the spectrum of observance one falls and is comfortable with that decision. This is the point of critical juncture, for the honeymoon is potentially over. Observance can become rote. Although satisfying, the thrill and sparkle of observance is gone. It is almost difficult to remember God amid all the rules and bustle of everyday Jewish life. We have appropriated Jewish observance so well that we take it for granted, just as we often take the ones we hold most dear for granted because we are already comfortable with them.

It is hard not to pay attention when one goes to *mikveh*. From the inconvenience of leaving the house at night to the warm flush of water against one's skin during the immersion, *mikveh* demands attention and awareness. So does *tefillin*, with its macramé of windings and pressure on the skin. *Tefillin* is our daily reminder of God and of our relationship with God.

I no longer see heavy black straps when I look at *tefillin* today. Instead, I see glistening ebony wedding bands that reflect in the morning sunlight for a service of the heart, my morning prayers.

F.   Judith Plaskow, *Standing Again at Sinai: Judaism from a Feminist Perspective*

Looking beyond issues of ritual innovation and egalitarian practice, some feminist thinkers have challenged approaches to Judaism that assume that male experience is universal. For Judith Plaskow, a central figure in the development of Jewish feminist theology, the future of Judaism demands profound transformations that recognize the full and equal humanity of all Jews, that reflect and voice the female experience, and that reintegrate the female aspects of the divine into Jewish conceptions of the Godhead. She writes of the need to incorporate women's history into the living memory of the Jewish people, noting that such knowledge cannot become transformative "until it becomes part of the community's collective memory." In the following passages, Plaskow discusses the centrality of human sexuality in her theological vision.

Toward a New Theology of Sexuality

Rethinking the categories Torah, Israel, and God provides the basic theological foundations for a feminist Judaism. There is a fourth category, however, which – while not foundational to Judaism in the same way – from a feminist perspective, equally requires reconceptualization. This is the category of sexuality. Jewish attitudes toward sexuality figure so significantly in the construction of women's position within Judaism that, on the one hand, much of the ground we have traveled is newly illuminated from the perspective this topic affords, and, on the other hand, it is simply not possible to create a feminist Judaism without transforming attitudes toward sexuality.

When Michael Wyschogrod depicts women as Israel's unredeemed flesh, or critics of female God-language link female images with fertility and sexuality, they are drawing on a long and deeply rooted history connecting women with sexuality in Judaism. Women have been associated with sexuality in Jewish law and legend (Torah), and this association has been the chief manifestation of women's Otherness both in Torah and in the community of Israel. Women have been

Source for reading F.:   Judith Plaskow, *Standing Again at Sinai: Judaism from a Feminist Perspective* (San Francisco: Harper & Row, 1990), pp. 170–1, 206–7, 208–9, 210.

separated from the (male) community in public prayer because of their supposed danger as sources of sexual temptation. Identification of women with sexuality, goddesses, and paganism contributed to the emergence of male God-language historically and is strongly linked to contemporary opposition to female images. Yet, while attitudes toward sexuality intersect with each of the three major categories of Jewish thought, they do not fit neatly under any one of them, and so I have considered these attitudes only indirectly. My discussion of Torah, Israel, and God now complete, it becomes essential to turn to sexuality as a subject in its own right, looking at the ways in which traditional understandings of sexuality have undergirded women's Otherness in each of these other areas.

In separating out sexuality as a special topic for consideration at this point, I mean to define the term in a particular and limited way. Sexuality as *gender* has been a central subject of this book. The neglect of women's experience, the normative status of maleness, the potential contribution of women's experience to the transformation of Judaism have been major ongoing issues. Now I intend to look at sexuality in its other significant sense: as the complex of attitudes and constructions around sexual orientation and desire, lovemaking and marriage, and as the social definition of licit and illicit sex.

When sexuality is defined in these terms, a series of questions emerges that can provide an agenda for feminist discussion of Judaism and sexuality. What is the relationship between Jewish understandings of women's sexuality and the persistent perception of women as Other? What is the connection between understandings of women's sexuality and the broader construction of sexuality within which women's sexuality finds its place? What is a feminist understanding of female sexuality, and what would it mean to transform Jewish attitudes toward sexuality in the context of a feminist Judaism? Examining these issues can make clear that women and sexuality have been a potent combination for Jewish practice and thought, a combination that intertwines with the themes of Torah, Israel, and God. . . .

To see sexuality as an aspect of our life energy, as part of a continuum with other ways of relating to the world and other people, is to insist that the norms of mutuality, respect for difference, and joint empowerment that characterize the larger feminist vision of community apply also – indeed especially – to the area of sexuality. If, in our general communal life, we seek to be present with each other in such a way that we can touch the greater power of being in which all communities dwell, how much more should this be true in those relationships which are potentially the most open, intimate, and vulnerable in our lives? The Song of Songs, because it unifies sensuality, spirituality, and profound mutuality, may offer us the finest Jewish vision of what our sexual relationships can be, a vision that at the same time points to the transformation of our common life. . . .

The same norms that apply to heterosexual relationships also apply to gay and lesbian relationships. Indeed, I have formulated them with both in mind. There are many issues that might be considered in reevaluating traditional Jewish rejection of homosexuality. But the central issue in the context of a feminist reconceptualization of sexuality is the relationship between homosexual choice and the continuity between sexual energy and embodied life energy. If we see sexuality as part of what enables us to reach out beyond ourselves, and thus as a fundamental ingredient in our spirituality, then the issue of homosexuality must be placed in a somewhat different framework from those in which it is most often discussed. The question of the morality of homosexuality becomes one not of halakhah or the right to privacy or freedom of choice, but the affirmation of the value to the individual and society of each of us being able to find that place within ourselves where sexuality and spirituality come together. It is possible that some or many of us for whom the connections between sexuality and deeper sources of personal and spiritual power emerge most richly, or only, with those of the same sex could choose to lead heterosexual lives for the sake of conformity to halakhah or wider social pressures and values. But this choice would then violate the deeper vision offered by the Jewish tradition that sexuality can be a medium for the experience and reunification of God. Historically, this vision has been expressed entirely in heterosexual terms. The reality is that for some Jews, however, it is realized only in relationships between two men or two women. Thus what calls itself the Jewish path to holiness in sexual relations is for some a cutting off of holiness – a sacrifice that comes at high cost for both the individual and community. Homosexuality, then, does not necessarily represent a rejection of Jewish values but the choice of certain Jewish values over others – where these conflict with each other, the choice of the possibility of holiness over control and law....

Lastly, but underlying all that I have said, sexuality as an aspect of our life energy and power connects us with God as the sustaining source of energy and power in the universe. In reaching out to another sexually with the total self, the boundaries between self and other can dissolve and we may feel ourselves united with larger currents of energy and sustenance. It is also the case, however, that even in ordinary, daily reachings out to others, we reach toward the God who is present in connection, in the web of relation with a wider world. On the one hand, the wholeness, the "all-embracing quality of sexual expression" that includes body, mind, and feeling, is for many people the closest we can come in this life to experiencing the embracing wholeness of God. On the other hand, the everyday bonds of community are also erotic bonds through which we touch the God of community, creating a place where the divine presence can rest. Feminist metaphors that name God not simply as female but sexual female – beautiful, filled with vitality, womb, birthgiver – seek to give imagistic expression to the continuity between our own sexual energy and the greater currents that nourish and renew it. Feminist images name female sexuality as powerful and legitimate and name sexuality as part of the image of God. They tell us that sexuality is not primarily a moral danger (though, of course, it can be that), but a source of energy and power that, schooled in the values of respect and mutuality, can lead us to the related, and therefore sexual, God.

G.   Rachel Adler, *Engendering Judaism: An Inclusive Theology and Ethics*

Rachel Adler's theological writings combine a deep knowledge of Jewish law and classical texts with an insistence that progressive Jewish communities be built on traditions and ordinances that emerge out of both female and male experience and insight. She believes that the formation of Jewish law must be a dynamic process, evolving from communities in dialogue with the divine, and that Jews themselves must "regenerate a world of legal meaning that fully, complexly, and inclusively integrates the stories and revelations, the duties and commitments of Jewish women and men."[1]

What does it mean to *engender* Judaism? Non-Orthodox Judaisms distinguish themselves from Orthodoxy by their belief that Jews beget Judaism; they reshape and renew Judaism in the various times and places they inhabit. If we accept this premise, it will lead us to a new sense in which Judaism needs to be engendered. Jews in the Western world live in societies where the ethical ideal is for women to be full and equal social participants. But Judaism has only just begun to reflect and to address the questions, understandings, and obligations of both Jewish women and Jewish men. It is not yet fully attentive to the impact of gender and sexuality either on the classical texts or on the lived experiences of the people Israel. Until progressive Judaisms engender themselves in this second sense, they cannot engender fully adequate Judaisms in the first sense. In this book, I propose a theology for engendering Judaism in both senses: a way of thinking about and practicing Judaism that men and women recreate and renew together as equals.

Engendering: Not for Women Only

All of us must participate in both kinds of engendering. Relegating gender issues to women alone perpetuates a fallacy about the nature of Judaism. It presumes that Judaism is a body of gender-neutral texts and traditions and that women constitute a special gendered addendum to the community of its transmitters. It further presumes that while women are represented in Jewish tradition they are separate from it. Scholarship about their representation is classified as "Women in ... " or "Women and ... " and is regarded as nonessential knowledge of interest only to women. Men do not need to consider these special topics; they can simply study "Judaism." The truth is that, to paraphrase an old spiritual, all God's chillun got gender. There is not and never was a Judaism unaffected by the

Source for reading G.:   Rachel Adler, *Engendering Judaism: An Inclusive Theology and Ethics* (Philadelphia: Jewish Publication Society, 1998), pp. xiv–xvi, xx, xxii–xxiii, xxviii.

gendered perspectives of its transmitters and augmenters. If, as progressive Judaisms argue, social and historical factors affect Judaism, then it is hardly tenable to argue that gender is the only variable to which this rule does not apply. The impact of gender on Judaism, then, is not a women's issue; it is an issue for everyone who seeks to understand Judaism.

Engendering Judaism requires two tasks. The *critical task* is to demonstrate that historical understandings of gender affect all Jewish texts and contexts and hence require the attention of all Jews. But this is only the first step. There is also an *ethical task*. That gender categories and distinctions have changed in the past tells us nothing about what sorts of changes we ought to make in the future. These changes must be negotiated in conversations where participants invoke and reexamine the values and priorities enunciated in Jewish tradition in the light of the current needs, injuries, or aspirations demanding to be addressed.

Every aspect of this undertaking is complex: applying traditional values and priorities while remaining conscious of their historical contingency and their possible gender biases; conducting conversations among Jews whose beliefs, institutional affiliations, and experiences (including gender) differ widely; identifying needs, wounds, and aspirations, now full-time enterprises for social scientists, jurists, philosophers, cultural critics, and psychologists; and, finally, characterizing an elusive "present time" in rapidly mutating, pluralistic, postindustrial societies. The method for engendering Judaism, then, will have to be as complex as the Jewish people and the world they inhabit.

People who undertake ethical tasks do not come as blank slates. We bring our lives and memories, our abilities and interests, our commitments and dreams. I bring my own complex identity and commitments to this book. I am a woman descended from five generations of Reform Jews. I lived as an Orthodox Jew for many years and learned both to love and to struggle with traditional texts and praxis. I brought these concerns with me when I returned to Reform Judaism.

I am also a feminist. That is, I believe that being a woman or a man is an intricate blend of biological predispositions and social constructions that varies greatly according to time and culture. Regardless of its cultural specifics, gender has been used to justify unequal distributions of social power and privilege. Feminists view these power disparities as a moral wrong and an obstacle to human flourishing. This moral evil can be overcome only with great effort because its distortions pervade social institutions, personal relationships, and systems of knowledge and belief, including religious traditions. My commitment to feminism is based on both objective and subjective factors. I find its analysis intellectually convincing, but it also profoundly affects how I value myself as a person and what impact I believe I can have upon those around me. If I were not a feminist, I would not feel entitled to make theology. Accepting feminism's premises leads me directly to the critical and ethical obligations to engender Jewish theology. Judaism, like most cultural and religious systems, assigns men the lion's share of social and religious goods. Yet, as I argue during the course of this book, Judaism's commitment to justice obligates it to understand and to redress gender inequity. By engendering theology and ethics, Judaism takes feminism to heart....

Halakhah as a Category Conundrum

Halakhah has been the lightning rod for these controversies from the beginning because women experience its oppression directly in communal praxis and because halakhic method and categories claim to be authoritative and are attractively well defined and systematic. In addition, halakhic texts offered precedent and categories for discussing feminist concerns such as the meanings attached to women's bodies and blood, for which no theological warrant existed. Consequently, some feminists optimistically believed that halakhic change alone would remedy gender injustice in Judaism. However, it is very difficult to argue in androcentric terms without being inexorably dragged to androcentric conclusions. Moreover, halakhah is not only a theoretical discourse but an institutional structure over which exclusively male decisors exercise authority. These decisors were not eager to correct the system that privileged them.

Whether gender justice is possible within halakhah and whether a feminist Judaism requires a halakhah at all are foundational questions for feminist Jewish theology that have no parallel in Christian feminist theology. A language for critique could not be borrowed from it. Appropriating the terms and method of halakhah itself, many feminists concluded, drew them into a game they could not win. In its infancy, Reform Judaism had embarked on a critique of halakhah, but it had simply abandoned this project, so it offered few resources for feminist critique. Halakhah became the feminists' elephant in the living room. Everyone agreed it was in the way, and no one knew how to get rid of it.

The debate over halakhah as a locus of authority and authenticity dramatically illustrates the struggle over categories and method for Jewish feminist theology....

Praxis is the issue that suffuses all theological categories; a theology requires a method that can connect what we believe with what we do. Such a method has to situate itself in time. It needs to inform itself with lived realities and yet commit its adherents to a moral vision in which these realities are contingent and open to transformation. Because it is so difficult to extricate thought from praxis in a living Judaism, the method must mirror the fluid boundaries that exist among theology, halakhah and ethics, liturgy, and textual exegesis. The special problem for an engendered theology of Judaism is how to construct such a method in conversation with a tradition compromised by gender injustice.

An engendered Judaism needs the materials of the tradition to make credible theology. It will have to critique halakhah, and yet it must not leave itself without a basis for a praxis. It must rigorously interrogate the theological languages of the past while illuminating vocabularies of metaphor and devotion through which God and the people Israel can continue to reveal themselves to one another. It must also be able to interpret classical texts without rejecting them, apologizing for them, or merging with them. In other words, we will have to make the theological project as complicated as the world from which we launch it. This requires not *a* method but an entire repertory of methods for thinking, for reading, for describing, and for imagining how diversely situated and gendered people have lived, do live, and could live Jewish lives. In short, the method must be multidisciplinary....

Engendering the Jewish conversation is a project that will occupy many generations of Jews. I am grateful for the many conversations that have enriched this book – even those where the decibel level was rather high. Every one of them is precious. Speech creates the biblical world, and every part of the creation has something to say. The hills shout, the heavens and earth give testimony, and the days and nights speak to one another. May we too speak words of truth and joy.

Note

1   Rachel Adler, *Engendering Judaism: An Inclusive Theology and Ethics* (Philadelphia: Jewish Publication Society, 1998), p. 59.

Chapter 22

Judaism as a Theopolitical Phenomenon

Daniel J. Elazar

In a political tradition nearly four thousand years old, both rooted in a specific land and expressed through a worldwide diaspora, which has passed through manifestations as diverse as patriarchal tribalism, both dynastic and non-dynastic constitutional monarchy, nomocracy, trusteeship of those learned in the law, not to speak of the variants of aristocracy, oligarchy, and democracy, the documentary evidence available to us is massive.

The responsa literature (Hebrew: she'elot u'tshuvot) reflecting Jewish case law alone has well over twenty thousand written decisions, now computerized and hence immediately accessible. The published literature of Jewish thought, much of it containing material of political interest, from Philo Judaeus onward, occupies many linear feet of shelf space. Jewish histories with considerable attention to the political range from the classic works of the Bible and Flavius Josephus to the highly technical monographic studies of contemporary historians. Underlying all of this are the recognized classic texts of Jewish tradition, which contain extensive political material from a theopolitical perspective – the Bible, the Talmud, the literature of Kabbalah, and the great Codes the principal among them. Here we can barely scratch the surface, focusing on the modern period and briefly illustrating the main concepts of Judaism as a theopolitical phenomenon.

A. Certificate of Incorporation and Bylaws: Congregation Kehillat Jeshurun, New York (1972)

The constitutional documents of the last century presented in our selections reflect Jewish covenantal-constitutional expressions in both modern Israel and the American Jewish community. This constitution of a leading Orthodox congregation reflects the constitutional adaptation of the covenantal idea to the modern legal framework of an American state while at the same time attempting to adhere to traditional Jewish patterns.

CONGREGATION KEHILLAT JESHURUN,
New York, N.Y.

Certificate of Incorporation and Bylaws, 1972

WE HEREBY CERTIFY:

First: The name of this Corporation is Congregation Kehilath Jeshurun.

Second: The certificate of incorporation of this Corporation was duly executed on June 26, 1878, approved on October 17, 1878, by the Hon. George C. Barret, J.S.C., and recorded in the office of the Register of the City of New York, County of New York, in Liber 2 of Religious Corporations, at page 374, on January 17, 1884.

Third: This restated certificate restates the text of the certificate of incorporation of this Corporation, as amended and changed hereby, and the text of said certificate of incorporation as so restated and amended and changed, shall read as follows:

Article 1

Name

The name of the Corporation is Congregation Kehilath Jeshurun (For purposes of this Certificate of Incorporation, the Corporation shall, from time to time, be hereinafter referred to as the "Congregation").

Article II

Purposes

Section 1. The Congregation is a corporation as defined in subparagraph (a)(5) of Section 102 of the Not-for-Profit Corporation Law of the State of New York.

Section 2. The purpose of the Congregation is to maintain and conduct an Orthodox synagogue in conformance with the dictates of the Written and Oral Law, as articulated in the Shulchan Aruch and its commentaries, including, without limitations, the following:

a) Specific sections of the sanctuaries shall be designated for the separate and exclusive use of men and women at all religious services.

b) At no time shall instrumental music be played or caused to be heard during worship or prayer on the Sabbath or Festivals.

c) Decisions concerning religious worship and conduct shall be made by the Rabbis of the Synagogue.

Article III

Membership

Section 1. The Membership of the Congregation shall consist of the following classes:

   a) Regular Members: Any male Jew who has reached the age of twenty-one (21) years and, if married, has not been married contrary to Jewish Law, and is of good character shall be eligible to be a Regular Member of the Congregation.

   b) Special Members: Any unmarried female Jew who has reached the age of twenty-one (21) years and who shall be of good character shall be eligible to be a Special member of the Congregation.

   c) Such other class or classes of Members possessing such qualifications and enjoying such rights and privileges as shall be established or determined from time to time by the By-Laws or by a resolution or resolutions of the Board of Trustees authorized by the By-Laws.

Section 2. A Member shall be elected by vote of the Membership at the annual meeting of the Congregation.

Section 3. All Members of all classes (except for the class or classes specified in subsection 1(c) of this Article III, to whose members the applicable By-Laws and/or resolution or resolutions shall not have accorded voting rights) shall be entitled to vote at the meetings of the Congregation.

Section 4. Membership dues and other charges shall be assessed and collected as provided in the By-Laws.

Article IV

Trustees

Section 1. The affairs of the Congregation shall be managed by the board of directors (hereinafter referred to as "Trustees") of the Congregation, consisting of thirty (30) Regular Trustees and not more than fifteen (15) Associate Trustees.

Section 2. Regular Trustees shall be elected at annual meetings of the Congregation by a plurality of the Members present and entitled to vote at each meeting and shall serve for a term expiring the third annual meeting of the Congregation next succeeding their election or until their successors have been elected and shall have qualified. There shall be three classes of Regular Trustees consisting of ten (10) Regular Trustees each and, except as provided in Section 10 of this Article IV, only the vacancies created by the expiration on the date of an annual meeting of the Congregation, of the term of a particular class, shall be filled at such annual meeting.

Section 3. Associate Trustees shall be elected by the Congregation at the Annual Meeting of the Congregation upon the nomination of the President, for a term of one (1) year.

Section 4. No person may serve as a Trustee unless he has been a Regular Member of the Congregation for at least three (3) consecutive years prior to the date of his election or appointment, as the case may be.

Section 5. No person shall serve for more than nine (9) consecutive years as a Regular Trustee or for more than six (6) consecutive years as an Associate Trustee.

Section 6. If a person shall have served as a Regular Trustee for more than eight (8) consecutive years or as an Associate Trustee for more than five (5) consecutive years, he shall again become eligible to be elected as a Trustee (subject to the limitations contained in Section 5 of this Article IV) once two years have elapsed since the end of his most recent term. For purposes of this Section 6, in the case of a Trustee who has served during the period in question both as a Regular Trustee and as an Associate Trustee, in order to determine whether he has served for more than the requisite number of consecutive years, there shall be included his uninterrupted years of consecutive service in each capacity unless at least two years shall have elapsed between the end of the last term in one capacity and the commencement of the first term in the other capacity.

Section 7. The provisions of Section 5, and 6 of this Article IV shall not apply to Regular Trustees who were elected or re-elected at the annual meeting of the Congregation held in the year 5730/1970.

Section 8. The President, Vice-President, Treasurer and Secretary of the Congregation, if not Trustees, shall nevertheless it [sic] as members ex-officio of the Board of Trustees.

Section 9. Every Trustee (whether a Regular Trustee or an Associate Trustee) shall be entitled to vote at any meeting of the Board of Trustees.

Section 10. In the event or the resignation or death of a Regular Trustee, the vacancy then created shall not be filled until the next annual meeting of the Congregation, at which time a successor shall be elected to fill the unexpired portion (if any) of the term of such resigned or dead Regular Trustee.

Article V

Officers

Section 1. The officers of the Congregation shall consist of the President, the Vice-President, the Treasurer and the Secretary, who shall be elected by the Membership, and such other officers as shall be elected from time to time by the Board of Trustees. Each officer shall be a Regular Member and in the case of the President, Vice-President and Treasurer, shall have been a Trustee of the Congregation for at least one year.

Section 2. The President, Vice-President, Treasurer and Secretary shall be elected at annual meetings of the Congregation by a plurality of the Members present and entitled to vote at such meeting, and shall serve for a term expiring at the annual meeting of the Congregation next succeeding their election or until their respective successors shall have been elected and shall have qualified.

Section 3. No person shall serve as President for more than six consecutive years.

Section 4. If a person shall have served as President for six consecutive years, he shall again become eligible to be elected to such office (subject to the limitations contained in Section 3 of this Article V) after a lapse of two years since the end of his most recent term.

Section 5. The officers elected by the Board of Trustees shall serve at the pleasure of the Board except as provided in Section 6 of this Article V.

Section 6. In the event of the death or resignation of the President, Vice-President, Treasurer or Secretary of the Congregation, the vacancy created thereby may be filled by either of the following methods:

a) The Board of Trustees may elect a successor to fill the unexpired term, in which case the vote of a majority of the Board of Trustees shall be required for election;

b) The Board of Trustees may call a special meeting of the Membership to elect a successor to fill the unexpired term, in which case the vote of a plurality of the Members present and entitled to vote shall be required for election.

Article VI

Amendment

Section 1. Any provision of this Certificate of Incorporation, other than Article II and Section 2 of this Article VI may be amended at any regular or special meeting of the Membership by the affirmative vote of a majority of the Members present.

Section 2. The provisions of Article II of this Certificate of Incorporation and of this Section 2 may be amended only by the affirmative vote at two successive annual meetings of the Congregation of 90% of the total Members.

Article VII

Miscellaneous

Section 1. The office of the Congregation is to be located in the City and County of New York, State of New York, in which the activities of the Congregation are principally to be conducted.

Section 2. The post office address to which the Secretary of State shall mail a copy of any notice required by law is 125 East 85th Street, New York, New York 10028.

Section 3. The By-Laws of the Congregation may be adopted, amended or repealed either by the Membership or the Trustees; provided, however, that the Trustees shall not have the power to amend or repeal any By-Law adopted by the Membership.

Fourth: This restated certificate of incorporation and the amendments and changes therein contained were duly authorized by the unanimous vote of the Board of Trustees of said Corporation duly held on April 20, 1972, and by a vote of at least two-thirds majority of the members entitled to vote thereon at a meeting of said membership duly held on May 7, 1972.

BY-LAWS OF CONGREGATION KEHILATH JESHURUN

Article I

Purpose and Intent of By-Laws

It is the intent of these By-Laws to implement and to supplement the provisions of the restated Certificate of Incorporation (the "Certificate of Incorporation") of Congregation Kehilath Jeshurun (the "Congregation"). Matters there covered will not here be repeated except in the interests of clarity. Definitions contained therein are applicable to these By-Laws. Should there be any conflict between these By-Laws and the said restated Certificate, then the latter shall be supreme.

Article II

Membership

Section 1. The Membership of the Congregation shall include the following classes:

    a) Regular Members: Any male Jew who has reached the age of twenty-one (21) and, if married, has not been married contrary to Jewish law, and is of good character, shall be eligible to be a Regular Member of the Congregation. Regular Members shall be entitled to vote at the meetings of the Congregation.

    b) Special Members: Any unmarried female Jew who has reached the age of twenty-one (21), who shall be of good character, shall be eligible to be a Special Member of the Congregation. Special Members shall be entitled to vote at the meetings of the Congregation.

c) Associate Members: Any male Jew who has reached the age of twenty-one (21) but who has not yet reached the age of thirty (30) and, if married, has not been married contrary to Jewish law, who is of good character, and any unmarried female Jew who has reached the age of twenty-one (21) but who has not yet reached the age of thirty (30), who is of good character, if he or she, as the case may be, shall satisfy such other criteria as are established from time to time by the Board of Trustees of the Congregation shall, upon payment of dues which shall be no greater than one-half (1/2) the dues of Regular Members, be eligible to be an Associate Member of the Congregation. Associate Members shall be entitled to vote at meetings of the Congregation.

d) Junior Members: Any male Jew who has reached the age of thirteen (13) but who has not yet reached the age of twenty-one (21), and any female Jew who has reached the age of twelve (12) but has not yet reached the age of twenty-one (21) shall, if he or she satisfies the criteria established from time to time by the Board of Trustees of the Congregation, and pays the dues required, be eligible to be a Junior Member. Junior Members shall be elected by vote of the Board of Trustees of the Congregation. Junior Members shall not have the right to vote at meetings of the Congregation.

Section 2. A Member (other than a Junior Member) shall be elected by vote of Members entitled to vote at the annual meeting of the Congregation. Each candidate for Membership shall file a written application on such form as the Board of Trustees may prescribe, which form shall provide that, among other things, the applicant agrees to be bound by the Certificate of Incorporation of the Congregation and these By-Laws, and any amendments thereof, along with all rules, regulations and decisions duly adopted by the Board of Trustees of the Congregation. Each application shall be referred to the Membership Committee which shall investigate the application and report its findings to the Board of Trustees. Upon the approval of an application by the Board of Trustees, the application shall be referred to the next annual meeting of the Congregation for action by the Membership.

Section 3. Every Member, and, if married, his wife, shall be entitled to a seat at High Holiday services without further charges than payment of annual dues and assessments as hereinafter specified.

Section 4.

a) Annual Membership does shall be due and payable by each Member, as of each May 1st, in advance, in the following sums:

    Regular Members (married) – $300.00
    Regular Members (unmarried) – 150.00
    Special Members – 150.00
    Associate Members (married) – 150.00
    Associate Members (unmarried) – 75.00
    Junior Members – 50.00

The President shall have the power to arrange for installment payments of such dues in such fashion as may be just, based upon the financial need of the Member.

b) After having been recommended by the Board of Trustees, dues may be changed at a meeting of the Congregation held upon specific written notice of an intention to take such action, sent by mail to each Member entitled to vote thereon at least ten (10) days prior to such meeting.

c) After having been recommended by the Board of Trustees, special assessments may be levied by a two-thirds (2/3) majority vote of the Members voting at a meeting of the Congregation held upon specific written notice of an intention to take such action sent by mail to each Member entitled to vote thereon at least ten (10) days prior to such meeting. Special assessments shall be due and payable as may be provided for in the resolution adopting such assessment.

d) A Member who is delinquent in the payment of dues or assessments shall be subject to expulsion. No Member may be expelled for such delinquency without a prior written notice, giving him or her a reasonable opportunity to cure such delinquency.

Section 5.

a) A Member shall be subject to expulsion, suspension, or other disciplinary action if found guilty, as hereinbelow provided for (except with respect to a delinquency in paying dues or assessments) of violating any provision of the Certificate of Incorporation or these By-Laws, any duly adopted rule, regulation or decision of the Board of Trustees or the Congregation, or conduct detrimental to the Congregation.

b) A Member may be disciplined only by the action of a majority of the entire Board of Trustees upon a hearing, and after having first been served with written specific charges and given a reasonable opportunity to prepare his defense. Disciplinary action by the Board of Trustees shall be subject to appeal to the Membership, at the next meeting of the Congregation, provided that a written notice of intention to appeal shall have been filed with the officers of the Congregation within thirty (30) days of the action of the Board of Trustees.

Article III

Government

Section 1. The government of the Congregation shall be vested in the Membership of the Congregation, acting at Membership meetings. Between meetings, the government of the Congregation (except to the extent prohibited by the Certificate of Incorporation or the By-Laws) shall be vested in the Board of Trustees of the Congregation, acting at meetings called by the President from time to time. Between meetings of the Board of Trustees, the government in the ordinary course of affairs of the Congregation, and, except to the extent prohibited by the

Certificate of Incorporation or the By-Laws, shall be vested in the officers of the Congregation.

Section 2.

a) There shall be an annual Membership meeting which shall take place each year at 8:00 P.M. on the first Tuesday of May in the Congregation Assembly Hall, or at such other date, time or place as the Board of Trustees shall determine. At least ten (10) days' written notice of meeting shall be given by mail to every Member.

b) Special membership meetings shall be called by the President, or by direction of the Board of Trustees, or upon a written petition signed by at least fifty (50) Members of the Congregation entitled to vote thereat. At least ten (10) days' written notice of a special meeting shall be given by mail, which notice shall specify the business to be taken up and acted upon at such meeting.

c) There shall be no absentee or proxy voting on any question or matter.

d) One hundred (100) Members entitled to vote shall constitute a quorum.

Section 3. The Board of Trustees shall meet bi-monthly on the first Monday of the month, or such other date as the President may determine. Special meetings of the Board of Trustees may be called by the President and shall be called by him upon the written request of five (5) Trustees. All meetings of the Board of Trustees shall be called upon at least five (5) days' written notice. Ten (10) Trustees shall constitute a quorum.

Article IV

Elections

Section 1. All elections shall be conducted at annual meetings or at special meetings called for that purpose.

Section 2. At least two months before the annual meeting, the President shall designate a nominating committee. This committee shall nominate one candidate for each elective office, and shall file its report of nominations at least two weeks before the annual meeting, which report shall be open for inspection by any Member at the Congregation office during ordinary business hours. Any Member of the Congregation, not so nominated, qualified to be an officer or Regular Trustee, may be nominated in a writing signed after the nominating committee's report shall have been filed, by twenty-five (25) Members of the Congregation entitled to vote at meetings of the Congregation, which writing shall be filed in the Congregation's office at least five (5) days before the annual meeting. Persons not nominated by either of the two methods herein specified may not be otherwise nominated.

Section 3. Elections shall be conducted only among those nominated as herein provided for. Elections shall be conducted separately for each office in the following order: Regular Trustee; President, Vice President; Treasurer and Secretary. Votes shall be counted by three (3) tellers appointed by the President before the elections commence. The candidate receiving the majority of votes for each office shall be deemed elected. In the event that there are more than two candidates for any office or Trusteeship, and no candidate receives a majority on the first ballot, successive ballots shall be cast for all candidates excluding, in each instance, the candidate who received the fewest number of votes on the preceding ballot, until one candidate receives a majority of votes.

Article V

Duties of Officers

Section 1. The President shall be the Chief executive officer of the Congregation. He shall be Chairman of the Board of Trustees. He shall preside at all meetings of the Congregation and at all meetings of the Board of Trustees, but shall not vote except in case of a tie. He shall appoint all committees, special and standing, and shall be an ex-officio member of all such committees. He shall have such further powers and duties as are usual to his office.

Section 2. The Vice-President shall assist the President and in the absence of the President, the Vice-President shall perform all the duties of the President. In case of the disability, death, resignation or removal from office of the President, the Vice-President shall act as President until the vacancy so created is filled as provided for in the Certificate of Incorporation.

Section 3. The Treasurer shall collect and receive all moneys due the Congregation and shall deposit same in the name of the Congregation in such banks as the Board of Trustees shall determine. He shall keep the financial records of the Congregation. He shall have such further powers and duties as are usual to his office.

Section 4. The Secretary shall keep the correct minutes of all meetings of the Board of Trustees and of the Congregation. He shall keep the seal of the Congregation and be in charge of all files and correspondence.

Section 5. All checks, drafts, notes, bills of sale, contracts, mortgages, deeds and other documents relating to property or rights or interests therein, of the Congregation shall be signed jointly by at least two of the Congregation's officers, after having been duly authorized by resolution of the Board of Trustees, or, where otherwise required, by the membership at a meeting.

Article VI

Religious Officials

Section 1. The Congregation shall select as hereinafter provided, such number of Rabbis, Cantors and Ritual Directors as it shall determine it needs.

Section 2.

a)   Any Rabbi of the Congregation must be Orthodox and possess the required learning to enable him to decide questions of Jewish law. He should be duly ordained by a recognized Yeshiva or shall possess an Ordination Certificate signed by at least two recognized Rabbis. Ordination, whether by a Yeshiva or individual Rabbis, shall be in the form of Semicha for Hatarat Hora'ah (Ordination granting authority to decide matters of religious law).

b) Any Cantor or Ritual Director of the Congregation should, in addition to the usual qualifications associated with his office, be an Orthodox, observant Jew in keeping with the laws of the Shulchan Aruch.

Section 3. The Board of Trustees shall adopt such procedures as it deems necessary to select Rabbis, Cantors and Ritual Directors and to negotiate and fix the terms and conditions under which such religious officials serve.

Article VII

Property

Section 1. All property, real and personal, and all rights and interests in property belonging to the Congregation shall be held in the name of the Congregation and shall be used, sold, invested or otherwise disposed of as may be authorized by the Board of Trustees from time to time.

Section 2. The Congregation shall have the same power of investment as does a Trustee under the Estates, Powers and Trusts Law of the State of New York presently in effect and as may hereafter be amended.

Article VIII

Committees

Section 1. Promptly after his election, the President shall appoint a House Committee, Cemetery Committee, Membership Committee, Adult Education Committee and such other committees as he deems advisable, and define the duties and functions of each such committee.

Section 2. Committees shall report to the Board of Trustees from time to time, as required by the Board.

Article IX

Amendments

Section 1. The provisions of these By-Laws dealing with the qualifications of religious officials may only be amended by the affirmative vote of 90 percent of the total membership of the Congregation at two successive annual meetings of the Congregation.

Section 2. Dues as fixed by Article II, Section 4(a) of these By-Laws shall be subject to amendment as provided in Article II, Section 4(b).

Section 3. Except as provided for in Sections 1 and 2 of this Article IX, the other provisions of these By-Laws may be amended as follows:

a)   At any regular or special meeting of the membership, by the affirmative vote of a majority of the members present; or

b)   By the affirmative vote of a majority of the Board of Trustees present at two successive meetings of the Board.

B.   Constitution and Bylaws of Monmouth Reform Temple, Monmouth, New Jersey (1988)

The Monmouth Reform Temple, located in one of the exurbs of New York City, prides itself as being at the forefront of the changes taking place in American Jewish life. Its rabbi was the first woman to receive rabbinical ordination in the United States. Its constitution was developed over a period of two years by the congregational membership working hard to achieve a document that would reflect both their principles and interests. The result reflects the new openness of a non-insular Jewish community even as it represents an effort to protect those Jewish elements deemed to be for Jews only. What those elements are reveals much about American Jewish thinking towards the end of the twentieth century.

MONMOUTH REFORM TEMPLE
Monmouth, New Jersey

Constitution and By-Laws, 1988

PREAMBLE: In order to perpetuate and enhance the religion of our ancestors, to uphold, teach and foster the essential principles and moral and ethical values of Judaism, to encourage and provide opportunities for divine worship, education and service as a Reform Jewish Congregation and for the spread of enlightened religious sentiments, to promote a better understanding and relationship among all people of good will and to advance the welfare of all those who may come under its influence, we do dedicate ourselves to the task of establishing a Reform Jewish Congregation.

Article I

Section 1. *Name.* This Congregation shall be known as MONMOUTH REFORM TEMPLE.

Section 2. *Object and Purpose.* The purpose of the Congregation shall be to promote Judaism by means of public and private worship, by religious education, and through social welfare activities, by emphasizing the principles of righteousness and fellowship in society at large, and such other means as shall serve to convey the teachings of Judaism.

Section 3. *Forms, Interpretation, and Affiliation.* The Congregation shall follow the forms, practices, and usage of a liberal interpretation of Judaism and shall affiliate itself with the Union of American Hebrew Congregations (UAHC).

Article II

Membership

Section 1. *Members.* "Upon approval by the Board of Trustees, any person of the Jewish faith or any person seeking to be permanently identified with Judaism and not actively participating in another religion is a member of the Congregation of Monmouth Reform Temple. The Rabbi shall keep a record indicating who is Jewish and who is not. A child of any member is also a member, provided that the child is not practicing another religion. Any child who is a member and who either marries or attains age 21 and is self-supporting shall no longer be considered a member of the Congregation until such child has applied and been accepted for membership."

Section 2. *Dues.* Dues-paying-units shall be determined by the Board of Trustees, as shall annual dues and building fund obligation for the fiscal year. Dues shall be payable in advance on a monthly, quarterly, semiannual or annual basis at the option of the member. The fiscal year shall commence July 1st. Dues will be determined by the member according to a "Fair Share Program."

Section 3. *Delinquency.* Any dues-paying-unit which is in arrears on any obligation to the Congregation for over three months may be suspended by the Board of Trustees upon failure of such family to pay such obligation within 30 days from the date of a written request for payment. For the purpose of this section, dues are considered payable in advance on a monthly basis; Building Fund obligation is considered payable as determined by the Board of Trustees.

Section 4. *Resignation.* Any member may resign from the Congregation by submitting a resignation in writing subject to the approval of the Board of Trustees.

Article III

Privileges of Membership

"A non-delinquent member of the Congregation shall be entitled to privileges of membership, subject to the rules, regulations and fees prescribed by the Board of Trustees.

Section 1. These privileges shall include:

a. The right to enjoy the fellowship of the Congregation.
b. The right to receive education in the Jewish tradition.
c. The right to be seated in the House of Worship of the Congregation at all times including the High Holy Days.
d. The right to participate in ritual practices, the specifics of which will be determined by the Ritual Committee and Rabbi.
e. The right to vote at all meetings of the Congregation, if either Confirmed or over the age of 18.
f. The right to use the Temple building for approved functions.

Section 2. The following privileges require membership in the Jewish faith, through either birth or conversion:

a. The right to receive religious education in preparation for Bar/Bat Mitzvah and/or Confirmation, and to receive same in the House of Worship of the Congregation.
b. The right to be elected as an officer or trustee of the Congregation.
c. The right to chair a Standing Committee.
d. The right to be elected as president of an Auxiliary of the Congregation.
e. The right to be appointed to the following Standing Committees: Israel, Jewish Philanthropy, Religious Education, Ritual, UAHC."

Article IV

Board of Trustees

Section 1. *Members of the Board.* The Board of Trustees shall be composed of the eight officers of the Congregation, the twelve Trustees, the President of Sisterhood, the President of Brotherhood, the President of the Senior Youth Group and any eligible past Presidents of the Congregation.

Section 2. *Conduct.* The Board of Trustees shall conduct their meetings in accordance with:

a. The Laws of the State of New Jersey.
b. The Constitution and By-Laws of the Temple.
c. Roberts' Rules of Parliamentary Procedure.

Section 3. *General Powers.* The Board of Trustees shall govern the affairs of the Congregation, control its revenue and property, and take such action as shall in its judgment best promote the welfare thereof.

Section 4. *Special Powers.* The Board of Trustees shall have the power to:

a. Elect members of the Congregation, in accordance with these By-Laws.
b. Determine and fix all dues and assessments including the fees to be paid for Religious School.
c. Remit or waive the whole or any portion of such dues and assessments according to its best judgment in hardship cases.

d. Select such employees as may be necessary, fix their duties and compensation; or remove such employees, unless otherwise prescribed by these By-Laws.

e. Prepare and submit an annual budget for the approval of the Congregation at its regular annual meeting.

f. Order a special meeting of the Congregation whenever it may be deemed necessary on its own motion or on the written request of ten percent of the qualified voters of the Congregation.

g. Expel or separate from service any member, officer or trustee as provided in Section 8 of this Article and in Article XIII.

h. Purchase, mortgage, or lease, subject to the approval of a majority of the Congregation present at a meeting of said Congregation, real estate for the purpose of providing a House of Worship, cemetery land or plots, or any other purpose incidental to the operation of the Congregation.

i. Authorize expenditures of monies from the funds of the Congregation in payment of any debts lawfully incurred on behalf of and for the Congregation.

j. Provide for an examination of the financial records of the Congregation.

k. Determine the terms and conditions to be observed by members and nonmembers of the Congregation for obtaining seats in the Congregation's House of Worship on the High Holy Days of Rosh Hashanah and Yom Kippur.

l. Authorize the formation and termination of any auxiliary or activity units of the Congregation.

m. Authorize any committee in charge of any of the functions of the Temple to solicit funds for its activities, to appoint its own treasurer and disburse such funds. Said committee should render an accounting of all receipts and disbursements whenever requested by the Board.

Section 5. Specification of the aforementioned powers shall in no way be construed to be a limitation of any of the general powers inherent in the Board of Trustees and necessary for the proper conduct in the affairs of the Congregation, except those powers specifically reserved to the Congregation.

Section 6. *Meetings*. The Board of Trustees shall meet at least once every month, and at the call of the President upon two days notice. Five Trustees may call a meeting of the Board of Trustees by giving at least twenty-four hours notice thereof, personally or by mail to all other Trustees and stating the purpose thereof. All meetings of the Board of Trustees shall be open to all members of the Congregation with the exception of those meetings or portions of meetings at which matters are discussed for which confidentiality is appropriate. In case of a tie vote at a meeting of the Board of Trustees, the presiding officer of such meeting even though having voted previously shall have an additional vote.

Section 7. *Quorum*. A majority of the Board of Trustees shall constitute a quorum.

Section 8. *Absence from Board Meetings.* A majority of the members of the Board of Trustees may remove any Officer or Trustee who has been absent without reasonable cause from three successive regular Board meetings.

Section 9. *Vacancy.* Should a vacancy occur on the Board of Trustees, the President with the approval of the Board of Trustees shall immediately fill such vacancy until the next annual meeting of the Congregation when the office of such Officer or Trustee shall then be filled, by election, for its unexpired term.

Section 10. *Eligible Past Presidents.* The President of the Congregation, having served for at least one full fiscal year, shall, upon election of a new President, become a member of the Board of Trustees with all the privileges pertaining thereto for a period of two years.

Section 11. *Presidents of Certain Temple Auxiliaries.* The Presidents of the Brotherhood, Sisterhood and the Senior Youth Group must be members of the Congregation.

Section 12. The President of the Congregation shall chair the Board of Trustees and it shall be the President's duty to preside at meetings of the Board of Trustees, decide all questions of order, and appoint such committees of the Board of Trustees as may from time to time be required.

Article V

Officers

Section 1. *Duties of the President.* The President shall preside at all meetings of the Congregation and of the Board of Trustees, shall enforce the By-Laws; and shall sign all checks jointly with the Treasurer, and official documents; and shall be an ex-officio member of all standing committees other than the Nominating Committee. It shall be the President's duty also to

a.   Decide all questions of order, subject to appeal by any Trustee or member, as the case may be, to the Congregation.

b.   Assign or designate an Officer or Trustee to sign all commitments and contracts over a specified amount. The specified amount shall be fixed by the Board of Trustees.

c.   Appoint such committees as may from time to time be required, except as otherwise provided.

d.   Call a special meeting of the Congregation or Board of Trustees, whenever, in the President's opinion, necessity therefor exists.

e.   Appoint with the advice and consent of the Board of Trustees, the representatives from the Congregation, to the UAHC and its subsidiary organizations.

f.   Appoint people to chair Standing Committees.

g.   Cast the deciding vote on all questions in which there may be an equal division of votes, except in the election of officers and appeals from the President's decision.

h.   Present a written report to the Congregation at its annual meeting of the state of affairs of the Congregation.

i.   The President shall assign a different Vice-President to oversee each group of standing committees designated in Article IX, Section 2.

Section 2. *Duties of the Senior Vice-President*. The Senior Vice-President shall in the absence of or vacancy in the office of the President assume all the duties and responsibilities incumbent upon the President. As assigned by the President, the Senior Vice-President shall oversee one group of standing committees designated in Article IX, Section 2.

Section 3. *Duties of the Second Vice-President*. The second Vice-President shall in the absence of or vacancy in the office of the Senior Vice-President assume all the duties and responsibilities incumbent upon the Senior Vice-President. As assigned by the President, the Second Vice-President shall oversee one group of standing committees designated in Article IX, Section 2.

Section 4. *Duties of the Third Vice-President*. The third Vice-President shall in the absence of or vacancy in the office of the second Vice-President assume all the duties and responsibilities incumbent upon the second Vice-President. As assigned by the President, the Third Vice-President shall oversee one group of standing committees designated in Article IX, Section 2.

Section 5. *Duties of the Treasurer*. It shall be the responsibility of the Treasurer to:

a.   Receive all money belonging to the Congregation, and give receipts therefore when necessary, and all money so received shall be deposited in the name of the Congregation in such bank or banks as the Board of Trustees may direct.

b.   Pay all orders, when attested in writing by authorized Board members, people who chair committees, the Rabbi or the Temple Administrator, as appropriate and sign all checks jointly with the President.

c.   The Treasurer shall be a member of the Finance Committee, attend its meetings, and have all relevant books and accounts ready for settlement at the expiration of the Treasurer's term or at any time the Board of Trustees may request upon two weeks' notice by mail.

d.   Perform such other duties as the office demands.

e.   Deliver to any successor Treasurer, when duly qualified, all money and other properties of the Congregation, and all books and papers pertaining to the office which may be in the Treasurer's possession.

f.   Make a written monthly report to the Board of Trustees and a written annual report to the Congregation at each annual meeting of the Congregation on the financial condition of the Congregation.

Section 6. *Duties of the Recording Secretary*. It shall be the responsibility of the Recording Secretary to:

a.   Attend all meetings, read the minutes and reports, and keep a correct record of the proceedings.

b.   Be the Custodian of the seal of the Congregation, and affix it to, and sign all documents emanating from the Congregation or Board of Trustees which require a seal.

c.   Perform such other duties as the office demands.

d.   Deliver to any successor Recording Secretary, when duly qualified, all property, including the Seal of the Congregation, and all relevant books and papers pertaining to the office, which may be in the Recording Secretary's possession.

Section 7. *Duties of Corresponding Secretary*. It shall be the responsibility of the Corresponding Secretary to:

a.   Attend all meetings and read the correspondence.

b.   Mail out all notices of meetings; both those of the Congregation and the Board of Trustees.

c.   Write all necessary letters for the Congregation.

d.   Perform such other duties as the office demands.

e.   Deliver to any successor Corresponding Secretary, when duly qualified, property, books and papers pertaining to the office which may be in the Corresponding Secretary's possession.

Section 8. *Duties of the Financial Secretary*. It shall be the responsibility of the Financial Secretary to:

a.   Keep a register of the names of all the members of the Congregation with complete data as to their membership.

b.   Keep a correct account between the Congregation and its members, make out and mail all bills for dues and assessments and other charges and supervise their collection.

c.   Deliver promptly to the Treasurer all money collected.

d.   Perform such other duties as the office demands.

e.   In the absence of the Treasurer, sign all checks jointly with the President.

f.   Deliver to any successor Financial Secretary, when duly qualified, all money and other property, and all books and papers pertaining to the office which may be in the Financial Secretary's possession.

g.   Be a regular member of the Finance Committee.

Article VI

Nomination and Election of Officers and Trustees

Section 1. The Congregation shall at the annual meeting in odd numbered years elect for a term of two years the Officers of the Congregation as follows: President, Senior Vice-President, Second Vice-President, Third Vice-President, Treasurer, Recording Secretary, Corresponding Secretary, and Financial Secretary. The Congregation shall at every annual meeting elect four trustees for a term of three years. The Congregation shall at every annual meeting elect Officers and

Trustees as needed to fill unexpired terms which have become vacant since the last annual meeting.

Section 2. No officer shall be elected for more than two consecutive terms in the same office, nor shall any trustee be elected for more than three consecutive terms. In any case, no one shall remain a member of the Board of Trustees for a period in excess of nine consecutive years except an immediate past president of the Congregation who may serve eleven consecutive years. Membership on the Board of Trustees as President of Brotherhood, Sisterhood, or Senior Youth Group shall not be counted in the nine or eleven year limitation.

Section 3. The terms of office of the Treasurer and Financial Secretary shall be concurrent with the Temple's fiscal year, July 1st to June 30th. The terms of all other Officers and Trustees shall end when their successors are elected.

Section 4. Nomination of members of the Congregation to serve on the Board of Trustees shall be made by the Nominating Committee appointed by the President with the consent of the Board of Trustees. The Nominating Committee shall consist of five members, two of whom shall be members of the Board of Trustees. No person who accepts appointment to the Nominating Committee shall be eligible for nomination by that committee. The President will notify each person offered appointment to the Committee of this provision.

Section 5. Nominations by the Nominating Committee shall be reported to the President of the Congregation and said slate shall be mailed to every member family at least 30 days prior to the date of election.

Section 6. Any further nominations of members of the Congregation to serve on the Board of Trustees may be made by written petition signed by at least ten (10) percent of the members eligible to vote and filed with the President at least fifteen days prior to the date of election.

Section 7. Notice of nominations by petition, if any, shall be mailed to every member family at least seven days prior to the date of election.

Section 8. In any contested election, the vote shall be by secret ballot, the nominees receiving the greatest number of votes to fill vacancies shall be declared elected.

Article VII

Rabbi

Section 1. *Election.* When a vacancy in the pulpit occurs, the President or the President's delegate(s) shall contact the Rabbinical Placement Commission of the UAHC and the Central Conference of American Rabbis (CCAR) to arrange to interview candidates for the pulpit. The Rabbi shall be elected by the Board of Trustees with such salary and for such period of time as may be determined, subject to the approval of a majority vote of the Congregation present at an annual or special meeting of the Congregation.

Section 2. *Affiliation to Congregation.* The Rabbi and the Rabbi's family shall be ex-officio members of the Congregation, enjoying all privileges of membership. They shall not pay dues or assessments, nor shall they be entitled to vote on congregational matters.

Section 3. *Duties.* The Rabbi shall perform all duties incumbent upon and in accordance with the office and as recommended by the guidelines for Rabbinical-Congregational Relationships established by the UAHC and the CCAR. The Rabbi shall be an ex-officio member of the Board of Trustees and all standing committees as described in Article IX, Section 2.

Section 4. *Congregational Relationship.* In the even that a serious disagreement occurs between the Rabbi and the Congregation, 15 percent of the Congregation may petition in writing and request the Board of Trustees to investigate. A copy of such petition stating the grievances shall be sent by the Secretary to the Rabbi by registered mail. At its first meeting after the receipt of such petition, the Board of Trustees shall select a committee to investigate. A member signing such a petition shall not serve on the investigating committee. The investigating committee will seek counsel from the National Commission of Rabbinical-Congregational Relationships and shall file a report with the Board of Trustees. If the Board of Trustees finds valid grievances, the Board of Trustees shall conduct a hearing, upon 20 days notice by registered mail to the Rabbi. At the hearing, the Rabbi shall have adequate opportunity to rebut the charges, and shall have the right to be represented by legal counsel at the hearing. Two-thirds of the members of the Board of Trustees may then request the resignation of the Rabbi before the termination of the Rabbi's contract. The Board of Trustees' request for resignation may be overridden by a majority of the Congregation at a regular or special Congregational meeting.

Article VIII

Seating

Section 1. *Unassigned Seats.* Seats in the synagogue shall be unassigned. It shall, however, be the duty of the Board of Trustees, whenever required on special occasions, to make a reservation sufficient to accommodate the membership: it being understood that no specific assignments to individuals shall be made within said reservation, except when in the judgement of the Board of Trustees necessity requires such assignment of seats. No charges or assessments of any kind shall be made for such assignment of seats.

Article IX

Committees

Section 1. *Executive Committee.* The Executive Committee shall consist of the President, the Vice-Presidents, and other members of the Board of Trustees as shall be appointed by the President with the approval of the Board of Trustees. The President shall act as chairman thereof. During the intervals between the meetings of the Board of Trustees, this committee shall have the powers of the Board of Trustees in emergency matters. All actions of this Committee on behalf of the Board of Trustees shall be reported to and subject to revision, alteration or approval by the Board of Trustees.

Section 2. *Standing Committees*. The standing committees of the Congregation are named in the following three lists. As shown in the lists, each standing committee belongs to one of three groups. Each standing committee indicated with the letter "B" must be chaired by an Officer or by a member of the Board of Trustees. The person who chairs each standing committee will appoint its members. In any case no one shall serve as a voting member on more than three standing committees.

Religious and Educational Practices Group: Adult Education (B), Library, Religious Education (B), Ritual (B), Scholarships, Youth Activities (B).

Finance and Operations Group: Arts and Decorations, Finance (B), House (B), Membership (B), Ways and Means (B).

Community and Religious Relations Group: Fellowship, Israel, Jewish Philanthropy, Outreach (B), Publicity, Social Action (B), UAHC.

a. *Adult Education Committee*. It shall be the responsibility of the Adult Education Committee to promote adult educational activities and programs for the Congregation and the Community.

b. *Arts and Decorations Committee*. It shall be the responsibility of the Arts and Decorations Committee to enhance the appearance of the Temple.

c. *Finance Committee*.

(a). It shall be the responsibility of the Finance Committee to make a detailed estimate of the income and expenses for the ensuing year and to furnish same to the Board of Trustees in writing at least fifteen (15) days prior to the annual meeting of the Congregation.

(b). It shall also be the responsibility of this committee to oversee compliance to the budget.

d. *House Committee*.

(a). It shall be the responsibility of the House Committee to find suitable and adequate quarters for the Congregation, to manage and keep the building and property of the Congregation in good order and repair. It shall have authority to grant permission to use the Temple building subject to such rules as may be adopted by the Board of Trustees.

(b). It shall also be the responsibility of this committee to maintain a continuing inventory of all property of the Congregation and to arrange for proper insurance coverage of said property.

e. *Membership Committee*. It shall be the responsibility of the Membership Committee to ascertain the eligibility of prospective members, to assist applicants for membership and propose them to the Board of Trustees, and to facilitate the participation of all members in Temple activities.

   f.   *Publicity Committee.*
        (a).   It shall be the responsibility of the Publicity and Public Relations
               Committee to promote the best interests of the Congregation by
               effective publicity in the press and other media and to seek out
               and maintain good and beneficial public relations with the com-
               munity.
        (b).   It shall also be the responsibility of this Committee to set up and
               maintain a calendar of Congregational events.
   g.   *Religious Education Committee.* It shall be the responsibility of the Religious
        Education Committee to make all regulations necessary to meet the reli-
        gious educational needs of member children, including the employment
        and compensation of qualified staff and the adoption of the course of study
        for the Religious School.
   h.   *Ritual Committee.* It shall be the responsibility of the Ritual Committee to
        establish and maintain the practices and procedures for the conduct of all
        religious services. This includes but is not limited to arranging for particip-
        ants, arranging for and maintaining music, arranging for seating, and
        having available for use all ceremonial objects essential for the conduct of
        the services.
   i.   *Social Action Committee.* It shall be the responsibility of the Social Action
        Committee to promote the Temple's commitment to social ideals by pro-
        posing positions for consideration and adoption by the Board of Trustees,
        and by planning and undertaking appropriate actions.
   j.   *Youth Activities Committee.* It shall be the responsibility of the Youth
        Activities Committee to initiate and promote Youth Activities to further
        the religious and educational aims of the Temple and to coordinate the
        various Youth Activities of the Temple and its affiliated organizations.
   k.   *Ways and Means Committee.*
        (a).   To assure that the fund raising activities of Sisterhood, Brotherhood
               and Senior Youth Group are consistent with Temple policy.
        (b).   To administer all other fund raising activities of the Temple.
   l.   *UAHC Committee.* It shall be the responsibility of the UAHC Committee to
        provide liaison with the UAHC.
   m.   *Jewish Philanthropy Committee.* It shall be the responsibility of the Jewish
        Philanthropy Committee to provide liaison with Jewish philanthropic
        organizations.
   n.   *Fellowship Committee.* It shall be the responsibility of the Fellowship Com-
        mittee to plan and supervise programs to enhance the social aspects of
        Temple life.
   o.   *Israel Committee.* It shall be the responsibility of the Israel Committee to
        coordinate and develop Temple participation and involvement in Reform
        Jewish commitment to the State of Israel.
   p.   *Library Committee.* It shall be the responsibility of the Library Committee to
        maintain and administer the Temple Library.

q. *Outreach Committee*. It shall be the responsibility of the Outreach Committee to plan and administer programs pertaining to interfaith relationships.

r. *Scholarships Committee*. It shall be the responsibility of the Scholarships Committee to administer and raise funds for scholarships that support Temple member involvement in Jewish education beyond that offered by the Temple.

Section 3. *Special Committees*. The President shall have the power to appoint such other committees as may be deemed necessary or desirable to carry out the purpose of the Congregation.

Article X

Meetings

Section 1. *Annual Meeting.*

a. An annual meeting of the Congregation shall be held in each year on the last Sunday in April or the first Sunday in May at such place and at such hour as designated by the Board of Trustees.

b. At this meeting the reports of all officers whose responsibility it is to make reports shall be submitted; all Standing Committees shall present a report; all Special Committees shall present a report; a budget for the coming year shall be adopted; all officers, necessary Trustees and Rabbi shall be elected.

c. If at such meeting, Trustees, Officers and Rabbi are not duly elected, within the provisions of these By-Laws, the meeting shall stand adjourned to be called again for such election, at a time to be designated by the Board of Trustees, within thirty (30) days after the adjourned meeting.

d. Every member of the Congregation shall be notified by mail, at least ten (10) days prior to the annual meeting, and five (5) days prior to any adjournment thereof.

e. At all annual meetings, business shall be conducted in accordance with the provisions contained in these By-Laws, or in the absence of same, according to the Laws of the State of New Jersey or Roberts' Rules of Parliamentary Procedure.

Section 2. *Special Meetings*.

a. Special meetings of the Congregation: 1. may be called by the Board of Trustees on its own motion and 2. must be called by the Board of Trustees on the written application of ten percent (10%) of the members of the Congregation.

b. The call for the Special Meeting shall set forth the purpose of the meeting and written notice thereof shall be mailed to all members at least ten days prior to the time of such meeting and no business shall be transacted except that specified in the call. The Corresponding Secretary shall be required to send out the notices for any such special meetings.

Section 3. *Quorum.* A quorum for voting at regular or special meetings of the Congregation shall consist of at least one member who is eligible to vote from twenty (20) percent of the dues-paying-units. In the event a quorum is not obtained, then the members present at the meeting may vote to take tentative action provided that at least one member who is eligible to vote from ten (10) percent of the dues-paying-units is present. Such a vote, or votes, must be ratified by the rest of the Congregation by mail. Failure to receive a reply by the date specified on the ballot will result in a vote for the position taken by the majority vote at the meeting.

Article XI

Amendments

Procedure for Amendments. Amendments to these by-Laws must be in writing and must be proposed by the Board of Trustees or by at least ten percent of the members of the Congregation and filed with the Board of Trustees. Such amendments may be acted on at any regular meeting of the Congregation or at any special meeting called for that purpose. Copies of proposed amendments shall be mailed to each member with the notice of the meeting at least ten days prior thereto. An affirmative vote of two-thirds of the members present who are eligible to vote shall be necessary to adopt any amendment.

Article XII

Saving Clause

Section 1. A majority of the members of the Board of Trustees shall determine any dispute as to the interpretation of any of these By-Laws.

Section 2. At any regular or special meeting of the Congregation, decisions of the Board of Trustees can be overridden by a two-thirds vote of those members present who are eligible to vote.

Article XIII

Discipline

Section 1. *Expulsion.* A member, officer, or Trustee, may be expelled from membership in the Congregation or separated from service to the Congregation, as the case may be, for a willful violation of the By-Laws of the Congregation or for any conduct prejudicial to the interests and welfare of the Congregation.

Section 2. *Presentment of Charges for Expulsion.* A member, officer, or Trustee, shall not be expelled or separated from service to the Congregation, as the case may be, except upon written charges and specifications preferred by 15 percent of the members of the Congregation and presented to the Board of Trustees who shall thereupon cause the Corresponding Secretary to serve a copy of such charges and specifications upon the accused by registered mail.

Section 3. *Procedure for Expulsion.*

a.   In case charges shall be so preferred by fifteen (15) percent of the Members of the Congregation against an officer, Trustee or member, then the Board of Trustees shall at its first meeting after the receipt of such charges and specifications, select a committee of three members to investigate the case. A member preferring such charges shall not serve on the investigating Committee.

b.   The Investigating Committee shall examine the matter and file its report with the Board of Trustees. If the Board of Trustees shall find a basis for the charge, then there shall be a hearing, upon 20 days notice by registered mail to the accused, before the Board of Trustees, at which the accused is present and permitted adequate opportunity to rebut the charges. Two-thirds of the members of the Board of Trustees shall have the power to make the decision concerning expulsion. The accused shall have the right of legal counsel at the hearing.

Article XIV

Inspector of Election

Appointment of Inspectors of Election. At any meeting at which Elections are to be held or any Amendment to these By-Laws voted upon, two Inspectors shall not be nominees for any office to be voted upon at that meeting. At the discretion of the President, two additional Inspectors of Election can be appointed and such additional inspectors shall not be nominees for any office to be voted on at that meeting.

Article XV

Notices

Services of Notices. Whenever under the provision of these By-Laws, notice is required to be given to anyone, it shall not be construed to mean personal notice, except when so specifically stated, but such notice may be given by ordinary mail and the time of giving such notice shall be 3 days after the time when the notice is mailed.

Article XVI

Definitions

Ex-Officio. This term, whenever used in these By-Laws, shall be construed to mean "non-voting."

C.   The Covenant of Petah Tikva (1878)

Petah Tikva was the first of the Zionist colonies established in Palestine in the latter part of the nineteenth century. It was actually established by Jews from Jerusalem who were determined to begin the agricultural resettlement of the land of Israel. Significantly, they chose to call their founding document "The Covenant of Petah Tikva," undoubtedly a reflection of their sense of continuity with traditional Jewish life. Nor were they alone. In essence, almost all of the *moshavot*, the settlements established between 1878 and World War I, adopted covenants or used similar terms familiar from traditional diaspora Jewish community constitutions. Indeed, the documents themselves and the settlements attempted to combine a basic traditionalism with the modernism and even revolutionary character of Zionism.

We, the undersigned, whom G-d has merited to be among the first to open the "gates of hope" (*petakh tikvah*) to return the Children of Israel to their land, purchased two large pieces of land in the portion of the tribe of Dan near the River Yarkon, adjacent to Lod and Jaffa, measuring more than one thousand hectares of good fields, fertile from the abundance of Eretz Yisrael and invested in them more than one hundred thousand francs. We have seen [however] that we have not yet been successful in our deeds, since we had not chosen a good, pleasant, healthy, and undisputed place to settle.

We therefore took upon ourselves to search for such a place, adjacent to our land, and came as one union to buy a plot of land in Kefar Yehud, famous for its clean and healthy air and good water. For this purpose, we insisted that each of our brethren as well as each of our older and newer members whom we agreed to have join us, give one hundred francs to our group in order to receive a portion of the settlement (*yishuv*). The money that remains after the purchase of this field will be spent on digging a well and improving the settlement in general.

In our little experience, we have seen that our group lacks permanent *takanot* and proper codes of behavior according to which its members shall live. This shall surely become a stumbling block for us, as each person will follow his own path and quarelling and arguing will ensue until the small settlement we have established is uprooted. Therefore, we have decided today to establish certain *takanot*, as our experience has taught us and we have taken it upon ourselves to live according to these rules and to not accept any new member until he and his offspring agree to follow all that has been decided upon and written in the Book of the Covenant.

The following is the Covenant:

CHAPTER ONE: IN THE TAKANAH OF THE *YISHUV*

CHAPTER TWO: THAT WHICH PERTAINS TO THE LAND

D.   The Scroll of Independence of the State of Israel (1948)

The Declaration of the State of Israel in 1948 as a document was framed to incorporate a series of compromises. First of all, it was framed in the modern style of a declaration of independence for modern statehood rather than the traditional style of a covenant. This was the case even though it serves the purposes of a covenant representing a consensus document to which all the parties participating in the new political entity agree, embodying their consent to the polity's basic principles. Second, it reflects and attempts to bridge the conflicts within the Zionist movement and its Yishuv (settled community) in the land of Israel – between the religious and secular, between socialists and liberals. Thus, God is referred to by a traditional designation, the Rock of Israel, which militant atheists could interpret in a secular fashion if they so chose. Similarly, the historic background emphasizes the social justice of the prophets rather than the Jewish law of the Torah. Finally, the Declaration embraces the universalism of the postwar world along with the particularism of a Jewish state. These compromises produce a document that has grown in stature in the minds of Israelis in the intervening fifty years.

Declaration of the Establishment of the State of Israel

ERETZ-ISRAEL (Land of Israel) was the birthplace of the Jewish people. Here their spiritual, religious and political identity was shaped. Here they first attained statehood, created cultural values of national and universal significance and gave to the world the eternal Book of Books.

After being forcibly exiled from their land, the people kept faith with it throughout their Dispersion and never ceased to pray and to hope for their return to it and for the restoration in it of their political freedom.

Impelled by this historic and traditional attachment, Jews strove in every successive generation to re-establish themselves in their ancient homeland.

In recent decades they returned in their masses. Pioneers, immigrants and defenders, they made deserts bloom, revived the Hebrew language, built villages and towns, and created a thriving community, controlling its own economy and culture, loving peace but knowing how to defend itself, bringing the blessings of progress to all the country's inhabitants, and aspiring towards independent nationhood.

In the year 5657 (1897), at the summons of the spiritual father of the Jewish State, Theodor Herzl, the First Zionist Congress convened and proclaimed the right of the Jewish people to national rebirth in its own country.

This right was recognised in the Balfour Declaration of the 2nd November, 1917, and re-affirmed in the Mandate of the League of Nations which, in particular, gave international sanction to the historic connection between the Jewish people and Eretz-Israel and to the right of the Jewish people to rebuild its National Home.

The catastrophe which recently befell the Jewish people – the massacre of millions of Jews in Europe – was another clear demonstration of the urgency of solving the problem of its homelessness by re-establishing in Eretz-Israel the Jewish State, which would open wide to every Jew the gates of the homeland and confer upon the Jewish people the status of a fully-privileged member of the family of nations.

Survivors of the Nazi holocaust in Europe, as well as Jews from other parts of the world, continued to immigrate to Israel, undaunted by difficulties, restrictions and dangers, and never ceased to assert their right to a life of dignity, freedom and honest toil in their national homeland.

In the Second World War, the Jewish community of this country contributed its full share to the struggle of freedom- and peace-loving nations against the forces of Nazi wickedness and, by the blood of its soldiers and its war effort, gained the right to be reckoned among the peoples who founded the United Nations.

On the 29th November, 1947, the United Nations General Assembly passed a resolution calling for the establishment of a Jewish State in Eretz-Israel; the General Assembly required the inhabitants of Eretz-Israel to take such steps as were necessary on their part for the implementation of that resolution. This recognition by the United Nations of the right of the Jewish people to establish their State is irrevocable.

This right is the natural right of the Jewish people to be masters of their own fate, like all other nations, in their own sovereign State. ACCORDINGLY WE, MEMBERS OF THE PEOPLE'S COUNCIL, REPRESENTATIVES OF THE JEWISH COMMUNITY OF ERETZ-ISRAEL AND OF THE ZIONIST MOVEMENT, ARE HERE ASSEMBLED ON THE DAY OF THE TERMINATION OF THE BRITISH MANDATE OVER ERETZ-ISRAEL AND, BY VIRTUE OF OUR NATURAL AND HISTORIC RIGHT AND ON THE STRENGTH OF THE RESOLUTION OF THE UNITED NATIONS GENERAL ASSEMBLY, HEREBY DECLARE THE ESTABLISHMENT OF A JEWISH STATE IN ERETZ-ISRAEL, TO BE KNOWN AS THE STATE OF ISRAEL.

WE DECLARE that, with effect from the moment of the termination of the Mandate, being tonight, the eve of Sabbath, the 6th of Iyar, 5708 (15th May, 1948), until the establishment of the elected, regular authorities of the State in accordance with the Constitution which shall be adopted by the Elected Constituent Assembly not later than the 1st October, 1948, the People's Council shall act as a Provisional Council of State, and its executive organ, the People's Administration, shall be the Provisional Government of the Jewish State, to be called "Israel."

THE STATE OF ISRAEL will be open for Jewish immigration and for the Ingathering of the Exiles; it will foster the development of the country for the benefit of all its inhabitants; it will be based on freedom, justice and peace as envisaged by the prophets of Israel; it will ensure complete equality of social and political rights to all its inhabitants irrespective of religion, race or sex; it will guarantee freedom of religion, conscience, language, education and culture; it will safeguard the Holy Places of all religions; and it will be faithful to the principles of the Charter of the United Nations.

THE STATE OF ISRAEL is prepared to cooperate with the agencies and representatives of the United Nations in implementing the resolution of the General Assembly of the 29th November, 1947, and will take steps to bring about the economic union of the whole of Eretz-Israel.

WE APPEAL to the United Nations to assist the Jewish people in the upbuilding of its State and to receive the State of Israel into the family of nations.

WE APPEAL – in the very midst of the onslaught launched against us now for months – to the Arab inhabitants of the State of Israel to preserve peace and participate in the upbuilding of the State on the basis of full and equal citizenship and due representation in all its provisional and permanent institutions.

WE EXTEND our hand to all neighbouring states and their peoples in an offer of peace and good neighbourliness, and appeal to them to establish bonds of cooperation and mutual help with the sovereign Jewish people settled in its own land. The State of Israel is prepared to do its share in a common effort for the advancement of the entire Middle East.

WE APPEAL to the Jewish people throughout the Diaspora to rally round the Jews of Eretz-Israel in the tasks of immigration and upbuilding and to stand by them in the great struggle for the realization of the age-old dream – the redemption of Israel.

PLACING OUR TRUST IN THE ROCK OF ISRAEL, WE AFFIX OUR SIGNATURES TO THIS PROCLAMATION AT THIS SESSION OF THE PROVISIONAL COUNCIL OF STATE, ON THE SOIL OF THE HOMELAND, IN THE CITY OF TEL-AVIV, ON THIS SABBATH EVE, THE 5TH DAY OF IYAR, 5708 (14TH MAY, 1948).

DAVID BEN-GURION
DANIEL AUSTER
MORDEKHAI BENTOV
YITZCHAK BEN ZVI
ELIYAHU BERLIGNE
FRITZ BERNSTEIN
RABBI WOLF GOLD
MEIR GRABOVSKY
YITZCHAK GRUENBAUM
DR ABRAHAM
   GRANOVSKY
ELIYAHU DOBKIN
MEIR WILNERKOVNER
ZERACH WAHRHAFTIG

HERZL VARDI
RACHEL COHEN
RABBI KALMAN KAHANA
SAADIA KOBASHI
RABBI YITZCHAK MEIR
   LEVIN
MEIR DAVID
   LOEWENSTEIN
ZVI LURIA
GOLDA MYERSON
NACHUM NIR
ZVI SEGAL
RABBI YEHUDA LEIB
   HACOHEN FISHMAN

DAVID ZVI PINKAS
AHARON ZISLING
MOSHE KOLODNY
ELIEZER KAPLAN
ABRAHAM KATZNELSON
FELIX ROSENBLUETH
DAVID REMEZ
BERL REPETUR
MORDEKHAI SHATTNER
BEN ZION STERNBERG
BEHOR SHITREET
MOSHE SHAPIRA
MOSHE SHERTOK

Chapter 23

Theology in Contemporary Judaism

Neil Gillman

The following selections, listed in alphabetical order, impress with the range of issues covered, the richness of the discussion, and, most important, with their concern about the issues. Theology, it has often been maintained, does not come intuitively to Jews or to Judaism. That claim, if it was ever true, is certainly disproved by these texts. It is not true in our day.

Why? Maybe because our day sharpens the sense of marginality for contemporary Jews. We live in an open society, an age of fierce competition between ideologies, with a pervasive sense of both moral and ideological relativism and of an aggressive scientism. In this era, none of the traditional ways of making sense of the world can automatically compel allegiance. Each has to be defended, and theology is the discipline that strives to supply that defense for an ancient religious tradition. Theology addresses the state of marginality. That may be why, in our day, it is a discipline whose time has come.

A.   Eugene Borowitz, *Renewing the Covenant: A Theology for the Postmodern Jew*

Borowitz, long identified with Reform Judaism's emphasis on individual autonomy in matters of Jewish belief and practice, now balances autonomy with other broader theological and communal norms. The result is that Jewish decision-making is the result of a complex process in which the tensions between the individual and the community are resolved.

Source for reading A.:   Philadelphia: The Jewish Publication Society of America, p. 288.

In contrast to contemporary privatistic notions of selfhood, the Jewish self, responding to God in Covenant, acknowledges its essential historicity and sociality. One did not begin the Covenant and one remains its conduit only as part of the ongoing people of Israel. Here, tradition and ethnicity round out the universal solidarity of humankind which this particularity grounds in its myth of the Noahide covenant. With heritage and folk essential to Jewishness, with the Jewish service of God directed to historic continuity lasting until messianic days, the Covenanted self knows that Jewish existence must be structured. Yet as long as we honor each Jew's selfhood with a contextually delimited measure of autonomy, this need for communal forms cannot lead us back to law as a required, corporately determined regimen. Instead, we must think in terms of a self-discipline that, because of the sociality of the Jewish self, becomes communally focused and shaped. The result is a dialectical autonomy, a life of freedom-exercised-in-Covenant

B.   Emil Fackenheim, *Quest for Past and Future*

The issue here is the verification of theological claims. Fackenheim argues that neither the believer nor the atheist can use observable data to substantiate their respective claims. Faith or non-faith is a decision. Hovering over the discussion are the theological implications of the Holocaust.

In such manner does faith refute the refutation proposed by subjectivist reductionism. But this is not to say that faith can prove its own case against subjectivist reductionism. It cannot refute but only reject it; and it can testify against it. For the argument cuts both ways. The reductionist cannot use observable data – religious images and feelings – to demonstrate the subjectivity of faith. But neither can the believer use these same data to demonstrate the objectivity of faith. For not only is it the case that the reductionist critic cannot or will not enter into the actual relation of openness to God; it is also the case that for the believer himself the "knowledge" obtained is shot through with the gravest of risks. After all, does not disguised self-love, being disguised, mistake itself for love of God? Are not god-projections, being unconscious, mistaken for real gods by those who are prey to them?

Some part of this risk has always been understood by believers in the Biblical tradition, who realized that false prophets, no less than true, can be sincere. The full extent of the risk, however, has become obvious only to the modern believer. His ancestor rarely doubted that man was in principle open to the Divine; hence the risk of which he was aware extended for the most part only to deciding when

Source for reading B.:   Bloomington: Indiana University Press, 1968, pp. 242–3.

and how such openness was truly manifest. The modern believer, by contrast, has glimpsed the possibility that all openness to the Divine may be pseudo – openness only – that man may be radically alone. He does not stand in immediate openness to the Divine. He seeks, in Kierkegaard's expression, an immediacy after reflection. The Psalmist in extremis experienced an eclipse of God. The extremity of faith in the modern age is uncertainty as to whether what is experienced is an eclipse of God, or the final exposure of an illusion.

C.   Neil Gillman, *Sacred Fragments*

Here I appropriate the term "myth" to characterize both the Torah itself and theological language as well. A myth is a structure of meaning through which a community makes coherent sense of its distinctive experience. I trace the process by which myths are canonized in Scripture.

A myth should be understood as a structure through which a community organizes and makes sense of its experience. The world "out there" does not impinge itself on us in a totally objective way, tidily packaged and organized into meaningful patterns. Our experience of the world is a complex transaction between what comes to us from "out there" and the way we structure or "read" it. Myths are the spectacles that enable us to see order in what would otherwise be confusion. They are created, initially, by "reading" communities, beginning with their earliest attempts to shape, explain, or make some sense out of their experience of nature and history. Gradually, as the mythic structure seems to work, to be confirmed by ongoing experience, it is refined, shared, and transmitted to later generations. It becomes embodied in official, "canonical" texts and assumes authoritative power. In its final form, it becomes omnipresent and quasi-invisible, so much has it become our intuitive way of confronting the world. . . .

Religious myths do all of this for a religious community. They also convey the community's distinctive answers to ultimate human questions: Why am I here? What is the meaning or purpose of my existence? How do I handle guilt, suffering, sexuality, interpersonal relations? What happens when I die? Myths promote loyalty to the community, motivate behavior, generate a sense of belonging and kinship. Because they emerge from and speak to the most primitive layers of our being, they are capable of moving or touching us in the most profound way. People die for their myths, so coercive is their hold.

Source for reading C.:   Philadelphia: The Jewish Publication Society of America, 1990, pp. 26, 28.

D. Arthur Green, *Seek My Face, Speak My Name*

As a true religious experientialist, Green insists that Jews have always "seen" God in the world. But he acknowledges that this "seeing" is in tension with God's intrinsic invisibility. The believer must walk that "tightrope."

Seeing God. The Torah itself seems to be conflicted on the question of whether such a thing can happen, or ever has happened, even at Sinai. Moses asks to see God's face and is told, "No human may see Me and live." Not that there is nothing to see; the point here seems to be that the experience of seeing God is so intense and powerful that it will bring on death. When God passes by the cleft of the rock where Moses is hidden at Sinai, he is told "You will see My back, but My face may not be seen." And yet in another chapter, also describing the Sinai experience, the text says quite clearly of Moses, Aaron, and the seventy elders, "They saw the God of Israel." The book of Deuteronomy, in recounting the Sinai experience, severely warns the reader that there was no visual component to that experience, lest future generations be led into an attempt to represent that vision of God in material form. Yet, it is that same book that concludes by describing Moses as one whom God had known "face to face." There are some who claim that the name Israel itself means "those who see God" as well as "those who struggle with God." Surely both of these readings are based in reality.

The warning of Deuteronomy against visual depiction of God must be seen in context. The Bible still saw itself as fighting a surrounding pagan culture in which such depictions were rampant. But even within Israel, the conflict among these Biblical sources may indicate that there was a debate among our most ancient thinkers over the question of God's visibility. This is a debate that accompanies Judaism throughout its history. Philosophers, sages, mystics, and visionaries through the ages have all had their say. In doing so, each of them has added something to the portrait, which still remains unfinished. To be a religious Jew is to walk the tightrope between knowing the invisibility of God and seeing the face of God everywhere. Y-H-W-H is but a breath, utterly without form, the essence of abstraction itself. And yet that same abstraction is the face of God that "peers out from the windows, peeks through the lattice-work." That face contains within it all the faces of humanity, and each of them contains the face of God.

Source for reading D.:   Northvale: Jason Aronson, 1992, pp. 36–7.

E.   Irving Greenberg, "Voluntary Covenant"

This is one of the more radical theological responses to the Holocaust. Greenberg argues that after the Holocaust, Israel's covenant with God can no longer compel allegiance. Rather, Jews may or may not accept their covenantal obligations in a totally voluntary way and in any way they choose to express their sense of being covenanted. He concludes by suggesting that this new covenantal theology can form the basis for a genuine Jewish theological and religious pluralism.

In the age of voluntary covenant, every person who steps forward to live as a Jew can be compared to a convert insofar as a convert, one who voluntarily opts to be a Jew, must make certain commitments and express certain beliefs. Then the classic conversion ceremony may guide us to contemporary Jews' proper affirmations. Through the conversion process, the convert testifies that although the Jews are driven, tormented, and persecuted to this very day, the convert still wants to be a Jew, that is, wants to offer the testimony of hope anyway. The convert learns the unity of God and the denial of idolatry; the analogue in our time is the affirmation of God's presence which is witnessed by Jewish existence itself.

The convert must affirm some of the weighty commandments/obligations of a Jew and some of the lighter ones. In this generation, all who opt to live as Jews automatically state their readiness for martyrdom, not only for themselves but for their children and grandchildren as well. There can be no "weightier" commitment than this. A decision to live in Israel and to a lesser extent, a commitment to support it, constitutes acceptance of the mitzvah to witness, to build a redeeming social reality, even to bring the Messiah. The appropriate range of "lighter" commandments obligations to be undertaken can be explored or debated between the denominations. But morally speaking, the simple observance of all the classical mitzvot can hardly be the only option offered under the covenantal definition.

While the covenant is now voluntary, birth into it remains an important statement. By being born a Jew, a person summons up all the associations and statements implicit in Jewish existence, including the Jewish testimony to a God who cares. One may opt out by refusing to live as a visible Jew, by trying to escape the fate of a Jew, by trying to deny. However, if one chooses to continue living as a Jew, one makes all the fundamental affirmations implicit in Jewish existence. This is true even if one does not use the officially articulated ways of making one's statements such as bearing witness to creation through Shabbat observance or expressing the messianic hope through prayers such as Aleinu.

As long as the covenant was involuntary, it could be imposed from above in a unitary way. This corresponds with the image and role of revelation in the Biblical

Source for reading E.:   In *Perspectives: A CLAL Thesis* (New York: CLAL: The National Center for Learning and Leadership, 1982), p. 38.

period, which includes unequivocal command and visible reward and punishment for obedience and disobedience. With the shift in covenantal relationship which characterizes the Rabbinic era, the revelation becomes more hidden, more subject to pluralist interpretation. Focus on reward and punishment shifts from the worldly toward the otherworldly hidden realm.

In the new era, the voluntary covenant is the theological base of a genuine pluralism. Pluralism is not a matter of tolerance made necessary by living in a non-Jewish reality, nor is it pity for one who does not know any better. It is a recognition that all Jews have chosen to make the fundamental Jewish statement at great personal risk and cost.

F.   David Hartman, *A Living Covenant*

An articulate traditionalist voice among contemporary Jewish theologians, Hartman argues for the legitimacy of a broadly-based interpretive freedom in matters of belief and practice, all within the context of a binding commitment to the Sinai covenant. What are the parameters of interpretive freedom? Whatever the community is prepared to accept.

Nor should the halakhic Jew's legislative and interpretive independence be identified with Kantian autonomy. Rabbinic acknowledgment of the inviolable content of revelation ("heteronomy") did not inhibit the intellectual freedom of Jews to interpret and apply the law in ways that not only extended beyond the literal constraints of biblical revelation, but also often made the text appear subservient to its commentators. The autonomy of rabbinic Judaism was expressed within a framework of divine authority rooted in the revelation at Sinai. As talmudic Judaism indicates, the model of the prophet who directly mediates between God and human beings (the heteronomous spirit) is not the only way of dramatically capturing the experience of God's commanding presence. The living word of God can be mediated through the application of human reason (the autonomous spirit) to the revealed norms of Torah. This is the essence of the dialectical vitality of talmudic Judaism.

G.   Will Herberg, *Judaism and Modern Man* – God

Herberg, true to his existentialist convictions and echoing the view of his mentor, Martin Buber, stresses the personal nature of the biblical God. God

Source for reading F.:   New York: The Free Press, 1985, pp. 40.
Source for reading G.:   New York: Farrar Straus and Young, 1951, pp. 60–1.

enters into personal relationships with people. Note the echo of Heschel's understanding of the divine pathos, a view that is similar to this one.

The ascription of personality to God is thus an affirmation of the fact that in the encounter of faith God meets us as person to person. It means, too, that the divine Person we meet in this encounter confronts us as a source of free dynamic activity and purpose. It is this freedom and purpose that, within limits – for the human spirit is conditioned by all the circumstances of life – exhibits itself in our own existence as an essential part of the meaning of personality. In God, these limitations are, of course, stripped away, and the free activity of, personality manifests itself in consummate form. The Scriptural writers-whether legalist, priestly or prophetic-simply take the full personality of God as axiomatic. God speaks and is spoken to; he is jealous, angry, compassionate and forgiving; he acts and is acted upon; he has aims and purposes which he executes in history: he is, in short, a "decision-making person who has communication with and care for decision-making persons on this earth." Later philosophers and to some extent even rabbinic writers were embarrassed by biblical expressions reflecting this "conception" of God and tried to explain them away as merely figurative or poetical;" modem apologists have, generally followed the same line. But this will not do.

Remove the "anthropomorphic" – or rather anthropopathic-features – from the biblical account of God and nothing whatever is left, not even a philosophical concept. "The divine reveals itself," writes A. J. Heschel, discussing the prophetic experience, "in a characteristically conditioned manner. . . . It reveals itself in its 'pathetic,' that is, emotional-personal bearing. God does not merely command and require obedience, he is also moved and affected; he does not simply go on ruling the world impassively, he also experiences it." The God of Hebraic religion is either a living, active, "feeling" God or he is nothing.

H.   Will Herberg, *Judaism and Modern Man* – Faith

Herberg portrays faith as a "leap" beyond all experience and reason. He then traces the nature of this existentialist understanding of faith and its implications.

This affirmation – the "leap of faith" that springs out of the decision for God – is not a leap of despair but rather a leap in triumph over despair. It is a leap made not in order to search blindly for an unknown God somewhere on the other side; it is a leap that is made because – wonderfully enough – God has already been found. Faith is risk, venture, decision so it is for us while we are still on this side of

Source for reading H.:   New York: Farrar Straus and Young, 1951, pp. 39, 40.

the abyss. We must dare the leap if the gulf is ever to be crossed; but once the decision of faith has been made, it is seen that the leap was possible only because the gulf had already been bridged for us from the other side. The reality of the decision remains, but we now see that what we had to decide was whether or not to accept the outstretched hand offered us over the abyss as we stood bewildered, anxious and despairing at the brink.

The existential achievement of faith is never secure. Faith is not a particular psychological goal, intellectual or emotional, which, once attained, may be expected to remain a permanent acquisition. Faith is a never-ending battle against self-absolutization and idolatry; it is a battle which has to be rethought every moment of life because it is a battle in which the victory can never be final. But although never final, victory is always possible, for the outstretched hand over the abyss is always there for us to take hold of. The resources of divine grace are always available in the spontaneity of faith.

Faith is not mere "feeling;" nor is it intellectual assent to a creed. It is orientation of the whole man; it is a total existential commitment that brings with it a new way of seeing things new perspectives and categories in the confrontation of reality. Through faith, existence is transposed into a new key. Everything – the universe, man, human life – is transfigured.

I. Abraham Joshua Heschel, *God in Search of Man*

Heschel's characteristic approach to our awareness of God is experientialist. He designates three ways of sensing God's presence in the world: in nature, in the Bible, and in sacred deeds. His phenomenological analysis of the religious experience contrasts this experience with the experience of the beautiful. On the issue of revelation, Heschel argues for a view that sees Torah as both revealed by a transcendent God and yet couched in human language and conceptualization. This is the import of his view that the Bible we have is itself a midrash on God's own version of the Torah. Thus both human and divine authority are manifest in the text. But Heschel does not trace the implications of this position. See the Eugene Borowitz reading above on this issue.

There are three starting points of contemplation about God; three trails that lead to Him. The first is the way of sensing the presence of God in the world, in things;' the second is the way of sensing His presence in the Bible; the third is the way of sensing His presence in sacred deeds.

These three ways are intimated in three Biblical passages:

Source for reading I.:   Philadelphia: The Jewish Publication Society of America, 1956, pp. 31, 39, 184–5.

Lift up your eyes on high and see, Who created these? Isaiah 40:26
I am the Lord thy God. Exodus 20:2
We shall do and we shall hear. Exodus 24:7

These three ways correspond in our tradition to the main aspects of religious existence: worship, learning, and action. The three are one, and we must go all three ways to reach the one destination. For this is what Israel discovered: the God of nature is the God of history, and the way to know Him is to do His will. . . .

The sublime is not opposed to the beautiful, and must not, furthermore, be considered an esthetic category. The sublime may be sensed in things of beauty as well as in acts of goodness and in the search for truth. The perception of beauty may be the beginning of the experience of the sublime. The sublime is that which we see and are unable to convey. It is the silent allusion of things to a meaning greater than themselves. It is that which all things ultimately stand for; "the inveterate silence of the world that remains immune to curiosity and inquisitiveness like distant foliage in the dusk." It is that which our words, our forms, our categories can never reach. This is why the sense of the sublime must be regarded as the root of man's creative activities in art, thought, and noble living. Just as no flora has ever fully displayed the hidden vitality of the earth, so has no work of art, no system of philosophy, no theory of science, ever brought to expression the depth of meaning, the sublimity of reality in the sight of which the souls of saints artists, and philosophers live . . .

The nature of revelation, being an event in the realm of the ineffable, is something which words cannot spell, which human language will never be able to portray. Our categories are not applicable to that which is both within and beyond the realm of matter and mind. In speaking about revelation, the more descriptive the terms, the less adequate is the description. The words in which the prophets attempted to relate their experiences were not photographs but illustrations, not descriptions but songs. A psychological reconstruction of the prophetic act is, therefore, no more possible than the attempt to paint a photographic likeness of a face on the basis of a song. The word "revelation" is like an exclamation; it is an indicative rather than a descriptive term. Like all terms that express the ultimate, it points to its meaning rather than fully rendering it. "It is very difficult to have a true conception of the events at Sinai, for there has never been before nor will there ever be again anything like it." "We believe," says Maimonides, "that the Torah has reached Moses from God in a manner which is described in Scripture figuratively by the term 'word,' and that nobody has ever known how that took place except Moses himself to whom that word reached."

We must not try to read chapters in the Bible dealing with the event at Sinai as if they were texts in systematic theology. Its intention is to celebrate the mystery, to introduce us to it rather than to penetrate or to explain it. As a report about revelation the Bible itself is a midrash.

J.   Mordecai Kaplan, *Questions Jews Ask: Reconstructionist Answers*

Kaplan is both a religious and theological naturalist. Religions emerge out of the thoroughly natural life-experience of human communities. And God is that power or impulse within the natural order that makes for fulfillment both for the individual and for society as a whole. In the second text, Kaplan answers a child who asked, "Why did God give me polio?" This is a classic statement of the naturalist limited-God theology.

The Basis in Experience of a Tenable Faith in God

Whatever general idea we hold in our minds and regard as pointing to, or representative of, Reality, or of any phase of it, derives from something seen, heard, felt, believed. It proceeds, in other words, from the known to the unknown. That fact is true also of the belief in God. In most religions of the past, that belief was derived from traditions concerning self-revelations of God through visions and oracles. Those traditions are now discounted by all who have become habituated to scientific and philosophic thought. Though such people are in the minority, their influence is bound to increase with time, and their rejection of the traditional basis of the belief in God is certain to be followed by a like attitude on the part of the multitude. This may take a long time, but it is bound to come sooner or later.

Those who are not content with the superficiality of merely rejecting a belief that has been so universal, spontaneous and persistent as the belief in God, have turned their attention to the study of human nature and its needs. They have rightly concluded that there must be something in the very nature of man which has led him to create that vast and complex edifice of religion with its creeds, rituals, institutions and polities. What is that something? Some maintain that religion is the product of fear of whatever is beyond man's control, and that it is nothing but a disguised form of primitive magic to which man resorted, expecting the supposed gods, demons, spirits and angels to fulfill his wishes. As man learns to bring under control more and more of the forces in his own body and in his environment, he feels he can dispense with religion, or belief in God; what he cannot control, he has to accept with resignation. Others, however, and I among them, assume that man, once his physiological needs are satisfied, begins to experience the need to overcome such traits as self-indulgence, arrogance, envy, exploitation and hatred, or to bring under control the aggressive forces of his nature. That constitutes man's true destiny. Therein lies his salvation.

Source for reading J.:   New York: Reconstructionist Press, 1956, pp. 82–4, 119–20.

From that point, it is natural to arrive at the next step, which requires no blind leap into the dark. The next step is to conclude that the cosmos is so constituted as to enable man to fulfill this highest human need of his nature.

A magnetic needle, hung on a thread or placed on a pivot, assumes of its own accord a position in which one end of the needle points north and the other south. So long as it is free to move about, all attempts to deflect it will not get it to remain away from its normal direction. Likewise, man normally veers in the direction of that which makes for the fulfillment of his destiny as a human being. That fact indicates the functioning of a cosmic Power which influences his behavior. What magnetism is to the magnetic needle, Godhood or God is to man.

To carry the analogy one step further, just as the magnetic needle is the source of our knowledge of the earth's magnetism, so is man's salvational behavior the source of our knowledge of God. And just as we learn from the action of the magnetic needle the laws of magnetism so do we learn from man's salvational behavior, which we come progressively really to understand, the law or will of God.

God did not make polio. God is always helping us humans to make this a better world, but the world cannot at once become the kind of world He would like it to be. When men make use of the intelligence God gave them, they learn more and more of the laws of health, by which all kinds of illness can be prevented or cured. When the doctor relieves your pain, when he helps you to get back more strength and better control over your muscles, it is with the intelligence that God gives him. When you use braces and other devices that help you get around and do some of the things you want to do, their manufacture is due to the intelligence and the concern for your welfare, that God puts into the minds of those who make these devices. Do not feel that God does not care for you. He is helping you now in many ways, and He will continue to help you. Maybe some day you will be restored by His help to perfect health. But if that does not happen, it is not because God does not love you. If He does not grant you all that you pray for, He will find other ways of enabling you to enjoy life. Be thankful to God for all the love and care that people show toward you, since all of that is part of God's love, and do not hesitate to ask God for further help. If the people around you are intelligent and loving, that help will come to you.

K.   Franz Rosenzweig, "The Builders: Concerning the Law"

One of the earliest and most influential of Jewish existentialists, Rosenzweig advocates a view of Jewish practice as subject to an entirely personal,

Source for reading K.:   In N. N. Glatzer, ed., *On Jewish Learning* (New York: Schocken Books, 1955), pp. 85–6.

individual decision which appropriates from the body of Jewish "laws" those the individual Jew can accept as a personal "command." This position, now widely accepted by modern Jews, inevitably diminishes the role of the community in formulating the set of obligations that are binding on contemporary Jews.

And again we have to realize that with this unifying and broadening of the Jewishly do-able, nothing has really been done. Whatever can and must be done is not yet done, whatever can and must be commanded is not yet commandment. Law [Gesetz] must again become commandment [Gebot] which seeks to be transformed into deed at the very moment it is heard. It must regain that living reality [Heutigkeit] in which all great Jewish periods have sensed the guarantee for its eternity. Like teaching, it must consciously start where its content stops being content and becomes inner power, our own inner power. Inner power which in turn is added to the substance of the law. For even if one should wish to do "everything" possible, he would still not fulfill the Law – he would not fulfill it in a way by which law would become commandment; a commandment which he must fulfil, simply because he cannot allow it to remain unfulfilled, as it was once expressed in Akiba's famous parable of the fishes. Thus what counts here too is not our will but our ability to act. Here too the decisive thing is the selection which our ability – without regard to our will – makes out of the wealth of the possible deeds. Since this selection does not depend on the will but on our ability, it is a very personal one, for while a general law can address itself with its demands to the will, ability carries in itself its own law; there is only my, your, his ability and, built upon them, ours; not everybody's. Therefore, whether much is done, or little, or maybe nothing at all, is immaterial in the face of the one and unavoidable demand; that whatever is being done, shall come from that inner power. As the knowledge of everything knowable is not yet wisdom, so the doing of everything do-able is not yet deed. The deed is created at the boundary of the merely do-able, where the voice of the commandment causes the spark to leap from "I must" to "I can." The Law is built on such commandments, and only on them.

L.   Richard Rubenstein, in *The Condition of Jewish Belief*

This is Rubenstein's theological response to the Holocaust, an event he views as totally unprecedented in human history. Hence none of the classical Jewish responses to suffering can work in this post-Holocaust age. In place of these, Rubenstein adopts the "death of God" theology that was popular in certain

Source for reading L.:   In *The Condition of Jewish Belief*, p. 199.

Protestant circles some decades ago. But what does it mean to claim that "God is dead"?

No man can really say that God is dead. How can we know that? Nevertheless, I am compelled to say that we live in the time of the "death of God." This is more a statement about man and his culture than about God. The death of God is a cultural fact. Buber felt this. He spoke of the eclipse of God. I can understand his reluctance to use the more explicitly Christian terminology. I am compelled to utilize it because of my conviction that the time which Nietzsche's madman said was too far off has come upon us. There is no way around Nietzsche. Had I lived in another time or another culture, I might have found some other vocabulary to express my meanings. I am, however, a religious existentialist after Nietzsche and after Auschwitz. When I say we live in the time of the death of God, I mean that the thread uniting God and man, heaven and earth has been broken. We stand in a cold, silent, unfeeling cosmos, unaided by any purposeful power beyond our own resources. After Auschwitz, what else can a Jew say about God?

M.   Harold M. Schulweis, *Evil and the Morality of God*

This book is an attempt to deal with the problem of human suffering from the perspective of a process or, to use the author's term, "predicate theology." This approach suggests that God should not be understood as a noun but rather as a verb or adverb. We begin, then, not with what God is, but rather with those activities that we claim to be divine or Godly. God is the accumulation of these divine predicates.

We consider Feuerbach's inversion proposal as a pedagogic and methodologic principle: "that which in religion is the predicate we must make the subject, and that which in religion is a subject we must make a predicate." The first shall become last and the last first. The predicates are no longer seen as qualities which derive their meaning from the subject. The predicates are now the proper subject of theology. They assume a new status. We look to them to understand the character of divinity.

The theological task changes accordingly. The aim is not to prove the existence of the subject but to demonstrate the reality of the predicates. For subject theology faith is belief in the subject and atheism is the denial of its existence. For predicate theology faith is belief in the reality of the predicates and atheism is their denial. The critical question for predicate theology is not "Do you believe that God is

Source for reading M.:   Cincinnati: Hebrew Union College Press, 1984, pp. 122–3.

merciful, caring, peacemaking?" but "Do you believe that doing mercy, caring, making peace are godly?" The energy of theology would be directed not toward convincing men that a subject possesses certain qualities themselves. Following the inversionary proposal, the religious contention is not that a subject is in some sense good or loving or intelligent or creator but that the humanly comprehensible qualities of goodness, love, intelligence, and creativity are godly; that they themselves are worthy of adoration, cultivation, and emulation in the lives of the believers. In Feuerbach's formulation, "God does not love, He is himself love; He does not live. He is life; He is not just but justice itself; not a person, but personality itself." What is important to note here is that the qualities do not derive their meaning and their worth from another realm of being. They are experienced and valued for themselves. They are not valued as appendages attached to a supersensible subject but are discovered in the course of man's transactions with his environment, human and nonhuman. They are not cast down from above or projected from below but revealed in the areas between persons and between persons and things. As we have seen, between man and the divine subject an unbridgeable qualitative gap exists. Between man and the divine predicates no such distance prevails.

N.   Michael Wyschogrod, *The Body of Faith: God in the People Israel*

Arguing from a traditionalist perspective on the binding quality of Jewish law, Wyschogrod nevertheless stresses that no human being can know with certainty what God really commands. His emphasis on the intrinsic insecurity of Jewish legal decision-making is a noteworthy corrective to the more fundamentalist tendency of Jewish traditionalism.

This is where the law comes in. The law is a guide to action in the absence of specific commands in specific situations. Each situation, after all, is different. Ideally, God would issue specific commands for each situation. Second best is the law. The law constructs abstractions such as theft, murder, animals that chew their cud, etc. Having studied the law, we then turn to specific cases. In view of what this animal does with its food, is it an animal that chews its cud? Given this particular action by this particular person, is it an action that constitutes theft? There are no perfectly certain answers to these question. By using our reason, we do the best we can, deciding that this particular case sufficiently resembles previous cases of theft to be classified as theft, while another case does not resemble them sufficiently and is therefore not theft. Legal reasoning is therefore

Source for reading N.:   San Francisco: Harper and Row, 1983, pp. 188–9.

an attempt to fathom the will of God when he has not specifically expressed it in the case under consideration.

If we see the law in this light, then all reasoning with respect to the law of God must be conducted with fear and trembling and with the constant awareness that what we take as the divine will may not be it. Such an Orthodox Judaism would lack security. It would lack the confidence with which the Orthodox Jew turns to his rabbi for an authoritative ruling on the law, thinking that if the rabbi's ruling is "wrong" (in some sense of that word), then it is the rabbi's responsibility and not that of the person posing the problem. In so doing, we overlook the basic truth that if each person is responsible to God, then dependence on the ruling of another is no absolute defense. Since ultimately it is conformity or nonconformity with God's will that is decisive, the religious life becomes a life of insecurity lived under the sense of divine judgment.

Chapter 24
Secular Forms of Jewishness

Paul Mendes-Flohr

A.   Michah Joseph Berdichevski, "Wrecking and Building"

Michah Joseph Berdichevski (also known by his Hebrew *nom de plume*, Bin-Gorion; 1865–1921), a descendent of a long line of illustrious hasidic rabbis, was himself renowned in his youth for his mastery of Talmud and mystical texts. Breaking with his family and traditional upbringing, he left his native Ukraine in 1890 for the "enlightened" West. Pursuing a secular education in Germany, he came under the influence of Nietzsche, whose teachings inspired his radical critique of traditional Judaism. Writing largely in Hebrew, Berdichevski called upon his fellow Jews to reject Rabbinic Judaism in the name of a life-affirming "transvaluation of values."

In the selection before us, Berdichevski advocates a deliberate secularization of Judaism, by virtue of which the individual Jew – and his or her legitimate need for earthly well-being and happiness – will take precedence. The Jew must no longer see him or herself as the mere servant of Judaism. An atavistic loyalty to the tradition may have preserved Judaism, but it has rendered the Jew a mere vehicle for preserving a basically moribund religion, utterly devoid of life-enhancing meaning. Indeed, as he put it, Judaism suffocates the Jews, transmogrifying them into a nation of "mummies" as opposed to living men and women. Hence, Berdichevski told his fellow Jews, either we are last of the Jews or we cast aside our ancestral faith and become the first of a new nation, the Hebrews. But the new Jew he envisioned was not to be a mere Hebrew-speaking heathen. Despite the radical secularization of Jewish culture and identity that they would represent, Berdichevski's Hebrews would

Source for reading A.:   Translated from the Hebrew by Ben Halpern and Arthur Hertzberg and included in the volume edited by the latter, *The Zionist Idea. A Historical Analysis and Reader* (New York: Atheneum, 1973), pp. 293–4.

remain beholden to the past or what may be called the cultural memory of Judaism.

This time in which we live is not like yesterday or the day before – it has no counterpart, for all the bases and conditions of our previous existence are now undermined and changed. The "long, dark night" is gone, and new days, with new circumstances, have replaced it. There is reason for the fear in our hearts – it is true that we are no longer standing on a clear road; we have come to a time of two worlds in conflict: To be or not to be! To be the last Jews or the first Hebrews.

Our people has come to its crisis, its inner and outer slavery has passed all bounds, and it now stands one step from spiritual and material annihilation. Is it any wonder that all who know in their hearts the burden, the implications, and the "dread" of such an hour should pit their whole souls on the side of life against annihilation? And this, too, such men must feel: that a new life must arise, broader in scope and different in condition from what has been. In devoting ourselves to the essential task, the resurrection of the people, we cannot even be indulgent to its tradition.

It is true that our past is that which gives us an historic claim and title to live on in the future; and as we go forward in our struggle for existence we look back to the day of Judah's bannered camp, to our heroes and ancient men of war, to our sages, the beacons of our spirit. Yet we cannot hide from ourselves that our ancestral heritage is not entirely an asset; it has also caused us great loss.

After the destruction of the Temple our political status declined and our independence came to an end. We ceased to be a people actively adding to its spiritual and material store and living in unbroken continuity with its earlier days. As our creativity diminished, the past – whatever had once been done and said among us, our legacy of thoughts and deeds – became the center of our existence, the main supports of our life. The Jews became secondary to Judaism.

All sentiments of survival, all vital desires that had swelled the hearts of Jacob's children in former times, sought an outlet through these channels. Many thought that they could satisfy the national conscience that lived in their hearts by preserving what had been handed down from their ancestors.

Apart from turning us into spiritual slaves, men whose natural forces had dried up and whose relation to life and to the world was no longer normal, this brought about the great interruption in our social and political development, an interruption that has almost led us to total decay.

Our young people were made to believe that spiritual attachment to the Jewish people necessarily meant faith in a fixed and parochial outlook, so they turned away and left us, for their souls sought another way.

We are torn to shreds: at one extreme, some leave the House of Israel to venture among foreign peoples, devoting to them the service of their hearts and spirits and offering their strength to strangers; while, at the other extreme, the pious sit in their gloomy caverns, obeying and preserving what God had commanded them. And the enlightened, standing between, are men of two faces: half Western – in their daily life and thoughts; and half Jews – in their synagogues. Our vital forces disperse while the nation crumbles.

For all the yearning for a revival which has begun to awaken in the hearts of the remaining few, we feel that such a revival must encompass both the inner and the outer life. It cannot arise other than by a total overturn, that is, by a transvaluation of the values which have been the guide lines of our lives in the past.

Our hearts, ardent for life, sense that the resurrection of Israel depends on a revolution – the Jews must come first, before Judaism – the living man, before the legacy of his ancestors.

We must cease to be Jews by virtue of an abstract Judaism and become Jews in our own right, as a living and developing nationality. The traditional "credo" is no longer enough for us.

We desire to elevate our powers of thought, to enrich our spirit, and to enlarge our capacity for action; but let us never force our spirits into set forms which prescribe for us what we may think and feel.

It is not reforms but transvaluations that we need – fundamental transvaluations in the whole course of our life, in our thoughts, in our very souls.

Jewish scholarship and religion are not the basic values – every man may be as much or as little devoted to them as he wills. But the people of Israel come before them – "Israel precedes the Torah."

The world about us, life in all its aspects, the many desires, resolves, and dispositions in our hearts – all these concern us as they would any man and affect the integrity of our soul. We can no longer solve the riddles of life in the old ways, or live and act as our ancestors did. We are the sons, and sons of sons, of older generations, but not their living monuments....

We must cease to be tablets on which books are transcribed and thoughts handed down to us – always handed down.

Through a basic revision of the very foundations of Israel's inner and outer life, our whole consciousness, our predispositions, thoughts, feelings, desires, and will and aim will be transformed: and we shall live and stand fast.

Such a fundamental revision in the people's condition, the basic drive toward freedom, and the boundless urge to new life will revive our souls. Transvaluation is like a flowing spring. It revives whatever is in us, in the secret places of the soul. Our powers are filled with a new, life-giving content.

Such a choice promises us a noble future; the alternative is to remain a straying people following its erring shepherds. A great responsibility rests upon us, for everything lies in our hands! We are the last Jews – or we are the first of a new nation.

B.   Ben Halpern, "Apologia Contra Rabbines"[1]

Prior to assuming a professorship in Jewish history at Brandeis University, Ben Halpern (1912–90) was the long-time editor of *Jewish Frontier*, the urbane organ of the Labor Zionism in the USA. In the selection presented here he defiantly defends himself as secular Jew (of socialist Zionist persuasion) against his many "Rabbinic" opponents. In developing his "apologia contra rabbines," he launches a scathing critique of American Jewry, which, especially since World War II and the establishment of the State of Israel, has found it necessary to abandon the secular Jewish culture of its elders, the immigrant generation. By retreating to the synagogue as a bastion that would presumably secure a tenable *American* Jewish identity, Halpern argues, Jews have in effect rendered the *Jewishness* of their parents, with its comprehensive culture, into a circumscribed religious cult. The extensive implications of this shift from culture to cult is that although Jewish identity might be secure in America, Judaism will cease to be a vital and creative reality. Although hardly sanguine about the prospects of sustaining a secular Jewish culture in America, Halpern insists that it is no less "authentic" than religious forms of Jewish association and practice.

Significantly Halpern does not exclude God and the mysteries of belief from the ambit of his Jewish cultural concern – but, given his agnosticism, he resolutely refuses to feign belief in order to shore up his Jewish identity. Here he echoes the words of his mentor at Harvard University, the eminent historian of Jewish philosophy, Harry A. Wolfson (1887–1970), who was wont scornfully to speak of "verbal theists," who for calculated social and political reason would dissimulate their unbelief.[2] Nonetheless, a Jewish secularism, Halpern conceded, is a "detour, if not a total departure, from the roads upon which the Jewish people historically have sought God." What the Jews sought in God they sought as a people, as a sort of "collective prayer," and they recorded "their joint findings" in their cultural memory – the "canonical literature and a normative set of folkways." In contrast to "verbal theists," secular Jews unflinchingly acknowledge that Jewish cultural memory has become strained ever since their tie "with God became evanescent." Accordingly, Jewish secularism "means not only freeing Jewish culture" from its traditional religious moorings, but also "the freeing of religion from the bonds of tradition." For the secularist borne by a religious impulse God may or may not be found in the traditional expressions of Judaism. "For better or worse, the Jewish secularist must find God on his own..." Halpern's quarrel with the verbal theists is, then, that "they offer us God too cheaply." Halpern adamantly refuses to turn

Source for reading B.:   This essay first appeared in *Midstream*, a journal sponsored by the Zionist Organization of America, in the Spring of 1956, pp. 12–22.

to God – that is God-talk – as a solution for the problem of contemporary Jewish identity, or for the sake of Jewish unity. "To make such a use of God seems to us [secularists] respectful neither to Him nor to our problems."

True to his Zionist convictions, Halpern affirms that a viable secular Jewish culture could ultimately only unfold in the State of Israel. In recent years, however, even in the sovereign Jewish state, secularists have increasingly found themselves on the defensive. Due to the peculiar constellations of Israeli parliamentary politics, Orthodox Jews, who regard themselves as the sole custodians of Jewish tradition, have become a dominant political force, aggressively challenging all alternative expressions of Judaism. In response, secular Jews – often in alliance with Reform and Conservative Jews – have rallied around the cause of "Jewish pluralism." With the context of this campaign, secular Israeli Jews find it necessary to articulate anew their vision of Jewish culture, which, while honoring their intellectual and spiritual autonomy, draws freely from the classical sources and teachings of the tradition.

I keep having the strange experience these days of finding myself talked at when I open a journal of Jewish discussion. Not talked to – talked *at*; I might even say scolded. Somehow I can't believe I deserve it.

I am not speaking as an individual now, of course, but as a representative type: as a "secularist," socialist, Zionist Jew. The triply qualified Jew that I represent has, I find, become a favorite target for sermons, expostulations, and reproofs ever since the establishment of the State of Israel caused American Jews, or their rabbis and ideologists, to reopen the discussion of the Jewish problem.

As a secularist, I find myself apostrophized by Will Herberg, Jacob B. Agus and a host of others who warn me that I am headed straight for paganism, for Nazi or Communist totalitarianism, for the idolatrous absolutization and deification of man, or society, or science. It does no good to protest that I don't feel like an idolater at all. This only leads to being told that I am in a transitional stage, that my so-called non-idolatrous secularism, inherently unstable and untenable, can be maintained only because of what I owe to inherited religious culture, that if not I, then my children or children's children, educated on secularist lines, will inevitably become idolaters – and that the only refuge is in the leap of faith to God. Even Mordecai M. Kaplan, who is considered by some to be almost a secularist himself, has this to tell me:

> faith in the highest potentialities of human nature and persistence in activating them cannot be sustained without a religious feeling for history and the time process or without a sense of destiny which transcends the life of individuals and societies.

This is not a line of argument that could inspire discussion. The answer to it is too ready; it takes the form of a rejoinder rather than a rebuttal. For the first, automatic reaction of a secularist is to retort that *religion* inherently tends to dogmatism, hence to intolerance, persecution, and theocratic totalitarianism –

and that if some "religionists" manage nevertheless to preserve a liberal tolerance, it is thanks only to the secular cultural tradition of the society they live in, for if religion were to succeed in overcoming secularism it would inevitably lead to the anti-humanist reaction that is the natural tendency of a religiously governed society. To this, no doubt, some "religionists" would hotly reply that absolutism is only a degeneration of and a departure from true religion; at which I should then cry out that totalitarianism, as the deification of secular values, is only a perversion of true secularism. And the argument would have degenerated into a quarrel.

Accordingly, I have not the remotest intention of discussing the general problem of secularism versus religiosity.

But the argument is brought much closer to home and, moreover, based on more or less controllable sociological and historical premises when the religious exhorters apply themselves to the contemporary Jewish problem in America. American Jewry, they contend, is basically defined as a religious community. This is the way Jews are regarded by the Gentiles, and the way, too, in which they regard themselves; taking into account, of course, that a "religious community" under American conditions represents the socially accepted legitimate form for the segregation of groups that differ from the older, settled, "Anglo-Saxon," Protestant community in ethnic origin and folkways as well as in creed. But in no other form than in a religious community, they insist, can ethnic differences be maintained in America. What, then, is demanded by our "existential" situation, ask these new ideologists. Since we Jews exist in America, and can only exist in America as a religious community under the established form of religious diversity through the division of church and state, and since this is so owing to the irresistible pressure of sociological laws, it is up to us to make our "existential" status "authentic": to realize our religious calling as individuals and collectively to accept our religious mission.

The argument goes on to this further conclusion: the chief antagonist who must be overcome so that American Jewry may live up to its mission is none other than myself – the secularist socialist Zionist. I am he who stands in the way, and I must go. To be more precise, I have two options. I am challenged to see the error of my ways and join a synagogue, or else I may consider myself to all intents and purposes excommunicated.

Mordecai M. Kaplan chastises me with the whips of kindness, Jacob B. Agus with the scorpions of wrath. "From the standpoint of ethical influence, which should be the true measure of religion," says Dr. Kaplan, "there is incomparably more of the truly religious spirit in the basic principles by which members of the *Histadrut* [the Labor Federations of Israel] are expected to regulate their daily lives than in the most devout worship and ritual practices. But in failing to recognize this, in the inability to see those transcendental or cosmic meanings which give point to its own ethical striving, the *Histadrut* is missing its opportunity to make Zionism the kind of humanist religious movement that it must become, if Zionism is to survive." Consequently, if I reform and recognize, first, that what the secular socialist Zionists in Israel are building is, in fact, a religion and, secondly, that American Jews can and should share in that religion while permanently established in America – then I am helping the Jews individually to achieve salvation and collectively to survive. If not, then "failing a Zionist philosophy that could make a difference in the personal and communal life of Diaspora Jewry, the steadily widening cultural and spiritual gap between the Jews in Israel and the rest of world Jewry is leading both groups from frustration to frustration."

Dr. Agus, on the other hand, neither wants nor expects anything from me. When one leading Zionist, Dr. Samuel Margoshes, recently showed an inclination to take Dr. Kaplan's advice, Dr. Agus reacted with a polite letter making, in substance, the rude suggestion that such a Zionist, now that he had come to his senses, should go the whole hog and stop calling himself a Zionist. To me (that is, to Zionists who show no desire to redefine themselves as suggested by Dr. Kaplan) he says this: *"Those who have no faith in America obviously cannot be trusted with the task of building the future of Jewry in America."* And, again: "[The community] need repudiate only such groups as negate the value of our continued existence in the Diaspora – whether in the name of a totalitarian Zionism or in the name of totalitarian Americanism."[3]

If I may now, for a moment, revert to my individual self, the reason I find these views require discussion is that I accept in all essentials the sociological and historical premises upon which they are based. I think it is correct that a "naturalized" Jewish community in America must tend more and more to define itself as a religious community, and that its right to remain permanently distinct from the Gentile Americans is most easily recognized as legitimate under the principle of freedom of worship. That is precisely why I have so little "faith in America" as the home of a creative Jewish community and a vital Jewish culture.

It is by no means *impossible*, of course, that a secular Jewish culture, such as our parental generation knew, should continue to be maintained in America. Yiddish, among other minority cultures, has flourished particularly in this country and still sustains a literary and social vitality deserving the utmost respect. The Hebrew-speaking and Hebrew-writing circles active in America are bent upon reproducing themselves, and one cannot safely predict their demise. America is large and free, and if any group is sufficiently devoted to a cult to contribute the necessary time and energy for its preservation, there is room for it to thrive.

To be sure, what we have in this instance is not a culture but only a cult: it is an artificial growth, and it can only complete its life cycle, run to seed, and sprout new growth if a loving hand supplies both fertilizer and topsoil, with no consideration of cost. Far from arising from the natural social conditions of our country, it requires special social conditions such as favor the segregation of a group of cultists. Such social conditions existed in the America of our parents' days because, as immigrants, their first habitat in America was the ethnically diverse immigrant ghetto. In our own largely native-born generation, which has emerged into America-at-large, religion alone establishes a natural and legitimate segregation of Jews from other Americans. Still, there is no reason why devotes of Yiddish and Hebrew culture should not by voluntary exertions maintain both the schooling and the type of segregation required to foster Yiddishism and/or Hebraism as one among America's many exotic cults.

Yet while not impossible such an effort is hardly likely to continue over a long stretch or on any significant scale. A secular cult, unable to exist by its own natural appeal, depends on ideological justification. There is ultimately only one justification for the survival of a secular cult. It can only command the enthusiasm and devotion required to foster it artificially if its adherents can believe that the time will come when their faith will prevail organically, as a natural culture. In short, a myth is required that envisions the ultimate triumphant enthronement of the cultists' exotic beliefs over historical society. In our specific case, the cult of Yiddishism in America, which once found a kind of natural habitat in the immigrant ghetto, could now thrive over the long stretch and on a significant scale among our own largely native-born generation only if it could successfully propagate the myth of an America-of-the-future based on a federalism of autonomous, secular, ethnic cultures. But we are unable to belive in such a myth for America; and the more we recognize the manifest destiny of America to be culturally federalistic on religious lines only, the less likelihood there is of working up popular enthusiasm for the cult of secular Jewish culture in America.

Religion stands superior to these difficulties. The very reason why religion is inherently cultist is that it is somehow above history. The religious myth is a trans-historical myth, and to have faith in it does not in any important degree require that history furnish some corroborative evidences of its probable, let alone imminent, materialization. The ideologists of a religious faith have, accordingly, a justification relatively easy to validate and popularize, and the creative devotees of the cult, while not really dependent on popular response at all, can also appeal to a response not essentially dependent on favorable conditions of immediate history and habitat. Thus, it is a fairly safe prediction that (barring catastrophes) there will "always" be something in the nature of Jewish traditional religion.

Moreover, Jewish religion does not have to rely on this exemption from the chances of history in order to survive in America. It is warranted as a legitimate American form of social diversity, and it stands in the direct line of the probable trends of contemporary history. I need not labor the point of the much-touted religious revival in this country. It is clear and accepted that for every real enthusiast and devotee of Judaism as a cult we have a far larger actual and potential throng of "religionists" simply conforming to current conventions.

Well, then, here am I (on behalf of all the secularists, socialists, Zionists among the Jews in America), confessing that I stand opposed to this wave of the future. I do not really think that what I represent offers so serious a threat to achieving the promise of this future that it should call for the kind of hectoring tone used in the current phillipics against me. But I can well understand that there may be some nuisance value to *any* nonconformity in these days. And I admit my obligation to offer some reason for persisting as a public nuisance.

The idea that I, the secularist socialist Zionist with "no faith in the *galut*," am a threat to American Jewry is not a new complaint first uttered by the religious ideologists. The same logic and the same tone of embittered anger are quite familiar from the old polemics of the Yiddishist-Hebraist *Sprachenkampf* and I find myself responding in the same weary and exasperated way. "Why is Yiddish having such a hard row to hoe in America?" we so often heard the Yiddishists moan. "Because the Zionists persecute Yiddish in Israel and leave it no hope for survival there, that is why it is impossible to win over the youth in America for Yiddish." When Yiddishists resorted to this argument in their anguish at the inexorable decline of the cult in which their whole lives had been invested, even our understanding the psychological sources of those futile recriminations could hardly make us suffer the foolishness gladly. *We* were responsible for thwarting the Yiddishists in their campaign to capture the hearts of American youth? Never were we aware of such influence over young America. But now the religious ideologists, riding their wave of the future, come too and complain that the pessimism of us here, the American secularist socialist Zionist *galut* negators, and of Ben Gurion in Israel, this is what is destroying the confidence upon which rests the whole future of American Jewry. Isn't this really too much? With the whole institutional set-up of America guaranteeing the viability and prevalence of their point of view, why do they still have to have us as their scapegoats? What are *they* afraid of?

But if I look closer at some of these writings, I see that the authors really are afraid, just as I am, and for just the same reasons. If they are angry at me, it is because I coldly entertain the very fears they are so hotly trying to overcome or repress. "Jews at present resemble a demobilized army," says Dr. Kaplan. "...With the decay of supernaturalistic religion as a uniting bond, no other inner cohesive force has thus far been generated. Jewish unity, whatever of it still exists, is buttressed from *without* by the Christian tradition and by its offspring Anti-Semitism, but its *inner* supports are crumbling." In order to escape from their "spiritual isolation and moral anomie," Jews "desperately" build synagogues and religious schools. They face "inevitable frustrations" in their flight to religion, because "though their spiritual leaders have long abandoned supernaturalism they have not replaced it with any other dedicated faith." As for the schools, "the number of men and women.... *qualified* to teach Jewish subject matter is shockingly small," and so low do American parents rate the degree of Jewish culture they need to transmit to their children that attendance is low, brief, and perfunctory: "The Jewish religious schools are like the subway trains, always full, with people constantly getting on and getting off at every station." What wonder then that the most gifted spirits among American Jews cannot "be associated with any type of normative Judaism," that "few of our bright young Jews are really interested in Judaism or Jewish culture," and that even among the "synagogued

Jews there are few who really live the Judaism that they profess to believe in." In other words, Dr. Kaplan does not feel comfortable sitting on the wave of the future; he is all too painfully aware that it is just so much froth and water. He is not content with having so many Jews come to roost under the wing of the synagogue, for what he earnestly wishes is that he could feel them to be real Jews.

How familiar is this melancholy outlook; so like our own – and yet so different! The secularist socialist Zionist in America has long been riding an ebbing rather than a rising tide. What we see flowing away from us is all that water upon which the new religious ideology floats; but what we are left with, and what we have always had, are, as we intensely feel, real and authentic Jews.

Why do we, the secularist socialist Zionists, have the sense of being real and authentic Jews, why have the Yiddishist groups always had it, and why, for that matter, do the Orthodox in their tight ghetto have it, while the Jews who accept most unreservedly the standard of American institutions have lost that feeling? Dr. Kaplan does not ask this question, but what his answer might be is obvious enough. It emerges quite clearly from the demands he makes upon us, as well as from the proposals he makes for the reconstruction of the American Jewish community. Israel must help save American Jews, according to Kaplan, by not only living a full ethical, Jewishly inspired life-in-this-world, as it has begun to do, but by formulating its practices as principles and expressing these as ceremonies which could be adopted by the Jewish cult in America: in other words, he asks the Israelis to create that *culture* that could give body and substance and vitality to Judaism as a *cult*. The same tendency is apparent in Dr. Kaplan's proposals for an "organic" Jewish community in America. He cannot be satisfied with a synagogue Judaism alone, even though (since Jewishness must be defined mainly as a cult in America) he defends the centrality of the synagogue. But, clustered around the synagogue, he demands that there be maintained in organic relationship – that is to say, in some sort of organized, democratically responsible unity – a whole array of "legislative" and administrative, social, economic, educational, welfare and civic defense activities. In other words, he wishes to give even American Jewry, as far as possible, the scope and aspect of a culture, not only a cult.

That is the crux of the question. To become a mere cult would make of American Jewry a collection of something less than real Jews; this is a truth that all these religious ideologists themselves cannot help but feel. The most consistent and ruthlessly logical partisan of the new ideological anti-Zionism, the one who is just about ready to call it by that very name, Dr. Jacob B. Agus, defines his position in these words:

> In any synthesis of national sentiments with religious values it is the latter that must be raised to the supreme level of importance; the former may be allowed but a subsidiary role, and encouraged only as they remain in accord with the standards and ideals of ethics and religion. . . . But when subordinated to higher considerations Jewish nationalism may continue to be a powerful creative force, serving the ends of

Jewish religion, as it did in the past, by bringing to the aid of piety additional motivation, and by supplying foci of sentimental loyalty within the Jewish community.

These are strange and discordant notes in the otherwise almost monotonously harmonic logic of Dr. Agus' essays. But what they express is the irrepressible sense that the price of Judaism as a pure cult is the inability of Jews to be real Jews.

A signal characteristic of the new cultist ideologies is that they are all bothered by a serious problem of definition. At least, what is characteristic is that *they* consider the question of defining "Jew" and "Judaism" to be of critical and fundamental importance – as one well may if he is dealing no longer with real Jews but with Jews who still have to be converted into the real thing. Thus Dr. Agus realizes that "the most telling objection raised against the conception of a religious status for American Jewry is the indubitable fact of its limited inclusiveness." He suggests that one could adopt "two complementary definitions" demarcating "nuclear and protoplasmic sections" of Jewry, the former consisting of strict observers, the latter distinguished from Gentiles only by the "inexorable hairline of conversion." Still, this would leave in the outer darkness of the protoplasmic section "many spiritually sensitive people unaffiliated with the synagogue, yet...profoundly stirred by Jewish associations"; and it would include in the inner circle of the nucleus "masses of indifferent materialists...cold and unmoved by any appeal to spiritual values." Nevertheless, when facts fail to accord with the definition, all Dr. Agus can suggest is that we are obliged to bring them into conformity. So seriously does he take the definition! Dr. Kaplan's view is well known. He has always felt that one could almost reduce the entire Jewish problem to one cardinal difficulty: we have lost a defined status as a community.

This is a difficulty that never really bothered the Orthodox Jews, the Yiddishists and ethnic autonomists, and the old-line Zionists, for all of these never doubted that they constituted groups of real Jews. As a result, whatever the disapproval and outright hostility each may have felt toward the other at times, or in general to other kinds of Jews outside their own party, they never viewed them with that peculiar troubled irritability of the religious ideologists towards Jews who escape their definitions; they never doubted the validity of other Jews' credentials or the reality behind their own. There was an underlying sense of easy brotherhood towards all Jews, precisely because it was so obvious the Jews were a real thing. The Orthodox knew beyond question that all the seed of Abraham were included in the Covenant, and if they rebelled against God, they were simply bad Jews – *poshei Yisrael* – but as real as any other. The Yiddishists and ethnic autonomists were, perhaps, somewhat limited in their Jewish perception, effectively feeling as their fellow Jews mainly the Yiddish-speaking community, but though the historic bond that bound them to Sephardim or to the "assimilated" Jews of the West may have grown thin, it was of such a kind that by extension it could include them, too: if *history* made one a Jew, all who shared it were indubitably real Jews. We, lastly, the Zionists, felt most keenly the critical and problematic state of Jewish existence. We arose out of a sense of the disintegration and collapse of the Jewish people. But by our very rise, by our assertion and drive toward a common destiny, we overcame the problem in the moment of grasping it, we gave body to the Jewish people in the moment of evoking its national will – and in that moment, too, we (together with the Yiddishists) gave freedom and creative *élan* to Jewish culture.

This, too, is a source of great perplexity to the new religious ideologists, for it is not only "Jew" but "Judaism" which appears to them to be seriously in need of redefinition. They are afflicted here, too, by severe doubt that what really exists as Jewish religious culture is valid, and driven to anxious efforts to conjure into reality that which by their definition Judaism ideally is. I need not quote from Dr. Kaplan, since it is well-known that his whole life has been given over to the passion of reconstructing Judaism in order to shape it into something that would fit his definition of a contemporary "salvational" system.

Dr. Agus is in the so-called right wing of American Conservative Judaism, yet he too is unable to accept Jewish tradition simply as it has been handed down to us by what Solomon Schechter called Catholic Israel – namely the consensus of generations upon generations of pious Jews. While accepting the Law as given – at least to start with – Dr. Agus refuses to accept the methods of reasoning through which the rabbis formerly derived the laws. He is very actively concerned with *rethinking* the body of law, just as is Dr. Kaplan, and he applies the same methods of thought, namely the universal logic of all men and not the traditional logic of the Talmud; he differs from Dr. Kaplan in that the aim he ultimately accepts is not "this-worldly" but (superficially, at least) "other-worldly." To be recognized by him as valid for Judaism today, any traditional practice (or proposed departure from it) must be shown to conduce toward making contemporary American Jews more pious.

Thus Catholic Israel has in effect been reduced to contemporary American Jewry – or rather, to a small committee of rabbis in the Conservative movement who undertake to revise Jewish religious culture in line with what they think is likely to make their congregations (given their temperaments, distractions, level of knowledge and commitment, and other circumstances) more pious. That there has indeed been a major shrinkage of Solomon Schechter's original (undoubtedly rather vague) conception of Catholic Israel is stated quite explicitly by Robert Gordis: "Catholic Israel must be conceived of differently from hitherto accepted views. Catholic Israel embraces all those who observe Jewish law in general, although they may violate one or another segment of it, and who are sensitive to the problem of their non-observance because they wish to respect the authority of Jewish law." What better description could one ask of Conservative Judaism in America – or, even more particularly, of the "group mind" emerging from the collective cogitations of the Law Committee of the Rabbinical Assembly? And Catholic Israel, so defined, has only one function, that of reducing the traditional religious culture of Judaism to the dimensions of a contemporary American cult.

It may be asked why I, the self-confessed secularist, am apparently so exercised over the matter? The question is certainly a fair and pertinent one. Just to make it even more pointed, let me make this further confession: I find far more *sympathiques* those ideologists of neo-Orthodoxy, like Will Herberg or Abraham J. Heschel, who try to persuade me to leap to God and land in the age-old net of *halachah* than I do the ideologists of the new Catholic Israel. For I find in the former, who seem hardly concerned with rewinding the springs of our rundown *halachic* system so that it may tell time for the new era, a breadth and freedom of culture that are, to my mind, notably lacking in the latter, absorbed as they are in tinkering with the works to make *halachah* run in a new tempo.

I say this in spite of the fact that it has been a major achievement of secularist *Yiddishkeit*, and above all of Zionism, to break the mold within which religious tradition had frozen Jewish culture, and to let the creative stream flow freely once more. We have given even to Orthodoxy a future, for the history that Zionism has made can go unmarked by no Jewish doctrine that experiences as its core the great Jewish theme of Exile and Redemption. But it was Orthodoxy that gave us a past. This past we wished to expand, to open up, to unfold, to expose to the light, to explore and find in it colors suppressed, rebellions forgotten, nuances denied by Catholic Israel in the course of its massive flow. Upon this past we still stand and reach out to new, it may be extravagant, it may even be illusory perspectives. And they who would bring us back to it, regarding us as straying children, they, too, know that we belong together however opposed, just as we feel akin to them. For the old Jewish values were the values of a *people*, they constituted a culture – a religious culture, to be sure, but not the bare bones of a cult. The attempt to redefine Judaism as a cult, to make it over into an intelligently engineered curriculum for training in piety, to reduce it to the scale of experience of no more than the contemporary synagogue, not only in principle excludes us secularists; it constitutes an assault upon our past. Much could be said on this point, but I will only add that to a secularist socialist Zionist *galut* negator like myself, any version of Judaism which tries to dispense with the concept of Exile and Redemption from Exile is attempting nothing less than a divorce from our central historic experience as a people. Such a Judaism (if it could ever exist) would have cut itself off from its memory, and could have no Jewish future. To be sure, the awareness of Exile is today merely repressed, not effectively expunged, but even this much success of the American ideology can hardly fail to estrange us.

The Neo-Orthodox offer me *halachah* as a mystery which they themselves do not pretend to understand, and they ask me to take it on faith, as I should God. But they offer me my Jewish past whole and complete[4] – and they would have me accept it with all of me, just as I am, with my sense of Exile and my will to Redemption. Orthodox Judaism is, of course, "normative," like any religious doctrine, which means that there are always some spontaneous cultural expressions that it would suppress as heretical. Moreover, in Eastern Europe the "Orthodox"[5] Jews lived in a community which, because of the sluggish pulse of all history in that part of the world and because of the high degree of Jewish isolation, allowed its religious culture, intense as it was, to become hemmed in and crabbed by conventions. It was precisely this constriction against which Zionism and Jewish secularism revolted. But, however straitjacketed "Orthodox" Judaism was in Eastern Europe, it still functioned as an expression of a people, not of a union of congregations. It had in it the inherent freedom and responsiveness of a culture, not the automatism of a cult. It is not surprising, then, if after the emergence of Orthodox Jewry into the Western world, its intellectual adherents, even while taking up the old ritual life unaltered, live in free communication with all of Western culture, just as had Jews before them in Spain, Italy, the Moslem countries, and wherever the Gentiles around them had a significant culture.

It may seem a paradox to charge Conservative Judaism and its new ideologists even by implication with being anything but completely open to all the winds of contemporary culture. Is it not, after all, their major preoccupation to pull in the slack of that cultural lag with which Jewish tradition seems to be afflicted? But precisely this seems to me to be a basic error, an atrocious lapse of the instinct for culture. The Jewish religious folkways may or may not be out of tune with contemporary social conditions – if they are, rely on it that the Orthodox Jews will eventually alter them both here and in Israel by a movement almost glacial in its massiveness and imperceptibility, or, when they are good and ready, by some more abrupt transition acceptable to themselves. But what is quite clear is that these folkways cannot be incompatible with any true culture, whether contemporary or futurist. Such products of a massive cultural experience can be out of fashion culturally, just as they can be "out of adjustment" socially; but these are two distinct and separate phenomena. That a cultural expression may have gone out of fashion means that men have lost a capacity to appreciate its intrinsic merit – a merit it nevertheless still possesses, as it always has, if it were indeed ever anything more than a fashionable novelty. The time may come when new men with new capacities will appreciate it in new ways. But even when, in the autonomous development of culture itself, men turn from the old to the unexplored new – if this is a process of authentic culture, not of socio-cultural engineering – they leave intact what they reject and they simply burst beyond its bounds along a line of flight contained potentially within the parent mass.

The real root of my objections may be, of course, that the new religious ideologists cannot accept such an "aberration" as myself – at least, they cannot if they adhere rigorously to their doctrine. It may seem as though I am putting too much emphasis on what is, after all, a merely academic question, for in spite of polemics the new ideologists have always been closely connected, in actuality, with us secularist socialist Zionists; so closely, indeed, that Dr. Kaplan, for one, wishes to call his doctrine the "New Zionism." If there have been occasions when this group viewed some cultural development in American Jewry with a censorious eye, it was usually a development with which we, too, had scant sympathy. But the point is not only that this group occasionally did show censorious tendencies, but that censoriousness is far more characteristic of them in principle than it has ever been (or, let us hope, ever will be) in practice. For the new doctrine is normative in a much more serious sense than Orthodox Judaism ever was, regardless of the incomparably worse actual record of the Orthodox as an obscurantist force. The Orthodox normative technique used a logic and method so "unscientific" that almost anything could in theory be justified by it, no matter how much was in fact, and on non-cultural grounds, excluded. But the new ideology operates with a precisely defined objective and a rigorous method: to cut and trim Jewish religious culture to a cult whose doctrines and practices can be shown by experimental evidence and logical inference to conduce to the attachment of the average American Jew to his synagogue.

As for God Himself, in whose name all the religious ideologists of whatever coloration join in chiding us [secularists], I have no doubt, on the strength of our acquaintanceship with Him through the medium of the vast, many-sided Jewish tradition, that He will be indulgent enough to let us make our way to Him through whatever detours we may each chance to find on our several routes. For it is clear enough that, in terms of normative Jewish tradition, Jewish secularism represents at least a detour, if not a total departure, from the roads upon which the Jewish people historically have sought God. What was characteristic of the Jews was that they sought God collectively, as a people, and incorporated their joint findings in a canonical literature and a normative set of folkways. The individual God-seeker, of course, always had his place in Judaism, whether as a prophet, cabbalist mystic, or ethical and ritual rigorist. But the "religious virtuoso" among Jews not only guarded himself to an unusual degree from a break with the community; the community went with him an extraordinarily long way on the road of devotion. Jewish culture, accordingly, was a religious culture, a form of collective prayer in fact.

Contemporary Jewish secularism means a twofold break with this background. It means not only freeing Jewish culture from religious forms which we felt had become hidebound; it also means freeing religion from the bonds of tradition. By the latter, however, are implied not only the bonds of the tradition formed in Eastern Europe and corresponding to conditions there. Whatever religious impulse secularists experience feels itself quite as free from all those new traditions that are being reconstructed for us with scissors and paste in America. For better or worse, the Jewish secularist must find God out of his own, free individual experience. He may not even find Him as easily in the forms of Jewish tradition (and this can be true of men by whom the values of Jewish culture are profoundly experienced) as in quite unrelated forms. He may never find Him in any clear and distinct vision – but he cannot on that account abandon his Jewishness or his concern with Jewish culture!

Nothing the religious ideologists may say can affect one hard fact with which we secularists in the Jewish community – that is, we committed but extra-synagogue Jews – are continually confronted. Both by will and by force of circumstances, we are Jews, real, unquestionable Jews. In America, in the exile generally, our Jewishness has become a problem ever since its tie with God became evanescent. We find ourselves, moreover, in the self-defeating position of turning our secular Jewishness into a cult. Only in the movement to concentrate the Jewish people in Israel do we sense a real possibility that our Jewishness may strike roots as a natural culture. But there, too, we realize that the lost tie with God stands as a challenge to Jewish culture.

What, then, is our quarrel with the American religious ideologists? Paradoxically enough (if they will only believe us) it is that they offer us God too cheaply. We do not want Him as a solution for the problem of the Jewish Diaspora in America, nor as a least common denominator to reduce the differences between Israel and the Diaspora, or between contemporary and traditional Jewish culture. To make such a use of God seems to us respectful neither to Him nor to our problems. The latter we wish to solve in their own terms. As to God, again I say, we have faith that He will be indulgent enough to let us, individually and collectively, make our way to Him by whatever detours we chance to meet on the road that we must travel.

Notes

1   Halpern's principal antagonists in the essay are Jacob B. Agus (1911–1986), a leader of Conservative Judaism, Will Herberg (1901–77), who had abandoned the Communism of his youth for Jewish religious faith, and Mordecai M. Kaplan (1881–1983), the founder of Reconstructionist Judaism.

2   See Harry A. Wolfson, "Sermonette: The Professed Atheist and the Verbal Theist," in Wolfson, *Religious Philosophy. A Group of Essays* (Cambridge, 1961), pp. 270–1. [Ben Halpern]

3   Everything italicized in the above quotations, by the way, was italicized in the sources, as though conveying instructions that here the sermon is to be read in a raised voice and more deliberate tempo, for emphasis. [Ben Halpern]

4   I would make this assertion even of such neo-Orthodox apologists as Will Herberg who, coming back to Judaism from estrangement, must themselves slowly acquire the whole of Jewish culture, and may, at first, fail to appreciate some of its central themes. [Ben Halpern]

5   I use quotation marks around this expression because it is really a misnomer. It is my impression that it never occurred to anyone to call a particular version of Judaism "Orthodox" until Reform Judaism arose and its opponents in Central Europe adopted this name in contradistinction. [Ben Halpern]

C.   Yaakov Malkin, "The Faith of Secular Jews"

The Israeli educator Yaakov Malkin (b. 1926), who is also a professor of aesthetics and rhetoric at the University of Tel Aviv, recently founded in Jerusalem a College of Pluralistic Judaism to promote dialogue between secular and Orthodox Jews. In a booklet sponsored by the College, Malkin outlines for the broader public his "credo." In this selection, he presents the beliefs of secular – "free" – Jews.

What do secular Jews believe?

FREE JEWS – that is, Jews free from the dominion of Halachic religion, free from an exclusive religious interpretation of *mitzvot*, from a religious interpretation of Jewish celebration, traditions and culture, Jews free of one inflexible view of the Bible and post-biblical literature–such Jews believe in:

THE FREEDOM TO CHOOSE the ways of realizing one's Jewishness. Jews may not be the "Chosen People," but Jewishness involves the obligation to choose. Jewish culture has no one "form of practice"; the free Jew determines how, and through what forms, he or she will participate in the ethnic solidarity which distinguishes Jewish identity.

FREE JEWS BELIEVE IN GOD as the hero of their central book and of other classic works of Jewish literature. This literature created God – both in human images and in the formless abstractions of philosophical thought. God has been perceived by Jews as a living functioning agent in all the eras of our history and culture. In the minds of most twentieth century secular Jews, God continues to function as the emblem of a long literary tradition-though without any practical authority in our personal or political life.

FREE JEWS BELIEVE IN THE BIBLE as a literary and historical anthology which stands at the core of Jewish culture and identity. This book became the basis for all Judaisms. Within the Bible can be found all the literary genres of Western literature. The corpus of the Bible – books of literature, laws, history, chronicles, philosophy, and rhetoric – represents the first thousand years of Judaism as the pluralistic national culture of the Jewish people.

FREE JEWS BELIEVE IN HUMANISM AND DEMOCRACY as essential to Judaism. The ethics of humanism were defined by Hillel, and this is the light by which the secular Jew reads the laws and principles guiding his/her life. Hillelian values allow for a humanist reading of the Ten Commandments, the teachings of

Source for Reading C.:   What Do Secular Jews Believe (Jerusalem: Free Judaism, 1998), pp. 11–16. The volume is translated from the Hebrew by Batya Stein.

the Prophets, the controversies over interpretations of the Talmudic law. These values advocate the sanctity of majority rule – which the Talmud too upholds, even when contradicting the voice of God. Belief in human rights is fundamental to the secular Jew. These rights take precedence over all religious demands and restrictions. In Israel, they form the basis of the law, a law which strives to reinterpret Jewish heritage free from the anachronisms of Halachic rulings.

FREE JEWS BELIEVE IN PLURALISM as fundamental to Jewish identity and culture throughout its history. In the biblical period, monotheism and polytheism coexisted and clashed, as did various Jewish views regarding the ethical nature of God. In the Hellenistic period, a plurality of views found expression in Jewish culture and were battled over in civil wars. The Middle Ages offered a plurality of secular and religious Jewish literatures and of ethnic traditions, and the simultaneous existence of rationalism and mysticism.

FREE JEWS BELIEVE IN OPENNESS TO OTHER CULTURES. This openness and exchange characterized Judaisms throughout history. It was Judaism's receptiveness to Egyptian, Meso-potamian, Hellenistic, Muslim, Christian, European, and American cultures that enabled it to spread its influence and to endure. Cross-fertilization and cultural flexibility render Judaism one of the most influential – and influenced – cultures in the West.

FREE JEWS BELIEVE IN HOLIDAY CELEBRATIONS as expressions of unique family and community values. In each period, in each context, free Jews redefine the practice of Jewish holidays, "pouring new content into old vessels." The Sabbath and the national holidays are celebrated by secular Jews in forms free from the rigidity and exclusivity of religious interpretation. These secular celebrations play a central role in Jewish family and community life, and become points of reference and enrichment for Jewish culture.

FREE JEWS BELIEVE IN THE UNIQUENESS OF THE JEWS AS A NATION. This belief is rooted in the acceptance of all nations as unique and entitled to a self-determined identity. The definition of the Swiss nation will not be applicable to the Welsh or the Gypsy nations. So too, the definition of the Jews as a nation has its own uniqueness, determined by the unique history of Judaism, and by the fusion of its history and cultural heritage. The uniqueness of Judaism is the consequence of the way Jewish states and its exiled communities have evolved, of its pluralistic culture, and of the interrelations between that culture and other national languages and cultures.

FREE JEWS BELIEVE THAT JUDAISM IS PART OF WORLD CULTURE. Rather than stress the exclusivity of Judaism, secular Jews recognize that the masterpieces of biblical literature, together with the great works of Greece, had a determining influence on the development of Western culture. The Ten Commandments are recognized as the ethical basis of Western morality. The Bible underlies, too, for example, the invention of the week and the Sabbath as egalitarian concepts which enable leisure for all. The innovation of the synagogue as both religious center and a center for learning and social relations – influenced the Western concept of community.

FREE JEWS BELIEVE IN JEWISH EDUCATION as the vanguard of the socialization of all Jewish women and men, of all ages. Secular Judaism teaches pluralism and humanism; it also teaches that these humanizing forces are possible only within a national and cultural context. Jewish education is a source of individual, family and community enrichment – and cohesion. It enables Jews to know and formulate their national culture. It stresses the participatory role of the individual in the interpretation and modes of practice which, in their many interrelated forms, define the Jews as a nation. Most important, secular Jews see education as one of the factors which determine the quality of individual life, and of the community within which the secular Jew functions as a free and committed part of the Jewish nation.

Chapter 25
Judaism and Zionism

Yosef Gorny

There is no doubt that after a hundred years of existence, Zionism has arrived at a crossroads, the result not of its failures but of its achievements. The question now is: "Quo vadis Zionism?" and to this question there are two positive "post-Zionist" answers.

One group views Zionism as having arrived at the end of the road. These post-Zionists are satisfied with Zionist national achievements, and at this point they want to see the State of Israel and its society become a normal citizen-state following the model of western countries in Europe and North America.

The second group views Zionism as having reached a crossroads in its long history. For this group, post-Zionism is only partial. While these individuals agree that a certain kind of Zionist era has reached its culmination, they are convinced that the Jewish people needs to move forward toward a new Zionist era. Existentially, to stand at a crossroads is more difficult and more problematic than to stand at the end of a road.

The following selections express this Zionist position: "Reflections at a Crossroads." The opening essay is a provocative assertion by Professor David Vital that the Jewish nation today lies shattered. The readings that follow may be seen as responses to that predicament. They offer constructive proposals for how to establish new relations between Israel and the Jewish diaspora on the basis of a new kind of Zionism. To present the broadest possible spectrum of ideas, I have chosen extracts from nine thinkers who belong to the two "competing" centers – USA and Israel. Additionally, all expressions of Zionist thought are represented – secular, Reform, Conservative, and religious Orthodox Zionists.

A.   David Vital, *The Future of the Jews: A People at the Crossroads?*

That the Jews, historically, were a "nation" in every important sense of that infinitely tricky and provocative term can hardly be gainsaid. Some historians have gone so far as to argue that it was the Jews (with the Greeks) who were the original inventors of the concept, at any rate in the western world, apart from constituting the prototypical case of the actual phenomenon. That, of course, is not the whole of the – and their – story. That the religion and culture (high as well as low) of the Jews were intimately and inextricably bound up with their nationhood over very many centuries is beyond question. What can be seriously, if somewhat fruitlessly, debated is only the subsidiary question whether their ancient faith should be seen primarily as the instrument of their national preservation, or contrariwise, whether it is their peoplehood that should be seen as the means whereby their religion was defended and preserved, and not without success, against successive, near fatal onslaughts by pagan, Christian, and Muslim rivals.

But these matters, it is contended, have now been relegated to the shade by a larger and vastly more urgent one. It is that of the very survival of Jewry as a people at all – at any rate in anything like the form in which traditionally and historically it had functioned and in which it had most commonly been recognized by Jew and non-Jew alike. Today, at the end of the unspeakable twentieth century, it is not too much to say that the survival of Jewry as a discrete people, its various branches bound to each other by common ties of culture, responsibility, and loyalty, is entirely in doubt. It is with the reasons for such doubt and with the salient causes of the changes and contradictions which have undermined the ancient structure of Jewry in the course of these past two centuries that this book is concerned.

Inevitably, the discussion has led to the matter of the relations between Diaspora Jewry and what might be termed the Jewry of Israel. While it is right to say that the roots of the present malaise (if not disorientation) which characterizes world Jewry today do not lie exclusively in that domain, still, plainly, the rise of an independent Jewish state has both revolutionized and destabilized the Jewish world. It was inevitable, therefore, that a good part of the essay be devoted to a consideration of its consequences. But let it be clear: my purpose is not so much to bring the viability or legitimacy of the Diaspora into question as to argue that the *interests*, and therefore the underlying tendencies and viewpoints, of American and other Jewries, cannot fail to differ crucially from those of Israeli Jewry. And that is one key reason, quite conceivably the chief reason, why willy-nilly the Jewish world – beaten by assimilation on the one hand and by destruction and

Source for Reading A.:   Cambridge, MA: Harvard University Press, 1990.

threats of further punishment on the other – is not coming apart. Where there was once a single, if certainly a scattered and far from monolithic people – indeed, a nation – there is now a sort of archipelago of discrete islands composed of rather shaky communities of all qualities, shapes, and sizes, in which the Island of Israel, as it were, is fated increasingly to be in a class by itself.

In sum, the old unity of Jewry, however fragile, however problematic, essentially a function of the old sense and, yes, the old reality of nationhood, lies shattered today, almost beyond repair. But my intention here is by no means to complain about this or any other feature of Jewish life, either in the Diaspora or in Israel. It is to explore and, if possible, account for what is now before us: the waning of the Jewish nation.

I.   *Galut*: The Centrality of Israel

B.   Ben Halpern, "Exile – Abstract Condition and Concrete Community"

It might help to still the interminable controversy about *Shlilat hagalut* (negation of the exile) and *hiyyuv hagolah* (affirmation of the exile), or at least confine it within sensible bounds, if people were more careful in their usage. The Hebrew *galut* means the abstract condition of exile, or bondage. *Golah* refers to a concrete community in exile. If the strict sense of these terms were respected, any normal person would have to repudiate the abstract condition of bondage; and few people would normally disapprove of a community because it is oppressed. Because this distinction is not always noted, the quarrel often degenerates into a verbal misunderstanding between those who are accused of loving bondage and those who are accused of hating Jews. If there is to be any fruitful discussion, it ought to begin with the stipulation by both sides that *sholelei* (negators) *hagalut* (not *sholelei hagolah*) need not hate any Jewish community and *mehayyevei* (affirmers) *hagolah* (not *mehayyevei hagalut*) need not love the condition of bondage.

Jewish tradition made sense of Jewish experience when the *galut* was in a state of palpable oppression. It sustained Jewish life as an exercise of passive, heroic resistance which was to be redeemed in the restoration to Zion. After the emancipation of Jewry the *galut* is not, at any rate, in a state of harsh oppression; particularly not when Israel exists as an always available opportunity for

Source for Reading B.:   In: Carol Diament, ed., *Zionism the Sequel* (New York: Hadassah, 1998), pp. 73–5.

redemption – which so few choose to make use of. Contemporary Jewish experience in America, accordingly, is not such that Jewish tradition can make sense of it. Attachment to Jewish tradition has consequently become, for some, an exercise of sheer otherworldly piety, and for others, a nostalgic or deliberately-cultivated sentimentalism seeking to cover the nakedness of an identity accepted by force of circumstances alone, without the inherent meaningfulness that it once had.

Such an identity may well survive. But for many who find themselves sharing it, the question of whether it is worth keeping may well arise. That this question in fact does arise is an accepted fact of contemporary Jewish life in America. It is the basis for many a Jewish parent's anxieties about exotic cults which attract young Jews in deplorable numbers. It is also the reason that a relatively small number of young Jews still experience diaspora Jewishness as oppressive, as *galut*, and wish to opt for redemption – or, if you wish, for the solution of their Jewish problem – by *aliyah* to Israel.

As one who believes that, wherever possible, problems ought to be solved, and who shares their *shlilat hagalut*, I believe they are right.

C.   Nathan Rotenstreich, "The Present-Day Relationship"

The creation of the State of Israel does not and cannot correspond to the idyllic model envisaged by Ahad Ha'Am, that the center to be established in Israel would be a continuation of the literary creativity previously centered in Odessa and Warsaw. This is not possible. Things do not develop in that fashion – they are accompanied by catastrophes, difficulties and stresses, by demographic and international problems; the ideal Jew does not emerge; no ideal type materializes. We must, therefore, see matters in a completely different light.

I suggest that the concept of Israel's centrality in relation to the diaspora be replaced by Israel's preferential status, its *primacy*, over the diaspora. The idea of primacy seems preferable to that of centrality; the former metaphor indicates that if there are conflicts of interest between the diaspora and the State of Israel, the interests of the State would be preferred. However, I do not wish to deal specifically with conflict situations, even though we have to take them into consideration as possibilities of historical processes. I would rather consider the primacy of the State of Israel from the viewpoint of its status.

The State of Israel, as such, is, first of all, the culmination of purposeful efforts by Jews; therein lies its basic difference from Jewish existence in the diaspora. It is the outcome of conscious decisions taken by Jews. It is not a reality created by force of circumstances, but a reality which we wanted to create and establish from

Source for Reading C.: In Carol Diament, ed., *Zionism the Sequel* (New York: Hadassah, 1998), pp. 82–4.

the outset. Someone skeptically disposed toward the State of Israel phrased it thus: "It was literally built into existence." I assert: Therein lies its *greatness*. The asserted element of artificial construction should, I suggest, be seen as the essential element. Essential is surely the opposite of artificial.

A second point – closely linked to the first – is that the State of Israel is the realization of the collective existence *ab initio* of the Jewish people. It was originally established in order that the Jewish people should have a defined and cohesive collective existence: not a *post factum* collective existence, in which Jews come together as individuals, and the enlightened world allows them to form social units and organizations which the world finds congenial, but a concentrated Jewish world which is defined by its collective character.... A collective, established as such from the very beginning, stands on a higher level than collectives which come into being incidentally.

Many of the difficulties that we encounter are essentially caused by the fact that the world has accepted the reality of Jews establishing collectives *post factum*, but it has not yet accepted the position that the Jews existed as a collective from the very beginning....

We can convey this to the diaspora without any embellishment.... We may say that there is a difference between helping brothers in distress and obeying the commandment to redeem captives, and supporting the effort for the historical collective home of the Jewish people. The second alternative possibly calls for a longer and more sustained effort, but we know that some aspirations which appear to be long-range are actually short-range. That is [my] second point in this concept of the primacy of the State of Israel.

D.   Shlomo Avineri, "Israel – A Normative Value of Jewish Existence"

Regardless of the concrete expressions of the relationship between the Jewish polity in the land of Israel and the Jewish communities in the diaspora, there is a *qualitative* difference between the two components in the relationship – Israel is a value, the diaspora is a mere fact. To put it differently: the existence of Israel has a normative status in Jewish consciousness, while the various diasporas – even if one grants, as Ahad Ha'Am did, their future continuous existence – have no such normative status.

There are nowadays, and have been in the past, societies that have been extremely hospitable and tolerant to Jewish existence and creativity: the Babylonian diaspora in talmudic times, Ptolemaic Egypt, the Roman Empire

Source for Reading D.: In Carol Diament, ed., *Zionism the Sequel* (New York: Hadassah, 1998), pp. 85–8.

(most of the time), Muslim and pre 1492 Christian Spain, the pre-partition Polish-Lithuanian Commonwealth, Austro-Hungary, pre-Nazi Germany, contemporary America. But anything achieved Jewishly in these societies could have been achieved in another diaspora; and when, for historical reasons, Jewish life became threatened or came to an end in any of these societies, Jews, so far as they did survive, were able to move to another diaspora in more hospitable countries and start again from scratch. This is the epic story of Jewish survival.

Israel, however, is different; its very existence as a Jewish society in the ancestral Jewish homeland gives it public standing – in Jewish and non-Jewish eyes – and hence a normative value as such.

This difference between the mere facticity of the diaspora and the normative nature of the existence of Israel was very clearly evident in the obvious distinctions made by western Jewry in the seventies and eighties in dealing with twin concerns that were then central to the Jewish agenda: Israel and Soviety Jewry. In the latter case, Jews worldwide were concerned about the life conditions of two to three million Jews in the Soviet Union: that they should not be persecuted, that they should be allowed to practice their religion and culture, and that they should be able to emigrate. The concern was for these Jews as individuals, and if their freedom and welfare as Jewish persons could not be achieved within the Soviet Union but only through emigration – so be it. The existence of a Jewish community in the Soviet Union as such was of no value; the life and freedom of its Jews were.

In the case of Israel, it was the public and corporate existence of Israel as a polity, not just as an agglomeration of four million individual Jews, that was, and still is, at stake. For if just the physical security and existence of Jewish individuals in Israel were the concern of world Jewry, then an evacuation to safer shores could become an option. This was, and is, obviously not the case, because it is the corporate existence of Israel as a Jewish public space (*parhessia* in Aramaic) that is of normative value; and hence the disappearance of Israel, even if all of its Jews were to be somehow saved, would be a major historical calamity, analogous to the destruction of the Second Temple.

It is this qualitative difference between Israel as incorporating Jewish space and the existence of individual Jews and Jewish communities in the diaspora that is at the center of Israel–diaspora relations. This is so because it is in Israel, through the integrative instrumentality of the Hebrew language and Israeli culture, despite all its pluralism, that Jews have been united as a nation; military service and paying taxes are also part of that public aspect of Jewish life in Israel. In the diaspora, on the other hand, there are many Jewish *communities*, not a Jewish *people*. A people needs a public corporate existence, and this can exist only in Israel. Hence all the attempts to create such a Jewish worldwide representation have failed in the past (from the Alliance Israelite Universelle to the World Jewish Congress), and will fail in the future.

II.   Zionist Religious Thinking

E.   Ismar Schorsch, "Making Israel a Light unto the Nations: Conservative Zionism Reconsidered"

I believe there are at least four cogent reasons why Conservative Jews ought to be active in Israel on a large scale.

First, Israel embodies a unique historical achievement which remains undimmed after forty years: namely, the reversal of two millennia of national homelessness. The recover of political sovereignty in the very land in which it was lost to the Romans in the year 63 BCE is a singular expression of unbroken historical consciousness steeled by religious faith. What is more, Israel's sterling record of commitment to democracy, political stability, absorption of refugees, social equity, agricultural development, scientific excellence, cultural creativity, and military prowess, compiled under the most adverse conditions, is unmatched by any other state founded after World War II. For Conservative Jews to observe this adventure from the sidelines is a travesty.

Second, Israel still represents the most potent force for unity in a secular age in which the Jewish people is deeply fragmented religiously. Israel stirs the emotions of secular and religious Jews alike, especially in moments of crises. Its very existence, according to Abraham Joshua Heschel, helped alleviate the anguish of the Holocaust, and its stunning accomplishments inspired diaspora Jews with awe, pride, and ethnic commitment.

The Vision We Can Offer

Third, as Conservative Jews, we are in Israel to offer an alternative Judaism. The vast majority of Israelis have been religiously disenfranchised, severed from their spiritual roots. To be sure, they are secular by choice, but also in part by lack of choice. How many Jews would be left in the open society of Canada or the United States if Orthodoxy were the only religious option? The national definition of Jewishness in a Jewish State has concealed the catastrophic failure of Orthodoxy to expose some 80 percent of Israeli society to even a modicum of religious vocabulary, study, and observance. And the more introverted and coercive it becomes, the greater the alienation. The introduction of genuine religious pluralism is vital not only to improve Israel–diaspora relations, but also to reconnect Israelis to Judaism. The inroads into Israeli society that we have already made, convince me that Conservatism is ideally suited for that historic task.

Source for Reading E.:   In Carol Diament, ed., *Zionism the Sequel* (New York: Hadassah, 1998), pp. 225–33.

Fourth and finally, our deepening involvement in Israel is motivated by loyalty to democratic ideals. The pervasive political ethos of modern Jewry since the emancipation has been democratic and not authoritarian for very good reason. The extension of varying degrees of equality to Jews in countries like England, France, Prussia, and Russia was always related to a broader revolutionary thrust to restructure the body politic, and hence the advocates of Jewish emancipation were never to be found among the defenders of the old order. Not surprisingly, Jews aligned themselves with the politics of their benefactors and embraced the vision of a free society based on the rule of law. Today Jews in the diaspora remain viscerally committed to the political culture of Western democracy....

As Conservative Jews, we must loudly reaffirm that Judaism and democracy are compatible, both in Israel and America. Right-wing extremism should not be countered by legal restrictions on free speech, but by a resounding consensus articulated in resolution that Israel's democracy is firmly rooted in the millennial experience of Jewish self-government and in the history of Zionism.

F.   Eugene B. Borowitz, "What Is Reform Religious Zionism?"

What constitutes Zionism never has been very clear, and since the establishment of *Medinat Yisrael* some Israelis have questioned whether or not the idea of Zionism makes any sense. Over the decades, the only constant has been that Zionists seem never to tire of talking about what Zionism really is, a tradition we now carry on.

For many of us the people of Israel is more than rewarding; it is important, essential, and not just to us, we believe, but to the world, perhaps even to human history. Suddenly Zionism changes from a religious possibility to a religious necessity. Someone who believes there is something special about the Jewish people – without thereby casting aspersions on any other group – will care passionately about its collective welfare: biological, physical, cultural, and spiritual. This understanding of our collectivity produces a close identification with the State of Israel in tranquil as in troubled times. It feeds the sentiment that no diaspora community is as important to our people's contemporary well-being and morale as is the State of Israel. Zionism, most richly understood, is the movement dedicated to assuring the Jewish State's multileveled well-being and our widespread Jewish people's continued flourishing. No wonder, then, that for many colleagues of the generation before mine, Zionism was as good as their entire religion.

Source for Reading F.:   In Carol Diament, ed., *Zionism the Sequel* (New York: Hadassah, 1998), pp. 234–40.

Reform Zionist Tasks

Although I do not view the State of Israel as central to my Jewish existence – and I don't know many diaspora Jews for whom it is – I believe that we must make the State of Israel a vital part of Reform Jewish consciousness; I do not think it is such at present for many of our rabbis (and certainly not for most lay people). Covenant makes the land of Israel highly important and contemporary political reality makes the State of Israel close to indispensable. . . .

The preferred form of fulfilling the covenant is social, not just personal. This makes *aliyah* a central Jewish demand. I pray that one benefit of ever greater peace will be an increase in the number of Reform Jews settling in Israel. For the rest of us, visits and sojourns must serve as a modest surrogate. We also need to help rabbis who hesitate to take groups of their congregants on tour there to do so. Moreover, the College and Conference need to set up a welcoming and useful sabbatical program for rabbis at our Jerusalem school. Both programs might also get more retired congregants and colleagues to live in the State of Israel. . . .

Our congregations and institutions in the State of Israel still struggle against heavy economic odds. They need more money, and while all of us have been badly pinched by a budgetary crunch, special causes still draw forth extra funds.

It is time to begin paying more attention to what Israeli Progressive Jews can do for us. They live Judaism in community much more intensively than we do, so they have something critical to teach us. . . .

We must be vigilant that the political interests of the State of Israel are presented in full virtue and that attacks on Israel's political interests are thoroughly refuted. Of course, as religious Zionists we come to this task with our great commitment to the ethics of a universal reach. An ethical politics is not easy, but it must apply to the causes projected by the State of Israel as it does to the social welfare of our North American fellow citizens.

G.   Isadore Twersky, "Survival, Normalcy, Modernity"

Have the goals of Zionism been completely fulfilled, or has its program been only partially realized? Clarification of this issue hinges on an indispensable differentiation between two definitions of Zionism: a bare-bones, essential, even monolithic conception which concentrates on a political objective, and a many-tiered, hyphenated conception which includes social, cultural, spiritual, ethical, and religious aspirations.

Source for Reading G.:   In Carol Diament, ed., *Zionism the Sequel* (New York: Hadassah, 1998), pp. 348–54.

We must return to the second conception of Zionism, the many-tiered, hyphen-ated one. If Zionism is a utopian adventure and an experiment in social engineering, the road to fulfillment is still a long one. If Zionism is a secular revolution and negation of *all* exilic history, it has not achieved its goal and its dream remains (I would interject, happily) unfulfilled. If Zionism is a romantic revolution against petrified *halakhah* and an attempted liberation of *all* modern Jews from the stultification of religion, it has been aborted. If, in short, Zionism has metapolitical aspirations and pretensions, its saga can only be described as a fusion of frustration and fulfillment, failure and triumph. Adherents of these various ideologies therefore contend that Zionism is in need of reformulation and revitalization.

Zionism in this broad metapolitical sense is often equated with modern Judaism, and their destinies are linked, yet proper historical perspective requires that Zionism be viewed and assessed as one of many competing ideologies. Zionists were not the only ones to grapple with the problems of the modern age. Moreover, Zionism in this spiritual/historical/cultural sense, unlike the political sense, did not develop new teaching *ex nihilo*.

Much of what is presented as Zionist ideology is actually a continuation of tendencies, attitudes, and criticism begun by the Englightenment and sustained throughout the nineteenth century.... The notion that there is no creativity, no challenge, no dynamism, no romance, no opportunity for self-expression and self-renewal in traditional Judaism of the modern age is neither novel nor correct....

I mean to suggest that the medley of contemporary spiritual–historical–cultural problems is best defined as the general concern of Judaism rather than an exclusive concern of Zionism. A revitalization of Zionism will be a part of a rejuvenation of Judaism – *biklal matayim manah* (the greater includes the lesser). [Note: B. B.B. 41b; B. San. 31a; and B. B.Q. 74a. The literal translation is: two hundred includes one hundred. This legal principle is applied in the Talmud to reconcile conflicting testimony by different witnesses.] It follows that the problems of diaspora Jewry and those of Israeli Jewry, the crucial political difference notwithstanding, have much in common. They should not be separated but be analyzed together. Moreover, those engaged in the process of analysis and reflection, of prescription and decision, need not – I would say, should not – confine themselves to the works of the "founding fathers" of Zionism. Clearly we must turn to pre-modern and pre-Zionist sources as well as to non-Zionist writings in our quest for renewed vision, strengthened dedication, and unswerving commitment – a quest for *klal Yisrael* in Israel and elsewhere.

III.   Constructive Ideas for a New Zionism

H.   Henry L. Feingold, "Zionism: A New Course Needed"

What Zionism will be in the next century we cannot fully know. But we can be certain that it will continue to possess a bedrock concern for Zion as represented by Israel. One can no longer imagine a Judaism without Zion. That is the gift and formidable resource bestowed on the Jewish enterprise by the Zionism of my generation. Its longing for Zion was intensified by the Holocaust, and its objective to build the State was nurtured by practical philanthropy. For many Jews in America giving to Israel became a way of retaining their link to Judaism. Now my generation is leaving the historical stage. The new Jewish generation does not even enjoy the thrill and the drama and, yes, the need to give of their wealth, all of which bound them to the Jewish future. What is needed is an idea and a movement strong enough to break through the privatism of our modern lives. Since the Emancipation that idea has emanated from a Zionism so multifaceted that it has thus far avoided the fate of other twentieth-century ideologies.

It is conceivable that the next idea to energize Judaism would market itself with a different product name. For those of us who take the broad view of Zionism, it doesn't really matter what it calls itself. Each epoch develops its own Zionism depending on the twist that its survival problem has taken. Still the term post-Zionism is particularly misleading, since it contains the unfortunate implication that Judaism itself is coming to an end. The way most living secular Jews have come to terms with their Judaism is through some form of Zionism. The only thing "post" the reuniversalized Zionism proposed here is that it is post the Zionism of state, blood, and soil that stemmed from the Holocaust. We are as much pre-the Zionism of tomorrow as we are post-the Zionism of yesterday.

There is some apprehension that the continuing crisis will rob Zionism of the multifacetedness on which its plasticity is based, thereby preventing it from confronting the crisis in the diaspora. If it is too rigid to become again the leader of a world movement concerned with the survival of Judaism everywhere, then it will become irrelevant and go the way of all the failed ideologies of the twentieth century. That may already be happening. But if it can recast itself and reclaim those universal aspects of Zionist ideology subsumed under the crisis of the Holocaust, if it can once again speak with passion about a renaissance of the Jewish people wherever they may find themselves, then we can face the problems of the next century with the same confidence.

It is, then, not only for the sake of American Jewry and other diaspora communities that the world Zionist movement must be restructured, but for its own

Source for Reading H.:   In Carol Diament, ed., *Zionism the Sequel* (New York: Hadassah, 1998), pp. 355–60.

continued viability. The next generation, like previous generations of Jews, will become the heirs of an extraordinarily difficult and challenging history. But it is also a history full of achievement and promise. Surely we have not taken this extraordinary millennial journey only to watch the Jewish presence vanish from the historical stage. There are still things Jews must do. We need a new Zionism to do them.

I.   Eliezer Schweid, "The Major Goal of Zionism Today: To Build the Spiritual Center"

What must be done in order to build Israel as a Jewish spiritual center?

First and foremost is the struggle for the Jewish identity of the State. The question is whether Israel will continue to be a Jewish and democratic state as set forth in the Declaration of Independence. That is, will Israel continue to be defined as the State of the Jewish people as a whole?

This definition is given a basis in the Law of Return. The significance of this law is that all Jews are deemed to be potential citizens of Israel, and are considered as repatriates. As soon as Jews arrive in Israel, they exercise the privilege to be citizens in their own country. Beyond the Law of Return, a covenant was ordained between the Jewish Agency, as the legally recognized representative of the interests of Israeli Jewry in Israel, and the World Zionist Organization.

The covenant states:

> The State of Israel considers itself a creation of the entire Jewish people, and its gates are kept open, in keeping with its laws, to every Jew who wishes to immigrate thereto.... The goal of the ingathering of the exiles, a central fixture in the tasks of the State of Israel and the Zionist movement in our days, requires constant efforts by the Jewish people in the diaspora, and therefore the State of Israel expects all Jews, singly and collectively, to participate in building the State and facilitating mass immigration of Jews thereto and believes it necessary to unify all Jewish groupings behind this goal.

This law, which gives the World Zionist Organization its status in Israel, makes Israel a Zionist State, that is, the State of the entire Jewish people.

The same conception is evident in the passage of the Yad Vashem Law. According to this statute, the role of Yad Vashem is to extend a "citizenship of remembrance" in Israel to all those annihilated in the Holocaust. In other words, the State of Israel regards itself as the State of all Jewish victims of the Holocaust.

Source for Reading I.:   In Carol Diament, ed., *Zionism the Sequel* (New York: Hadassah, 1998), pp. 332–41.

They are its citizens. In this law, the State of Israel plays the symbolic role of the redeemer of Jewish history and historical memory. Such an action expresses profound affiliation and identification with the Jewish heritage.

At the root of these laws is the State's commitment to and responsibility for all Jews, both by virtue of the State being the place where Jewish collective identity is manifested, and through the State's ongoing connection with the Jewish people's origins. The Declaration of Independence notes the prophets' vision of Israel as a source for basic social, national, and democratic perspectives. Israel is democratic not because of an exogenous idea, but because of its association with the prophetic principles of justice and peace.

This hands us a monumental Zionist task: to ensure that Israel remains a Jewish State in the foregoing senses and that it implements its commitment to Judaism in its educational, creative, and spiritual processes.

Since the establishment of the State of Israel, the Zionist movement has communicated only with Jews in the diaspora, not with those of us in Israel. Here it is just a bureaucracy. Furthermore, we do not elect the leaders of and delegates to the institutions of the Zionist movement; we merely appoint them through the mechanism of Knesset elections. As a movement that provides education and cultural activity and raises donations for its aims, there is no Zionist movement in Israel.

It is time for Israeli Jews to realize that today we are no poorer, and may even be richer, than much of diaspora Jewry. It is time for us, too, to contribute to Jewish educational and cultural endeavors through a Zionist fund-raising appeal.

The central message in a year dedicated to Zionism should be as follows: The mission of Zionism, which we have hardly begun to pursue, is the creation of a Jewish spiritual center that will fashion the educational and cultural tools necessary for the sustenance of the Jewish nation.

J.   Yosef Gorny, "The Need for a New *Hibbat Zion*"

I believe that we are now on the threshold of a new movement – postsovereignty. As we approach the year 2000, Jewish life is characterized worldwide by two conflicting features. On the one hand, world Jewry has never been so united in the political sense, and on the other hand, Judaism has never before been so divided culturally.

One hundred years ago, the Hebrew writer M. Z. Feuerberg wrote an essay entitled "Where To?" ("Le'an?"). The question reverberated in the world of eastern European Jewish intellectuals. The answer proposed by Hibbat Zion saved the national identity of the Jewish people. I believe that the time has come to rouse a new Hibbat Zion movement. Ostensibly this is a paradoxical and nonhistorical

Source for Reading J.:   In Carol Diament, ed., *Zionism the Sequel* (New York: Hadassah, 1998), pp. 364–9.

thought. The Jewish people are now living under totally different conditions from those of the 1880s, when Hibbat Zion came into being. At the same time – although the past century has witnessed the creation of large Jewish concentrations in the West, the Holocaust which destroyed both Jews and the Jewish predicament, and the establishment of a State which bestowed a measure of normality on Jewish existence – there is a certain resemblance between the two historical conditions, reflected in the choice granted to the Jewish masses. In the past, they were free to choose between emigration and *aliyah*; now they are free to choose between Judaism and assimilation.

In this situation where freedom of choice is compounded by the relative ease of assimilation, the predicament of the Jews is easing, and the predicament of Judaism, as Ahad Ha'Am called it, is growing more acute. What is needed is a new Hibbat Zion, in Ahad Ha'Am's version, meaning primarily to relieve the plight of Judaism in the face of the danger of individual assimilation, detachment of Jewish centers from one another, and loss of individual and group self-respect. In no previous period in our history have these dangers been as real as today.

At the same time, let it be pointed out that this call for a new Hibbat Zion is directed toward the idea rather than the movement, since the historical Hibbat Zion was a movement that failed and an idea that triumphed. It failed because it did not produce from its midst a national leadership, failed to unite Jews of eastern and western Europe in a joint endeavor, and was unable to recruit the required funds in order to help the First *Aliyah* settlers, who were eventually saved by Baron Rothschild. As an idea, however, it succeeded, and to this very day its national principles are valid and lie at the core of Jewish public discussion. These principles should be reconsolidated and the relevant organizational and practical conclusions drawn.

Three of Hibbat Zion's principles are of vital significance for present-day Zionism. This movement removed the meaning of Jewish identity from the exclusive sphere of religious definition, by determining that Judaism is a national entity with its own distinctive social, cultural, and spiritual character. Religion was perceived in this context as a spiritual/cultural element, but not as a faith on which Jewishness is dependent. The second principle is the assumption that the national cohesion of the dispersed and divided Jewish people will be achieved through the settlement of the land of Israel, which will be gradual, protracted, and perhaps never-ending. The third principle was the attribution of supreme importance to national education, both as the conduit of Jewish culture to the individual and as a barrier against mass assimilation. These ideas are as valid today as they ever were.

These principles hold out the hope that Zionism, which was once a movement for the liberation of the Jewish people – which freed them from forced exile, from humiliation and persecution, from self-hatred and inferior status – can become a movement for national united existence, fortifying the rebellious desire of those Jews who wish to be Jews.

Chapter 26

The "Return" to Traditional Judaism at the End of the Twentieth Century: Cross-Cultural Comparisons

M. Herbert Danzger

These selections, drawn from my Returning to Tradition, *describe aspects of the contemporary return to traditional Judaism in the United States and Israel. They define the problematics of this phenomenon and describe the processes that enable or retard the return. While there are some comparative elements in these materials that take into account the different contexts in which return occurs, the major focus here is on the processes that characterizes all: men and women, Israelis and Americans.*

A. Return: An Unanticipated Development

This first selection simply suggests what is problematic about the return. The reader should know that my re-analysis of a survey demonstrates that about one in four people following what is clearly Orthodox religious practice was reared in a family that did not follow the full measure of these practices. Twenty-four percent of "high observance" Jews (those who do not even handle money on the Sabbath) came from families whose observance was less careful. In fact, 10 percent of the "high observers" came from "non-observant" families or from ones that had "low observance" (fasted on Yom Kippur and lit Hanukah candles but did not follow the laws of kashrut at home or light Sabbath candles). The analysis here is not concerned with changed

Source for readings in Chapter 27:   M. Herbert Danziger, *Returning to Tradition: The Contemporary Revival of Orthodox Judaism* (New Haven, 1989); page numbers are given separately for each reading. *Source for reading A.:*   pp. 196–7.

"self-definition," i.e., from "Reform" or "Conservative" to "Orthodox," but rather with changed practices that indicate a changed involvement in religion.

Typically, the sequence of roles in a person's life is anticipated and prepared for. The twelve-year-old boy anticipates his young manhood, learns about it, and seeks role models. Parents, friends, and neighbors, as well as relevant organizations, anticipate the coming change in status, attempt to inform the boy of how to play the role of young man, define when it shall begin and how it shall be done. Certainly people do not march through this sequence in lockstep. But there are many ordered sequences, particularly in areas most crucial to defining a person. Thus there are educational sequences (elementary school, high school, possibly college and professional training), marital sequences (courtship, marriage, widowhood), developmental sequences (childhood, youth, adulthood, middle age, old age), occupational sequences (novice, young Turk, old hand, retiree).

But the ba'al t'shuva disrupts the anticipated ordered sequence. Whereas religious convictions were peripheral they now become central. This reorders life's priorities, requiring the adoption of a new rhythm of life with no work on Saturdays, the adoption of a new holiday calendar celebrating a different set of events, the eating of different foods (and scrupulous avoidance of other foods), and the developing of new friends. It may even require a different mate than was anticipated earlier. In these ways, becoming a ba'al t'shuva may be radically different from becoming a reborn Christian. Although Christian rebirth may also require sharp changes in patterns of life, they are not likely to be so radical because, as we have seen, Christianity requires belief primarily and action only secondarily and because to become Christian in America is to emphasize dominant cultural themes whereas to become more Jewish is to estrange oneself from the mainstream and to embrace a different set of values, rituals, and life-styles.

The ba'al t'shuva thus moves on an uncharted and unexpected course. Parents and friends anticipate a given progression – college, job, marriage – and most people move through this sequence as expected. The ba'al t'shuva has also been socialized into this sequence, not into the role of a practicing Jew. His every encounter with Judaism is fresh. He sees it with an adult's eyes and subjects it to critical if not cynical scrutiny. His Orthodoxy is unlike that of those reared in Orthodoxy, who have learned to accept behaviors and beliefs in unquestioning childish innocence that carries over to adulthood.

Just as Orthodox Jews continue in their practice in part as a result of the momentum of their childhood experience and social pressure, so most people reject this different practice as a result of their socialization to the dominant set of values and their desire to conform to the expectations of peers. Separating the force of this momentum and the power of the social bonds that tie one to continued rejection of Judaism from the experience of encountering Judaism is difficult. That experience may be positive but not sufficiently powerful to overcome the social ties. Or the symbols and values of Judaism themselves may drive off potential returnees.

The essential attractiveness of Jewish rituals, values, and symbols has been under scrutiny from within Judaism for over a hundred years. Reform Judaism in particular (but also Conservative and to a far smaller degree Orthodox Judaism) has attempted to eliminate "crude" or "primitive" rituals and to introduce more appealing ones. But what is attractive to people, what is unattractive, and why remain an enigma. The ba'al t'shuva offers a unique opportunity to view Judaism with mature eyes, unclouded by the social ties and presocialized attitudes that help keep the Orthodox from birth within the fold. Although Jews have learned through millennia of experience how to unfold Judaism for the young, the ba'al t'shuva challenges them to do this for adults. In the process, Judaism is itself articulated and clarified.

B.   Religious Authority in Judaism

A major difference between traditionalists and modernists, concerning the nature of religious authority, is the least visible, yet, paradoxically, is the most crucial point of conflict between the camps. This difference is explored here.

The nature of religious authority, the conception of what guides a Jew's actions, differs for each of Judaism's wings. For Reform Judaism the source of religious authority is the ethical and universalistic teachings of the prophets. Because conscience is a reflection of the Godhead for Reform, the ultimate authority is man's own conscience, guided by the moral and ethical teachings of the Bible.

Conservative Judaism finds the core of religious authority in Jewish peoplehood – the culture, customs, and practices of the Jewish people throughout the ages. Judaism is a tradition that includes not only the Bible, the Talmud, and the Codes but also the practices of Jews, the traditions of "catholic Israel,"[1] the entire "civilization of Judaism."[2] The ultimate source of religious authority for Conservative Judaism is the Jewish people and its tradition.

Orthodoxy views the halakhah as the essence of Judaism. Conformity to these norms (which include traditions and community practice), decided on by a majority of scholars in the past and codified into religious law, is obligatory. Religious authority is to be found in the Codes and Responsa, the body of legal decisions and precedents. Not surprisingly, therefore, the focus of Judaic studies for Reform is philosophy, for Conservatism is history, and for Orthodoxy is Talmud.

Source for reading B.:   pp. 166–76.

But if halakhah is the source of authority for all Orthodox Jews, why are there differences among the Orthodox? The answer is that even a detailed legal system needs interpreters. In Orthodoxy the question is "who shall be the interpreters of halakhah?" For chasidic Jews, the rebbe, the scholar-saint of the community, the person those knowledge and holiness set him above others so that his decisions, behaviors, and advice are to be followed, is the interpreter. In the case of the rebbe, saintliness is manifested not only by saintly behavior but occasionally also by reputation as a *ba'al mofsim* (literally, a performer of miracles) or more frequently a *po'el yeshu'ot* (literally, a provider of salvations), whose prayers affect the higher spheres and who is aware of heaven's plans for men.

The eighteenth-century opponents of Chasidism (mitnaggedim), who founded the great European yeshivot, insisted on the primacy of halakhah and the technical halakhic expertise of the pious person[3] as the bases of religious authority. In the past two or three decades traditionalistic yeshivot have been claiming that the basis for religious authority is not only halakhah but also *da'at Torah*, "the Torah perspective."

Both modernistic and traditionalistic yeshivot are committed to halakhah, including norms regulating dress, sexual relations, diet, work, and ethical behavior. Regarding the authority of contemporary rabbis, modernistic and traditionalistic yeshivot differ. The traditionalistic refer the student to the *da'at Torah* of the gedolim (great talmudic sages), arguing that gedolim may address any issue, halakhic or nonhalakhic, and claim the authority of Torah.[4] Traditionalists argue that even if modernists do not violate halakhah in any way, nevertheless the modernistic stance is in violation of *da'at Torah*. Modernistic yeshivot reject this view.

Religious Authority and Potential Returnees

Religious authority is a special problem for ba'alei t'shuva, whose situation requires that values be articulated fully and quickly "lest the potential recruit misunderstand and leave." Although they tend to accept the binding authority of the Bible, the major intellectual problem they face concerns the authority of the oral tradition (*Torah sheh ba'al peh*), which involves humans in determining the scope and application of Divine laws. In yeshivot for ba'alei t'shuva the issue is twofold: (1) What authority do the oral law and extensions of the laws of the Bible have? (2) What authority do contemporary rabbis have, and does rabbinic authority extend beyond the specifics of the Codes?

Yeshivot respond to the first question by teaching students the Talmud, which elucidates the connection between biblical and rabbinic law. The oral tradition claims authority contemporaneous with the Revelation at Sinai, and the Talmud applies and explicates the oral tradition. For example, the Pentateuch forbids work on the Sabbath, but apart from the lighting of fires, it does not define "work." Yet there must have been a tradition as to what constitutes work. The

Talmud defines the nature of work through a process of biblical exegesis. The Talmud's candid style does not hide from the students disagreements over the nature of the tradition and its applications.

The Talmud wrestles with a paradox: on one hand it holds that the oral tradition starts with the Revelation at Sinai; on the other hand it presents disagreements, extensions, and new applications of the law. The Talmud distinguishes between laws based on "tradition from Moses who received it at Sinai" and those parts of the law developed by rabbis. The Talmud insists on the Divine nature of the law and at the same time on the authority of the rabbis to continue to develop and shape halakhah. The law is Divine in its source, yet humans develop and extend it,[5] and disagreements arise about elements of the law.

This paradox is not openly addressed, but the entire thrust of the Talmud is to attempt to resolve apparent inconsistencies and disagreements by seeking the reasoning behind contradictory statements that might explain how both could apply or by demonstrating that they derive from different but equally valid traditions. The underlying message of the effort is that this tradition has been taken seriously since the beginnings of rabbinic Judaism and must be taken seriously by those who would follow it now. Yeshivot believe that studying the Talmud powerfully demonstrates to students the authoritativeness of the oral tradition. In this, all yeshivot, modernist and traditionalist, are in agreement.

How are the different views of authority taught in modernist and traditionalist yeshivot? The answer to this lies not in what is taught but in *how* it is taught.

Approaches to the Talmud at Ba'al T'shuva Yeshivot

Traditionalistic

There are striking differences between modernist and traditionalist yeshivot in their respective *approaches* to the study of Talmud. Surprisingly, the modernists first attempt to teach the student to master the text, whereas traditionalists are more concerned that the student comprehend the logic of the arguments.

Rabbi Mendel Weinbach reports that at Ohr Someyach (traditionalistic) students are presented almost immediately with abstract and complex issues, leaving the task of mastering the text for a later time.

> I'll start by presenting to the students the major ideas of the Gemara's discussion. For students who have just come in and who don't have the background I won't use a text, but I'll present the Gemara and the Rashi and Tosafot. We'll be doing a kind of mental acrobatics, moving from one view to another and to the commentaries. But we really don't cover the text.
>
> They may have the same Gemara a few months later, when they've become acquainted with the language and can follow the argument inside the Gemara. If they are around long enough they may even have it a third time, when I cover the Gemara, Rashi, Tosafot, and other sources inside. It's not always the same people

that go through all three levels; it depends in part on how much they knew when they came in. There are three levels of shi'urim (lectures), and as they advance they learn more of the text and more on their own.

In regular yeshivot Gemara is also studied on several levels. For the first few years students study Gemara using only the Rashi commentary. Similarly, laymen studying Gemara typically read only the Rashi commentary. Tosafot is generally reserved for advanced classes at yeshivot. Yet in Ohr Someyach and other traditionalistic ba'al t'shuva yeshivot students are introduced to the questions raised by Tosafot soon after they start their studies. They are involved in highly abstract discussions of talmudic points before they have mastered the text.

Modernistic

At Yeshivat Hamivtar (modernistic) students first spend a number of weeks studying the language of the text itself and the simple meanings of the words. They are then ready to move to the next higher level, the structure of the argument on the page. Only after several months of wrestling with the text at this level do the students proceed to the logic of the argument as it is presented on the page as well as in commentaries and discussion elsewhere in the Talmud.

For example, at Yeshivat Hamivtar (Modernist) the text was *Pesahim* 8a; the students were beginners in the program. The point under consideration in the Gemara was where one is *not* required to search for leaven prior to Passover, when all bread and leaven are forbidden.

A potential confusion in the text illustrates this technique. The unvocalized text reads "if a MTH divides a house . . . further search for leaven is required." Vocalized one way (*Meetah*), the phrase refers to a bed that divides the area within a house. Vocalized another way (*Mateh*), it refers to a stick or a staff. The student reading the phrase was uncertain about the correct reading. Rather than provide the answer, the rebbi prodded the students to draw the logical conclusions of each interpretation. An animated discussion ensued. "Staff," it was argued, implied that a slight object would not divide a room, but a large one might; "bed" implied that even a large, heavy object does not divide a room and further search was still required. The rebbi was not as interested in the correct answer as he was in whether students were learning to apply the logic of the Talmud to the problem. He complimented the students on their ability to consider the implication of each interpretation, briefly demonstrated why bed was the correct reading, and went on.

This approach gives the students confidence that they can deal with the texts. They are asked to hold Rashi and Tosafot in abeyance until they have at least attempted to understand the text on their own. They are not there to learn what Rashi or Tosafot think; they are attempting to understand the Gemara. After they have tried it themselves they turn to the great interpreters of the Talmud to see what others have said. In a sense, this approach puts them on a footing with the commentaries in the great enterprise of interpreting the Talmud. It not only provides the student with skills in interpreting and understanding the Talmud but also builds the feeling of being a colleague of Rashi and Tosafot and other commentaries, although admittedly a junior colleague, rather than simply a student.[6] Nothing to this effect is stated in the process of study.[7]

Approaches to Other Subjects Differences between yeshivot can be seen in their approaches to other studies as well. Charismatics redirect the life of followers in a wide range of areas, and relationships are not ordinarily limited to a specific role. This implies an emotional attachment on the part of the follower to the charismatic.

Halakhic Decisions

How students learn the halakhically required behaviors for different situations also distinguishes modernistic and traditionalistic yeshivot. This difference was illustrated by Rabbi Brovender's (modernistic) response to the question of how students learn which ruling is to be followed.

Q. What do you tell someone who comes to you with a question about halakhah?
A. We don't tell him what to do.
Q. But then how does he know what to do?
A. We have him look it up himself.
Q. But how can a person who is just beginning look up something? How will they know the sources? How can they read the material? How is the newcomer here supposed to learn about whether or not he can turn on a light on Shabbat or when he is supposed to wash his hands? Do you have them look it all up?
A. No. When it comes to telling a person that turning a light is forbidden on Shabbat we simply tell them that. That's easy enough to follow. I'm not talking about that. I'm talking about a situation where someone wants to know the *reasons* for something, or the point of view to follow where there is a difference of opinion. I'll tell them where it can be found and have them read it themselves.
Q. And if they can't?
A. Then I'll help them. But I don't give them the answers. That's something they have to work out for themselves.

Consider, in contrast, the following quotation drawn from the introduction to the English translation of the *Mishnah Berurah* (the authoritative halakhic code of liturgical and holiday observances) by Rabbi Aharon Feldman, a rosh yeshiva at Ohr Someyach. "IMPORTANT ADVICE: *No one should ever on his own decide a halakhah problem from a printed text without first consulting a proper authority. This is true for any work and especially for the Mishnah Berurah."*

Notes

1   Solomon Schechter's phrase denoting *all* of the Jewish people.

2   Mordecai Kaplan's descriptive term (1934) for the essence of Judaism.

3   A rabbi's reputation for personal piety is an important factor affecting acceptance of his halakhic decisions. The rabbi's authority derives from his role as both scholar and saint (Carlin and Mendlowitz 1958).

4   This formulation leans primarily on Rabbi Elchonon Wasserman (1875–1941), who claimed *da'at Torah* as the moral authority for his opposition to Zionism, Communism, and secular education and for his views on other contemporary issues. Those claiming the authority of *da'at Torah* also question the legitimacy of modernistic yeshivot. Rabbi Wasserman was rosh yeshiva at Baranowicz, Poland, and the leader of Agudat Yisrael, the traditionalistic and at that time anti-Zionist Orthodox party. See Helmreich 1982, 68–9 for a discussion of the traditionalistic view of *da'at Torah*.

   The response that modernistic yeshivot make to this attack is that (1) even on halakhah, gedolim are not infallible; (2) if there is room for legitimate differences of opinion on halakhic matters, where gedolim are expert, they cannot be infallible in areas where they possess no special expertise (for example, on whether the Soviet Union will respond to public pressures for Jewish immigration); (3) gedolim differ on major issues such as Zionism and secular education. (See *Hamevaser*, the student publication of Yeshiva University, 11 Jan. 1984, citing Rabbi Moshe Feinstein's introduction to his *Igros Moshe*. Rabbi Feinstein [1895–1986] was the most highly regarded *posek* (halakhic decisor) in America in the post-World War II period and a gadol accepted by modernists and traditionalists.)

5   By and large this issue is not confronted in Orthodox yeshivot, although it is addressed by such innovative thinkers as Rabbi Joseph B. Soloveitchik at Yeshiva University and Rabbi Eliezer Berkowitz at the Hebrew College of Skokie. See the latter's *Not in Heaven*, 1984.

6   In distinguishing the styles of study of the two yeshivot one needs to be mindful that Ohr Someyach and other yeshivot must catch the interest and loyalty of the student as quickly as possible, lest the student simply leave. Some of these students are people who have been met at the Kotel or at the bus stop by recruiters and invited to a meal or a Shabbat at the yeshiva.

   Yeshivat Hamivtar, on the other hand, has until recently been reluctant to attempt to persuade the uncommitted. In the early 1970s Brovender evidenced almost a distaste for this task, although lately his views have softened. Students at Hamivtar are not ordinarily drop-ins but have committed themselves to study for six months to a year. This program, then, was based on the assumption that there will be sufficient time to teach, and that the student's interest is already there.

   The programs of Ohr Someyach and Hamivtar are thus not fully comparable. Yet they do reflect the difference between the modernist and traditionalist approaches.

7   This difference in approaches to the study of Gemara is far less apparent at regular yeshivot than at ba'al t'shuva yeshivot. Students at regular yeshivot will have learned

the reading and translation skills at much younger ages, beginning at age ten. Over the next several years emphasis will slowly shift from the text to the logic of the argument, as the students become more capable of grasping the intricacies of the discussions. The subtle differences in attitude that lead to differences in the conception of religious authority are harder to demonstrate, although they are there. For an illustration of the approach to a page of the Talmud in a traditionalist yeshiva, see Helmreich 1982, 98–103. For a discussion of Talmud study in informal study groups outside the yeshiva, see Heilman 1983.

C.   Action and Study

The major mechanism for return to tradition is involvement in ritual action rather than ideological persuasion. Commitment to belief follows rather than proceeds religious acts. This is illustrated by the reading on action and study, which relates study to ritual.

That religious acts rather than beliefs are the core of Judaism raises several questions. First, are these acts merely mechanically performed, or do they contribute to the formation of a meaning system and a set of beliefs? If the latter, how does this happen? Second, if acts are the core, why the emphasis on study? Finally, is the study of Gemara understandable simply as a way of acquiring knowledge for the performance of religious acts?

Understanding through the Act

In Judaism's philosophy of education, acts come first, and beliefs and commitment follow. This position is stated succinctly in *Sefer Hakhinukh* (literally, *The Book of Education*), purportedly written by Rabbi Aharon Halevi of Toledo in the thirteenth century.

> Know that man is formed by his actions. His heart and all his thoughts follow after the actions he engages in, whether they be good or evil. Even if a person's heart is totally evil...if his spirit is awakened and he puts his effort and his activities diligently in Torah and the mitzvot, even though he does not do it for the sake of heaven, he will immediately turn to the good, and from having acted with no concern for God he will come to act for His Name. And because of the power of his actions his evil inclination will die. *Because the heart is drawn after the deeds.*
>
> And even if a person is totally righteous, and his heart is straight and innocent and desires Torah and Mitzvot, if he is involved constantly in foolish things...he

Source for reading C.:   pp. 128–33.

will turn, after a given time, from righteous heartedness to being totally evil. For *a person is formed by his actions*. (Sixteenth Commandment, emphasis added)

This lesson is taught in many ways in all yeshivot. For the more advanced students the words of the *Sefer Hakhinukh* may be used. But even young children are taught that in observing the commandments one must first do and then understand. They are taught that just as Jews responded at Mount Sinai when accepting the Torah, saying, "We will do and we will listen" (Ex. 14:23), so in observing the commandments, the ritual actions are required first. Explanations may follow, and they may be accepted or rejected.

This perspective was demonstrated at a t'shuva meeting in an Orthodox synagogue in Queens, New York in spring 1987. The featured speaker was Uri Zohar, a former Israeli television personality who had become Orthodox in 1977, had since been ordained as a rabbi, and for some years had been a leading speaker at meetings for return to Orthodoxy. In the lecture Zohar addressed the question of what is a Jew. He insisted that to be a Jew one had to *act* like a Jew, and that meant observing the commandments of the Torah as defined by the rabbis. In the question and answer period following the lecture, a member of the audience suggested that Zohar's position left no room for the importance of faith, for belief in God; all was simply action. Zohar insisted that concern with faith and belief was a Christian concept. Suppose, he said, one compares two people. One calculates that there is a 50 percent chance that God exists and has revealed His law to Israel at Sinai, and as a consequence – as "insurance" against the possibility that this might be true – he observes the commandments of the Torah. The other professes complete faith in the existence of God yet does not observe the commandments. Which of the two is the good Jew? He insisted that without a doubt the rabbis and sages would choose the observant Jew, not the believer.

In presenting this argument Zohar was articulating the perpective of many yeshivot for the newly Orthodox, in particular Yeshivat Aish Hatorah in Jerusalem. In this view, Orthodoxy can be a rational choice. Faith is not essential. But how then is commitment to Orthodoxy developed?

Social-psychological studies cast light on this question. Role-playing, for example, has been shown to influence opinion change (Janis and King 1954). People who pretend to take a role advocating a point of view come to accept this view. Those who passively listen to or read about a point of view are far less likely to do so.

Festinger (1962) and others (Festinger, Riecken, and Schachter 1956) have demonstrated that actions involving expenditures or commitments are often rationalized after the action has been taken.[1] The less the external pressures (such as coercion or remuneration) to justify behaviors or value choices, the more will the activity or value choice be seen as sufficient justification for the action. Furthermore, the more costly the action or value choice in terms of time, expenditure, or conflict with other values, the greater will be the weight attributed to the chosen values or actions. In this way the person reduces the "dissonance" of the choice. In other words, a person who makes a choice or by action demonstrates a commitment will then rationalize that choice or action to himself or others. The thought process of justification occurs *after*, not before, the choice or act of commitment.

Zohar's description of his own experience with prayer is a paradigm of this response. "The first time I tried to pray I wrapped myself in a prayer shawl, I faced the wall so nothing would distract me and tried to speak words of prayer. But I couldn't. I felt I was talking to the wall. I felt foolish. I just stood there and wished for a long time that I could experience the feeling of prayer. And then it came to me and I could pray in sincerity and not feel foolish."[2]

In yeshivot, then, the object of the curriculum is not to learn *about* the rituals but to learn to *perform* the rituals. That the person first performs the action and only afterward speculates on its inner meaning may provide a psychological impetus to accept an explanation and allows the development of a range of explanations, as the act, not the explanation, is primary.

Study as an Act in Itself

If action is required and beliefs and meaning are only accidental characteristics, then ritual would seem wooden and empty. Yet Jews attribute meaning to rituals, and Jews have beliefs. How are the rituals given meaning? The answer is by study.

To be sure, one studies to know how to perform the commandments. But many rituals could be taught more easily through observation. Moreover, why spend many hours in study when one simply wishes to *behave* as an Orthodox Jew? In fact the majority of the newly Orthodox never study at a yeshiva. If knowing the rituals is all that is required, why study the Talmud? Anyone who is familiar with the Talmud knows that the digressions, minority opinions, logical distinctions, and the often ambiguous conclusions sometimes leave students at all levels without a clear sense of what the final ruling is. Why then is Talmud the major part of the curriculum at the ba'al t'shuva yeshivot?

In part the answer is that study itself is an ultimate value. A person who studies is religionizing, is involved in a holy act that gives him a sense of worth. The fact that time was spent in study is enough (see Heilman 1983).

The head of one yeshiva described it as follows: "Religious experiences are fairly universal, whereas this notion of being able to learn and turning that into a religious experience is somewhat unique to Judaism. The notion that there is a Torah which God gave us and that by learning Torah you somehow involve yourself in this process of the giving of the Torah and delving into the will of God is fairly unique."

Study facilitates the performance of rituals, and it is a religious act in itself. Beyond this it has the latent function of providing an opportunity for reflection on the meanings of rituals and commandments. It gives ritual acts a surprising elasticity of meaning, so that contrary to the assumption that the acts are wooden and crumble when tested by modern ideas – an argument that Glazer (1957, 69) offers to explain the decline of Orthodoxy in America – ritual acts provide the space and forms on which to reflect and draw meaning. Constructing a new meaning system may take time, and during that time ritual practice and religious commitment may indeed decline. But they need not remain empty. Ritual acts provide opportunities to develop meanings, and study groups are the plausibility structures that support these meanings.

How does one get from study, seemingly an individual act, to group-supported meanings? The structures of study provide the answer. Although individual study often occurs, great weight is placed on group study. The school on various levels and the public reading of the Torah in synagogues provide opportunities for communal learning.

More interesting are the informal study groups for the study of Talmud, such as those described by Heilman (1983). These groups develop into powerful plausibility structures, not only mentally recreating the life and times of the Bible, the Mishnah, and the Talmud but also providing an opportunity to reflect on the meaning of the rituals, to reinterpret them in light of the experience of the group, and to develop a new bond.

In the ba'al t'shuva yeshiva this development occurs with particular clarity. Students are taught the rituals and norms of Judaism and spend time deeply involved in study. They are soon reflecting on the meaning of the rituals. As we shall see, some explanations offered have a surprisingly modern cast.

Interestingly, in yeshivot different subjects are typically studied in different structures. Jewish philosophy is most often studied alone, the Bible sometimes alone and sometimes in groups, and the Talmud most often in groups. This difference suggests another important consequence of study, the construction of religious authority.

Typically, a teacher (rebbi) offers a *shi'ur*, or lecture, which covers a page of the Talmud. A student may read the page and related commentaries with the help of the teacher. The teacher will then elucidate and comment on the arguments presented. The Talmud's style of argument is question and answer, and it lends itself to question and answer by teacher and student. The teacher may ask students a question the Talmud itself asks, and the student may give an answer provided by the Talmud or by one of the commentaries, with or without being aware that others have suggested it. Giving the answer in the latter case indicates that the student has fully understood the discussion, as does asking a question that the Gemara or a commentary asks. Both a *guteh kasha* (a good question) and a *guteh teretz* (a good answer) are highly valued. A *shi'ur* in Talmud, then, typically requires more active involvement by the student than a college lecture.

The character of talmudic study is evident in student preparation and review. Talmud is studied with a *chavruta*, a study partner. The students correct each other's mistakes, try to explain the argument to each other, and sometimes find themselves gesticulating and shouting at each other. A bet midrash, or study hall, is not at all the silent contemplative place one might expect. It is full of shouting and vociferous argument, a marketplace of ideas, not an ivory tower. A ranking system based on scholastic abilities is built, and at the apex of this system is the rosh yeshiva, the head of the yeshiva, the leading teacher and scholar. The scholar becomes the authoritative interpreter of the laws and rituals, and the group becomes an authority structure. Yet scholarship alone is not sufficient; piety is also required, as the emphasis on ritual practice suggests. In essence the scholar-saint is the leading authority.

Study and Commitment: Summing up

Judaism's approach to religion is experiential. Acts or religious practices constitute the core, and carrying out these acts – that is, playing the role of practicing Jew – leads one to become Jewish in soul or personality. In this framework, study has two objectives. One is to learn the halakhah, the rules that should be followed. Simple observation or experience of Judaism, although important, may be insufficient in new circumstances. Study, which teaches the principles behind the action, is therefore also important for action.

Study is also a religious act. To study is not simply to learn and know but also to religionize.[3] For this reason yeshivot – places where one practices Judaism as well as learns to practice it – spend so much time on study.

Beyond this, study is an opportunity to develop a plausibility structure, a network that supports the common meanings in ritual and at the same time facilitates a search for additional interpretations and understandings of the meaning of rituals.

Notes

1   Festinger (1962) reported that people offered two equally attractive objects tend to value the one they keep more highly after their choice than before it. The more costly the choice or the fewer the rewards for it, the more powerful the efforts to rationalize it. This has come to be known as "the theory of cognitive dissonance."

Psychologist Roger Brown sums up this theory as follows: "If action cannot be adequately accounted for by factors other than a favorable judgment, then there is a very great need to make the judgment favorable in order to justify or explain the motivation for what has been done ... The poorer the excuse for an action, the greater the need to make it 'rational' by means of attitude change" (Brown 1965, 585).

2   This is also consonant with Eliade's (1959) explanation for why ancient religions began with rituals and only later developed the myths and beliefs that explained them. Himmelfarb (1975, 615) has demonstrated that action is more important than belief in predicting religious involvement. Based on a factor analysis of data gathered from a sample of Jewish adults in Chicago, he concludes that "in some respects the more efficient measures of religious involvement for American Jews are behavioral rather than ideational measures." He further notes, "This is especially interesting because the

literature on Christians concentrates predominantly on ideational measures – particularly orthodoxy (doctrinal beliefs).

3   Outside of yeshivot only a minority of Orthodox Jews are involved in study circles. Those who observe kashrut, Shabbat, family purity, and required prayers are "good Jews" even if they do not study. Those who also study are further honored for the additional hours they spend "religionizing."

Perhaps many Orthodox Jews are content to rely on the rabbis to provide explanations when necessary, much as laymen are confident that scientists have rational explanations of puzzling phenomena. They implicitly rely on a system that legitimates some ideas as truths. This trust is expressed by the term *emunat chachamim*, "belief in the sages." Instilling this trust is one of the critical tasks of yeshivot.

D.   Why They Return

The last selection explains how to understand the return to tradition within the specific context of Judaism. It addresses the question of how the specifically Judaic system of thought affects the "motives" or accounts of returnees and processes of return to tradition.

Why do people change their attitudes and beliefs and become Orthodox Jews? Answers to this question are suggested by the actions of those who become Orthodox, the groups they join, and the stages by which the process occurs. The reasons the returnees themselves offer to explain their behavior are important data for understanding how they see their own actions and how they are viewed by others, but they may not be sufficient to explain why they changed.[1]

A person's reconstruction of the events leading to his return reflects the pattern that he has learned is appropriate. Events or stages that have no place in prevalent paradigms of return pass unnoticed. Other experiences, which at the time of their occurrence were hardly noticed or felt, may take on new and weightier significance so as to be consistent with acceptable patterns of return. This is characteristic of all of us in a variety of situations, not only of ba'alei t'shuva. We construct a biography of our occupational development, our marriage, our very selves in much the same manner. These reconstructed biographies are referred to in sociology as "accounts" (Scott and Lyman 1968). They are stories that "account for" our present situation.

These accounts are not false or intended to mislead, although indeed they may at times mislead. But even when they are intended to be faithful accounts of a person's progress from the past to the present or explanations of how one came to be a ba'al t'shuva, the *explanation must be accepted by others in that social situation, and only certain accounts are acceptable*. Much of the welter of past experience will

Source for reading D.:   pp. 222–30.

be overlooked in the construction of the biography. The account is thus a reflection of the group's values and self-perception, as well as the individual's.

The Rhetoric of Return

Inauthentic and authentic rhetoric

In January 1975 the Young Israel of Hillcrest, Queens, sponsored a Friday night forum on "Returning to Judaism," at which Sara, the daughter of Rebbitzin Esther Jungreis, chaired the forum and two newly Orthodox Jews described how and why they became Orthodox. One of the returnees was a young, pretty girl of about eighteen or nineteen. The other was a young man of twenty-three or twenty-four. After some brief opening remarks, the young woman was introduced as a former "Jesus Freak" who had been "saved" by Rebbitzin Esther Jungreis. She rose and told her story.

She had grown up in Miami and had known nothing more about her Jewishness than that she was Jewish. On hearing that the Rebbitzin was holding a Jewish revival meeting in Miami, she and three friends, also Jesus Freaks, determined to challenge the Rebbetzin with their new-found religion.

The disruption they caused during the meeting led to a discussion afterward, which continued into the night. In the next several days, she, her friends, and the Rebbitzin met for many hours of heated discussion, much of it centering around the martyrdom of the Jewish people for their religion and the Holocaust experience. Toward the end of these sessions, the Rebbitzin invited her to come to New York to continue the discussions, and in a few more days she "became convinced of the Truth." She called her parents who cried for joy over her new-found commitment.

In closing, she said, "I found *Ha-Shem*.[2] I was at peace, I felt great joy. I felt Ha-Shem was in me, that He loved me and cared for me." Turning to the audience she said, "You have to find Ha-Shem, to feel His love, to let Him come into your heart."

Somehow this struck a false note with the audience of modernistic Orthodox ranging in age from fifteen to about fifty-five, with most in the thirty-five to forty-five age bracket. Many were professionals, both men and women. Those who were more involved and educated in Judaism were particularly skeptical of the young woman. They doubted that she would long remain Orthodox.

The young man followed with a description of his return. He had become friendly with a neighbor who was Orthodox. His neighbor's practices intrigued him. He enjoyed the warmth and family life that accompanied the observance of the Sabbath and the holidays. Slowly he began some of these practices himself. His neighbor, while not affiliated with Lubavitch, admired the group's welcoming approach to other Jews and suggested that he contact Lubavitch to learn more about Orthodox Judaism. Through his neighbor and Lubavitcher tutors he has learned about Orthodoxy. He currently observes the laws of Shabbat and kashrut and continues to study with Lubavitch.

This young man's talk was accepted by the audience as the story of someone who would probably remain Orthodox. Somehow his story was authentic while hers was inauthentic. Her story attaches her to Ha-Shem; his attaches him to the Jewish people, to community. Her story speaks of the sense of being loved by God; his speaks of study, of growing knowledge and awareness of Jewish law and practice. Her transformation was swift; his was slow. Finally, his story leaves him a beginner, one still learning from others. Her story places her in a position to proclaim a message to others, to be a leader.

Both, of course, are telling their own stories as they knew them. Inquiry several years later revealed that both had remained Orthodox. But whereas her story was acceptable in Christianity, it was not acceptable in Judaism. The audience considered it false because it did not fit into the patterns of accepted motivation for Judaism. Ba'alei t'shuva who tell such stories describing their motivation meet with incredulity. The repetition of such stories is discouraged, and a different account or biography of return is constructed, with neither the community nor the returnee aware of this process.

The following excerpt from a paper by a graduate student in sociology (Kramer 1972), himself a ba'al t'shuva, describes the leader of a ba'al t'shuva settlement established on an old deserted kibbutz, referred to here as "K."

> Reuben M. is a ba'al t'shuva and his wife is a convert to Judaism. Reuben M. once ran a radio station in the United States, and his public voice makes itself obvious after one speaks to him for a few minutes. He is a professional and has succeeded in gaining the sympathy and support of the Israeli public and the Jewish Agency. Contributions come in the form of voluntary labor from nearby settlements, individual financial donations, and, recently, government aid to his ba'al t'shuva kibbutz. He and his settlement have appeared in all the Israeli newspapers, plus French television and foreign publications in many parts of the world. Reuben doesn't care what is said about him as long as he is publicized. According to the newspaper clipping collection I saw at "K," he has been quite successful.
>
> Not only does Reuben utilize his charisma for the outside world, but he manages "K" with it internally as well. He strictly prohibits promiscuity and drugs, which has resulted in his expelling a few people. Other people have left because of dissension with Reuben. His personality is overpowering and what he says goes.
>
> Most of the people in "K" at first are willing to submit to his charisma since usually they are too unsure of themselves and their new Judaism to assert themselves about anything. Later as people pull themselves together some find Reuben's charisma unbearable.
>
> As inevitably happens when a yippie [politically activist hippie in the 1970s] establishment is too hippie, people go elsewhere. Two couples have married in "K" and both have left to continue learning in a more stable religious environment.
>
> The most unusual aspect of "K" is Reuben's ignorance of Judaism and his unwillingness to admit it. He speaks with a general sense of jubilance about Torah and mitzvot, but after a few minutes it becomes obvious that he has only the most

rudimentary idea about what he's saying. At one point I corrected him on something he plainly misunderstood; he countered by telling me to go and learn. He
continued talking, and several knowledgeable yeshiva students again corrected him.
He countered this by saying that today Judaism must be rediscovered. His enthusiasm, like his confidence, gives him a striking resemblance to a Baptist evangelist
from Alabama.

He has refused offers of help from the chasidim of Lubavitch and others. Many feel
the reason is that he fears others will eventually run the show. He has so far only
accepted aid in religious instruction from individuals, not from organizations. He is
very critical of the religious establishment in Israel without any real knowledge of
the situation.

The critical point is that the observer – himself a ba'al t'shuva – associates
charisma and enthusiasm with "a Baptist evangelist" in contrast to knowledge,
which he sees as essential to practice and leadership in Judaism. This observer
rejects claims to authority based on personal experience or religious feelings. The
only authority acceptable to him is that of the Torah, the religious literature that
has grown up around it, and implicitly the interpretation of this literature by the
Orthodox establishment. Personal salvation and religious experience are not a
source of authority.

The emphasis on rationality in teaching and in the experience of ba'alei t'shuva
can also be seen in the following discussion with the deans of Yeshiva Ohr
Someyach. Commenting on what a student entering the yeshiva is told, one of
the deans said: "You tell the guy very simply, you're coming into a rough regimen. It's an all-day program. If you're not inclined to it, this is not the place for
you. Our appeal is academic and intellectual, not one of emotion, music, or an
extended family relationship."

He was interrupted by another of the deans: "One moment. There is a certain
paradox, because although the approach here is intellectually rigorous, TLC
[tender loving care] is certainly an important part of this process, as is visiting
someone's home. They are not intellectual activities. Both are happening at the
same time." In this context the emotional and supportive elements are continually downplayed in the rhetoric, to the point where even the teachers and deans
forget their importance. The intellectual and cognitive aspects are thought to be
the only basis for religious authority.

The Lack of Miracles and Divine Intervention

In contrast to converts to Christian groups and born-again Christians, ba'alei
t'shuva place little emphasis on miraculous events as having influenced their new
commitment. There are no stories of having been persuaded to become Orthodox
as a result of some miraculous cure or of hearing once more from a lost relative
or of having a dream about someone dear to them or of having a prayer answered

– experiences that are quite commonly reported by Christian converts and born-again Christians.[3] Ba'alei t'shuva describe a search for meaning in life, a search for God, a feeling of having found the truth. But they do not report miracles.[4]

One does find reports of chance experiences that are interpreted as evidence of Divine Providence.[5] Most often these stories are presented with much drama; every detail is considered important and at the same time not the normal pattern for that person. The out-of-the-ordinary character of the activity is stressed, making the chance element in the story stand out. The conclusion that this event implies some Divine Providence is not stated, as this would indicate a degree of hubris not readily accepted by the teachers and guides of the ba'al t'shuva. Rather than affirm the individual's commitment, such stories engender skepticism about his "fitness" to function normally in the Orthodox community, although these questions are not raised directly to the ba'al t'shuva.

The "evidences" of Divine intervention which brought the ba'al t'shuva into his religious commitment lose their vigor as the person remains in the Orthodox community. In essence one may say that ba'alei t'shuva rarely if ever cite Divine Providence when explaining their new commitment. This is consistent with the rationalistic perspectives of both the society they leave and the society of the Orthodox, in which miracles play a limited role. (And, more important, it avoids the grandiose claim that one was worthy of a miracle.)

Even those living hippie life-styles, those who sought mind expansion, those who were "into" astrology, tarot, and the like, those who were Jesus Freaks, even these people are likely to reconstruct their biographies slowly as they come to understand Judaism better. At the outset of their "conversion" they may tell others that they have experienced special events, more than mere coincidences, which persuaded them to begin learning about Judaism. These people will be eager to learn about Kabbalah and particularly about magical lore associated with this mysticism. (Most of their knowledge of the existence of such a body of magical lore will have been gleaned from non-Jewish sources.) Such inquiry as we have seen will be discouraged by schools for ba'alei t'shuva, for they hold that such holy powers are granted only rarely, perhaps to one in a generation, and are only for the extremely pious, after long years of practice of Judaism. The ba'al t'shuva will be bidden to put off such goals and to start the study and practice of Orthodox Judaism. After he has learned the *Niglah*,[6] the required codes, etc., he may then choose to pursue his studies in Kabbalah.

Thus, although at an early stage in the process of change ba'alei t'shuva may claim that they were motivated to become Orthodox through some Divine sign, as they are socialized into Orthodoxy failure to mute this element in the account of their change leads to the assessment of the conversion as inauthentic or at least incomplete. Slowly, it becomes clear to the ba'al t'shuva that only the extraordinarily pious and learned may exercise holy powers or experience the Divine presence. He therefore reconstructs the biography of his journey in terms of what is acceptable as a motivation.

But Judaism and Christianity share a Bible replete with stories of miracles.[7] How is it, then, that the motivational vocabulary associated with Christian conversion and rebirth emphasizes miracles while Judaism de-emphasizes it?

What distinguishes Judaism from Christianity in this respect is that miracles are interpreted differently. To both Christians and Jews, miracles are signs of Divine intervention in the world, but in Christianity they are believed to be instrumental in persuading people to follow God, whereas in Judaism they are not, nor is it believed that they ever were. In the last analysis, for Judaism miracles do not make one faithful. The philosophical principle is "All is in the hands of Heaven save fear of God." Miracles did not engender faith even for the generation that Moses led out of Egypt with "the Hand of God." The Pentateuch makes it clear in the account in Exodus and elsewhere that immediately after being saved by miracles or chastised by God's intervention the Jews would turn and sin again. In Judaism's view faith and commitment depend on man's own will. They are not molded, nor should they be, by Divine intervention.[8]

Notes

1   Answers to such questions as "How did you come to be attracted to Orthodoxy?" or "Why did you become a ba'al t'shuva?" are usually framed in terms of motivation or attitudes. But motives are understood differently by social scientists than by the public at large.

When one's actions belie the words used to explain the actions (as when revolutionaries claim to be robbing the rich to further the revolution but use the booty to live the high life), the motives offered may be questioned. When they are meant to deceive others they are termed lies. When they are perceived to deceive the self they are called rationalizations. In both cases another motive is sought based on the evidence of the actions. But whether a motive in fact explains the act depends on whether the society is willing to accept it as an explanation. As C. Wright Mills (1940) has taught us, "What is reason for one man is rationalization for another." The difference depends on whether the group to which one is relating is willing to accept it.

Thus individualistic, sexual, hedonistic, and pecuniary vocabularies of motives are acceptable in twentieth-century urban America. But we would be skeptical of a billionaire businessman who claimed religious motives for his business conduct, because such motives are not *now* accepted as business motives. Similarly, a medieval monk who wrote that he gave food to a poor but pretty woman "for the salvation of his soul" would probably be disbelieved in the twentieth century. Demonic possession might be a satisfactory "motive" for action in the medieval world; it is not in ours. Nor would a Freudian or Marxist interpretation of behavior have been accepted in the medieval world.

Max Weber defines motive as the meaning that appears to the actor or the observer to be an adequate ground for his conduct (Mills 1940, 906). The motive, or reason, for an action is not the same as the cause of action. Motives are justifications of actions.

This approach to motives, which is widely accepted in social psychology, suggests that we will not find a motive or motives to explain why a person becomes a ba'al t'shuva any more than the motive for voting Republican or Democrat can be fully explained by the voter's description of a candidate's attractiveness. In both cases the dominant theoretical perspective in social psychology would suggest that we look instead toward group affiliations, position in the social structure, or past experiences that have left their mark on the individual. Social class, income, and education are excellent predictors of voting tendency, even though the voter may not be aware of their impact on his behavior.

Experimental evidence demonstrates the extent to which situational factors affect a person's actions. College students subjected to group pressures deny the evidence of their own eyes and agree with a group's definition of the length of a line (Asch 1958). People obey authority even when no sanctions are applied or threatened and will attempt to administer painful, even dangerous electric shocks to others at the simple but firm request of a person in authority (Milgram 1964). Whether a person helps another in distress varies with whether the person is alone or in the presence of someone else. In one experiment 70 percent of subjects attempted to provide assistance when they were alone, but if another person present ignored the cries only 7 percent tried to help (Latane and Rodin 1969).

Identity is itself viewed as an amalgam of responses of the individual in various situated activities (Alexander and Wiley 1981). Attitude is a problematic concept with implications for behavior that are not entirely clear. If anything, it is viewed as a dependent variable emerging from the pressures exerted on the individual that force compliance as a result of sanctions or that he espouses in order to remain a member of a group. Kelman (1961), who has developed this view of attitudes systematically, holds that some attitudes are internalized and, once internalized, are partially independent of social structure. But internalized attitudes seem to constitute a small part of the attitude set. From Kelman's perspective, most attitudes are simply reflective of the pressures of social structure.

Social psychologists generally view attitudes as dependent factors caused by other factors rather than as independent factors that cause behaviors. Studies indicate that attitude changes may occur if one changes one's group or simply plays a different role. The most convincing explanation for this is the theory of cognitive dissonance, which says that people justify their actions after the fact by attributing value to their choices that they themselves did not hold prior to the actions.

This brings us once again back to the perspective that the stated motives of people are less explanations of their behavior than rationalization. Festinger (1962) and Mills (1940), though starting from different perspectives, seem in complete agreement on this.

2   Hebrew for "the Name," a reference to God, whose name is ineffable.

3   See, for example, Westley 1977 for reports of miracles inducing faith among Catholic charismatics. This pattern is also widely observed among Protestant Pentacostals. Stories of miracles in Judaism generally emphasize the spiritual powers of the miracle worker, typically a rebbe.

4   Glanz and Harrison (1978) are not in full agreement with me in this.

5   For example, a ba'al t'shuva at Ohr Someyach reported that he first became involved with Orthodoxy when on his way to visit a friend in Jerusalem he stopped at a grocery store to buy a bottle of wine as a gift. Rabbi Nota Schiller of Ohr Somayach was there and asked if he was buying the wine for Kiddush. They talked, and he was persuaded

to come to Ohr Someyach. He felt that meeting Rabbi Schiller was a sign of *hashgacha*, of God's concern for each individual, and in this case for him in particular. Other ba'alei t'shuva gave similar interpretations to their encounters with recruiters.

6   Niglah literally means the exoteric or public knowledge. This refers to the Bible, the Talmud and the Codes, in contrast to *Nistar*, which literally means the Hidden or esoteric knowledge (Kabbalah).

7   Although the demonology of Christianity finds no parallel in Judaism, miracles are an essential element in Jewish belief as in Christian belief. Moreover, the Jewish tradition of miracles continued beyond the period of the closing of the canon in about 135 CE. One finds the continuation of this tradition in the Talmud and *aggadic* literature (narrative and homilies of the Oral Law) developed in the first three centuries of the common era and continuing as a minor theme throughout Jewish history to the story of the Golem of Prague, the miracles of the Ba'al Shem Tov, and the miraculous powers of other chasidic rebbes.

Abbreviations

A.Z.	Avodah Zarah	Gen.	Genesis
Ah.	Ahilot	Git.	Gittin
Ar.	Arakhin	Gk.	Greek
Aram.	Aramaic	Hab.	Habakuk
B.	Babli, Babylonian Talmud	Hag.	Haggai
b.	*ben*, "son of"	Hag.	Hagigah
B.B.	Baba Batra	hal.	Hallah
B.M.	Baba Mesia	Heb.	Hebrew
B.Q.	Baba Qamma	Hor.	Horayot
Bek.	Bekhorot	Hos.	Hosea
Ber.	Berakhot	Hul.	Hullin
Bes.	Besah	Is.	Isaiah
Bik.	Bikkurim	Jer.	Jeremiah
Cant.	Canticles (Song of Songs)	Josh.	Joshua
ch(s).	chapter(s)	Judg.	Judges
Chr.	Chronicles	Kel.	Kelim
col(s).	column(s)	Ker.	Keritot
Cor.	Corinthians	Ket.	Ketuvot
Dan.	Daniel	Kgs.	Kings
Dem.	Demai	Kil.	Kilaim
Deut.	Deuteronomy	Lat.	Latin
Eccl.	Ecclesiastes	Lev.	Leviticus
Ed.	Eduyyot	M.	Mishnah
Erub.	Erubin	M.Q.	Moed Qatan
Esdr.	Esdras	M.S.	Maaser Sheni
Esth.	Esther	Ma.	Maaserot
Exod.	Exodus	Macc.	Maccabees
Ezek.	Ezekiel	Mak.	Makkot
Gal.	Galatians	Makh.	Makhshirin

Matt.	Matthew	Rom.	Romans
Mal.	Malachi	Sam.	Samuel
Me.	Meilah	San.	Sanhedrin
Meg.	Megillah	Shab.	Shabbat
Men.	Menahot	Shav.	Shavuot
Mic.	Micah	Sheb.	Shebiit
Mid.	Middot	Sheq.	Sheqalim
Miq.	Miqvaot	Sir.	Sirach
MS(S).	Manuscript(s)	Sot.	Sotah
Naz.	Nazir	Suk.	Sukkah
Ned.	Nedarim	T.	Tosefta
Neg.	Negaim	T.Y.	Tebul Yom
Neh.	Nehemiah	Ta.	Taanit
Nid.	Niddah	Tam.	Tamid
Num.	Numbers	Tan.	Tanhuma
Obad.	Obadiah	Tem.	Temurah
Oh.	Ohalot	Ter.	Terumot
Or.	Orlah	Toh.	Toharot
Par.	Parah	Uqs.	Uqsin
Pes.	Pesahim	Y.	Yerushalmi, Palestinian
Phil.	Philemonians		Talmud
Prov.	Proverbs	Y.T.	Yom Tob
Ps(s).	Psalm(s)	Yad.	Yadaim
Qid.	Qiddushin	Yeb.	Yebamot
Qin.	Qinnim	Yom.	Yoma
R.	Rabbi	Zab.	Zabbim
R.H.	Rosh Hashanah	Zeb.	Zebahim
Rab.	Rabbah	Zech.	Zechariah
Rev.	Revelation	Zeph.	Zepheniah

Index

Note: Within the text of this book, distinctive spellings of names and places have been retained as they appear in the original sources. For purposes of indexing, only the single most common spelling is used.

Aaron, 366
Abba bar Kahana, 84
Abba Saul, 187
Abba Siqara, 60–1
Abba the therapeutic bleeder, 291
Abbahu, 210
Abel, 40–1
Abot D'Rabbi Nathan, 161
Abot Tractate, 62–3, 102, 146, 161, 164
Abrabanel, Isaac, 6, 163, 166–7, 171
Abraham, 325
  binding of Isaac, 33–5, 322–3
  biography as history of Israel, 80, 190, 196, 197
  covenant with YHWH, 19–20, 194
  Genesis Rabbah, 82, 83, 85, 190, 191, 192, 194, 196, 199
  God's call, 35–9
  Hatam Sofer, 233
  Leviticus Rabbah, 68
  Torah, 82
Abraham ben David of Posquières, 6
absolutism, 382
Abyss, 237, 238
Adah, 41
Adam, 307, 309, 317
  Genesis Rabbah, 83, 85
  Targum Pseudo-Jonathan, 40, 41

Adler, Rachel, 271, 329–32
Adret, Solomon ben Abraham, 124–6, 161
adultery, 5
Africa, 14, 15
aggadah, 164, 233, 431
agricultural tithes, 75–9
Agudat Yisrael, 418
Agus, Jacob B., 382, 383, 384, 387–8, 389, 393
Aha, Rabbi, 206, 209
Ahab, King, 187
Ahad Ha'am, 5, 168, 172, 400, 401, 410
ahavat olam, 229
Ahaz, King, 27
Ahio, 25
Ahitophel, 187
Air, 213–14
Akedah, 33
Akiba, Rabbi, 61, 66, 122, 161, 164, 183, 187, 189, 210, 312
Albalag, Isaac, 166
Albo, Joseph, 6, 131, 163, 166, 171
Alexander of Macedonia, 191, 192, 193
Alexandria pogroms, 133
Alfasi, Isaac, 222
allegory, Philo of Alexandria, 35–9
Alliance Israelite Universelle, 402
Almohades, 105

Alshekh, Moses, 163, 166–7
Alter, Rabbi Avraham Mordechai, 241
Ambrose, Bishop, 98
Amidah, 204, 205
Amram, 85
androcentrism, 11
anthropology, 304
anti-intellectualism, 271
anti-nomianism, 271
Antigonus of Sokho, 62
Antiochus IV, 47, 50, 52–4, 177
Antonius Pius, 91
apocalyptic literature *see* Baruch, Books of;
    Daniel, Book of; Fourth Ezra; Jubilees,
    Book of
Apocrypha, 11
apologetics, 91–2
apostasy, 16
Arakhin Tractate, 152
Arama, Isaac, 6, 163, 166–7
archeological finds, 11
Aristeas, 163, 179
Aristotelianism, 124, 125, 138
Aristotle, 104, 121, 128, 129, 132, 166
arithmetic, 103
Ark of YHWH, 25–6
art, 124
Artaxerxes, King, 43–4
asceticism, 8
Asia, 14
Assaf, 69
astrology, 103
astronomy, 103
atheism, 174
attitudes, 430
Augustine, 98–100
authenticity, models of, 269
autonomy, 363–4, 368
Avin, Rabbi, 64
Avineri, Shlomo, 401–2
Avodah Zarah, 164
Avtalyon, 63

Ba, Rabbi, 66
ba'al mofsim, 414
Ba'al Shem Tov, 431
baalei teshuvah, 325, 411–31
Baba Batra, 148, 251, 406
Baba Mesia, 147, 170
Baba Qamma, 70–2, 406

Babli *see* Babylonian Talmud
Babylonia, 68, 69, 70, 79, 198
Babylonian Talmud
    Baba Batra Tractate, 148, 251, 406
    Baba Qamma Tractate, 70–2, 406
    Berakhot Tractate, 147, 182
    blessings, 16
    Gittin Tractate, 17, 60–1, 160
    Megillah Tractate, 204–6
    Qiddushin Tractate, 207
    Sanhedrin Tractate, 114, 406
    Shabbat Tractate, 4, 148, 164, 307
    women, 11
Baeck, Leo, 7
Bahya ibn Paquda, 8, 165
Balaam, 187
Balfour Declaration, 360
Bar Hutah, 209
Bar Kokhba rebellion, 13
bar mitzvah ceremony, 146
Barcelona, Disputation at, 116–17
Barnabas, 89
Baruch, Books of, 170, 178
Bavli *see* Babylonian Talmud
Bayme, Dr. Steven, 222
Beer Heteb, 146, 151, 152
behavioral model, 269–70
being, 104
Beirur, 253
ben Azzai, Simeon, 164
Ben Gurion, David, 386
benevolence, 5
Berakhot Tractate, 147, 182
Berdichevski, Michah Joseph, 378–80
Berekiah, Rabbi, 210
Bereshit, 147
Berkowitz, Rabbi Eliezer, 418
Bible *see* Gospels; Hebrew Bible (Tanakh);
    New Testament
biblical religion, 4–5, 9
bioethics, 287–306
birkat ha-minim, 16
blessings
    Encyclopedia of Religion, 16
    feminist values, 318–20
    Mishnah Sotah, 202, 203
    Reform Judaism, 217–18, 219–20
    Tosefta Sotah, 204
B'nai Jeshurun (New York), 268–9
body

Body (*cont.*)
  Philo of Alexandria, 36–9
  Torah, 165
BonJour, Laurence, 289
Booths Festival *see* Sukkot
Borowitz, Eugene, 217–20, 295–6, 304, 363–4, 404–5
Boyd, Richard, 294
Brovender, Rabbi, 417, 418
Brown, Roger, 423
Buber, Martin, 168–9, 248, 276, 314, 368, 375
Buddhism, 16, 17, 276
business, 306–15

Cain, 40–1, 85
Calami, 129
Canaanites, 191, 192, 193
captives, redemption of, 297–8
Cardin, Nina Beth, 271
Caro, Joseph, 15, 222
Catholic Israel, 389–90, 413
CCAR, 225
celibacy, 317
Centenary Perspective, 228
Central Conference of American Rabbis (CCAR), 225
chaos, 242–3
charismatics, 417
charity, 17, 122–3, 313
Chasidism *see* hasidic movement
Christianity
  claim to be a new Israel, 196, 197
  doctrine of two powers, 176
  Encyclopedia of Religion, 16, 17
  and Judaism, 8, 9, 86–100, 114–27
  miracles, 427–8, 429, 430
  reborn Christians, 412, 427–8
  see also Gospels; Jesus Christ; New Testament
Chronicles, Books of, 21, 180, 188, 197, 200
Chrysostom, Saint John, 16
Church Fathers, 13
Cicero, 98
Clement of Alexandria, 35, 92–4
Cochin, 14
codes and codification, 16
cognitive dissonance, theory of, 423, 430
cognitive intuitionism, 293–4

Cohen, Henry, 225–7
Cohen, Hermann, 141–2, 168, 254
coherence reasoning, 289–90, 302
Columbus Platform (1937), 228
commandments, 22–3, 395, 420
common-sense rationale, 248–51
competition, 311
confession, 17
Confucianism, 17
Congregation Kehillat Jeshurun, 333–44
conscience, 293–5, 304, 413
Conservative Judaism, 256–67, 281, 282, 389, 391
  Halakhah, 257–8
  homosexuality, 266–7
  Jewish pluralism, 382
  religious authority, 413
  revelation, 257
  rituals, 413
  Sabbath, 260–2
  statement of principles, 256–9
  synagogues, 269
  women, 262–5, 316
Conservative Judaism (Journal), 269
Conservative Zionism, 403–4
Constantine, 79, 97
constitutions
  Kehillat Jeshurun, 333–44
  Monmouth Reform Temple, 344–58
contradictions, unity of, 237–9
conversion, 114–15, 191, 367
Corinthians, Epistle to, 93
corruption, 314
covenantal theory, 10, 363–4
  between God and "Israel" at Sinai, 13, 160, 161, 366, 371
  voluntary covenant, 367–8
  YHWH's covenant with Abraham, 19–20
creation
  Genesis Rabbah, 79, 80, 83
  human being's place in, 309
  Philo of Alexandria, 133–4
  rites and festivals, 13
Crescas, Hasdai, 162–3, 166, 167, 171
Crusades, 17, 114
cultural flexibility, 395
Cumanus, 57
curses, 202, 203
Cyrus, 42, 43

da'at, 248–51
Daniel, Book of, 11, 47–9
  Genesis Rabbah, 211
  God, 177
  Leviticus Rabbah, 68, 69
  Yerushalmi Yebamot, 66–7
Daniels, Norman, 298, 306
Darius I, King of Persia, 43, 69
David
  Ark of YHWH brought to Jerusalem, 25–6
  basic principles, 5
  Genesis Rabbah, 81, 83
  Hatam Sofer, 233
  regarded as prophet, 31
  as sage of the Torah, 200
  Yerushalmi Sanhedrin, 200
  Yerushalmi Sheqalim, 200–1
  YHWH's promise, 26–7, 30
David ben Solomon ibn Abi Zimra, 6–7
day school movement, 223
death
  burial procedures, 149–52
  care for a dying patient, 293
  criteria for determination of, 291–2
  Genesis Rabbah, 81
debt, 23–4
Delmedigo, Joseph Solomon, 163
Demetrius, 94
demiurge, 176
democracy
  Conservative Zionism, 404
  secular Jews, 394–5
Derekh ha-Hayyim, 149, 150
Deuteronomy, Book of, 4, 280
  agricultural tithes, 75
  Baba Qamma, 72
  burial of the dead, 150
  debt remission, 23–4
  Encyclopedia of Religion, 16
  festivals, 24–5
  Genesis Rabbah, 192
  Gittin Tractate, 61
  God, 178, 179, 180, 182
  "Israel," 189, 190, 195
  Leviticus Rabbah, 69
  Maimonides' *Guide for the Perplexed*, 107
  Megillah, 205
  Mishnah Sotah, 202–3
  needs/lacks, 298
  Peah Tractate, 64, 65

  revelation by God at Sinai, 366
  sacrifice of first-born, 20
  teaching of children, 102
  ten commandments, 22
  Torah, 29, 64, 65, 163, 164, 170
  Tosefta Sotah, 204
  Yebamot Tractate, 66
  see also Sifre Deuteronomy
diaspora
  Orthodox Judaism, 252
  philosophy, 130
  Reform Judaism, 231
  state of Israel, 398–9, 400–2
Diocletian, 97
divorcement, 114–15, 116
Doeg, 187
Donatists, 98
Dorff, Elliot, 266–7
dualism, 176–7

Ecclesiastes, Book of, 81, 109
Ecclesiastes Rabbah, 170
economic justice, 306–15
economics
  anthropology of, 309–11, 313
  ethics of, 311–13
  theology of, 309, 313
Edom, 68, 69, 198
education
  day school movement, 223
  Joseph ibn Caspi, 121
  Judah ibn Tibbon, 119–20
  Judaism in Muslim World, 101–5
  rabbinic, 271
  religious schools, 386
  secular Jews, 396
  see also yeshivot
ego enhancement, 310, 311, 313
Egypt/Egyptians, 191, 193
  Exodus from, 13, 20–2
Elat Chayyim, 281, 283
elders, 62
Eleazar ben Abinah, 209
Eleazar ben Pedat, 178, 183
Eleazar ben Shammua, 164
Eleazar of Mayence, 122–3
Eleazar, Rabbi, 64, 206, 210
Eliade, Mircea, 13, 423
Eliezer ben Hyrcanus, 170
Eliezer ben Yose, 161

Eliezer, Rabbi, 61, 66, 126, 189, 190
Ellenson, David, 288
emancipation, 7, 234–7
Emet Ve-Emunah, 256–9
emotions, 248–50, 280
Encyclopaedia Judaica, 3–8
The Encyclopedia of Religion, 9, 10–18
Enoch, 41
Enosh, 41
Erubin Tractate, 164
Esau, 197, 198
eschatological prophets, 57–8
eschatology, 17
Esther, Book of, 4, 68, 198, 205, 206
ethics, 141–2, 287–315
    Halakhah, 287, 295, 296, 302
    Kantian ethics, 293, 304
    Orthodox Judaism, 288
    Reform Judaism, 218, 221, 288
    Talmud, 291, 296
Ethics of the Fathers, 110, 111
ethnicity, 8–15
Euphrates, 68
Europe, 14, 15
Eusebius, 94, 96–8
Eve, 40, 41, 309, 317
evil, 176, 238, 253, 310–11
exile, 399–400
    return from with Persian permission,
        42–3
    see also diaspora
Exodus, Book of
    compensation for injury, 70, 71
    crossing of Red Sea, 21–2
    essence of Judaism, 5
    Genesis Rabbah, 193, 197, 199, 209
    God, 177, 179, 180
    Hatam Sofer, 233
    "Israel," 187, 195, 196
    justice, 313
    Maimonides' *Guide of the Perplexed*, 107
    making of images, 124
    Philo of Alexandria, 37, 38, 39
    revelation by God at Sinai, 420
    sacrifice of first-born, 20–1
    sensing the presence of God, 371
    ten commandments, 22–3
    Torah, 64, 65, 160, 163, 164, 170
Exodus from Egypt, 13, 20–2
Exodus Rabbah, 164

extremism, 245–6
Ezekiel, Book of, 69, 182, 195
Ezra, 17, 43–4
IV Ezra, 58–9
Ezra, Book of, 42–4, 160

Fackenheim, Emil, 364–5
Fadus, 58
faith
    Encyclopedia of Religion, 17
    Emil Fackenheim, 364–5
    Judah Halevi, 137–8
    Orthodox Judaism, 420
    passive spirituality, 278
    Solomon ben Adret, 124–5
    Will Herberg, 369–70
Falashas, 14
Falk, Marcia, 318–20
family metaphor, 80, 190–9
Al-Farabi, 101
Feingold, Henry L., 407–8
Feinstein, Rabbi Moshe, 418
Feld, Merle, 320–2
Feldman, Rabbi Aharon, 417–18
feminism, 270–1, 316, 326–8, 330–1
Festinger, Leon, 420, 423, 430
festivals, 12–13, 24–5, 229, 395
    Shavuot(Weeks Festival), 12, 24–5,
        204
    Sukkot (Booths Festival), 12, 25, 204
    see also Passover; Sabbath
Feuerbach, Ludwig, 375, 376
Feuerberg, M. Z., 409
Fire, 213–14
foundationalism, 288, 291–3, 300
Fourth Ezra, 58–9
Frankiel, Tamar, 316–18
Friedman, Rabbi Raphi, 283
Frymer-Kensky, Tikva, 271

Gaius, Emperor, 133
Galatians, 3, 88–90
Galileo, 250
galut, 235–6, 399–400
Gamaliel, Rabban, 61, 63, 64, 182
gay culture, 266–7, 327–8
Gebiah ben Qosem, 191–2, 193
gedolim, 414, 418
Gehazi, 187
Geiger, Abraham, 167

Genesis, Book of
  Abraham's sons of his concubines,
    191, 192
  binding of Isaac, 33, 322–3
  death of Jacob, 80–1
  God, 177, 180, 183
  God curses serpent, 84
  God's call of Abraham, 36–9
  Hatam Sofer, 233
  "Israel," 189, 195–6, 197, 198, 199
  Jacob takes away birthright, 82
  Leviticus Rabbah, 68, 69
  Maimonides' *Guide of the Perplexed*,
    107, 109
  man's creation after image of God, 133
  Mishnah Sotah, 203
  Noah finds grace, 83
  Philo of Alexandria, 37, 38, 39
  Targum Pseudo-Jonathan, 39–41
  Torah, 160, 164
  Torah in Hebrew language, 210, 211
  YHWH's covenant with Abraham,
    19–20, 194
Genesis Rabbah
  Hebrew language, 207, 208–11
  "Israel," 79–85, 190–9
  Torah, 161, 164, 170
Gentiles, 12, 16
geometry, 103
Gihon, 68
Gikatilla, Joseph, 166
Gillman, Neil, 268–71, 365
Gittin Tractate, 17, 60–1, 160
Glazer, Nathan, 422
gnosis, 88
God, 173–86
  agricultural tithes, 75–9
  Ark of YHWH, 25–6
  binding of Isaac, 33–5
  call of Abraham, 35–9
  choice of David as king, 26–7
  Cohen on, 141–2
  as common denominator of all religions,
    253–4
  covenant with "Israel" at Sinai, 13, 160,
    161, 366, 371
  crossing of Red Sea, 21–2
  death of God theology, 374–5
  debt remission, 23–4
  essence of Judaism, 6
  gives Moses precepts, 5
  Green on, 366
  Halpern on, 381–2, 392–3
  Herberg on, 368–9
  Heschel on, 370–1
  identification with Torah, 166
  Jewish Renewal movement, 281–2
  justice, 313, 314
  Kaplan on, 372–3
  Maimonides' Thirteen Principles, 6
  man's creation as image of, 133–4
  Orthodox Judaism, 253–5
  personal nature of, 368–9
  Reform Judaism, 218, 228–9
  relationship to Israel, 82–3, 324
  ritual, 219–20
  Rubenstein on, 374–5
  sacrifice of first-born, 20–1
  Schulweis on, 375–6
  secular Jews, 394
  "seeing," 366
  sensing the presence of, 370–1
  sexuality, 328
  ten commandments, 22–3
  two authorities theory, 176–7
  unity of contradictions, 238
  Wyschogrod on, 376–7
  YHWH as creator and giver of Torah,
    29–30
  YHWH's covenant with Abraham, 19–20
  YHWH's relationship to Davidic kings, 30
Golah, 399
Goldin, Rabbi Hyman, 145
Golem of Prague, 431
goodness, 253, 310–11
Gordis, Daniel, 291–2
Gordis, Robert, 389
Gorny, Yosef, 409–10
goses, 292
Gospels, 86–8
Graetz, Heinrich, 5
grammar, 102
Greece/Greek culture
  Genesis Rabbah, 79, 198
  Leviticus Rabbah, 68, 69, 70
  philosophy, 130, 132–4
Greek language, 206
Green, Arthur, 269, 271–7, 366
Green, William Scott, 8–18
Greenberg, Irving, 367–8

Grossman, Susan, 323–6
grudges, 121–2
Guttmann, Julius, 129–31

Habad Lubavitch *see* Lubavitch Hasidism
Habakkuk, 5, 31–3, 68
Hadassi, Judah, 162
Haggai the prophet, 45–6
Haggai, Rabbi, 65
Hagigah, 107
Halakhah
    Conservative Judaism, 257–8
    Encyclopedia of Religion, 16
    ethics, 287, 295, 296, 302
    feminism, 331–2
    Megillah Tractate, 206
    neo-Orthodoxy, 390
    Orthodox Judaism, 247–51, 413–14
    Reform Judaism, 221, 331
    religious authority, 413–14, 417–18
    tzedakah, 297
Halevi, Judah, 17
    faith, 137–8
    The Kuzari, 115, 136–8, 162, 165
    man is formed by actions, 419–20
    poem on Return to Zion, 115
    Torah, 162, 163, 165, 166, 167, 169
halisah, 202, 203
Hallel, 204, 205
Halpern, Ben, 381–93, 399–400
Hamadrikh, 145
Haman, 68
Hampshire, Stuart, 296, 305
Hanina ben Dosa, 182
Hannah, 199
Hanukkah, 51, 204
Haredi community, 244, 245, 246
Hartman, David, 305, 368
Harvey, Warren (Zev), 159–72
hasid, emergence of, 14
hasidic movement, 126, 237, 246, 414
    avodah be-gashmiyut doctrine, 280
    evil, 253
    Lubavitch Hasidism, 251–3, 425–6
    meditations, 279
    renewed interest in, 269
    Torah, 168
Hatam Sofer, 232–3
Hazon Ish Karelitz, 244–6
healing, 268

health care, 297–300
heathenism, 176
heaven, 177–8
Hebrew Bible (Tanakh)
    agricultural tithes, 75, 78–9
    Baruch Spinoza, 140
    blessings, 16
    conflict with reason, 11
    Encyclopedia of Religion, 17
    ethics, 291
    Hatam Sofer, 232
    "Israel," 190–1
    and Judaism, 8–9, 16–18
    Philo of Alexandria, 132–4
    religious authority, 413
    sages, 79, 80, 83, 190, 197, 199–200
    secular Jews, 394, 395–6
    sensing the presence of God, 370–1
    study of, 102, 422
    theopolitical perspective, 333
    Torah, 160
    tzedakah, 297
    Yahadut, 4
    see also Deuteronomy; Exodus; Genesis;
        Leviticus; *Midrash*; Numbers; Psalms,
        Book of; Torah
Hebrew language, 202–14, 229
Hebrew Union College–Jewish Institute of
        Religion (HUC–JIR), 228
Hebrews, Epistle to, 90–1
Heidegger, Martin, 142
Heilman, Samuel, 421, 422
Hekhalot literature, 211–14
Hekhalot Rabbati, 126
Heliodorus, 53, 54
Helkiah, Rabbi, 69, 210–11
Hellenism *see* Greece/Greek culture
Hellenistic Reform, 52–3
Herberg, Will, 368–70, 382, 390, 393
heretics, 177
Herod the Great, 56, 176
Herzl, Theodor, 360
Heschel, Abraham Joshua, 280, 313, 369,
        370–1, 390, 403
Hibbat Zion, 409–10
hiddush, 249
Hillel, 4, 5, 63, 164, 394
Hillel, House of, 73–4
Hilqiah, Rabbi, 69, 210–11
Himmelfarb, Milton, 423, 424

Hinduism, 16, 276
Hirsch, Rabbi Samson Raphael, 234–7
Histadrut, 383
Hiyya bar Aba, Rabbi, 200, 209
Hokhmah, 162, 250
Hokhmat Adam, 149, 150, 151
holiday celebrations *see* festivals
holiness, 5, 228, 229, 279–80, 317, 328
Holocaust, 224, 246–7, 374–5, 407,
    408–9
    see also Shoah
Holy, 239–41
holy days *see* festivals
Holy of Holies, 239
homosexuality, 266–7, 327–8
Hosea, Book of, 64, 83, 323–4
Hoshaiah, Rabbi, 161, 163
Hoshen ha-Mishpat, 148
house, dedication of, 146–7
HUC–JIR, 228
humanism, secular Jews, 394–5
Humanity, 239–41
humility, 5
Huna, Rabbi, 68, 211
Huna bar Idi, Rabbi, 207
hupah ceremony, 152–6
huqqim, 123
Husik, Isaac, 131–2
Husserl, Edmund, 142

ibn 'Aqnin, Joseph ben Judah, 101–5
ibn Caspi, Joseph, 121
ibn Daud, Abraham, 118, 165, 171
ibn Ezra, Abraham, 162, 165
ibn Ezra, Moses, 4, 115–16
ibn Habib, Jacob ben Solomon, 163
ibn Latif, Isaac, 162, 163
ibn Tibbon, Judah, 119–20
ibn Tibbon, Samuel ben Judah, 119, 166
idolatry, 5, 6, 124, 166, 175–6
incest, 5
inferential knowledge, 135–6
inscriptional records, 11
intellectual model, 269–70
intermarriage, 225–7, 272
intuitive cognition, 293–4
invalids, laws for visiting, 147–9
Irad, 41
Isaac, 325
    binding of, 33–5, 198, 322–3

biography as history of Israel, 80, 190,
    196, 197, 198
Genesis Rabbah, 82, 85, 190, 191, 192,
    196, 197, 198
Torah, 82
Isaac, Rabbi, 180, 199, 201
Isaiah, Book of, 27–8, 171, 243
    essence of Judaism, 5
    Genesis Rabbah, 210
    Gittin Tractate, 61
    God, 177, 178, 179, 183, 371
    "Israel," 187, 195, 196, 199
Ishmael ben R. Nehemiah, Rabbi, 67–8
Ishmaelites, 191–2, 193
Islam
    Encyclopedia of Religion, 16, 17
    incompatibility with Judaism, 8
    philosophy, 130
Israel, Land of
    holiness of, 11
    Jewish philosophy, 129
    Judah ha-Levi's poem on Return to Zion,
        115
    as Torah center, 244
Israel, State of
    centrality of, 399–402
    Conservative Zionism, 403–4
    Declaration of Independence, 359–62, 408,
        409
    diaspora, 398–9, 400–2
    as Jewish spiritual center, 408–9
    Law of Return, 408
    normative status, 401–2
    Orthodox Judaism, 382, 403
    primacy of, 400–1
    Reform Judaism, 231, 404–5
    Yad Vashem Law, 408–9
"Israel" (the holy community), 187–201
    covenant with God at Sinai, 13, 160, 161,
        366, 371
    Encyclopedia of Religion, 15
    family metaphor, 80, 190–9
    Genesis Rabbah, 79–85, 190–9
    God's relationship to, 82–3, 324
    Orthodox Judaism, 234–7
    Rabbinic literature, 12
    Reform Judaism, 230–1
    sages, 190, 193–4, 197, 199–200, 201
    as *sui generis* in the Mishnah, 187–90
    as *sui generis* in the Yerushalmi, 199–201

"Israel" (the holy community) (*cont*)
  and Torah, 164, 168–9
  women's otherness, 326

Jabal, 41
Jacob, 325
  biography as history of Israel, 80, 83, 190, 196, 197, 198
  death, 80–1
  Genesis Rabbah, 80, 81, 82, 83, 85, 190, 196
  Torah, 82
Jacob, Walter, 220–2
Jacobs, Rabbi Louis, 3–8
Jaffee, Martin, 75–9
Jason, 52–3
Jeremiah, Book of, 304
  call to observe Torah, 28–9
  duty of "Israel," 234
  endurance of Jewish nation, 170
  Genesis Rabbah, 83, 211
  Gittin Tractate, 61
  God, 179
  Leviticus Rabbah, 69
Jeroboam, King, 187
Jerusalem, 25–6
Jerusalem Talmud (Yerushalmi)
  blessings, 16
  Israel as *sui generis*, 199–201
  Peah Tractate, 63–5, 147
  Sanhedrin Tractate, 65–6, 200
  Sheqalim Tractate, 161, 200–1
  Yebamot Tractate, 66–7
Jeshua, 43
Jesse, 27–8
Jesus Christ
  Gospel according to Matthew, 86–7
  Gospel according to Thomas, 88
  Maimonides' Thirteen Principles, 6
  Moses ben Nahman, 116–17
  "Q" source, 86
  see also Christianity
Jewish Agency, 408, 426
Jewish community
  ethnic group, 8–15
  see also diaspora
Jewish emancipation, 7, 234–7
Jewish Frontier, 381
Jewish Quarterly Review, 5
Jewish Renewal movement, 280–3

Jewish self-identity, 143–4
Jewish Theological Seminary, 262
Jewish Week, 273
Job, Book of, 108, 179, 180, 183, 210, 212
John, father of Eupolemus, 53
Joseph, 38, 80–1
Joseph, Rabbi, 61, 205
Josephus Flavius, 11, 55–8, 60, 333
  Against Apion, 128–9, 165, 170
  Jewish Antiquities, 33–5, 56–8
  Jewish War, 55, 57
  Torah, 165, 170
Joshua, 46–7, 62
Joshua ben Hananiah, 170
Joshua ben Levi, 65, 183
Joshua ben Perahyah, 62
Joshua, Book of, 114, 160, 163, 203
Joshua, Rabbi, 61, 66
Joshua of Sikhnin, Rabbi, 81
Josiah, 28
Jubal, 41
Jubilees, Book of, 169
Judaei, 129
Judah ben Barzillai, 161
Judah ben Jehiel, 167
Judah ben R. Simon, 69, 210
Judah ben Tabbai, 63
Judah, Kingdom of
  exiles allowed to return, 42–3
  Ezra brings Torah to, 43–4
Judah Loew ben Bezalel, 163, 166–7
Judah the Maccabee, 51
Judah the Prince, 66–7, 203, 210
Judaism
  concept of normative Judaism, 7–8
  definition, 3–18
  distinction from Torah, 4–5
  Encyclopedia of Religion, 9, 10–18
  essence of, 5–8
  recognition of constant ideas, 8
Judas the Gaulanite, 56
judgments, 293–5, 300, 304
Jungreis, Esther, 425
Jungreis, Sara, 425
Jupiter Dolichenus, 177
Jupiter Heliopolitanus, 177
justice, 5, 297, 299
  economic, 306–15
  for all, 313–15

justification, 288, 301, 302
Justin Martyr, 91–2

Kabbalah, 126–7, 237–9, 277
    baalei teshuvah, 428
    evil, 253
    Lurianic Kabbalah, 241–2
    theopolitical perspective, 333
    Torah, 162, 166, 169, 171–2
Kahath, 85
Kant, Immanuel, 141, 142, 294
Kantian ethics, 293, 304
Kaplan, Rabbi Aryeh, 269, 318
Kaplan, Rabbi Mordecai, 383–4, 386–7, 388
    faith, 382
    God, 372–3
    New Zionism doctrine, 391–2
    Reconstructionism, 271, 281, 282, 389,
        393
    Torah, 168
Karelitz, Rabbi Avraham Yeshayahu
    see Hazon Ish Karelitz
Karo, Joseph see Caro
kavannot, 279
kedushah (holiness), 228, 229
Kehillat Jeshurun, 333–44
kelim, 238
Kelman, Herbert, 430
Ketubah, 152, 154–6
Ketuvot Tractate, 4
kiddush, 319–20
Kierkegaard, Soren, 365
King Jr., Martin Luther, 280, 290, 291,
    302–3
Kings, Books of, 28, 81, 178
kinyan, 148, 152, 155
kippah, 323
Kitzur Shulhan Arukh, 148, 149,
    151, 152
knowledge, 135–6, 237, 238
Kook, Rabbi Abraham Isaac, 169,
    237–43, 244
Korah, 248, 249–50, 251
Kristol, Irving, 225
Krochmal, Nachman, 163, 167
Kushner, Lawrence, 269
The Kuzari, 115, 136–8, 162, 165

Lamech, 41
Law of Return, 408

laws
    Judah Halevi on, 138
    Maimonides on, 123, 139
    unjustness of, 290, 302
    Wyschogrod on, 376–7
    see also Halakhah; Mishnah; Torah
Lazarus, Moritz, 168
League of Nations, 360
Leah, 191, 325
Leibowitz, Yeshaayahu, 169, 253–5
lesbianism, 266–7, 327–8
Letter of Aristeas, 163, 179
Levi, 85
Levi bar Sisi, 66–7
Levi ben Gershom, 166
Levi, Rabbi, 81, 84, 178, 208–9
Levi tribe, 20
Levinas, Emmanuel, 142–4, 169
Leviticus, Book of, 69, 70
    agricultural tithes, 75
    Baba Qamma, 71
    Genesis Rabbah, 195
    God, 174
    Torah, 160, 164, 169
    uncleanness, 74
    vengeance, 121
Leviticus Rabbah
    four kingdoms, 67–70
    Hebrew language, 207–8, 211
    Torah, 161, 170
Levy, Rabbi Richard, 227–8
lexical ordering, 296, 305
Liberal party, 240
liberalism, 314
Lichtenstein, Aharon, 295, 296
liturgy
    Reform Judaism, 221–2
    translation, 202–4
    women, 318–22
logic, 103, 105
logos, 161
love, 5, 162–3, 308, 314
Lubavitch Hasidism, 251–3, 425–6
Lucius, 91
Luke, Gospel of, 86, 88
Luria, Isaac, 15
Lurianic Kabbalah, 241–2
Luzzatto, Moses Hayyim, 8
Luzzatto, Samuel David, 167–8
Lydda, Council of, 5

Ma'abar Yabbok, 150, 151
Ma'aseh Merkavah, 126
Maaserot Tractate, 75–9
Maccabees, Books of the, 3, 49–54, 177
Mackler, Rabbi Aaron L., 287–306
Magen Abraham, 151
Maimonides, Moses, 132, 222
   art and idolatry, 124
   attack by Solomon ben Adret, 124–5
   charity, 17, 313
   ethics, 291
   Gentiles, 12
   Guide of the Perplexed, 105–13, 118–19,
      138–9, 162, 165
   law, 123, 139
   needs/lacks, 306
   redemption of captives, 297
   thirteen principles, 6
   Torah, 6, 162, 165–6, 167, 170–1
Mainz martyrs, 117
Makkot Tractate, 5
Malachi, Book of, 160, 170
Malkhut, 162
Malkin, Yaakov, 394–6
Manasseh, King, 187
Manicheanism, 98
Margoshes, Dr. Samuel, 384
marriage
   importance of, 317
   intermarriage, 225–7, 272
marriage ceremony, 152–6
martyrdom, 5, 97–8, 117
Marxism, 304
Maslow, Abraham H., 279
mathematics, 103, 105
matriarchs, 191, 194, 325
Mattathias, 50–1
Matthew, Gospel of, 86–7
Mayer, Egon, 226
mechanics, 104
Media, 68, 69, 70, 79, 198
medicine, 104, 126
   see also health care
meditations, 279
Megillah Tractate, 204–6
Mehujael, 41
Meir, Rabbi, 66, 208, 312
Mekilta, 164, 177, 179
Mendelssohn, Moses, 167, 168, 232
menuchah, 229

mercy, prayers for, 148
Merkavah, 126
messiah
   Maimonides' Thirteen Principles, 6
   Psalms of Solomon, 54–5
metaphysics, 103, 104–5
Methushael, 41
mezuzah/mezuzot, 204, 220
Miasha, Rabbi, 64
Micah, Book of, 5, 196, 283
Michael, 48, 49
Michal, daughter of Saul, 26
Middle East, 15
midrash
   Hebrew language, 207–11
   Maimonides' *Guide of the Perplexed*, 109
   Tanhuma, 147, 161, 164
   see also Genesis Rabbah; Leviticus Rabbah;
      Sifre Deuteronomy
migration, 17
mikvah, 228, 317–18, 324, 325
Milgram, Stanley, 430
Mills, C. Wright, 429, 430
Minhage Yeshurun, 149
minyan, 264–5
miracles, 181–3, 414, 427–9, 430, 431
Miriam the prophetess, 22
Mishnah, 73–9
   blessings, 16, 202, 203
   commentaries to, 15
   heathenism, 176
   Israel as *sui generis*, 187–90
   Maaserot Tractate, 75–9
   Megillah Tractate, 204
   priorities of rescue, 299
   sanctification, 13
   Sanhedrin Tractate, 6, 16, 171, 187–90
   Sotah Tractate, 202–3
   study of, 102
   Terumot Tractate, 77
   Uqsin Tractate, 73–5
   women, 11
   Yadaim Tractate, 162, 166, 239
   see also Abot Tractate; Babylonian Talmud;
      Jerusalem Talmud (Yerushalmi); Talmud
Mishnah Berurah, 417–18
mishpatim, 123
mitzvah/mitzvot, 221, 228, 229, 248–50,
   263–4, 323–4
Modeh Ani, 219

Moed Katan, 149
Moline, Jack, 280–3
monism, 175
Monmouth Reform Temple, 344–58
monopolies, 311
monotheism, 174–5, 176–7
Moore, George Foot, 173–86
morality, 141–2, 168, 306–15
Moses
    ascent to heaven to capture Torah, 164
    crossing of Red Sea, 21–2
    Exodus from Egypt, 20–2
    faith of, 278
    four kingdoms, 69
    Genesis Rabbah, 81, 85
    God reveals Torah at Sinai, 13, 160, 161,
        366, 371
    God's call of Abraham, 36–7, 39
    hands Torah to Joshua, 62
    Hatam Sofer, 233
    and Korah, 248, 249–50, 251
    Maimonides' Thirteen Principles, 6
    male youth subject to punishment, 146
    man's creation after image of God, 133
    receives precepts from God, 5
    seeing God, 366
    student of Torah, 200
moshavot, 358
motives, 424–30
Motsi, 219
Muhammad, 6
murder, 5
music, 104
Muslim world, 101–13
mysticism, 211–14, 224, 277
    Encyclopedia of Religion, 13, 17
    Lubavitch Hasidism, 251–3, 425–6
    renewed interest in, 269
    union of husband and wife, 317
    Zohar, 8, 126, 162, 166
    see also Kabbalah
myths, 365

Naamah, 41
Nahmanides, Rabbi Moses ben, 116–17,
    124, 166
Nahum the Scribe, 63, 64
Nathan (prophet), 26
Nathan, Rabbi, 177, 197
Nation, 239–41

Nationalist party, 240
nature, 181–2
Nebuchadnezzar, 68
Nedarim, 147, 148, 164
needs, 298
Nehemiah, Book of, 44–5, 83
Nehemiah, Rabbi, 189
Nehunyah ben Ha-Qanah, 126
Neo-Orthodoxy, 234, 390
Neo-Platonism, 98, 126
New Age Judaism, 268–83
New Moons, 204
New Testament, 11, 86–91
Newton, Sir Isaac, 250
niddah, 317–18
Nietzsche, Friedrich Wilhelm, 375, 378
Niglah, 428, 431
Nissim ben Reuben Gerondi, 163
Nistar, 431
Nittai the Arbelite, 62
Noah, 80, 83
normative Judaism, 7–8
North Africa, 15
Numbers, Book of
    Baba Qamma, 71, 72
    Genesis Rabbah, 81
    "Israel," 189, 195, 196
    Maimonides' *Guide of the Perplexed*, 107
    Mishnah Sotah, 202
    Moses and Korah, 248
    sacrifice of first-born, 20
    Torah, 160, 162, 164

Obed-edom the Gittite, 25–6
obedience, 17
Ohr Someyach, 415–16, 418, 427,
    430–1
Olam ha-Tikkun, 241–2
Olam ha-Tohu, 241–2
Omer-man, Rabbi Jonathan, 281
oneg, 229
optics, 103
oral Torah, 17, 63–5, 159, 160, 167, 169,
    414–15
    see also Babylonian Talmud; Halakhah;
        Jerusalem Talmud (Yerushalmi);
        midrash; Mishnah; Talmud; Torah
order, 242–3
Orenstein, Deborah, 271
Origen, 35, 94–6

Orthodox Judaism, 232–55
  authoritative rulings on the law, 377
  dominant political force in Israel, 382
  emancipation, 234–7
  ethics, 288
  extremism, 245–6
  faith, 420
  God, 253–5
  Halakhah, 247–51, 413–14
  Holocaust, 246–7
  ideological diversity and unity, 239–41
  "Israel," 234–7
  Kehillat Jeshurun, 333–44
  normative technique, 390–1, 392
  redemption, 251–3
  religious authority, 413–15
  return to, 411–31
  rituals, 413, 419–23
  science, 253–5
  secular Zionist idealism, 241–3
  state of Israel, 403
  status as a community, 388
  study, 415–17, 418–19, 421–4
  Torah, 172, 235, 244
  unity of contradictions, 237–9
  women, 262, 316
  see also Haredi community
Otto, Rudolf, 129, 219
Ovedei Kokhavim, 166

paganism, 250
Palestinian Talmud see Jerusalem Talmud
  (Yerushalmi)
Pamphilus, 96–7
Pantaenus, 94
pantheism, 175
papal encyclicals, 314
Pappos, 183
parables, 106, 108–10
paradise, 13
Passover (Pesach), 12, 278
  clash with Romans under Cumanus, 57
  Deuteronomy, 24
  Ezra, 43
  Hallel recitation, 204
  Jerusalem Temple defiled by
    Samaritans, 56
  Philo of Alexandria, 39
patriarchs, 79, 191, 194–5, 196–8, 308
  see also Abraham; Isaac; Jacob

Paul, 88–90, 93, 95, 196
peace, 237–9
Peah Tractate, 63–5, 147
Pelagians, 98
Pentateuch, 160, 414, 429
  see also Deuteronomy; Exodus; Genesis;
    Leviticus; Numbers; Torah
Persia/Persians, Jews allowed to return, 42–3
Pesach see Passover
Pesahim Tractate, 161, 163, 164, 416
pesher commentaries, 31–3
Pesiqta Rabbati, 164
Petah Tikva, 358–9
Peter, 88–9
Pharaoh, 21
Pharisees, 11, 58
philanthropy, 310–13
Philo of Alexandria, 132–4, 333
  God, 174, 179–80
  man last in world's creation, 134
  man's creation after image of God, 133–4
  migration of Abraham, 35–9
  Torah, 35–9, 161, 164–5, 166, 170
philosophy, 128–44
  Encyclopedia of Religion, 13, 15
  Greece/Greek culture, 130, 132–4
  Joseph ibn Caspi, 121
  medieval period, 130, 135–9
  modern period, 130, 139–44
  Solomon ben Adret, 125–6
  study of, 102–3, 422
  Torah, 159
Phineas, 81
Phineas, Rabbi, 69, 210–11
phylacteries (tefillin), 204, 228, 323–6
piety, 13, 122–3, 145–56
Pilate, Pontius, 176
Pishon, 68
Pittsburgh Platform (1885), 228
piyyutim, 17
Plaskow, Judith, 326–8
Plato, 36, 132, 164
pluralism, 395
po'el yeshu'ot, 414
poetry, 17, 102
polytheism, 174–5
post-modernity, 271–7
power, 314
prayer, 82, 421
  for mercy, 148

Reform Judaism, 221
  women, 262–3
predicate theology, 375–6
priests, blessings of, 202, 203, 204
profit system, 308, 311
Promethean myth, 309
prophets/prophecy
  economic justice, 308
  eschatological, 57–8
  essence of Judaism, 5
  Maimonides' *Guide of the Perplexed*, 106
  Maimonides' Thirteen Principles, 6
  pesharim, 31
  receive Torah, 62
  religious authority, 413
Proverbs, Book of
  ethics, 291
  Genesis Rabbah, 210
  Gittin Tractate, 61
  Torah, 161, 163
  Yebamot Tractate, 67
Psalms, Book of
  dedication of a house, 147
  Encyclopedia of Religion, 17
  essence of Judaism, 5
  ethics, 291
  Genesis Rabbah, 82, 83, 84, 85, 199,
    209, 210
  God, 179, 181, 183
  Hatam Sofer, 233
  House of David and Jerusalem
    Temple, 30
  "Israel," 189, 195, 196
  Leviticus Rabbah, 69
  Maimonides' *Guide of the Perplexed*, 107,
    108, 110, 111
  Megillah Tractate, 205
  pesharim, 31
  Sefer Yetzirah, 213
  Sheqalim Tractate, 200
  Torah, 29–30, 163, 170
  YHWH as creator and giver of Torah,
    29–30
Psalms of Solomon, 54–5, 170
Pseudepigrapha, 11, 17
psycho-analysis, 304
punishment, 6, 49, 368
purification laws, 149–52
Purim, 278
purity/impurity, 11

Pythagoras, 129

"Q" source, 86
Qiddushin Tractate, 207
Qumran pesher, 31–3
Qumran Scrolls, 11

Rab, 206
Raba, 205
Rabbinic Judaism, 60–72
  autonomy, 368
  benedictions, 16
  Berdichevski's call to reject, 378–80
  democratic nature of, 12
  Encyclopedia of Religion, 11–13, 16
  origins of, 11
  tzedakah, 297
  women, 11
  see also sages
Rabbinic literature
  collectivity of, 11
  distinctive character of Judaism, 9
  ethics, 291
  "Israel," 12
  Yahadut, 4
  see also Abot Tractate; Babylonian Talmud;
    Genesis Rabbah; Jerusalem Talmud
    (Yerushalmi); Leviticus Rabbah; *midrash*;
    Mishnah; Talmud
rabbis
  education in liberal movements, 271
  ordination, 65–6
  religious authority, 414
  in service of community, 66–7
  supernatural abilities, 11, 12
  Torah, 169–70
Rabina, 206
Rachel, 191, 325
racial segregation, 290
rain, 182
Ramban, 232
Rashi, 114–15, 116, 121–2, 146, 232,
    249, 415–17
Rawls, John, 288, 289, 301, 302, 303, 305
reading, 101–2
reason
  Baruch Spinoza, 140
  Encyclopedia of Religion, 11
  Judah Halevi, 138
  Saadia Gaon, 135–6, 165

reason (*cont*)
  Solomon ben Adret, 124–5
  Torah, 159, 165
reasoning, 289–90, 302, 376–7
Rebecca, 190, 325
Recanati, Menaham, 166
Reconstructionist Judaism, 271, 281, 282,
    316, 389, 393
Red Sea, 21–2
redemption, Orthodox Judaism, 251–3
Refaenu Conferences, 270
reflective equilibrium, 289, 301, 302, 306
Reform Judaism, 217–31, 281, 282
  blessings, 217–18, 219–20
  ethics, 218, 221, 288
  God, 218, 228–9
  Halakhah, 221, 331
  intermarriage, 225–7
  "Israel," 230–1
  Jewish pluralism, 382
  Monmouth Reform Temple, 344–58
  outreach, 222–5
  religious authority, 413
  rituals, 217–20, 413
  standards, 220–2
  state of Israel, 231, 404–5
  statement of principles, 227–31
  synagogues, 269
  Torah, 229–30
  women, 224, 262, 316
religious authority, 413–19
religious experience, 143
religious schools, 386
religious Zionism, 404–5
Responsa literature, 15, 291, 333
resurrection
  Augustine, 99–100
  Book of Daniel, 49
  Maimonides' Thirteen Principles, 6
  miracle of rain, 182
  Origen, 95
Reuben, 82
Reuben M., 426–7
revelation
  Conservative Judaism, 257
  Encyclopedia of Religion, 17
  Irving Greenberg, 367–8
  Abraham Joshua Heschel, 370, 371
  of Torah by God at Sinai, 13, 160, 161,
    366, 371

rewards, 6, 49, 368
riddles, 108–9
Riecken, Henry W., 420
rituals, 145–56
  Conservative Judaism, 413
  Encyclopedia of Religion, 12–13
  niddah, 317–18
  Orthodox Judaism, 413, 419–23
  Reform Judaism, 217–20, 413
  study, 421–3
  understanding through action, 419–21
role-playing, 420
Rome/Romans, 55–8, 68, 69–70, 79, 194,
    197
Rosenzweig, Franz, 129, 163, 168–9, 373–4
Rosh Hodesh, 319–20
Rotenstreich, Nathan, 400–1
Roth, Joel, 262–5
Rothschild, Baron, 410
Rubenstein, Richard, 374–5

Saadia Gaon, 135–6, 161, 165, 167, 170
Sabbath
  changing people's views of time, 219
  Conservative Judaism, 260–2
  laws for visiting the sick, 148, 149
  observance as an act of YHWH's creation,
    22–3
  Pentateuch forbids work on, 414–15
  Reform Judaism, 229
  secular Jews, 395, 396
Sachs, Nelly, 17
sacred scrolls, 204
Saddok, 56
Sadducees, 11, 58
Sadoq, Rabbi, 61
sages
  Abot Tractate, 62
  Encyclopedia of Religion, 11, 12
  Genesis Rabbah, 79–85
  Gentiles, 12
  Hebrew Scriptures, 79, 80, 83, 190, 197,
    199–200
  "Israel," 190, 193–4, 197, 199–200, 201
  Maimonides' *Guide of the Perplexed*, 107,
    108, 109
  Torah, 11, 200
  Yerushalmi, 201
  see also Abot Tractate
Saladin, 138

Salkin, Jeffrey K., 277–80
salvation
   anthropocentric religions, 253
   Encyclopedia of Religion, 11
   Genesis Rabbah, 79, 80, 83, 85
   Torah, 82
Samaritans, 56, 193
Samuel, 206, 207
Samuel bar Nahman, Rabbi, 65, 183,
      210, 211
Samuel ben Yehuda *see* ibn Tibbon
Samuel, Books of
   Ark of YHWH brought to Jerusalem, 25–6
   Encyclopedia of Religion, 17
   faith, 17
   Genesis Rabbah, 199
   Jeremiah, 28
   Mishnah, 189
   YHWH chooses David as king, 26–7
Samuel ha-Nagid, 118
sanctification, 11, 13, 319–20
Sanctuaries, 90–1
Sanhedrin Tractate, 152, 164
   Babylonian Talmud, 114, 406
   Jerusalem Talmud (Yerushalmi), 65–6, 200
   Mishnah, 6, 16, 171, 187–90
Sarah, 190, 191, 322–3, 325
Satan, 47
Schachter, Stanley, 420
Schechinah, 224
Schechter, Dr. Solomon, 6, 281, 389
Schiller, Rabbi Nota, 430–1
Schneersohn, Rabbi Menachem Mendel,
      251–3
scholasticism, 142
schools, 223, 386
Schorsch, Ismar, 403
Schulweis, Harold M., 375–6
Schweid, Eliezer, 408–9
science
   Maimonides' *Guide of the Perplexed*,
      107, 108
   Orthodox Judaism, 253–5
   Solomon ben Adret, 125–6
   study in Muslim World, 103, 104, 105
sciolists, 121
Scott, Marvin B., 424
Second Temple period, 42–59
secularism, 4, 129, 274, 378–96
   democracy, 394–5

education, 396
Encyclopedia of Religion, 13–14
God, 394
Hebrew Bible, 394, 395–6
humanism, 394–5
Sabbath, 395, 396
Zionism, 168–9, 241–3
seers, 5
Sefer ha-Hayyim, 149, 150
Sefer ha-Temunah, 171
Sefer Yetzirah, 161, 211–14
Sefirot, 162, 166
segregation, 290
Seleucus, 52, 54
selfishness, 6
Semahot, 149
sense perception, 36–7, 135–6
Sephirot, 238
Septimus Severus, 92, 94
Septuagint, 163
Seth, 41
sexuality, 5, 266–7, 282–3, 317, 326–8
Shabbat *see* Sabbath
Shabbat Tractate, 4, 148, 164, 307
Shabbetai Zevi, 15, 172
shalom, 238
Shalom, Abraham, 162, 171
Shammai, 63
Shammai, House of, 73–4
Shavuot (Weeks Festival), 12, 24–5, 204
sheheheyanu blessing, 319, 320
Shema, 202, 204, 205
Shemaiah, 63
Sheqalim Tractate, 200–1
Shevuot Tractate, 247
Shiloh sanctuary, 29
Shin, 213–14
Shir ha-Shirim Rabbah, 238
Shoah, 224
   see also Holocaust
shrouds, 149–52
Shulhan Arukh, 254, 292, 305
Sibyl, 175
sick, laws for visiting, 147–9
Sidgwick, Henry, 294
Siegel, Seymour, 306–15
Sifra Be-Hukkotai, 170
Sifre Deuteronomy, 164, 170, 177, 207, 208
Sifra Kedoshim, 164
Sifre Numbers, 166

INDEX

...ver, Abba Hillel, 8
Simeon, 66, 78, 83, 209, 211
Simeon ben Laqish, 69, 161
Simeon ben Nazira, 201
Simeon ben Shetah, 63
Simeon the Just (Righteous), 62, 164
Simeon of Mispah, 64
Simeon (son of Gamaliel), 63, 126, 204,
    206, 311
Simon, 51–2
sin, 307–8
Sinai, Mount, God's covenant with "Israel,"
    13, 160, 161, 366, 371
Sirach, 180
skepticism, 174
slavery, 23–4
Smith, Adam, 311
socialism, 314
Sofer, Moshe see Hatam Sofer
Solomon, 109, 178, 238
Solomon bar Simson, 117
Solomon ben Isaac of Troyes see Rashi
Soloveitchik, Rabbi Joseph Baer, 247–51, 418
Song of Songs, 201, 238, 327
Sotah Tractate, 202–3
soul, 165, 179, 238
souls, transmigration of, 5
Soviet Union, 402
speculation, 136
speech, Philo of Alexandria, 36–7
Spinoza, Baruch, 139–40, 167, 168, 172
spirituality, 268–71, 273–4
    feminine, 316–18
    and work, 277–80
Steinheim, Salomon Ludwig, 167–8
Stoics, 36
Strauss, Bruno, 141
subjectivist reductionism, 364
Sukkot (Booths Festival), 12, 25, 204
Supernal Holiness, 239–41
Suryah, 126
synagogues, 386–7
    Conservative Judaism, 269
    needs of modern young Jews, 268, 273–4
    Reform Judaism, 269
    secular Jews, 396
    use of motor vehicle to attend, 261–2
Synoptic Gospels, 86–7, 88

tabernacle, 178

Tabernacles Festival see Sukkot
takanot, 358–9
tallith, 149, 323
Talmud
    attempts to state essence, 5–6
    commentaries to, 15
    ethics, 291, 296
    gift of fire to Adam, 309
    language of liturgy, 204–6
    miracles, 431
    needs/lacks, 298
    opposition to, 222
    redemption of captives, 305
    religious authority, 413, 414–17, 418–19
    sanctity of majority rule, 395
    study of, 102, 415–17, 418–19, 421–4
    theopolitical perspective, 333
    tzedakah, 305
    see also Babylonian Talmud; Jerusalem
        Talmud (Yerushalmi)
Talmud scholar, emergence of, 14
Tanakh see Hebrew Bible (Tanakh)
Tanhuma, 147, 161, 164
Tarfon, Rabbi, 307
Targum Pseudo-Jonathan, 39–41
"Teacher of Righteousness," 31, 32
tefillin (phylacteries), 204, 228, 323–6
Tehom, 238
Teitlbaum, Rabbi Moshe, 246
Teitlbaum, Rabbi Yoel, 246–7
Temple, Jerusalem
    defiled by Samaritans, 56
    destruction (70 CE), 13
    as God's earthly dwelling place, 178
    and ruling House of David, 30
    Second Temple period, 42–3, 45–6
    suffering at loss of, 58–9
Temurah Tractate, 170
Terumot Tractate, 77
Teshubat Rabbenu Asher, 146
theology, contemporary, 363–77
theopolitical phenomenon, 333–62
Theudas, 58
Thomas, Gospel of, 88
Tiferet, 162
Tigris, 68
tikkun olam, 224, 230
time, 12–13
tithes, 75–9
Titus, 89

Torah, 159–72
  Abot Tractate, 62–3
  Abraham Joshua Heschel, 370, 371
  belief in divinity of, 6–7
  Book of Deuteronomy, 29, 64, 65, 163,
    164, 170
  Book of Exodus, 64, 65, 160, 163, 164,
    170
  Book of Genesis, 160, 164
  Book of Leviticus, 160, 164, 169
  Book of Numbers, 160, 162, 164
  Book of Proverbs, 161, 163
  Book of Psalms, 29–30, 163, 170
  definition, 160
  distinction from Judaism, 4–5
  Encyclopedia of Religion, 11, 15
  eternity/non-abrogability of, 169–72
  Ezra brings to Judah, 43–4
  Genesis Rabbah, 161, 164, 170
  Hatam Sofer, 232
  identification with God, 166
  "Israel," 164, 168–9
  Israel as New Torah Center, 244
  Jeremiah's call to observe, 28–9
  Jewish Renewal movement, 282
  Josephus Flavius, 165, 170
  Judah Halevi, 162, 163, 165, 166,
    167, 169
  Kabbalah, 162, 166, 169, 171–2
  Leviticus Rabbah, 161, 170
  Maimonides, 6, 162, 165–6, 167, 170–1
  Moses ascends to heaven to capture, 164
  Moses hands to Joshua, 62
  nature and purpose, 163–9
  New Age Judaism, 277
  origin and pre-existence, 161–3
  Orthodox Judaism, 172, 235, 244
  Pharisees, 58
  Philo of Alexandria, 35–9, 161, 164–5,
    166, 170
  Reform Judaism, 229–30
  religious authority, 414, 418
  revealed in multiple languages, 207, 208
  revelation by God at Sinai, 13, 160, 161,
    366, 371
  Sadducees, 58
  sages, 11, 200
  salvation, 82
  scroll as sacred object in Rabbinic
    Judaism, 11
  seeing God, 366
  study of, 102
  as whole body of Jewish teaching, 4
  women's otherness, 326
  written and oral, 17, 63–5, 159, 160, 167,
    169, 414–15
  YHWH as creator and giver of, 29–30
  see also Babylonian Talmud; Halakhah;
    Hebrew Bible; Hebrew Scriptures;
    Jerusalem Talmud; midrash; Mishnah;
    Talmud
Tosafot, 415–17
Tosefta Sotah, 204
totalitarianism, 382–3
trade unions, 314
tradition, 135–6
transcendence, 143
translation, 202–4
transmigration, 5
Treitschke, Heinrich von, 141
Trinity, 142
tshuvah, 224
Tubal-cain, 41
Turnus Rufus, 312
Twersky, Isadore, 405–6
tyranny, 314
tzedakah, 230, 297, 305, 310–11, 312
tzedek, 230

UAHC, 228
Umansky, Ellen, 271, 322–3
unchastity, 6
Union of American Hebrew
  Congregations (UAHC), 228
United Nations, 360
United States
  Encyclopedia of Religion, 14, 15
  Jewish commitment to family and
    community, 14
  rabbinical seminaries, 15
Uqsin Tractate, 73–5
utopianism, 314
Uzzah, 25

Vedanta, 276
vengeance, 121–2
Verissimus, 91
Vital, David, 397, 398–9

Wasserman, Rabbi Elchonon, 418

ater, 213–14
Weber, Max, 429
wedding ceremony, 152–6
Weeks Festival *see Shavuot*
Weinbach, Rabbi Mendel, 415–16
Wikler, Daniel, 299, 306
wisdom, 161, 162, 163
Wisdom of Ben Sira, 161, 163, 169
Wisdom of Solomon, 175
Wise, Isaac Meyer, 281
Wissenschaft des Judentums movement, 7, 167
Wolfson, Harry A., 381
Wolpe, David, 269
women, 316–32
    Babylonian Talmud, 11
    Conservative Judaism, 262–5, 316
    Hatam Sofer, 233
    liturgy, 318–22
    Mishnah, 11
    Orthodox Judaism, 262, 316
    prayer, 262–3
    Rabbinic Judaism, 11
    Reform Judaism, 224, 262, 316
    sexuality, 326–8
    transfer of, 11
    see also feminism
work, 277–80, 414–15
World Jewish Congress, 402
World Zionist Organization, 408
worldliness, 115–16, 279–80
writing, 101–2
Wyschogrod, Michael, 326, 376–7

Yad Vashem Law, 408–9
Yadaim Tractate, 162, 166, 239
Yahadut, 4
Yebamot Tractate, 66–7

Yehoshua ben Levi, Rabbi, 209
Yehoshua, Rabbi, 210
Yeshiva Ohr Someyach, 415–16, 418, 427, 430–1
Yeshivat Aish Hatorah, 420
Yeshivat Hamivtar, 416–17, 418
yeshivot, 244, 414–17, 418–19, 421–3
yetsers, 309–10
Yiddishism cult, 384–5, 386, 388
Yidishkeyt, 4, 224
Yirmiya, Rabbi, 209
Yoffie, Eric, 222–5
Yohanan ben Zakkai, 60–1, 66, 182
Yohanan, Rabbi, 64, 65, 69, 210, 211
Yoma Tractate, 160
Yonah, Rabbi, 208–9
Yoreh Deah, 147, 148, 149, 150, 151, 152
Yose ben Yoezer of Zeredah, 62
Yose ben Yohanan of Jerusalem, 62
Yudan ben R. Simeon, Rabbi, 65

Zaddik, Joseph ibn, 165
Zechariah, Book of, 46–7, 63, 195, 198, 233
Zeira, Rabbi, 64
Zerubbabel, 43, 46, 47
Zeus, 177
Zillah, 41
Zimri, 81
Zionism, 383–4, 388–9, 397–410
    secularism, 168–9, 241–3
    Torah, 159
Zionist colonies, 358–9
Zionist Congress (1897), 360
Zionist Religious Movement, 237, 245
Zohar, 8, 126, 162, 166
Zohar, Uri, 420, 421